COMPILATION OF SELECTED
PUBLIC BUILDINGS RELATED LAWS

As amended through the 118th Congress.

Prepared By M. TWINCHEK

2025

Forward

This Compilation of Selected United States laws related to public buildings is a resource for those interested in U.S. laws governing public buildings; their creation and maintenance.

The materials included come from publicly available, open source information, prepared for the public by the Office of the Legislative Counsel of the U.S. House of Representatives and the Office of the Law Revision Counsel.

Items listed as a Statute Compilation do not appear in the U.S. Code or that have been classified to a title of the U.S. Code that has not been enacted into positive law. Each Statute Compilation incorporates the amendments made to the underlying statute since it was originally enacted and are current as of the date noted.

This compilation is not an official document and should not be cited as evidence of any law. The official version of Federal law is found in the United States Statutes at Large and in the U.S. Code, the legal effect of which is established in sections 112 and 204, respectively, of title 1, United States Code.

A special thanks is extended to the Office of Law Revision Counsel and the House Office of the Legislative Counsel for providing the U.S. Code and statute compilations; and to the Government Publications Office for hosting and making these available for use to the public. An additional thank you is offered to the staff of the House Committee who were gracious in responding to inquiries and providing background information on the legislation included. Questions and comments may be directed to:

M. Twinchek
Email: mtwinchek@outlook.com

Contents

Laws Relating to the General Services Administration

Provisions of Title 40 U.S.C.– Public Buildings, Property, and Works

TITLE 40—PUBLIC BUILDINGS, PROPERTY, AND WORKS

This title was enacted by Pub. L. 107–217, §1, Aug. 21, 2002, 116 Stat. 1062

SUBTITLE I—FEDERAL PROPERTY AND ADMINISTRATIVE SERVICES

CHAPTER 1—GENERAL

SUBCHAPTER I—PURPOSE AND DEFINITIONS

SUBCHAPTER I—PURPOSE AND DEFINITIONS

§101. PURPOSE

The purpose of this subtitle is to provide the Federal Government with an economical and efficient system for the following activities:

(1) Procuring and supplying property and nonpersonal services, and performing related functions including contracting, inspection, storage, issue, setting specifications, identification and classification, transportation and traffic management, establishment of pools or systems for transportation of Government personnel and property by motor vehicle within specific areas, management of public utility services, repairing and converting, establishment of inventory levels, establishment of forms and procedures, and representation before federal and state regulatory bodies.

(2) Using available property.

(3) Disposing of surplus property.

(4) Records management.

(Pub. L. 107–217, Aug. 21, 2002, 116 Stat. 1063.)

§102. DEFINITIONS

Except as provided in subchapter VII of chapter 5 of this title, the following definitions apply in chapters 1 through 7 of this title and in division C (except sections 3302, 3501(b), 3509, 3906, 4710, and 4711) of subtitle I of title 41:

(1) CARE AND HANDLING.—The term "care and handling" includes—

(A) completing, repairing, converting, rehabilitating, operating, preserving, protecting, insuring, packing, storing, handling, conserving, and transporting excess and surplus property; and

(B) rendering innocuous, or destroying, property that is dangerous to public health or safety.

(2) CONTRACTOR INVENTORY.—The term "contractor inventory" means—

(A) property, in excess of amounts needed to complete full performance, that is acquired by and in possession of a contractor or subcontractor under a contract pursuant to which title is vested in the Federal Government; and

(B) property that the Government is obligated or has the option to take over, under any type of contract, as a result of changes in specifications or plans under the contract, or as a result of termination of the contract (or a subcontract), prior to completion of the work, for the convenience or at the option of the Government.

(3) EXCESS PROPERTY.—The term "excess property" means property under the control of a federal agency that the head of the agency determines is not required to meet the agency's needs or responsibilities.

(4) EXECUTIVE AGENCY.—The term "executive agency" means—

(A) an executive department or independent establishment in the executive branch of the Government; and

(B) a wholly owned Government corporation.

(5) FEDERAL AGENCY.—The term "federal agency" means an executive agency or an establishment in the legislative or judicial branch of the Government (except the Senate, the House of Representatives, and the Architect of the Capitol, and any activities under the direction of the Architect of the Capitol).

(6) FOREIGN EXCESS PROPERTY.—The term "foreign excess property" means excess property that is not located in the States of the United States, the District of Columbia, Puerto Rico, American Samoa, Guam, the Northern Mariana Islands, the Federated States of Micronesia, the Marshall Islands, Palau, and the Virgin Islands.

(7) MOTOR VEHICLE.—The term "motor vehicle" means any vehicle, self-propelled or drawn by mechanical power, designed and operated principally for highway transportation of property or passengers, excluding—

(A) a vehicle designed or used for military field training, combat, or tactical purposes, or used principally within the confines of a regularly established military post, camp, or depot; and

(B) a vehicle regularly used by an agency to perform investigative, law enforcement, or intelligence duties, if the head of the agency determines that exclusive control of the vehicle is essential for effective performance of duties.

(8) NONPERSONAL SERVICES.—The term "nonpersonal services" means contractual services designated by the Administrator of General Services, other than personal and professional services.

(9) PROPERTY.—The term "property" means any interest in property except—

(A)(i) the public domain;

(ii) land reserved or dedicated for national forest or national park purposes;

(iii) minerals in land or portions of land withdrawn or reserved from the public domain which the Secretary of the Interior determines are suitable for disposition under the public land mining and mineral leasing laws; and

(iv) land withdrawn or reserved from the public domain except land or portions of land so withdrawn or reserved which the Secretary, with the concurrence of the Administrator, determines are not suitable for return to the public domain for disposition under the general public land laws because the lands are substantially changed in character by improvements or otherwise;

(B) naval vessels that are battleships, cruisers, aircraft carriers, destroyers, or submarines; and

(C) records of the Government.

(10) SURPLUS PROPERTY.—The term "surplus property" means excess property that the Administrator determines is not required to meet the needs or responsibilities of all federal agencies.

(Pub. L. 107–217, Aug. 21, 2002, 116 Stat. 1063; Pub. L. 111–350, §5(l)(2), Jan. 4, 2011, 124 Stat. 3850; Pub. L. 114–318, §3(b)(2), Dec. 16, 2016, 130 Stat. 1613.)

SUBCHAPTER II—SCOPE

§111. APPLICATION TO DIVISION C (EXCEPT SECTIONS 3302, 3501(B), 3509, 3906, 4710, AND 4711) OF SUBTITLE I OF TITLE 41

In the following provisions, the words "this subtitle" are deemed to refer also to division C (except sections 3302, 3501(b), 3509, 3906, 4710, and 4711) of subtitle I of title 41:

(1) Section 101 of this title.
(2) Section 112(a) of this title.
(3) Section 113 of this title.
(4) Section 121(a) of this title.
(5) Section 121(c)(1) of this title.
(6) Section 121(c)(2) of this title.
(7) Section 121(d)(1) and (2) of this title.
(8) Section 121(e)(1) of this title.
(9) Section 121(f) of this title.
(10) Section 121(g) of this title.
(11) Section 122(a) of this title.
(12) Section 123(a) of this title.
(13) Section 123(c) of this title.
(14) Section 124 of this title.
(15) Section 126 of this title.
(16) Section 311(c) of this title.
(17) Section 313(a) of this title.
(18) Section 528 of this title.
(19) Section 541 of this title.
(20) Section 549(e)(3)(H)(i)(II) of this title.
(21) Section 557 of this title.
(22) Section 558(a) of this title.
(23) Section 559(f) of this title.
(24) Section 571(b) of this title.
(25) Section 572(a)(2)(A) of this title.
(26) Section 572(b)(4) of this title.

(Pub. L. 107–217, Aug. 21, 2002, 116 Stat. 1065; Pub. L. 111–350, §5(l)(3), Jan. 4, 2011, 124 Stat. 3850.)

§112. APPLICABILITY OF CERTAIN POLICIES, PROCEDURES, AND DIRECTIVES IN EFFECT ON JULY 1, 1949

(a) IN GENERAL.—A policy, procedure, or directive described in subsection (b) remains in effect until superseded or amended under this subtitle or other appropriate authority.

(b) DESCRIPTION.—A policy, procedure, or directive referred to in subsection (a) is one that was in effect on July 1, 1949, and that was prescribed by—

(1) the Director of the Bureau of Federal Supply or the Secretary of the Treasury and that related to a function transferred to or vested in the Administrator of General Services on June 30, 1949, by the Federal Property and Administrative Services Act of 1949; [1]

(2) an officer of the Federal Government under authority of the Surplus Property Act of 1944 (ch. 479, 58 Stat. 765) or other authority related to surplus property or foreign excess property;

(3) the Federal Works Administrator or the head of a constituent agency of the Federal Works Agency; or

(4) the Archivist of the United States or another officer or body whose functions were transferred on June 30, 1949, by title I [1] of the Federal Property and Administrative Services Act of 1949.

(Pub. L. 107–217, Aug. 21, 2002, 116 Stat. 1065.)

[1] See References in Text note below.

§113. LIMITATIONS

(a) IN GENERAL.—Except as otherwise provided in this section, the authority conferred by this subtitle is in addition to any other authority conferred by law and is not subject to any inconsistent provision of law.

(b) LIMITATION REGARDING DIVISION B (EXCEPT SECTIONS 1704 AND 2303) OF SUBTITLE I OF TITLE 41.—The authority conferred by this subtitle is subject to division B (Except [1] Sections [1] 1704 and 2303) of subtitle I of title 41.

(c) LIMITATION REGARDING CERTAIN GOVERNMENT CORPORATIONS AND AGENCIES.—Sections 121(b) and 506(c) of this title do not apply to a Government corporation or agency that is subject to chapter 91 of title 31.

(d) LIMITATION REGARDING CONGRESS.—This subtitle does not apply to the Senate or the House of Representatives (including the Architect of the Capitol and any building, activity, or function under the direction of the Architect). However, services and facilities authorized by this subtitle shall, as far as practicable, be made available to the Senate, the House of Representatives, and the Architect of the Capitol on their request. If payment would be required for providing a similar service or facility to an executive agency, payment shall be made by the recipient, on presentation of proper vouchers, in advance or by reimbursement (as may be agreed upon by the Administrator of General Services and the officer or body making the request). The payment may be credited to the applicable appropriation of the executive agency receiving the payment.

(e) OTHER LIMITATIONS.—Nothing in this subtitle impairs or affects the authority of—

(1) the President under the Philippine Property Act of 1946 (22 U.S.C. 1381 et seq.);

(2) an executive agency, with respect to any program conducted for purposes of resale, price support, grants to farmers, stabilization, transfer to foreign governments, or foreign aid, relief, or rehabilitation, but the agency carrying out the program shall, to the maximum extent practicable, consistent with the purposes of the program and the effective, efficient conduct of agency business, coordinate its operations with the requirements of this subtitle and with policies and regulations prescribed under this subtitle;

(3) an executive agency named in section 3063 of title 10, and the head of the agency, with respect to the administration of the provisions of that title referred to in section 3016 of such title as "chapter 137 legacy provisions";

(4) the Secretary of Defense with respect to property required for or located in occupied territories;

(5) the Secretary of Defense with respect to the administration of section 4881 of title 10;

(6) the Secretary of Defense and the Secretaries of the Army, Navy, and Air Force with respect to the administration of the Strategic and Critical Materials Stock Piling Act (50 U.S.C. 98 et seq.);

(7) the Secretary of State under the Foreign Service Buildings Act, 1926 (22 U.S.C. 292 et seq.);

(8) the Secretary of Agriculture under—

(A) the Richard B. Russell National School Lunch Act (42 U.S.C. 1751 et seq.);

(B) the Farmers Home Administration Act of 1946 (ch. 964, 60 Stat. 1062);

(C) section 32 of the Act of August 24, 1935 (7 U.S.C. 612c), with respect to the exportation and domestic consumption of agricultural products;

(D) section 201 of the Agricultural Adjustment Act of 1938 (7 U.S.C. 1291); or

(E) section 203(j) of the Agricultural Marketing Act of 1946 (7 U.S.C. 1622(j));

(9) an official or entity under the Farm Credit Act of 1971 (12 U.S.C. 2001 et seq.), with respect to the acquisition or disposal of property;

(10) the Secretary of Housing and Urban Development or the Federal Deposit Insurance Corporation (or an officer of the Corporation) with respect to the disposal of—

(A) residential property; or

(B) other property—

(i) acquired or held as part of, or in connection with, residential property; or

(ii) held in connection with the insurance of mortgages, loans, or savings association accounts under the National Housing Act (12 U.S.C. 1701 et seq.), the Federal Deposit Insurance Act (12 U.S.C. 1811 et seq.), or any other law;

(11) the Tennessee Valley Authority with respect to nonpersonal services, with respect to section 501(c) of this title, and with respect to property acquired in connection with a program of processing, manufacture, production, or force account construction, but the Authority shall, to the maximum extent it considers practicable,

consistent with the purposes of its program and the effective, efficient conduct of its business, coordinate its operations with the requirements of this subtitle and with policies and regulations prescribed under this subtitle;

(12) the Secretary of Energy with respect to atomic energy;

(13) the Secretary of Transportation or the Secretary of Commerce with respect to the disposal of airport property and airway property (as those terms are defined in section 47301 of title 49) for use as such property;

(14) the United States Postal Service;

(15) the Maritime Administration with respect to the acquisition, procurement, operation, maintenance, preservation, sale, lease, charter, construction, reconstruction, or reconditioning (including outfitting and equipping incidental to construction, reconstruction, or reconditioning) of a merchant vessel or shipyard, ship site, terminal, pier, dock, warehouse, or other installation necessary or appropriate for carrying out a program of the Administration authorized by law or nonadministrative activities incidental to a program of the Administration authorized by law, but the Administration shall, to the maximum extent it considers practicable, consistent with the purposes of its programs and the effective, efficient conduct of its activities, coordinate its operations with the requirements of this subtitle and with policies and regulations prescribed under this subtitle;

(16) the Central Intelligence Agency;

(17) the Joint Committee on Printing, under title 44 or any other law;

(18) the Secretary of the Interior with respect to procurement for program operations under the Bonneville Project Act of 1937 (16 U.S.C. 832 et seq.);

(19) the Secretary of State with respect to the furnishing of facilities in foreign countries and reception centers within the United States; or

(20) the Office of the Director of National Intelligence.

(Pub. L. 107–217, Aug. 21, 2002, 116 Stat. 1066; Pub. L. 108–458, title I, §1080, Dec. 17, 2004, 118 Stat. 3696; Pub. L. 111–350, §5(l)(4), Jan. 4, 2011, 124 Stat. 3851; Pub. L. 117–81, div. A, title XVII, §1702(g)(1), Dec. 27, 2021, 135 Stat. 2157.)

¹ *So in original. Probably should not be capitalized.*

SUBCHAPTER III—ADMINISTRATIVE AND GENERAL

§121. ADMINISTRATIVE

(a) POLICIES PRESCRIBED BY THE PRESIDENT.—The President may prescribe policies and directives that the President considers necessary to carry out this subtitle. The policies must be consistent with this subtitle.

(b) ACCOUNTING PRINCIPLES AND STANDARDS.—

(1) PRESCRIPTION.—The Comptroller General, after considering the needs and requirements of executive agencies, shall prescribe principles and standards of accounting for property.

(2) PROPERTY ACCOUNTING SYSTEMS.—The Comptroller General shall cooperate with the Administrator of General Services and with executive agencies in the development of property accounting systems and approve the systems when they are adequate and in conformity with prescribed principles and standards.

(3) COMPLIANCE REVIEW.—From time to time the Comptroller General shall examine the property accounting systems established by executive agencies to determine the extent of compliance with prescribed principles and standards and approved systems. The Comptroller General shall report to Congress any failure to comply with the principles and standards or to adequately account for property.

(c) REGULATIONS BY ADMINISTRATOR.—

(1) GENERAL AUTHORITY.—The Administrator may prescribe regulations to carry out this subtitle.

(2) REQUIRED REGULATIONS AND ORDERS.—The Administrator shall prescribe regulations that the Administrator considers necessary to carry out the Administrator's functions under this subtitle and the head of each executive agency shall issue orders and directives that the agency head considers necessary to carry out the regulations.

(d) DELEGATION OF AUTHORITY BY ADMINISTRATOR.—

(1) IN GENERAL.—Except as provided in paragraph (2), the Administrator may delegate authority conferred on the Administrator by this subtitle to an official in the General Services Administration or to the head of another federal agency. The Administrator may authorize successive redelegation of authority conferred by this subtitle.

(2) EXCEPTIONS.—The Administrator may not delegate—

(A) the authority to prescribe regulations on matters of policy applying to executive agencies;

(B) the authority to transfer functions and related allocated amounts from one component of the Administration to another under paragraphs (1)(C) and (2)(A) of subsection (e); or

(C) other authority for which delegation is prohibited by this subtitle.

(3) RETENTION AND USE OF RENTAL PAYMENTS.—A department or agency to which the Administrator has delegated authority to operate, maintain or repair a building or facility under this subsection shall retain the portion of the rental payment that the Administrator determines is available to operate, maintain or repair the building or facility. The department or agency shall directly expend the retained amounts to operate, maintain, or repair the building or facility. Any amounts retained under this paragraph shall remain available until expended for these purposes.

(e) ASSIGNMENT OF FUNCTIONS BY ADMINISTRATOR.—

(1) IN GENERAL.—The Administrator may provide for the performance of a function assigned under this subtitle by any of the following methods:

(A) The Administrator may direct the Administration to perform the function.

(B) The Administrator may designate or establish a component of the Administration and direct the component to perform the function.

(C) The Administrator may transfer the function from one component of the Administration to another.

(D) The Administrator may direct an executive agency to perform the function for itself, with the consent of the agency or by direction of the President.

(E) The Administrator may direct one executive agency to perform the function for another executive agency, with the consent of the agencies concerned or by direction of the President.

(F) The Administrator may provide for performance of a function by a combination of the methods described in this paragraph.

(2) TRANSFER OF RESOURCES.—

(A) WITHIN ADMINISTRATION.—If the Administrator transfers a function from one component of the Administration to another, the Administrator may also provide for the transfer of appropriate allocated amounts from the component that previously carried out the function to the component being directed to carry out the function. A transfer under this subparagraph must be reported to the Director of the Office of Management and Budget.

(B) BETWEEN AGENCIES.—If the Administrator transfers a function from one executive agency to another (including a transfer to or from the Administration), the Administrator may also provide for the transfer of appropriate personnel, records, property, and allocated amounts from the executive agency that previously carried out the function to the executive agency being directed to carry out the function. A transfer under this subparagraph is subject to approval by the Director.

(f) ADVISORY COMMITTEES.—The Administrator may establish advisory committees to provide advice on any function of the Administrator under this subtitle. Members of the advisory committees shall serve without compensation but are entitled to transportation and not more than $25 a day instead of expenses under section 5703 of title 5.

(g) CONSULTATION WITH FEDERAL AGENCIES.—The Administrator shall advise and consult with interested federal agencies and seek their advice and assistance to accomplish the purposes of this subtitle.

(h) ADMINISTERING OATHS.—In carrying out investigative duties, an officer or employee of the Administration, if authorized by the Administrator, may administer an oath to an individual.

(Pub. L. 107–217, Aug. 21, 2002, 116 Stat. 1068.)

1–1. SPACE ACQUISITION

1–101. Federal facilities and Federal use of space in urban areas shall serve to strengthen the Nation's cities and to make them attractive places to live and work. Such Federal space shall conserve existing urban resources and encourage the development and redevelopment of cities.

1–102. Procedures for meeting space needs in urban areas shall give serious consideration to the impact a site selection will have on improving the social, economic, environmental, and cultural conditions of the communities in the urban area.

1–103. Except where such selection is otherwise prohibited, the process for meeting Federal space needs in urban areas shall give first consideration to a centralized community business area and adjacent areas of similar character, including other specific areas which may be recommended by local officials.

1–104. The process of meeting Federal space needs in urban areas shall be consistent with the policies of this Order and shall include consideration of the following criteria:

(a) Compatability [sic] of the site with State, regional, or local development, redevelopment, or conservation objectives.

(b) Conformity with the activities and programs of other Federal agencies.

(c) Impact on economic development and employment opportunities in the urban area, including the utilization of human, natural, cultural, and community resources.

(d) Availability of adequate low and moderate income housing for Federal employees and their families on a nondiscriminatory basis.

(e) Availability of adequate public transportation and parking and accessibility to the public.

1–105. Procedures for meeting space needs in urban areas shall be consistent with the policies of this Order and shall include consideration of the following alternatives:

(a) Availability of existing Federally controlled facilities.

(b) Utilization of buildings of historic, architectural, or cultural significance within the meaning of section 105 of the Public Buildings Cooperative Use Act of 1976 (90 Stat. 2507, 40 U.S.C. 612a) [now 40 U.S.C. 3306].

(c) Acquisition or utilization of existing privately owned facilities.

(d) Construction of new facilities.

(e) Opportunities for locating cultural, educational, recreational, or commercial activities within the proposed facility.

1–106. Site selection and space assignments shall take into account the management needs for consolidation of agencies or activities in common or adjacent space in order to improve administration and management and effect economies.

1–2. ADMINISTRATOR OF GENERAL SERVICES

1–201. The Administrator of General Services shall develop programs to implement the policies of this Order through the efficient acquisition and utilization of Federally owned and leased space. In particular, the Administrator shall:

(a) Select, acquire, and manage Federal space in a manner which will foster the policies and programs of the Federal government and improve the management and administration of government activities.

(b) Issue regulations, standards, and criteria for the selection, acquisition, and management of Federally owned and leased space.

(c) Periodically undertake surveys of space requirements and space utilization in the executive agencies.

(d) Ensure, in cooperation with the heads of Executive agencies, that their essential space requirements are met in a manner that is economically feasible and prudent.

(e) Make maximum use of existing Federally controlled facilities which, in his judgment, are adequate or economically adaptable to meeting the space needs of executive agencies.

(f) Annually submit long–range plans and programs for the acquisition, modernization, and use of space for approval by the President.

1–202. The Administrator is authorized to request from any Executive agency such information and assistance deemed necessary to carry out his functions under this Order. Each agency shall, to the extent not prohibited by law, furnish such information and assistance to the Administrator.

1–203. In the process of meeting Federal space needs in urban areas and implementing the policies of this Order, the Administrator shall:

(a) Consider the efficient performance of the missions and programs of the agencies, the nature and function of the facilities involved, the convenience of the public served, and the maintenance and improvement of safe and healthful working conditions for employees.

(b) Coordinate proposed programs and plans for facilities and space with the Director of the Office of Management and Budget.

(c) Consult with appropriate Federal, State, regional, and local government officials and consider their recommendations for and objections to a proposed selection site or space acquisition.

(d) Coordinate proposed programs and plans for facilities and space in a manner designed to implement the purposes of this Order.

(e) Prior to making a final determination concerning the location of Federal facilities, notify the concerned Executive agency of an intended course of action and take into account any additional information provided.

1–204. In ascertaining the social, economic, environmental and other impacts which site selection would have on a community, the Administrator shall, when appropriate, obtain the advice of interested agencies.

1–3. GENERAL PROVISIONS

1–301. The heads of Executive agencies shall cooperate with the Administrator in implementing the policies of this Order and shall economize on their use of space. They shall ensure that the Administrator is given early notice of new or changing missions or organizational realignments which affect space requirements.

1–302. Executive agencies which acquire or utilize Federally owned or leased space under authority other than the Federal Property and Administrative Services Act of 1949, as amended [now chapters 1 to 11 of this title and division C (except sections 3302, 3307(e), 3501(b), 3509, 3906, 4710, and 4711) of subtitle I of Title 41], shall conform to the provisions of this Order to the extent they have the authority to do so.

1–303. Executive Order No. 11512 of February 27, 1970, is revoked.

§122. PROHIBITION ON SEX DISCRIMINATION

(a) PROHIBITION.—With respect to a program or activity carried on or receiving federal assistance under this subtitle, an individual may not be excluded from participation, denied benefits, or otherwise discriminated against based on sex.

(b) ENFORCEMENT.—Subsection (a) shall be enforced through agency provisions and rules similar to those already established with respect to racial and other discrimination under title VI of the Civil Rights Act of 1964 (42 U.S.C. 2000d et seq.). However, this remedy is not exclusive and does not prejudice or remove any other legal remedies available to an individual alleging discrimination.

(Pub. L. 107–217, Aug. 21, 2002, 116 Stat. 1070.)

§123. CIVIL REMEDIES FOR FRAUD

(a) IN GENERAL.—In connection with the procurement, transfer or disposition of property under this subtitle, a person that uses or causes to be used, or enters into an agreement, combination, or conspiracy to use or cause to be used, a fraudulent trick, scheme, or device for the purpose of obtaining or aiding to obtain, for any person, money, property, or other benefit from the Federal Government—

(1) shall pay to the Government an amount equal to the sum of—

(A) $2,000 for each act;

(B) two times the amount of damages sustained by the Government because of each act; and

(C) the cost of suit;

(2) if the Government elects, shall pay to the Government, as liquidated damages, an amount equal to two times the consideration that the Government agreed to give to the person, or that the person agreed to give to the Government; or

(3) if the Government elects, shall restore to the Government the money or property fraudulently obtained, with the Government retaining as liquidated damages, the money, property, or other consideration given to the Government.

(b) ADDITIONAL REMEDIES AND CRIMINAL PENALTIES.—The civil remedies provided in this section are in addition to all other civil remedies and criminal penalties provided by law.

(c) IMMUNITY OF GOVERNMENT OFFICIALS.—An officer or employee of the Government is not liable (except for an individual's own fraud) or accountable for collection of a purchase price that is determined to be uncollectible by the federal agency responsible for property if the property is transferred or disposed of in accordance with this subtitle and with regulations prescribed under this subtitle.

(d) JURISDICTION AND VENUE.—

(1) DEFINITION.—In this subsection, the term "district court" means a district court of the United States or a district court of a territory or possession of the United States.

(2) IN GENERAL.—A district court has original jurisdiction of an action arising under this section, and venue is proper, if at least one defendant resides or may be found in the court's judicial district. Jurisdiction and venue are determined without regard to the place where acts were committed.

(3) ADDITIONAL DEFENDANT OUTSIDE JUDICIAL DISTRICT.—A defendant that does not reside and may not be found in the court's judicial district may be brought in by order of the court, to be served personally, by publication, or in another reasonable manner directed by the court.

(Pub. L. 107–217, Aug. 21, 2002, 116 Stat. 1070.)

§124. AGENCY USE OF AMOUNTS FOR PROPERTY MANAGEMENT

Amounts appropriated, allocated, or available to a federal agency for purposes similar to the purposes in section 121 of this title or subchapter I (except section 506), II, or III of chapter 5 of this title may be used by the agency for the disposition of property under this subtitle, and for the care and handling of property pending the disposition, if the Director of the Office of Management and Budget authorizes the use.

(Pub. L. 107–217, Aug. 21, 2002, 116 Stat. 1071.)

§125. LIBRARY MEMBERSHIPS

Amounts appropriated may be used, when authorized by the Administrator of General Services, for payment in advance for library memberships in societies whose publications are available to members only, or to members at a lower price than that charged to the general public.

(Pub. L. 107–217, Aug. 21, 2002, 116 Stat. 1071.)

§126. Reports to Congress

The Administrator of General Services, at times the Administrator considers desirable, shall submit a report to Congress on the administration of this subtitle. The report shall include any recommendation for amendment of this subtitle that the Administrator considers appropriate and shall identify any law that is obsolete because of the enactment or operation of this subtitle.

(Pub. L. 107–217, Aug. 21, 2002, 116 Stat. 1071.)

CHAPTER 3—ORGANIZATION OF GENERAL SERVICES ADMINISTRATION

SUBCHAPTER I—GENERAL

[1] *Section repealed by Pub. L. 111–8 without corresponding amendment of chapter analysis.*

SUBCHAPTER I—GENERAL

§301. ESTABLISHMENT

The General Services Administration is an agency in the executive branch of the Federal Government.

(Pub. L. 107–217, Aug. 21, 2002, 116 Stat. 1071.)

REORGANIZATION PLAN NO. 18 OF 1950

EFF. JULY 1, 1950, 15 F.R. 3177, 64 STAT. 1270

Prepared by the President and transmitted to the Senate and the House of Representatives in Congress assembled, March 13, 1950, pursuant to the provisions of the Reorganization Act of 1949, approved June 20, 1949 [see 5 U.S.C. 901 et seq.].

BUILDING AND SPACE MANAGEMENT FUNCTIONS

MESSAGE OF THE PRESIDENT

To the Congress of the United States:

I transmit herewith Reorganization Plan No. 18 of 1950, prepared in accordance with the provisions of the Reorganization Act of 1949. The plan transfers to the Administrator of General Services the functions of the various Federal agencies with respect to leasing and assigning general-purpose space in buildings and the operation, maintenance, and custody of office buildings. Since such authority is already largely concentrated in the General Services Administration with respect to the District of

Columbia, the plan principally relates to the administration of these functions in the field.

The transfers made by this plan will promote more economical leasing, better utilization of building space, and more efficient operation of Government-controlled office buildings. They will effectuate the recommendations of the Commission on Organization of the Executive Branch of the Government with respect to concentrating in the General Services Administration the responsibility for space allotment and the operation of Government buildings outside of the District of Columbia. Likewise, they will extend the principles laid down by the Congress in enacting the Federal Property and Administrative Services Act of 1949 to another important area of Government-wide administrative services—the administration of Government office buildings and general-purpose building space in the field.

Within the District of Columbia, one agency, the Public Buildings Service of the General Services Administration, has long had the operation and custody of most Government buildings and the leasing and assignment of space for executive agencies. Thus, nearly all requests for building space are handled by a single organization which is responsible for seeing that agencies are properly and efficiently housed. This arrangement has proved its worth and has repeatedly been approved by the Congress.

Outside of the National Capital, however, responsibility for the acquisition and control of building space and the operation of Government buildings is widely diffused. A variety of agencies operate and control general-purpose buildings. If quarters are not available in Federal buildings, each agency ordinarily does its own leasing. As a result, in some cases Federal agencies have contracted for space at high rentals at the very time that other agencies have been giving up surplus low-cost space.

The assignment of space in Government-owned buildings outside of Washington is also divided among a number of agencies. While the Public Buildings Service constructs a large part of the Government buildings, it operates and controls the assignment of space in only a small proportion of them. The Post Office Department operates and allocates the space in post-office buildings, several hundred of which contain substantial amounts of office space available for other agencies. During and immediately after the war several other Federal agencies acquired office buildings in the field. As their activities have contracted, surplus space in many of these structures has become available for other uses.

This plan concentrates in the General Services Administration the responsibility for the leasing and assignment of what is termed general-purpose building space; that is, space which is suitable for the uses of a number of Federal agencies. It specifically excludes space in buildings at military posts, arsenals, navy yards, and similar defense installations and space in hospitals, laboratories, factories, and other special-purpose buildings.

Also, the plan excludes the Post Office Department from the transfer of leasing authority since the Department has a highly developed organization for this purpose, and it limits the transfer of space assignment authority in post-office buildings to the space not occupied by the Department. Further, it gives the needs of the Post Office Department priority in the assignment of space in post-office buildings. Thus, the plan amply safeguards the interests of the Post Office Department while making it possible to include the general office space in post-office buildings in any given city with other similar space under Federal control in planning and executing an efficient program for housing Government agencies in that area.

In addition, the plan transfers to the General Services Administration the operation, maintenance, and custody of office buildings owned or leased by the Government, including those post-office buildings which are not used predominantly for post-office purposes. This will make it possible to establish a single organization for the operation and maintenance of Government office buildings in principal cities in the field as has proved desirable in the National Capital. Since many post offices are in fact primarily large office buildings, the plan includes in this transfer the post-office buildings which are not used predominantly for post-office purposes. This will relieve the Post Office Department of a considerable expenditure for building operation and maintenance which properly should not be charged against postal revenues.

While the plan effects a broad transfer of functions with respect to leasing and assignment of space and the operation and maintenance of office buildings, it specifically authorizes the Administrator of General Services to delegate the performance of any part of these functions to other agencies subject to such regulations as he deems desirable for economical and effective administration. In this the plan follows the pattern adopted by the Federal Property and Administrative Services Act of 1949 for other branches of property management. In large urban centers where numerous Federal units are located unified administration of space activities by the General Services Administration will normally be advantageous. On the other hand, in the smaller communities it will no doubt be desirable to delegate the work back to the agencies directly affected, to be carried on under standards laid down by the Administrator of General Services. The plan provides ample flexibility for working out the most effective administrative arrangement for each type of situation.

The fundamental soundness and economy of centralized administration of building space have been amply demonstrated in the National Capital. By virtue of unified control it has been possible since the war to accomplish far-reaching changes which have consolidated agencies in much fewer locations, released many of the rented buildings, and greatly reduced the cost of housing the Government establishment. Similar procedures applied in the larger centers of field activity should produce substantial savings.

After investigation, I have found, and hereby declare, that each reorganization contained in this plan is necessary to accomplish one or more of the purposes set forth in section 2(a) of the Reorganization Act of 1949.

While it is not possible at this time to calculate the reduction in expenditures which will result from this plan, it can safely be predicted that it will produce substantial savings. I am confident that this reorganization plan will constitute a significant improvement in Federal business practice and will bring about an important increase in efficiency in housing Government agencies.

HARRY S TRUMAN.

§302. ADMINISTRATOR AND DEPUTY ADMINISTRATOR

(a) ADMINISTRATOR.—The Administrator of General Services is the head of the

General Services Administration. The Administrator is appointed by the President with the advice and consent of the Senate. The Administrator shall perform functions subject to the direction and control of the President.

(b) DEPUTY ADMINISTRATOR.—The Administrator shall appoint a Deputy Administrator of General Services. The Deputy Administrator shall perform functions designated by the Administrator. The Deputy Administrator is Acting Administrator of General Services during the absence or disability of the Administrator and, unless the President designates another officer of the Federal Government, when the office of Administrator is vacant.

(Pub. L. 107–217, Aug. 21, 2002, 116 Stat. 1072.)

§303. FEDERAL ACQUISITION SERVICE

(a) ESTABLISHMENT.—There is established in the General Services Administration a Federal Acquisition Service. The Administrator of General Services shall appoint a Commissioner of the Federal Acquisition Service, who shall be the head of the Federal Acquisition Service.

(b) FUNCTIONS.—Subject to the direction and control of the Administrator of General Services, the Commissioner of the Federal Acquisition Service shall be responsible for carrying out functions related to the uses for which the Acquisition Services Fund is authorized under section 321 of this title, including any functions that were carried out by the entities known as the Federal Supply Service and the Federal Technology Service and such other related functions as the Administrator considers appropriate.

(c) REGIONAL EXECUTIVES.—The Administrator may appoint Regional Executives in the Federal Acquisition Service, to carry out such functions within the Federal Acquisition Service as the Administrator considers appropriate.

(Pub. L. 107–217, Aug. 21, 2002, 116 Stat. 1072; Pub. L. 109–313, §2(a)(1), Oct. 6, 2006, 120 Stat. 1734.)

§304. FEDERAL INFORMATION CENTERS

The Administrator of General Services may establish within the General Services Administration a nationwide network of federal information centers for the purpose of providing the public with information about the programs and procedures of the Federal Government and for other appropriate and related purposes.

(Pub. L. 107–217, Aug. 21, 2002, 116 Stat. 1072.)

§305. ELECTRONIC GOVERNMENT AND INFORMATION TECHNOLOGIES

The Administrator of General Services shall consult with the Administrator of the Office of Electronic Government on programs undertaken by the General Services Administration to promote electronic Government and the efficient use of information technologies by Federal agencies.

(Added Pub. L. 107–347, title I, §102(a)(1), Dec. 17, 2002, 116 Stat. 2910.)

SUBCHAPTER II—ADMINISTRATIVE

§311. PERSONNEL

(a) APPOINTMENT AND COMPENSATION.—The Administrator of General Services,

§312. Repealed. Pub. L. 111–8, div. D, title V,
518(c)(1), Mar. 11, 2009, 123 Stat. 665]

CHAPTER 3—ORGANIZATION OF
GENERAL SERVICES ADMINISTRATION

subject to chapters 33 and 51 and subchapter III of chapter 53 of title 5, may appoint and fix the compensation of personnel necessary to carry out chapters 1, 3, and 5 of this title and division C (except sections 3302, 3501(b), 3509, 3906, 4710, and 4711) of subtitle I of title 41.

(b) TEMPORARY EMPLOYMENT.—The Administrator may procure the temporary or intermittent services of experts or consultants under section 3109 of title 5 to the extent the Administrator finds necessary to carry out chapters 1, 3, and 5 of this title and division C (except sections 3302, 3501(b), 3509, 3906, 4710, and 4711) of subtitle I of title 41.

(c) PERSONNEL FROM OTHER AGENCIES.—Notwithstanding section 973 of title 10 or any other law, in carrying out functions under this subtitle the Administrator may use the services of personnel (including armed services personnel) from an executive agency other than the General Services Administration with the consent of the head of the agency.

(d) DETAIL OF FIELD PERSONNEL TO DISTRICT OF COLUMBIA.—The Administrator, in the Administrator's discretion, may detail field personnel of the Administration to the District of Columbia for temporary duty for a period of not more than 30 days in any one case. Subsistence or similar expenses may not be allowed for an employee on temporary duty in the District of Columbia under this paragraph.

(Pub. L. 107–217, Aug. 21, 2002, 116 Stat. 1072; Pub. L. 111–350, §5(l)(5), Jan. 4, 2011, 124 Stat. 3851.)

[§312. REPEALED. PUB. L. 111–8, DIV. D, TITLE V, §518(C)(1), MAR. 11, 2009, 123 STAT. 665]

Section, Pub. L. 107–217, Aug. 21, 2002, 116 Stat. 1073, related to transfer and use of amounts for major equipment acquisitions.

§313. TESTS OF MATERIALS

(a) SCOPE.—This section applies to any article or commodity tendered by a producer or vendor for sale or lease to the General Services Administration or to any procurement authority acting under the direction and control of the Administrator of General Services pursuant to this subtitle.

(b) AUTHORITY TO CONDUCT TESTS.—The Administrator, in the Administrator's discretion and with the consent of the producer or vendor, may have tests conducted, in a manner the Administrator specifies, to—

(1) determine whether an article or commodity conforms to prescribed specifications and standards; or

(2) aid in the development of specifications and standards.

(c) FEES.—

(1) IN GENERAL.—The Administrator shall charge the producer or vendor a fee for the tests.

(2) AMOUNT OF FEE IF TESTS PREDOMINANTLY SERVE INTEREST OF PRODUCER OR VENDOR.—If the Administrator determines that conducting the tests predominantly serves the interest of the producer or vendor, the Administrator shall fix the fee in an amount that will recover the costs of conducting the tests, including all components of the costs, determined in accordance with accepted accounting principles.

(3) AMOUNT OF FEE IF TESTS DO NOT PREDOMINANTLY SERVE INTEREST OF PRODUCER OR VENDOR.—If the Administrator determines that conducting the tests does not predominantly serve the interest of the producer or vendor, the Administrator shall fix the fee in an amount the Administrator determines is reasonable for furnishing the testing service.

(Pub. L. 107–217, Aug. 21, 2002, 116 Stat. 1073.)

SUBCHAPTER III—FUNDS

§321. ACQUISITION SERVICES FUND

(a) EXISTENCE.—The Acquisition Services Fund is a special fund in the Treasury.

(b) COMPOSITION.—

(1) IN GENERAL.—The Fund is composed of amounts authorized to be transferred to the Fund or otherwise made available to the Fund.

(2) OTHER CREDITS.—The Fund shall be credited with all reimbursements, advances, and refunds or recoveries relating to personal property or services procured through the Fund, including—

(A) the net proceeds of disposal of surplus personal property; and

(B) receipts from carriers and others for loss of, or damage to, personal property; and

(C) receipts from agencies charged fees pursuant to rates established by the Administrator.

(3) COST AND CAPITAL REQUIREMENTS.—The Administrator shall determine the cost and capital requirements of the Fund for each fiscal year and shall develop a plan concerning such requirements in consultation with the Chief Financial Officer of the General Services Administration. Any change to the cost and capital requirements of the Fund for a fiscal year shall be approved by the Administrator. The Administrator shall establish rates to be charged agencies provided, or to be provided, supply of personal property and non-personal services through the Fund, in accordance with the plan.

(4) DEPOSIT OF FEES.—Fees collected by the Administrator under section 313 of this title may be deposited in the Fund to be used for the purposes of the Fund.

(c) USES.—

(1) IN GENERAL.—The Fund is available for use by or under the direction and control of the Administrator for—

(A) procuring, for the use of federal agencies in the proper discharge of their responsibilities—

(i) personal property (including the purchase from or through the Director of the Government Publishing Office, for warehouse issue, of standard forms, blankbook work, standard specifications, and other printed material in common use by federal agencies and not available through the Superintendent of Documents);

(ii) nonpersonal services; and

(iii) personal services related to the provision of information technology (as defined in section 11101(6) of this title);

(B) paying the purchase price, cost of transportation of personal property and services, and cost of personal services employed directly in the repair, rehabilitation, and conversion of personal property; and

(C) paying other direct costs of, and indirect costs that are reasonably related to, contracting, procurement, inspection, storage, management, distribution, and accountability of property and nonpersonal services provided by the General Services Administration or by special order through the Administration.

(2) OTHER USES.—The Fund may be used for the procurement of personal property and nonpersonal services authorized to be acquired by—

(A) mixed-ownership Government corporations;

(B) the municipal government of the District of Columbia; or

(C) a requisitioning non-federal agency when the function of a federal agency authorized to procure for it is transferred to the Administration.

(d) PAYMENT FOR PROPERTY AND SERVICES.—

(1) IN GENERAL.—For property or services procured through the Fund for requisitioning agencies, the agencies shall pay prices the Administrator fixes under this subsection.

(2) PRICES FIXED BY ADMINISTRATOR.—The Administrator shall fix prices at levels sufficient to recover—

(A) so far as practicable—

(i) the purchase price;

(ii) the transportation cost;

(iii) inventory losses;

(iv) the cost of personal services employed directly in the repair, rehabilitation, and conversion of personal property;

(v) the cost of personal services employed directly in providing information technology (as defined in section 11101(6) of this title); and

(vi) the cost of amortization and repair of equipment used for lease or rent to executive agencies; and

(B) properly allocable costs payable by the Fund under subsection (c)(1)(C).

(3) TIMING OF PAYMENTS.—

(A) PAYMENT IN ADVANCE.—A requisitioning agency shall pay in advance when the Administrator determines that there is insufficient capital otherwise available in the Fund. Payment in advance may also be made under an agreement between a requisitioning agency and the Administrator.

(B) PROMPT REIMBURSEMENT.—If payment is not made in advance, the Administration shall be reimbursed promptly out of amounts of the requisitioning agency in accordance with accounting procedures approved by the Comptroller General.

(C) FAILURE TO MAKE PROMPT REIMBURSEMENT.—The Administrator may obtain reimbursement by the issuance of transfer and counterwarrants, or other lawful transfer documents, supported by itemized invoices, if payment is not made by a requisitioning agency within 45 days after the later of—

(i) the date of billing by the Administrator; or

(ii) the date on which actual liability for personal property or services is incurred by the Administrator.

(e) REIMBURSEMENT FOR EQUIPMENT PURCHASED FOR CONGRESS.—The Administrator may accept periodic reimbursement from the Senate and from the House of Representatives for the cost of any equipment purchased for the Senate or the House of Representatives with money from the Fund. The amount of each periodic reimbursement shall be computed by amortizing the total cost of each item of equipment over the useful life of the equipment, as determined by the Administrator, in consultation with the Sergeant at Arms and Doorkeeper of the Senate or the Chief Administrative Officer of the House of Representatives, as appropriate.

(f) TRANSFER OF UNCOMMITTED BALANCES.—Following the close of each fiscal year, after making provision for a sufficient level of inventory of personal property to meet the needs of Federal agencies, the replacement cost of motor vehicles, and other anticipated operating needs reflected in the cost and capital plan developed under subsection (b), the uncommitted balance of any funds remaining in the Fund shall be transferred to the general fund of the Treasury as miscellaneous receipts.

(g) AUDITS.—The Comptroller General shall audit the Fund in accordance with the provisions of chapter 35 of title 31 and report the results of the audits.

(h) [1] REQUIREMENT FOR ANNUAL REPORT TO CONGRESS.—Not later than September 30 of each year, the Administrator shall submit to the Committee on Oversight and Accountability of the House of Representatives and the Committee on Homeland Security and Governmental Affairs of the Senate a report that includes, at a minimum, a list of each program within the Technology Transformation Services funded by expenditures during the previous fiscal year, or that have been funded by expenditures in the previous 5-year period, including the following:

(1) An explanation of the program.

(2) Information about how the program is funded, including the amount of expenditures the program received in the previous fiscal year and total amount.

(3) The amount of reimbursements associated with or anticipated to be associated with the program from another source of funds or another agency, if applicable.

(4) A description of projects or initiatives associated with the program, including—

(A) information about when the projects or initiatives were initiated and completed; and

(B) funding information, to the extent practicable.

(5) Any additional information, data, or analysis used to determine the information estimated within the report, if applicable.

(i) [1] DEFINITIONS.—In this section:

(1) ADMINISTRATOR.—The term "Administrator" means the Administrator of General Services.

(2) EXPENDITURE.—The term "expenditure" means any obligation of funds from the Acquisition Services Fund for programs referenced in subsection (h).

(Pub. L. 107–217, Aug. 21, 2002, 116 Stat. 1074; Pub. L. 109–313, §3(d)–(g), (h)(2), Oct. 6, 2006, 120 Stat. 1735, 1736; Pub. L. 113–235, div. H, title I, §1301(d), Dec. 16, 2014, 128 Stat. 2537; Pub. L. 118–182, §2(b), Dec. 23, 2024, 138 Stat. 2624.)

[1] *See Delayed Effective Date of Amendment note below.*

§322. Repealed. Pub. L. 109–313, §3(h)(1), Oct. 2006, 120 Stat. 1736]

CHAPTER 3—ORGANIZATION OF
GENERAL SERVICES ADMINISTRATION

[§322. REPEALED. PUB. L. 109–313, §3(H)(1), OCT. 6, 2006, 120 STAT. 1736]

Section, Pub. L. 107–217, Aug. 21, 2002, 116 Stat. 1076, related to an Information Technology Fund in the Treasury.

§323. CONSUMER INFORMATION CENTER FUND [1]

(a) EXISTENCE.—There is in the Treasury a Federal Citizen Services Fund, General Services Administration, for the purpose of disseminating Federal Government information to the public and for other related purposes.

(b) DEPOSITS.—Money shall be deposited into the Fund from—

(1) appropriations from the Treasury for Federal Citizen Services activities;

(2) user fees from the public;

(3) reimbursements from other federal agencies for costs of distributing publications; and

(4) any other income incident to Center [2] activities.

(c) EXPENDITURES.—Money deposited into the Fund is available for expenditure for Center [2] activities in amounts specified in appropriation laws. The Fund shall assume all liabilities, obligations, and commitments of the Center [2] account.

(d) UNOBLIGATED BALANCES.—Any unobligated balances at the end of a fiscal year remain in the Fund and are available for authorization in appropriation laws for subsequent fiscal years.

(e) GIFT ACCOUNT.—The Center [2] may accept and deposit to this account gifts for purposes of defraying the costs of printing, publishing, and distributing consumer information and educational materials and undertaking other consumer information activities. In addition to amounts appropriated or otherwise made available, the Center [2] may expend the gifts for these purposes and any balance remains available for expenditure.

(f) The Administrator may enter into agreements with federal agencies to provide services through the Fund on a fully reimbursable basis.

(Pub. L. 107–217, Aug. 21, 2002, 116 Stat. 1077; Pub. L. 111–8, div. D, title V, §516, Mar. 11, 2009, 123 Stat. 664; Pub. L. 117–103, div. E, title V, §527, Mar. 15, 2022, 136 Stat. 276; Pub. L. 118–182, §2(a), Dec. 23, 2024, 138 Stat. 2623.)

[1] So in original. Probably should be "Federal Citizen Services Fund".

[2] So in original. See 2009 Amendment notes below.

CHAPTER 5—PROPERTY MANAGEMENT

SUBCHAPTER I—PROCUREMENT AND WAREHOUSING

SUBCHAPTER I—PROCUREMENT AND WAREHOUSING

§501. SERVICES FOR EXECUTIVE AGENCIES

(a) AUTHORITY OF ADMINISTRATOR OF GENERAL SERVICES.—

(1) IN GENERAL.—The Administrator of General Services shall take action under this subchapter for an executive agency—

(A) to the extent that the Administrator of General Services determines that the action is advantageous to the Federal Government in terms of economy, efficiency, or service; and

(B) with due regard to the program activities of the agency.

(2) EXEMPTION FOR DEFENSE.—The Secretary of Defense may exempt the Department of Defense from an action taken by the Administrator of General Services under this subchapter, unless the President directs otherwise, whenever the Secretary determines that an exemption is in the best interests of national security.

(b) PROCUREMENT AND SUPPLY.—

(1) FUNCTIONS.—

(A) IN GENERAL.—The Administrator of General Services shall procure and supply personal property and nonpersonal services for executive agencies to use in the proper discharge of their responsibilities, and perform functions related to procurement and supply including contracting, inspection, storage, issue, property identification and classification, transportation and traffic management, management of public utility services, and repairing and converting.

(B) PUBLIC UTILITY CONTRACTS.—A contract for public utility services may be made for a period of not more than 10 years.

(2) POLICIES AND METHODS.—

(A) IN GENERAL.—The Administrator of General Services shall prescribe policies and methods for executive agencies regarding the procurement and supply of personal property and nonpersonal services and related functions.

(B) CONTROLLING REGULATION.—Policies and methods prescribed by the Administrator of General Services under this paragraph are subject to regulations prescribed by the Administrator for Federal Procurement Policy under division B (except sections 1704 and 2303) of subtitle I of title 41.

(c) REPRESENTATION.—(1) For transportation and other public utility services used by executive agencies, the Administrator of General Services shall represent the agencies—

(A) in negotiations with carriers and other public utilities; and

(B) in proceedings involving carriers or other public utilities before federal and state regulatory bodies.

(2) Prior to representing any installation of the Department of Defense in any proceeding under this subsection, the Administrator or any persons or entities acting on behalf of the Administrator shall—

(A) notify the senior mission commander of the installation; and

(B) solicit and represent the interests of the installation as determined by the installation's senior mission commander.

(d) FACILITIES.—The Administrator of General Services shall operate, for executive agencies, warehouses, supply centers, repair shops, fuel yards, and other similar facilities. After consultation with the executive agencies affected, the Administrator of General Services shall consolidate, take over, or arrange for executive agencies to operate the facilities.

(Pub. L. 107–217, Aug. 21, 2002, 116 Stat. 1079; Pub. L. 111–350, §5(l)(6), Jan. 4, 2011, 124 Stat. 3851; Pub. L. 115–232, div. B, title XXVIII, §2826, Aug. 13, 2018, 132 Stat. 2270.)

§502. SERVICES FOR OTHER ENTITIES

(a) FEDERAL AGENCIES, MIXED-OWNERSHIP GOVERNMENT CORPORATIONS, AND THE DISTRICT OF COLUMBIA.—On request, the Administrator of General Services shall provide, to the extent practicable, any of the services specified in section 501 of this title to—

(1) a federal agency;

(2) a mixed-ownership Government corporation (as defined in section 9101 of title 31); or

(3) the District of Columbia.

(b) QUALIFIED NONPROFIT AGENCIES.—

(1) IN GENERAL.—On request, the Administrator may provide, to the extent practicable, any of the services specified in section 501 of this title to an agency that is—

(A)(i) a qualified nonprofit agency for the blind (as defined in section 8501(7) of title 41); or

(ii) a qualified nonprofit agency for other severely disabled (as defined in section 8501(6) of title 41); and

(B) providing a commodity or service to the Federal Government under chapter 85 of title 41.

(2) USE OF SERVICES.—A nonprofit agency receiving services under this subsection shall use the services directly in making or providing to the Government a commodity or service that has been determined by the Committee for Purchase From People Who Are Blind or Severely Disabled under section 8503 of title 41 to be suitable for procurement by the Government.

(c) USE OF CERTAIN SUPPLY SCHEDULES.—

(1) IN GENERAL.—The Administrator may provide for the use by State or local governments of Federal supply schedules of the General Services Administration for the following:

(A) Automated data processing equipment (including firmware), software, supplies, support equipment, and services (as contained in Federal supply classification code group 70).

(B) Alarm and signal systems, facility management systems, firefighting and rescue equipment, law enforcement and security equipment, marine craft and related equipment, special purpose clothing, and related services (as contained in Federal supply classification code group 84 or any amended or subsequent version of that Federal supply classification group).

(2) VOLUNTARY USE.—In any case of the use by a State or local government of a Federal supply schedule pursuant to paragraph (1), participation by a firm that sells to the Federal Government through the supply schedule shall be voluntary with respect to a sale to the State or local government through such supply schedule.

(3) DEFINITIONS.—In this subsection:

(A) The term "State or local government" includes any State, local, regional, or tribal government, or any instrumentality thereof (including any local educational agency or institution of higher education).

(B) The term "tribal government" means—

(i) the governing body of any Indian tribe, band, nation, or other organized group or community located in the continental United States (excluding the State of Alaska) that is recognized as eligible for the special programs and services provided by the United States to Indians because of their status as Indians, and

(ii) any Alaska Native regional or village corporation established pursuant to the Alaska Native Claims Settlement Act (43 U.S.C. 1601 et seq.).

(C) The term "local educational agency" has the meaning given that term in section 7013 of the Elementary and Secondary Education Act of 1965.

(D) The term "institution of higher education" has the meaning given that term in section 101(a) of the Higher Education Act of 1965 (20 U.S.C. 1001(a)).

(d) USE OF SUPPLY SCHEDULES FOR CERTAIN GOODS AND SERVICES.—

(1) IN GENERAL.—The Administrator may provide for the use by State or local governments of Federal supply schedules of the General Services Administration for goods or services that are to be used to facilitate recovery from a major disaster declared by the President under the Robert T. Stafford Disaster Relief and Emergency Assistance Act (42 U.S.C. 5121 et seq.), to facilitate disaster preparedness or response, or to facilitate recovery from terrorism or nuclear, biological, chemical, or radiological attack.

(2) DETERMINATION BY SECRETARY OF HOMELAND SECURITY.—The Secretary of Homeland Security shall determine which goods and services qualify as goods and services described in paragraph (1) before the Administrator provides for the use of the Federal supply schedule relating to such goods and services.

(3) VOLUNTARY USE.—In the case of the use by a State or local government of a Federal supply schedule pursuant to paragraph (1), participation by a firm that sells to the Federal Government through the supply schedule shall be voluntary with respect to a sale to the State or local government through such supply schedule.

(4) DEFINITIONS.—The definitions in subsection (c)(3) shall apply for purposes of this subsection.

(e) USE OF SUPPLY SCHEDULES BY THE RED CROSS AND OTHER QUALIFIED ORGANIZATIONS.—

(1) IN GENERAL.—The Administrator may provide for the use by the American National Red Cross and other qualified organizations of Federal supply schedules. Purchases under this authority by the American National Red Cross shall be used in furtherance of the purposes of the American National Red Cross set forth in section 300102 of title 36, United States Code. Purchases under this authority by other qualified organizations shall be used in furtherance of purposes determined to be appropriate to facilitate emergency preparedness and disaster relief and set forth in guidance by the Administrator of General Services, in consultation with the Administrator of the Federal Emergency Management Agency.

(2) LIMITATION.—The authority under this subsection may not be used to purchase supplies for resale.

(3) QUALIFIED ORGANIZATION.—In this subsection, the term "qualified organization" means a relief or disaster assistance organization as described in section 309 of the Robert T. Stafford Disaster Relief and Emergency Assistance Act (42 U.S.C. 5152).

(f) DUTY OF USERS REGARDING USE OF SUPPLY SCHEDULES.—All users of Federal supply schedules, including non-Federal users, shall use the schedules in accordance with the ordering guidance provided by the Administrator of General Services.

(Pub. L. 107–217, Aug. 21, 2002, 116 Stat. 1080; Pub. L. 107–347, title II, §211(a), Dec. 17, 2002, 116 Stat. 2939; Pub. L. 109–364, div. A, title VIII, §833(a), Oct. 17, 2006, 120 Stat. 2332; Pub. L. 110–248, §2, June 26, 2008, 122 Stat. 2316; Pub. L. 111–263, §§2–4, Oct. 8, 2010, 124 Stat. 2787, 2788; Pub. L. 111–350, §5(l)(7), Jan. 4, 2011, 124 Stat. 3851; Pub. L. 114–95, title IX, §9215(www), Dec. 10, 2015, 129 Stat. 2191.)

§503. EXCHANGE OR SALE OF SIMILAR ITEMS

(a) AUTHORITY OF EXECUTIVE AGENCIES.—In acquiring personal property, an executive agency may exchange or sell similar items and may apply the exchange allowance or proceeds of sale in whole or in part payment for the property acquired.

(b) Applicable Regulation and Law.—

(1) Regulations prescribed by administrator of general services.—A transaction under subsection (a) must be carried out in accordance with regulations the Administrator of General Services prescribes, subject to regulations prescribed by the Administrator for Federal Procurement Policy under division B (except sections 1704 and 2303) of subtitle I of title 41.

(2) In writing.—A transaction under subsection (a) must be evidenced in writing.

(3) Section 6101(b) to (d) of title 41.—Section 6101(b) to (d) of title 41 applies to a sale of property under subsection (a), except that fixed price sales may be conducted in the same manner and subject to the same conditions as are applicable to the sale of property under section 545(d) of this title.

(Pub. L. 107–217, Aug. 21, 2002, 116 Stat. 1081; Pub. L. 111–350, §5(l)(8), Jan. 4, 2011, 124 Stat. 3851.)

§504. Agency cooperation for inspection

(a) Receiving Assistance.—An executive agency may use the services, work, materials, and equipment of another executive agency, with the consent of the other executive agency, to inspect personal property incident to procuring the property.

(b) Providing Assistance.—Notwithstanding section 1301(a) of title 31 or any other law, an executive agency may provide services, work, materials, and equipment for purposes of this section without reimbursement or transfer of amounts.

(c) Policies and Methods.—The use or provision of services, work, materials, and equipment under this section must be in conformity with policies and methods the Administrator of General Services prescribes under section 501 of this title.

(Pub. L. 107–217, Aug. 21, 2002, 116 Stat. 1081.)

§505. Exchange or transfer of medical supplies

(a) Excess Property Determination.—

(1) In general.—Medical materials or supplies an executive agency holds for national emergency purposes are considered excess property for purposes of subchapter II when the head of the agency determines that—

(A) the remaining storage or shelf life is too short to justify continued retention for national emergency purposes; and

(B) transfer or other disposal is in the national interest.

(2) Timing.—To the greatest extent practicable, the head of the agency shall make the determination in sufficient time to allow for the transfer or other disposal and use of medical materials or supplies before their shelf life expires and they are rendered unfit for human use.

(b) Transfer or Exchange.—

(1) In general.—In accordance with regulations the Administrator of General Services prescribes, medical materials or supplies considered excess property may be transferred to another federal agency or exchanged with another federal agency for other medical materials or supplies.

(2) Use of proceeds.—Any proceeds derived from a transfer under this section

may be credited to the current applicable appropriation or fund of the transferor agency and shall be available only to purchase medical materials or supplies to be held for national emergency purposes.

(3) DISPOSAL AS SURPLUS PROPERTY.—If the materials or supplies are not transferred to or exchanged with another federal agency, they shall be disposed of as surplus property.

(Pub. L. 107–217, Aug. 21, 2002, 116 Stat. 1081.)

§506. INVENTORY CONTROLS AND SYSTEMS

(a) ACTIVITIES OF THE ADMINISTRATOR OF GENERAL SERVICES.—

(1) IN GENERAL.—Subject to paragraph (2), and after adequate advance notice to affected executive agencies, the Administrator of General Services may undertake the following activities as necessary to carry out functions under this chapter:

(A) SURVEYS AND REPORTS.—Survey and obtain executive agency reports on Federal Government property and property management practices.

(B) INVENTORY LEVELS.—Cooperate with executive agencies to establish reasonable inventory levels for property stocked by them, and report any excessive inventory levels to Congress and to the Director of the Office of Management and Budget.

(C) FEDERAL SUPPLY CATALOG SYSTEM.—Establish and maintain a uniform federal supply catalog system that is appropriate to identify and classify personal property under the control of federal agencies.

(D) STANDARD PURCHASE SPECIFICATIONS AND STANDARD FORMS AND PROCEDURES.—Prescribe standard purchase specifications and standard forms and procedures (except forms and procedures that the Comptroller General prescribes by law) subject to regulations the Administrator for Federal Procurement Policy prescribes under division B (except sections 1704 and 2303) of subtitle I of title 41.

(E) CAPITALIZATION THRESHOLDS.—Establish thresholds for acquisitions of personal property for which executive agencies shall capitalize the personal property.

(F) ACCOUNTABILITY THRESHOLDS.—Notwithstanding section 121(b), for the management and accountability of personal property, establish thresholds for acquisitions of personal property for which executive agencies shall establish and maintain property records in a centralized system.

(2) SPECIAL CONSIDERATIONS REGARDING DEPARTMENT OF DEFENSE.—

(A) IN GENERAL.—The Administrator of General Services shall carry out activities under paragraph (1) with due regard to the requirements of the Department of Defense, as determined by the Secretary of Defense.

(B) FEDERAL SUPPLY CATALOG SYSTEM.—In establishing and maintaining a uniform federal supply catalog system under paragraph (1)(C), the Administrator of General Services and the Secretary shall coordinate to avoid unnecessary duplication.

(b) ACTIVITIES OF FEDERAL AGENCIES.—Each federal agency shall use the uniformed federal supply catalog system, the standard purchase specifications, and the standard forms and procedures established under subsection (a), except as the Administrator of General Services, considering efficiency, economy, or other interests of the Government, may otherwise provide.

(c) AUDIT OF PROPERTY ACCOUNTS.—The Comptroller General shall audit all types of property accounts and transactions. Audits shall be conducted at the time and in the manner the Comptroller General decides and as far as practicable at the place where the property or records of the executive agencies are kept. Audits shall include an evaluation of the effectiveness of internal controls and audits, and a general audit of the discharge of accountability for Government-owned or controlled property, based on generally accepted principles of auditing.

(Pub. L. 107–217, Aug. 21, 2002, 116 Stat. 1082; Pub. L. 111–350, §5(l)(9), Jan. 4, 2011, 124 Stat. 3852; Pub. L. 115–419, §2(b), Jan. 3, 2019, 132 Stat. 5443.)

SUBCHAPTER II—USE OF PROPERTY

§521. POLICIES AND METHODS

Subject to section 523 of this title, in order to minimize expenditures for property, the Administrator of General Services shall—

(1) prescribe policies and methods to promote the maximum use of excess property by executive agencies; and

(2) provide for the transfer of excess property—

(A) among federal agencies; and

(B) to the organizations specified in section 321(c)(2) of this title.

(Pub. L. 107–217, Aug. 21, 2002, 116 Stat. 1083.)

§522. REIMBURSEMENT FOR TRANSFER OF EXCESS PROPERTY

(a) IN GENERAL.—Subject to subsections (b) and (c), the Administrator of General Services, with the approval of the Director of the Office of Management and Budget, shall prescribe the amount of reimbursement required for a transfer of excess property.

(b) REIMBURSEMENT AT FAIR VALUE.—The amount of reimbursement required for a transfer of excess property is the fair value of the property, as determined by the Administrator, if—

(1) net proceeds are requested under section 574(a) of this title; or

(2) either the transferor or the transferee agency (or the organizational unit affected) is—

(A) subject to chapter 91 of title 31; or

(B) an organization specified in section 321(c)(2) of this title.

(c) DISTRIBUTION THROUGH GENERAL SERVICES ADMINISTRATION SUPPLY CENTERS.—Excess property determined by the Administrator to be suitable for distribution through the supply centers of the General Services Administration shall be retransferred at prices set by the Administrator with due regard to prices established under section 321(d) of this title.

(Pub. L. 107–217, Aug. 21, 2002, 116 Stat. 1083; Pub. L. 109–284, §6(1), (2), Sept. 27, 2006, 120 Stat. 1212.)

§523. EXCESS REAL PROPERTY LOCATED ON INDIAN RESERVATIONS

(a) PROCEDURES FOR TRANSFER.—The Administrator of General Services shall prescribe procedures necessary to transfer to the Secretary of the Interior, without compensation, excess real property located within the reservation of any group, band, or tribe of Indians that is recognized as eligible for services by the Bureau of Indian Affairs.

(b) PROPERTY HELD IN TRUST.—

(1) IN GENERAL.—Except as provided in paragraph (2), the Secretary shall hold excess real property transferred under this section in trust for the benefit and use of the group, band, or tribe of Indians, within whose reservation the excess real property is located.

(2) SPECIAL REQUIREMENT FOR OKLAHOMA.—The Secretary shall hold excess real property that is located in Oklahoma and transferred under this section in trust for Oklahoma Indian tribes recognized by the Secretary if the real property—

(A) is located within boundaries of former reservations in Oklahoma, as defined by the Secretary, and was held in trust by the Federal Government for an Indian tribe when the Government acquired it; or

(B) is contiguous to real property presently held in trust by the Government for an Oklahoma Indian tribe and was held in trust by the Government for an Indian tribe at any time.

(Pub. L. 107–217, Aug. 21, 2002, 116 Stat. 1083.)

§524. DUTIES OF EXECUTIVE AGENCIES

(a) REQUIRED.—Each executive agency shall—

(1) maintain adequate inventory controls and accountability systems for property under its control;

(2) continuously survey property under its control to identify excess property;

(3) promptly report excess property to the Administrator of General Services;

(4) perform the care and handling of excess property;

(5) transfer or dispose of excess property as promptly as possible in accordance with authority delegated and regulations prescribed by the Administrator;

(6) develop current and future workforce projections so as to have the capacity to assess the needs of the Federal workforce regarding the use of real property;

(7) establish goals and policies that will lead the executive agency to reduce excess property and underutilized property in the inventory of the executive agency;

(8) submit to the Federal Real Property Council an annual report on all excess property that is real property and underutilized property in the inventory of the executive agency, including—

(A) whether underutilized property can be better utilized, including through collocation with other executive agencies or consolidation with other facilities; and

(B) the extent to which the executive agency believes that retention of the underutilized property serves the needs of the executive agency;

(9) adopt workplace practices, configurations, and management techniques that can achieve increased levels of productivity and decrease the need for real property assets;

(10) assess leased space to identify space that is not fully used or occupied;

(11) on an annual basis and subject to the guidance of the Federal Real Property Council—

(A) conduct an inventory of real property under control of the executive agency; and

(B) make an assessment of each property, which shall include—

(i) the age and condition of the property;

(ii) the size of the property in square footage and acreage;

(iii) the geographical location of the property, including an address and description;

(iv) the extent to which the property is being utilized;

(v) the actual annual operating costs associated with the property;

(vi) the total cost of capital expenditures incurred by the Federal Government associated with the property;

(vii) sustainability metrics associated with the property;

(viii) the number of Federal employees and contractor employees and functions housed at the property;

(ix) the extent to which the mission of the executive agency is dependent on the property;

(x) the estimated amount of capital expenditures projected to maintain and operate the property during the 5-year period beginning on the date of enactment of this paragraph; and

(xi) any additional information required by the Administrator of General Services to carry out section 623;

(12) provide to the Federal Real Property Council and the Administrator of General Services the information described in paragraph (11)(B) to be used for the establishment and maintenance of the database described in section 21 of the Federal Assets Sale and Transfer Act of 2016; and

(13) in accordance with guidance from the Administrator of General Services—

(A) on an annual basis, conduct an inventory and assessment of capitalized personal property to identify excess capitalized personal property under its control, including evaluating—

(i) the age and condition of the personal property;

(ii) the extent to which the executive agency utilizes the personal property;

(iii) the extent to which the mission of the executive agency is dependent on the personal property; and

(iv) any other aspect of the personal property that the Administrator determines is useful or necessary for the executive agency to evaluate; and

(B) on a regular basis, conduct an inventory and assessment of accountable personal property under its control, including evaluating—

(i) the age and condition of the personal property;

(ii) the extent to which the executive agency utilizes the personal property;

(iii) the extent to which the mission of the executive agency is dependent on the personal property; and

(iv) any other aspect of the personal property that the Administrator determines is useful or necessary for the executive agency to evaluate.

(b) REQUIRED AS FAR AS PRACTICABLE.—Each executive agency, as far as practicable, shall—

(1) reassign property to another activity within the agency when the property is no longer required for the purposes of the appropriation used to make the purchase;

(2) transfer excess property under its control to other federal agencies and to organizations specified in section 321(c)(2) of this title; and

(3) obtain excess property from other federal agencies.

(c) DEFINITION OF EXECUTIVE AGENCY.—For the purpose of paragraphs (6) through (12) of subsection (a), the term "executive agency" shall have the meaning given the term "Federal agency" in section 621.

(Pub. L. 107–217, Aug. 21, 2002, 116 Stat. 1084; Pub. L. 114–318, §6, Dec. 16, 2016, 130 Stat. 1615; Pub. L. 115–419, §2(a), Jan. 3, 2019, 132 Stat. 5442.)

§525. EXCESS PERSONAL PROPERTY FOR FEDERAL AGENCY GRANTEES

(a) GENERAL PROHIBITION.—A federal agency is prohibited from obtaining excess personal property for the purpose of furnishing the property to a grantee of the agency, except as provided in this section.

(b) EXCEPTION FOR PUBLIC AGENCIES AND TAX-EXEMPT NONPROFIT ORGANIZATIONS.—

(1) IN GENERAL.—Under regulations the Administrator of General Services may prescribe, a federal agency may obtain excess personal property for the purpose of furnishing it to a public agency or an organization that is nonprofit and exempt from taxation under section 501 of the Internal Revenue Code of 1986 (26 U.S.C. 501), if—

(A) the agency or organization is conducting a federally sponsored project pursuant to a grant made for a specific purpose with a specific termination provision;

(B) the property is to be furnished for use in connection with the grant; and

(C)(i) the sponsoring federal agency pays an amount equal to 25 percent of the original acquisition cost (except for costs of care and handling) of the excess property; and

(ii) the amount is deposited in the Treasury as miscellaneous receipts.

(2) TITLE.—Title to excess property obtained under this subsection vests in the grantee. The grantee shall account for and dispose of the property in accordance with procedures governing accountability for personal property acquired under grant agreements.

(c) EXCEPTION FOR CERTAIN PROPERTY FURNISHED BY SECRETARY OF AGRICULTURE.—

(1) DEFINITION.—In this subsection, the term "State" means a State of the United States, Puerto Rico, Guam, American Samoa, the Northern Mariana Islands, the Federated States of Micronesia, the Marshall Islands, Palau, the Virgin Islands, and the District of Columbia.

(2) IN GENERAL.—Under regulations and restrictions the Administrator may prescribe, subsection (a) does not apply to property furnished by the Secretary of Agriculture to—

(A) a state [1] or county extension service engaged in cooperative agricultural extension work under the Smith-Lever Act (7 U.S.C. 341 et seq.);

(B) a state [1] experiment station engaged in cooperative agricultural research work under the Hatch Act of 1887 (7 U.S.C. 361a et seq.); or

(C) an institution engaged in cooperative agricultural research or extension work under section 1433, 1434, 1444, or 1445 of the National Agricultural Research, Extension, and Teaching Policy Act of 1977 (7 U.S.C. 3195, 3196, 3221, or 3222), or the Act of October 10, 1962 (16 U.S.C. 582a et seq.), if the Federal Government retains title.

(d) OTHER EXCEPTIONS.—Under regulations and restrictions the Administrator may prescribe, subsection (a) does not apply to—

(1) property furnished under section 608 of the Foreign Assistance Act of 1961 (22 U.S.C. 2358), to the extent that the Administrator determines that the property is not needed for donation under section 549 of this title;

(2) scientific equipment furnished under section 11(e) of the National Science Foundation Act of 1950 (42 U.S.C. 1870(e));

(3) property furnished under section 203 of the Department of Agriculture Organic Act of 1944 (16 U.S.C. 580a), in connection with the Cooperative Forest Fire Control Program, if the Government retains title; or

(4) property furnished in connection with a grant to a tribe, as defined in section 3(c) of the Indian Financing Act of 1974 (25 U.S.C. 1452(c)).

(Pub. L. 107–217, Aug. 21, 2002, 116 Stat. 1084.)

[1] *So in original. Probably should be capitalized.*

§526. TEMPORARY ASSIGNMENT OF EXCESS REAL PROPERTY

(a) ASSIGNMENT OF SPACE.—The Administrator of General Services may temporarily assign or reassign space in excess real property to a federal agency, for use as office or storage space or for a related purpose, if the Administrator determines that assignment or reassignment is more advantageous than permanent transfer. The Administrator shall determine the duration of the assignment or reassignment.

(b) REIMBURSEMENT FOR MAINTENANCE.—If there is no appropriation available to the Administrator for the expense of maintaining the space, the Administrator may obtain appropriate reimbursement from the federal agency.

(Pub. L. 107–217, Aug. 21, 2002, 116 Stat. 1085.)

§527. ABANDONMENT, DESTRUCTION, OR DONATION OF PROPERTY

The Administrator of General Services may authorize the abandonment or destruction of property, or the donation of property to a public body, if—

(1) the property has no commercial value; or

(2) the estimated cost of continued care and handling exceeds the estimated proceeds from sale.

(Pub. L. 107–217, Aug. 21, 2002, 116 Stat. 1086.)

§528. UTILIZATION OF EXCESS FURNITURE

A department or agency of the Federal Government may not use amounts provided by law to purchase furniture if the Administrator of General Services determines that requirements can reasonably be met by transferring excess furniture, including rehabilitated furniture, from other departments or agencies pursuant to this subtitle.

(Pub. L. 107–217, Aug. 21, 2002, 116 Stat. 1086.)

§529. ANNUAL EXECUTIVE AGENCY REPORTS ON EXCESS PERSONAL PROPERTY

(a) IN GENERAL.—During the calendar quarter following the close of each fiscal year, each executive agency shall submit to the Administrator of General Services and the Committee on Homeland Security and Governmental Affairs of the Senate and the Committee on Oversight and Accountability of the House of Representatives a report on personal property—

    (1) obtained as—

        (A) excess property; or

        (B) personal property determined to be no longer required for the purpose of the appropriation used to make the purchase; and

    (2) furnished within the United States to a recipient other than a federal agency.

(b) REQUIRED INFORMATION.—The report must set out the categories of equipment and show—

    (1) the acquisition cost of the property;

    (2) the recipient of the property; and

    (3) other information the Administrator may require.

(c) COMPILATION OF DATA.—Not later than 180 days following the close of a fiscal year, the Administrator shall compile the data in the reports submitted under subsection (a) and submit to the Committee on Homeland Security [1] Governmental Affairs of the Senate and the Committee on Oversight and Accountability of the House of Representatives and publish on a centralized online website a publicly available report, which shall include—

    (1) the complete data provided in each report in a user-friendly format;

    (2) a summary of the findings of each report, including the aggregate dollar amount of personal property determined to be no longer required for the purpose of the appropriation used to make the purchase; and

    (3) any other recommendations from the Administrator.

(Pub. L. 107–217, Aug. 21, 2002, 116 Stat. 1086; Pub. L. 118–99, §2(a)(1), (e)(1), Oct. 1, 2024, 138 Stat. 1578, 1579.)

----

[1] *So in original. The word "and" probably should appear.*

§530. INTERNAL GUIDANCE ON EXCESS PERSONAL PROPERTY

(a) INITIAL REPORT.—Not later than 180 days after the date of enactment of this section, each executive agency shall submit to the Administrator of General Services and make publicly available on the website of the executive agency the internal guidance of the executive agency on considering using excess personal property to meet the needs of the executive agency, which shall include—

    (1) a requirement to consider excess personal property before buying new;

    (2) when it is practicable to check for and obtain excess personal property;

    (3) how to evaluate the suitability of excess personal property for use; and

    (4) defined roles and responsibilities relevant to considering the use of excess personal property, including the designation of an employee as responsible for searching through available excess personal property for items that meet the needs of

the executive agency.

(b) UPDATES.—Each executive agency shall submit to the Administrator of General Services and update on the website of the executive agency any changes to the internal guidance submitted and made available under subsection (a).

(Pub. L. 118–99, §2(a)(2), (e)(2), Oct. 1, 2024, 138 Stat. 1578, 1579.)

SUBCHAPTER III—DISPOSING OF PROPERTY

§541. SUPERVISION AND DIRECTION

Except as otherwise provided in this subchapter, the Administrator of General Services shall supervise and direct the disposition of surplus property in accordance with this subtitle.

(Pub. L. 107–217, Aug. 21, 2002, 116 Stat. 1086.)

§542. CARE AND HANDLING

The disposal of surplus property, and the care and handling of the property pending disposition, may be performed by the General Services Administration or, when the Administrator of General Services decides, by the executive agency in possession of the property or by any other executive agency that agrees.

(Pub. L. 107–217, Aug. 21, 2002, 116 Stat. 1086.)

§543. METHOD OF DISPOSITION

An executive agency designated or authorized by the Administrator of General Services to dispose of surplus property may do so by sale, exchange, lease, permit, or transfer, for cash, credit, or other property, with or without warranty, on terms and conditions that the Administrator considers proper. The agency may execute documents to transfer title or other interest in the property and may take other action it considers necessary or proper to dispose of the property under this chapter.

(Pub. L. 107–217, Aug. 21, 2002, 116 Stat. 1086.)

§544. VALIDITY OF TRANSFER INSTRUMENTS

A deed, bill of sale, lease, or other instrument executed by or on behalf of an executive agency purporting to transfer title or other interest in surplus property under this chapter is conclusive evidence of compliance with the provisions of this chapter concerning title or other interest of a bona fide grantee or transferee for value and without notice of lack of compliance.

(Pub. L. 107–217, Aug. 21, 2002, 116 Stat. 1087.)

§545. PROCEDURE FOR DISPOSAL

(a) PUBLIC ADVERTISING FOR BIDS.—

(1) REQUIREMENT.—

(A) IN GENERAL.—Except as provided in subparagraph (B), the Administrator of General Services may make or authorize a disposal or a contract for disposal of surplus property only after public advertising for bids, under regulations the Administrator prescribes.

(B) EXCEPTIONS.—This subsection does not apply to disposal or a contract for disposal of surplus property—

(i) under subsection (b) or (d); or

(ii) by abandonment, destruction, or donation or through a contract broker.

(2) TIME, METHOD, AND TERMS.—The time, method, and terms and conditions of advertisement must permit full and free competition consistent with the value and nature of the property involved.

(3) PUBLIC DISCLOSURE.—Bids must be publicly disclosed at the time and place stated in the advertisement.

(4) AWARDS.—An award shall be made with reasonable promptness by notice to the responsible bidder whose bid, conforming to the invitation for bids, is most advantageous to the Federal Government, price and other factors considered. However, all bids may be rejected if it is in the public interest to do so.

(b) NEGOTIATED DISPOSAL.—Under regulations the Administrator prescribes, disposals and contracts for disposal may be negotiated without regard to subsection (a), but subject to obtaining competition that is feasible under the circumstances, if—

(1) necessary in the public interest—

(A) during the period of a national emergency declared by the President or Congress, with respect to a particular lot of personal property; or

(B) for a period not exceeding three months, with respect to a specifically described category of personal property as determined by the Administrator;

(2) the public health, safety, or national security will be promoted by a particular disposal of personal property;

(3) public exigency will not allow delay incident to advertising certain personal property;

(4) the nature and quantity of personal property involved are such that disposal under subsection (a) would impact an industry to an extent that would adversely affect the national economy, and the estimated fair market value of the property and other satisfactory terms of disposal can be obtained by negotiation;

(5) the estimated fair market value of the property involved does not exceed $15,000;

(6) after advertising under subsection (a), the bid prices for the property, or part of the property, are not reasonable or have not been independently arrived at in open competition;

(7) with respect to real property, the character or condition of the property or unusual circumstances make it impractical to advertise publicly for competitive bids and the fair market value of the property and other satisfactory terms of disposal can be obtained by negotiation;

(8) the disposal will be to a State, territory, or possession of the United States, or to a political subdivision of, or a tax-supported agency in, a State, territory, or possession, and the estimated fair market value of the property and other satisfactory terms of disposal are obtained by negotiation; or

(9) otherwise authorized by law.

(c) DISPOSAL THROUGH CONTRACT BROKERS.—Disposals and contracts for disposal of surplus real and related personal property through contract realty brokers employed by the Administrator shall be made in the manner followed in similar commercial transactions under regulations the Administrator prescribes. The regulations must require that brokers give wide public notice of the availability of the property for disposal.

(d) NEGOTIATED SALE AT FIXED PRICE.—

(1) AUTHORIZATION.—The Administrator may make a negotiated sale of personal property at a fixed price, either directly or through the use of a disposal contractor, without regard to subsection (a). However, the sale must be publicized to an extent consistent with the value and nature of the property involved and the price established must reflect the estimated fair market value of the property. Sales under this subsection are limited to categories of personal property for which the Administrator determines that disposal under this subsection best serves the interests of the Government.

(2) FIRST OFFER.—Under regulations and restrictions the Administrator prescribes, an opportunity to purchase property at a fixed price under this subsection may be offered first to an entity specified in subsection (b)(8) that has expressed an interest in the property.

(e) EXPLANATORY STATEMENTS FOR NEGOTIATED DISPOSALS.—

(1) REQUIREMENT.—

(A) IN GENERAL.—Except as provided in subparagraph (B), an explanatory statement of the circumstances shall be prepared for each disposal by negotiation of—

(i) personal property that has an estimated fair market value in excess of $15,000;

(ii) real property that has an estimated fair market value in excess of $100,000, except that real property disposed of by lease or exchange is subject only to clauses (iii)–(v) of this subparagraph;

(iii) real property disposed of by lease for a term of not more than 5 years, if the estimated fair annual rent is more than $100,000 for any year;

(iv) real property disposed of by lease for a term of more than 5 years, if the total estimated rent over the term of the lease is more than $100,000; or

(v) real property or real and related personal property disposed of by exchange, regardless of value, or any property for which any part of the consideration is real property.

(B) EXCEPTION.—An explanatory statement is not required for a disposal of personal property under subsection (d), or for a disposal of real or personal property authorized by any other law to be made without advertising.

(2) TRANSMITTAL TO CONGRESS.—The explanatory statement shall be transmitted to the appropriate committees of Congress in advance of the disposal, and a copy of the statement shall be preserved in the files of the executive agency making the disposal.

(3) LISTING IN REPORT.—A report of the Administrator under section 126 of this title must include a listing and description of any negotiated disposals of surplus property having an estimated fair market value of more than $15,000, in the case of real property, or $5,000, in the case of any other property, other than disposals for which an explanatory statement has been transmitted under this subsection.

(f) APPLICABILITY OF OTHER LAW.—Section 6101(b)–(d) of title 41 does not apply to a disposal or contract for disposal made under this section.

(Pub. L. 107–217, Aug. 21, 2002, 116 Stat. 1087; Pub. L. 111–350, §5(l)(10), Jan. 4, 2011, 124 Stat. 3852.)

§546. CONTRACTOR INVENTORIES

Subject to regulations of the Administrator of General Services, an executive agency may authorize a contractor or subcontractor with the agency to retain or dispose of contractor inventory.

(Pub. L. 107–217, Aug. 21, 2002, 116 Stat. 1089.)

§547. AGRICULTURAL COMMODITIES, FOODS, AND COTTON OR WOOLEN GOODS

(a) POLICIES.—The Administrator of General Services shall consult with the Secretary of Agriculture to formulate policies for the disposal of surplus agricultural commodities, surplus foods processed from agricultural commodities, and surplus cotton or woolen goods. The policies shall be formulated to prevent surplus agricultural commodities, or surplus foods processed from agricultural commodities, from being dumped on the market in a disorderly manner and disrupting the market prices for agricultural commodities.

(b) TRANSFERS TO DEPARTMENT OF AGRICULTURE.—

(1) IN GENERAL.—The Administrator shall transfer without charge to the Department of Agriculture any surplus agricultural commodities, foods, and cotton or woolen goods for disposal, when the Secretary determines that a transfer is necessary for the Secretary to carry out responsibilities for price support or stabilization.

(2) DEPOSIT OF RECEIPTS.—Receipts resulting from disposal by the Department under this subsection shall be deposited pursuant to any authority available to the Secretary. When applicable, however, net proceeds from the sale of surplus property transferred under this subsection shall be credited pursuant to section 572(a) of this title.

(3) LIMITATION OF SALES.—Surplus farm commodities transferred under this subsection may not be sold, other than for export, in quantities exceeding, or at prices less than, the applicable quantities and prices for sales of those commodities by the Commodity Credit Corporation.

(Pub. L. 107–217, Aug. 21, 2002, 116 Stat. 1089.)

§548. SURPLUS VESSELS

The Maritime Administration shall dispose of surplus vessels of 1,500 gross tons or more which the Administration determines to be merchant vessels or capable of conversion to merchant use. The vessels shall be disposed of in accordance with part F of subtitle V of title 46 and other laws authorizing the sale of such vessels.

(Pub. L. 107–217, Aug. 21, 2002, 116 Stat. 1090; Pub. L. 109–304, §17(g)(1), Oct. 6, 2006, 120 Stat. 1708.)

§549. DONATION OF PERSONAL PROPERTY THROUGH STATE AGENCIES

(a) DEFINITIONS.—In this section, the following definitions apply:

(1) PUBLIC AGENCY.—The term "public agency" means—

(A) a State;

(B) a political subdivision of a State (including a unit of local government or economic development district);

(C) a department, agency, or instrumentality of a State (including instrumentalities created by compact or other agreement between States or political subdivisions); or

(D) an Indian tribe, band, group, pueblo, or community located on a state reservation.

(2) STATE.—The term "State" means a State of the United States, the District of Columbia, Puerto Rico, the Virgin Islands, Guam, the Northern Mariana Islands, and American Samoa.

(3) STATE AGENCY.—The term "state agency" means an agency designated under state law as the agency responsible for fair and equitable distribution, through donation, of property transferred under this section.

(b) AUTHORIZATION.—

(1) IN GENERAL.—The Administrator of General Services, in the Administrator's discretion and under regulations the Administrator may prescribe, may transfer property described in paragraph (2) to a state agency.

(2) PROPERTY.—

(A) IN GENERAL.—Property referred to in paragraph (1) is any personal property that—

(i) is under the control of an executive agency; and

(ii) has been determined to be surplus property.

(B) SPECIAL RULE.—In determining whether the property is to be transferred for donation under this section, no distinction may be made between property capitalized in a working-capital fund established under section 2208 of title 10 (or similar fund) and any other property.

(3) NO COST.—Transfer of property under this section is without cost, except for any costs of care and handling.

(c) ALLOCATION AND TRANSFER OF PROPERTY.—

(1) IN GENERAL.—The Administrator shall allocate and transfer property under this section in accordance with criteria that are based on need and use and that are established after consultation with state agencies to the extent feasible. The Administrator shall give fair consideration, consistent with the established criteria, to an expression of need and interest from a public agency or other eligible institution within a State. The Administrator shall give special consideration to an eligible recipient's request, transmitted through the state agency, for a specific item of property.

(2) ALLOCATION AMONG STATES.—The Administrator shall allocate property among the States on a fair and equitable basis, taking into account the condition of the property as well as the original acquisition cost of the property.

(3) RECIPIENTS AND PURPOSES.—The Administrator shall transfer to a state agency property the state agency selects for distribution through donation within the State—

(A) to a public agency for use in carrying out or promoting, for residents of a given political area, a public purpose, including conservation, economic development, education, parks and recreation, public health, and public safety;

(B) for purposes of education or public health (including research), to a nonprofit educational or public health institution or organization that is exempt from taxation under section 501 of the Internal Revenue Code of 1986 (26 U.S.C. 501), including—

(i) a medical institution, hospital, clinic, health center, or drug abuse treatment center;

(ii) a provider of assistance to homeless individuals or to families or individuals whose annual incomes are below the poverty line (as that term is defined in section 673 of the Community Services Block Grant Act (42 U.S.C. 9902));

(iii) a school, college, or university;

(iv) a school for the mentally retarded or physically handicapped;

(v) a child care center;

(vi) a radio or television station licensed by the Federal Communications Commission as an educational radio or educational television station;

(vii) a museum attended by the public, and, for purposes of determining whether a museum is attended by the public, the Administrator shall consider a museum to be public if the nonprofit educational or public health institution or organization, at minimum, accedes to any request submitted for access during business hours;

(viii) a library serving free all residents of a community, district, State, or region; or

(ix) a historic light station as defined under section 305101(4) of title 54, including a historic light station conveyed under section 305103 of title 54, notwithstanding the number of hours that the historic light station is open to the public; or

(C) for purposes of providing services to veterans (as defined in section 101 of title 38), to an organization whose—

(i) membership comprises substantially veterans; and

(ii) representatives are recognized by the Secretary of Veterans Affairs under section 5902 of title 38.

(4) EXCEPTION.—This subsection does not apply to property transferred under subsection (d).

(d) DEPARTMENT OF DEFENSE PROPERTY.—

(1) DETERMINATION.—The Secretary of Defense shall determine whether surplus personal property under the control of the Department of Defense is usable and necessary for educational activities which are of special interest to the armed services, including maritime academies, or military, naval, Air Force, or Coast Guard preparatory schools.

(2) PROPERTY USABLE FOR SPECIAL INTEREST ACTIVITIES.—If the Secretary of Defense determines that the property is usable and necessary for educational activities which are of special interest to the armed services, the Secretary shall allocate the property for transfer by the Administrator to the appropriate state agency for distribution through donation to the educational activities.

(3) PROPERTY NOT USABLE FOR SPECIAL INTEREST ACTIVITIES.—If the Secretary of

Defense determines that the property is not usable and necessary for educational activities which are of special interest to the armed services, the property may be disposed of in accordance with subsection (c).

(e) STATE PLAN OF OPERATION.—

(1) IN GENERAL.—Before property may be transferred to a state agency, the State shall develop a detailed state plan of operation, in accordance with this subsection and with state law.

(2) PROCEDURE.—

(A) CONSIDERATION OF NEEDS AND RESOURCES.—In developing and implementing the state plan of operation, the relative needs and resources of all public agencies and other eligible institutions in the State shall be taken into consideration. The Administrator may consult with interested federal agencies to obtain their views concerning the administration and operation of this section.

(B) PUBLICATION AND PERIOD FOR COMMENT.—The state plan of operation, and any major amendment to the plan, may not be filed with the Administrator until 60 days after general notice of the proposed plan or amendment has been published and interested persons have been given at least 30 days to submit comments.

(C) CERTIFICATION.—The chief executive officer of the State shall certify and submit the state plan of operation to the Administrator.

(3) REQUIREMENTS.—

(A) STATE AGENCY.—The state plan of operation shall include adequate assurance that the state agency has—

(i) the necessary organizational and operational authority and capability including staff, facilities, and means and methods of financing; and

(ii) established procedures for accountability, internal and external audits, cooperative agreements, compliance and use reviews, equitable distribution and property disposal, determination of eligibility, and assistance through consultation with advisory bodies and public and private groups.

(B) EQUITABLE DISTRIBUTION.—The state plan of operation shall provide for fair and equitable distribution of property in the State based on the relative needs and resources of interested public agencies and other eligible institutions in the State and their abilities to use the property.

(C) MANAGEMENT CONTROL AND ACCOUNTING SYSTEMS.—The state plan of operation shall require, for donable property transferred under this section, that the state agency use management control and accounting systems of the same type as systems required by state law for state-owned property. However, with approval from the chief executive officer of the State, the state agency may elect to use other management control and accounting systems that are effective to govern the use, inventory control, accountability, and disposal of property under this section.

(D) RETURN AND REDISTRIBUTION FOR NON-USE.—The state plan of operation shall require the state agency to provide for the return and redistribution of donable property if the property, while still usable, has not been placed in use for the purpose for which it was donated within one year of donation or ceases to be used by the donee for that purpose within one year of being placed in use.

(E) REQUEST BY RECIPIENT.—The state plan of operation shall require the state agency, to the extent practicable, to select property requested by a public agency or other eligible institution in the State and, if requested by the recipient, to arrange shipment of the property directly to the recipient.

(F) SERVICE CHARGES.—If the state agency is authorized to assess and collect service charges from participating recipients to cover direct and reasonable indirect costs of its activities, the method of establishing the charges shall be set out in the state plan of operation. The charges shall be fair and equitable and shall be based on services the state agency performs, including screening, packing, crating, removal, and transportation.

(G) TERMS, CONDITIONS, RESERVATIONS, AND RESTRICTIONS.—

(i) IN GENERAL.—The state plan of operation shall provide that the state agency—

(I) may impose reasonable terms, conditions, reservations, and restrictions on the use of property to be donated under subsection (c); and

(II) shall impose reasonable terms, conditions, reservations, and restrictions on the use of a passenger motor vehicle and any item of property having a unit acquisition cost of $5,000 or more.

(ii) SPECIAL LIMITATIONS.—If the Administrator finds that an item has characteristics that require special handling or use limitations, the Administrator may impose appropriate conditions on the donation of the property.

(H) UNUSABLE PROPERTY.—

(i) DISPOSAL.—The state plan of operation shall provide that surplus personal property which the state agency determines cannot be used by eligible recipients shall be disposed of—

(I) subject to the disapproval of the Administrator within 30 days after notice to the Administrator, through transfer by the state agency to another state agency or through abandonment or destruction if the property has no commercial value or if the estimated cost of continued care and handling exceeds estimated proceeds from sale; or

(II) under this subtitle, on terms and conditions and in a manner the Administrator prescribes.

(ii) PROCEEDS FROM SALE.—Notwithstanding subchapter IV of this chapter and section 702 of this title, the Administrator, from the proceeds of sale of property described in subsection (b), may reimburse the state agency for expenses that the Administrator considers appropriate for care and handling of the property.

(f) COOPERATIVE AGREEMENTS WITH STATE AGENCIES.—

(1) PARTIES TO THE AGREEMENT.—For purposes of carrying out this section, a cooperative agreement may be made between a state surplus property distribution agency designated under this section and—

(A) the Administrator;

(B) the Secretary of Education, for property transferred under section 550(c) of this title;

(C) the Secretary of Health and Human Services, for property transferred under section 550(d) of this title; or

(D) the head of a federal agency designated by the Administrator, the Secretary of Education, or the Secretary of Health and Human Services.

(2) SHARED RESOURCES.—The cooperative agreement may provide that the property, facilities, personnel, or services of—

(A) a state agency may be used by a federal agency; and

(B) a federal agency may be made available to a state agency.

(3) REIMBURSEMENT.—The cooperative agreement may require payment or reimbursement for the use or provision of property, facilities, personnel, or services. Payment or reimbursement received from a state agency shall be credited to the fund or appropriation against which charges would otherwise be made.

(4) SURPLUS PROPERTY TRANSFERRED TO STATE AGENCY.—

(A) IN GENERAL.—Under the cooperative agreement, surplus property transferred to a state agency for distribution pursuant to subsection (c) may be retained by the state agency for use in performing its functions. Unless otherwise directed by the Administrator, title to the retained property vests in the state agency.

(B) CONDITIONS.—Retention of surplus property under this paragraph is subject to conditions that may be imposed by—

(i) the Administrator;

(ii) the Secretary of Education, for property transferred under section 550(c) of this title; or

(iii) the Secretary of Health and Human Services, for property transferred under section 550(d) of this title.

(Pub. L. 107–217, Aug. 21, 2002, 116 Stat. 1090; Pub. L. 109–313, §5, Oct. 6, 2006, 120 Stat. 1737; Pub. L. 111–338, §2, Dec. 22, 2010, 124 Stat. 3590; Pub. L. 113–26, §2, Aug. 9, 2013, 127 Stat. 502; Pub. L. 113–287, §5(j)(1), Dec. 19, 2014, 128 Stat. 3269; Pub. L. 114–287, §23, Dec. 16, 2016, 130 Stat. 1479.)

§549A. DONATION OF PERSONAL PROPERTY THROUGH NONPROFIT REFURBISHERS

(a) AUTHORIZATION.—Not later than 30 days after the date on which the Administrator provides State agencies for surplus property an opportunity to review surplus computer or technology equipment under section 549, the Administrator shall, as appropriate, transfer full title to such surplus computer or technology equipment that is determined to be eligible under subsection (b)(1) to nonprofit computer refurbishers for repair, distribution, and subsequent transfer of full title of the equipment to eligible recipients under this section.

(b) ELIGIBILITY, PARTICIPATION, AND DUTIES.—

(1) ELIGIBILITY.—Surplus computer or technology equipment is eligible for transfer under this section if a Federal agency determines that—

(A) the surplus computer or technology equipment is repairable; and

(B) the surplus computer or technology equipment meets the Guidelines for Media Sanitization issued by the National Institute of Standards and Technology (NIST Special Publication 800–88), or any successor thereto.

(2) PARTICIPATION.—The Administrator may establish partnerships with nongovernmental entities, at no cost and through cooperative agreements, to facilitate the identification and participation of nonprofit computer refurbishers under this section.

(3) DUTIES OF REFURBISHERS.—A nonprofit computer refurbisher that receives

surplus computer or technology equipment under this section shall—

(A) make necessary repairs to restore the surplus computer or technology equipment to working order;

(B) distribute the repaired surplus computer or technology equipment to eligible recipients at no cost, except to the extent—

(i) necessary to facilitate shipping and handling of such equipment; and

(ii) that such cost is consistent with any regulations promulgated by the Administrator under subsection (d);

(C) offer training programs on the use of the repaired computers and technology equipment for the recipients of the equipment; and

(D) use recyclers to the maximum extent practicable in the event that surplus computer or technology equipment transferred under this section cannot be repaired or reused.

(c) REPORTING REQUIREMENTS.—

(1) REFURBISHER REPORTS.—A nonprofit computer refurbisher that receives surplus computer or technology equipment under this section shall provide the Administrator with any information the Administrator determines to be necessary for required reporting—

(A) including information about the distribution of such equipment; and

(B) which shall not include any personal identifying information about the recipient of such equipment apart from whether a recipient is an educational institution, individual with disabilities, low-income individual, student, senior in need, or veteran for the purposes of eligibility under this section.

(2) ADMINISTRATOR REPORTS.—Annually and consistent with reporting requirements for transfers of Federal personal property to non-Federal entities, the Administrator shall submit to Congress and make publicly available a report that includes, for the period covered by the report—

(A) a description of the efforts of the Administrator under this section;

(B) a list of nongovernmental entities with which the Administrator had a partnership described in subsection (b)(2);

(C) a list of nonprofit computer refurbishers that received, made repairs to, and distributed surplus computer and technology equipment, including disclosure of any foreign ownership interest in a nonprofit computer refurbisher; and

(D) a list of donated and subsequently repaired surplus computer or technology equipment identifying—

(i) the Federal agency that donated the surplus computer or technology equipment;

(ii) the State and county (or similar unit of local government) where the recipient is located; and

(iii) whether the recipient is an educational institution, individual with disabilities, low-income individual, student, senior in need, or veteran.

(3) AGENCY REPORTS.—Not later than 5 years after the date of enactment of this section, and annually thereafter, the head of each Federal agency shall make publicly available a report on the number of pieces of repairable surplus computer or technology equipment that were sent to recycling, abandoned, or destroyed.

(d) REGULATIONS.—The Administrator shall issue regulations that are necessary and appropriate to implement this section, including—

(1) allowing nonprofit computer refurbishers to assess nominal fees (which shall not exceed fair market value) on recipients of refurbished surplus computer or technology equipment to facilitate shipping and handling of the surplus computer or technology equipment;

(2) determining, in coordination with other relevant Federal agencies, eligibility and certification requirements for nongovernmental entities and nonprofit computer refurbishers to participate in the program established under this section, including whether the participation of a nongovernmental entity or nonprofit computer refurbisher poses any actual or potential harm to the national security interests of the United States;

(3) establishing an efficient process for identifying eligible recipients; and

(4) determining appropriate recyclers to dispose of surplus computer or technology equipment if it cannot be repaired or refurbished under this section.

(e) JUDICIAL REVIEW.—Nothing in this section shall be construed to create any substantive or procedural right or benefit enforceable by law by a party against the United States, its agencies, its officers, or its employees.

(f) RULE OF CONSTRUCTION.—Nothing in this section may be construed to supersede the requirements of the Stevenson-Wydler Technology Innovation Act of 1980 (Public Law 96–480; 15 U.S.C. 3701 et seq.).

(g) DEFINITIONS.—In this section:

(1) ADMINISTRATOR.—The term "Administrator" means the Administrator of General Services.

(2) DIGITAL DIVIDE.—The term "digital divide" means the gap between those who have an internet-connected computer and the skills to use the computer and those who do not.

(3) DISABILITY.—The term "disability" has the meaning given that term in section 3 of the Americans with Disabilities Act of 1990 (42 U.S.C. 12102).

(4) EDUCATIONAL INSTITUTION.—The term "educational institution" means—

(A) any public or private child care center, preschool, elementary school, secondary school, accredited institution of vocational or professional education, or institution of higher education;

(B) in the case of an accredited institution of vocational or professional education or an institution of higher education composed of more than 1 school, college, or department that is administratively a separate unit, each such school, college, or department; and

(C) a home school (whether treated as a home school or private school for the purposes of applicable State law).

(5) ELIGIBLE RECIPIENT.—The term "eligible recipient" means an educational institution, individual with a disability, low-income individual, student, senior in need, or veteran that is residing or based in the United States.

(6) INSTITUTION OF HIGHER EDUCATION.—The term "institution of higher education" has the meaning given that term in section 101 of the Higher Education Act of 1965 (20 U.S.C. 1001).

(7) Low-income individual.—The term "low-income individual" has the meaning given that term in section 351 of the Small Business Investment Act of 1958 (15 U.S.C. 689).

(8) Nongovernmental entity.—The term "nongovernmental entity" means an organization or group of organizations that—

(A) are not part of a Federal, State, local, Tribal, or territorial government; and

(B) are nonprofit computer refurbishers or other industry participants that—

(i) primarily work to improve access to information and communication technology in their mission to bridge the digital divide through coordination and oversight of computer refurbishment and repair; and

(ii) operate in the United States.

(9) Nonprofit computer refurbisher.—The term "nonprofit computer refurbisher" means a nonprofit organization that—

(A) primarily works to improve access to information and communication technology in their mission to bridge the digital divide; and

(B) operates in the United States.

(10) Nonprofit organization.—The term "nonprofit organization" means an organization that is described under section 501(c)(3) of the Internal Revenue Code of 1986 and is exempt from taxation under section 501(a) of such Code.

(11) Repairable.—The term "repairable" means property that is unusable in its current state but can be economically repaired.

(12) Secondary school.—The term "secondary school" has the meaning given that term in section 8101 of the Elementary and Secondary Education Act of 1965 (20 U.S.C. 7801).

(13) Senior.—The term "senior" means an individual who is 65 years of age or older.

(14) Senior in need.—The term "senior in need" means a senior who experiences cultural, social, or geographical isolation that—

(A) restricts the ability of the senior to perform normal daily tasks; or

(B) threatens the capacity of the senior to live independently.

(15) State agency for surplus property.—The term "State agency for surplus property" has the meaning given the term "state agency" under section 549(a).

(16) Student.—The term "student" means any individual enrolled in an educational institution, but not a public or private child care center.

(17) Surplus computer or technology equipment.—The term "surplus computer or technology equipment" means computer or technology equipment that is property described under section 549(b)(2).

(18) Technology equipment.—The term "technology equipment" means any physical asset related to a computer or information technology, including any peripheral component, tablet, communication device (such as a router, server, or cell phone), printer, scanner, uninterruptible power source, cable, or connection.

(19) Veteran.—The term "veteran" has the meaning given that term in section 101 of title 38.

(Added Pub. L. 117–328, div. Z, §103(a), Dec. 29, 2022, 136 Stat. 5524.)

§550. Disposal of real property for certain purposes

(a) DEFINITION.—In this section, the term "State" includes the District of Columbia, Puerto Rico, and the territories and possessions of the United States.

(b) ENFORCEMENT AND REVISION OF INSTRUMENTS TRANSFERRING PROPERTY UNDER THIS SECTION.—

(1) IN GENERAL.—Subject to disapproval by the Administrator of General Services within 30 days after notice of a proposed action to be taken under this section, except for personal property transferred pursuant to section 549 of this title, the official specified in paragraph (2) shall determine and enforce compliance with the terms, conditions, reservations, and restrictions contained in an instrument by which a transfer under this section is made. The official shall reform, correct, or amend the instrument if necessary to correct the instrument or to conform the transfer to the requirements of law. The official shall grant a release from any term, condition, reservation or restriction contained in the instrument, and shall convey, quitclaim, or release to the transferee (or other eligible user) any right or interest reserved to the Federal Government by the instrument, if the official determines that the property no longer serves the purpose for which it was transferred or that a release, conveyance, or quitclaim deed will not prevent accomplishment of that purpose. The release, conveyance, or quitclaim deed may be made subject to terms and conditions that the official considers necessary to protect or advance the interests of the Government.

(2) SPECIFIED OFFICIAL.—The official referred to in paragraph (1) is—

(A) the Secretary of Education, for property transferred under subsection (c) for school, classroom, or other educational use;

(B) the Secretary of Health and Human Services, for property transferred under subsection (d) for use in the protection of public health, including research;

(C) the Secretary of the Interior, for property transferred under subsection (e) for public park or recreation area use;

(D) the Secretary of Housing and Urban Development, for property transferred under subsection (f) to provide housing or housing assistance for low-income individuals or families; and

(E) the Secretary of the Interior, for property transferred under subsection (h) for use as a historic monument for the benefit of the public.

(c) PROPERTY FOR SCHOOL, CLASSROOM, OR OTHER EDUCATIONAL USE.—

(1) ASSIGNMENT.—The Administrator, in the Administrator's discretion and under regulations that the Administrator may prescribe, may assign to the Secretary of Education for disposal surplus real property, including buildings, fixtures, and equipment situated on the property, that the Secretary recommends as needed for school, classroom, or other educational use.

(2) SALE OR LEASE.—Subject to disapproval by the Administrator within 30 days after notice to the Administrator by the Secretary of Education of a proposed transfer, the Secretary, for school, classroom, or other educational use, may sell or lease property assigned to the Secretary under paragraph (1) to a State, a political subdivision or instrumentality of a State, a tax-supported educational institution, or a nonprofit educational institution that has been held exempt from taxation under section 501(c)(3) of the Internal Revenue Code of 1986 (26 U.S.C. 501(c)(3)).

(3) FIXING VALUE.—In fixing the sale or lease value of property disposed of under paragraph (2), the Secretary of Education shall take into consideration any benefit which has accrued or may accrue to the Government from the use of the property by the State, political subdivision or instrumentality, or institution.

(d) PROPERTY FOR USE IN THE PROTECTION OF PUBLIC HEALTH, INCLUDING RESEARCH.—

(1) ASSIGNMENT.—The Administrator, in the Administrator's discretion and under regulations that the Administrator may prescribe, may assign to the Secretary of Health and Human Services for disposal surplus real property, including buildings, fixtures, and equipment situated on the property, that the Secretary recommends as needed for use in the protection of public health, including research.

(2) SALE OR LEASE.—Subject to disapproval by the Administrator within 30 days after notice to the Administrator by the Secretary of Health and Human Services of a proposed transfer, the Secretary, for use in the protection of public health, including research, may sell or lease property assigned to the Secretary under paragraph (1) to a State, a political subdivision or instrumentality of a State, a tax-supported medical institution, or a hospital or similar institution not operated for profit that has been held exempt from taxation under section 501(c)(3) of the Internal Revenue Code of 1986 (26 U.S.C. 501(c)(3)).

(3) FIXING VALUE.—In fixing the sale or lease value of property disposed of under paragraph (2), the Secretary of Health and Human Services shall take into consideration any benefit which has accrued or may accrue to the Government from the use of the property by the State, political subdivision or instrumentality, or institution.

(e) PROPERTY FOR USE AS A PUBLIC PARK OR RECREATION AREA.—

(1) ASSIGNMENT.—The Administrator, in the Administrator's discretion and under regulations that the Administrator may prescribe, may assign to the Secretary of the Interior for disposal surplus real property, including buildings, fixtures, and equipment situated on the property, that the Secretary recommends as needed for use as a public park or recreation area.

(2) SALE OR LEASE.—Subject to disapproval by the Administrator within 30 days after notice to the Administrator by the Secretary of the Interior of a proposed transfer, the Secretary, for public park or recreation area use, may sell or lease property assigned to the Secretary under paragraph (1) to a State, a political subdivision or instrumentality of a State, or a municipality.

(3) FIXING VALUE.—In fixing the sale or lease value of property disposed of under paragraph (2), the Secretary of the Interior shall take into consideration any benefit which has accrued or may accrue to the Government from the use of the property by the State, political subdivision or instrumentality, or municipality.

(4) DEED OF CONVEYANCE.—The deed of conveyance of any surplus real property disposed of under this subsection—

(A) shall provide that all of the property be used and maintained for the purpose for which it was conveyed in perpetuity, and that if the property ceases to be used or maintained for that purpose, all or any portion of the property shall, in its then existing condition, at the option of the Government, revert to the Government; and

(B) may contain additional terms, reservations, restrictions, and conditions the Secretary of the Interior determines are necessary to safeguard the interests of the Government.

(f) PROPERTY FOR LOW INCOME HOUSING ASSISTANCE.—

(1) ASSIGNMENT.—The Administrator, in the Administrator's discretion and under regulations that the Administrator may prescribe, may assign to the Secretary of Housing and Urban Development for disposal surplus real property, including buildings, fixtures, and equipment situated on the property, that the Secretary recommends as needed to provide housing or housing assistance for low-income individuals or families.

(2) SALE OR LEASE.—Subject to disapproval by the Administrator within 30 days after notice to the Administrator by the Secretary of Housing and Urban Development of a proposed transfer, the Secretary, to provide housing or housing assistance for low-income individuals or families, may sell or lease property assigned to the Secretary under paragraph (1) to a State, a political subdivision or instrumentality of a State, or a nonprofit organization that exists for the primary purpose of providing housing or housing assistance for low-income individuals or families.

(3) SELF-HELP HOUSING.—

(A) IN GENERAL.—The Administrator shall disapprove a proposed transfer of property under this subsection unless the Administrator determines that the property will be used for low-income housing opportunities through the construction, rehabilitation, or refurbishment of self-help housing, under terms requiring that—

(i) subject to subparagraph (B), an individual or family receiving housing or housing assistance through use of the property shall contribute a significant amount of labor toward the construction, rehabilitation, or refurbishment; and

(ii) dwellings constructed, rehabilitated, or refurbished through use of the property shall be quality dwellings that comply with local building and safety codes and standards and shall be available at prices below prevailing market prices.

(B) GUIDELINES FOR CONSIDERING DISABILITIES.—For purposes of fulfilling self-help requirements under paragraph (3)(A)(i), the Administrator shall ensure that nonprofit organizations receiving property under paragraph (2) develop and use guidelines to consider any disability (as defined in section 3(2) of the Americans with Disabilities Act of 1990 (42 U.S.C. 12102(2)).

(4) FIXING VALUE.—

(A) IN GENERAL.—In fixing the sale or lease value of property disposed of under paragraph (2), the Secretary of Housing and Urban Development shall take into consideration and discount the value for any benefit which has accrued or may accrue to the Government from the use of the property by the State, political subdivision or instrumentality, or nonprofit organization.

(B) AMOUNT OF DISCOUNT.—The amount of the discount under subparagraph (A) is 75 percent of the market value of the property, except that the Secretary of Housing and Urban Development may discount by a greater percentage if the Secretary, in consultation with the Administrator, determines that a higher percentage is justified.

(g) PROPERTY FOR NATIONAL SERVICE ACTIVITIES.—

(1) ASSIGNMENT.—The Administrator, in the Administrator's discretion and under regulations that the Administrator may prescribe, may assign to the Chief Executive Officer of the Corporation for National and Community Service for disposal surplus property that the Chief Executive Officer recommends as needed for national service activities.

(2) SALE, LEASE, OR DONATION.—Subject to disapproval by the Administrator within 30 days after notice to the Administrator by the Chief Executive Officer of a proposed transfer, the Chief Executive Officer, for national service activities, may sell, lease, or donate property assigned to the Chief Executive Officer under paragraph (1) to an entity that receives financial assistance under the National and Community Service Act of 1990 (42 U.S.C. 12501 et seq.).

(3) FIXING VALUE.—In fixing the sale or lease value of property disposed of under paragraph (2), the Chief Executive Officer shall take into consideration any benefit which has accrued or may accrue to the Government from the use of the property by the entity receiving the property.

(h) PROPERTY FOR USE AS A HISTORIC MONUMENT.—

(1) CONVEYANCE.—

(A) IN GENERAL.—Without monetary consideration to the Government, the Administrator may convey to a State, a political subdivision or instrumentality of a State, or a municipality, the right, title, and interest of the Government in and to any surplus real and related personal property that the Secretary of the Interior determines is suitable and desirable for use as a historic monument for the benefit of the public.

(B) RECOMMENDATION BY NATIONAL PARK SYSTEM ADVISORY BOARD.—Property may be determined to be suitable and desirable for use as a historic monument only in conformity with a recommendation by the National Park System Advisory Board established under section 102303 of title 54. Only the portion of the property that is necessary for the preservation and proper observation of the property's historic features may be determined to be suitable and desirable for use as a historic monument.

(2) REVENUE-PRODUCING ACTIVITY.—

(A) IN GENERAL.—The Administrator may authorize use of any property conveyed under this subsection for revenue-producing activities if the Secretary of the Interior—

(i) determines that the activities are compatible with use of the property for historic monument purposes;

(ii) approves the grantee's plan for repair, rehabilitation, restoration, and maintenance of the property;

(iii) approves the grantee's plan for financing the repair, rehabilitation, restoration, and maintenance of the property; and

(iv) examines and approves the accounting and financial procedures used by the grantee.

(B) USE OF EXCESS INCOME.—The Secretary of the Interior may approve a grantee's financial plan only if the plan provides that the grantee shall use income exceeding the cost of repair, rehabilitation, restoration, and maintenance only for public historic preservation, park, or recreational purposes.

(C) AUDITS.—The Secretary of the Interior may periodically audit the records of the grantee that are directly related to the property conveyed.

(3) DEED OF CONVEYANCE.—The deed of conveyance of any surplus real property disposed of under this subsection—

(A) shall provide that all of the property be used and maintained for historical monument purposes in perpetuity, and that if the property ceases to be used or maintained for historical monument purposes, all or any portion of the property shall, in its then existing condition, at the option of the Government, revert to the Government; and

(B) may contain additional terms, reservations, restrictions, and conditions the Administrator determines are necessary to safeguard the interests of the Government.

(Pub. L. 107–217, Aug. 21, 2002, 116 Stat. 1094; Pub. L. 113–287, §5(j)(2), Dec. 19, 2014, 128 Stat. 3269.)

§551. DONATIONS TO AMERICAN RED CROSS

The Administrator of General Services, in the Administrator's discretion and under regulations that the Administrator may prescribe, may donate to the American National Red Cross for charitable purposes property that the American National Red Cross processed, produced, or donated and that has been determined to be surplus property.

(Pub. L. 107–217, Aug. 21, 2002, 116 Stat. 1099.)

§552. ABANDONED OR UNCLAIMED PROPERTY ON GOVERNMENT PREMISES

(a) AUTHORITY TO TAKE PROPERTY.—The Administrator of General Services may take possession of abandoned or unclaimed property on premises owned or leased by the Federal Government and determine when title to the property vests in the Government. The Administrator may use, transfer, or otherwise dispose of the property.

(b) CLAIM FILED BY FORMER OWNER.—If a former owner files a proper claim within three years from the date that title to the property vests in the Government, the former owner shall be paid an amount—

(1) equal to the proceeds realized from the disposition of the property less costs incident to care and handling as determined by the Administrator; or

(2) if the property has been used or transferred, equal to the fair value of the property as of the time title vested in the Government less costs incident to care and handling as determined by the Administrator.

(Pub. L. 107–217, Aug. 21, 2002, 116 Stat. 1099; Pub. L. 109–284, §6(3), Sept. 27, 2006, 120 Stat. 1212.)

§553. PROPERTY FOR CORRECTIONAL FACILITY, LAW ENFORCEMENT, AND EMERGENCY MANAGEMENT RESPONSE PURPOSES

(a) DEFINITION.—In this section, the term "State" includes the District of Columbia, Puerto Rico, Guam, American Samoa, the Virgin Islands, the Federated States of Micronesia, the Marshall Islands, Palau, and, the Northern Mariana Islands.

(b) AUTHORITY TO TRANSFER PROPERTY.—The Administrator of General Services, in the Administrator's discretion and under regulations that the Administrator may prescribe, may transfer or convey to a State, or political subdivision or instrumentality of a State, surplus real and related personal property that—

(1) the Attorney General determines is required by the transferee or grantee for correctional facility use under a program approved by the Attorney General for the care or rehabilitation of criminal offenders;

(2) the Attorney General determines is required by the transferee or grantee for law enforcement purposes; or

(3) the Administrator of the Federal Emergency Management Agency determines is required by the transferee or grantee for emergency management response purposes including fire and rescue services.

(c) NO MONETARY CONSIDERATION.—A transfer or conveyance under this section shall be made without monetary consideration to the Federal Government.

(d) DEED OF CONVEYANCE.—The deed of conveyance of any surplus real and related personal property disposed of under this section—

(1) shall provide that all of the property be used and maintained for the purpose for which it was conveyed in perpetuity, and that if the property ceases to be used or maintained for that purpose, all or any portion of the property shall, in its then existing condition, at the option of the Government, revert to the Government; and

(2) may contain additional terms, reservations, restrictions, and conditions that the Administrator determines are necessary to safeguard the interests of the Government.

(e) ENFORCEMENT AND REVISION OF INSTRUMENTS TRANSFERRING PROPERTY UNDER THIS SECTION.—The Administrator shall determine and enforce compliance with the terms, conditions, reservations, and restrictions contained in an instrument by which a transfer or conveyance under this section is made. The Administrator shall reform, correct, or amend the instrument if necessary to correct the instrument or to conform the transfer to the requirements of law. The Administrator shall grant a release from any term, condition, reservation or restriction contained in the instrument, and shall convey, quitclaim, or release to the transferee (or other eligible user) any right or interest reserved to the Government by the instrument, if the Administrator determines that the property no longer serves the purpose for which it was transferred or that a release, conveyance, or quitclaim deed will not prevent accomplishment of that purpose. The release, conveyance, or quitclaim deed may be made subject to terms and conditions that the Administrator considers necessary to protect or advance the interests of the Government.

(Pub. L. 107–217, Aug. 21, 2002, 116 Stat. 1099; Pub. L. 109–295, title VI, §612(c), Oct. 4, 2006, 120 Stat. 1410.)

§554. PROPERTY FOR DEVELOPMENT OR OPERATION OF A PORT FACILITY

(a) DEFINITIONS.—In this section, the following definitions apply:

(1) BASE CLOSURE LAW.—The term "base closure law" has the meaning given that term in section 101(a)(17) of title 10.

(2) STATE.—The term "State" includes the District of Columbia, Puerto Rico, Guam, American Samoa, the Virgin Islands, the Federated States of Micronesia, the Marshall Islands, Palau, and the Northern Mariana Islands.

(b) AUTHORITY FOR ASSIGNMENT TO THE SECRETARY OF TRANSPORTATION.—Under regulations that the Administrator of General Services, after consultation with the Secretary of Defense, may prescribe, the Administrator, or the Secretary of Defense in the case of property located at a military installation closed or realigned pursuant to a base closure law, may assign to the Secretary of Transportation for disposal surplus real property, including buildings, fixtures, and equipment situated on the property, that the Secretary of Transportation recommends as needed for the development or operation of a port facility.

(c) AUTHORITY FOR CONVEYANCE BY THE SECRETARY OF TRANSPORTATION.—

(1) IN GENERAL.—Subject to disapproval by the Administrator or the Secretary of Defense within 30 days after notice of a proposed conveyance by the Secretary of Transportation, the Secretary of Transportation, for the development or operation of a port facility, may convey property assigned to the Secretary of Transportation under subsection (b) to a State or political subdivision, municipality, or instrumentality of a State.

(2) CONVEYANCE REQUIREMENTS.—A transfer of property may be made under this section only after the Secretary of Transportation has—

(A) determined, after consultation with the Secretary of Labor, that the property to be conveyed is located in an area of serious economic disruption;

(B) received and, after consultation with the Secretary of Commerce, approved an economic development plan submitted by an eligible grantee and based on assured use of the property to be conveyed as part of a necessary economic development program; and

(C) transmitted to Congress an explanatory statement that contains information substantially similar to the information contained in statements prepared under section 545(e) of this title.

(d) NO MONETARY CONSIDERATION.—A conveyance under this section shall be made without monetary consideration to the Federal Government.

(e) DEED OF CONVEYANCE.—The deed of conveyance of any surplus real and related personal property disposed of under this section shall—

(1) provide that all of the property be used and maintained for the purpose for which it was conveyed in perpetuity, and that if the property ceases to be used or maintained for that purpose, all or any portion of the property shall, in its then existing condition, at the option of the Government, revert to the Government; and

(2) contain additional terms, reservations, restrictions, and conditions that the Secretary of Transportation shall by regulation require to ensure use of the property for the purposes for which it was conveyed and to safeguard the interests of the Government.

(f) ENFORCEMENT AND REVISION OF INSTRUMENTS TRANSFERRING PROPERTY UNDER THIS SECTION.—The Secretary of Transportation shall determine and enforce compliance with the terms, conditions, reservations, and restrictions contained in an instrument by which a transfer or conveyance under this section is made. The Secretary shall reform, correct, or amend the instrument if necessary to correct the instrument or to conform the transfer to the requirements of law. The Secretary shall grant a release from any term, condition, reservation or restriction contained in the instrument, and shall convey, quitclaim, or release to the grantee any right or interest reserved to the Government by the instrument, if the Secretary determines that the property no longer serves the purpose for which it was transferred or that a release, conveyance, or quitclaim deed will not prevent accomplishment of that purpose. The release, conveyance, or quitclaim deed may be made subject to terms and conditions that the Secretary considers necessary to protect or advance the interests of the Government.

(Pub. L. 107–217, Aug. 21, 2002, 116 Stat. 1100; Pub. L. 109–163, div. A, title X, §1056(a)(5)(A), Jan. 6, 2006, 119 Stat. 3439; Pub. L. 109–284, §6(4), Sept. 27, 2006, 120 Stat. 1212.)

§555. DONATION OF LAW ENFORCEMENT CANINES TO HANDLERS

The head of a federal agency having control of a canine that has been used by a federal agency in the performance of law enforcement duties and that has been determined by the agency to be no longer needed for official purposes may donate the canine to an individual who has experience handling canines in the performance of those duties.

(Pub. L. 107–217, Aug. 21, 2002, 116 Stat. 1102.)

§556. DISPOSAL OF DREDGE VESSELS

(a) IN GENERAL.—The Administrator of General Services, pursuant to sections 521 through 527, 529, and 549 of this title, may dispose of a United States Army Corps of Engineers vessel used for dredging, together with related equipment owned by the Federal Government and under the control of the Chief of Engineers, if the Secretary of the Army declares the vessel to be in excess of federal needs.

(b) RECIPIENTS AND PURPOSES.—Disposal under this section is accomplished—
    (1) through sale or lease to—
        (A) a foreign government as part of a Corps of Engineers technical assistance program;
        (B) a federal or state maritime academy for training purposes; or
        (C) a non-federal public body for scientific, educational, or cultural purposes; or
    (2) through sale solely for scrap to foreign or domestic interests.

(c) NO DREDGING ACTIVITIES.—A vessel described in subsection (a) shall not be disposed of under any law for the purpose of engaging in dredging activities within the United States.

(d) DEPOSIT OF AMOUNTS COLLECTED.—Amounts collected from the sale or lease of a vessel or equipment under this section shall be deposited into the revolving fund authorized by section 101 (9th par.) of the Civil Functions Appropriation [1] Act, 1954 (33 U.S.C. 576), to be available, as provided in appropriation laws, for the operation and maintenance of vessels under the control of the Corps of Engineers.

(Pub. L. 107–217, Aug. 21, 2002, 116 Stat. 1102.)

[1] So in original. Probably should be "Appropriations".

§557. DONATION OF BOOKS TO FREE PUBLIC LIBRARY

Subject to regulations under this subtitle, a book that is no longer needed by an executive department, bureau, or commission of the Federal Government, and that is not an advisable addition to the Library of Congress, shall be turned over to the Free Public

Library of the District of Columbia for general use if the book is appropriate for the Free Public Library.

(Pub. L. 107–217, Aug. 21, 2002, 116 Stat. 1102.)

§558. DONATION OF FORFEITED VESSELS

(a) IN GENERAL.—A vessel that is forfeited to the Federal Government may be donated, in accordance with procedures under this subtitle, to an eligible institution described in subsection (b).

(b) ELIGIBLE INSTITUTION.—An eligible institution referred to in subsection (a) is an educational institution with a commercial fishing vessel safety program or other vessel safety, education and training program. The institution must certify to the federal officer making the donation that the program includes, at a minimum, all of the following courses in vessel safety:

(1) Vessel stability.

(2) Firefighting.

(3) Shipboard first aid.

(4) Marine safety and survival.

(5) Seamanship rules of the road.

(c) TERMS AND CONDITIONS.—The donation of a vessel under this section shall be made on terms and conditions considered appropriate by the federal officer making the donation. All of the following terms and conditions are required:

(1) NO WARRANTY.—The institution must accept the vessel as is, where it is, and without warranty of any kind and without any representation as to its condition or suitability for use.

(2) MAINTENANCE.—The institution is responsible for maintaining the vessel.

(3) INSTRUCTION ONLY.—The vessel may be used only for instructing students in a vessel safety education and training program.

(4) DOCUMENTATION.—If the vessel is eligible to be documented, it must be documented by the institution as a vessel of the United States under chapter 121 of title 46. The requirements of paragraph (5) must be noted on the permanent record of the vessel.

(5) DISPOSAL.—The institution must obtain prior approval from the Administrator of General Services before disposing of the vessel and any proceeds from disposal shall be payable to the Government.

(6) INSPECTION OR REGULATION.—The vessel shall be inspected or regulated in the same manner as a nautical school vessel under chapter 33 of title 46.

(d) GOVERNMENT LIABILITY.—The Government is not liable in an action arising out of the transfer or use of a vessel transferred under this section.

(Pub. L. 107–217, Aug. 21, 2002, 116 Stat. 1103.)

§559. ADVICE OF ATTORNEY GENERAL WITH RESPECT TO ANTITRUST LAW

(a) DEFINITION.—In this section, the term "antitrust law" includes—

(1) the Sherman Act (15 U.S.C. 1 et seq.);

(2) the Clayton Act (15 U.S.C. 12 et seq., 29 U.S.C. 52, 53);

(3) the Federal Trade Commission Act (15 U.S.C. 41 et seq.); and

(4) sections 73 and 74 of the Wilson Tariff Act (15 U.S.C. 8, 9).

(b) ADVICE REQUIRED.—

(1) IN GENERAL.—An executive agency shall not dispose of property to a private interest until the agency has received the advice of the Attorney General on whether the disposal to a private interest would tend to create or maintain a situation inconsistent with antitrust law.

(2) EXCEPTION.—This section does not apply to disposal of—

(A) real property, if the estimated fair market value is less than $3,000,000; or

(B) personal property (other than a patent, process, technique, or invention), if the estimated fair market value is less than $3,000,000.

(c) NOTICE TO ATTORNEY GENERAL.—

(1) IN GENERAL.—An executive agency that contemplates disposing of property to a private interest shall promptly transmit notice of the proposed disposal, including probable terms and conditions, to the Attorney General.

(2) COPY.—Except for the General Services Administration, an executive agency that transmits notice under paragraph (1) shall simultaneously transmit a copy of the notice to the Administrator of General Services.

(d) ADVICE FROM ATTORNEY GENERAL.—Within a reasonable time, not later than 60 days, after receipt of notice under subsection (c), the Attorney General shall advise the Administrator and any interested executive agency whether, so far as the Attorney General can determine, the proposed disposition would tend to create or maintain a situation inconsistent with antitrust law.

(e) REQUEST FOR INFORMATION.—On request from the Attorney General, the head of an executive agency shall furnish information the agency possesses that the Attorney General determines is appropriate or necessary to—

(1) give advice required by this section; or

(2) determine whether any other disposition or proposed disposition of surplus property violates antitrust law.

(f) NO EFFECT ON ANTITRUST LAW.—This subtitle does not impair, amend, or modify antitrust law or limit or prevent application of antitrust law to a person acquiring property under this subtitle.

(Pub. L. 107–217, Aug. 21, 2002, 116 Stat. 1103.)

SUBCHAPTER IV—PROCEEDS FROM SALE OR TRANSFER

§571. GENERAL RULES FOR DEPOSIT AND USE OF PROCEEDS

(a) DEPOSIT IN TREASURY AS MISCELLANEOUS RECEIPTS.—

(1) IN GENERAL.—Except as otherwise provided in this subchapter, proceeds described in paragraph (2) shall be deposited in the Treasury as miscellaneous receipts.

(2) PROCEEDS.—The proceeds referred to in paragraph (1) are proceeds under this chapter from a—

(A) transfer of excess property to a federal agency for agency use; or

(B) sale, lease, or other disposition of surplus property.

(b) PAYMENT OF EXPENSES OF SALE BEFORE DEPOSIT.—Subject to regulations under this subtitle, the expenses of the sale of old material, condemned stores, supplies, or other public property may be paid from the proceeds of sale so that only the net proceeds are deposited in the Treasury. This subsection applies whether proceeds are deposited as miscellaneous receipts or to the credit of an appropriation as authorized by law.

(Pub. L. 107–217, Aug. 21, 2002, 116 Stat. 1104; Pub. L. 114–287, §20(a), Dec. 16, 2016, 130 Stat. 1477; Pub. L. 114–318, §7(c)(1), Dec. 16, 2016, 130 Stat. 1616.)

§572. REAL PROPERTY

(a) IN GENERAL.—

(1) SEPARATE FUND.—Except as provided in subsection (b), proceeds of the disposition of surplus real and related personal property by the Administrator of General Services shall be set aside in a separate fund in the Treasury.

(2) PAYMENT OF EXPENSES FROM THE FUND.—

(A) AUTHORITY.—From the fund described in paragraph (1), the Administrator may obligate an amount to pay the following direct expenses incurred for the use of excess property and the disposal of surplus property under this subtitle:

(i) Fees of appraisers, auctioneers, and realty brokers, in accordance with the scale customarily paid in similar commercial transactions.

(ii) Costs of environmental and historic preservation services, highest and best use of property studies, utilization of property studies, deed compliance inspection, and the expenses incurred in a relocation.

(iii) Advertising and surveying.

(B) LIMITATIONS.—

(i) PERCENTAGE LIMITATION.—In each fiscal year, no more than 12 percent of the proceeds of all dispositions of surplus real and related personal property may be paid to meet direct expenses incurred in connection with the dispositions.

(ii) DETERMINATION OF MAXIMUM AMOUNT.—The Director of the Office of Management and Budget each quarter shall determine the maximum amount that may be obligated under this paragraph.

(C) DIRECT PAYMENT OR REIMBURSEMENT.—An amount obligated under this paragraph may be used to pay an expense directly or to reimburse a fund or appropriation that initially paid the expense.

(3) TRANSFER TO MISCELLANEOUS RECEIPTS.—At least once each year, excess amounts beyond current operating needs shall be transferred from the fund described in paragraph (1) to miscellaneous receipts.

(4) REPORT.—A report of receipts, disbursements, and transfers to miscellaneous receipts under this subsection shall be made annually, in connection with the budget estimate, to the Director and to Congress.

(b) REAL PROPERTY UNDER CONTROL OF A MILITARY DEPARTMENT.—

(1) DEFINITIONS.—In this subsection, the following definitions apply:

(A) MILITARY INSTALLATION.—The term "military installation" has the meaning given that term in section 2687(e)(1) [1] of title 10.

(B) BASE CLOSURE LAW.—The term "base closure law" has the meaning given that term in section 101(a)(17) of title 10.

(2) APPLICATION.—

(A) IN GENERAL.—This subsection applies to real property, including any improvement on the property, that is under the control of a military department and that the Secretary of the department determines is excess to the department's needs.

(B) EXCEPTIONS.—This subsection does not apply to—

(i) damaged or deteriorated military family housing facilities conveyed under section 2854a of title 10; or

(ii) property at a military installation designated for closure or realignment pursuant to a base closure law.

(3) TRANSFER BETWEEN MILITARY DEPARTMENTS.—The Secretary of Defense shall provide that property described in paragraph (2) is available for transfer, without reimbursement, to other military departments within the Department of Defense.

(4) ALTERNATIVE DISPOSITION BY ADMINISTRATOR OF GENERAL SERVICES.—If property is not transferred pursuant to paragraph (3), the Secretary of the military department with the property under its control shall request the Administrator to transfer or dispose of the property in accordance with this subtitle or other applicable law.

(5) PROCEEDS.—

(A) DEPOSIT IN SPECIAL ACCOUNT.—For a transfer or disposition of property pursuant to paragraph (4), the Administrator shall deposit any proceeds (less expenses of the transfer or disposition as provided in subsection (a)) in a special account in the Treasury.

(B) AVAILABILITY OF AMOUNT DEPOSITED.—To the extent provided in an appropriation law, an amount deposited in a special account under subparagraph (A) is available for facility maintenance and repair or environmental restoration as follows:

(i) In the case of property located at a military installation that is closed, the amount is available for facility maintenance and repair or environmental restoration by the military department that had jurisdiction over the property before the closure of the military installation.

(ii) In the case of property located at any other military installation—

(I) 50 percent of the amount is available for facility maintenance and repair or environmental restoration at the military installation where the property was located before it was disposed of or transferred; and

(II) 50 percent of the amount is available for facility maintenance and repair and for environmental restoration by the military department that had jurisdiction over the property before it was disposed of or transferred.

(6) REPORT.—As part of the annual request for authorizations of appropriations to the Committees on Armed Services of the Senate and the House of Representatives, the Secretary of Defense shall include an accounting of each transfer and disposal made in accordance with this subsection during the fiscal year preceding the fiscal year in which the request is made. The accounting shall include a detailed explanation of each transfer and disposal and of the use of the proceeds received from it by the Department of Defense.

(Pub. L. 107–217, Aug. 21, 2002, 116 Stat. 1105; Pub. L. 108–447, div. H, title IV, §408, Dec. 8, 2004, 118 Stat. 3258; Pub. L. 109–13, div. A, title VI, §6068, May 11, 2005, 119 Stat. 299; Pub. L. 109–163, div. A, title X, §1056(a)(5)(B), Jan. 6, 2006, 119 Stat. 3439.)

[1] See References in Text note below.

§573. PERSONAL PROPERTY

The Administrator of General Services may retain from the proceeds of sales of personal property the Administrator conducts amounts necessary to recover, to the extent practicable, costs the Administrator (or the Administrator's agent) incurs in conducting the sales. The Administrator shall deposit amounts retained into the Acquisition Services Fund established under section 321(a) of this title. From the amounts deposited, the Administrator may pay direct costs and reasonably related indirect costs incurred in conducting sales of personal property. At least once each year, amounts retained that are not needed to pay the direct and indirect costs shall be transferred from the Acquisition Services Fund to the general fund or another appropriate account in the Treasury.

(Pub. L. 107–217, Aug. 21, 2002, 116 Stat. 1107; Pub. L. 109–313, §3(h)(4), Oct. 6, 2006, 120 Stat. 1736.)

§574. OTHER RULES REGARDING PROCEEDS

(a) CREDIT TO REIMBURSABLE FUND OR APPROPRIATION.—

(1) APPLICATION.—This subsection applies to property acquired with amounts—

(A) not appropriated from the general fund of the Treasury; or

(B) appropriated from the general fund of the Treasury but by law reimbursable from assessment, tax, or other revenue or receipts.

(2) IN GENERAL.—The net proceeds of a disposition or transfer of property described in paragraph (1) shall be—

(A) credited to the applicable reimbursable fund or appropriation; or

(B) paid to the federal agency that determined the property to be excess.

(3) CALCULATION OF NET PROCEEDS.—For purposes of this subsection, the net proceeds of a disposition or transfer of property are the proceeds less all expenses incurred for the disposition or transfer, including care and handling.

(4) ALTERNATIVE CREDIT TO MISCELLANEOUS RECEIPTS.—If the agency that determined the property to be excess decides that it is uneconomical or impractical to ascertain the amount of net proceeds, the proceeds shall be credited to miscellaneous receipts.

(b) SPECIAL ACCOUNT FOR REFUNDS OR PAYMENTS FOR BREACH.—

(1) DEPOSITS.—A federal agency that disposes of surplus property under this chapter may deposit, in a special account in the Treasury, amounts of the proceeds of the dispositions that the agency decides are necessary to permit—

(A) appropriate refunds to purchasers for dispositions that are rescinded or that do not become final; and

(B) payments for breach of warranty.

(2) WITHDRAWALS.—A federal agency that deposits proceeds in a special account under paragraph (1) may withdraw amounts to be refunded or paid from the account without regard to the origin of the amounts withdrawn.

(c) CREDIT TO COST OF CONTRACTOR'S WORK.—If a contract made by an executive agency, or a subcontract under that contract, authorizes the proceeds of a sale of property in the custody of a contractor or subcontractor to be credited to the price or cost of work covered by the contract or subcontract, then the proceeds of the sale shall be credited in accordance with the contract or subcontract.

(d) ACCEPTANCE OF PROPERTY INSTEAD OF CASH.—An executive agency entitled to receive cash under a contract for the lease, sale, or other disposition of surplus property may accept property instead of cash if the President determines that the property is strategic or critical material. The property is valued at the prevailing market price when the cash payment becomes due.

(e) MANAGEMENT OF CREDIT, LEASES, AND PERMITS.—For a disposition of surplus property under this chapter, if credit has been extended, or if the disposition has been by lease or permit, the Administrator of General Services, in a manner and on terms the Administrator determines are in the best interest of the Federal Government—

(1) shall administer and manage the credit, lease, or permit, and any security for the credit, lease, or permit; and

(2) may enforce, adjust, and settle any right of the Government with respect to the credit, lease, or permit.

(Pub. L. 107–217, Aug. 21, 2002, 116 Stat. 1107.)

SUBCHAPTER V—OPERATION OF BUILDINGS AND RELATED ACTIVITIES

§581. GENERAL AUTHORITY OF ADMINISTRATOR OF GENERAL SERVICES

[(a) Repealed. Pub. L. 107–296, title XVII, §1706(a)(1), Nov. 25, 2002, 116 Stat. 2316.]

(b) PERSONNEL AND EQUIPMENT.—The Administrator of General Services may—

(1) employ and pay personnel at per diem rates approved by the Administrator, not exceeding rates currently paid by private industry for similar services in the place where the services are performed; and

(2) purchase, repair, and clean uniforms for civilian employees of the General Services Administration who are required by law or regulation to wear uniform clothing.

(c) ACQUISITION AND MANAGEMENT OF PROPERTY.—

(1) REAL ESTATE.—The Administrator may acquire, by purchase, condemnation, or otherwise, real estate and interests in real estate.

(2) GROUND RENT.—The Administrator may pay ground rent for buildings owned by the Federal Government or occupied by federal agencies, and pay the rent in advance if required by law or if the Administrator determines that advance payment is in the public interest.

(3) RENT AND REPAIRS UNDER A LEASE.—The Administrator may pay rent and make repairs, alterations, and improvements under the terms of a lease entered into by, or transferred to, the Administration for the housing of a federal agency.

(4) REPAIRS THAT ARE ECONOMICALLY ADVANTAGEOUS.—The Administrator may repair, alter, or improve rented premises if the Administrator determines that doing so is advantageous to the Government in terms of economy, efficiency, or national security. The Administrator's determination must—

(A) set forth the circumstances that make the repair, alteration, or improvement advantageous; and

(B) show that the total cost (rental, repair, alteration, and improvement) for the expected life of the lease is less than the cost of alternative space not needing repair, alteration, or improvement.

(5) INSURANCE PROCEEDS FOR DEFENSE INDUSTRIAL RESERVE.—At the direction of the Secretary of Defense, the Administrator may use insurance proceeds received for damage to property that is part of the Defense Industrial Reserve to repair or restore the property.

(6) MAINTENANCE CONTRACTS.—The Administrator may enter into a contract, for a period not exceeding five years, for the inspection, maintenance, and repair of fixed equipment in a federally owned building.

(d) LEASE OF FEDERAL BUILDING SITES.—

(1) IN GENERAL.—The Administrator may lease a federal building site or addition, including any improvements, until the site is needed for construction purposes. The lease must be for fair rental value and on other terms and conditions the Administrator considers to be in the public interest pursuant to section 545 of this title.

(2) NEGOTIATION WITHOUT ADVERTISING.—A lease under this subsection may be negotiated without public advertising for bids if—

(A) the lessee is—

(i) the former owner from whom the Government acquired the property; or

(ii) the former owner's tenant in possession; and

(B) the lease is negotiated incident to or in connection with the acquisition of the property.

(3) DEPOSIT OF RENT.—Rent received under this subsection may be deposited into the Federal Buildings Fund.

(e) ASSISTANCE TO THE INAUGURAL COMMITTEE.—The Administrator may provide direct assistance and special services for the Inaugural Committee (as defined in section 501 of title 36) during an inaugural period in connection with Presidential inaugural operations and functions. Assistance and services under this subsection may include—

(1) employment of personal services without regard to chapters 33 and 51 and subchapter III of chapter 53 of title 5;

(2) providing Government-owned and leased space for personnel and parking;

(3) paying overtime to guard and custodial forces;

(4) erecting and removing stands and platforms;

(5) providing and operating first-aid stations;

(6) providing furniture and equipment; and

(7) providing other incidental services in the discretion of the Administrator.

(f) UTILITIES FOR DEFENSE INDUSTRIAL RESERVE AND SURPLUS PROPERTY.—The Administrator may—

(1) provide utilities and services, if the utilities and services are not provided by other sources, to a person, firm, or corporation occupying or using a plant or portion of a plant that constitutes—

(A) any part of the Defense Industrial Reserve pursuant to section 4881 of title 10; or

(B) surplus real property; and

(2) credit an amount received for providing utilities and services under this

subsection to an applicable appropriation of the Administration.

(g) OBTAINING PAYMENTS.—The Administrator may—

(1) obtain payments, through advances or otherwise, for services, space, quarters, maintenance, repair, or other facilities furnished, on a reimbursable basis, to a federal agency, a mixed-ownership Government corporation (as defined in chapter 91 of title 31), or the District of Columbia; and

(2) credit the payments to the applicable appropriation of the Administration.

(h) COOPERATIVE USE OF PUBLIC BUILDINGS.—

(1) LEASING SPACE FOR COMMERCIAL AND OTHER PURPOSES.—The Administrator may lease space on a major pedestrian access level, courtyard, or rooftop of a public building to a person, firm, or organization engaged in commercial, cultural, educational, or recreational activity (as defined in section 3306(a) of this title). The Administrator shall establish a rental rate for leased space equivalent to the prevailing commercial rate for comparable space devoted to a similar purpose in the vicinity of the public building. The lease may be negotiated without competitive bids, but shall contain terms and conditions and be negotiated pursuant to procedures that the Administrator considers necessary to promote competition and to protect the public interest.

(2) OCCASIONAL USE OF SPACE FOR NON-COMMERCIAL PURPOSES.—The Administrator may make available, on occasion, or lease at a rate and on terms and conditions that the Administrator considers to be in the public interest, an auditorium, meeting room, courtyard, rooftop, or lobby of a public building to a person, firm, or organization engaged in cultural, educational, or recreational activity (as defined in section 3306(a) of this title) that will not disrupt the operation of the building.

(3) DEPOSIT AND CREDIT OF AMOUNTS RECEIVED.—The Administrator may deposit into the Federal Buildings Fund an amount received under a lease or rental executed pursuant to paragraph (1) or (2). The amount shall be credited to the appropriation from the Fund applicable to the operation of the building.

(4) FURNISHING UTILITIES AND MAINTENANCE.—The Administrator may furnish utilities, maintenance, repair, and other services to a person, firm, or organization leasing space pursuant to paragraph (1) or (2). The services may be provided during and outside of regular working hours of federal agencies.

(Pub. L. 107–217, Aug. 21, 2002, 116 Stat. 1108; Pub. L. 107–296, title XVII, §1706(a), Nov. 25, 2002, 116 Stat. 2316; Pub. L. 109–284, §6(5), Sept. 27, 2006, 120 Stat. 1212; Pub. L. 117–81, div. A, title XVII, §1702(g)(2), Dec. 27, 2021, 135 Stat. 2158.)

§582. MANAGEMENT OF BUILDINGS BY ADMINISTRATOR OF GENERAL SERVICES

(a) REQUEST BY FEDERAL AGENCY OR INSTRUMENTALITY.—At the request of a federal agency, a mixed-ownership Government corporation (as defined in chapter 91 of title 31), or the District of Columbia, the Administrator of General Services may operate, maintain, and protect a building that is owned by the Federal Government (or, in the case of a wholly owned or mixed-ownership Government corporation, by the corporation) and occupied by the agency or instrumentality making the request.

(b) TRANSFER OF FUNCTIONS BY DIRECTOR OF THE OFFICE OF MANAGEMENT AND BUDGET.—

(1) IN GENERAL.—When the Director of the Office of Management and Budget

determines that it is in the interest of economy or efficiency, the Director shall transfer to the Administrator all functions vested in a federal agency with respect to the operation, maintenance, and custody of an office building owned by the Government or a wholly owned Government corporation, or an office building, or part of an office building, that is occupied by a federal agency under a lease.

(2) EXCEPTION FOR POST-OFFICE BUILDINGS.—A transfer of functions shall not be made under this subsection for a post-office building, unless the Director determines that the building is not used predominantly for post-office purposes. The Administrator may delegate functions with respect to a post-office building that are transferred to the Administrator under this subsection only to another officer or employee of the General Services Administration or to the Postmaster General.

(3) EXCEPTION FOR BUILDINGS IN A FOREIGN COUNTRY.—A transfer of functions shall not be made under this subsection for a building located in a foreign country.

(4) EXCEPTION FOR DEPARTMENT OF DEFENSE BUILDINGS.—A transfer of functions shall not be made under this subsection for a building located on the grounds of a facility of the Department of Defense (including a fort, camp, post, arsenal, navy yard, naval training station, airfield, proving ground, military supply depot, or school) unless and only to the extent that the Secretary of Defense has issued a permit for use by another agency.

(5) EXCEPTION FOR GROUPS OF SPECIAL PURPOSE BUILDINGS.—A transfer of functions shall not be made under this subsection for a building that the Director finds to be a part of a group of buildings that are—

(A) located in the same vicinity;

(B) used wholly or predominantly for the special purposes of the agency with custody of the buildings; and

(C) not generally suitable for use by another agency.

(6) EXCEPTION FOR CERTAIN GOVERNMENT BUILDINGS.—A transfer of functions shall not be made under this subsection for the Treasury Building, the Bureau of Engraving and Printing Building, the buildings occupied by the National Institute of Standards and Technology, and the buildings under the jurisdiction of the regents of the Smithsonian Institution.

(Pub. L. 107–217, Aug. 21, 2002, 116 Stat. 1110.)

§583. CONSTRUCTION OF BUILDINGS

(a) AUTHORITY.—At the request of a federal agency, a mixed-ownership Government corporation (as defined in chapter 91 of title 31), or the District of Columbia, the Administrator of General Services may—

(1) acquire land for a building or project authorized by Congress;

(2) make or cause to be made (under contract or otherwise) surveys and test borings and prepare plans and specifications for a building or project prior to the Attorney General's approval of the title to the site; and

(3) contract for, and supervise, the construction, development, and equipping of a building or project.

(b) TRANSFER OF AMOUNTS.—An amount available to a federal agency or instrumentality for a building or project may be transferred, in advance, to the General

Services Administration for purposes the Administrator determines are necessary, including payment of salaries and expenses for preparing plans and specifications and for field supervision.

(Pub. L. 107–217, Aug. 21, 2002, 116 Stat. 1111.)

§584. ASSIGNMENT AND REASSIGNMENT OF SPACE

(a) AUTHORITY.—

(1) IN GENERAL.—Subject to paragraph (2), the Administrator of General Services may assign or reassign space for an executive agency in any Federal Government-owned or leased building.

(2) REQUIREMENTS.—The Administrator's authority under paragraph (1) may be exercised only—

(A) in accordance with policies and directives the President prescribes under section 121(a) of this title;

(B) after consultation with the head of the executive agency affected; and

(C) on a determination by the Administrator that the assignment or reassignment is advantageous to the Government in terms of economy, efficiency, or national security.

(b) PRIORITY FOR PUBLIC ACCESS.—In assigning space on a major pedestrian access level (other than space leased under section 581(h)(1) or (2) of this title), the Administrator shall, where practicable, give priority to federal activities requiring regular contact with the public. If the space is not available, the Administrator shall provide space with maximum ease of access to building entrances.

(Pub. L. 107–217, Aug. 21, 2002, 116 Stat. 1112.)

§585. LEASE AGREEMENTS

(a) IN GENERAL.—

(1) AUTHORITY.—The Administrator of General Services may enter into a lease agreement with a person, copartnership, corporation, or other public or private entity for the accommodation of a federal agency in a building (or improvement) which is in existence or being erected by the lessor to accommodate the federal agency. The Administrator may assign and reassign the leased space to a federal agency.

(2) TERMS.—A lease agreement under this subsection shall be on terms the Administrator considers to be in the interest of the Federal Government and necessary for the accommodation of the federal agency. However, the lease agreement may not bind the Government for more than 20 years and the obligation of amounts for a lease under this subsection is limited to the current fiscal year for which payments are due without regard to section 1341(a)(1)(B) of title 31.

(b) SUBLEASE.—

(1) APPLICATION.—This subsection applies to rent received if the Administrator—

(A) determines that an unexpired portion of a lease of space to the Government is surplus property; and

(B) disposes of the property by sublease.

(2) USE OF RENT.—Notwithstanding section 571(a) of this title, the Administrator may deposit rent received into the Federal Buildings Fund. The Administrator may defray from the fund any costs necessary to provide services to the Government's

lessee and to pay the rent (not otherwise provided for) on the lease of the space to the Government.

(c) AMOUNTS FOR RENT AVAILABLE FOR LEASE OF BUILDINGS ON GOVERNMENT LAND.—Amounts made available to the General Services Administration for the payment of rent may be used to lease space, for a period of not more than 30 years, in buildings erected on land owned by the Government.

(d) Any bargain-price option to purchase at less than fair market value contained in any lease agreement entered into on or after January 1, 2021, pursuant to this section may be exercised only to the extent specifically provided for in subsequent appropriation Acts or other Acts of Congress.

(Pub. L. 107–217, Aug. 21, 2002, 116 Stat. 1112; Pub. L. 117–257, §1, Dec. 21, 2022, 136 Stat. 2371.)

§586. CHARGES FOR SPACE AND SERVICES

(a) DEFINITION.—In this section, "space and services" means space, services, quarters, maintenance, repair, and other facilities.

(b) CHARGES BY ADMINISTRATOR OF GENERAL SERVICES.—

(1) IN GENERAL.—The Administrator of General Services shall impose a charge for furnishing space and services.

(2) RATES.—The Administrator shall, from time to time, determine the rates to be charged for furnishing space and services and shall prescribe regulations providing for the rates. The rates shall approximate commercial charges for comparable space and services. However, for a building for which the Administrator is responsible for alterations only (as the term "alter" is defined in section 3301(a) of this title), the rates shall be fixed to recover only the approximate cost incurred in providing alterations.

(3) EXEMPTIONS.—The Administrator may exempt anyone from the charges required by this subsection when the Administrator determines that charges would be infeasible or impractical. To the extent an exemption is granted, appropriations to the General Services Administration are authorized to reimburse the Federal Buildings Fund for any loss of revenue.

(c) CHARGES BY EXECUTIVE AGENCIES.—

(1) IN GENERAL.—An executive agency, other than the Administration, may impose a charge for furnishing space and services at rates approved by the Administrator.

(2) CREDITING AMOUNTS RECEIVED.—An amount an executive agency receives under this subsection shall be credited to the appropriation or fund initially charged for providing the space or service. However, amounts in excess of actual operating and maintenance costs shall be credited to miscellaneous receipts unless otherwise provided by law.

(d) RENT PAYMENTS FOR LEASE SPACE.—An agency may make rent payments to the Administration for lease space relating to expansion needs of the agency. Payment rates shall approximate commercial charges for comparable space as provided in subsection (b). Payments shall be deposited into the Federal Buildings Fund. The Administration may use amounts received under this subsection, in addition to amounts received as New Obligational Authority, in the Rental of Space activity of the Fund.

(Pub. L. 107–217, Aug. 21, 2002, 116 Stat. 1113.)

§587. Telecommuting and other alternative workplace arrangements

(a) Definition.—In this section, the term "telecommuting centers" means flexiplace work telecommuting centers.

(b) Telecommuting Centers Established by Administrator of General Services.—

(1) Establishment.—The Administrator of General Services may acquire space for, establish, and equip telecommuting centers for use in accordance with this subsection.

(2) Use.—A telecommuting center may be used by employees of federal agencies, state and local governments, and the private sector. The Administrator shall give federal employees priority in using a telecommuting center. The Administrator may make a telecommuting center available for use by others to the extent it is not fully utilized by federal employees.

(3) User fees.—The Administrator shall charge a user fee for the use of a telecommuting center. The amount of the user fee shall approximate commercial charges for comparable space and services. However, the user fee may not be less than necessary to pay the cost of establishing and operating the telecommuting center, including the reasonable cost of renovation and replacement of furniture, fixtures, and equipment.

(4) Deposit and use of fees.—The Administrator may—

(A) deposit user fees into the Federal Buildings Fund and use the fees to pay costs incurred in establishing and operating the telecommuting center; and

(B) accept and retain income received by the General Services Administration, from federal agencies and non-federal sources, to defray costs directly associated with the functions of telecommuting centers.

(c) Development of Alternative Workplace Arrangements by Executive Agencies and Others.—

(1) Definition.—In this subsection, the term "alternative workplace arrangements" includes telecommuting, hoteling, virtual offices, and other distributive work arrangements.

(2) Consideration by executive agencies.—In considering whether to acquire space, quarters, buildings, or other facilities for use by employees, the head of an executive agency shall consider whether needs can be met using alternative workplace arrangements.

(3) Guidance from administrator.—The Administrator may provide guidance, assistance, and oversight to any person regarding the establishment and operation of alternative workplace arrangements.

(d) Amounts Available for Flexiplace Work Telecommuting Programs.—

(1) Definition.—In this subsection, the term "flexiplace work telecommuting program" means a program under which employees of a department or agency set out in paragraph (2) are permitted to perform all or a portion of their duties at a telecommuting center established under this section or other federal law.

(2) Minimum funding.—For each of the following departments and agencies, in each fiscal year at least $50,000 of amounts made available for salaries and expenses is available only for carrying out a flexiplace work telecommuting program:

(A) Department of Agriculture.

(B) Department of Commerce.

(C) Department of Defense.

(D) Department of Education.

(E) Department of Energy.

(F) Department of Health and Human Services.

(G) Department of Housing and Urban Development.

(H) Department of the Interior.

(I) Department of Justice.

(J) Department of Labor.

(K) Department of State.

(L) Department of Transportation.

(M) Department of the Treasury.

(N) Department of Veterans Affairs.

(O) Environmental Protection Agency.

(P) General Services Administration.

(Q) Office of Personnel Management.

(R) Small Business Administration.

(S) Social Security Administration.

(T) United States Postal Service.

(Pub. L. 107–217, Aug. 21, 2002, 116 Stat. 1113.)

§588. MOVEMENT AND SUPPLY OF OFFICE FURNITURE

(a) DEFINITION.—In this section, the term "controlled space" means a substantial and identifiable segment of space (such as a building, floor, or wing) in a location that the Administrator of General Services controls for purposes of assignment of space.

(b) APPLICATION.—This section applies if an agency (or unit of the agency), moves from one controlled space to another, whether in the same or a different location.

(c) MOVING EXISTING FURNITURE.—The furniture and furnishings used by an agency (or organizational unit of the agency) shall be moved only if the Administrator determines, after consultation with the head of the agency and with due regard for the program activities of the agency, that it would not be more economical and efficient to make suitable replacements available in the new controlled space.

(d) PROVIDING REPLACEMENT FURNITURE.—In the absence of a determination under subsection (c), suitable furniture and furnishings for the new controlled space shall be provided from stocks under the control of the moving agency or from stocks available to the Administrator, whichever the Administrator determines to be more economical and efficient. However, the same or similar items may not be provided from both sources.

(e) CONTROL OF REPLACEMENT FURNITURE.—If furniture and furnishings for a new controlled space are provided from stocks available to the Administrator, the items being provided remain in the control of the Administrator.

(f) CONTROL OF FURNITURE NOT MOVED.—

(1) IN GENERAL.—If furniture and furnishings for a new controlled space are provided from stocks available to the Administrator, the furniture and furnishings that were previously used by the moving agency (or unit of the agency) pass to the control

of the Administrator.

(2) REIMBURSEMENT.—

(A) IN GENERAL.—Furniture and furnishings passing to the control of the Administrator under this section pass without reimbursement.

(B) EXCEPTION FOR TRUST FUND.—If furniture and furnishings that were purchased from a trust fund pass to the control of the Administrator under this section, the Administrator shall reimburse the trust fund for the fair market value of the furniture and furnishings.

(3) REVOLVING OR WORKING CAPITAL FUND.—If furniture and furnishings are carried as assets of a revolving or working capital fund at the time they pass to the control of the Administrator under this section, the net book value of the furniture and furnishings shall be written off and the capital of the fund is diminished by the amount of the write-off.

(Pub. L. 107–217, Aug. 21, 2002, 116 Stat. 1115.)

§589. INSTALLATION, REPAIR, AND REPLACEMENT OF SIDEWALKS

(a) IN GENERAL.—An executive agency may install, repair, and replace sidewalks around buildings, installations, property, or grounds that are—

(1) under the agency's control;

(2) owned by the Federal Government; and

(3) located in a State, the District of Columbia, Puerto Rico, or a territory or possession of the United States.

(b) REIMBURSEMENT.—Subsection (a) may be carried out by—

(1) reimbursement to a State or political subdivision of a State, the District of Columbia, Puerto Rico, or a territory or possession of the United States; or

(2) a means other than reimbursement.

(c) REGULATIONS.—Subsection (a) shall be carried out in accordance with regulations the Administrator of General Services prescribes with the approval of the Director of the Office of Management and Budget.

(d) USE OF AMOUNTS.—Amounts appropriated to an executive agency for installation, repair, and maintenance, generally, are available to carry out this section.

(e) LIABILITY.—This section does not increase or enlarge the tort liability of the Government for injuries to individuals or damages to property.

(Pub. L. 107–217, Aug. 21, 2002, 116 Stat. 1116.)

§590. CHILD CARE

(a) GUIDANCE, ASSISTANCE, AND OVERSIGHT.—Through the General Services Administration's licensing agreements, the Administrator of General Services shall provide guidance, assistance, and oversight to federal agencies for the development of child care centers to provide economical and effective child care for federal workers.

(b) ALLOTMENT OF SPACE IN FEDERAL BUILDINGS.—

(1) DEFINITIONS.—In this subsection, the following definitions apply:

(A) CHILD CARE PROVIDER.—The term "child care provider" means an individual or entity that provides or proposes to provide child care services for federal employees.

(B) ALLOTMENT OFFICER.—The term "allotment officer" means an officer or agency of the Federal Government charged with the allotment of space in federal buildings.

(2) ALLOTMENT.—A child care provider may be allotted space in a federal building by an allotment officer if—

(A) the child care provider applies to the allotment officer in the community or district in which child care services are to be provided;

(B) the space is available; and

(C) the allotment officer determines that—

(i) the space will be used to provide child care services to children of whom at least 50 percent have one parent or guardian employed by the Government; and

(ii) the child care provider will give priority to federal employees for available child care services in the space.

(c) PAYMENT FOR SPACE AND SERVICES.—

(1) DEFINITION.—For purposes of this subsection, the term "services" includes the providing of lighting, heating, cooling, electricity, office furniture, office machines and equipment, classroom furnishings and equipment, kitchen appliances, playground equipment, telephone service (including installation of lines and equipment and other expenses associated with telephone services), and security systems (including installation and other expenses associated with security systems), including replacement equipment, as needed.

(2) NO CHARGE.—Space allotted under subsection (b) may be provided without charge for rent or services.

(3) REIMBURSEMENT FOR COSTS.—For space allotted under subsection (b), if there is an agreement for the payment of costs associated with providing space or services, neither title 31, nor any other law, prohibits or restricts payment by reimbursement to the miscellaneous receipts or other appropriate account of the Treasury.

(d) PAYMENT OF OTHER COSTS.—If an agency has a child care facility in its space, or is a sponsoring agency for a child care facility in other federal or leased space, the agency or the Administration may—

(1) pay accreditation fees, including renewal fees, for the child care facility to be accredited by a nationally recognized early-childhood professional organization;

(2) pay travel and per diem expenses for representatives of the child care facility to attend the annual Administration child care conference; and

(3) enter into a consortium with one or more private entities under which the private entities assist in defraying costs associated with the salaries and benefits for personnel providing services at the facility.

(e) REIMBURSEMENT FOR EMPLOYEE TRAINING.—Notwithstanding section 1345 of title 31, an agency, department, or instrumentality of the Government that provides or proposes to provide child care services for federal employees may reimburse a federal employee or any individual employed to provide child care services for travel, transportation, and subsistence expenses incurred for training classes, conferences, or other meetings in connection with providing the services. A per diem allowance made under this subsection may not exceed the rate specified in regulations prescribed under section 5707 of title 5.

(f) CRIMINAL HISTORY BACKGROUND CHECKS.—

(1) DEFINITION.—In this subsection, the term "executive facility" means a facility owned or leased by an office or entity within the executive branch of the Government. The term includes a facility owned or leased by the General Services Administration on behalf of an office or entity within the judicial branch of the Government.

(2) IN GENERAL.—All workers in a child care center located in an executive facility shall undergo a criminal history background check as defined in section 231 of the Crime Control Act of 1990 (42 U.S.C. 13041).[1]

(3) NONAPPLICATION TO LEGISLATIVE BRANCH FACILITIES.—This subsection does not apply to a facility owned by or leased on behalf of an office or entity within the legislative branch of the Government.

(g) APPROPRIATED AMOUNTS FOR AFFORDABLE CHILD CARE.—

(1) DEFINITION.—For purposes of this subsection, the term "Executive agency" has the meaning given that term in section 105 of title 5, but does not include the Government Accountability Office.

(2) IN GENERAL.—In accordance with regulations the Office of Personnel Management prescribes, an Executive agency that provides or proposes to provide child care services for federal employees may use appropriated amounts that are otherwise available for salaries and expenses to provide child care in a federal or leased facility, or through contract, for civilian employees of the agency.

(3) AFFORDABILITY.—Amounts used pursuant to paragraph (2) shall be applied to improve the affordability of child care for lower income federal employees using or seeking to use the child care services.

(4) ADVANCES.—Notwithstanding section 3324 of title 31, amounts may be paid in advance to licensed or regulated child care providers for services to be rendered during an agreed period.

(5) NOTIFICATION.—No amounts made available by law may be used to implement this subsection without advance notice to the Committees on Appropriations of the House of Representatives and the Senate.

(6) APPLICATION TO HOUSE OF REPRESENTATIVES.—This subsection shall apply with respect to the House of Representatives in the same manner as it applies to an Executive agency, except that—

(A) the authority granted to the Office of Personnel Management shall be exercised with respect to the House of Representatives by the Speaker of the House of Representatives in accordance with regulations promulgated by the Committee on House Administration; and

(B) amounts may be made available to implement this subsection with respect to the House of Representatives without advance notice to the Committee on Appropriations of the Senate.

(7) APPLICATION TO SENATE.—This subsection shall apply with respect to the Senate in the same manner as it applies to an Executive agency, except that—

(A) the authority granted to the Office of Personnel Management shall be exercised with respect to the Senate, by the Majority and Minority Leaders of the Senate, in accordance with regulations promulgated by the Committee on Rules and Administration of the Senate; and

(B) amounts may be made available to implement this subsection with respect to the Senate without advance notice to the Committee on Appropriations of the House of Representatives.

(Pub. L. 107–217, Aug. 21, 2002, 116 Stat. 1116; Pub. L. 108–271, §8(b), July 7, 2004, 118 Stat. 814; Pub. L. 117–328, div. I, title I, §117(a), Dec. 29, 2022, 136 Stat. 4924; Pub. L. 118–47, div. E, title I, §103(a), Mar. 23, 2024, 138 Stat. 712.)

[1] *See References in Text note below.*

§591. PURCHASE OF ELECTRICITY

(a) GENERAL LIMITATION ON USE OF AMOUNTS.—A department, agency, or instrumentality of the Federal Government may not use amounts appropriated or made available by any law to purchase electricity in a manner inconsistent with state law governing the provision of electric utility service, including—

(1) state utility commission rulings; and

(2) electric utility franchises or service territories established under state statute, state regulation, or state-approved territorial agreements.

(b) EXCEPTIONS.—

(1) ENERGY SAVINGS.—This section does not preclude the head of a federal agency from entering into a contract under section 801 of the National Energy Conservation Policy Act (42 U.S.C. 8287).

(2) ENERGY SAVINGS FOR MILITARY INSTALLATIONS.—This section does not preclude the Secretary of a military department from—

(A) entering into a contract under section 2394 [1] of title 10; or

(B) purchasing electricity from any provider if the Secretary finds that the utility having the applicable state-approved franchise (or other service authorization) is unwilling or unable to meet unusual standards of service reliability that are necessary for purposes of national defense.

(Pub. L. 107–217, Aug. 21, 2002, 116 Stat. 1118.)

[1] *See References in Text note below.*

§592. FEDERAL BUILDINGS FUND

(a) EXISTENCE.—There is in the Treasury a fund known as the Federal Buildings Fund.

(b) DEPOSITS.—

(1) IN GENERAL.—The following revenues and collections shall be deposited into the Fund:

(A) User charges under section 586(b) of this title, payable in advance or otherwise.

(B) Proceeds from the lease of federal building sites or additions under section 581(d) of this title.

(C) Receipts from carriers and others for loss of, or damage to, property belonging to the Fund.

(2) REIMBURSEMENTS FOR SPECIAL SERVICES.—This subchapter does not preclude the Administrator of General Services from providing special services, not included in the standard level user charge, on a reimbursable basis. The reimbursements may be

credited to the Fund.

(3) TRANSFER OF SURPLUS AMOUNTS.—To prevent the accumulation of excessive surpluses in the Fund, in any fiscal year an amount specified in an appropriation law may be transferred out of the Fund and deposited as miscellaneous receipts in the Treasury.

(c) USES.—

(1) IN GENERAL.—Deposits in the Fund are available for real property management and related activities in the amounts specified in annual appropriation laws without regard to fiscal year limitations.

(2) SALARIES AND EXPENSES RELATED TO CONSTRUCTION PROJECTS OR PLANNING PROGRAMS.—Deposits in the Fund that are available pursuant to annual appropriation laws may be transferred and consolidated on the books of the Treasury into a special account in accordance with, and for the purposes specified in, section 3176 of this title.

(3) REPAYMENT OF GENERAL SERVICES ADMINISTRATION BORROWING FROM FEDERAL FINANCING BANK.—The Administrator, in accordance with rules and procedures that the Office of Management and Budget and the Secretary of the Treasury establish, may transfer from the Fund an amount necessary to repay the principal amount of a General Services Administration borrowing from the Federal Financing Bank, if the borrowing is a legal obligation of the Fund.

(4) BUILDINGS DEEMED FEDERALLY OWNED.—For purposes of amounts authorized to be expended from the Fund, the following are deemed to be federally owned buildings:

(A) A building constructed pursuant to the purchase contract authority of section 5 of the Public Buildings Amendments of 1972 (Public Law 92–313, 86 Stat. 219).

(B) A building occupied pursuant to an installment purchase contract.

(C) A building under the control of a department or agency, if alterations of the building are required in connection with moving the department or agency from a former building that is, or will be, under the control of the Administration.

(d) ENERGY MANAGEMENT PROGRAMS.—

(1) RECEIVING CASH INCENTIVES.—The Administrator may receive amounts from rebates or other cash incentives related to energy savings and shall deposit the amounts in the Fund for use as provided in paragraph (4).

(2) RECEIVING GOODS OR SERVICES.—The Administrator may accept, from a utility, goods or services that enhance the energy efficiency of federal facilities.

(3) ASSIGNMENT OF ENERGY REBATES.—In the administration of real property that the Administrator leases and for which the Administrator pays utility costs, the Administrator may assign all or a portion of energy rebates to the lessor to underwrite the costs incurred in undertaking energy efficiency improvements in the real property if the payback period for the improvement is at least 2 years less than the remainder of the term of the lease.

(4) OBLIGATING AMOUNTS FOR ENERGY MANAGEMENT IMPROVEMENT PROGRAMS.—In addition to amounts appropriated for energy management improvement programs and without regard to subsection (c)(1), the Administrator may obligate for those programs—

(A) amounts received and deposited in the Fund under paragraph (1);

(B) goods and services received under paragraph (2); and

(C) amounts the Administrator determines are not needed for other authorized projects and that are otherwise available to implement energy efficiency programs.

(e) Recycling Programs.—

(1) Receiving amounts.—The Administrator may receive amounts from the sale of recycled materials and shall deposit the amounts in the Fund for use as provided in paragraph (2).

(2) Obligating amounts for recycling programs.—In addition to amounts appropriated for such purposes and without regard to subsection (c)(1), the Administrator may obligate amounts received and deposited in the Fund under paragraph (1) for programs which—

(A) promote further source reduction and recycling programs; and

(B) encourage employees to participate in recycling programs by providing financing for child care.

(f) Additional Authority Related to Energy Management and Recycling Programs.—The Fund may receive, in the form of rebates, cash incentives or otherwise, any revenues, collections, or other income related to energy savings or recycling efforts. Amounts received under this subsection remain in the Fund until expended and remain available for federal energy management improvement programs, recycling programs, or employee programs that are authorized by law or that the Administrator considers appropriate. The Administration may use amounts received under this subsection, in addition to amounts received as New Obligational Authority, in activities of the Fund as necessary.

(Pub. L. 107–217, Aug. 21, 2002, 116 Stat. 1118.)

§593. Protection for veterans preference employees

(a) Definitions.—In this section, the following definitions apply:

(1) Covered services.—The term "covered services" means any guard, elevator operator, messenger, or custodial services.

(2) Sheltered workshop.—The term "sheltered workshop" means a sheltered workshop employing the severely handicapped under chapter 85 of title 41.

(b) In General.—Except as provided in subsection (c), amounts made available to the General Services Administration pursuant to section 592 of this title may not be obligated or expended to procure covered services by contract if an employee who was a permanent veterans preference employee of the Administration on November 19, 1995, would be terminated as a result.

(c) Exception.—Amounts made available to the Administration pursuant to section 592 of this title may be obligated and expended to procure covered services by contract with a sheltered workshop or, if sheltered workshops decline to contract for the provision of covered services, by competitive contract for a period of no longer than 5 years. When a competitive contract expires, or is terminated for any reason, the Administration shall again offer to procure the covered services by contract with a sheltered workshop before procuring the covered services by competitive contract.

(Pub. L. 107–217, Aug. 21, 2002, 116 Stat. 1120; Pub. L. 109–284, §6(6), Sept. 27, 2006, 120 Stat. 1212;

Pub. L. 111–350, §5(l)(11), Jan. 4, 2011, 124 Stat. 3852.)

SUBCHAPTER VI—MOTOR VEHICLE POOLS AND TRANSPORTATION SYSTEMS

§601. PURPOSES

In order to provide an economical and efficient system for transportation of Federal Government personnel and property consistent with section 101 of this title, the purposes of this subchapter are—

(1) to establish procedures to ensure safe operation of motor vehicles on Government business;

(2) to provide for proper identification of Government motor vehicles;

(3) to establish an effective means to limit the use of Government motor vehicles to official purposes;

(4) to reduce the number of Government-owned vehicles to the minimum necessary to transact public business; and

(5) to provide wherever practicable for centrally operated interagency pools or systems for local transportation of Government personnel and property.

(Pub. L. 107–217, Aug. 21, 2002, 116 Stat. 1121.)

§602. AUTHORITY TO ESTABLISH MOTOR VEHICLE POOLS AND TRANSPORTATION SYSTEMS

(a) IN GENERAL.—Subject to section 603 of this title, and regulations issued under section 603, the Administrator of General Services shall—

(1) take over from executive agencies and consolidate, or otherwise acquire, motor vehicles and related equipment and supplies;

(2) provide for the establishment, maintenance, and operation (including servicing and storage) of motor vehicle pools or systems; and

(3) furnish motor vehicles and related services to executive agencies for the transportation of property and passengers.

(b) METHODS OF PROVIDING VEHICLES AND SERVICES.—As determined by the Administrator, motor vehicles and related services may be furnished by providing an agency with—

(1) Federal Government-owned motor vehicles;

(2) the use of motor vehicles, under rental or other arrangements, through private fleet operators, taxicab companies, or local or interstate common carriers; or

(3) both.

(c) RECIPIENTS OF VEHICLES AND SERVICES.—The Administrator shall, so far as practicable, furnish motor vehicles and related services under this section to any federal agency, mixed-ownership Government corporation (as defined in chapter 91 of title 31), or the District of Columbia, on its request.

(Pub. L. 107–217, Aug. 21, 2002, 116 Stat. 1121.)

§603. PROCESS FOR ESTABLISHING MOTOR VEHICLE POOLS AND TRANSPORTATION SYSTEMS

(a) DETERMINATION REQUIREMENT.—

(1) IN GENERAL.—The Administrator of General Services may carry out section 602 only if the Administrator determines, after consultation with the agencies concerned and with due regard to their program activities, that doing so is advantageous to the Federal Government in terms of economy, efficiency, or service.

(2) ELEMENTS OF THE DETERMINATION.—A determination under this section must be in writing. For each motor vehicle pool or system, the determination must set forth an analytical justification that includes—

(A) a detailed comparison of estimated costs for present and proposed modes of operation; and

(B) a showing that savings can be realized by the establishment, maintenance, and operation of a motor vehicle pool or system.

(b) REGULATIONS RELATED TO ESTABLISHMENT.—

(1) IN GENERAL.—The President shall prescribe regulations establishing procedures to carry out section 602 of this title.

(2) ELEMENTS OF THE REGULATIONS.—The regulations shall provide for—

(A) adequate notice to an executive agency of any determination that affects the agency or its functions;

(B) independent review and decision as directed by the President of any determination disputed by an agency, with the possibility that the decision may include a partial or complete exemption of the agency from the determination; and

(C) enforcement of determinations that become effective under the regulations.

(3) EFFECT OF THE REGULATIONS.—A determination under subsection (a) is binding on an agency only as provided in regulations issued under this subsection.

(Pub. L. 107–217, Aug. 21, 2002, 116 Stat. 1122.)

§604. TREATMENT OF ASSETS TAKEN OVER TO ESTABLISH MOTOR VEHICLE POOLS AND TRANSPORTATION SYSTEMS

(a) REIMBURSEMENT.—

(1) REQUIREMENT.—When the Administrator of General Services takes over motor vehicles or related equipment or supplies under section 602 of this title, reimbursement is required if the property is taken over from—

(A) a Government corporation; or

(B) an agency, if the agency acquired the property through unreimbursed expenditures made from a revolving or trust fund authorized by law.

(2) AMOUNT.—The Administrator shall reimburse a Government corporation, or a fund through which an agency acquired property, by an amount equal to the fair market value of the property. If the Administrator subsequently returns property of a similar kind under section 610 of this title, the Government corporation or the fund shall reimburse the Administrator by an amount equal to the fair market value of the property returned.

(b) ADDITION TO ACQUISITION SERVICES FUND.—If the Administrator takes over motor vehicles or related equipment or supplies under section 602 of this title but reimbursement is not required under subsection (a), the value of the property taken over, as determined by the Administrator, may be added to the capital of the Acquisition Services Fund. If the Administrator subsequently returns property of a similar kind under section 610 of this title, the value of the property may be deducted from the Fund.

(Pub. L. 107–217, Aug. 21, 2002, 116 Stat. 1122; Pub. L. 109–313, §3(h)(5), Oct. 6, 2006, 120 Stat. 1736.)

§605. PAYMENT OF COSTS

(a) USE OF ACQUISITION SERVICES FUND TO COVER COSTS.—The Acquisition Services Fund provided for in section 321 of this title is available for use by or under the direction and control of the Administrator of General Services to pay the costs of carrying out section 602 of this title, including the cost of purchasing or renting motor vehicles and related equipment and supplies.

(b) SETTING PRICES TO RECOVER COSTS.—

(1) IN GENERAL.—The Administrator shall set prices for furnishing motor vehicles and related services under section 602 of this title. Prices shall be set to recover, so far as practicable, all costs of carrying out section 602 of this title.

(2) INCREMENT FOR REPLACEMENT COST.—In the Administrator's discretion, prices may include an increment for the estimated replacement cost of motor vehicles and related equipment and supplies. Notwithstanding section 321(f) of this title, the increment may be retained as a part of the capital of the Acquisition Services Fund but is available only to replace motor vehicles and related equipment and supplies.

(c) ACCOUNTING METHOD.—The purchase price of motor vehicles and related equipment, and any increment for estimated replacement cost, shall be recovered only through charges for the cost of amortization. Costs shall be determined, and financial reports prepared, in accordance with the accrual accounting method.

(Pub. L. 107–217, Aug. 21, 2002, 116 Stat. 1123; Pub. L. 109–313, §3(h)(6), Oct. 6, 2006, 120 Stat. 1736.)

§606. REGULATIONS RELATED TO OPERATION

(a) IN GENERAL.—The Director of the Office of Personnel Management shall prescribe regulations to govern executive agencies in authorizing civilian personnel to operate Federal Government-owned motor vehicles for official purposes within the States of the United States, the District of Columbia, Puerto Rico, and the territories and possessions of the United States.

(b) ELEMENTS OF THE REGULATIONS.—The regulations shall prescribe standards of physical fitness for authorized operators. The regulations may require operators and prospective operators to obtain state and local licenses or permits that are required to operate similar vehicles for other than official purposes.

(c) AGENCY ORDERS.—The head of each executive agency shall issue orders and directives necessary for compliance with the regulations. The orders and directives shall provide for—

(1) periodically testing the physical fitness of operators and prospective operators; and

(2) suspension and revocation of authority to operate.

(Pub. L. 107–217, Aug. 21, 2002, 116 Stat. 1123.)

§607. RECORDS

The Administrator of General Services shall maintain an accurate record of the cost of establishing, maintaining, and operating each motor vehicle pool or system established under section 602 of this title.

(Pub. L. 107–217, Aug. 21, 2002, 116 Stat. 1124.)

§608. SCRIP, TOKENS, TICKETS

The Administrator of General Services, in the operation of motor vehicle pools or systems under this subchapter, may provide for the sale and use of scrip, tokens, tickets, and similar devices to collect payment.

(Pub. L. 107–217, Aug. 21, 2002, 116 Stat. 1124.)

§609. IDENTIFICATION OF VEHICLES

(a) IN GENERAL.—Under regulations prescribed by the Administrator of General Services, every motor vehicle acquired and used for official purposes within the United States, or the territories or possessions of the United States, by any federal agency or by the District of Columbia shall be conspicuously identified by showing, on the vehicle—

(1)(A) the full name of the department, establishment, corporation, or agency that uses the vehicle and the service for which the vehicle is used; or

(B) a title that readily identifies the department, establishment, corporation, or agency that uses the vehicle and that is descriptive of the service for which the vehicle is used; and

(2) the legend "For official use only".

(b) EXCEPTIONS.—The regulations prescribed pursuant to this section may provide for exemptions when conspicuous identification would interfere with the purpose for which a vehicle is acquired and used.

(Pub. L. 107–217, Aug. 21, 2002, 116 Stat. 1124.)

§610. DISCONTINUANCE OF MOTOR VEHICLE POOL OR SYSTEM

(a) IN GENERAL.—The Administrator of General Services shall discontinue a motor vehicle pool or system if there are no actual savings realized (based on accounting as provided in section 605 of this title) during a reasonable period of not longer than two successive fiscal years.

(b) RETURN OF COMPARABLE PROPERTY.—If a motor vehicle pool or system is discontinued, the Administrator shall return to each agency involved motor vehicles and related equipment and supplies similar in kind and reasonably comparable in value to any motor vehicles and related equipment and supplies which were previously taken over by the Administrator.

(Pub. L. 107–217, Aug. 21, 2002, 116 Stat. 1124.)

§611. DUTY TO REPORT VIOLATIONS

During the regular course of the duties of the Administrator of General Services, if the Administrator becomes aware of a violation of section 1343, 1344, or 1349(b) of title 31 or of section 641 of title 18 involving the conversion by a Federal Government official or employee of a Government-owned or leased motor vehicle to the official or employee's own use or to the use of others, the Administrator shall report the violation to the head of the agency in which the official or employee is employed, for further investigation and either appropriate disciplinary action under section 1343, 1344, or

1349(b) of title 31 or, if appropriate, referral to the Attorney General for prosecution under section 641 of title 18.

(Pub. L. 107–217, Aug. 21, 2002, 116 Stat. 1124; Pub. L. 109–284, §6(7), Sept. 27, 2006, 120 Stat. 1212.)

SUBCHAPTER VII—PROPERTY MANAGEMENT

§621. DEFINITIONS

In this subchapter:

(1) ADMINISTRATOR.—The term "Administrator" means the Administrator of General Services.

(2) COUNCIL.—The term "Council" means the Federal Real Property Council established by section 623(a).

(3) DIRECTOR.—The term "Director" means the Director of the Office of Management and Budget.

(4) FEDERAL AGENCY.—The term "Federal agency" means—

(A) an executive department or independent establishment in the executive branch of the Government; or

(B) a wholly owned Government corporation (other than the United States Postal Service).

(5) FIELD OFFICE.—The term "field office" means any office of a Federal agency that is not the headquarters office location for the Federal agency.

(6) POSTAL PROPERTY.—The term "postal property" means any property owned or leased by the United States Postal Service.

(7) PUBLIC-PRIVATE PARTNERSHIP.—The term "public-private partnership" means any partnership or working relationship between a Federal agency and a corporation, individual, or nonprofit organization for the purpose of financing, constructing, operating, managing, or maintaining one or more Federal real property assets.

(8) UNDERUTILIZED PROPERTY.—The term "underutilized property" means a portion or the entirety of any real property, including any improvements, that is used—

(A) irregularly or intermittently by the accountable Federal agency for program purposes of the Federal agency; or

(B) for program purposes that can be satisfied only with a portion of the property.

(Added Pub. L. 114–318, §3(a), Dec. 16, 2016, 130 Stat. 1608.)

§622. COLLOCATION AMONG UNITED STATES POSTAL SERVICE PROPERTIES

(a) IDENTIFICATION OF POSTAL PROPERTY.—Each year, the Postmaster General shall—

(1) identify a list of postal properties with space available for use by Federal agencies; and

(2) not later than September 30, submit the list to—

(A) the Committee on Homeland Security and Governmental Affairs of the Senate; and

(B) the Committee on Oversight and Government Reform of the House of Representatives.

(b) VOLUNTARY IDENTIFICATION OF POSTAL PROPERTY.—Each year, the Postmaster

General may submit the list under subsection (a) to the Council.

(c) SUBMISSION OF LIST OF POSTAL PROPERTIES TO FEDERAL AGENCIES.—

(1) IN GENERAL.—Not later than 30 days after the completion of a list under subsection (a), the Council shall provide the list to each Federal agency.

(2) REVIEW BY FEDERAL AGENCIES.—Not later than 90 days after the receipt of the list submitted under paragraph (1), each Federal agency shall—

(A) review the list;

(B) review properties under the control of the Federal agency; and

(C) recommend collocations if appropriate.

(d) TERMS OF COLLOCATION.—On approval of the recommendations under subsection (c) by the Postmaster General and the applicable agency head, the Federal agency or appropriate landholding entity may work with the Postmaster General to establish appropriate terms of a lease for each postal property.

(e) RULE OF CONSTRUCTION.—Nothing in this section exceeds, modifies, or supplants any other Federal law relating to any competitive bidding process governing the leasing of postal property.

(Added Pub. L. 114–318, §3(a), Dec. 16, 2016, 130 Stat. 1609.)

§623. ESTABLISHMENT OF A FEDERAL REAL PROPERTY COUNCIL

(a) ESTABLISHMENT.—There is established a Federal Real Property Council.

(b) PURPOSE.—The purpose of the Council shall be—

(1) to develop guidance and ensure implementation of an efficient and effective real property management strategy;

(2) to identify opportunities for the Federal Government to better manage property and assets of the Federal Government; and

(3) to reduce the costs of managing property of the Federal Government, including operations, maintenance, and security associated with Federal property.

(c) COMPOSITION.—

(1) IN GENERAL.—The Council shall be composed exclusively of—

(A) the senior real property officers of each Federal agency;

(B) the Deputy Director for Management of the Office of Management and Budget;

(C) the Controller of the Office of Management and Budget;

(D) the Administrator; and

(E) any other full-time or permanent part-time Federal officials or employees, as the Chairperson determines to be necessary.

(2) CHAIRPERSON.—The Deputy Director for Management of the Office of Management and Budget shall serve as Chairperson of the Council.

(3) EXECUTIVE DIRECTOR.—

(A) IN GENERAL.—The Chairperson shall designate an Executive Director to assist in carrying out the duties of the Council.

(B) QUALIFICATIONS.—The Executive Director shall—

(i) be appointed from among individuals who have substantial experience in the areas of commercial real estate and development, real property management, and Federal operations and management; and

(ii) hold no outside employment that may conflict with duties inherent to the position.

(d) MEETINGS.—

(1) IN GENERAL.—The Council shall meet subject to the call of the Chairperson.

(2) MINIMUM.—The Council shall meet not fewer than 4 times each year.

(e) DUTIES.—The Council, in consultation with the Director and the Administrator, shall—

(1) not later than 1 year after the date of enactment of this subchapter, establish a real property management plan template, to be updated annually, which shall include performance measures, specific milestones, measurable savings, strategies, and Government-wide goals based on the goals established under section 524(a)(7) to reduce surplus property or to achieve better utilization of underutilized property, and evaluation criteria to determine the effectiveness of real property management that are designed—

(A) to enable Congress and heads of Federal agencies to track progress in the achievement of property management objectives on a Government-wide basis;

(B) to improve the management of real property; and

(C) to allow for comparison of the performance of Federal agencies against industry and other public sector agencies;

(2) develop utilization rates consistent throughout each category of space, considering the diverse nature of the Federal portfolio and consistent with nongovernmental space use rates;

(3) develop a strategy to reduce the reliance of Federal agencies on leased space for long-term needs if ownership would be less costly;

(4) provide guidance on eliminating inefficiencies in the Federal leasing process;

(5) compile a list of field offices that are suitable for collocation with other property assets;

(6) research best practices regarding the use of public-private partnerships to manage properties and develop guidelines for the use of those partnerships in the management of Federal property; and

(7) not later than 1 year after the date of enactment of this subchapter and annually during the 4-year period beginning on the date that is 1 year after the date of enactment of this subchapter and ending on the date that is 5 years after the date of enactment of this subchapter, the Council shall submit to the Director a report that contains—

(A) a list of the remaining excess property that is real property, surplus property that is real property, and underutilized property of each Federal agency;

(B) the progress of the Council toward developing guidance for Federal agencies to ensure that the assessment required under section 524(a)(11)(B) is carried out in a uniform manner;

(C) the progress of Federal agencies toward achieving the goals established under section 524(a)(7);

(D) if necessary, recommendations for legislation or statutory reforms that would further the goals of the Council, including streamlining the disposal of excess or underutilized real property; and

(E) a list of entities that are consulted under subsection (f).

(f) CONSULTATION.—In carrying out the duties described in subsection (e), the Council shall also consult with representatives of—

(1) State, local, and tribal authorities, as appropriate, and other affected communities; and

(2) appropriate private sector entities and nongovernmental organizations that have expertise in areas of—

(A) commercial real estate and development;

(B) government management and operations;

(C) space planning;

(D) community development, including transportation and planning;

(E) historic preservation; and

(F) providing housing to the homeless population.

(g) COUNCIL RESOURCES.—The Director and the Administrator shall provide staffing, and administrative support for the Council, as appropriate.

(h) ACCESS TO REPORT.—The Council shall provide, on an annual basis, the real property management plan template required under subsection (e)(1) and the reports required under subsection (e)(7) to—

(1) the Committee on Homeland Security and Governmental Affairs of the Senate;

(2) the Committee on Environment and Public Works of the Senate;

(3) the Committee on Oversight and Government Reform of the House of Representatives;

(4) the Committee on Transportation and Infrastructure of the House of Representatives; and

(5) the Comptroller General of the United States.

(i) EXCLUSIONS.—In this section, surplus property shall not include—

(1) any military installation (as defined in section 2910 of the Defense Base Closure and Realignment Act of 1990 (10 U.S.C. 2687 note; Public Law 101–510));

(2) any property that is excepted from the definition of the term "property" under section 102;

(3) Indian and native Eskimo property held in trust by the Federal Government as described in section 3301(a)(5)(C)(iii);

(4) real property operated and maintained by the Tennessee Valley Authority pursuant to the Tennessee Valley Authority Act of 1933 (16 U.S.C. 831 et seq.);

(5) any real property the Director excludes for reasons of national security;

(6) any public lands (as defined in section 203 of the Public Lands Corps Act of 1993 (16 U.S.C. 1722)) administered by—

(A) the Secretary of the Interior, acting through—

(i) the Director of the Bureau of Land Management;

(ii) the Director of the National Park Service;

(iii) the Commissioner of Reclamation; or

(iv) the Director of the United States Fish and Wildlife Service; or

(B) the Secretary of Agriculture, acting through the Chief of the Forest Service; or

(7) any property operated and maintained by the United States Postal Service.

(Added Pub. L. 114–318, §3(a), Dec. 16, 2016, 130 Stat. 1609.)

§624. Information on certain leasing authorities

(a) In General.—Except as provided in subsection (b), not later than December 31 of each year following the date of enactment of this subchapter, a Federal agency with independent leasing authority shall submit to the Council a list of all leases, including operating leases, in effect on the date of enactment of this subchapter that includes—

(1) the date on which each lease was executed;

(2) the date on which each lease will expire;

(3) a description of the size of the space;

(4) the location of the property;

(5) the tenant agency;

(6) the total annual rental payment; and

(7) the amount of the net present value of the total estimated legal obligations of the Federal Government over the life of the contract.

(b) Exception.—Subsection (a) shall not apply to—

(1) the United States Postal Service; or

(2) any other property the Director excludes from subsection (a) for reasons of national security.

(Added Pub. L. 114–318, §3(a), Dec. 16, 2016, 130 Stat. 1612.)

CHAPTER 7—FOREIGN EXCESS PROPERTY

§701. ADMINISTRATIVE

(a) POLICIES PRESCRIBED BY THE PRESIDENT.—The President may prescribe policies that the President considers necessary to carry out this chapter. The policies must be consistent with this chapter.

(b) EXECUTIVE AGENCY RESPONSIBILITY.—

(1) IN GENERAL.—The head of an executive agency that has foreign excess property is responsible for the disposal of the property.

(2) CONFORMANCE TO POLICIES.—In carrying out functions under this chapter, the head of an executive agency shall—

(A) use the policies prescribed by the President under subsection (a) for guidance; and

(B) dispose of foreign excess property in a manner that conforms to the foreign policy of the United States.

(3) DELEGATION OF AUTHORITY.—The head of an executive agency may—

(A) delegate authority conferred by this chapter to an official in the agency or to the head of another executive agency; and

(B) authorize successive redelegation of authority conferred by this chapter.

(4) EMPLOYMENT OF PERSONNEL.—As necessary to carry out this chapter, the head of an executive agency may—

(A) appoint and fix the pay of personnel in the United States, subject to chapters 33 and 51 and subchapter III of chapter 53 of title 5; and

(B) appoint personnel outside the States of the United States and the District of Columbia, without regard to chapter 33 of title 5.

(c) SPECIAL RESPONSIBILITIES OF SECRETARY OF STATE.—

(1) USE OF FOREIGN CURRENCIES AND CREDITS.—The Secretary of State may use foreign currencies and credits acquired by the United States under section 704(b)(2) of this title—

(A) to carry out the Mutual Educational and Cultural Exchange Act of 1961 (22 U.S.C. 2451 et seq.);

(B) to carry out the Foreign Service Buildings Act, 1926 (22 U.S.C. 292 et seq.); and

(C) to pay other governmental expenses payable in local currencies.

(2) RENEWAL OF CERTAIN AGREEMENTS.—Except as otherwise directed by the President, the Secretary of State shall continue to perform functions under agreements in effect on July 1, 1949, related to the disposal of foreign excess property. The Secretary of State may amend, modify, and renew the agreements. Foreign currencies or credits the Secretary of State acquires under the agreements shall be administered

in accordance with procedures that the Secretary of the Treasury may establish. Foreign currencies or credits reduced to United States currency must be deposited in the Treasury as miscellaneous receipts.

(Pub. L. 107–217, Aug. 21, 2002, 116 Stat. 1125.)

§702. RETURN OF FOREIGN EXCESS PROPERTY TO UNITED STATES

(a) IN GENERAL.—Under regulations prescribed pursuant to subsection (b), foreign excess property may be returned to the United States for handling as excess or surplus property under subchapter II of chapter 5 of this title or section 549 or 551 of this title when the head of the executive agency concerned, or the Administrator of General Services after consultation with the agency head, determines that return of the property to the United States for such handling is in the interest of the United States.

(b) REGULATIONS.—The Administrator shall prescribe regulations to carry out this section. The regulations must require that transportation costs for returning foreign excess property to the United States are paid by the federal agency, state agency, or donee receiving the property.

(Pub. L. 107–217, Aug. 21, 2002, 116 Stat. 1126.)

§703. DONATION OF MEDICAL SUPPLIES FOR USE IN FOREIGN COUNTRY

(a) APPLICATION.—This section applies to medical materials or supplies that are in a foreign country but that would, if situated within the United States, be available for donation under subchapter III of chapter 5 of this title.

(b) IN GENERAL.—An executive agency may donate medical materials or supplies that are not disposed of under section 702 of this title.

(c) CONDITIONS.—A donation under this section is subject to the following conditions:

(1) The medical materials and supplies must be donated for use in a foreign country.

(2) The donation must be made to a nonprofit medical or health organization, which may be an organization qualified to receive assistance under section 214(b) or 607 of the Foreign Assistance Act of 1961 (22 U.S.C. 2174(b), 2357).

(3) The donation must be made without cost to the donee (except for costs of care and handling).

(Pub. L. 107–217, Aug. 21, 2002, 116 Stat. 1126.)

§704. OTHER METHODS OF DISPOSAL

(a) IN GENERAL.—Foreign excess property not disposed of under section 702 or 703 of this title may be disposed of as provided in this section.

(b) METHODS OF DISPOSAL.—

(1) SALE, EXCHANGE, LEASE, OR TRANSFER.—The head of an executive agency may dispose of foreign excess property by sale, exchange, lease, or transfer, for cash, credit or other property, with or without warranty, under terms and conditions the head of the executive agency considers proper.

(2) EXCHANGE FOR FOREIGN CURRENCY OR CREDIT.—If the head of an executive agency determines that it is in the interest of the United States, foreign excess property may be exchanged for—

(A) foreign currencies or credits; or

(B) substantial benefits or the discharge of claims resulting from the compromise or settlement of claims in accordance with law.

(3) ABANDONMENT, DESTRUCTION, OR DONATION.—The head of an executive agency may authorize the abandonment, destruction, or donation of foreign excess property if the property has no commercial value or if estimated costs of care and handling exceed the estimated proceeds from sale.

(c) ADVERTISING.—The head of an executive agency may dispose of foreign excess property without advertising if the head of the executive agency finds that disposal without advertising is the most practicable and advantageous means for the Federal Government to dispose of the property.

(d) TRANSFER OF TITLE.—The head of an executive agency may execute documents to transfer title or other interests in, and take other action necessary or proper to dispose of, foreign excess property.

(Pub. L. 107–217, Aug. 21, 2002, 116 Stat. 1126.)

§705. HANDLING OF PROCEEDS FROM DISPOSAL

(a) IN GENERAL.—This section applies to proceeds from the sale, lease, or other disposition of foreign excess property under this chapter.

(b) FOREIGN CURRENCIES OR CREDITS.—Proceeds in the form of foreign currencies or credits, must be administered in accordance with procedures that the Secretary of the Treasury may establish.

(c) UNITED STATES CURRENCY.—

(1) SEPARATE FUND IN TREASURY.—Section 572(a) of this title applies to proceeds of foreign excess property disposed of for United States currency under this chapter.

(2) DEPOSITED IN TREASURY AS MISCELLANEOUS RECEIPTS.—Except as provided in paragraph (1), proceeds in the form of United States currency, including foreign currencies or credits that are reduced to United States currency, must be deposited in the Treasury as miscellaneous receipts.

(d) SPECIAL ACCOUNT FOR REFUNDS OR PAYMENTS FOR BREACH.—

(1) DEPOSITS.—A federal agency that disposes of foreign excess property under this chapter may deposit, in a special account in the Treasury, amounts of the proceeds of the dispositions that the agency decides are necessary to permit—

(A) appropriate refunds to purchasers for dispositions that are rescinded or that do not become final; and

(B) payments for breach of warranty.

(2) WITHDRAWALS.—A federal agency that deposits proceeds in a special account under paragraph (1) may withdraw amounts to be refunded or paid from the account without regard to the origin of the amounts withdrawn.

(Pub. L. 107–217, Aug. 21, 2002, 116 Stat. 1127.)

CHAPTER 9—URBAN LAND USE

§901. PURPOSE AND POLICY

The purpose of this chapter is to promote harmonious intergovernmental relations and encourage sound planning, zoning, and land use practices by prescribing uniform policies and procedures for the Administrator of General Services to acquire, use, and dispose of land in urban areas. To the greatest extent practicable, urban land transactions entered into for the General Services Administration and other federal agencies shall be consistent with zoning and land use practices and with the planning and development objectives of local governments and planning agencies.

(Pub. L. 107–217, Aug. 21, 2002, 116 Stat. 1127.)

§902. DEFINITIONS

In this chapter, the following definitions apply:

(1) UNIT OF GENERAL LOCAL GOVERNMENT.—The term "unit of general local government" means a city, county, town, parish, village, or other general-purpose political subdivision of a State.

(2) URBAN AREA.—The term "urban area" means—

(A) a geographical area within the jurisdiction of an incorporated city, town, borough, village, or other unit of general local government, except a county or parish, having a population of at least 10,000 inhabitants;

(B) that portion of the geographical area within the jurisdiction of a county, town, township, or similar governmental entity which contains no incorporated unit of general local government but has a population density of at least 1,500 inhabitants per square mile; and

(C) that portion of a geographical area having a population density of at least 1,500 inhabitants per square mile and situated adjacent to the boundary of an incorporated unit of general local government which has a population of at least 10,000.

(Pub. L. 107–217, Aug. 21, 2002, 116 Stat. 1128.)

§903. ACQUISITION AND USE

(a) NOTICE TO LOCAL GOVERNMENT.—To the extent practicable, before making a commitment to acquire real property situated in an urban area, the Administrator of General Services shall give notice of the intended acquisition and the proposed use of the property to the unit of general local government exercising zoning and land use jurisdiction. If the Administrator determines that providing advance notice would adversely impact the acquisition, the Administrator shall give notice of the acquisition and the proposed use of the property immediately after the property is acquired.

(b) OBJECTIONS TO ACQUISITION OR CHANGE OF USE.—In the acquisition or change of use of real property situated in an urban area as a site for public building, if the unit of general local government exercising zoning and land use jurisdiction objects on grounds that the proposed acquisition or change of use conflicts with zoning regulations or planning objectives, the Administrator shall, to the extent the Administrator determines is practicable, consider all the objections and comply with the zoning regulations and planning objectives.

(Pub. L. 107–217, Aug. 21, 2002, 116 Stat. 1128.)

§904. DISPOSAL

(a) NOTICE TO LOCAL GOVERNMENT.—Before offering real property situated in an urban area for sale, the Administrator of General Services shall give reasonable notice to the unit of general local government exercising zoning and land use jurisdiction in order to provide an opportunity for zoning so that the property is used in accordance with local comprehensive planning described in subsection (c).

(b) NOTICE TO PROSPECTIVE PURCHASERS.—To the greatest extent practicable, the Administrator shall furnish to all prospective purchasers of real property situated in an urban area complete information concerning—

(1) current zoning regulations, prospective zoning requirements, and objectives for property if it is unzoned; and

(2)(A) the current availability of streets, sidewalks, sewers, water, street lights, and other service facilities; and

(B) the prospective availability of those service facilities if the property is included in local comprehensive planning described in subsection (c).

(c) LOCAL COMPREHENSIVE PLANNING.—Local comprehensive planning referred to in subsections (a) and (b) includes any of the following activities, to the extent the activity is directly related to the needs of a unit of general local government:

(1) As a guide for government policy and action, preparing general plans related to—

(A) the pattern and intensity of land use;

(B) the provision of public facilities (including transportation facilities) and other government services; and

(C) the effective development and use of human and natural resources.

(2) Preparing long-range physical and fiscal plans for government action.

(3) Programming capital improvements and other major expenditures, based on a determination of relative urgency, together with definitive financial planning for expenditures in the earlier years of a program.

(4) Coordinating related plans and activities of state and local governments and agencies.

(5) Preparing regulatory and administrative measures to support activities described in this subsection.

(Pub. L. 107–217, Aug. 21, 2002, 116 Stat. 1128.)

§905. WAIVER

The procedures prescribed in sections 903 and 904 of this title may be waived during a period of national emergency proclaimed by the President.

(Pub. L. 107–217, Aug. 21, 2002, 116 Stat. 1129.)

CHAPTER 11—SELECTION OF ARCHITECTS AND ENGINEERS

§1101. POLICY

The policy of the Federal Government is to publicly announce all requirements for architectural and engineering services and to negotiate contracts for architectural and engineering services on the basis of demonstrated competence and qualification for the type of professional services required and at fair and reasonable prices.

(Pub. L. 107–217, Aug. 21, 2002, 116 Stat. 1129.)

§1102. DEFINITIONS

In this chapter, the following definitions apply:

(1) AGENCY HEAD.—The term "agency head" means the head of a department, agency, or bureau of the Federal Government.

(2) ARCHITECTURAL AND ENGINEERING SERVICES.—The term "architectural and engineering services" means—

(A) professional services of an architectural or engineering nature, as defined by state law, if applicable, that are required to be performed or approved by a person licensed, registered, or certified to provide the services described in this paragraph;

(B) professional services of an architectural or engineering nature performed by contract that are associated with research, planning, development, design, construction, alteration, or repair of real property; and

(C) other professional services of an architectural or engineering nature, or incidental services, which members of the architectural and engineering professions (and individuals in their employ) may logically or justifiably perform, including studies, investigations, surveying and mapping, tests, evaluations, consultations, comprehensive planning, program management, conceptual designs, plans and specifications, value engineering, construction phase services, soils engineering, drawing reviews, preparation of operating and maintenance manuals, and other related services.

(3) FIRM.—The term "firm" means an individual, firm, partnership, corporation, association, or other legal entity permitted by law to practice the profession of architecture or engineering.

(Pub. L. 107–217, Aug. 21, 2002, 116 Stat. 1129.)

§1103. SELECTION PROCEDURE

(a) IN GENERAL.—These procedures apply to the procurement of architectural and engineering services by an agency head.

(b) ANNUAL STATEMENTS.—The agency head shall encourage firms to submit annually a statement of qualifications and performance data.

(c) EVALUATION.—For each proposed project, the agency head shall evaluate current statements of qualifications and performance data on file with the agency, together with statements submitted by other firms regarding the proposed project. The agency head shall conduct discussions with at least 3 firms to consider anticipated concepts and compare alternative methods for furnishing services.

(d) SELECTION.—From the firms with which discussions have been conducted, the agency head shall select, in order of preference, at least 3 firms that the agency head considers most highly qualified to provide the services required. Selection shall be based on criteria established and published by the agency head.

(Pub. L. 107–217, Aug. 21, 2002, 116 Stat. 1130.)

§1104. NEGOTIATION OF CONTRACT

(a) IN GENERAL.—The agency head shall negotiate a contract for architectural and engineering services at compensation which the agency head determines is fair and reasonable to the Federal Government. In determining fair and reasonable compensation, the agency head shall consider the scope, complexity, professional nature, and estimated value of the services to be rendered.

(b) ORDER OF NEGOTIATION.—The agency head shall attempt to negotiate a contract, as provided in subsection (a), with the most highly qualified firm selected under section 1103 of this title. If the agency head is unable to negotiate a satisfactory contract with the firm, the agency head shall formally terminate negotiations and then undertake negotiations with the next most qualified of the selected firms, continuing the process until an agreement is reached. If the agency head is unable to negotiate a satisfactory contract with any of the selected firms, the agency head shall select additional firms in order of their competence and qualification and continue negotiations in accordance with this section until an agreement is reached.

(Pub. L. 107–217, Aug. 21, 2002, 116 Stat. 1130.)

CHAPTER 13—PUBLIC PROPERTY

§1301. Charge of property transferred to the Federal Government

(a) In General.—Except as provided in subsection (b), the Administrator of General Services shall have charge of—

(1) all land and other property which has been or may be assigned, set off, or conveyed to the Federal Government in payment of debts;

(2) all trusts created for the use of the Government in payment of debts due the Government; and

(3) the sale and disposal of land—

(A) assigned or set off to the Government in payment of debt; or

(B) vested in the Government by mortgage or other security for the payment of debts.

(b) Nonapplication.—This section does not apply to—

(1) real estate which has been or shall be assigned, set off, or conveyed to the Government in payment of debts arising under the Internal Revenue Code of 1986 (26 U.S.C. 1 et seq.); or

(2) trusts created for the use of the Government in payment of debts arising under the Code and due the Government.

(Pub. L. 107–217, Aug. 21, 2002, 116 Stat. 1131.)

§1302. Lease of buildings

Except as otherwise specifically provided by law, the leasing of buildings and property of the Federal Government shall be for a money consideration only. The lease may not include any provision for the alteration, repair, or improvement of the buildings or property as a part of the consideration for the rent to be paid for the use and occupation of the buildings or property. Money derived from the rent shall be deposited in the Treasury as miscellaneous receipts.

(Pub. L. 107–217, Aug. 21, 2002, 116 Stat. 1131.)

§1303. DISPOSITION OF SURPLUS REAL PROPERTY

(a) DEFINITION.—In this section, the term "federal agency" means an executive department, independent establishment, commission, board, bureau, division, or office in the executive branch, or other agency of the Federal Government, including wholly owned Government corporations.

(b) ASSIGNMENT OF SPACE OR LEASE OR SALE OF PROPERTY.—

(1) ACTIONS OF ADMINISTRATOR.—When the President, on the recommendation of the Administrator of General Services, or the federal agency having control of any real property the agency acquires that is located outside of the District of Columbia, other than military or naval reservations, declares the property to be surplus to the needs of the agency, the Administrator—

(A) may assign space in the property to any federal agency;

(B) pending a sale, may lease the property for not more than 5 years and on terms the Administrator considers to be in the public interest; or

(C) may sell the property at public sale to the highest responsible bidder on terms and after public advertisement that the Administrator considers to be in the public interest.

(2) REVIEW OF DECISION TO ASSIGN SPACE.—If the federal agency to which space is assigned does not desire to occupy the space, the decision of the Administrator under paragraph (1)(A) is subject to review by the President.

(3) NEGOTIATED SALE.—If no bids which are satisfactory as to price and responsibility of the bidder are received as a result of public advertisement, the Administrator may sell the property by negotiation, on terms as may be considered to be to the best interest of the Government, but at a price not less than that bid by the highest responsible bidder.

(c) DEMOLITION.—The Administrator may demolish any building declared to be surplus to the needs of the Government under this section on deciding that demolition will be in the best interest of the Government. Before proceeding with the demolition, the Administrator shall inform the Secretary of the Interior in writing of the Administrator's intention to demolish the building, and shall not proceed with the demolition until receiving written notice from the Secretary that the building is not an historic building of national significance within the meaning of chapter 3201 of title 54. If the Secretary does not notify the Administrator of the Secretary's decision as to whether the building is an historic building of national significance within 90 days of the receipt of the notice of intention to demolish the building, the Administrator may proceed to demolish the building.

(d) REPAIRS AND ALTERATIONS TO ASSIGNED REAL PROPERTY.—When the Administrator, after investigation, decides that real property referred to in subsection (b) should be used for the accommodation of a federal agency, the Administrator may make any repairs or alterations that the Administrator considers necessary or advisable and may maintain and operate the property.

(e) PAYMENT BY FEDERAL AGENCIES.—

(1) ASSIGNED REAL PROPERTY.—To the extent that the appropriations of the General Services Administration not otherwise allocated are inadequate for repairs, alterations, maintenance, or operation, the Administrator may require each federal

agency to which space has been assigned to pay promptly by check to the Administrator out of its appropriation for rent any part of the estimated or actual cost of the repairs, alterations, maintenance, and operation. Payment may be either in advance of, or on or during, occupancy of the space. The Administrator shall determine and equitably apportion the total amount to be paid among the agencies to whom space has been assigned.

(2) LEASED SPACES.—To the extent that the appropriations of the Administration not otherwise required are inadequate, the Administrator may require each federal agency to which leased space has been assigned to pay promptly by check to the Administrator out of its available appropriations any part of the estimated cost of rent, repairs, alterations, maintenance, operation, and moving. Payment may be either in advance or during occupancy of the space. When space in a building is occupied by two or more agencies, the Administrator shall determine and equitably apportion rental, operation, and other charges on the basis of the total amount of space leased.

(f) AUTHORIZATION OF APPROPRIATIONS.—Necessary amounts may be appropriated to cover the costs incident to the sale or lease of real property, or authorized demolition of buildings on the property, declared to be surplus to the needs of any federal agency under this section, and the care, maintenance, and protection of the property, including pay of employees, travel of Government employees, brokers' fees not in excess of rates paid for similar services in the community where the property is situated, appraisals, photographs, surveys, evidence of title and perfecting of defective titles, advertising, and telephone and telegraph charges. However, the agency remains responsible for the proper care, maintenance, and protection of the property until the Administrator assumes custody or other disposition of the property is made.

(g) REGULATIONS.—The Administrator may prescribe regulations as necessary to carry out this section.

(Pub. L. 107–217, Aug. 21, 2002, 116 Stat. 1131; Pub. L. 113–287, §5(j)(3), Dec. 19, 2014, 128 Stat. 3269.)

§1304. TRANSFER OF FEDERAL PROPERTY TO STATES

(a) OBSOLETE BUILDINGS AND SITES.—

(1) IN GENERAL.—The Administrator of General Services, in the Administrator's discretion, on terms the Administrator considers proper, and under regulations the Administrator may prescribe, may sell property described in paragraph (2) to a State or a political subdivision of a State for public use if the Administrator considers the sale to be in the best interest of the Federal Government.

(2) APPLICABLE PROPERTY.—The property referred to in paragraph (1) is any federal building, building site, or part of a building site under the Administrator's control that has been replaced by a new structure and that the Administrator determines is no longer needed by the Government.

(3) PRICE.—The purchase price for a sale under this section must be at least 50 percent of the value of the land as appraised by the Administrator.

(4) PROCEEDS OF SALE.—The proceeds of a sale under this section shall be deposited in the Treasury as miscellaneous receipts.

(5) PAYMENT TERMS.—The Administrator may enter into a long term contract for the payment of the purchase price in installments that the Administrator considers fair

and reasonable. The Administrator may waive any requirement for interest charges on deferred payment.

(6) CONVEYANCE.—The Administrator may convey property sold under this section by the usual quitclaim deed.

(b) WIDENING OF PUBLIC ROADS.—

(1) DEFINITION.—In this subsection, the term "executive agency" means an executive department or independent establishment in the executive branch of the Government, including any wholly owned Government corporation.

(2) IN GENERAL.—When a State or a political subdivision of a State applies for a conveyance or transfer of real property of the Government in connection with an authorized widening of a public highway, street, or alley, the head of the executive agency that controls the affected real property may convey or transfer to the State or political subdivision, with or without consideration, an interest in the real property that the agency head determines is not adverse to the interests of the Government. A conveyance or transfer under this subsection is subject to terms and conditions the agency head considers necessary to protect the interests of the Government.

(3) LIMITATION ON TRANSFERS FOR HIGHWAY PURPOSES.—An interest in real property which can be transferred to a State or a political subdivision of a State for highway purposes under title 23 may not be conveyed or transferred under this subsection.

(4) LIMITATION ON ISSUANCE OF RIGHTS OF WAY.—Rights of way over, under, and through public lands and lands in the National Forest System may not be granted under this subsection.

(Pub. L. 107–217, Aug. 21, 2002, 116 Stat. 1133.)

§1305. DISPOSITION OF LAND ACQUIRED BY DEVISE

The General Services Administration may take custody, for disposal as excess property under this subtitle and division C (except sections 3302, 3501(b), 3509, 3906, 4710, and 4711) of subtitle I of title 41, of land acquired by the Federal Government by devise.

(Pub. L. 107–217, Aug. 21, 2002, 116 Stat. 1134; Pub. L. 111–350, §5(l)(12), Jan. 4, 2011, 124 Stat. 3852.)

§1306. DISPOSITION OF ABANDONED OR FORFEITED PERSONAL PROPERTY

(a) DEFINITIONS.—In this section—

(1) AGENCY.—The term "agency" includes any executive department, independent establishment, board, commission, bureau, service, or division of the Federal Government, and any corporation in which the Government owns at least a majority of the stock.

(2) PROPERTY.—The term "property" means all personal property, including vessels, vehicles, and aircraft.

(b) VOLUNTARILY ABANDONED PROPERTY.—Property voluntarily abandoned to any agency in a way that vests title to the property in the Government may be retained by the agency and devoted to official use only. If the agency does not desire to retain the property, the head of the agency immediately shall notify the Administrator of General Services to that effect, and the Administrator, within a reasonable time, shall—

(1) order the agency to deliver the property to another agency that requests the

property and that the Administrator believes should be given the property; or

(2) order disposal of the property as otherwise provided by law.

(c) FORFEITED PROPERTY.—

(1) AGENCY RETAINS PROPERTY.—An agency that seizes property that has been forfeited to the Government other than by court decree may retain the property and devote it only to official use instead of disposing of the property as otherwise provided by law if competent authority does not order the property returned to any claimant.

(2) AGENCY DOES NOT DESIRE TO RETAIN PROPERTY.—If the agency does not desire to retain the property, the head of the agency immediately shall notify the Administrator to that effect, and the property—

(A) if not ordered by competent authority to be returned to any claimant, or disposed of as otherwise provided by law, shall be delivered by the agency, on order of the Administrator given within a reasonable time, to another agency that requests the property and that the Administrator believes should be given the property; or

(B) on order of the Administrator given within a reasonable time, shall be disposed of as otherwise provided by law.

(d) PROPERTY SUBJECT TO COURT PROCEEDING FOR FORFEITURE.—

(1) NOTIFICATION OF ADMINISTRATOR.—If a proceeding has begun for the forfeiture of any property by court decree, the agency that seized the property immediately shall notify the Administrator and at the same time may file with the Administrator a request for the property for its official use.

(2) APPLICATION FOR COURT ORDER TO DELIVER PROPERTY.—

(A) IN GENERAL.—Before entry of a decree, the Administrator shall apply to the court to order delivery of the property in accordance with this paragraph.

(B) DELIVERY TO SEIZING AGENCY.—If the agency that seized the property files a request for the property under paragraph (1), the Administrator shall apply to the court to order delivery of the property to the agency that seized the property.

(C) DELIVERY TO OTHER REQUESTING AGENCY.—If the agency that seized the property does not file a request for the property under paragraph (1) but another agency requests the property, the Administrator shall apply to the court to order delivery of the property to the requesting agency if the Administrator believes that the requesting agency should be given the property.

(D) DELIVERY TO SEIZING AGENCY FOR TEMPORARY HOLDING.—If application to the court cannot be made under subparagraph (B) or (C) and the Administrator believes the property may later become necessary to any agency for official use, the Administrator shall apply to the court to order delivery of the property to the agency that seized the property, to be retained in its custody. Within a reasonable time, the Administrator shall order the agency to—

(i) deliver the property to another agency that requests the property and that the Administrator believes should be given the property; or

(ii) dispose of the property as otherwise provided by law.

(3) FORFEITURE DECREED.—If forfeiture is decreed and the property is not ordered by competent authority to be returned to any claimant, the court shall order delivery

as provided in paragraph (2).

(4) WHEN NO APPLICATION MADE.—The court shall dispose of property for which no application is made in accordance with law.

(e) RETENTION OR DELIVERY OF PROPERTY DEEMED SALE.—Retention or delivery of forfeited or abandoned property under this section is deemed to be a sale of the property for the purpose of laws providing for informer's fees or remission or mitigation of a forfeiture. Property acquired under this section when no longer needed for official use shall be disposed of in the same manner as other surplus property.

(f) PAYMENT OF COSTS RELATED TO PROPERTY.—

(1) AVAILABILITY OF APPROPRIATIONS.—The appropriation available to an agency for the purchase, hire, operation, maintenance, and repair of any property is available for—

(A) the payment of expenses of operation, maintenance, and repair of property of the same kind the agency receives under this section for official use;

(B) the payment of a lien recognized and allowed under law;

(C) the payment of amounts found to be due a person on the authorized remission or mitigation of a forfeiture; and

(D) reimbursement of other agencies as provided in paragraph (2).

(2) PAYMENT AND REIMBURSEMENT OF CERTAIN COSTS.—The agency that receives property under this section shall pay the cost of hauling, transporting, towing, and storing the property. If the property is later delivered to another agency for official use under this section, the agency to which the property is delivered shall make reimbursement for all of those costs incurred prior to the date the property is delivered.

(g) REPORT.—With the approval of the Secretary of the Treasury, the Administrator may require an agency to make a report of all property abandoned to it or seized and the disposal of the property.

(h) ADMINISTRATIVE.—

(1) REGULATIONS.—With the approval of the Secretary, the Administrator may prescribe regulations necessary to carry out this section.

(2) OTHER LAWS NOT REPEALED.—This section does not repeal any other laws relating to the disposition of forfeited or abandoned property, except provisions of those laws directly in conflict with this section which were enacted prior to August 27, 1935.

(3) PROPERTY NOT SUBJECT TO ALLOCATION UNDER THIS SECTION.—The following classes of property are not subject to allocation under this section, but shall be disposed of in the manner otherwise provided by law:

(A) narcotic drugs, as defined in the Controlled Substances Act (21 U.S.C. 801 et seq.).

(B) firearms, as defined in section 5845 of the Internal Revenue Code of 1986 (26 U.S.C. 5845).

(C) other classes or kinds of property the disposal of which the Administrator, with the approval of the Secretary, may consider in the public interest, and may by regulation provide.

(Pub. L. 107–217, Aug. 21, 2002, 116 Stat. 1134.)

§1307. DISPOSITION OF SECURITIES

The President, or an officer, agent, or agency the President may designate, may dispose of any securities acquired on behalf of the Federal Government under the provisions of the Transportation Act of 1920 (ch. 91, 41 Stat. 456), including any securities acquired as an incident to a case under title 11, under a receivership or reorganization proceeding, by assignment, transfer, substitution, or issuance, or by acquisition of collateral given for the payment of obligations to the Government, or may make arrangements for the extension of the maturity of the securities, in the manner, in amounts, at prices, for cash, securities, or other property or any combination of cash, securities, or other property, and on terms and conditions the President or designee considers advisable and in the public interest.

(Pub. L. 107–217, Aug. 21, 2002, 116 Stat. 1137.)

§1308. DISPOSITION OF UNFIT HORSES AND MULES

Subject to applicable regulations under this subtitle and division C (except sections 3302, 3501(b), 3509, 3906, 4710, and 4711) of subtitle I of title 41, horses and mules belonging to the Federal Government that have become unfit for service may be destroyed or put out to pasture, either on pastures belonging to the Government or those belonging to financially sound and reputable humane organizations whose facilities permit them to care for the horses and mules during the remainder of their natural lives, at no cost to the Government.

(Pub. L. 107–217, Aug. 21, 2002, 116 Stat. 1137; Pub. L. 111–350, §5(l)(13), Jan. 4, 2011, 124 Stat. 3852.)

§1309. PRESERVATION, SALE, OR COLLECTION OF WRECKED, ABANDONED, OR DERELICT PROPERTY

The Administrator of General Services may make contracts and provisions for the preservation, sale, or collection of property, or the proceeds of property, which may have been wrecked, been abandoned, or become derelict, if the Administrator considers the contracts and provisions to be in the interest of the Federal Government and the property is within the jurisdiction of the United States and should come to the Government. A contract may provide compensation the Administrator considers just and reasonable to any person who gives information about the property or actually preserves, collects, surrenders, or pays over the property. Under each specific agreement for obtaining, preserving, collecting, or receiving property or making property available, the costs or claim chargeable to the Government may not exceed amounts realized and received by the Government.

(Pub. L. 107–217, Aug. 21, 2002, 116 Stat. 1137.)

§1310. SALE OF WAR SUPPLIES, LAND, AND BUILDINGS

(a) IN GENERAL.—The President, through the head of any executive department and on terms the head of the department considers expedient, may sell to a person, another department of the Federal Government, or the government of a foreign country engaged in war against a country with which the United States is at war—

    (1) war supplies, material, and equipment;

    (2) by-products of the war supplies, material, and equipment; and

(3) any building, plant, or factory, including the land on which the plant or factory may be situated, acquired since April 6, 1917, for the production of war supplies, materials, and equipment that, during the emergency existing on July 9, 1918, may have been purchased, acquired, or manufactured by the Government.

(b) LIMITATION ON SALE OF GUNS AND AMMUNITION.—Sales of guns and ammunition authorized under any law shall be limited to—

(1) other departments of the Government;

(2) governments of foreign countries engaged in war against a country with which the United States is at war; and

(3) members of the National Rifle Association and of other recognized associations organized in the United States for the encouragement of small-arms target practice.

(Pub. L. 107–217, Aug. 21, 2002, 116 Stat. 1137.)

§1311. AUTHORITY OF PRESIDENT TO OBTAIN RELEASE

For the use or benefit of the Federal Government, the President may obtain from an individual or officer to whom land has been or will be conveyed a release of the individual's or officer's interest to the Government.

(Pub. L. 107–217, Aug. 21, 2002, 116 Stat. 1138.)

§1312. RELEASE OF REAL ESTATE IN CERTAIN CASES

(a) IN GENERAL.—Real estate that has become the property of the Federal Government in payment of a debt which afterward is fully paid in money and received by the Government may be conveyed by the Administrator of General Services to the debtor from whom it was taken or to the heirs or devisees of the debtor or the person that they may appoint.

(b) NONAPPLICATION.—This section does not apply to real estate the Government acquires in payment of any debt arising under the Internal Revenue Code of 1986 (26 U.S.C. 1 et seq.).

(Pub. L. 107–217, Aug. 21, 2002, 116 Stat. 1138.)

§1313. RELEASING PROPERTY FROM ATTACHMENT

(a) STIPULATION OF DISCHARGE.—

(1) PERSON ASSERTING CLAIM ENTITLED TO BENEFITS.—In a judicial proceeding under the laws of a State, district, territory, or possession of the United States, when property owned or held by the Federal Government, or in which the Government has or claims an interest, is seized, arrested, attached, or held for the security or satisfaction of a claim made against the property, the Attorney General may direct the United States Attorney for the district in which the property is located to enter a stipulation that on discharge of the property from the seizure, arrest, attachment, or proceeding, the person asserting the claim against the property becomes entitled to all the benefits of this section.

(2) NONAPPLICATION.—This subsection does not—

(A) recognize or concede any right to enforce by seizure, arrest, attachment, or any judicial process a claim against property—

(i) of the Government; or

(ii) held, owned, or employed by the Government, or by a department of the

Government, for a public use; or

(B) waive an objection to a proceeding brought to enforce the claim.

(b) PAYMENT.—After a discharge, a final judgment which affirms the claim for the security or satisfaction and the right of the person asserting the claim to enforce it against the property, notwithstanding the claims of the Government, is deemed to be a full and final determination of the rights of the person and entitles the person, as against the Government, to the rights the person would have had if possession of the property had not been changed. When the claim is for the payment of money found to be due, presentation of an authenticated copy of the record of the judgment and proceedings is sufficient evidence to the proper accounting officers for the allowance of the claim, which shall be allowed and paid out of amounts in the Treasury not otherwise appropriated. The amount allowed and paid shall not exceed the value of the interest of the Government in the property.

(Pub. L. 107–217, Aug. 21, 2002, 116 Stat. 1138.)

§1314. EASEMENTS

(a) DEFINITIONS.—In this section—

(1) EXECUTIVE AGENCY.—The term "executive agency" means an executive department or independent establishment in the executive branch of the Federal Government, including a wholly owned Government corporation.

(2) REAL PROPERTY OF THE GOVERNMENT.—The term "real property of the Government" excludes—

(A) public land (including minerals, vegetative, and other resources) in the United States, including—

(i) land reserved or dedicated for national forest purposes;

(ii) land the Secretary of the Interior administers or supervises in accordance with section 100101(a), chapter 1003, and sections 100751(a), 100752, 100753, and 102101 of title 54;

(iii) Indian-owned trust and restricted land; and

(iv) land the Government acquires primarily for fish and wildlife conservation purposes and the Secretary administers;

(B) land withdrawn from the public domain primarily under the jurisdiction of the Secretary; and

(C) land acquired for national forest purposes.

(3) STATE.—The term "State" means a State of the United States, the District of Columbia, Puerto Rico, and the territories and possessions of the United States.

(b) GRANT OF EASEMENT.—When a State, a political subdivision or agency of a State, or a person applies for the grant of an easement in, over, or on real property of the Government, the executive agency having control of the real property may grant to the applicant, on behalf of the Government, an easement that the head of the agency decides will not be adverse to the interests of the Government, subject to reservations, exceptions, limitations, benefits, burdens, terms, or conditions that the head of the agency considers necessary to protect the interests of the Government. The grant may be made without consideration, or with monetary or other consideration, including an interest in real property.

(c) RELINQUISHMENT OF LEGISLATIVE JURISDICTION.—In connection with the grant of an easement, the executive agency concerned may relinquish to the State in which the real property is located legislative jurisdiction that the executive agency considers necessary or desirable. Relinquishment of legislative jurisdiction may be accomplished by filing with the chief executive officer of the State a notice of relinquishment to take effect upon acceptance or by proceeding in the manner that the laws applicable to the State may provide.

(d) TERMINATION OF EASEMENT.—

(1) WHEN TERMINATION OCCURS.—The instrument granting the easement may provide for termination of any part of the easement if there has been—

(A) a failure to comply with a term or condition of the grant;

(B) a nonuse of the easement for a consecutive 2-year period for the purpose for which granted; or

(C) an abandonment of the easement.

(2) NOTICE REQUIRED.—If a termination provision is included, it shall require that written notice of the termination be given to the grantee, or its successors or assigns.

(3) EFFECTIVE DATE.—The termination is effective as of the date of the notice.

(e) ADDITIONAL EASEMENT AUTHORITY.—The authority conferred by this section is in addition to, and shall not affect or be subject to, any other law under which an executive agency may grant easements.

(f) LIMITATION ON ISSUANCE OF RIGHTS OF WAY.—Rights of way over, under, and through public lands and lands in the National Forest System may not be granted under this section.

(Pub. L. 107–217, Aug. 21, 2002, 116 Stat. 1139; Pub. L. 113–287, §5(j)(4), Dec. 19, 2014, 128 Stat. 3269.)

§1315. LAW ENFORCEMENT AUTHORITY OF SECRETARY OF HOMELAND SECURITY FOR PROTECTION OF PUBLIC PROPERTY

(a) IN GENERAL.—To the extent provided for by transfers made pursuant to the Homeland Security Act of 2002, the Secretary of Homeland Security (in this section referred to as the "Secretary") shall protect the buildings, grounds, and property that are owned, occupied, or secured by the Federal Government (including any agency, instrumentality, or wholly owned or mixed-ownership corporation thereof) and the persons on the property.

(b) OFFICERS AND AGENTS.—

(1) DESIGNATION.—The Secretary may designate employees of the Department of Homeland Security, including employees transferred to the Department from the Office of the Federal Protective Service of the General Services Administration pursuant to the Homeland Security Act of 2002, as officers and agents for duty in connection with the protection of property owned or occupied by the Federal Government and persons on the property, including duty in areas outside the property to the extent necessary to protect the property and persons on the property.

(2) POWERS.—While engaged in the performance of official duties, an officer or agent designated under this subsection may—

(A) enforce Federal laws and regulations for the protection of persons and property;

(B) carry firearms;

(C) make arrests without a warrant for any offense against the United States committed in the presence of the officer or agent or for any felony cognizable under the laws of the United States if the officer or agent has reasonable grounds to believe that the person to be arrested has committed or is committing a felony;

(D) serve warrants and subpoenas issued under the authority of the United States;

(E) conduct investigations, on and off the property in question, of offenses that may have been committed against property owned or occupied by the Federal Government or persons on the property; and

(F) carry out such other activities for the promotion of homeland security as the Secretary may prescribe.

(c) REGULATIONS.—

(1) IN GENERAL.—The Secretary, in consultation with the Administrator of General Services, may prescribe regulations necessary for the protection and administration of property owned or occupied by the Federal Government and persons on the property. The regulations may include reasonable penalties, within the limits prescribed in paragraph (2), for violations of the regulations. The regulations shall be posted and remain posted in a conspicuous place on the property.

(2) PENALTIES.—A person violating a regulation prescribed under this subsection shall be fined under title 18, United States Code, imprisoned for not more than 30 days, or both.

(d) DETAILS.—

(1) REQUESTS OF AGENCIES.—On the request of the head of a Federal agency having charge or control of property owned or occupied by the Federal Government, the Secretary may detail officers and agents designated under this section for the protection of the property and persons on the property.

(2) APPLICABILITY OF REGULATIONS.—The Secretary may—

(A) extend to property referred to in paragraph (1) the applicability of regulations prescribed under this section and enforce the regulations as provided in this section; or

(B) utilize the authority and regulations of the requesting agency if agreed to in writing by the agencies.

(3) FACILITIES AND SERVICES OF OTHER AGENCIES.—When the Secretary determines it to be economical and in the public interest, the Secretary may utilize the facilities and services of Federal, State, and local law enforcement agencies, with the consent of the agencies.

(e) AUTHORITY OUTSIDE FEDERAL PROPERTY.—For the protection of property owned or occupied by the Federal Government and persons on the property, the Secretary may enter into agreements with Federal agencies and with State and local governments to obtain authority for officers and agents designated under this section to enforce Federal laws and State and local laws concurrently with other Federal law enforcement officers and with State and local law enforcement officers.

(f) SECRETARY AND ATTORNEY GENERAL APPROVAL.—The powers granted to officers and agents designated under this section shall be exercised in accordance with guidelines approved by the Secretary and the Attorney General.

(g) LIMITATION ON STATUTORY CONSTRUCTION.—Nothing in this section shall be construed to—

(1) preclude or limit the authority of any Federal law enforcement agency; or

(2) restrict the authority of the Administrator of General Services to promulgate regulations affecting property under the Administrator's custody and control.

(Pub. L. 107–217, Aug. 21, 2002, 116 Stat. 1140; Pub. L. 107–296, title XVII, §1706(b)(1), Nov. 25, 2002, 116 Stat. 2316.)

SUBTITLE II—PUBLIC BUILDINGS AND WORKS

PART A—GENERAL

PART A—GENERAL

CHAPTER 31—GENERAL

SUBCHAPTER I—OVERSIGHT AND REGULATION OF PUBLIC BUILDINGS

Sec.

[1] *Section catchline amended by Pub. L. 113–50 without corresponding amendment of chapter analysis.*

[2] *Section catchline amended by Pub. L. 111–8 without corresponding amendment of chapter analysis.*

³ *Editorially supplied. Section 3177 added by Pub. L. 109–58 without corresponding amendment of chapter analysis.*

SUBCHAPTER I—OVERSIGHT AND REGULATION OF PUBLIC BUILDINGS

§3101. Public buildings under control of Administrator of General Services

All public buildings outside of the District of Columbia and outside of military reservations purchased or erected out of any appropriation under the control of the Administrator of General Services, and the sites of the public buildings, are under the exclusive jurisdiction and control, and in the custody of, the Administrator. The Administrator may take possession of the buildings and assign and reassign rooms in the buildings to federal officials, clerks, and employees that the Administrator believes should be furnished with offices or rooms in the buildings.

(Pub. L. 107–217, Aug. 21, 2002, 116 Stat. 1143.)

§3102. Naming or designating buildings

The Administrator of General Services may name or otherwise designate any building under the custody and control of the General Services Administration, regardless of whether it was previously named by statute.

(Pub. L. 107–217, Aug. 21, 2002, 116 Stat. 1143.)

§3103. Admission of guide dogs or other service animals accompanying individuals with disabilities

(a) In General.—Guide dogs or other service animals accompanying individuals with disabilities and especially trained and educated for that purpose shall be admitted to any building or other property owned or controlled by the Federal Government on the same terms and conditions, and subject to the same regulations, as generally govern the admission of the public to the property. The animals are not permitted to run free or roam in a building or on the property and must be in guiding harness or on leash and under the control of the individual at all times while in a building or on the property.

(b) Regulations.—The head of each department or other agency of the Government may prescribe regulations the individual considers necessary in the public interest to carry out this section as it applies to any building or other property subject to the individual's jurisdiction.

(Pub. L. 107–217, Aug. 21, 2002, 116 Stat. 1143.)

§3104. Furniture for new buildings

Furniture for all new public buildings shall be acquired in accordance with plans and specifications approved by the Administrator of General Services.

(Pub. L. 107–217, Aug. 21, 2002, 116 Stat. 1143.)

§3105. Buildings not to be draped in mourning

No building owned, or used for public purposes, by the Federal Government shall be draped in mourning nor may public money be used for that purpose.

(Pub. L. 107–217, Aug. 21, 2002, 116 Stat. 1143.)

SUBCHAPTER II—ACQUIRING LAND

§3111. APPROVAL OF SUFFICIENCY OF TITLE PRIOR TO ACQUISITION

(a) APPROVAL OF ATTORNEY GENERAL REQUIRED.—Public money may not be expended to purchase land or any interest in land unless the Attorney General gives prior written approval of the sufficiency of the title to the land for the purpose for which the Federal Government is acquiring the property.

(b) DELEGATION.—

(1) IN GENERAL.—The Attorney General may delegate the responsibility under this section to other departments and agencies of the Government, subject to general supervision by the Attorney General and in accordance with regulations the Attorney General prescribes.

(2) REQUEST FOR OPINION OF ATTORNEY GENERAL.—A department or agency of the Government that has been delegated the responsibility to approve land titles under this section may request the Attorney General to render an opinion as to the validity of the title to any real property or interest in the property, or may request the advice or assistance of the Attorney General in connection with determinations as to the sufficiency of titles.

(c) PAYMENT OF EXPENSES FOR PROCURING CERTIFICATES OF TITLE.—Except where otherwise authorized by law or provided by contract, the expenses of procuring certificates of titles or other evidences of title as the Attorney General may require may be paid out of the appropriations for the acquisition of land or out of the appropriations made for the contingencies of the acquiring department or agency of the Government.

(d) NONAPPLICATION.—This section does not affect any provision of law in effect on September 1, 1970, that is applicable to the acquisition of land or interests in land by the Tennessee Valley Authority.

(Pub. L. 107–217, Aug. 21, 2002, 116 Stat. 1144.)

§3112. FEDERAL JURISDICTION

(a) EXCLUSIVE JURISDICTION NOT REQUIRED.—It is not required that the Federal Government obtain exclusive jurisdiction in the United States over land or an interest in land it acquires.

(b) ACQUISITION AND ACCEPTANCE OF JURISDICTION.—When the head of a department, agency, or independent establishment of the Government, or other authorized officer of the department, agency, or independent establishment, considers it desirable, that individual may accept or secure, from the State in which land or an interest in land that is under the immediate jurisdiction, custody, or control of the individual is situated, consent to, or cession of, any jurisdiction over the land or interest not previously obtained. The individual shall indicate acceptance of jurisdiction on behalf of the Government by filing a notice of acceptance with the Governor of the State or in another manner prescribed by the laws of the State where the land is situated.

(c) PRESUMPTION.—It is conclusively presumed that jurisdiction has not been accepted until the Government accepts jurisdiction over land as provided in this section.

(Pub. L. 107–217, Aug. 21, 2002, 116 Stat. 1144.)

§3113. Acquisition by condemnation

An officer of the Federal Government authorized to acquire real estate for the erection of a public building or for other public uses may acquire the real estate for the Government by condemnation, under judicial process, when the officer believes that it is necessary or advantageous to the Government to do so. The Attorney General, on application of the officer, shall have condemnation proceedings begun within 30 days from receipt of the application at the Department of Justice.

(Pub. L. 107–217, Aug. 21, 2002, 116 Stat. 1144.)

§3114. Declaration of taking

(a) Filing and Content.—In any proceeding in any court of the United States outside of the District of Columbia brought by and in the name of the United States and under the authority of the Federal Government to acquire land, or an easement or right of way in land, for the public use, the petitioner may file, with the petition or at any time before judgment, a declaration of taking signed by the authority empowered by law to acquire the land described in the petition, declaring that the land is taken for the use of the Government. The declaration of taking shall contain or have annexed to it—

(1) a statement of the authority under which, and the public use for which, the land is taken;

(2) a description of the land taken that is sufficient to identify the land;

(3) a statement of the estate or interest in the land taken for public use;

(4) a plan showing the land taken; and

(5) a statement of the amount of money estimated by the acquiring authority to be just compensation for the land taken.

(b) Vesting of Title.—On filing the declaration of taking and depositing in the court, to the use of the persons entitled to the compensation, the amount of the estimated compensation stated in the declaration—

(1) title to the estate or interest specified in the declaration vests in the Government;

(2) the land is condemned and taken for the use of the Government; and

(3) the right to just compensation for the land vests in the persons entitled to the compensation.

(c) Compensation.—

(1) Determination and award.—Compensation shall be determined and awarded in the proceeding and established by judgment. The judgment shall include interest, in accordance with section 3116 of this title, on the amount finally awarded as the value of the property as of the date of taking and shall be awarded from that date to the date of payment. Interest shall not be allowed on as much of the compensation as has been paid into the court. Amounts paid into the court shall not be charged with commissions or poundage.

(2) Order to pay.—On application of the parties in interest, the court may order that any part of the money deposited in the court be paid immediately for or on account of the compensation to be awarded in the proceeding.

(3) Deficiency judgment.—If the compensation finally awarded is more than the amount of money received by any person entitled to compensation, the court shall enter judgment against the Government for the amount of the deficiency.

(d) AUTHORITY OF COURT.—On the filing of a declaration of taking, the court—

(1) may fix the time within which, and the terms on which, the parties in possession shall be required to surrender possession to the petitioner; and

(2) may make just and equitable orders in respect of encumbrances, liens, rents, taxes, assessments, insurance, and other charges.

(e) VESTING NOT PREVENTED OR DELAYED.—An appeal or a bond or undertaking given in a proceeding does not prevent or delay the vesting of title to land in the Government.

(Pub. L. 107–217, Aug. 21, 2002, 116 Stat. 1145.)

§3115. IRREVOCABLE COMMITMENT OF FEDERAL GOVERNMENT TO PAY ULTIMATE AWARD WHEN FIXED

(a) REQUIREMENT FOR IRREVOCABLE COMMITMENT.—Action under section 3114 of this title irrevocably committing the Federal Government to the payment of the ultimate award shall not be taken unless the head of the executive department or agency or bureau of the Government empowered to acquire the land believes that the ultimate award probably will be within any limits Congress prescribes on the price to be paid.

(b) AUTHORIZED PURPOSES OF EXPENDITURES AFTER IRREVOCABLE COMMITMENT MADE.—When the Government has taken or may take title to real property during a condemnation proceeding and in advance of final judgment in the proceeding and has become irrevocably committed to pay the amount ultimately to be awarded as compensation, and the Attorney General believes that title to the property has been vested in the Government or that all persons having an interest in the property have been made parties to the proceeding and will be bound by the final judgment, the Government may expend amounts appropriated for that purpose to demolish existing structures on the property and to erect public buildings or public works on the property.

(Pub. L. 107–217, Aug. 21, 2002, 116 Stat. 1146.)

§3116. INTEREST AS PART OF JUST COMPENSATION

(a) CALCULATION.—The district court shall calculate interest required to be paid under this subchapter as follows:

(1) PERIOD OF NOT MORE THAN ONE YEAR.—Where the period for which interest is owed is not more than one year, interest shall be calculated from the date of taking at an annual rate equal to the weekly average one-year constant maturity Treasury yield, as published by the Board of Governors of the Federal Reserve System, for the calendar week preceding the date of taking.

(2) PERIOD OF MORE THAN ONE YEAR.—Where the period for which interest is owed is more than one year, interest for the first year shall be calculated in accordance with paragraph (1) and interest for each additional year shall be calculated on the amount by which the award of compensation is more than the deposit referred to in section 3114 of this title, plus accrued interest, at an annual rate equal to the weekly average one-year constant maturity Treasury yield, as published by the Board of Governors of the Federal Reserve System, for the calendar week preceding the beginning of each additional year.

(b) DISTRIBUTION OF NOTICE OF RATES.—The Director of the Administrative Office of the United States Courts shall distribute to all federal courts notice of the rates described in paragraphs (1) and (2) of subsection (a).

(Pub. L. 107–217, Aug. 21, 2002, 116 Stat. 1146.)

§3117. Exclusion of certain property by stipulation of Attorney General

In any condemnation proceeding brought by or on behalf of the Federal Government, the Attorney General may stipulate or agree on behalf of the Government to exclude any part of the property, or any interest in the property, taken by or on behalf of the Government by a declaration of taking or otherwise.

(Pub. L. 107–217, Aug. 21, 2002, 116 Stat. 1147.)

§3118. Right of taking as addition to existing rights

The right to take possession and title in advance of final judgment in condemnation proceedings as provided by section 3114 of this title is in addition to any right, power, or authority conferred by the laws of the United States or of a State, territory, or possession of the United States under which the proceeding may be conducted, and does not abrogate, limit, or modify that right, power, or authority.

(Pub. L. 107–217, Aug. 21, 2002, 116 Stat. 1147.)

SUBCHAPTER III—BONDS

§3131. Bonds of contractors of public buildings or works

(a) Definition.—In this subchapter, the term "contractor" means a person awarded a contract described in subsection (b).

(b) Type of Bonds Required.—Before any contract of more than $100,000 is awarded for the construction, alteration, or repair of any public building or public work of the Federal Government, a person must furnish to the Government the following bonds, which become binding when the contract is awarded:

(1) Performance bond.—A performance bond with a surety satisfactory to the officer awarding the contract, and in an amount the officer considers adequate, for the protection of the Government.

(2) Payment bond.—A payment bond with a surety satisfactory to the officer for the protection of all persons supplying labor and material in carrying out the work provided for in the contract for the use of each person. The amount of the payment bond shall equal the total amount payable by the terms of the contract unless the officer awarding the contract determines, in a writing supported by specific findings, that a payment bond in that amount is impractical, in which case the contracting officer shall set the amount of the payment bond. The amount of the payment bond shall not be less than the amount of the performance bond.

(c) Coverage for Taxes in Performance Bond.—

(1) In general.—Every performance bond required under this section specifically shall provide coverage for taxes the Government imposes which are collected, deducted, or withheld from wages the contractor pays in carrying out the contract with respect to which the bond is furnished.

(2) Notice.—The Government shall give the surety on the bond written notice, with respect to any unpaid taxes attributable to any period, within 90 days after the date when the contractor files a return for the period, except that notice must be given

no later than 180 days from the date when a return for the period was required to be filed under the Internal Revenue Code of 1986 (26 U.S.C. 1 et seq.).

(3) CIVIL ACTION.—The Government may not bring a civil action on the bond for the taxes—

(A) unless notice is given as provided in this subsection; and

(B) more than one year after the day on which notice is given.

(d) WAIVER OF BONDS FOR CONTRACTS PERFORMED IN FOREIGN COUNTRIES.—A contracting officer may waive the requirement of a performance bond and payment bond for work under a contract that is to be performed in a foreign country if the officer finds that it is impracticable for the contractor to furnish the bonds.

(e) AUTHORITY TO REQUIRE ADDITIONAL BONDS.—This section does not limit the authority of a contracting officer to require a performance bond or other security in addition to those, or in cases other than the cases, specified in subsection (b).

(Pub. L. 107–217, Aug. 21, 2002, 116 Stat. 1147; Pub. L. 109–284, §6(8), Sept. 27, 2006, 120 Stat. 1213.)

§3132. ALTERNATIVES TO PAYMENT BONDS PROVIDED BY FEDERAL ACQUISITION REGULATION

(a) IN GENERAL.—The Federal Acquisition Regulation shall provide alternatives to payment bonds as payment protections for suppliers of labor and materials under contracts referred to in section 3131(a) of this title that are more than $25,000 and not more than $100,000.

(b) RESPONSIBILITIES OF CONTRACTING OFFICER.—The contracting officer for a contract shall—

(1) select, from among the payment protections provided for in the Federal Acquisition Regulation pursuant to subsection (a), one or more payment protections which the offeror awarded the contract is to submit to the Federal Government for the protection of suppliers of labor and materials for the contract; and

(2) specify in the solicitation of offers for the contract the payment protections selected.

(Pub. L. 107–217, Aug. 21, 2002, 116 Stat. 1148.)

§3133. RIGHTS OF PERSONS FURNISHING LABOR OR MATERIAL

(a) RIGHT OF PERSON FURNISHING LABOR OR MATERIAL TO COPY OF BOND.—The department secretary or agency head of the contracting agency shall furnish a certified copy of a payment bond and the contract for which it was given to any person applying for a copy who submits an affidavit that the person has supplied labor or material for work described in the contract and payment for the work has not been made or that the person is being sued on the bond. The copy is prima facie evidence of the contents, execution, and delivery of the original. Applicants shall pay any fees the department secretary or agency head of the contracting agency fixes to cover the cost of preparing the certified copy.

(b) RIGHT TO BRING A CIVIL ACTION.—

(1) IN GENERAL.—Every person that has furnished labor or material in carrying out work provided for in a contract for which a payment bond is furnished under section 3131 of this title and that has not been paid in full within 90 days after the day on

which the person did or performed the last of the labor or furnished or supplied the material for which the claim is made may bring a civil action on the payment bond for the amount unpaid at the time the civil action is brought and may prosecute the action to final execution and judgment for the amount due.

(2) PERSON HAVING DIRECT CONTRACTUAL RELATIONSHIP WITH A SUBCONTRACTOR.—A person having a direct contractual relationship with a subcontractor but no contractual relationship, express or implied, with the contractor furnishing the payment bond may bring a civil action on the payment bond on giving written notice to the contractor within 90 days from the date on which the person did or performed the last of the labor or furnished or supplied the last of the material for which the claim is made. The action must state with substantial accuracy the amount claimed and the name of the party to whom the material was furnished or supplied or for whom the labor was done or performed. The notice shall be served—

(A) by any means that provides written, third-party verification of delivery to the contractor at any place the contractor maintains an office or conducts business or at the contractor's residence; or

(B) in any manner in which the United States marshal of the district in which the public improvement is situated by law may serve summons.

(3) VENUE.—A civil action brought under this subsection must be brought—

(A) in the name of the United States for the use of the person bringing the action; and

(B) in the United States District Court for any district in which the contract was to be performed and executed, regardless of the amount in controversy.

(4) PERIOD IN WHICH ACTION MUST BE BROUGHT.—An action brought under this subsection must be brought no later than one year after the day on which the last of the labor was performed or material was supplied by the person bringing the action.

(5) LIABILITY OF FEDERAL GOVERNMENT.—The Government is not liable for the payment of any costs or expenses of any civil action brought under this subsection.

(c) WAIVER OF RIGHT TO CIVIL ACTION.—A waiver of the right to bring a civil action on a payment bond required under this subchapter is void unless the waiver is—

(1) in writing;

(2) signed by the person whose right is waived; and

(3) executed after the person whose right is waived has furnished labor or material for use in the performance of the contract.

(Pub. L. 107–217, Aug. 21, 2002, 116 Stat. 1148; Pub. L. 109–284, §6(9), (10), Sept. 27, 2006, 120 Stat. 1213.)

§3134. WAIVERS FOR CERTAIN CONTRACTS

(a) MILITARY.—The Secretary of the Army, the Secretary of the Navy, the Secretary of the Air Force, or the Secretary of Transportation may waive this subchapter with respect to cost-plus-a-fixed fee and other cost-type contracts for the construction, alteration, or repair of any public building or public work of the Federal Government and with respect to contracts for manufacturing, producing, furnishing, constructing, altering, repairing, processing, or assembling vessels, aircraft, munitions, materiel, or supplies for the Army, Navy, Air Force, or Coast Guard, respectively, regardless of the terms of the contracts as to payment or title.

(b) TRANSPORTATION.—The Secretary of Transportation may waive this subchapter with respect to contracts for the construction, alteration, or repair of vessels when the contract is made under sections 1535 and 1536 of title 31 or subtitle V of title 46, regardless of the terms of the contracts as to payment or title.

(c) NATIONAL OCEANIC AND ATMOSPHERIC ADMINISTRATION.—The Secretary of Commerce may waive this subchapter with respect to contracts for the construction, alteration, or repair of vessels, regardless of the terms of the contracts as to payment or title, when the contract is made under the Act entitled "An Act to define the functions and duties of the Coast and Geodetic Survey, and for other purposes", approved August 6, 1947 (33 U.S.C. 883a et seq.).

(Pub. L. 107–217, Aug. 21, 2002, 116 Stat. 1149; Pub. L. 109–304, §17(g)(2), Oct. 6, 2006, 120 Stat. 1709; Pub. L. 115–91, div. C, title XXXV, §3502(b)(2), Dec. 12, 2017, 131 Stat. 1910; Pub. L. 115–232, div. C, title XXXV, §3515(c), Aug. 13, 2018, 132 Stat. 2313.)

SUBCHAPTER IV—WAGE RATE REQUIREMENTS

§3141. DEFINITIONS

In this subchapter, the following definitions apply:

(1) FEDERAL GOVERNMENT.—The term "Federal Government" has the same meaning that the term "United States" had in the Act of March 3, 1931 (ch. 411, 46 Stat. 1494) (known as the Davis-Bacon Act).

(2) WAGES, SCALE OF WAGES, WAGE RATES, MINIMUM WAGES, AND PREVAILING WAGES.—The terms "wages", "scale of wages", "wage rates", "minimum wages", and "prevailing wages" include—

(A) the basic hourly rate of pay; and

(B) for medical or hospital care, pensions on retirement or death, compensation for injuries or illness resulting from occupational activity, or insurance to provide any of the forgoing, for unemployment benefits, life insurance, disability and sickness insurance, or accident insurance, for vacation and holiday pay, for defraying the costs of apprenticeship or other similar programs, or for other bona fide fringe benefits, but only where the contractor or subcontractor is not required by other federal, state, or local law to provide any of those benefits, the amount of—

(i) the rate of contribution irrevocably made by a contractor or subcontractor to a trustee or to a third person under a fund, plan, or program; and

(ii) the rate of costs to the contractor or subcontractor that may be reasonably anticipated in providing benefits to laborers and mechanics pursuant to an enforceable commitment to carry out a financially responsible plan or program which was communicated in writing to the laborers and mechanics affected.

(Pub. L. 107–217, Aug. 21, 2002, 116 Stat. 1150; Pub. L. 109–284, §6(11), Sept. 27, 2006, 120 Stat. 1213.)

§3142. RATE OF WAGES FOR LABORERS AND MECHANICS

(a) APPLICATION.—The advertised specifications for every contract in excess of $2,000, to which the Federal Government or the District of Columbia is a party, for construction, alteration, or repair, including painting and decorating, of public buildings and public works of the Government or the District of Columbia that are located in a State or the District of Columbia and which requires or involves the employment of mechanics or laborers shall contain a provision stating the minimum wages to be paid various classes of laborers and mechanics.

(b) BASED ON PREVAILING WAGE.—The minimum wages shall be based on the wages the Secretary of Labor determines to be prevailing for the corresponding classes of laborers and mechanics employed on projects of a character similar to the contract work in the civil subdivision of the State in which the work is to be performed, or in the District of Columbia if the work is to be performed there.

(c) STIPULATIONS REQUIRED IN CONTRACT.—Every contract based upon the specifications referred to in subsection (a) must contain stipulations that—

(1) the contractor or subcontractor shall pay all mechanics and laborers employed directly on the site of the work, unconditionally and at least once a week, and without subsequent deduction or rebate on any account, the full amounts accrued at time of payment, computed at wage rates not less than those stated in the advertised specifications, regardless of any contractual relationship which may be alleged to exist between the contractor or subcontractor and the laborers and mechanics;

(2) the contractor will post the scale of wages to be paid in a prominent and easily accessible place at the site of the work; and

(3) there may be withheld from the contractor so much of accrued payments as the contracting officer considers necessary to pay to laborers and mechanics employed by the contractor or any subcontractor on the work the difference between the rates of wages required by the contract to be paid laborers and mechanics on the work and the rates of wages received by the laborers and mechanics and not refunded to the contractor or subcontractors or their agents.

(d) DISCHARGE OF OBLIGATION.—The obligation of a contractor or subcontractor to make payment in accordance with the prevailing wage determinations of the Secretary of Labor, under this subchapter and other laws incorporating this subchapter by reference, may be discharged by making payments in cash, by making contributions described in section 3141(2)(B)(i) of this title, by assuming an enforceable commitment to bear the costs of a plan or program referred to in section 3141(2)(B)(ii) of this title, or by any combination of payment, contribution, and assumption, where the aggregate of the payments, contributions, and costs is not less than the basic hourly rate of pay plus the amount referred to in section 3141(2)(B) of this title.

(e) OVERTIME PAY.—In determining the overtime pay to which a laborer or mechanic is entitled under any federal law, the regular or basic hourly rate of pay (or other alternative rate on which premium rate of overtime compensation is computed) of the laborer or mechanic is deemed to be the rate computed under section 3141(2)(A) of this title, except that where the amount of payments, contributions, or costs incurred with respect to the laborer or mechanic exceeds the applicable prevailing wage, the regular or basic hourly rate of pay (or other alternative rate) is the amount of payments, contributions, or costs actually incurred with respect to the laborer or mechanic minus the greater of the amount of contributions or costs of the types described in section 3141(2)(B) of this title actually incurred with respect to the laborer or mechanic or the amount determined under section 3141(2)(B) of this title but not actually paid.

(Pub. L. 107–217, Aug. 21, 2002, 116 Stat. 1150; Pub. L. 109–284, §6(12), (13), Sept. 27, 2006, 120 Stat. 1213.)

§3143. TERMINATION OF WORK ON FAILURE TO PAY AGREED WAGES

Every contract within the scope of this subchapter shall contain a provision that if the contracting officer finds that any laborer or mechanic employed by the contractor or any subcontractor directly on the site of the work covered by the contract has been or is being paid a rate of wages less than the rate of wages required by the contract to be paid, the Federal Government by written notice to the contractor may terminate the contractor's right to proceed with the work or the part of the work as to which there has been a failure to pay the required wages. The Government may have the work completed, by contract or otherwise, and the contractor and the contractor's sureties shall be liable to the Government for any excess costs the Government incurs.

(Pub. L. 107–217, Aug. 21, 2002, 116 Stat. 1151.)

§3144. AUTHORITY TO PAY WAGES AND LIST CONTRACTORS VIOLATING CONTRACTS

(a) PAYMENT OF WAGES.—

(1) IN GENERAL.—The Secretary of Labor shall pay directly to laborers and mechanics from any accrued payments withheld under the terms of a contract any wages found to be due laborers and mechanics under this subchapter.

(2) RIGHT OF ACTION.—If the accrued payments withheld under the terms of the contract are insufficient to reimburse all the laborers and mechanics who have not been paid the wages required under this subchapter, the laborers and mechanics have the same right to bring a civil action and intervene against the contractor and the contractor's sureties as is conferred by law on persons furnishing labor or materials. In those proceedings it is not a defense that the laborers and mechanics accepted or agreed to accept less than the required rate of wages or voluntarily made refunds.

(b) LIST OF CONTRACTORS VIOLATING CONTRACTS.—

(1) IN GENERAL.—The Comptroller General shall distribute to all departments of the Federal Government a list of the names of persons whom the Comptroller General has found to have disregarded their obligations to employees and subcontractors.

(2) RESTRICTION ON AWARDING CONTRACTS.—No contract shall be awarded to persons appearing on the list or to any firm, corporation, partnership, or association in which the persons have an interest until three years have elapsed from the date of publication of the list.

(Pub. L. 107–217, Aug. 21, 2002, 116 Stat. 1152; Pub. L. 113–50, §2(a), Nov. 21, 2013, 127 Stat. 578.)

§3145. REGULATIONS GOVERNING CONTRACTORS AND SUBCONTRACTORS

(a) IN GENERAL.—The Secretary of Labor shall prescribe reasonable regulations for contractors and subcontractors engaged in constructing, carrying out, completing, or repairing public buildings, public works, or buildings or works that at least partly are financed by a loan or grant from the Federal Government. The regulations shall include a provision that each contractor and subcontractor each week must furnish a statement on the wages paid each employee during the prior week.

(b) APPLICATION.—Section 1001 of title 18 applies to the statements.

(Pub. L. 107–217, Aug. 21, 2002, 116 Stat. 1152.)

§3146. EFFECT ON OTHER FEDERAL LAWS

This subchapter does not supersede or impair any authority otherwise granted by federal law to provide for the establishment of specific wage rates.

(Pub. L. 107–217, Aug. 21, 2002, 116 Stat. 1152.)

§3147. SUSPENSION OF THIS SUBCHAPTER DURING A NATIONAL EMERGENCY

The President may suspend the provisions of this subchapter during a national emergency.

(Pub. L. 107–217, Aug. 21, 2002, 116 Stat. 1153.)

§3148. APPLICATION OF THIS SUBCHAPTER TO CERTAIN CONTRACTS

This subchapter applies to a contract authorized by law that is made without regard to section 6101(b) to (d) of title 41, or on a cost-plus-a-fixed-fee basis or otherwise without advertising for proposals, if this subchapter otherwise would apply to the contract.

(Pub. L. 107–217, Aug. 21, 2002, 116 Stat. 1153; Pub. L. 111–350, §5(l)(14), Jan. 4, 2011, 124 Stat. 3852.)

SUBCHAPTER V—VOLUNTEER SERVICES

§3161. PURPOSE

It is the purpose of this subchapter to promote and provide opportunities for individuals who wish to volunteer their services to state or local governments, public agencies, or nonprofit charitable organizations in the construction, repair, or alteration (including painting and decorating) of public buildings and public works that at least partly are financed with federal financial assistance authorized under certain federal programs and that otherwise might not be possible without the use of volunteers.

(Pub. L. 107–217, Aug. 21, 2002, 116 Stat. 1153.)

§3162. WAIVER FOR INDIVIDUALS WHO PERFORM VOLUNTEER SERVICES

(a) CRITERIA FOR RECEIVING WAIVER.—The requirement that certain laborers and mechanics be paid in accordance with the wage-setting provisions of subchapter IV of this chapter as set forth in the Indian Self-Determination and Education Assistance Act (25 U.S.C. 450 et seq.),[1] the Indian Health Care Improvement Act (25 U.S.C. 1601 et seq.), and the Housing and Community Development Act of 1974 (42 U.S.C. 5301 et seq.) does not apply to an individual—

(1) who volunteers to perform a service directly to a state or local government, a public agency, or a public or private nonprofit recipient of federal assistance—

(A) for civic, charitable, or humanitarian reasons;

(B) only for the personal purpose or pleasure of the individual;

(C) without promise, expectation, or receipt of compensation for services rendered, except as provided in subsection (b); and

(D) freely and without pressure or coercion, direct or implied, from any employer;

(2) whose contribution of service is not for the direct or indirect benefit of any contractor otherwise performing or seeking to perform work on the same project for which the individual is volunteering;

(3) who is not employed by and does not provide services to a contractor or subcontractor at any time on the federally assisted or insured project for which the individual is volunteering; and

(4) who otherwise is not employed by the same public agency or recipient of federal assistance to perform the same type of services as those for which the individual proposes to volunteer.

(b) PAYMENTS.—

(1) IN ACCORDANCE WITH REGULATIONS.—Volunteers described in subsection (a) who are performing services directly to a state or local government or public agency may receive payments of expenses, reasonable benefits, or a nominal fee only in accordance with regulations the Secretary of Labor prescribes. Volunteers who are performing services directly to a public or private nonprofit entity may not receive those payments.

(2) CRITERIA AND CONTENT OF REGULATIONS.—In prescribing the regulations, the Secretary shall consider criteria such as the total amount of payments made (relating to expenses, benefits, or fees) in the context of the economic realities. The regulations shall include provisions that provide that—

(A) a payment for an expense may be received by a volunteer for items such as uniform allowances, protective gear and clothing, reimbursement for approximate out-of-pocket expenses, or the cost or expense of meals and transportation;

(B) a reasonable benefit may include the inclusion of a volunteer in a group insurance plan (such as a liability, health, life, disability, or worker's compensation plan) or pension plan, or the awarding of a length of service award; and

(C) a nominal fee may not be used as a substitute for compensation and may not be connected to productivity.

(3) NOMINAL FEE.—The Secretary shall decide what constitutes a nominal fee for purposes of paragraph (2)(C). The decision shall be based on the context of the economic realities of the situation involved.

(c) ECONOMIC REALITY.—In determining whether an expense, benefit, or fee described in subsection (b) may be paid to volunteers in the context of the economic realities of the particular situation, the Secretary may not permit any expense, benefit, or fee that has the effect of undermining labor standards by creating downward pressure on prevailing wages in the local construction industry.

(Pub. L. 107–217, Aug. 21, 2002, 116 Stat. 1153.)

[1] *See References in Text note below.*

SUBCHAPTER VI—MISCELLANEOUS

§3171. CONTRACT AUTHORITY WHEN APPROPRIATION IS FOR LESS THAN FULL AMOUNT

Unless specifically directed otherwise, the Administrator of General Services may make a contract within the full limit of the cost fixed by Congress for the acquisition of land for sites, or for the enlargement of sites, for public buildings, or for the erection, remodeling, extension, alteration, and repairs of public buildings, even though an appropriation is made for only part of the amount necessary to carry out legislation authorizing that purpose.

(Pub. L. 107–217, Aug. 21, 2002, 116 Stat. 1154.)

§3172. EXTENSION OF STATE WORKERS' COMPENSATION LAWS TO BUILDINGS, WORKS, AND PROPERTY OF THE FEDERAL GOVERNMENT

(a) AUTHORIZATION OF EXTENSION.—The state authority charged with enforcing and requiring compliance with the state workers' compensation laws and with the orders, decisions, and awards of the authority may apply the laws to all land and premises in the State which the Federal Government owns or holds by deed or act of cession, and to all projects, buildings, constructions, improvements, and property in the State and belonging to the Government, in the same way and to the same extent as if the premises were under the exclusive jurisdiction of the State in which the land, premises, projects, buildings, constructions, improvements, or property are located.

(b) LIMITATION ON RELINQUISHING JURISDICTION.—The Government under this section does not relinquish its jurisdiction for any other purpose.

(c) NONAPPLICATION.—This section does not modify or amend subchapter I of chapter 81 of title 5.

(Pub. L. 107–217, Aug. 21, 2002, 116 Stat. 1154.)

§3173. WORKING CAPITAL FUND FOR GENERAL SERVICES ADMINISTRATION

(a) ESTABLISHMENT AND PURPOSE.—There is a working capital fund for the necessary expenses of administrative support services including accounting, budget, personnel, legal support and other related services; and the maintenance and operation of printing and reproduction facilities in support of the functions of the General Services Administration, other Federal agencies, and other entities; and other such administrative and management services that the Administrator of GSA deems appropriate and advantageous (subject to prior notice to the Office of Management and Budget).

(b) COMPOSITION.—

(1) IN GENERAL.—Amounts received, including advance payments, shall be credited to and merged with the Fund, to remain available until expended, for operating costs and capital outlays of the Fund: *Provided*, That entities for which such services are performed shall be charged at rates which will return in full all costs of providing such services.

(2) COST AND CAPITAL REQUIREMENTS.—The Administrator shall determine the cost and capital requirements of the Fund for each fiscal year and shall develop a plan concerning such requirements in consultation with the Chief Financial Officer of the General Services Administration. Any change to the cost and capital requirements of the Fund for a fiscal year shall be approved by the Administrator. The Administrator shall establish rates to be charged to entities for which services are performed, in accordance with the plan.

(c) DEPOSIT OF EXCESS AMOUNTS IN THE TREASURY.—At the close of each fiscal year, after making provision for anticipated operating needs reflected in the cost and capital plan developed under subsection (b), the uncommitted balance of any funds remaining in the Fund shall be transferred to the general fund of the Treasury as miscellaneous receipts.

(d) TRANSFER AND USE OF AMOUNTS FOR MAJOR EQUIPMENT ACQUISITIONS.—

(1) IN GENERAL.—Subject to subparagraph (2), unobligated balances of amounts

appropriated or otherwise made available to the General Services Administration for operating expenses and salaries and expenses may be transferred and merged into the "Major equipment acquisitions and development activity" of the working capital fund of the General Services Administration for agency-wide acquisition of capital equipment, automated data processing systems and financial management and management information systems: *Provided*, That acquisitions are limited to those needed to implement the Chief Financial Officers Act of 1990 (Public Law 101–576, 104 Stat. 2838) and related laws or regulations or for agency-wide acquisition of equipment or systems or the acquisition of services in lieu thereof, as necessary to implement the Act.

(2) REQUIREMENTS AND AVAILABILITY.—

(A) TIME FOR TRANSFER.—Transfer of an amount under this section must be done no later than the end of the fifth fiscal year after the fiscal year for which the amount is appropriated or otherwise made available.

(B) APPROVAL FOR USE.—An amount transferred under this section may be used only with the advance approval of the Committees on Appropriations of the House of Representatives and the Senate.

(C) AVAILABILITY.—An amount transferred under this section remains available until expended.

(Pub. L. 107–217, Aug. 21, 2002, 116 Stat. 1155; Pub. L. 111–8, div. D, title V, §518(a), (b), (c)(2), Mar. 11, 2009, 123 Stat. 664, 665; Pub. L. 117–103, div. E, title V, §§528, 529, Mar. 15, 2022, 136 Stat. 276.)

§3174. OPERATION OF PUBLIC UTILITY COMMUNICATIONS SERVICES SERVING GOVERNMENTAL ACTIVITIES

The Administrator of General Services may provide and operate public utility communications services serving any governmental activity when the services are economical and in the interest of the Federal Government. This section does not apply to communications systems for handling messages of a confidential or secret nature, the operation of cryptographic equipment or transmission of secret, security, or coded messages, or buildings operated or occupied by the United States Postal Service, except on request of the department or agency concerned.

(Pub. L. 107–217, Aug. 21, 2002, 116 Stat. 1155.)

§3175. ACCEPTANCE OF GIFTS OF PROPERTY

The Administrator of General Services, and the United States Postal Service where that office is concerned, may accept on behalf of the Federal Government unconditional gifts of property in aid of any project or function within their respective jurisdictions.

(Pub. L. 107–217, Aug. 21, 2002, 116 Stat. 1155.)

§3176. ADMINISTRATOR OF GENERAL SERVICES TO FURNISH SERVICES IN CONTINENTAL UNITED STATES TO INTERNATIONAL BODIES

Sections 1535 and 1536 of title 31 are extended so that the Administrator of General Services, at the request of the Secretary of State, may furnish services in the continental United States, on a reimbursable basis, to any international body with which the Federal Government is affiliated.

(Pub. L. 107–217, Aug. 21, 2002, 116 Stat. 1156.)

§3177. USE OF PHOTOVOLTAIC ENERGY IN PUBLIC BUILDINGS

(a) PHOTOVOLTAIC ENERGY COMMERCIALIZATION PROGRAM.—

(1) IN GENERAL.—The Administrator of General Services may establish a photovoltaic energy commercialization program for the procurement and installation of photovoltaic solar electric systems for electric production in new and existing public buildings.

(2) PURPOSES.—The purposes of the program shall be to accomplish the following:

(A) To accelerate the growth of a commercially viable photovoltaic industry to make this energy system available to the general public as an option which can reduce the national consumption of fossil fuel.

(B) To reduce the fossil fuel consumption and costs of the Federal Government.

(C) To attain the goal of installing solar energy systems in 20,000 Federal buildings by 2010, as contained in the Federal Government's Million Solar Roof Initiative of 1997.

(D) To stimulate the general use within the Federal Government of life-cycle costing and innovative procurement methods.

(E) To develop program performance data to support policy decisions on future incentive programs with respect to energy.

(3) ACQUISITION OF PHOTOVOLTAIC SOLAR ELECTRIC SYSTEMS.—

(A) IN GENERAL.—The program shall provide for the acquisition of photovoltaic solar electric systems and associated storage capability for use in public buildings.

(B) ACQUISITION LEVELS.—The acquisition of photovoltaic electric systems shall be at a level substantial enough to allow use of low-cost production techniques with at least 150 megawatts (peak) cumulative acquired during the 5 years of the program.

(4) ADMINISTRATION.—The Administrator shall administer the program and shall—

(A) issue such rules and regulations as may be appropriate to monitor and assess the performance and operation of photovoltaic solar electric systems installed pursuant to this subsection;

(B) develop innovative procurement strategies for the acquisition of such systems; and

(C) transmit to Congress an annual report on the results of the program.

(b) PHOTOVOLTAIC SYSTEMS EVALUATION PROGRAM.—

(1) IN GENERAL.—Not later than 60 days after the date of enactment of this section, the Administrator shall establish a photovoltaic solar energy systems evaluation program to evaluate such photovoltaic solar energy systems as are required in public buildings.

(2) PROGRAM REQUIREMENT.—In evaluating photovoltaic solar energy systems under the program, the Administrator shall ensure that such systems reflect the most advanced technology.

(c) AUTHORIZATION OF APPROPRIATIONS.—

(1) PHOTOVOLTAIC ENERGY COMMERCIALIZATION PROGRAM.—There are authorized to be appropriated to carry out subsection (a) $50,000,000 for each of fiscal years 2006 through 2010. Such sums shall remain available until expended.

(2) PHOTOVOLTAIC SYSTEMS EVALUATION PROGRAM.—There are authorized to be

appropriated to carry out subsection (b) $10,000,000 for each of fiscal years 2006 through 2010. Such sums shall remain available until expended.

(Added Pub. L. 109–58, title II, §204(a), Aug. 8, 2005, 119 Stat. 653.)

CHAPTER 33—ACQUISITION, CONSTRUCTION, AND ALTERATION

[1] *So in original. Two sections 3318 have been enacted.*

§3301. DEFINITIONS AND NONAPPLICATION

(a) DEFINITIONS.—In this chapter—

(1) ALTER.—The term "alter" includes—

(A) preliminary planning, engineering, architectural, legal, fiscal, and economic investigations and studies, surveys, designs, plans, working drawings, specifications, procedures, and other similar actions necessary for the alteration of a public building; and

(B) repairing, remodeling, improving, or extending, or other changes in, a public building.

(2) CONSTRUCT.—The term "construct" includes preliminary planning, engineering, architectural, legal, fiscal, and economic investigations and studies, surveys, designs, plans, working drawings, specifications, procedures, and other similar actions necessary for the construction of a public building.

(3) EXECUTIVE AGENCY.—The term "executive agency" means an executive department or independent establishment in the executive branch of the Federal Government, including—

(A) any wholly owned Government corporation;

(B) the Central-Bank for Cooperatives and the regional banks for cooperatives;

(C) federal land banks;

(D) federal intermediate credit banks;

(E) the Federal Deposit Insurance Corporation; and

(F) the Government National Mortgage Association.

(4) FEDERAL AGENCY.—The term "federal agency" means an executive agency or an establishment in the legislative or judicial branch of the Government (except the Senate, the House of Representatives, and the Architect of the Capitol and any activities under the direction of the Architect).

(5) PUBLIC BUILDING.—The term "public building"—

(A) means a building, whether for single or multitenant occupancy, and its grounds, approaches, and appurtenances, which is generally suitable for use as office or storage space or both by one or more federal agencies or mixed-ownership Government corporations;

(B) includes—

(i) federal office buildings;

(ii) post offices;

(iii) customhouses;

(iv) courthouses;

(v) appraisers stores;

(vi) border inspection facilities;

(vii) warehouses;

(viii) record centers;

(ix) relocation facilities;

(x) telecommuting centers;

(xi) similar federal facilities; and

(xii) any other buildings or construction projects the inclusion of which the President considers to be justified in the public interest; but

(C) does not include a building or construction project described in subparagraphs (A) and (B)—

(i) that is on the public domain (including that reserved for national forests and other purposes);

(ii) that is on property of the Government in foreign countries;

(iii) that is on Indian and native Eskimo property held in trust by the Government;

(iv) that is on land used in connection with federal programs for agricultural, recreational, and conservation purposes, including research in connection with the programs;

(v) that is on or used in connection with river, harbor, flood control, reclamation or power projects, for chemical manufacturing or development projects, or for nuclear production, research, or development projects;

(vi) that is on or used in connection with housing and residential projects;

(vii) that is on military installations (including any fort, camp, post, naval training station, airfield, proving ground, military supply depot, military school, or any similar facility of the Department of Defense);

(viii) that is on installations of the Department of Veterans Affairs used for hospital or domiciliary purposes; or

(ix) the exclusion of which the President considers to be justified in the public interest.

(6) UNITED STATES.—The term "United States" includes the States of the United States, the District of Columbia, Puerto Rico, and the territories and possessions of the United States.

(b) NONAPPLICATION.—This chapter does not apply to the construction of any public building to which section 241(g) of the Immigration and Nationality Act (8 U.S.C. 1231(g)) or section 1 of the Act of June 26, 1930 (19 U.S.C. 68) applies.

(Pub. L. 107–217, Aug. 21, 2002, 116 Stat. 1156.)

§3302. PROHIBITION ON CONSTRUCTION OF BUILDINGS EXCEPT BY ADMINISTRATOR OF GENERAL SERVICES

Only the Administrator of General Services may construct a public building. The Administrator shall construct a public building in accordance with this chapter.

(Pub. L. 107–217, Aug. 21, 2002, 116 Stat. 1158.)

§3303. CONTINUING INVESTIGATION AND SURVEY OF PUBLIC BUILDINGS

(a) CONDUCTED BY ADMINISTRATOR.—The Administrator of General Services shall—

(1) make a continuing investigation and survey of the public buildings needs of the Federal Government so that the Administrator may carry out the duties of the Administrator under this chapter; and

(2) submit to Congress prospectuses of proposed projects in accordance with section 3307(a) and (b) of this title.

(b) COOPERATION WITH FEDERAL AGENCIES.—

(1) DUTIES OF ADMINISTRATOR.—In carrying out the duties of the Administrator under this chapter, the Administrator—

(A) shall cooperate with all federal agencies in order to keep informed of their needs;

(B) shall advise each federal agency of the program with respect to the agency; and

(C) may request the cooperation and assistance of each federal agency in carrying out duties under this chapter.

(2) DUTY OF FEDERAL AGENCIES.—Each federal agency shall cooperate with, advise, and assist the Administrator in carrying out the duties of the Administrator under this chapter as determined necessary by the Administrator to carry out the purposes of this chapter.

(c) REQUEST FOR IDENTIFICATION OF EXISTING BUILDINGS OF HISTORICAL, ARCHITECTURAL, OR CULTURAL SIGNIFICANCE.—When the Administrator undertakes a survey of the public buildings needs of the Government within a geographical area, the Administrator shall request that, within 60 days, the Advisory Council on Historic Preservation established by section 304101 of title 54 identify any existing buildings in the geographical area that—

(1) are of historical, architectural, or cultural significance (as defined in section 3306(a) of this title); and

(2) whether or not in need of repair, alteration, or addition, would be suitable for acquisition to meet the public buildings needs of the Government.

(d) STANDARD FOR CONSTRUCTION AND ACQUISITION OF PUBLIC BUILDINGS.—In carrying out the duties of the Administrator under this chapter, the Administrator shall provide for the construction and acquisition of public buildings equitably throughout the United States with due regard to the comparative urgency of the need for each particular building. In developing plans for new buildings, the Administrator shall give due consideration to excellence of architecture and design.

(Pub. L. 107–217, Aug. 21, 2002, 116 Stat. 1158; Pub. L. 113–287, §5(j)(5), Dec. 19, 2014, 128 Stat. 3269.)

§3304. ACQUISITION OF BUILDINGS AND SITES

(a) IN GENERAL.—The Administrator of General Services may acquire, by purchase, condemnation, donation, exchange, or otherwise, any building and its site which the Administrator decides is necessary to carry out the duties of the Administrator under this chapter.

(b) ACQUISITION OF LAND OR INTEREST IN LAND FOR USE AS SITES.—The Administrator may acquire, by purchase, condemnation, donation, exchange, or otherwise, land or an interest in land the Administrator considers necessary for use as sites, or additions to sites, for public buildings authorized to be constructed or altered under this chapter.

(c) PUBLIC BUILDINGS USED FOR POST OFFICE PURPOSES.—When any part of a public building is to be used for post office purposes, the Administrator shall act jointly with the United States Postal Service in selecting the town or city where the building is to be constructed, and in selecting the site in the town or city for the building.

(d) SOLICITATION OF PROPOSALS FOR SALE, DONATION, OR EXCHANGE OF REAL PROPERTY.—When the Administrator is to acquire a site under subsection (b), the Administrator, if the Administrator considers it necessary, by public advertisement may solicit proposals for the sale, donation, or exchange of real property to the Federal Government to be used as the site. In selecting a site under subsection (b) the Administrator (with the concurrence of the United States Postal Service if any part of the public building to be constructed on the site is to be used for post office purposes) may—

(1) select the site that the Administrator believes is the most advantageous to the Government, all factors considered; and

(2) acquire the site without regard to division C (except sections 3302, 3501(b), 3509, 3906, 4710, and 4711) of subtitle I of title 41.

(Pub. L. 107–217, Aug. 21, 2002, 116 Stat. 1158; Pub. L. 108–178, §3(1), Dec. 15, 2003, 117 Stat. 2640; Pub. L. 111–350, §5(l)(15), Jan. 4, 2011, 124 Stat. 3852.)

§3305. CONSTRUCTION AND ALTERATION OF BUILDINGS

(a) CONSTRUCTION.—

(1) REPLACEMENT OF EXISTING BUILDINGS.—When the Administrator of General Services considers it to be in the best interest of the Federal Government to construct a new public building to take the place of an existing public building, the Administrator may demolish the existing building and use the site on which it is located for the site of the proposed public building. If the Administrator believes that it is more advantageous to construct the public building on a different site in the same city, the Administrator may exchange the building and site, or the site, for another site, or may sell the building and site in accordance with subtitle I of this title and division C

(except sections 3302, 3501(b), 3509, 3906, 4710, and 4711) of subtitle I of title 41.

(2) SALE OR EXCHANGE OF SITES.—When the Administrator decides that a site acquired for the construction of a public building is not suitable for that purpose, the Administrator may exchange the site for another site, or may sell it in accordance with subtitle I of this title and division C (except sections 3302, 3501(b), 3509, 3906, 4710, and 4711) of subtitle I of title 41.

(3) COMMITTEE APPROVAL REQUIRED.—This subsection does not permit the Administrator to use any land as a site for a public building if the project has not been approved in accordance with section 3307 of this title.

(b) ALTERATION OF BUILDINGS.—

(1) AUTHORITY TO ALTER BUILDINGS AND ACQUIRE LAND.—The Administrator may—

(A) alter any public building; and

(B) acquire in accordance with section 3304(b)–(d) of this title land necessary to carry out the alteration.

(2) COMMITTEE APPROVAL NOT REQUIRED.—

(A) THRESHOLD AMOUNT.—Approval under section 3307 of this title is not required for any alteration and acquisition authorized by this subsection for which the estimated maximum cost does not exceed $1,500,000.

(B) DOLLAR AMOUNT ADJUSTMENT.—The Administrator annually may adjust the dollar amount referred to in subparagraph (A) to reflect a percentage increase or decrease in construction costs during the prior calendar year, as determined by the composite index of construction costs of the Department of Commerce. Any adjustment shall be expeditiously reported to the Committee on Environment and Public Works of the Senate and the Committee on Transportation and Infrastructure of the House of Representatives.

(c) CONSTRUCTION OR ALTERATION BY CONTRACT.—The Administrator may carry out any construction or alteration authorized by this chapter by contract if the Administrator considers it to be most advantageous to the Government.

(Pub. L. 107–217, Aug. 21, 2002, 116 Stat. 1159; Pub. L. 111–350, §5(l)(16), Jan. 4, 2011, 124 Stat. 3852.)

§3306. ACCOMMODATING FEDERAL AGENCIES

(a) DEFINITIONS.—In this section—

(1) COMMERCIAL ACTIVITIES.—The term "commercial activities" includes the operations of restaurants, food stores, craft stores, dry goods stores, financial institutions, and display facilities.

(2) CULTURAL ACTIVITIES.—The term "cultural activities" includes film, dramatic, dance, and musical presentations, and fine art exhibits, whether or not those activities are intended to make a profit.

(3) EDUCATIONAL ACTIVITIES.—The terms "educational activities" includes the operations of libraries, schools, day care centers, laboratories, and lecture and demonstration facilities.

(4) HISTORICAL, ARCHITECTURAL, OR CULTURAL SIGNIFICANCE.—The term "historical, architectural, or cultural significance" includes buildings listed or eligible to be listed on the National Register established under chapter 3021 of title 54.

(5) RECREATIONAL ACTIVITIES.—The term "recreational activities" includes the operations of gymnasiums and related facilities.

(6) UNIT OF GENERAL LOCAL GOVERNMENT.—The term "unit of general local government" means a city, county, town, parish, village, or other general-purpose political subdivision of a State.

(b) DUTIES OF ADMINISTRATOR.—To carry out the duties of the Administrator of General Services under sections 581(h), 584(b), 3303(c), and 3307(b)(3) and (5) of this title and under any other authority with respect to constructing, operating, maintaining, altering, and otherwise managing or acquiring space necessary to accommodate federal agencies and to accomplish the purposes of sections 581(h), 584(b), 3303(c), and 3307(b)(3) and (5), the Administrator shall—

(1) acquire and utilize space in suitable buildings of historical, architectural, or cultural significance, unless use of the space would not prove feasible and prudent compared with available alternatives;

(2) encourage the location of commercial, cultural, educational, and recreational facilities and activities in public buildings;

(3) provide and maintain space, facilities, and activities, to the extent practicable, that encourage public access to, and stimulate public pedestrian traffic around, into, and through, public buildings, permitting cooperative improvements to and uses of the area between the building and the street, so that the activities complement and supplement commercial, cultural, educational, and recreational resources in the neighborhood of public buildings; and

(4) encourage the public use of public buildings for cultural, educational, and recreational activities.

(c) CONSULTATION AND SOLICITATION OF COMMENTS.—In carrying out the duties under subsection (b), the Administrator shall—

(1) consult with chief executive officers of the States, areawide agencies established pursuant to title II of the Demonstration Cities and Metropolitan Development Act of 1966 (42 U.S.C. 3331 et seq.) and section 6506 of title 31, and chief executive officers of those units of general local government in each area served by an existing or proposed public building; and

(2) solicit the comments of other community leaders and members of the general public as the Administrator considers appropriate.

(Pub. L. 107–217, Aug. 21, 2002, 116 Stat. 1160; Pub. L. 113–287, §5(j)(6), Dec. 19, 2014, 128 Stat. 3269.)

§3307. CONGRESSIONAL APPROVAL OF PROPOSED PROJECTS

(a) RESOLUTIONS REQUIRED BEFORE APPROPRIATIONS MAY BE MADE.—The following appropriations may be made only if the Committee on Environment and Public Works of the Senate and the Committee on Transportation and Infrastructure of the House of Representatives adopt resolutions approving the purpose for which the appropriation is made:

(1) An appropriation to construct, alter, or acquire any building to be used as a public building which involves a total expenditure in excess of $1,500,000, so that the equitable distribution of public buildings throughout the United States with due regard for the comparative urgency of need for the buildings, except as provided in

section 3305(b) of this title, is ensured.

(2) An appropriation to lease any space at an average annual rental in excess of $1,500,000 for use for public purposes.

(3) An appropriation to alter any building, or part of the building, which is under lease by the Federal Government for use for a public purpose if the cost of the alteration will exceed $750,000.

(b) TRANSMISSION TO CONGRESS OF PROSPECTUS OF PROPOSED PROJECT.—To secure consideration for the approval referred to in subsection (a), the Administrator of General Services (referred to in this section as the "Administrator") shall transmit to Congress a prospectus of the proposed facility, including—

(1) a brief description of the building to be constructed, altered, or acquired, or the space to be leased, under this chapter;

(2) the location of the building or space to be leased and an estimate of the maximum cost to the Government of the facility to be constructed, altered, or acquired, or the space to be leased;

(3) a comprehensive plan for providing space for all Government officers and employees in the locality of the proposed facility or the space to be leased, having due regard for suitable space which may continue to be available in existing Government-owned or occupied buildings, especially those buildings that enhance the architectural, historical, social, cultural, and economic environment of the locality;

(4) with respect to any project for the construction, alteration, or acquisition of any building, a statement by the Administrator that suitable space owned by the Government is not available and that suitable rental space is not available at a price commensurate with that to be afforded through the proposed action;

(5) a statement by the Administrator of the economic and other justifications for not acquiring a building identified to the Administrator under section 3303(c) of this title as suitable for the public building needs of the Government;

(6) a statement of rents and other housing costs currently being paid by the Government for federal agencies to be housed in the building to be constructed, altered, or acquired, or the space to be leased;

(7) with respect to any prospectus for the construction, alteration, or acquisition of any building or space to be leased, an estimate of the future energy performance of the building or space and a specific description of the use of energy efficient and renewable energy systems, including photovoltaic systems, in carrying out the project;

(8) a statement of how the proposed project is consistent with the standards and criteria developed under section 11(b) of the Federal Assets Sale and Transfer Act of 2016;

(9) information on any space occupied by the relevant agency in the geographical area of the proposed facility, including uses, utilization rates, any proposed consolidations, and, if not proposed to be consolidated, a justification for such determination;

(10) a statement by the Administrator of whether the public building needs of the Government for the proposed space to be leased were formerly met by a federally owned building, including any building identified for disposal or sale; and

(11) details on actual utilization rates, including number of personnel assigned to the facility, number of personnel expected to work in-person at the facility and whether all personnel identified reflect filled and authorized positions.

(c) INCREASE OF ESTIMATED MAXIMUM COST.—The estimated maximum cost of any project approved under this section as set forth in any prospectus may be increased by an amount equal to any percentage increase, as determined by the Administrator, in construction or alteration costs from the date the prospectus is transmitted to Congress. The increase authorized by this subsection may not exceed 10 percent of the estimated maximum cost. The Administrator shall notify, in writing, the Committee on Transportation and Infrastructure of the House of Representatives and the Committee on Environment and Public Works of the Senate of any increase of more than 5 percent of an estimated maximum cost or of any increase or decrease in the scope or size of a project of 5 or more percent. Such notification shall include an explanation regarding any such increase or decrease. The scope or size of a project shall not increase or decrease by more than 10 percent unless an amended prospectus is submitted and approved pursuant to this section.

(d) RESCISSION OF APPROVAL.—If an appropriation is not made within one year after the date a project for construction, alteration, or acquisition is approved under subsection (a), the Committee on Environment and Public Works of the Senate or the Committee on Transportation and Infrastructure of the House of Representatives by resolution may rescind its approval before an appropriation is made.

(e) EMERGENCY LEASES BY THE ADMINISTRATOR.—This section does not prevent the Administrator from entering into emergency leases during any period declared by the President to require emergency leasing authority. An emergency lease may not be for more than 180 days without approval of a prospectus for the lease in accordance with subsection (a).

(f) MINIMUM PERFORMANCE REQUIREMENTS FOR LEASED SPACE.—With respect to space to be leased, the Administrator shall include, to the maximum extent practicable, minimum performance requirements requiring energy efficiency and the use of renewable energy.

(g) LIMITATION ON LEASING CERTAIN SPACE.—

(1) IN GENERAL.—The Administrator may not lease space to accommodate any of the following if the average rental cost of leasing the space will exceed $1,500,000:

(A) Computer and telecommunications operations.

(B) Secure or sensitive activities related to the national defense or security, except when it would be inappropriate to locate those activities in a public building or other facility identified with the Government.

(C) A permanent courtroom, judicial chamber, or administrative office for any United States court.

(2) EXCEPTION.—The Administrator may lease space with respect to which paragraph (1) applies if the Administrator—

(A) decides, for reasons set forth in writing, that leasing the space is necessary to meet requirements which cannot be met in public buildings; and

(B) submits the reasons to the Committee on Environment and Public Works of the Senate and the Committee on Transportation and Infrastructure of the House of

Representatives.

(h) DOLLAR AMOUNT ADJUSTMENT.—The Administrator annually may adjust any dollar amount referred to in this section to reflect a percentage increase or decrease in construction costs during the prior calendar year, as determined by the composite index of construction costs of the Department of Commerce. Any adjustment shall be expeditiously reported to the Committee on Environment and Public Works of the Senate and the Committee on Transportation and Infrastructure of the House of Representatives.

(i) NOTIFICATION REQUIRED.—For each project approved under this section, the Administrator shall notify, in writing, the Committee on Transportation and Infrastructure of the House of Representatives and the Committee on Environment and Public Works of the Senate of any project milestones that are accomplished, including—

(1) the solicitation and award of design and construction services;

(2) the completion of any actions required for the project pursuant to the National Environmental Policy Act of 1969 (42 U.S.C. 4321 et seq.);

(3) any ceremonies for the beginning or completion of the project;

(4) a naming ceremony for the project; and

(5) the completion of the project.

(j) EXPIRATION OF COMMITTEE RESOLUTIONS.—

(1) IN GENERAL.—Unless a lease is awarded or a construction, alteration, repair, design, or acquisition project is initiated not later than 5 years after the resolution approvals adopted by the Committee on Transportation and Infrastructure of the House of Representatives and the Committee on Environment and Public Works of the Senate pursuant to subsection (a), the resolutions shall be deemed expired.

(2) APPLICATION.—This subsection shall only apply to resolutions approved after the date of enactment of this subsection.

(Pub. L. 107–217, Aug. 21, 2002, 116 Stat. 1161; Pub. L. 110–140, title III, §323(a), (b), Dec. 19, 2007, 121 Stat. 1589, 1590; Pub. L. 114–287, §17, Dec. 16, 2016, 130 Stat. 1476; Pub. L. 118–272, div. B, title III, §§2304(a), (c), (f), 2310, Jan. 4, 2025, 138 Stat. 3223, 3224, 3227.)

§3308. ARCHITECTURAL OR ENGINEERING SERVICES

(a) EMPLOYMENT BY ADMINISTRATOR.—When the Administrator of General Services decides it to be necessary, the Administrator may employ, by contract or otherwise, without regard to chapters 33 and 51 and subchapter III of chapter 53 of title 5, civil service rules and regulations, or section 6101(b) to (d) of title 41, the services of established architectural or engineering corporations, firms, or individuals, to the extent the Administrator may require those services for any public building authorized to be constructed or altered under this chapter.

(b) EMPLOYMENT ON PERMANENT BASIS NOT PERMITTED.—A corporation, firm, or individual shall not be employed under authority of subsection (a) on a permanent basis.

(c) RESPONSIBILITY OF ADMINISTRATOR.—Notwithstanding any other provision of this section, the Administrator is responsible for all construction authorized by this chapter, including the interpretation of construction contracts, approval of material and workmanship supplied under a construction contract, approval of changes in the construction contract, certification of vouchers for payments due the contractor, and final settlement of the contract.

(Pub. L. 107–217, Aug. 21, 2002, 116 Stat. 1163; Pub. L. 111–350, §5(l)(17), Jan. 4, 2011, 124 Stat. 3852.)

§3309. Buildings and sites in the District of Columbia

(a) In General.—The purposes of this chapter shall be carried out in the District of Columbia as nearly as may be practicable in harmony with the plan of Peter Charles L'Enfant. Public buildings shall be constructed or altered to combine architectural beauty with practical utility.

(b) Closing of Streets and Alleys.—When the Administrator of General Services decides that constructing or altering a public building under this chapter in the District of Columbia requires using contiguous squares as a site for the building, parts of streets that lie between the squares, and alleys that intersect the squares, may be closed and vacated if agreed to by the Administrator, the Council of the District of Columbia, and the National Capital Planning Commission. Those streets and alleys become part of the site.

(c) Consultations Prior to Acquisitions.—

(1) With house office building commission.—The Administrator must consult with the House Office Building Commission created by the Act of March 4, 1907 (ch. 2918, 34 Stat. 1365), before the Administrator may acquire land located south of Independence Avenue, between Third Street SW and Eleventh Street SE, in the District of Columbia, for use as a site or an addition to a site.

(2) With architect of capitol.—The Administrator must consult with the Architect of the Capitol before the Administrator may acquire land located in the area extending from the United States Capitol Grounds to Eleventh Street NE and SE and bounded by Independence Avenue on the south and G Street NE on the north, in the District of Columbia, for use as a site or an addition to a site.

(d) Contracts for Events in Stadium.—Notwithstanding the District of Columbia Stadium Act of 1957 (Public Law 85–300, 71 Stat. 619) or any other provision of law, the Armory Board may make contracts to conduct events in Robert F. Kennedy Stadium.

(Pub. L. 107–217, Aug. 21, 2002, 116 Stat. 1163.)

§3310. Special rules for leased buildings

For any building to be constructed for lease to, and for predominant use by, the Federal Government, the Administrator of General Services—

(1) notwithstanding section 585(a)(1) of this title, shall not make any agreement or undertake any commitment which will result in the construction of the building until the Administrator has established detailed specification requirements for the building;

(2) may acquire a leasehold interest in the building only by the use of competitive procedures required by sections 3105, 3301, and 3303 to 3305 of title 41;

(3) shall include in the solicitation for any lease requiring a prospectus under section 3307 an evaluation factor considering the extent to which the offeror will promote energy efficiency and the use of renewable energy;

(4) shall inspect every building during construction to establish that the specifications established for the building are complied with;

(5) on completion of the building, shall evaluate the building to determine the extent of failure to comply with the specifications referred to in clause (1); and

(6) shall ensure that any contract entered into for the building shall contain provisions permitting a reduction of rent during any period when the building is not in compliance with the specifications.

(Pub. L. 107–217, Aug. 21, 2002, 116 Stat. 1164; Pub. L. 110–140, title III, §323(d), Dec. 19, 2007, 121 Stat. 1591; Pub. L. 111–350, §5(l)(18), Jan. 4, 2011, 124 Stat. 3852.)

§3311. STATE ADMINISTRATION OF CRIMINAL AND HEALTH AND SAFETY LAWS

When the Administrator of General Services considers it desirable, the Administrator may assign to a State or a territory or possession of the United States any part of the authority of the Federal Government to administer criminal laws and health and safety laws with respect to land or an interest in land under the control of the Administrator and located in the State, territory, or possession. Assignment of authority under this section may be accomplished by filing with the chief executive officer of the State, territory, or possession a notice of assignment to take effect on acceptance, or in another manner as may be prescribed by the laws of the State, territory, or possession in which the land or interest is located.

(Pub. L. 107–217, Aug. 21, 2002, 116 Stat. 1164.)

§3312. COMPLIANCE WITH NATIONALLY RECOGNIZED CODES

(a) APPLICATION.—

(1) IN GENERAL.—This section applies to any project for construction or alteration of a building for which amounts are first appropriated for a fiscal year beginning after September 30, 1989.

(2) NATIONAL SECURITY WAIVER.—This section does not apply to a building for which the Administrator of General Services or the head of the federal agency authorized to construct or alter the building decides that the application of this section to the building would adversely affect national security. A decision under this subsection is not subject to administrative or judicial review.

(b) BUILDING CODES.—Each building constructed or altered by the General Services Administration or any other federal agency shall be constructed or altered, to the maximum extent feasible as determined by the Administrator or the head of the federal agency, in compliance with one of the nationally recognized model building codes and with other applicable nationally recognized codes, including electrical codes, fire and life safety codes, and plumbing codes, as the Administrator decides is appropriate. In carrying out this subsection, the Administrator or the head of the federal agency shall use the latest edition of the nationally recognized codes.

(c) ZONING LAWS.—Each building constructed or altered by the Administration or any other federal agency shall be constructed or altered only after consideration of all requirements (except procedural requirements) of the following laws of a State or a political subdivision of a State, which would apply to the building if it were not a building constructed or altered by a federal agency:

(1) Zoning laws.

(2) Laws relating to landscaping, open space, minimum distance of a building from the property line, maximum height of a building, historic preservation, esthetic qualities of a building, and other similar laws.

(d) COOPERATION WITH STATE AND LOCAL OFFICIALS.—

(1) STATE AND LOCAL GOVERNMENT CONSULTATION, REVIEW, AND INSPECTIONS.—To meet the requirements of subsections (b) and (c), the Administrator or the head of the federal agency authorized to construct or alter the building—

(A) in preparing plans for the building, shall consult with appropriate officials of the State or political subdivision of a State, or both, in which the building will be located;

(B) on request shall submit the plans in a timely manner to the officials for review by the officials for a reasonable period of time not exceeding 30 days; and

(C) shall permit inspection by the officials during construction or alteration of the building, in accordance with the customary schedule of inspections for construction or alteration of buildings in the locality, if the officials provide to the Administrator or the head of the federal agency—

(i) a copy of the schedule before construction of the building is begun; and

(ii) reasonable notice of their intention to conduct any inspection before conducting the inspection.

(2) LIMITATION ON RESPONSIBILITIES.—This section does not impose an obligation on any State or political subdivision to take any action under paragraph (1).

(e) STATE AND LOCAL GOVERNMENT RECOMMENDATIONS.—Appropriate officials of a State or political subdivision of a State may make recommendations to the Administrator or the head of the federal agency authorized to construct or alter a building concerning measures necessary to meet the requirements of subsections (b) and (c). The officials also may make recommendations to the Administrator or the head of the federal agency concerning measures which should be taken in the construction or alteration of the building to take into account local conditions. The Administrator or the head of the agency shall give due consideration to the recommendations.

(f) EFFECT OF NONCOMPLIANCE.—An action may not be brought against the Federal Government and a fine or penalty may not be imposed against the Government for failure to meet the requirements of subsection (b), (c), or (d) or for failure to carry out any recommendation under subsection (e).

(g) LIMITATION ON LIABILITY.—The Government and its contractors shall not be required to pay any amount for any action a State or a political subdivision of a State takes to carry out this section, including reviewing plans, carrying out on-site inspections, issuing building permits, and making recommendations.

(Pub. L. 107–217, Aug. 21, 2002, 116 Stat. 1165.)

§3313. PROCUREMENT OF LIFE-CYCLE COST EFFECTIVE AND ENERGY EFFICIENT LIGHTING SYSTEMS

(a) DEFINITIONS.—In this section:

(1) ADMINISTRATOR.—The term "Administrator" means the Administrator of General Services.

(2) LIGHTING SYSTEM.—The term "lighting system" means the elements required to maintain a desired light level, including lamps, light fixtures, fixture distribution, sensors and control technologies, interior design elements, and daylighting sources.

(b) PROCUREMENT.—

(1) IN GENERAL.—To the maximum extent practicable, the Administrator shall—

(A) procure the most life-cycle cost effective and energy efficient lighting systems; and

(B) ensure that procurements after the date of enactment of the BRIGHT Act of lighting systems or the individual components of lighting systems maximize life-cycle cost effectiveness and energy efficiency.

(2) USE.—Each public building constructed, altered, acquired, or leased by the Administrator shall be equipped, to the maximum extent practicable as determined by the Administrator, with the most life-cycle cost effective and energy efficient lighting systems for each application.

(c) MAINTENANCE OF PUBLIC BUILDINGS.—Each individual component of a lighting system, including a lamp or fixture, that is replaced by the Administrator in the normal course of maintenance of public buildings shall be replaced, to the maximum extent practicable, with the most life-cycle cost effective and energy efficient lighting system possible for the application.

(d) CONSIDERATIONS.—

(1) CONTRACTING OPTIONS.—In carrying out this section, the Administrator shall consider appropriate contracting options for the procurement of the most life-cycle cost effective and energy efficient lighting systems.

(2) PROCUREMENT AND USE.—In making a determination under this section concerning the practicability of procuring and installing the most life-cycle cost effective and energy efficient lighting system, the Administrator shall consider—

(A) the compatibility of the lighting system with existing equipment, including consideration of a cost effective retrofit;

(B) whether procurement and use of the lighting system could result in interference with productivity;

(C) the aesthetics relating to the use of the lighting system; and

(D) such other factors as the Administrator determines to be appropriate.

(e) LIFE-CYCLE COST EFFECTIVE.—The Administrator shall use the procedures and methods established under section 544(a) of the National Energy Conservation Policy Act (42 U.S.C. 8254(a)) in determining whether a lighting system is life-cycle cost effective.

(f) ENERGY STAR.—A lighting system shall be treated as being energy efficient for purposes of this section if—

(1) the lighting system or the individual components of the lighting system are certified under the Energy Star program established by section 324A of the Energy Policy and Conservation Act (42 U.S.C. 6294a);

(2) in the case of all light-emitting diode (LED) luminaires, lamps, and systems whose efficacy (lumens per watt) and Color Rendering Index (CRI) meet the Department of Energy requirements for minimum luminaire efficacy and CRI for the Energy Star certification, as verified by an independent third-party testing laboratory that the Administrator and the Secretary of Energy determine conducts its tests according to the procedures and recommendations of the Illuminating Engineering Society of North America, even if the luminaires, lamps, and systems have not received such certification; or

(3) the Administrator and the Secretary of Energy have otherwise determined that

the lighting system is energy efficient.

(g) ADDITIONAL ENERGY EFFICIENT LIGHTING DESIGNATIONS.—The Administrator of the Environmental Protection Agency and the Secretary of Energy shall give priority to establishing Energy Star performance criteria or Federal Energy Management Program designations for additional lighting product categories that are appropriate for procurement and use in public buildings.

(h) GUIDELINES.—The Administrator shall develop guidelines for the procurement and use of energy efficient lighting technologies that contain mercury in child care centers in public buildings.

(i) APPLICABILITY OF BUY AMERICAN ACT.—Acquisitions carried out pursuant to this section shall be subject to the requirements of the Buy American Act [1] (41 U.S.C. 10c et seq.).

(Added Pub. L. 110–140, title III, §323(c)(1)(B), Dec. 19, 2007, 121 Stat. 1590; amended Pub. L. 117–202, §3(a), Oct. 17, 2022, 136 Stat. 2224.)

[1] *See References in Text note below.*

§3314. BABY CHANGING FACILITIES IN RESTROOMS

(a) ADDITIONAL REQUIREMENT FOR THE CONSTRUCTION, ALTERATION, AND ACQUISITION OF PUBLIC BUILDINGS.—Except as provided in subsection (b) and subject to any reasonable accommodations that may be made for individuals in accordance with the Americans with Disabilities Act (42 U.S.C. 12101 et seq.) restrooms in a public building shall be equipped with baby changing facilities that the Administrator determines are physically safe, sanitary, and appropriate.

(b) EXCEPTIONS.—The requirement under subsection (a) shall not apply—

(1) to a restroom in a public building that is not available or accessible for public use;

(2) to a restroom in a public building that contains clear and conspicuous signage indicating where a restroom with a baby changing table is located on the same floor of such public building;

(3) if new construction would be required to install a baby changing facility in the public building and the cost of such construction is unfeasible; or

(4) to a building not subject to an alteration as set forth in section 3307.

(c) DEFINITIONS.—In this section:

(1) BABY CHANGING FACILITY.—The term "baby changing facility" means a table or other device suitable for changing the diaper of a child age 3 or under.

(2) PUBIC [1] building.—The term "public building" means a public building as defined in section 3301 and controlled by the Public Building Service of the General Services Administration.

(Added Pub. L. 114–235, §2(a)(2), Oct. 7, 2016, 130 Stat. 964.)

[1] *So in original. Probably should be "PUBLIC".*

§3315. DELEGATION

(a) WHEN ALLOWED.—The carrying out of the duties and powers of the

Administrator of General Services under this chapter, in accordance with standards the Administrator prescribes—

(1) shall, except for the authority contained in section 3305(b) of this title, be delegated on request to the appropriate executive agency when the estimated cost of the project does not exceed $100,000; and

(2) may be delegated to the appropriate executive agency when the Administrator determines that delegation will promote efficiency and economy.

(b) NO EXEMPTION FROM OTHER PROVISIONS OF CHAPTER.—Delegation under subsection (a) does not exempt the person to whom the delegation is made, or the carrying out of the delegated duty or power, from any other provision of this chapter.

(Pub. L. 107–217, Aug. 21, 2002, 116 Stat. 1166, §3313; Pub. L. 109–304, §17(g)(3), Oct. 6, 2006, 120 Stat. 1709; renumbered §3314, Pub. L. 110–140, title III, §323(c)(1)(A), Dec. 19, 2007, 121 Stat. 1590; renumbered §3315, Pub. L. 114–235, §2(a)(1), Oct. 7, 2016, 130 Stat. 964.)

§3316. REPORT TO CONGRESS

(a) REQUEST BY EITHER HOUSE OF CONGRESS OR ANY COMMITTEE.—Within a reasonable time after a request of either House of Congress or any committee of Congress, the Administrator of General Services shall submit a report showing the location, space, cost, and status of each public building the construction, alteration, or acquisition of which—

(1) is to be under authority of this chapter; and

(2) was uncompleted as of the date of the request, or as of another date the request may designate.

(b) REQUEST OF COMMITTEE ON PUBLIC WORKS AND ENVIRONMENT OR COMMITTEE ON TRANSPORTATION AND INFRASTRUCTURE.—The Administrator and the United States Postal Service shall make building project surveys requested by resolution by the Committee on Environment and Public Works of the Senate or the Committee on Transportation and Infrastructure of the House of Representatives, and within a reasonable time shall make a report on the survey to Congress. The report shall contain all other information required to be included in a prospectus of the proposed public building project under section 3307(b) of this title.

(Pub. L. 107–217, Aug. 21, 2002, 116 Stat. 1166, §3314; renumbered §3315, Pub. L. 110–140, title III, §323(c)(1)(A), Dec. 19, 2007, 121 Stat. 1590; renumbered §3316, Pub. L. 114–235, §2(a)(1), Oct. 7, 2016, 130 Stat. 964.)

§3317. CERTAIN AUTHORITY NOT AFFECTED

This chapter does not limit or repeal the authority conferred by law on the United States Postal Service.

(Pub. L. 107–217, Aug. 21, 2002, 116 Stat. 1167, §3315; renumbered §3316, Pub. L. 110–140, title III, §323(c)(1)(A), Dec. 19, 2007, 121 Stat. 1590; renumbered §3317, Pub. L. 114–235, §2(a)(1), Oct. 7, 2016, 130 Stat. 964.)

§3318.[1] LACTATION ROOM IN PUBLIC BUILDINGS

(a) DEFINITIONS.—In this section:

(1) APPROPRIATE AUTHORITY.—The term "appropriate authority" means the head of a Federal agency, the Architect of the Capitol, or other official authority responsible

for the operation of a public building.

(2) COVERED PUBLIC BUILDING.—The term "covered public building" means a public building (as defined in section 3301) that is open to the public and contains a public restroom, and includes a building listed in section 6301 or 5101.

(3) LACTATION ROOM.—The term "lactation room" means a hygienic place, other than a bathroom, that—

(A) is shielded from view;

(B) is free from intrusion; and

(C) contains a chair, a working surface, and, if the public building is otherwise supplied with electricity, an electrical outlet.

(b) LACTATION ROOM REQUIRED.—Except as provided in subsection (c), the appropriate authority of a covered public building shall ensure that the building contains a lactation room that is made available for use by members of the public to express breast milk.

(c) EXCEPTIONS.—A covered public building may be excluded from the requirement in subsection (b) at the discretion of the appropriate authority if—

(1) the public building—

(A) does not contain a lactation room for employees who work in the building; and

(B) does not have a room that could be repurposed as a lactation room or a space that could be made private using portable materials, at a reasonable cost; or

(2) new construction would be required to create a lactation room in the public building and the cost of such construction is unfeasible.

(d) NO UNAUTHORIZED ENTRY.—Nothing in this section shall be construed to authorize an individual to enter a public building or portion thereof that the individual is not otherwise authorized to enter.

(Added Pub. L. 116–30, §2(a), July 25, 2019, 133 Stat. 1032.)

___

[1] Another section 3318 is set out after this section.

§3318.[1] AVAILABILITY OF FEDERAL BUILDING PROJECT INFORMATION

(a) IN GENERAL.—Not later than 180 days after the date of enactment of this section, and, at a minimum, on a quarterly basis thereafter, the Administrator shall make publicly available on a subpage of the website of the General Services Administration all prospectuses submitted pursuant to sections 3307 and 3316, and associated information subject to the following requirements:

(1) The Administrator shall maintain such information in an easily accessible and readable, organized, downloadable, and searchable format.

(2) The Administrator shall ensure the information is current and prospectuses and associated information updated on a regular basis.

(3) The information required under this section shall be inclusive for a period of not less than 10 years.

(4) The information shall include—

(A) the last date on which the relevant webpage was updated;

(B) approval dates of respective authorizing resolutions by each committee of jurisdiction, if applicable;

(C) copies of respective committee of jurisdiction resolutions authorizing such prospectuses, as appropriate;

(D) cross-references to any resubmitted or amended prospectuses and associated resolutions; and

(E) such other information as determined by the Administrator.

(b) DEFINITIONS.—In this section, the following definitions apply:

(1) PROSPECTUS.—The term "prospectus" means prospectuses, building surveys, and factsheets submitted to the committees of jurisdiction pursuant to sections 3307 and 3316.

(2) COMMITTEES OF JURISDICTION.—The term "committees of jurisdiction" means the Committee on Transportation and Infrastructure of the House of Representatives and the Committee on Environment and Public Works of the Senate.

(3) ASSOCIATED INFORMATION.—The term "associated information" means resolutions approved by the committees of jurisdiction and other information as required pursuant to subsection (a).

(Added Pub. L. 116–333, §2(a), Jan. 13, 2021, 134 Stat. 5113.)

[1] *Another section 3318 is set out preceding this section.*

§3319. INTERAGENCY SPACE COORDINATION

Unless a Federal agency specifically restricts the sharing of the information described in this section for national security purposes, the Administrator of General Services shall share with tenant Federal agencies pursuing new or replacement office space information on any other Federal agencies located in the same geographical area for purposes of determining opportunities for consolidations, collocations, or other space sharing to reduce the costs of space and maximize space utilization.

(Added Pub. L. 118–272, div. B, title III, §2304(e)(1), Jan. 4, 2025, 138 Stat. 3224.)

★

28 U.S.C. §464–Court Accommodations

TITLE 28—JUDICIARY AND JUDICIAL PROCEDURE

This title was enacted by act June 25, 1948, ch. 646, §1, 62 Stat. 869

* * * * * * *

PART I—ORGANIZATION OF COURTS

* * * * * * *

CHAPTER 21—GENERAL PROVISIONS APPLICABLE TO COURTS AND JUDGES

* * * * * * *

§462. Court accommodations

(a) Sessions of courts of the United States (except the Supreme Court) shall be held only at places where the Director of the Administrative Office of the United States Courts provides accommodations, or where suitable accommodations are furnished without cost to the judicial branch.

(b) The Director of the Administrative Office of the United States Courts shall provide accommodations, including chambers and courtrooms, only at places where regular sessions of court are authorized by law to be held, but only if the judicial council of the appropriate circuit has approved the accommodations as necessary.

(c) The limitations and restrictions contained in subsection (b) of this section shall not prevent the Director from furnishing chambers to circuit judges at places within the circuit other than where regular sessions of court are authorized by law to be held, when the judicial council of the circuit approves.

(d) The Director of the Administrative Office of the United States Courts shall provide permanent accommodations for the United States Court of Appeals for the Federal Circuit and for the United States Court of Federal Claims only at the District of Columbia. However, each such court may hold regular and special sessions at other places utilizing the accommodations which the Director provides to other courts.

(e) The Director of the Administrative Office of the United States Courts shall provide accommodations for probation officers, pretrial service officers, and Federal Public Defender Organizations at such places as may be approved by the judicial council of the appropriate circuit.

(f) Upon the request of the Director, the Administrator of General Services is authorized and directed to provide the accommodations the Director requests, and to close accommodations which the Director recommends for closure with the approval of the Judicial Conference of the United States.

(Added Pub. L. 97–164, title I, §115(c)(1), Apr. 2, 1982, 96 Stat. 31; amended Pub. L. 100–702, title X, §1015, Nov. 19, 1988, 102 Stat. 4669; Pub. L. 102–572, title IX, §902(b)(1), Oct. 29, 1992, 106 Stat. 4516.)

★

HOMELAND SECURITY ACT OF 2002 SUBTITLE G OF TITLE IV–U.S. CUSTOMS AND BORDER PROTECTION PUBLIC PRIVATE PARTNERSHIPS

PUBLIC LAW 107–296
AS AMENDED THROUGH PUB. L. 119–4

HOMELAND SECURITY ACT OF 2002

[Public Law 107–296; Approved November 25, 2002]

[As Amended Through P.L. 119–4, Enacted March 15, 2025]

AN ACT To establish the Department of Homeland Security, and for other purposes.

Be it enacted by the Senate and House of Representatives of the United States of America in Congress assembled,

SECTION 1. SHORT TITLE; TABLE OF CONTENTS.

(a) **[6 U.S.C. 101 note]** SHORT TITLE.— This Act may be cited as the "Homeland Security Act of 2002".

(b) TABLE OF CONTENTS.— The table of contents for this Act is as follows:

* * * * * * *

TITLE IV—BORDER, MARITIME, AND TRANSPORTATION SECURITY

* * * * * * *

Subtitle G—U.S. CUSTOMS AND BORDER PROTECTION PUBLIC

PRIVATE PARTNERSHIPS

SEC. 481. [6 U.S.C. 301] FEE AGREEMENTS FOR CERTAIN SERVICES AT PORTS OF ENTRY.

(a) IN GENERAL.—Notwithstanding section 13031(e) of the Consolidated Omnibus Budget Reconciliation Act of 1985 (19 U.S.C. 58c(e)) and section 451 of the Tariff Act of 1930 (19 U.S.C. 1451), the Commissioner of U.S. Customs and Border Protection, upon the request of any entity, may enter into a fee agreement with such entity under which—

(1)   U.S. Customs and Border Protection shall provide services described in subsection (b) at a United States port of entry or any other facility at which U.S. Customs and Border Protection provides or will provide such services;

(2)   such entity shall remit to U.S. Customs and Border Protection a fee imposed under subsection (h) in an amount equal to the full costs that are incurred or will be incurred in providing such services; and

(3)   if space is provided by such entity, each facility at which U.S. Customs and Border Protection services are performed shall be maintained and equipped by such entity, without cost to the Federal Government, in accordance with U.S. Customs and Border Protection specifications.

(b) SERVICES DESCRIBED.— The services described in this subsection are any activities of any employee or Office of Field Operations contractor of U.S. Customs and Border Protection (except employees of the U.S. Border Patrol, as established under section 411(e)) pertaining to, or in support of, customs, agricultural processing, border security, or immigration inspection-related matters at a port of entry or any other facility at which U.S. Customs and Border Protection provides or will provide services.

(c) MODIFICATION OF PRIOR AGREEMENTS.— The Commissioner of U.S. Customs and Border Protection, at the request of an entity who has previously entered into an agreement with U.S. Customs and Border Protection for the reimbursement of fees in effect on the date of enactment of this section, may modify such agreement to implement any provisions of this section.

(d) LIMITATIONS.—

(1) IMPACTS OF SERVICES.—The Commissioner of U.S. Customs and Border Protection—

(A) may enter into fee agreements under this section only for services that—

(i)   will increase or enhance the operational capacity of U.S. Customs and Border Protection based on available staffing and workload; and

(ii)   will not shift the cost of services funded in any appropriations Act, or provided from any account in the Treasury of the United States derived by the collection of fees, to entities under this Act; and

(B)   may not enter into a fee agreement under this section if such agreement would unduly and permanently impact services funded in any appropriations Act, or provided from any account in the Treasury of the United States, derived by the collection of fees.

(2) NUMBER.— There shall be no limit to the number of fee agreements that the

Commissioner of U.S. Customs and Border Protection may enter into under this section.

(e) AIR PORTS OF ENTRY.—

(1) FEE AGREEMENT.— Except as otherwise provided in this subsection, a fee agreement for U.S. Customs and Border Protection services at an air port of entry may only provide for the payment of overtime costs of U.S. Customs and Border Protection officers and salaries and expenses of U.S. Customs and Border Protection employees to support U.S. Customs and Border Protection officers in performing services described in subsection (b).

(2) SMALL AIRPORTS.— Notwithstanding paragraph (1), U.S. Customs and Border Protection may receive reimbursement in addition to overtime costs if the fee agreement is for services at an air port of entry that has fewer than 100,000 arriving international passengers annually.

(3) COVERED SERVICES.—In addition to costs described in paragraph (1), a fee agreement for U.S. Customs and Border Protection services at an air port of entry referred to in paragraph (2) may provide for the reimbursement of—

(A) salaries and expenses of not more than five full-time equivalent U.S. Customs and Border Protection Officers beyond the number of such officers assigned to the port of entry on the date on which the fee agreement was signed;

(B) salaries and expenses of employees of U.S. Customs and Border Protection, other than the officers referred to in subparagraph (A), to support U.S. Customs and Border Protection officers in performing law enforcement functions; and

(C) other costs incurred by U.S. Customs and Border Protection relating to services described in subparagraph (B), such as temporary placement or permanent relocation of employees, including incentive pay for relocation, as appropriate.

(f) PORT OF ENTRY SIZE.— The Commissioner of U.S. Customs and Border Protection shall ensure that each fee agreement proposal is given equal consideration regardless of the size of the port of entry.

(g) DENIED APPLICATION.—

(1) IN GENERAL.—If the Commissioner of U.S. Customs and Border Protection denies a proposal for a fee agreement under this section, the Commissioner shall provide the entity submitting such proposal with the reason for the denial unless—

(A) the reason for the denial is law enforcement sensitive; or

(B) withholding the reason for the denial is in the national security interests of the United States.

(2) JUDICIAL REVIEW.— Decisions of the Commissioner of U.S. Customs and Border Protection under paragraph (1) are in the discretion of the Commissioner and are not subject to judicial review.

(h) FEE.—

(1) IN GENERAL.— The amount of the fee to be charged under an agreement authorized under subsection (a) shall be paid by each entity requesting U.S. Customs and Border Protection services, and shall be for the full cost of providing such services, including the salaries and expenses of employees and contractors of U.S. Customs and Border Protection, to provide such services and other costs incurred by U.S. Customs and Border Protection relating to such services, such as temporary placement or permanent relocation of such employees and contractors.

(2) TIMING.— The Commissioner of U.S. Customs and Border Protection may require that the fee referred to in paragraph (1) be paid by each entity that has entered into a fee agreement under subsection (a) with U.S. Customs and Border Protection in advance of the performance of U.S. Customs and Border Protection services.

(3) OVERSIGHT OF FEES.—The Commissioner of U.S. Customs and Border Protection shall develop a process to oversee the services for which fees are charged pursuant to an agreement under subsection (a), including—

(A) a determination and report on the full costs of providing such services, and a process for increasing such fees, as necessary;

(B) the establishment of a periodic remittance schedule to replenish appropriations, accounts, or funds, as necessary; and

(C) the identification of costs paid by such fees.

(i) DEPOSIT OF FUNDS.—

(1) ACCOUNT.—Funds collected pursuant to any agreement entered into pursuant to subsection (a)—

(A) shall be deposited as offsetting collections;

(B) shall remain available until expended without fiscal year limitation; and

(C) shall be credited to the applicable appropriation, account, or fund for the amount paid out of such appropriation, account, or fund for any expenses incurred or to be incurred by U.S. Customs and Border Protection in providing U.S. Customs and Border Protection services under any such agreement and any other costs incurred or to be incurred by U.S. Customs and Border Protection relating to such services.

(2) RETURN OF UNUSED FUNDS.— The Commissioner of U.S. Customs and Border Protection shall return any unused funds collected and deposited into the account described in paragraph (1) if a fee agreement entered into pursuant to subsection (a) is terminated for any reason or the terms of such fee agreement change by mutual agreement to cause a reduction of U.S. Customs and Border Protections services. No interest shall be owed upon the return of any such unused funds.

(j) TERMINATION.—

(1) IN GENERAL.— The Commissioner of U.S. Customs and Border Protection shall terminate the services provided pursuant to a fee agreement entered into under subsection (a) with an entity that, after receiving notice from the Commissioner that a fee under subsection (h) is due, fails to pay such fee in a timely manner. If such

services are terminated, all costs incurred by U.S. Customs and Border Protection that have not been paid shall become immediately due and payable. Interest on unpaid fees shall accrue based on the rate and amount established under sections 6621 and 6622 of the Internal Revenue Code of 1986.

(2) PENALTY.— Any entity that, after notice and demand for payment of any fee under subsection (h), fails to pay such fee in a timely manner shall be liable for a penalty or liquidated damage equal to two times the amount of such fee. Any such amount collected under this paragraph shall be deposited into the appropriate account specified under subsection (i) and shall be available as described in such subsection.

(3) TERMINATION BY THE ENTITY.— Any entity who has previously entered into an agreement with U.S. Customs and Border Protection for the reimbursement of fees in effect on the date of enactment of this section, or under the provisions of this section, may request that such agreement be amended to provide for termination upon advance notice, length, and terms that are negotiated between such entity and U.S. Customs and Border Protection.

(k) ANNUAL REPORT.—The Commissioner of U.S. Customs and Border Protection shall—

(1) submit an annual report identifying the activities undertaken and the agreements entered into pursuant to this section to—

(A)   the Committee on Appropriations of the Senate;

(B)   the Committee on Finance of the Senate;

(C)   the Committee on Homeland Security and Governmental Affairs of the Senate;

(D)   the Committee on the Judiciary of the Senate;

(E)   the Committee on Appropriations of the House of Representatives;

(F)   the Committee on Homeland Security of the House of Representatives;

(G)   the Committee on the Judiciary of the House of Representatives; and

(H)   the Committee on Ways and Means of the House of Representatives; and

(2)   not later than 15 days before entering into a fee agreement, notify the members of Congress that represent the State or Congressional District in which the affected port of entry or facility is located of such agreement.

(l) RULE OF CONSTRUCTION.— Nothing in this section may be construed as imposing on U.S. Customs and Border Protection any responsibilities, duties, or authorities relating to real property.

SEC. 482. [6 U.S.C. 301a] PORT OF ENTRY DONATION AUTHORITY.

(a) PERSONAL PROPERTY DONATION AUTHORITY.—

(1) IN GENERAL.—The Commissioner of U.S. Customs and Border Protection, in consultation with the Administrator of General Services, may enter into an agreement with any entity to accept a donation of personal property, money, or

nonpersonal services for the uses described in paragraph (3) only with respect to the following locations at which U.S. Customs and Border Protection performs or will be performing inspection services:

(A)   A new or existing sea or air port of entry.

(B)   An existing Federal Government-owned or -leased land port of entry.

(C) A new Federal Government-owned or -leased land port of entry if—

(i)   the fair market value of the donation is $75,000,000 or less; and

(ii)   the fair market value of donations with respect to the land port of entry total $75,000,000 or less over the preceding five years.

(2) Limitation on monetary donations.— Any monetary donation accepted pursuant to this subsection may not be used to pay the salaries of U.S. Customs and Border Protection employees performing inspection services.

(3) Uses.—Donations accepted pursuant to this subsection may be used for activities of the Office of Field Operations set forth in subparagraphs (A) through (F) of section 411(g)(3), which are related to a new or existing sea or air port of entry or a new or existing Federal Government-owned or -leased land port of entry described in paragraph (1), including expenses related to—

(A)   furniture, fixtures, equipment, or technology, including the installation or deployment of such items; and

(B)   the operation and maintenance of such furniture, fixtures, equipment, or technology.

(b) Real Property Donation Authority.—

(1) In general.—Subject to paragraph (3), the Commissioner of U.S. Customs and Border Protection, and the Administrator of General Services[7], as applicable, may enter into an agreement with any entity to accept a donation of real property or money for uses described in paragraph (2) only with respect to the following locations at which U.S. Customs and Border Protection performs or will be performing inspection services:

---

[7]   Section 6410(2)(A) of division F of Public Law 117–81 provides for an amendment to strike Administrator of the General Services Administration and insert Administrator of General Services in the matter preceding paragraph (1). Such amendment should have been made to paragraph (1) in the matter preceding subparagraph (A); however, it was carried out according to the probable intent of Congress.

(A)   A new or existing sea or air port of entry.

(B)   An existing Federal Government-owned land port of entry.

(C) A new Federal Government-owned land port of entry if—

(i)   the fair market value of the donation is $75,000,000 or less; and

(ii)   the fair market value of donations with respect to the land port of entry total $75,000,000 or less over the preceding five years.

(2) Use.—Donations accepted pursuant to this subsection may be used for activities of the Office of Field Operations set forth in section 411(g), which are

related to the construction, alteration, operation, or maintenance of a new or existing sea or air port of entry or a new or existing a Federal Government-owned land port of entry described in paragraph (1), including expenses related to—

(A)   land acquisition, design, construction, repair, or alteration; and

(B)   operation and maintenance of such port of entry facility.

(3) LIMITATION ON REAL PROPERTY DONATIONS.— A donation of real property under this subsection at an existing land port of entry owned by the General Services Administration may only be accepted by the Administrator of General Services.

(4) SUNSET.—

(A) IN GENERAL.— The authority to enter into an agreement under this subsection shall terminate on December 31, 2026.

(B) RULE OF CONSTRUCTION.— The termination date referred to in subparagraph (A) shall not apply to a proposal accepted for consideration by U.S. Customs and Border Protection or the General Services Administration pursuant to this section or a prior pilot program prior to such termination date.

(c) GENERAL PROVISIONS.—

(1) DURATION.— An agreement entered into under subsection (a) or (b) (and, in the case of such subsection (b), in accordance with paragraph (4) of such subsection) may last as long as required to meet the terms of such agreement.

(2) CRITERIA.—In carrying out an agreement entered into under subsection (a) or (b), the Commissioner of U.S. Customs and Border Protection, in consultation with the Administrator of General Services, shall establish criteria regarding—

(A)   the selection and evaluation of donors;

(B)   the identification of roles and responsibilities between U.S. Customs and Border Protection, the General Services Administration, and donors;

(C)   the identification, allocation, and management of explicit and implicit risks of partnering between the Federal Government and donors;

(D)   decision-making and dispute resolution processes; and

(E)   processes for U.S. Customs and Border Protection, and the General Services Administration, as applicable, to terminate agreements if selected donors are not meeting the terms of any such agreement, including the security standards established by U.S. Customs and Border Protection.

(3) EVALUATION PROCEDURES.—

(A) IN GENERAL.—The Commissioner of U.S. Customs and Border Protection, in consultation with the Administrator of General Services, as applicable, shall—

(i)   establish criteria for evaluating a proposal to enter into an agreement under subsection (a) or (b); and

(ii)   make such criteria publicly available.

(B) CONSIDERATIONS.—Criteria established pursuant to subparagraph (A) shall consider—

(i)   the impact of a proposal referred to in such subparagraph on the land, sea, or air port of entry at issue and other ports of entry or similar facilities or other infrastructure near the location of the proposed donation;

(ii)   such proposal's potential to increase trade and travel efficiency through added capacity;

(iii)   such proposal's potential to enhance the security of the port of entry at issue;

(iv)   the impact of the proposal on reducing wait times at that port of entry or facility and other ports of entry on the same border;

(v) for a donation under subsection (b)—

(I)   whether such donation satisfies the requirements of such proposal, or whether additional real property would be required; and

(II)   how such donation was acquired, including if eminent domain was used;

(vi)   the funding available to complete the intended use of such donation;

(vii)   the costs of maintaining and operating such donation;

(viii)   the impact of such proposal on U.S. Customs and Border Protection staffing requirements; and

(ix)   other factors that the Commissioner or Administrator determines to be relevant.

(C) DETERMINATION AND NOTIFICATION.—

(i) INCOMPLETE PROPOSALS.—

(I) IN GENERAL.—   Not later than 60 days after receiving the proposals for a donation agreement from an entity, the Commissioner of U.S. Customs and Border Protection shall notify such entity as to whether such proposal is complete or incomplete.

(II) RESUBMISSION.—If the Commissioner of U.S. Customs and Border Protection determines that a proposal is incomplete, the Commissioner shall—

(aa)   notify the appropriate entity and provide such entity with a description of all information or material that is needed to complete review of the proposal; and

(bb)   allow the entity to resubmit the proposal with additional information and material described in item (aa) to complete the proposal.

(ii) COMPLETE PROPOSALS.—Not later than 180 days after receiving a completed proposal to enter into an agreement under subsection (a) or (b), the Commissioner of U.S. Customs and Border Protection, with the concurrence of the Administrator of General Services, as applicable, shall—

(I)   determine whether to approve or deny such proposal; and

(II) notify the entity that submitted such proposal of such determination.

(4) SUPPLEMENTAL FUNDING.— Except as required under section 3307 of title 40, United States Code, real property donations to the Administrator of General Services made pursuant to subsection (a) and (b) at a GSA-owned land port of entry may be used in addition to any other funding for such purpose, including appropriated funds, property, or services.

(5) RETURN OF DONATIONS.— The Commissioner of U.S. Customs and Border Protection, or the Administrator of General Services, as applicable, may return any donation made pursuant to subsection (a) or (b). No interest shall be owed to the donor with respect to any donation provided under such subsections that is returned pursuant to this subsection.

(6) PROHIBITION ON CERTAIN FUNDING.—

(A) IN GENERAL.— Except as provided in subsections (a) and (b) regarding the acceptance of donations, the Commissioner of U.S. Customs and Border Protection and the Administrator of General Services, as applicable, may not, with respect to an agreement entered into under either of such subsections, obligate or expend amounts in excess of amounts that have been appropriated pursuant to any appropriations Act for purposes specified in either of such subsections or otherwise made available for any of such purposes.

(B) CERTIFICATION REQUIREMENT.—Before accepting any donations pursuant to an agreement under subsection (a) or (b), the Commissioner of U.S. Customs and Border Protection shall certify to the congressional committees set forth in paragraph (7) that[8]

(i) the donation will not be used for the construction of a detention facility or a border fence or wall; and

(ii) the donor will be notified in the Donations Acceptance Agreement that the donor shall be financially responsible for all costs and operating expenses related to the operation, maintenance, and repair of the donated real property until such time as U.S. Customs and Border Protection provides the donor written notice otherwise.

---

[8] A missing em dash after paragraph (7) that is so in law. See amendment made by section 6410(3) of division F of Public Law 117–81.

---

(7) ANNUAL REPORTS.—The Commissioner of U.S. Customs and Border Protection, in collaboration with the Administrator of General Services, as applicable, shall submit an annual report identifying the activities undertaken and agreements entered into pursuant to subsections (a) and (b) to—

(A) the Committee on Appropriations of the Senate;

(B) the Committee on Environment and Public Works of the Senate;

(C) the Committee on Finance of the Senate;

(D) the Committee on Homeland Security and Governmental Affairs of the Senate;

(E) the Committee on the Judiciary of the Senate;

(F) the Committee on Appropriations of the House of Representatives;

(G) the Committee on Homeland Security of the House of Representatives;

(H) the Committee on the Judiciary of the House of Representatives;

(I) the Committee on Transportation and Infrastructure of the House of Representatives; and

(J) the Committee on Ways and Means of the House of Representatives.

(d) GAO REPORT.—The Comptroller General of the United States shall submit an biennial report to the congressional committees referred to in subsection (c)(7) that evaluates—

(1) fee agreements entered into pursuant to section 481;

(2) donation agreements entered into pursuant to subsections (a) and (b); and

(3) the fees and donations received by U.S. Customs and Border Protection pursuant to such agreements.

(e) JUDICIAL REVIEW.— Decisions of the Commissioner of U.S. Customs and Border Protection and the Administrator of General Services under this section regarding the acceptance of real or personal property are in the discretion of the Commissioner and the Administrator and are not subject to judicial review.

(f) RULE OF CONSTRUCTION.— Except as otherwise provided in this section, nothing in this section may be construed as affecting in any manner the responsibilities, duties, or authorities of U.S. Customs and Border Protection or the General Services Administration.

SEC. 483. [6 U.S.C. 301b] CURRENT AND PROPOSED AGREEMENTS.

Nothing in this subtitle or in section 4 of the Cross-Border Trade Enhancement Act of 2016 may be construed as affecting—

(1) any agreement entered into pursuant to section 560 of division D of the Consolidated and Further Continuing Appropriations Act, 2013 (Public Law 113–6) or section 559 of title V of division F of the Consolidated Appropriations Act, 2014 (6 U.S.C. 211 note; Public Law 113–76), as in existence on the day before the date of the enactment of this subtitle, and any such agreement shall continue to have full force and effect on and after such date; or

(2) a proposal accepted for consideration by U.S. Customs and Border Protection pursuant to such section 559, as in existence on the day before such date of enactment.

SEC. 484. [6 U.S.C. 301c] DEFINITIONS.

In this subtitle:

(1) DONOR.— The term donor means any entity that is proposing to make a donation under this Act.

(2) ENTITY.—The term entity means any—

(A) person;

(B) partnership, corporation, trust, estate, cooperative, association, or any other organized group of persons;

(C) Federal, State or local government (including any subdivision, agency or instrumentality thereof); or

(D) any other private or governmental entity.

★

SELECTED PROVISIONS OF THE INDEPENDENT AGENCIES APPROPRIATIONS ACT, 1988

PUBLIC LAW 100–202

INDEPENDENT AGENCIES APPROPRIATIONS ACT, 1988

[(Public Law 100–202; 101 Stat. 1329–405)]

[As Amended Through P.L. 100–202, Enacted December 22, 1987]

* * * * * * *

TITLE IV—INDEPENDENT AGENCIES

* * * * * * *

GENERAL SERVICES ADMINISTRATION

FEDERAL BUILDING FUND

LIMITATIONS ON AVAILABILITY OF REVENUE

* * * * * * *

Provided further, That the Administrator of the GSA is hereby directed to enter into an agreement, pursuant to a competitive selection process, for the lease-purchase of a building in San Francisco, California, during fiscal year 1988 of approximately 430,000 office occupiable square feet on a site donated by that city: Provided further, That the agreement shall provide for annual lease or installment payments from funds available for the rental of space in the Federal Buildings Fund over a period not to exceed 30 years for the payment of the purchase price of such building, and shall provide for title to the building to vest in the United States on or before the expiration of the contract term upon fulfillment of the terms and conditions of the agreement: Provided further, That additional space may be acquired if the Administrator finds such space to be in the public interest and will not reduce the occupiable Federal space to be available in the Oakland Federal Building. The Oakland Building shall, when completed be fully occupied by federal agencies and continued full occupancy shall have the highest priority consistent with the Federal interest: Provided further, That for the purposes of this authorization, buildings constructed pursuant to the Public Buildings Purchase Contract Act of 1954 (40 U.S.C. 356), the Public Buildings Amendments of 1972 (40 U.S.C. 490), and buildings under the control of another department or agency where alterations of such buildings are required in connection with the moving of such other department or agency from buildings then, or thereafter to be, under the control of the General Services Administration shall be considered to be federally owned buildings: *Provided further*, That none of the funds available to the General Services Administration with the exception of those for Capital Improvements for United States-Mexico Border Facilities; Other Approved Border Facility projects; and the San Francisco, California Federal building project, shall be available for expenses in connection with any construction, repair, alteration, and acquisition project for which a prospectus, if required by the Public Buildings Act of 1959, as amended, has not been approved, except that necessary funds may be expended for each project for required expenses in connection with the development of a proposed prospectus: *Provided further*, That notwithstanding any other provision of law, the Administrator of General Services is authorized, under section 210(h) of the Federal Property and Administrative Services Act of 1949, to acquire the building in Chicago, Illinois, approved under this heading in fiscal year 1987, from any commercial or private entity, through a lease to ownership transaction. Said lease shall not exceed 30 years, on such terms and conditions as he deems appropriate. These terms and conditions may include an option to permit the Federal Government, if the Administrator deems that it is in the best interest of the Federal Government, to execute a succeeding lease: *Provided further*, That funds available in the Federal Buildings Fund may be expended for emergency repairs when advance approval is obtained from the Committees on Appropriations of the House and Senate: *Provided further*, That not later than 60 days after the date of the enactment of this Act, the Administrator of General Services shall submit under the Public Buildings Act of 1959, a prospectus for acquiring by purchase or lease-purchase (1) a building which is not to exceed 1,400,000 occupiable square feet for the Environmental Protection Agency in the Washington metropolitan area, and (2) a building which is not to exceed 1,800,000 occupiable square feet for the Department of Transportation. The lease-purchase shall provide for annual lease or installment payments from funds available for the rental of space in the Federal Buildings Fund over a period not to exceed 30 years for the payment of the purchase price of such building and reasonable interest thereon and shall provide for title to the building to vest in the United States on or before the last day of the term of the lease-purchase transaction. If a lease-purchase prospectus for a building described in this paragraph is approved under the Public Buildings Act of 1959, the Administrator of General Services may enter into a transaction for the lease-purchase of such building in accordance with the terms specified in such approved prospectus and applicable provisions of law and may make annual lease or installment payments from funds available for the rental of space in such fund: *Provided further*, That amounts necessary to provide reimbursable special services to other agencies under section 210(f)(6) of the Federal Property and Administrative Services Act of 1949, as amended (40 U.S.C. 490(f)(6)) and amounts to provide such reimbursable fencing, lighting, guard booths, and other facilities on private or other property not in Government ownership or control as may be appropriate to enable the United States Secret Service to perform its protective functions pursuant to 18 U.S.C. 3056, as amended, shall be available from such revenues and collections: *Provided further*, That revenues and collections and any other sums accruing to this fund during fiscal year 1988 excluding reimbursements under section 210(f)(6) of the Federal Property and Administrative Services Act of 1949 (40 U.S.C. 490(f)(6)) in excess of $2,854,052,000 shall remain in the Fund and shall not be available for expenditure except as authorized in appropriation Acts.

* * * * * * *

GENERAL SERVICES ADMINISTRATION—GENERAL PROVISION

* * * * * * *

SEC. 8.   The Administrator of General Services is hereby directed to submit a prospectus to the Congress within 60 days to enable the Administrator to contract for construction of two buildings not to exceed a total of 1,600,000 gross square feet of office space, plus additional parking and retail space, in New York City on sites to be acquired from the city of New York. The contracts shall provide, by lease or installment payments over a period not to exceed 30 years, from funds available for the rental of space in the Federal Buildings Fund for the payment of the purchase price, and reasonable interest thereon. The contracts shall further provide that title to the buildings shall vest in the United States at or before expiration of the contract term upon fulfillment of the terms and conditions of the contracts. If a lease-purchase prospectus for a building described in this paragraph is approved under the Public Buildings Act of 1959, the Administrator of General Services may enter into a transaction for the lease-purchase of such building in accordance with the terms specified in such approved prospectus and applicable provisions of law and may make annual lease or installment payments from the funds available for the rental of space in such Fund. The General Services Administration shall lease up to 400,000 square feet of office space and associated parking to the city of New York at rates that reflect an appropriate portion of the construction and related costs of the projects, adjusted for the value of the land acquired from the city. In addition, income accrued by the General Services Administration from the outlease of office space to the city as well as retail and related space to private organizations shall be used to offset GSA's installment payments for the cost of the facilities. Obligations of funds under these transactions shall be limited to the current fiscal year for which payments are due without regard to 31 U.S.C. 1341(a)(1)(B).

★

INDEPENDENT AGENCIES APPROPRIATIONS ACT, 1989

PUBLIC LAW 100–440

INDEPENDENT AGENCIES APPROPRIATIONS ACT, 1989

[Public Law 100–440; 101 Stat. 1737]

[As Amended Through P.L. 100–440, Enacted September 22, 1988]
[Missing Amendments Made by Sec. 9 of P.L. 101–136 (103 Stat. 803), Enacted
November 3, 1989]

* * * * * * *

TITLE IV—INDEPENDENT AGENCIES

* * * * * * *

GENERAL SERVICES ADMINISTRATION
FEDERAL BUILDINGS FUND
LIMITATIONS ON AVAILABILITY OF REVENUE

Provided further, That obligations of funds for lease, lease purchase, or installment purchase public buildings projects authorized in Public Law 100–202 for the General Services Administration at Oakland, California and San Francisco, California, and for the Environmental Protection Agency and Department of Transportation shall be limited to the current fiscal year for which payments are due without regard to 31 U.S.C. 1341(a)(1)(B): Provided further, That for the purposes of this authorization, buildings constructed pursuant to the Public Buildings Purchase Contract Act of 1954 (40 U.S.C. 356), the Public Buildings Amendments of 1972 (40 U.S.C. 490), and buildings under the control of another department or agency where alterations of such buildings are required in connection with the moving of such other department or agency from buildings then, or thereafter to be, under the control of the General Services Administration shall be considered to be federally owned buildings:

GENERAL SERVICES ADMINISTRATION—GENERAL PROVISIONS

SEC. 5. [40 U.S.C. 490d]
[Section 5 was repealed by section 6 of P.L. 107–217 (116 Stat. 1062).]

SEC. 6. The Administrator of General Services shall proceed with the site selection and design for construction of a facility of not less than 182,000 usable square feet for the Social Security Administration in Wilkes-Barre, Pennsylvania, pursuant to section 115 of the joint resolution entitled Joint resolution making continuing appropriations for the fiscal year 1987 and for other purposes, approved October 30, 1986 (100 Stat. 3341–49; Public Law 99–591).

SEC. 7.   Notwithstanding any provisions of this Act or any other Act in any fiscal year, the Administrator of General Services is authorized and directed to charge the Department of the Interior for design and alterations to the Avondale, Maryland property at rates so as to recover the approximate applicable cost incurred by General Services Administration in providing such alterations, and the Department of the Interior is authorized to repay such charges out of any appropriation available to the department and the payments shall be deposited in the fund established by 40 U.S.C. 490(f).

SEC. 8. (a) LEASE-PURCHASE AGREEMENT.— The Administrator of General Services shall acquire from the State of Tennessee or a political subdivision thereof by lease-purchase a building to house the Internal Revenue Service Center in Memphis, Tennessee, and such other Federal agencies as may be appropriate.

(b) LIMITATIONS.—

(1) SIZE.— The building to be acquired under subsection (a) may not exceed 600,000 gross square feet in size plus such additional space as may be necessary for parking.

(2) COST.— The total cost of the lease-purchase agreement under this section to the United States may not exceed $36,000,000, plus reasonable interest thereon, as well as operating costs, if applicable.

(3) TERM.— The term of the lease-purchase agreement under this section may not exceed thirty years. The agreement shall provide that ownership of the building will vest in the United States on or before the end of such term.

(4) OBLIGATION OF FUNDS.— Obligations of funds under this section shall be limited to the current fiscal year for which payments are due without regard to section 1341(a)(1)(B) of title 31, United States Code.

(c) SALE OF LEASEHOLD INTEREST.— The Administrator of General Services shall sell any leasehold or other interest which the United States has in the building which is providing office space for the Internal Revenue Service Center in Memphis, Tennessee, and shall deposit the proceeds from such sale in the Federal Buildings Fund established by section 210(f) of the Federal Property and Administrative Services Act of 1949.

9.   The General Services Administration is directed to construct under their lease-purchase authority, a 40,000 net square foot office building at the CDC campus in Chamblee, Georgia, designed with funds which Congress provided the Center for Disease Control in the fiscal year 1987 Department of Labor, Health and Human Services, and Education, and Related Agencies Appropriations, and shall be acquired without regard to the provisions of the Public Buildings Act of 1959 regarding prospectus approval by lease-purchase contracts entered into by the General Services Administration prior to their construction using funds appropriated annually to the General Services Administration from the Federal Buildings Fund for the rental of space which shall hereafter be available for this purpose. The contracts shall provide for the payment of the purchase price and reasonable interest thereon by lease or installment payments over a period not to exceed thirty years. The contracts shall further provide that title to the buildings shall vest in the United States at or before expiration of the contract term upon fulfillment of the terms and conditions of the contracts. The Federal Buildings Fund shall be reimbursed from the annual appropriation to the Centers for

Disease Control—Disease Control, Research, and Training (or any other appropriation hereafter made available to the CDC for construction of research facilities) and such appropriations shall hereafter be available for the purpose of reimbursing the Federal Buildings Fund. Obligations of funds under these transactions shall be limited to the current fiscal year for which payments are due without regard to 31 U.S.C. 1502 and 1341(a)(1)(B).

10.   The Administrator of General Services is authorized and directed to hire up to and maintain an annual average of not less than one thousand full-time equivalent positions for Federal Protective Officers. This shall be accomplished by increasing existing staff levels at the end of fiscal year 1988 at a rate of not less than fifty positions per year until the full-time equivalency of one thousand is attained by not later than fiscal year 1992.

11. [40 U.S.C. 490a–1]
[Section 11 was repealed by section 6 of P.L. 107–217 (116 Stat. 1062).]

★

SELECTED PROVISIONS OF THE INDEPENDENT AGENCIES APPROPRIATIONS ACT, 1991

PUBLIC LAW 101–509
AS AMENDED THROUGH PUB. L. 107–217

[Public Law 101–509; 104 Stat. 1412]

[As Amended Through P.L. 107–217, Enacted August 21, 2002]

TITLE IV—
INDEPENDENT AGENCIES

* * * * * * *

GENERAL SERVICES ADMINISTRATION—GENERAL PROVISIONS

8. [40 U.S.C. 490f]
[Section 8 was repealed by section 6 of P.L. 107–217 (116 Stat. 1062).]

11.   Notwithstanding any other provision of law, the Administrator of General Services is authorized to sell by publicly advertising for bids and on such terms and conditions as the Administrator deems proper, the John W. McCormack Post Office and Courthouse located at One Post Office Square in Boston, Massachusetts. All proceeds from such sale, less direct expenses incurred in the sale, shall be deposited into the fund established under section 210(f) of the Federal Property and Administrative Services Act.

12.   Notwithstanding any other provision of law, the Administrator of General Services is authorized and directed to provided not less than 120,000 square feet of storage space, together with additional space as necessary for office use, to establish a National Long Term Records Center in Pittsfield, Massachusetts for the specialized storage of Federal agency records by the National Archives and Records Administration: Provided, That notwithstanding any other provision of law, the Administrator of General Services is authorized and directed to provide not less than 3,000 square feet of public space in Pittsfield, Massachusetts for a satellite facility of the New England Regional Archives: Provided further, That the Archivist of the United States shall assign adequate personnel to operate the satellite facility established by this section: Provided further, That the Administrator of General Services and the Archivist of the United States shall report on a quarterly basis to the House and Senate Committees on Appropriations on the progress made to implement the directives in this section and the resources necessary to complete the Long Term Records Center and the satellite facility.

13.   Notwithstanding the provisions of the Act of September 13, 1982 (Public Law 97–258, 31 U.S.C. 1345), any agency, department or instrumentality of the United States

15. [Section 15 was repealed by section 6 of P.L. 107–217 (116 Stat. 1062).]

Independent Agencies Appropriations Act, 19

which provides or proposes to provide child care services for Federal employees may reimburse any Federal employee or any person employed to provide such services for travel, transportation and subsistence expenses incurred for training classes, conferences or other meetings in connection with the provision of such services: Provided, That any per diem allowance made pursuant to this section shall not exceed the rate specified in regulations prescribed pursuant to section 5707 of title 5, United States Code.

* * * * * * *

15. [Section 15 was repealed by section 6 of P.L. 107–217 (116 Stat. 1062).]

16. Notwithstanding any other provision of law, the General Services Administration is hereby authorized to sell, at competitive bid, the Federal Building located at 500 Quarrier Street in Charleston, West Virginia, and to deposit such proceeds into the Federal Buildings Fund.

17. (a) Notwithstanding any other provision of law, the Administrator of General Services is authorized to sell on such terms and conditions as the Administrator deems proper, the Federal Building and United States Courthouse located at 110 South Fourth Street in Minneapolis, Minnesota. All proceeds from such sale, less direct expenses, shall be deposited into the fund established under section 210(f) of the Federal Property and Administrative Services Act, and the General Services Administration is authorized to use such funds, in addition to amounts received as New Obligational Authority in the Construction and Acquisition of Facilities activity of the Federal Buildings Fund for the construction of a new Federal Building and United States Courthouse in Minneapolis, Minnesota.

(b) In addition, the General Services Administration is hereby authorized to accept donations from the City of Minneapolis, Minnesota and to deposit such donations into the fund established under section 210(f) of the Federal Property and Administrative Services Act, and the General Services Administration is authorized to use such funds, in addition to the amount received as New Obligational Authority in the Construction and Acquisition of Facilities activity of the Federal Buildings Fund for the construction of a new Federal Building and United States Courthouse in Minneapolis, Minnesota.

(c) There are hereby appropriated, out of the Federal Buildings Fund, such sums as may be necessary for carrying out the purposes of subsections (a) and (b).

★

ARCHITECTURAL BARRIERS ACT OF 1968

SUBTITLE F OF PUBLIC LAW 90–480
AS AMENDED THROUGH PUB. L. 103–437

ARCHITECTURAL BARRIERS ACT OF 1968

[Public Law 90-480]
[Popularly known as the Architectural Barriers Act of 1968]

[As Amended Through P.L. 103–437, Enacted November 2, 1994]

AN ACT To insure that certain buildings financed with Federal funds are so designed and constructed as to be accessible to the physically handicapped.

Be it enacted by the Senate and House of Representatives of the United States of America in Congress assembled,

[42 U.S.C. 4151] That, as used in this Act, the term building means any building or facility (other than (A) a privately owned residential structure not leased by the Government for subsidized housing programs and (B) any building or facility on a military installation designed and constructed primarily for use by able bodied military personnel) the intended use for which either will require that such building or facility be accessible to the public, or may result in the employment or residence therein of physically handicapped persons, which building or facility is—

(1) to be constructed or altered by or on behalf of the United States;

(2) to be leased in whole or in part by the United States after the date of enactment of this Act;

(3) to be financed in whole or in part by a grant or a loan made by the United States after the date of enactment of this Act if such building or facility is subject to standards for design, construction, or alteration issued under authority of the law authorizing such grant or loan; or

(4) to be constructed under authority of the National Capital Transportation Act of 1960, the National Capital Transportation Act of 1965, or title III of the Washington Metropolitan Area Transit Regulation Compact.

SEC. 2. [42 U.S.C. 4152]   The Administrator of General Services, in consultation with the Secretary of Health, Education, and Welfare, shall prescribe standards for the design, construction, and alteration of buildings (other than residential structures subject to this Act and buildings, structures, and facilities of the Department of Defense and of the United States Postal Service subject to this Act) to insure whenever possible that physically handicapped persons will have ready access to, and use of, such buildings.

SEC. 3. [42 U.S.C. 4153]   The Secretary of Housing and Urban Development, in consultation with the Secretary of Health, Education, and Welfare, shall prescribe standards for the design, construction, and alteration of buildings which are residential structures subject to this Act to insure whenever possible that physically handicapped persons will have ready access to, and use of, such buildings.

SEC. 4. [42 U.S.C. 4154]   The Secretary of Defense, in consultation with the Secretary of Health, Education, and Welfare, shall prescribe standards for the design, construction, and alteration of buildings, structures, and facilities of the Department of Defense subject to this Act to insure whenever possible that physically handicapped persons will have ready access to, and use of, such buildings.

SEC. 4A. [42 U.S.C. 4154a]   The United States Postal Service, in consultation with the Secretary of Health, Education, and Welfare, shall prescribe such standards for the design, construction, and alteration of its buildings to insure whenever possible that physically handicapped persons will have ready access to, and use of, such buildings.

SEC. 5. [42 U.S.C. 4155]   Every building designed, constructed, or altered after the effective date of a standard issued under this Act which is applicable to such building, shall be designed, constructed, or altered in accordance with such standard.

SEC. 6. [42 U.S.C. 4156] The Administrator of General Services, with respect to standards issued under section 2 of this Act, and the Secretary of Housing and Urban Development, with respect to standards issued under section 3 of this Act, and the Secretary of Defense with respect to standards issued under section 4 of this Act, and the United States Postal Service with respect to standards issued under section 4a of this Act—

(1)   is authorized to modify or waive any such standard, on a case-by-case basis, upon application made by the head of the department, agency, or instrumentality of the United States concerned, and upon a determination by the Administrator or Secretary, as the case may be, that such modification or waiver is clearly necessary, and

(2)   shall establish a system of continuing surveys and investigations to insure compliance with such standards.

SEC. 7. [42 U.S.C. 4157] (a)   The Administrator of General Services shall report to Congress during the first week of January of each year on his activities and those of other departments, agencies, and instrumentalities of the Federal Government under this Act during the preceding fiscal year including, but not limited to, standards issued, revised, amended, or repealed under this Act and all case-by-case modifications, and waivers of such standards during such year.

(b)   The Architectural and Transportation Barriers Compliance Board established by section 502 of the Rehabilitation Act of 1973 (Public Law 93–112) shall report to the Public Works and Transportation Committee of the House of Representatives and the Environment and Public Works Committee of the Senate during the first week of January of each year on its activities and actions to insure compliance with the standards prescribed under this Act.

★

36 U.S.C. CH. 3001–THE AMERICAN RED CROSS

CHAPTER 3001—THE AMERICAN NATIONAL RED CROSS

Sec.
300108. Buildings.

* * * * * * *

NOTES

PERMANENT BUILDING FOR DISTRICT OF COLUMBIA CHAPTER

Act July 1, 1947, ch. 195, 61 Stat. 241, as amended by Pub. L. 100–637, §1, Nov. 8, 1988, 102 Stat. 3325, provided:

* * * * * * *

"SEC. 11. (a) Notwithstanding any other provision of law, the Administrator of the General Services Administration shall enter into a lease of the real property described in the first section of this Act with the American National Red Cross, District of Columbia Chapter. Such lease shall provide that such property shall be used as an office, medical and scientific facility by such Red Cross Chapter and the tenants of such Chapter on such terms and conditions as shall be customary and necessary, including that—

"(1) the lease shall be triple net to the United States and such Red Cross Chapter shall pay all taxes, insurance, and operating costs, and a rent of $1.00 for the term of the lease;

"(2) the lease term shall be for 99 years, and all improvements on such property shall revert to the ownership of the United States at the conclusion of the term;

"(3) such Red Cross Chapter may (at the expense of such Chapter) demolish the improvements on such property or any improvements constructed on such property after the date of enactment of this section [Nov. 8, 1988], build, own, operate, and maintain new improvements, enter into leases, finance improvements (and mortgage any improvements and the leasehold estate), and in all manner deal with the property subject only to the condition that the ownership interest of the United States in the land shall not be adversely affected;

"(4) any space not needed for the operations of such Red Cross Chapter or the American National Red Cross in any building or improvement constructed on such property shall be first made available for use by Federal agencies at rental rates and other related expenses that are less than fair market value and reflect the value of the property provided to such Red Cross Chapter under the provisions of this Act;

"(5) the United States shall cooperate with such Red Cross Chapter with respect to any zoning or other matters relating to the development or improvement of such

195

property; and

"(6) the plans of any proposed building or improvement for construction after the date of the enactment of this section shall first be approved by the American National Red Cross, the Commission of Fine Arts, and the National Capital Planning Commission.

"(b) The enactment of this section may not be construed as establishing a policy of the United States Government to furnish building sites for Red Cross chapters or any eleemosynary institution at any other place."

★

Laws Relating to the Architect of the Capitol and Use of the Capitol Grounds

40 U.S.C. Ch. 51–United States Capitol

SUBTITLE II—PUBLIC BUILDINGS AND WORKS

PART B—UNITED STATES CAPITOL

Chapter   Sec.

51.   UNITED STATES CAPITOL BUILDINGS AND GROUNDS   5101

PART B—UNITED STATES CAPITOL

CHAPTER 51—UNITED STATES CAPITOL BUILDINGS AND GROUNDS

§5101. DEFINITION

In this chapter, the term "Capitol Buildings" means the United States Capitol, the Senate and House Office Buildings and garages, the Capitol Power Plant, all buildings on the real property described under section 5102(c) (including the Administrative Building of the United States Botanic Garden) [1] all buildings on the real property described under section 5102(d), all subways and enclosed passages connecting two or more of those structures, and the real property underlying and enclosed by any of those structures.

(Pub. L. 107–217, Aug. 21, 2002, 116 Stat. 1174; Pub. L. 108–7, div. H, title I, §1016(a), Feb. 20, 2003, 117 Stat. 364; Pub. L. 110–161, div. H, title I, §1004(d)(2)(A)(i), Dec. 26, 2007, 121 Stat. 2233; Pub. L. 110–178, §4(b)(1)(A), Jan. 7, 2008, 121 Stat. 2551; Pub. L. 111–145, §6(d)(1), Mar. 4, 2010, 124 Stat.

54.)

¹ So in original. Probably should be followed by a comma.

§5102. Legal description and jurisdiction of United States Capitol Grounds

(a) Legal Description.—The United States Capitol Grounds comprises all squares, reservations, streets, roadways, walks, and other areas as defined on a map entitled "Map showing areas comprising United States Capitol Grounds", dated June 25, 1946, approved by the Architect of the Capitol, and recorded in the Office of the Surveyor of the District of Columbia in book 127, page 8, including all additions added by law after June 25, 1946.

(b) Jurisdiction.—

(1) Architect of the capitol.—The jurisdiction and control over the Grounds, vested prior to July 31, 1946, by law in the Architect, is extended to the entire area of the Grounds. Except as provided in paragraph (2), the Architect is responsible for the maintenance and improvement of the Grounds, including those streets and roadways in the Grounds as shown on the map referred to in subsection (a) as being under the jurisdiction and control of the Commissioners of the District of Columbia.

(2) Mayor of the district of columbia.—

(A) In general.—The Mayor of the District of Columbia is responsible for the maintenance and improvement of those portions of the following streets which are situated between the curblines of those streets: Constitution Avenue from Second Street Northeast to Third Street Northwest, First Street from D Street Northeast to D Street Southeast, D Street from First Street Southeast to Washington Avenue Southwest, and First Street from the north side of Louisiana Avenue to the intersection of C Street and Washington Avenue Southwest, Pennsylvania Avenue Northwest from First Street Northwest to Third Street Northwest, Maryland Avenue Southwest from First Street Southwest to Third Street Southwest, Second Street Northeast from F Street Northeast to C Street Southeast; C Street Southeast from Second Street Southeast to First Street Southeast; that portion of Maryland Avenue Northeast from Second Street Northeast to First Street Northeast; that portion of New Jersey Avenue Northwest from D Street Northwest to Louisiana Avenue; that portion of Second Street Southwest from the north curb of D Street to the south curb of Virginia Avenue Southwest; that portion of Virginia Avenue Southwest from the east curb of Second Street Southwest to the west curb of Third Street Southwest; that portion of Third Street Southwest from the south curb of Virginia Avenue Southwest to the north curb of D Street Southwest; that portion of D Street Southwest from the west curb of Third Street Southwest to the east curb of Second Street Southwest; that portion of Washington Avenue Southwest, including sidewalks and traffic islands, from the south curb of Independence Avenue Southwest to the west curb of South Capitol Street.

(B) Repair and maintenance of utility services.—The Mayor may enter any part of the Grounds to repair or maintain or, subject to the approval of the Architect, construct or alter, any utility service of the District of Columbia Government.

(c) National Garden of the United States Botanic Garden.—

(1) In general.—Except as provided under paragraph (2), the United States

Capitol Grounds shall include—

(A) the National Garden of the United States Botanic Garden;

(B) all grounds contiguous to the Administrative Building of the United States Botanic Garden, including Bartholdi Park; and

(C) all grounds bounded by the curblines of First Street, Southwest on the east; Washington Avenue, Southwest to its intersection with Independence Avenue, and Independence Avenue from such intersection to its intersection with Third Street, Southwest on the south; Third Street, Southwest on the west; and Maryland Avenue, Southwest on the north.

(2) MAINTENANCE AND IMPROVEMENTS.—Notwithstanding subsections (a) and (b), jurisdiction and control over the buildings on the grounds described in paragraph (1) shall be retained by the Joint Committee on the Library, and the Joint Committee on the Library shall continue to be solely responsible for the maintenance and improvement of the grounds described in such paragraph.

(3) AUTHORITY NOT LIMITED.—Nothing in this subsection shall limit the authority of the Architect of the Capitol under section 307E of the Legislative Branch Appropriations Act, 1989 (40 U.S.C. 216c).[1]

(d) LIBRARY OF CONGRESS BUILDINGS AND GROUNDS.—

(1) IN GENERAL.—Except as provided under paragraph (2), the United States Capitol Grounds shall include the Library of Congress grounds described under section 11 of the Act entitled "An Act relating to the policing of the buildings [2] of the Library of Congress", approved August 4, 1950 (2 U.S.C. 167j).

(2) AUTHORITY OF LIBRARIAN OF CONGRESS.—Notwithstanding subsections (a) and (b), the Librarian of Congress shall retain authority over the Library of Congress buildings and grounds in accordance with section 1 of the Act of June 29, 1922 (2 U.S.C. 141; 42 Stat. 715).

(Pub. L. 107–217, Aug. 21, 2002, 116 Stat. 1175; Pub. L. 108–7, div. H, title I, §1016(b), Feb. 20, 2003, 117 Stat. 364; Pub. L. 110–161, div. H, title I, §1004(d)(2)(A)(ii), Dec. 26, 2007, 121 Stat. 2233; Pub. L. 110–178, §4(b)(1)(B), Jan. 7, 2008, 121 Stat. 2551; Pub. L. 111–145, §6(d)(1), Mar. 4, 2010, 124 Stat. 54.)

DEFINITION OF UNITED STATES CAPITOL GROUNDS

For provisions directing amendment of this section (or section 1 of the Act of July 31, 1946, as amended (former 40 U.S.C. 193a), which was repealed and reenacted by Pub. L. 107–217, §§1, 6(b), Aug. 21, 2002, 116 Stat. 1062, 1304, as this section) to include within or exclude from the definition of the United States Capitol Grounds certain parcels or areas.

[1] *See References in Text note below.*

[2] *So in original. Probably should be followed by "and grounds".*

§5103. RESTRICTIONS ON PUBLIC USE OF UNITED STATES CAPITOL GROUNDS

Public travel in, and occupancy of, the United States Capitol Grounds is restricted to the roads, walks, and places prepared for that purpose.

(Pub. L. 107–217, Aug. 21, 2002, 116 Stat. 1176.)

§5104. UNLAWFUL ACTIVITIES

(a) DEFINITIONS.—In this section—

(1) ACT OF PHYSICAL VIOLENCE.—The term "act of physical violence" means any act involving—

(A) an assault or other infliction or threat of infliction of death or bodily harm on an individual; or

(B) damage to, or destruction of, real or personal property.

(2) DANGEROUS WEAPON.—The term "dangerous weapon" includes—

(A) all articles enumerated in section 14(a) of the Act of July 8, 1932 (ch. 465, 47 Stat. 654); and

(B) a device designed to expel or hurl a projectile capable of causing injury to individuals or property, a dagger, a dirk, a stiletto, and a knife having a blade over three inches in length.

(3) EXPLOSIVES.—The term "explosives" has the meaning given that term in section 841(d) of title 18.

(4) FIREARM.—The term "firearm" has the meaning given that term in section 921(3) [1] of title 18.

(b) OBSTRUCTION OF ROADS.—A person may not occupy the roads in the United States Capitol Grounds in a manner that obstructs or hinders their proper use, or use the roads in the area of the Grounds, south of Constitution Avenue and B Street and north of Independence Avenue and B Street, to convey goods or merchandise, except to or from the United States Capitol on Federal Government service.

(c) SALE OF ARTICLES, DISPLAY OF SIGNS, AND SOLICITATIONS.—A person may not carry out any of the following activities in the Grounds:

(1) offer or expose any article for sale.

(2) display a sign, placard, or other form of advertisement.

(3) solicit fares, alms, subscriptions, or contributions.

(d) INJURIES TO PROPERTY.—A person may not step or climb on, remove, or in any way injure any statue, seat, wall, fountain, or other erection or architectural feature, or any tree, shrub, plant, or turf, in the Grounds.

(e) CAPITOL GROUNDS AND BUILDINGS SECURITY.—

(1) FIREARMS, DANGEROUS WEAPONS, EXPLOSIVES, OR INCENDIARY DEVICES.—An individual or group of individuals—

(A) except as authorized by regulations prescribed by the Capitol Police Board—

(i) may not carry on or have readily accessible to any individual on the Grounds or in any of the Capitol Buildings a firearm, a dangerous weapon, explosives, or an incendiary device;

(ii) may not discharge a firearm or explosives, use a dangerous weapon, or ignite an incendiary device, on the Grounds or in any of the Capitol Buildings; or

(iii) may not transport on the Grounds or in any of the Capitol Buildings explosives or an incendiary device; or

(B) may not knowingly, with force and violence, enter or remain on the floor of either House of Congress.

(2) VIOLENT ENTRY AND DISORDERLY CONDUCT.—An individual or group of

individuals may not willfully and knowingly—

(A) enter or remain on the floor of either House of Congress or in any cloakroom or lobby adjacent to that floor, in the Rayburn Room of the House of Representatives, or in the Marble Room of the Senate, unless authorized to do so pursuant to rules adopted, or an authorization given, by that House;

(B) enter or remain in the gallery of either House of Congress in violation of rules governing admission to the gallery adopted by that House or pursuant to an authorization given by that House;

(C) with the intent to disrupt the orderly conduct of official business, enter or remain in a room in any of the Capitol Buildings set aside or designated for the use of—

(i) either House of Congress or a Member, committee, officer, or employee of Congress, or either House of Congress; or

(ii) the Library of Congress;

(D) utter loud, threatening, or abusive language, or engage in disorderly or disruptive conduct, at any place in the Grounds or in any of the Capitol Buildings with the intent to impede, disrupt, or disturb the orderly conduct of a session of Congress or either House of Congress, or the orderly conduct in that building of a hearing before, or any deliberations of, a committee of Congress or either House of Congress;

(E) obstruct, or impede passage through or within, the Grounds or any of the Capitol Buildings;

(F) engage in an act of physical violence in the Grounds or any of the Capitol Buildings; or

(G) parade, demonstrate, or picket in any of the Capitol Buildings.

(3) EXEMPTION OF GOVERNMENT OFFICIALS.—This subsection does not prohibit any act performed in the lawful discharge of official duties by—

(A) a Member of Congress;

(B) an employee of a Member of Congress;

(C) an officer or employee of Congress or a committee of Congress; or

(D) an officer or employee of either House of Congress or a committee of that House.

(f) PARADES, ASSEMBLAGES, AND DISPLAY OF FLAGS.—Except as provided in section 5106 of this title, a person may not—

(1) parade, stand, or move in processions or assemblages in the Grounds; or

(2) display in the Grounds a flag, banner, or device designed or adapted to bring into public notice a party, organization, or movement.

(Pub. L. 107–217, Aug. 21, 2002, 116 Stat. 1176; Pub. L. 110–161, div. H, title I, §1004(d)(2)(A)(iii), Dec. 26, 2007, 121 Stat. 2234; Pub. L. 110–178, §4(b)(1)(C), Jan. 7, 2008, 121 Stat. 2552; Pub. L. 111–145, §6(d)(1), Mar. 4, 2010, 124 Stat. 54.)

[1] So in original. Probably should be "921(a)(3)".

§5105. ASSISTANCE TO AUTHORITIES BY CAPITOL EMPLOYEES

Each individual employed in the service of the Federal Government in the United States Capitol or within the United States Capitol Grounds shall prevent, as far as may be in the individual's power, a violation of a provision of this chapter or section 9, 9A, 9B, 9C, or 14 of the Act of July 31, 1946 (ch. 707, 60 Stat. 719, 720), and shall aid the police in securing the arrest and conviction of the individual violating the provision.

(Pub. L. 107–217, Aug. 21, 2002, 116 Stat. 1178.)

§5106. SUSPENSION OF PROHIBITIONS

(a) AUTHORITY TO SUSPEND.—To allow the observance in the United States Capitol Grounds of occasions of national interest becoming the cognizance and entertainment of Congress, the President of the Senate and the Speaker of the House of Representatives concurrently may suspend any of the prohibitions contained in sections 5103 and 5104 of this title that would prevent the use of the roads and walks within the Grounds by processions or assemblages, and the use in the Grounds of suitable decorations, music, addresses, and ceremonies, if responsible officers have been appointed and the President and the Speaker determine that adequate arrangements have been made to maintain suitable order and decorum in the proceedings and to guard the United States Capitol and its grounds from injury.

(b) POWER TO SUSPEND PROHIBITIONS IN ABSENCE OF PRESIDENT OR SPEAKER.—If either the President or Speaker is absent from the District of Columbia, the authority to suspend devolves on the other officer. If both officers are absent, the authority devolves on the Capitol Police Board.

(c) AUTHORITY OF MAYOR TO PERMIT USE OF LOUISIANA AVENUE.—Notwithstanding subsection (a) and section 5104(f) of this title, the Capitol Police Board may grant the Mayor of the District of Columbia authority to permit the use of Louisiana Avenue for any of the purposes prohibited by section 5104(f).

(Pub. L. 107–217, Aug. 21, 2002, 116 Stat. 1178.)

§5107. CONCERTS ON GROUNDS

Sections 5102, 5103, 5104(b)–(f), 5105, 5106, and 5109 of this title and sections 9, 9A, 9B, and 9C of the Act of July 31, 1946 (ch. 707, 60 Stat. 719, 720), do not prohibit a band in the service of the Federal Government from giving concerts in the United States Capitol Grounds at times which will not interfere with Congress and as authorized by the Architect of the Capitol.

(Pub. L. 107–217, Aug. 21, 2002, 116 Stat. 1178; Pub. L. 108–178, §3(2), Dec. 15, 2003, 117 Stat. 2640.)

§5108. AUDIT OF PRIVATE ORGANIZATIONS

A private organization (except a political party or committee constituted for the election of federal officials), whether or not organized for profit and whether or not any of its income inures to the benefit of any person, that performs services or conducts activities in the United States Capitol Buildings or Grounds is subject to a special audit of its accounts for each year in which it performs those services or conducts those activities. The Comptroller General shall conduct the audit and report the results of the audit to the Senate and the House of Representatives.

(Pub. L. 107–217, Aug. 21, 2002, 116 Stat. 1178.)

The words "as defined by or pursuant to law" are omitted as unnecessary because of sections 5101 and 5102 of the revised title. The words "Comptroller General" are substituted for "General Accounting Office" because of 31:702 and for consistency in the revised title.

§5109. PENALTIES

(a) FIREARMS, DANGEROUS WEAPONS, EXPLOSIVES, OR INCENDIARY DEVICE OFFENSES.—An individual or group violating section 5104(e)(1) of this title, or attempting to commit a violation, shall be fined under title 18, imprisoned for not more than five years, or both.

(b) OTHER OFFENSES.—A person violating section 5103 or 5104(b), (c), (d), (e)(2), or (f) of this title, or attempting to commit a violation, shall be fined under title 18, imprisoned for not more than six months, or both.

(c) PROCEDURE.—

(1) IN GENERAL.—An action for a violation of this chapter or section 9, 9A, 9B, 9C or 14 of the Act of July 31, 1946 (ch. 707, 60 Stat. 719, 720), including an attempt or a conspiracy to commit a violation, shall be brought by the Attorney General in the name of the United States. This chapter and sections 9, 9A, 9B, 9C and 14 do not supersede any provision of federal law or the laws of the District of Columbia. Where the conduct violating this chapter or section 9, 9A, 9B, 9C or 14 also violates federal law or the laws of the District of Columbia, both violations may be joined in a single action.

(2) VENUE.—An action under this section for a violation of—

(A) section 5104(e)(1) of this title or for conduct that constitutes a felony under federal law or the laws of the District of Columbia shall be brought in the United States District Court for the District of Columbia; and

(B) any other section referred to in subsection (a) may be brought in the Superior Court of the District of Columbia.

(3) AMOUNT OF PENALTY.—The penalty which may be imposed on a person convicted in an action under this subsection is the highest penalty authorized by any of the laws the defendant is convicted of violating.

(Pub. L. 107–217, Aug. 21, 2002, 116 Stat. 1178.)

★

TRANSFER OF O'NEILL BUILDING TO HOUSE OF REPRESENTATIVES

SECTION 176 OF PUBLIC LAW 114–223
AS AMENDED THROUGH PUB. L. 116–6

CONTINUING APPROPRIATIONS AND MILITARY CONSTRUCTION, VETERANS AFFAIRS, AND RELATED AGENCIES APPROPRIATIONS ACT, 2017, AND ZIKA RESPONSE AND PREPAREDNESS ACT

[(Public Law 114–223)]

[As Amended Through P.L. 116–6, Enacted February 15, 2019]

AN ACT Making continuing appropriations for fiscal year 2017, and for other purposes.

Be it enacted by the Senate and House of Representatives of the United States of America in Congress assembled,

SECTION 1. SHORT TITLE.

This Act may be cited as the "Continuing Appropriations and Military Construction, Veterans Affairs, and Related Agencies Appropriations Act, 2017, and Zika Response and Preparedness Act".

* * * * * * *

Division C—CONTINUING APPROPRIATIONS ACT, 2017

* * * * * * *

SEC. 176. TRANSFER OF O'NEILL BUILDING TO HOUSE OF REPRESENTATIVES.— (a) TRANSFER.— Effective upon the expiration of the 180-day period that begins on the date of the enactment of this section—

(1) the building described in subsection (e) shall become an office building of the House of Representatives;

(2) the Administrator of General Services shall transfer custody, control, and administrative jurisdiction over the building to the Architect of the Capitol; and

(3) the Architect of the Capitol shall exercise custody, control, and administrative jurisdiction over the building subject to the direction of the House Office Building Commission.

(b) TREATMENT AS HOUSE OFFICE BUILDING AND PART OF CAPITOL GROUNDS .—Upon the transfer of custody, control, and administrative jurisdiction under subsection (a), the building and grounds described in subsection (e) shall be treated as a House Office Building and as part of the United States Capitol Grounds for purposes of all laws,

Sec. 176.

Cont. Approps and Mil. Const., VA, and R
Agencies Approps. Act, 2017, and Zi

rules, and regulations applicable to the House Office Buildings and the Capitol Grounds, including—

(1) chapter 51 of title 40, United States Code (relating to the administration of the United States Capitol Buildings and Grounds); and

(2) section 9 of the Act entitled An Act to define the area of the United States Capitol Grounds, to regulate the use thereof, and for other purposes, approved July 31, 1946 (2 U.S.C. 1961) (relating to the authority of the United States Capitol Police to police the United States Capitol Buildings and Grounds).

(c) AUTHORITY OF ARCHITECT OF THE CAPITOL TO ENTER INTO LEASES AND OTHER AGREEMENTS WITH FEDERAL DEPARTMENTS AND AGENCIES FOR USE OF BUILDING.—

(1) AUTHORITY DESCRIBED.— The Architect of the Capitol is authorized to enter into leases and other agreements with departments and agencies of the Federal Government for the use of the building described in subsection (e) (or portions thereof), subject to the approval of the House Office Building Commission.

(2) COLLECTION OF PAYMENTS.— Pursuant to a lease or other agreement entered into between the Architect of the Capitol and a department or agency of the Federal Government under the authority described in paragraph (1), the Architect of the Capitol is authorized to collect payments from such department or agency and such department or agency is authorized to make payments to the Architect of the Capitol, including payments of commercially-equivalent rent.

(3) TREATMENT OF PAYMENTS.— Any payments received by the Architect of the Capitol pursuant to any lease or other agreement entered into under this subsection shall be deposited to the appropriation available to the Architect of the Capitol from the House Office Buildings Fund established under subsection (d) and shall be subject to future appropriation.

(d) HOUSE OFFICE BUILDINGS FUND.—

(1) ESTABLISHMENT.— There is established in the Treasury of the United States a fund to be known as the House Office Buildings Fund (hereafter in this section referred to as the Fund).

(2) CONTENTS OF FUND.— The Fund shall consist of the following amounts:

(A) Amounts transferred by the Architect of the Capitol under paragraph (3) of subsection (c).

(B) Interest earned on the balance of the Fund.

(C) Such other amounts as may be appropriated by law.

(3) USE OF FUND.— Amounts in the Fund shall be available to the Architect of the Capitol for the maintenance, care, and operation of the House office buildings, and may be used to reimburse the United States Capitol Police, the House of Representatives, or any other office of the legislative branch which provides goods or services for the maintenance, care, and operation of the building and grounds described in subsection (e), in such amounts as may be appropriated under law.

(4) NOTIFICATION TO COMMITTEE ON APPROPRIATIONS.— Upon making any obligation or expenditure of any amount in the Fund, the Architect of the Capitol

c. 176.

Cont. Approps and Mil. Const., VA, and Rel.
Agencies Approps. Act, 2017, and Zika

shall notify the Committee on Appropriations of the House of Representatives of the amount and purpose of the obligation or expenditure.

(5) CONTINUING AVAILABILITY OF FUNDS.— Amounts in the Fund are available without regard to fiscal year limitation.

(e) DESCRIPTION OF BUILDING AND GROUNDS.—

(1) DESCRIPTION.— The building and grounds described in this subsection is the Federal building located in the District of Columbia which is commonly known as the Thomas P. O'Neill Jr. Federal Building, and which is more particularly described as follows: Square 579, Lot 827, at 200 C Street Southwest, bounded by C Street Southwest on the north, by 2nd Street Southwest on the east, by D Street Southwest on the south, and by 3rd Street Southwest on the west, and by all that area contiguous to and surrounding Square 579 from the property line thereof to the west curb of 3rd Street Southwest, the north curb of C Street Southwest, the east curb of 2nd Street Southwest, and the south curb of D Street Southwest.

(2) RETENTION OF RESPONSIBILITIES OF DISTRICT OF COLUMBIA.— The Mayor of the District of Columbia will retain responsibility for the maintenance and improvement of those portions of the streets which are situated between the curb lines of the streets referenced in paragraph (1).

★

DETAIL OF CAPITOL POLICE

2 U.S.C. 1962

TITLE 2—THE CONGRESS

* * * * * * *

CHAPTER 29—CAPITOL POLICE

* * * * * * *

SUBCHAPTER II—POWERS AND DUTIES

* * * * * * *

§1962. DETAIL OF POLICE

The Capitol Police Board is authorized to detail police from the House Office, Senate Office, and Capitol Buildings for police duty on the Capitol Grounds and on the Library of Congress Grounds.

(Pub. L. 96–432, §5, Oct. 10, 1980, 94 Stat. 1853.)

CODIFICATION

Section was classified to section 212a–1 of former Title 40, prior to the enactment of Title 40, Public Buildings, Property, and Works, by Pub. L. 107–217, §1, Aug. 21, 2002, 116 Stat. 1062.

★

SELECTED PROVISIONS OF THE SECOND DEFICIENCY APPROPRIATION ACT, 1948

ACT OF JUNE 25, 1948
AS AMENDED THROUGH P.L. 107–249

SECOND DEFICIENCY APPROPRIATION ACT, 1948

(Additional Office Building for the United States Senate)

[Ch. 658; 62 Stat. 1029]

[As Amended Through P.L. 107–249, Enacted October 23, 2002]

ARCHITECT OF THE CAPITOL

* * * * * * *

ADDITIONAL OFFICE BUILDING FOR THE UNITED STATES SENATE

* * * * * * *

Provided further, [40 U.S.C. 174b–1] That upon completion of the project, the building and the grounds and sidewalks surrounding the same shall be subject to the provisions of the Act of June 8, 1942 (U.S.C., title 40, sec. 174 (c) and (d)) and the Act of July 31, 1946 (60 Stat. 718), in the same manner and to the same extent as the present Senate Office Building and the grounds and sidewalks surrounding the same.

★

SELECTED PROVISION OF THE ACT OF JULY 31, 1946

ACT OF JULY 31, 1946
AS AMENDED THROUGH P.L. 111–145

ACT OF JULY 31, 1946

(United States Capitol Grounds)

[Chapter 707 of the 79th Congress; 60 Stat. 719]

[As Amended Through P.L. 111–145, Enacted March 4, 2010]

AN ACT To define the area of the United States Capitol Grounds, to regulate the use thereof, and for other purposes.

Be it enacted by the Senate and House of Representatives of the United States of America in Congress assembled,

* * * * * * *

[Sections 1–8 were repealed by section 6 of P.L. 107–217 (116 Stat. 1062).]

SEC. 9. [2 U.S.C. 1961] (a)   The Capitol Police shall police the United States Capitol Buildings and Grounds under the direction of the Capitol Police Board, consisting of the Sergeant at Arms of the United States Senate, the Sergeant at Arms of the House of Representatives, and the Architect of the Capitol, and shall have the power to enforce the provisions of this Act (and regulations promulgated under section 14 of this Act (2 U.S.C. 1969)), and chapter 51 of title 40, United States Code, and to make arrests within the United States Capitol Buildings and Grounds for any violations of any law of the United States, of the District of Columbia, or of any State, or any regulation promulgated pursuant thereto: *Provided,* That for the fiscal year for which appropriations are made by this Act the Capitol Police shall have the additional authority to make arrests within the District of Columbia for crimes of violence, as defined in section 16 of title 18, committed within the Capitol Buildings and Grounds and shall have the additional authority to make arrests, without a warrant, for crimes of violence, as defined in section 16 of title 18, committed in the presence of any member of the Capitol Police performing official duties: *Provided further,* That the Metropolitan Police force of the District of Columbia are authorized to make arrests within the United States Capitol Buildings and Grounds for any violation of any such laws or regulations, but such authority shall not be construed as authorizing the Metropolitan Police force, except with the consent or upon the request of the Capitol Police Board, to enter such buildings to make arrests in response to complaints or to serve warrants or to patrol the United States Capitol Buildings and Grounds. For the purpose of this section, the word grounds shall include the House Office Buildings parking areas and that part or parts of property which have been or hereafter are acquired in the District of Columbia by the Architect of the Capitol, or by an officer of the Senate or the House, by lease, purchase, intergovernment transfer, or otherwise, for the use of the Senate, the House, or the Architect of the Capitol.

(b)   For purposes of this section, the United States Capitol Buildings and Grounds shall include any building or facility acquired by the Sergeant at Arms of the Senate for the use of the Senate for which the Sergeant at Arms of the Senate has entered into an agreement with the United States Capitol Police for the policing of the building or facility.

(c)   For purposes of this section, the United States Capitol Buildings and Grounds shall include any building or facility acquired by the Chief Administrative Officer of the House of Representatives for the use of the House of Representatives for which the Chief Administrative Officer has entered into an agreement with the United States Capitol Police for the policing of the building or facility.

(d)   For purposes of this section, United States Capitol Buildings and Grounds shall include the Library of Congress buildings and grounds described under section 11 of the Act entitled An Act relating to the policing of the buildings of the Library of Congress, approved August 4, 1950 (2 U.S.C. 167j), except that in a case of buildings or grounds not located in the District of Columbia, the authority granted to the Metropolitan Police Force of the District of Columbia shall be granted to any police force within whose jurisdiction the buildings or grounds are located.

* * * * * * *

SEC. 9B. [40 U.S.C. 212a–3] (a) Subject to such regulations as may be prescribed by the Capitol Police Board and approved by the Committee on House Oversight of the House of Representatives and the Committee on Rules and Administration of the Senate, a member of the Capitol Police shall have authority to make arrests and otherwise enforce the laws of the United States, including the laws of the District of Columbia—

(1)   within the District of Columbia, with respect to any crime of violence committed within the United States Capitol Grounds;

(2)   within the District of Columbia, with respect to any crime of violence committed in the presence of the member, if the member is in the performance of official duties when the crime is committed;

(3)   within the District of Columbia, to prevent imminent loss of life or injury to person or property, if the officer is in the performance of official duties when the authority is exercised;

(4)   within the area described under subsection (b)(1); and[1]

---

[1]   Section 1003 of the Legislative Branch Appropriations Act, 2004 (P.L. 108–83; 117 Stat. 1021) amended paragraph (4) by striking in subsection (b) of this section. and inserting under subsection (b)(1); and. The amendment probably should not have included of this section in the matter to be struck. The amendment made by such public law was executed to reflect the probable intent of Congress.

(5) within the area described under subsection (b)(2)—

(A)   with respect to any crime of violence committed in the presence of the member, if the member is in the performance of official duties, as defined under such regulations, when the crime is committed; and

(B) to prevent imminent loss of life or injury to person or property, if the officer is in the performance of official duties, as defined under such regulations, when the authority is exercised.

(b)(1) The area referred to in subsection (a)(4) is that area bounded by the north curb of H Street from 3rd Street, N.W. to 7th Street, N.E., the east curb of 7th Street from H Street, N.E., to M Street, S.E., the south curb of M Street from 7th Street, S.E. to 1st Street, S.E., the east curb of 1st Street from M Street, S.E. to Potomac Avenue S.E., the southeast curb of Potomac Avenue from 1st Street, S.E. to South Capitol Street, S.W., the west curb of South Capitol Street from Potomac Avenue, S.W. to P Street, S.W., the north curb of P Street from South Capitol Street, S.W. to 3rd Street, S.W., and the west curb of 3rd Street from P Street, S.W. to H Street, N.W.

(2) The area referred to under subsection (a)(5) is that area bounded by the north curb of Constitution Avenue from 14th Street, N.W., to 3rd Street, N.W., the east curb of 3rd Street from Constitution Avenue, N.W., to Independence Avenue, S.W., the south curb of Independence Avenue from 3rd Street, S.W., to 14th Street, S.W., and the west curb of 14th Street from Independence Avenue, S.W., to Constitution Avenue, N.W.

(c) This section does not affect the authority of the Metropolitan Police force of the District of Columbia with respect to the area described in subsection (b).

(d) As used in this section, the term crime of violence has the meaning given that term in section 16 of title 18, United States Code.

SEC. 9C. [40 U.S.C. 207a] Payroll administration for the Capitol Police and civilian support personnel of the Capitol Police shall be carried out on a unified basis by a single disbursing authority. The Capitol Police Board, with the approval of the Committee on House Oversight of the House of Representatives and the Committee on Rules and Administration of the Senate, acting jointly, shall, by contract or otherwise, provide for such unified payroll administration.[Sections 10–13 were repealed by section 6 of P.L. 107–217 (116 Stat. 1062).]

SEC. 14. [40 U.S.C. 212b] (a) The Capitol Police Board, consisting of the Sergeant at Arms of the United States Senate, the Sergeant at Arms of the House of Representatives, and the Architect of the Capitol, shall have exclusive charge and control of the regulation and movement of all vehicular and other traffic, including the parking and impounding of vehicles and limiting the speed thereof, within the United States Capitol Grounds; and said Board is hereby authorized and empowered to make and enforce all necessary regulations therefor and to prescribe penalties for violation of such regulations, such penalties not to exceed a fine of $300 or imprisonment for not more than ninety days. Notwithstanding the foregoing provisions of this section those provisions of the District of Columbia Traffic Act of 1925, as amended, for the violation of which specific penalties are provided in said Act, as amended, shall be applicable to the United States Capitol Grounds. Prosecutions for violation of such regulations shall be in The Municipal Court for the District of Columbia, upon information by the Corporation Counsel of the District of Columbia or any of his assistants.

(b)   Regulations authorized to be promulgated under this section shall be promulgated by the Capitol Police Board and such regulations may be amended from time to time by the Capitol Police Board whenever it shall deem it necessary: *Provided,* That until such regulations are promulgated and become effective, the traffic regulations of the District of Columbia shall be applicable to the United States Capitol Grounds.

(c)   All regulations promulgated under the authority of this section shall, when adopted by the Capitol Police Board, be printed in one or more of the daily newspapers published in the District of Columbia, and shall not become effective until the expiration of ten days after the date of such publication, except that whenever the Capitol Police Board deems it advisable to make effective immediately any regulation relating to parking, diverting of vehicular traffic, or the closing of streets to such traffic, the regulation shall be effective immediately upon placing at the point where it is to be in force conspicuous signs containing a notice of the regulation. Any expenses incurred under this subsection shall be payable from the appropriation Uniforms and Equipment, Capitol Police.

(d)   It shall be the duty of the Commissioners of the District of Columbia, or any officer or employee of the government of the District of Columbia designated by said Commissioners, upon request of the Capitol Police Board, to cooperate with the Board in the preparation of the regulations authorized to be promulgated under this section, and any future amendments thereof.

   [Sections 15 and 16(a) were repealed by section 6 of P.L. 107–217 (116 Stat. 1062).]

★

SELECTED PROVISIONS OF THE LEGISLATIVE BRANCH APPROPRIATION ACT, 1942

PUBLIC LAW 85–95
AS AMENDED THROUGH P.L. 107–249

LEGISLATIVE BRANCH APPROPRIATION ACT, 1942

(Architect of the Capitol)

[Public Law 85-95]

[As Amended Through P.L. 107–249, Enacted October 23, 2002]

* * * * * * *

ARCHITECT OF THE CAPITOL

* * * * * * *

CAPITOL BUILDINGS AND GROUNDS

* * * * * * *

* * * Provided, [40 U.S.C. 174b] That structural changes in the Senate Office Building shall only be made with the approval of the Architect of the Capitol: * * *

* * * * * * *

★

SELECTED PROVISION TITLE 2 U.S.C. RELATING TO THE CAPITOL POWER PLANT

2 U.S. CODE §2162

SELECT PROVISIONS OF THE U.S. CODE RELATING TO THE CAPITOL POWER PLANT

TITLE 2—THE CONGRESS

* * * * * * *

CHAPTER 30—OPERATION AND MAINTENANCE OF CAPITOL COMPLEX

* * * * * * *

SUBCHAPTER VII—OTHER ENTITIES AND SERVICES

* * * * * * *

§2162. CAPITOL POWER PLANT

(A) DESIGNATION

The heating, lighting, and power plant constructed under the terms of the Act approved April 28, 1904 (33 Stat. 479, chapter 1762) shall be known as the "Capitol Power Plant".

(B) DEFINITION

In this section, the term "carbon dioxide energy efficiency" means the quantity of electricity used to power equipment for carbon dioxide capture and storage or use.

(C) FEASIBILITY STUDY

The Architect of the Capitol shall conduct a feasibility study evaluating the available methods to capture, store, and use carbon dioxide emitted from the Capitol Power Plant as a result of burning fossil fuels. In carrying out the feasibility study, the Architect of the Capitol is encouraged to consult with individuals with expertise in carbon capture and storage or use, including experts with the Environmental Protection Agency, Department of Energy, academic institutions, non-profit organizations, and industry, as appropriate. The study shall consider—

(1) the availability of technologies to capture and store or use Capitol Power Plant carbon dioxide emissions;

(2) strategies to conserve energy and reduce carbon dioxide emissions at the Capitol Power Plant; and

(3) other factors as determined by the Architect of the Capitol.

(D) DEMONSTRATION PROJECTS

(1) IN GENERAL

If the feasibility study determines that a demonstration project to capture and store or use Capitol Power Plant carbon dioxide emissions is technologically feasible and economically justified (including direct and indirect economic and environmental benefits), the Architect of the Capitol may conduct 1 or more demonstration projects to capture and store or use carbon dioxide emitted from the Capitol Power Plant as a result of burning fossil fuels.

(2) FACTORS FOR CONSIDERATION

In carrying out such demonstration projects, the Architect of the Capitol shall consider—

(A) the amount of Capitol Power Plant carbon dioxide emissions to be captured and stored or used;

(B) whether the proposed project is able to reduce air pollutants other than carbon dioxide;

(C) the carbon dioxide energy efficiency of the proposed project;

(D) whether the proposed project is able to use carbon dioxide emissions;

(E) whether the proposed project could be expanded to significantly increase the amount of Capitol Power Plant carbon dioxide emissions to be captured and stored or used;

(F) the potential environmental, energy, and educational benefits of demonstrating the capture and storage or use of carbon dioxide at the U.S. Capitol; and

(G) other factors as determined by the Architect of the Capitol.

(3) TERMS AND CONDITIONS

A demonstration project funded under this section shall be subject to such terms and conditions as the Architect of the Capitol may prescribe.

(E) AUTHORIZATION OF APPROPRIATIONS

There is authorized to be appropriated to carry out the feasibility study and demonstration project $3,000,000. Such sums shall remain available until expended.

(Mar. 4, 1911, ch. 285, 36 Stat. 1414; Mar. 3, 1921, ch. 124, 41 Stat. 1291; Pub. L. 110–140, title V, §505(2), Dec. 19, 2007, 121 Stat. 1657.)

EDITORIAL NOTES

* * * * * * *

STATUTORY NOTES AND RELATED SUBSIDIARIES

CHANGE OF NAME

Change of name of Architect of the Capitol, functions abolished, transferred, etc., by prior acts, see Prior Provisions and Change of Name notes set out under former section

1801 of this title.

* * * * * * *

MANAGEMENT AND OPERATION OF THE CAPITOL POWER PLANT

Pub. L. 108–447, div. G, title I, §1101, Dec. 8, 2004, 118 Stat. 3185, provided that:

"(a) DEFINITION.—In this section, the term 'appropriate congressional committees' means—

"(1) the Committee on Appropriations of the Senate and the House of Representatives;

"(2) the Committee on Rules and Administration of the Senate; and

"(3) the House Office Building Commission.

"(b) STUDY OF CONTRACT WITH A PRIVATE ENTITY.—Not later than 180 days after the date of enactment of this Act [Dec. 8, 2004], the Comptroller General shall conduct a study and submit to the appropriate congressional committees and the Architect of the Capitol a report that—

"(1) analyzes the costs, cost effectiveness, benefits, and feasibility of the Architect of the Capitol entering into a contract with a private entity for the management and operation of the Capitol Power Plant; and

"(2) makes a recommendation on whether the Architect of the Capitol should enter into such a contract.

"(c) IMPLEMENTATION PLAN.—If the Comptroller General makes a recommendation under subsection (b)(2) in favor of entering into a contract, the Architect of the Capitol shall submit an implementation plan for that contract to the appropriate congressional committees not later than the later of—

"(1) 270 days after the date of enactment of this Act [Dec. 8, 2004]; or

"(2) the date of the completion of the West Refrigeration Plant.

"(d) CONTRACT.—Subject to the approval of the appropriate congressional committees, the Architect of the Capitol shall enter into a contract with a private entity for the management and operation of the Capitol Power Plant.

"(e) EFFECTIVE DATE.—This section shall apply to fiscal year 2005 and each fiscal year thereafter."

GENERAL SERVICES ADMINISTRATION COAL YARD

Pub. L. 100–458, title I, Oct. 1, 1988, 102 Stat. 2170, provided: "That appropriations under this head ["CAPITOL POWER PLANT"] shall hereafter be available for maintenance, alterations, personal and other services, and for all other necessary expenses of the Government owned property, buildings and facilities located in Lot 803, Square 695, formerly known as the General Services Administration Coal Yard at 42 I Street, S.E., in the District of Columbia."

* * * * * * *

★

SELECTED PROVISIONS OF 2 U.S.C. RELATING TO THE LIBRARY OF CONGRESS

2 U.S.C. SS142NOTE

SELECT PROVISIONS OF THE U.S. CODE RELATING TO THE ARCHITECT OF THE CAPITOL

TITLE 2—THE CONGRESS

* * * * * * *

CHAPTER 28—ARCHITECT OF THE CAPITOL

* * * * * * *

SUBCHAPTER I—GENERAL

§1801. Repealed. Pub. L. 118–31, div. E, title LVII, §5702(d)(1), Dec. 22, 2023, 137 Stat. 960

Section, Pub. L. 101–163, title III, §319, Nov. 21, 1989, 103 Stat. 1068; Pub. L. 104–19, title I, §701, July 27, 1995, 109 Stat. 220, related to appointment of Architect of the Capitol by the President by and with the advice and consent of the Senate for a term of 10 years. See section 1801a of this title.

Editorial Notes

Codification

Section was classified to section 162–1 of former Title 40, prior to the enactment of Title 40, Public Buildings, Property, and Works, by Pub. L. 107–217, §1, Aug. 21, 2002, 116 Stat. 1062.

Prior Provisions

Act Aug. 15, 1876, ch. 287, 19 Stat. 147, transferred duties relative to the Capitol theretofore performed by Commissioner of Public Buildings and Grounds to Architect of the Capitol.

Act Mar. 2, 1867, ch. 167, §2, 14 Stat. 466, abolished office of Commissioner of Public Buildings and Grounds referred to in section 1811 of this title, and transferred the duties of that office to the Chief of Engineers of the Army.

Act Sept. 30, 1850, ch. 90, §1, 9 Stat. 538, made appropriation for "the extension of the Capitol" according to the plan as might be approved by the President, to be expended under his direction, "by such architect as he may appoint to execute the same." Subsequent acts frequently referred to the Architect of the Capitol or to the Architect of the Capitol Extension.

Act Mar. 3, 1829, ch. 51, §2, 4 Stat. 363, authorized President to continue office of Architect of the Capitol long enough to complete work in progress.

Act May 2, 1828, ch. 45, §3, 4 Stat. 266, abolished office of Architect of the Capitol. The duties of that office were transferred to Commissioner of Public Buildings and Grounds, appointed by President under act April 29, 1816, ch. 150, §2, 3 Stat. 324, to succeed a previously existing board of three commissioners of Public Buildings and Grounds.

STATUTORY NOTES AND RELATED SUBSIDIARIES

CHANGE OF NAME

The name of Superintendent of the Capitol Building and Grounds was changed to Architect of the Capitol by Act Mar. 3, 1921, ch. 124, 41 Stat. 1291, the Legislative, Executive, and Judicial Appropriation Act Mar. 3, 1921, fiscal year 1922.

The name of Architect of the Capitol was changed to Superintendent of the Capitol Building and Grounds, by act Feb. 14, 1902, ch. 17, 32 Stat. 20, popularly known as the "Urgent Deficiency Appropriation Act for 1902".

* * * * * * *

SUBCHAPTER II—GENERAL POWERS AND DUTIES

§1811. POWERS AND DUTIES

The Architect of the Capitol shall perform all the duties relative to the Capitol Building performed prior to August 15, 1876, by the Commissioner of Public Buildings and Grounds: *Provided*, That no change in the architectural features of the Capitol Building or in the landscape features of the Capitol Grounds shall be made except on plans to be approved by Congress.

(Aug. 15, 1876, ch. 287, 19 Stat. 147; Feb. 14, 1902, ch. 17, 32 Stat. 20; Mar. 3, 1921, ch. 124, 41 Stat. 1291; Pub. L. 118–31, div. E, title LVII, §5702(d)(2), Dec. 22, 2023, 137 Stat. 961.)

EDITORIAL NOTES

CODIFICATION

Section was classified to section 162 of former Title 40, prior to the enactment of Title 40, Public Buildings, Property, and Works, by Pub. L. 107–217, §1, Aug. 21, 2002, 116 Stat. 1062.

Section is a composite of the acts of Aug. 15, 1876, and Feb. 14, 1902, cited in the credits.

* * * * * * *

STATUTORY NOTES AND RELATED SUBSIDIARIES

CHANGE OF NAME

Change of name of Architect of the Capitol, functions abolished, transferred, etc., by prior acts, see Prior Provisions and Change of Name notes set out under former section

1801 of this title.

EFFECTIVE DATE OF 2023 AMENDMENT

Amendment by Pub. L. 118–31 applicable with respect to appointments made on or after Dec. 22, 2023, see section 1801a(e) of this title.

TRANSFER TO ARCHITECT OF THE CAPITOL

Pub. L. 112–74, div. G, title I, §1202, Dec. 23, 2011, 125 Stat. 1129, provided that:

"(a) TRANSFER.—To the extent that the Director of the National Park Service has jurisdiction and control over any portion of the area described in subsection (b) and any monument or other facility which is located within such area, such jurisdiction and control is hereby transferred to the Architect of the Capitol as of the date of the enactment of this Act [Dec. 23, 2011].

"(b) AREA DESCRIBED.—The area described in this subsection is the property which is bounded on the north by Pennsylvania Avenue Northwest, on the east by First Street Northwest and First Street Southwest, on the south by Maryland Avenue Southwest, and on the west by Third Street Southwest and Third Street Northwest."

ACQUISITION OF PROPERTY BY ARCHITECT OF THE CAPITOL

Pub. L. 107–68, title I, §128, Nov. 12, 2001, 115 Stat. 579, provided that: "Notwithstanding any other provision of law and subject to the availability of appropriations, the Architect of the Capitol is authorized to secure, through multi-year rental, lease, or other appropriate agreement, the property located at 67 K Street, S.W., Washington, D.C., for use of Legislative Branch agencies, and to incur any necessary incidental expenses including maintenance, alterations, and repairs in connection therewith: *Provided*, That in connection with the property referred to under the preceding proviso, the Architect of the Capitol is authorized to expend funds appropriated to the Architect of the Capitol for the purpose of the operations and support of Legislative Branch agencies, including the United States Capitol Police, as may be required for that purpose."

* * * * * * *

§1812. CARE AND SUPERINTENDENCE OF CAPITOL

The Architect of the Capitol shall on and after March 3, 1977, have the care and superintendence of the Capitol, including lighting. His office shall be in the Capitol Building.

(Aug. 15, 1876, ch. 287, 19 Stat. 147; Mar. 3, 1877, ch. 102, 19 Stat. 298; Oct. 31, 1951, ch. 654, §3(14), 65 Stat. 708.)

EDITORIAL NOTES

CODIFICATION

Section was classified to section 163 of former Title 40, prior to the enactment of Title 40, Public Buildings, Property, and Works, by Pub. L. 107–217, §1, Aug. 21, 2002, 116 Stat. 1062.

The first sentence of this section is from act Mar. 3, 1877. The second sentence of this section is from act Aug. 15, 1876, popularly known as the "Sundry Civil Appropriation Act".

PRIOR PROVISIONS

Provisions similar to those comprising the first sentence of this section were contained in act Aug. 15, 1876, ch. 287, 19 Stat. 147.

AMENDMENTS

1951—Act Oct. 31, 1951, struck out ", and shall submit through the Secretary of the Interior estimates thereof" at end of first sentence.

STATUTORY NOTES AND RELATED SUBSIDIARIES

CHANGE OF NAME

Change of name of Architect of the Capitol, functions abolished, transferred, etc., by prior acts, see Prior Provisions and Change of Name notes set out under former section 1801 of this title.

§1813. EXTERIOR OF CAPITOL

On and after July 7, 1884, it shall be the duty of the Architect to clean and keep in proper order the exterior of the Capitol.

(July 7, 1884, ch. 332, 23 Stat. 209.)

EDITORIAL NOTES

REFERENCES IN TEXT

The Architect, referred to in text, means the Architect of the Capitol.

CODIFICATION

Section was classified to section 163a of former Title 40, prior to the enactment of Title 40, Public Buildings, Property, and Works, by Pub. L. 107–217, §1, Aug. 21, 2002, 116 Stat. 1062.

Section is from the Sundry Civil Appropriation Act July 7, 1884, fiscal year 1885.

* * * * * * *

§1814. REPAIRS OF CAPITOL

All improvements, alterations, additions, and repairs of the Capitol Building shall be made by the direction and under the supervision of the Architect of the Capitol.

(R.S. §1816; Feb. 14, 1902, ch. 17, 32 Stat. 20; Mar. 3, 1921, ch. 124, 41 Stat. 1291; Oct. 31, 1951, ch. 654, §3(15), 65 Stat. 708.)

EDITORIAL NOTES

CODIFICATION

Section was classified to section 166 of former Title 40, prior to the enactment of Title 40, Public Buildings, Property, and Works, by Pub. L. 107–217, §1, Aug. 21, 2002, 116 Stat. 1062.

R.S. §1816 derived from Res. Apr. 16, 1862, No. 28, 12 Stat. 617; acts Mar. 30, 1867, ch. 24, §2, 15 Stat. 13; July 20, 1868, ch. 177, §1, 15 Stat. 115; Mar. 3, 1869, ch. 121, §1, 15 Stat. 283, 284; Mar. 3, 1871, ch. 114, §1, 16 Stat. 500; Aug. 15, 1876, ch. 287, 19 Stat. 147.

Provision of R.S. §1816 relating to purchase of furniture or carpets for House or Senate is classified to section 2184 of this title.

* * * * * * *

Change of Name

Change of name of Architect of the Capitol, functions abolished, transferred, etc., by prior acts, see Prior Provisions and Change of Name notes set out under former section 1801 of this title.

* * * * * * *

Codification

Section was classified to section 166i of former Title 40, prior to the enactment of Title 40, Public Buildings, Property, and Works, by Pub. L. 107–217, §1, Aug. 21, 2002, 116 Stat. 1062.

* * * * * * *

★

SELECTED PROVISIONS OF 2 U.S.C. RELATING TO THE LIBRARY OF CONGRESS

2 U.S.C. §142NOTE

SELECT PROVISIONS OF THE U.S. CODE RELATING TO THE LIBRARY OF CONGRESS

TITLE 2—THE CONGRESS

* * * * * * *

CHAPTER 5—LIBRARY OF CONGRESS

* * * * * * *

§141. ALLOCATION OF RESPONSIBILITIES FOR LIBRARY BUILDINGS AND GROUNDS

* * * * * * *

STATUTORY NOTES AND RELATED SUBSIDIARIES

* * * * * * *

Amendment by Pub. L. 101–520 and 101–562 effective on date [Nov. 6, 1991] Architect of the Capitol acquires the property and improvements described in Pub. L. 101–520, §205(a), and Pub. L. 101–562, §1, see section 205(e) of Pub. L. 101–520 and former section 2(d) of Pub. L. 101–562, set out as a Special Facilities Center; Acquisition note below.

* * * * * * *

ACQUISITION OF REAL PROPERTY FOR LIBRARY OF CONGRESS

Pub. L. 105–144, Dec. 15, 1997, 111 Stat. 2667, as amended by Pub. L. 106–554, §1(a)(2) [title II, §207], Dec. 21, 2000, 114 Stat. 2763, 2763A–114; Pub. L. 108–83, title I, §1203(a), Sept. 30, 2003, 117 Stat. 1031, provided that:

"SECTION 1. ACQUISITION OF FACILITY IN CULPEPER, VIRGINIA.

"(a) ACQUISITION.—The Architect of the Capitol may acquire on behalf of the United States Government by transfer of title, without reimbursement or transfer of funds, the following property:

"(1) Three parcels totaling approximately 45 acres, more or less, located in Culpeper County, Virginia, and identified as Culpeper County Tax Parcel Numbers 51–80B, 51–80C, and 51–80D, further described as real estate (consisting of 40.949 acres) conveyed to David and Lucile Packard Foundation by deed from Federal

Reserve Bank of Richmond, dated May 15, 1998, and recorded May 19, 1998, in the Clerk's Office, Circuit Court of Culpeper County, Virginia, in Deed Book 644, page 372; and real estate (consisting of 4.181 acres) conveyed to Packard Humanities Institute by deed from Russell H. Inskeep, dated February 13, 2002, and recorded February 13, 2002, in the Clerk's Office, Circuit Court of Culpeper County, Virginia, as instrument number 020001299.

"(2) Improvements to such real property.

"(b) Uses.—Effective on the date on which the Architect of the Capitol acquires the property under subsection (a), such property shall be available to the Librarian of Congress for use as a national audiovisual conservation center.

"(c) Transfer Payment by Architect.—Notwithstanding the limitation on reimbursement or transfer of funds under subsection (a) of this section, the Architect of the Capitol may, not later than 90 days after acquisition of the property under this section, transfer funds to the entity from which the property was acquired by the Architect of the Capitol. Such transfers may not exceed a total of $16,500,000.

* * * * * * *

"SEC. 3. ACCEPTANCE OF TRANSFERRED GIFTS OR TRUST FUNDS.

"Gifts or trust funds given to the Library or the Library of Congress Trust Fund Board for the structural and mechanical work and refurbishment of Library buildings and grounds specified in section 1 shall be transferred to the Architect of the Capitol to be spent in accordance with the provisions of the first section of the Act of June 29, 1922 (2 U.S.C. 141).

"SEC. 4. FUND FOR TRANSFERRED FUNDS.

"There is established in the Treasury of the United States a fund consisting of those gifts or trust funds transferred to the Architect of the Capitol under section 3. Upon prior approval of the Committee on House Oversight [now Committee on House Administration] of the House of Representatives and Committee on Rules and Administration of the Senate, amounts in the fund shall be available to the Architect of the Capitol, subject to appropriation, to remain available until expended, for the structural and mechanical work and refurbishment of Library buildings and grounds. Such funds shall be available for expenditure in fiscal year 1998, subject to the prior approval of the Committee on House Oversight of the House of Representatives and the Committee on Rules and Administration of the Senate.

"SEC. 5. EFFECTIVE DATE.

"(a) In General.—Except as provided in subsection (b), the provisions of this Act shall take effect on the date of the enactment of this Act [Dec. 15, 1997].

* * * * * * *

Special Facilities Center; Temporary Restriction on Evening Use

Pub. L. 102–451, §4, Oct. 23, 1992, 106 Stat. 2253, provided that: "No evening meetings may be held at the Library of Congress Special Facilities Center until an on-site parking plan for the property is approved by the Joint Committee on the Library."

SPECIAL FACILITIES CENTER; ACQUISITION

Pub. L. 101–520, title II, §205, Nov. 5, 1990, 104 Stat. 2272, as amended by Pub. L. 102–451, §§1–3, Oct. 23, 1992, 106 Stat. 2253, provided that:

"(a) The Architect of the Capitol may acquire on behalf of the United States Government by purchase, condemnation, transfer, or otherwise (1) all publicly or privately owned real property in lot 51 in square 869 in the District of Columbia, as that lot appears on the records in the office of the Surveyor of the District of Columbia on August 1, 1990, extending to the outer face of the curbs of the square in which it is located and including all alleys or parts of alleys and streets within the lot lines and curb lines surrounding such real property, and (2) improvements to such real property. The property acquired under this section shall be known as the 'Library of Congress Special Facilities Center' (hereinafter in this section referred to as the 'Center').

* * * * * * *

"(c) The property and improvements acquired under subsection (a) shall be repaired and altered, to the maximum extent feasible as determined by the Architect of the Capitol, in compliance with one of the nationally recognized model building codes and with other applicable nationally recognized codes (including electrical codes, fire and life safety codes, plumbing codes, as determined appropriate by the Architect), using the latest edition of the nationally recognized codes referred to in this paragraph.

* * * * * * *

"(e) Subsections (b) and (c) and the amendment made by subsection (d) shall take effect on the date [Nov. 6, 1991] the Architect of the Capitol acquires the property and improvements described in subsection (a).

"(f) There is authorized to be appropriated to the Architect of the Capitol $5,000,000 for carrying out the purposes of this section, to remain available until expended.

"(g) Effective on the date [Nov. 6, 1991] on which the Architect of the Capitol acquires the property known as St. Cecilia's School (Lot 51 in square 869) in the District of Columbia, as provided by law, such property shall be available to the Librarian of Congress for use—

"(1) as a day care center for children of employees of the Library of Congress and children of other employees of the legislative branch of the Government;

"(2) for staff training and development for employees of the Library of Congress;

"(3) for external training;

"(4) for general assembly and education programs of the Library;

"(5) for temporary living quarters and common areas for visiting scholars using the collections of the Library or participating in the programs of the Library; and

"(6) for other purposes relating to the operations of the Library of Congress.

Any use of such property shall be subject to approval by the Joint Committee on the Library, the Committee on House Administration of the House of Representatives, and the Committee on Rules and Administration of the Senate.

"(h)(1) The Librarian of Congress—

"(A) may charge fees for use of the Center under paragraphs (3), (4), and (5) of subsection (g); and

"(B) shall deposit the fees in the fund under paragraph (2).

"(2) There is established in the Treasury a fund which shall consist of amounts deposited under paragraph (1) and such other amounts as may be appropriated to the fund. The fund shall be—

"(A) available to the Librarian of Congress, in amounts specified in appropriations Acts, for the expenses of the Center; and

"(B) subject to audit by the Comptroller General at the discretion of the Comptroller General."

Similar provisions were contained in Pub. L. 101–562, §§1, 2, 4, Nov. 15, 1990, 104 Stat. 2780, 2781, which was repealed by Pub. L. 102–451, §5, Oct. 23, 1992, 106 Stat. 2254, eff. Nov. 15, 1990.

* * * * * * *

★

SELECTED PROVISIONS OF 2 U.S.C. RELATING TO THE SENATE PAGE SCHOOL

2 U.S.C. SS2021

SELECT PROVISIONS OF THE U.S. CODE RELATING TO THE SENATE PAGE SCHOOL

TITLE 2—THE CONGRESS

* * * * * * *

CHAPTER 30—OPERATION AND MAINTENANCE OF CAPITOL COMPLEX

* * * * * * *

SUBCHAPTER II—SENATE

§2021. ADDITIONAL SENATE OFFICE BUILDING

Upon completion of the additional office building for the United States Senate, the building and the grounds and sidewalks surrounding the same shall be subject to the provisions of sections 1922, 1961, 1966, 1967, 1969, 2023, and 2024 of this title and sections 5101 to 5107 and 5109 of title 40, in the same manner and to the same extent as the present Senate Office Building and the grounds and sidewalks surrounding the same.

(June 25, 1948, ch. 658, title I, 62 Stat. 1029.)

EDITORIAL NOTES

REFERENCES IN TEXT

Sections 1922, 1961, 1966, 1967, and 1969 of this title and sections 5101 to 5107 and 5109 of title 40, referred to in text, was in the original a reference to the Act of July 31, 1946, ch. 707, 60 Stat. 718. Sections 9, 9A, 9B, 9C, and 14 of the Act are classified, respectively, to sections 1961, 1966, 1967, 1922, and 1969 of this title, and section 16(b) of the Act is set out as a note under section 1961 of this title. Sections 1 to 8, 10 to 13, and 16(a) of the Act, which were classified to sections 193a to 193m of former Title 40, Public Buildings, Property, and Works, were repealed and reenacted as sections 5101 to 5107 and 5109 of Title 40, Public Buildings, Property, and Works, by Pub. L. 107–217, §§1, 6(b), Aug. 21, 2002, 116 Stat. 1062, 1312, the first section of which enacted Title 40. Section 5(c) of Pub. L. 107–217, set out as a note preceding section 101 of Title 40, provides that a reference to a law replaced by section 1 of Pub. L. 107–217 is deemed to refer to the corresponding provision enacted by Pub. L. 107–217.

For complete classification of the act of July 31, 1946, to the Code, see Tables. For disposition of sections of former Title 40, see table at the beginning of Title 40.

Sections 2023 and 2024 of this title, referred to in text, was in the original a reference to "the Act of June 8, 1942 (U.S.C., title 40, sec. 174(c) and (d))", which, to reflect the probable intent of Congress, was translated as meaning the provisions of the act of June 8, 1942, ch. 396, 56 Stat. 330, which were classified to sections 174c and 174d of former Title 40, Public Buildings, Property, and Works. Sections 174c and 174d of former Title 40 have been transferred to sections 2023 and 2024, respectively, of this title.

CODIFICATION

Section was classified to section 174b–1 of former Title 40, prior to the enactment of Title 40, Public Buildings, Property, and Works, by Pub. L. 107–217, §1, Aug. 21, 2002, 116 Stat. 1062.

* * * * * * *

STATUTORY NOTES AND RELATED SUBSIDIARIES

ACQUISITION OF PROPERTY FOR USE AS RESIDENTIAL FACILITY FOR UNITED STATES SENATE PAGES

Pub. L. 102–330, §1, Aug. 3, 1992, 106 Stat. 849, as amended by Pub. L. 103–50, ch. XII, §1202, July 2, 1993, 107 Stat. 267, provided that:

"(a) ACQUISITION OF PROPERTY.—(1) The Architect of the Capitol, under the direction of the Senate Committee on Rules and Administration, may acquire, on behalf of the United States Government, by purchase, condemnation, transfer or otherwise, as an addition to the United States Capitol Grounds, such real property in the District of Columbia as may be necessary to carry out the provisions of this Act [this note]. Real property acquired for purposes of this Act, may, in the discretion of the Architect of the Capitol, extend to the outer face of the curbs of such property so acquired, including alleys or parts of alleys and streets within the lot lines and curblines surrounding such real property, together with any or all improvements thereon.

"(2) Subject to the approval by the Committee on Appropriations of the Senate, an amount necessary to enable the Architect of the Capitol to carry out the provisions of this section may be transferred from any appropriation under the heading 'SENATE' and the subheadings 'SALARIES, OFFICERS AND EMPLOYEES', and 'OFFICE OF THE SERGEANT AT ARMS AND DOORKEEPER', and the subheadings 'CONTINGENT EXPENSES OF THE SENATE' and 'SERGEANT AT ARMS AND DOORKEEPER OF THE SENATE' to the account appropriated under the heading 'ARCHITECT OF THE CAPITOL' and the subheadings 'CAPITOL BUILDINGS AND GROUNDS' and 'SENATE OFFICE BUILDINGS'.

"(b) UNITED STATES CAPITOL GROUNDS AND BUILDINGS.—Immediately upon the acquisition by the Architect of the Capitol, on behalf of the United States, of the real property, and the improvements thereon, as provided under subsection (a), the real property acquired shall be a part of the United States Capitol Grounds, and the improvements on such real property shall be a part of the Senate Office Buildings. Such real property and improvements shall be subject to the Act of July 31, 1946 (40 U.S.C. 193a et seq.) [2 U.S.C. 1922, 1961, 1966, 1967, 1969; 40 U.S.C. 5101 to 5107, 5109], and the Act of June 8, 1942 (40 U.S.C. 174c) [2 U.S.C. 2023, 2024].

"(c) BUILDING CODES.—The real property and improvements acquired in accordance with subsection (a) shall be repaired and altered, to the maximum extent feasible as determined by the Architect of the Capitol, in accordance with a nationally recognized model building code, and other applicable nationally recognized codes (including electrical codes, fire and life safety codes, and plumbing codes, as determined by the Architect of the Capitol), using the most current edition of the nationally recognized codes referred to in this subsection.

"(d) REPAIRS; EXPENDITURES.—The Architect of the Capitol is authorized, without regard to the provisions of section 3709 of the Revised Statutes of the United States [see 41 U.S.C. 6101], to enter into contracts and to make expenditures for (1) necessary repairs to, and refurbishment of, the real property and the improvements on such real property acquired in accordance with subsection (a), including expenditures for personal and other services as may be necessary to carry out the purposes of this Act; and (2) for the construction on such real property of any facilities thereon as authorized under subsection (f). In no event shall the aggregate value of contracts and expenditures under this subsection exceed an amount equal to that authorized to be appropriated pursuant to subsection (e).

"(e) AUTHORIZATION.—There is authorized to be appropriated to the account under the heading 'Architect of the Capitol' and the subheadings 'Capitol Buildings and Grounds' and 'Senate Office Buildings', $2,000,000 for carrying out the purposes of this Act. Moneys appropriated pursuant to this authorization may remain available until expended.

"(f) USE OF PROPERTY.—The real property, and improvements thereon, acquired in accordance with subsection (a) shall be available to the Sergeant at Arms and Doorkeeper of the Senate for use as a residential facility for United States Senate Pages, and for such other purposes as the Senate Committee on Rules and Administration may provide."

* * * * * * *

★

JAPANESE AMERICAN PATRIOTISM MEMORIAL
SEC. 514 OF THE OMNIBUS PARKS AND PUBLIC LANDS MANAGEMENT ACT OF 1996

PUBLIC LAW 104–333
AS AMENDED THROUGH P.L. 117–339

OMNIBUS PARKS AND PUBLIC LANDS MANAGEMENT ACT OF 1996

(Japanese American Patriotism Memorial)

Public Law 104–333, Enacted November 12, 1996; 110 Stat. 4156]

[As Amended Through P.L. 117–339, Enacted January 5, 2023]

DIVISION I—

* * * * * * *

TITLE V—HISTORIC AREAS AND CIVIL RIGHTS

* * * * * * *

SEC. 514. [40 U.S.C. 5102 note] JAPANESE AMERICAN PATRIOTISM MEMORIAL.

(a) PURPOSE.—It is the purpose of this section—

(1) to assist in the effort to timely establish within the District of Columbia a national memorial to Japanese American patriotism in World War II; and

(2) to improve management of certain parcels of Federal real property located within the District of Columbia,
by the transferring jurisdiction over such parcels to the Architect of the Capitol, the Secretary of the Interior, and the Government of the District of Columbia.

(b) TRANSFERS OF JURISDICTION.—

(1) IN GENERAL.— Effective on the date of the enactment of this Act and notwithstanding any other provision of law, jurisdiction over the parcels of Federal real property described in paragraph (2) is transferred without additional consideration as provided by paragraph (2).

(2) SPECIFIC TRANSFERS.—

(A) TRANSFERS TO SECRETARY OF THE INTERIOR.—

(i) IN GENERAL.—Jurisdiction over the following parcels is transferred to the Secretary of the Interior:

(I) That triangle of Federal land, including any contiguous sidewalks and tree space, that is part of the United States Capitol Grounds under the jurisdiction of the Architect of the Capitol bound by D Street, N.W., New Jersey Avenue, N.W., and Louisiana Avenue, N.W., in square W632

SEC. 514. [40 U.S.C. 5102 note] JAPANESE
AMERICAN PATRIOTISM MEMORIAL.

Omnibus Parks and Public Lands Managem●
Act of 1●

in the District of Columbia, as shown on the Map Showing Properties Under Jurisdiction of the Architect of the Capitol, dated November 8, 1994.

(II) That triangle of Federal land, including any contiguous sidewalks and tree space, that is part of the United States Capitol Grounds under the jurisdiction of the Architect of the Capitol bound by C Street, N.W., First Street, N.W., and Louisiana Avenue, N.W., in the District of Columbia, as shown on the Map Showing Properties Under Jurisdiction of the Architect of the Capitol, dated November 8, 1994.

(ii) LIMITATION.— The parcels transferred by clause (i) shall not include those contiguous sidewalks
abutting Louisiana Avenue, N.W., which shall remain part of the United States Capitol Grounds under the jurisdiction of the Architect of the Capitol.

(iii) CONSIDERATION AS MEMORIAL SITE.— The
parcels transferred by subclause (I) of clause (i) may be considered as a site for a national memorial to Japanese American patriotism in World War II.

(B) TRANSFERS TO ARCHITECT OF THE CAPITOL.—
Jurisdiction over the following parcels is transferred to the Architect of the Capitol:

(i) That portion of the triangle of Federal land in Reservation No. 204 in the District of Columbia under the jurisdiction of the Secretary of the Interior, including any contiguous sidewalks, bound by Constitution Avenue, N.E., on the north, the branch of
Maryland Avenue, N.E., running in a northeast direction on the west, the major portion of Maryland Avenue, N.E., on the south, and 2nd Street, N.E., on the east, including the contiguous sidewalks.

(ii) That irregular area of Federal land in Reservation No. 204 in the District of Columbia under the jurisdiction of the Secretary of the Interior, including any contiguous sidewalks, northeast of the real property described in clause (i) bound by Constitution Avenue, N.E., on the north, the branch of Maryland Avenue, N.E., running to the northeast on the south, and the private property on the west known as lot 7, in square 726.

(iii) The two irregularly shaped medians lying north and east of the property described in clause (i), located between the north and south curbs of
Constitution Avenue, N.E., west of its intersection with Second Street, N.E., all as shown in Land Record No. 268, dated November 22, 1957, in the Office of the Surveyor, District of Columbia, in Book 138, Page 58.

(iv) All sidewalks under the jurisdiction of the District of Columbia abutting on and contiguous to the land described in clauses (i), (ii), and (iii).

(C) TRANSFERS TO DISTRICT OF COLUMBIA.—Jurisdiction over the following parcels is transferred to the Government of the District of Columbia:

(i) That portion of New Jersey Avenue, N.W., between the northernmost

SC. 514. [40 U.S.C. 5102 note] JAPANESE
AMERICAN PATRIOTISM MEMORIAL.

Omnibus Parks and Public Lands Management
Act of 1996

point of the intersection of New Jersey Avenue, N.W., and D Street, N.W., and the northernmost point of the intersection of New Jersey Avenue, N.W., and Louisiana Avenue, N.W., between squares 631 and W632, which remains Federal property.

(ii) That portion of D Street, N.W., between its intersection with New Jersey Avenue, N.W., and its intersection with Louisiana Avenue, N.W., between squares 630 and W632, which remains Federal
property.

(c) MISCELLANEOUS.—

(1) COMPLIANCE WITH OTHER LAWS.— Compliance with this section shall be deemed to satisfy the requirements of all laws otherwise applicable to transfers of jurisdiction over parcels of Federal real property.

(2) LAW ENFORCEMENT RESPONSIBILITY.— Law enforcement responsibility for the parcels of Federal real property for which jurisdiction is transferred by subsection (b) shall be assumed by the person acquiring such jurisdiction.

(3) UNITED STATES CAPITOL GROUNDS.—

(A) DEFINITION.— The first section of the Act entitled An Act to define the United States Capitol Grounds, to regulate the use thereof, and for other purposes, approved July 31, 1946 (40 U.S.C. 193a), is amended to include within the definition of the United States Capitol Grounds the parcels of Federal real property described in subsection (b)(2)(B).

(B) JURISDICTION OF CAPITOL POLICE.— The United States Capitol Police shall have jurisdiction over the parcels of Federal real property described in subsection (b)(2)(B) in accordance with section 9 of such Act of July 31, 1946 (40 U.S.C. 212a).

(4) EFFECT OF TRANSFERS.— A person relinquishing jurisdiction over a parcel of Federal real property transferred by subsection (b) shall not retain any interest in the parcel except as specifically provided by this section.

★

SELECTED PROVISIONS OF 2 U.S.C. RELATING TO THE CAPITOL VISITOR CENTER

2 U.S.C. §2201 TO 2281

SELECT PROVISIONS OF THE U.S. CODE RELATING TO THE CAPITOL VISITOR CENTER

TITLE 2—THE CONGRESS

* * * * * * *

CHAPTER 31—CAPITOL VISITOR CENTER

* * * * * * *

SUBCHAPTER I—IN GENERAL

§2201. DESIGNATION OF FACILITY AS CAPITOL VISITOR CENTER; PURPOSES OF FACILITY; TREATMENT OF THE CAPITOL VISITOR CENTER

(A) DESIGNATION

The facility authorized for construction under the heading "Capitol Visitor Center" under chapter 5 of title II of division B of the Omnibus Consolidated and Emergency Supplemental Appropriations Act, 1999 (Public Law 105–277; 112 Stat. 2681–569) is designated as the Capitol Visitor Center and is a part of the Capitol.

(B) PURPOSES OF THE FACILITY

The Capitol Visitor Center shall be used—

(1) to provide enhanced security for persons working in or visiting the United States Capitol;

(2) to improve the visitor experience by providing a structure that will afford improved visitor orientation and enhance the educational experience of those who have come to learn about the Congress and the Capitol; and

(3) for other purposes as determined by Congress or the Committee on Rules and Administration of the Senate and the Committee on House Administration of the House of Representatives.

(C) TREATMENT OF THE CAPITOL VISITOR CENTER

(1) OVERSIGHT

The Committee on Rules and Administration of the Senate and the Committee on House Administration of the House of Representatives shall have oversight of the Capitol Visitor Center.

(2) TREATMENT OF EXPANSION SPACE OF THE SENATE AND HOUSE OF REPRESENTATIVES IN THE CAPITOL VISITOR CENTER

(A) SENATE

The expansion space of the Senate described as unassigned space under the heading "Capitol Visitor Center" under the heading "ARCHITECT OF THE CAPITOL" under title II of the Act entitled "An Act making appropriations for the Legislative Branch for the fiscal year ending September 30, 2002, and for other purposes", approved November 12, 2001 (Public Law 107–68; 115 Stat. 588) shall be part of the Senate wing of the Capitol.

(B) HOUSE OF REPRESENTATIVES

The expansion space of the House of Representatives described as unassigned space under the heading "Capitol Visitor Center" under the heading "ARCHITECT OF THE CAPITOL" under title II of the Act entitled "An Act making appropriations for the Legislative Branch for the fiscal year ending September 30, 2002, and for other purposes", approved November 12, 2001 (Public Law 107–68; 115 Stat. 588) shall be part of the House of Representatives wing of the Capitol.

(D) TREATMENT OF CONGRESSIONAL AUDITORIUM AND RELATED ADJACENT AREAS

(1) IN GENERAL

The Committee on Rules and Administration of the Senate and the Committee on House Administration of the House of Representatives shall jointly prescribe regulations for the assignment of the space in the Capitol Visitor Center known as the Congressional Auditorium and the related adjacent areas.

(2) RELATED ADJACENT AREAS

The regulations under paragraph (1) shall include a designation of the areas that are related adjacent areas to the Congressional Auditorium.

(E) OMITTED

(F) EXHIBITS FOR DISPLAYS

(1) IN GENERAL

(A) LOAN AGREEMENTS

Subject to subparagraph (B), the Architect of the Capitol may enter into loan agreements to place historical objects for display in the Exhibition Hall of the Capitol Visitor Center.

(B) CONSULTATION AND APPROVAL

The Architect of the Capitol may exercise the authority under subparagraph (A) with respect to each loan agreement—
    (i) after consultation with—
        (I) the Senate Commission on Art; and
        (II) the House of Representatives Fine Arts Board; and
    (ii) subject to the approval of—

(I) the Committee on Rules and Administration of the Senate; and

(II) the Committee on House Administration of the House of Representatives.

(C) Effective date

This paragraph shall take effect on December 3, 2008.

(2) Omitted

(3) Exceptions to exhibition prohibition

Section 2134 of this title shall not apply to any historical object placed within an exhibit in the Exhibition Hall of the Capitol Visitor Center that—

(A)(i) is directly related to the purpose of the Capitol Visitor Center under subsection (b)(2);

(ii) is the subject of a loan agreement entered into by the Architect of the Capitol before December 2, 2008; and

(iii) has been approved by the Capitol Preservation Commission; or

(B) is the subject of a loan agreement described under paragraph (1)(A).

(4) Substitution of historical object

A loan agreement described under paragraph (3)(A)(ii) may provide for the removal of an historical object from exhibition for preservation purposes and the substitution of that object with another historical object having a comparable educational purpose.

(Pub. L. 110–437, title I, §101, Oct. 20, 2008, 122 Stat. 4984.)

* * * * * * *

Statutory Notes and Related Subsidiaries

Short Title

Pub. L. 110–437, §1(a), Oct. 20, 2008, 122 Stat. 4983, provided that: "This Act [enacting this chapter, amending sections 130e, 1301, 1331, 1341, and 2134 of this title and sections 2107 and 5379 of Title 5, Government Organization and Employees, repealing sections 1806, 1807, 1825, 2165, and 2166 of this title, enacting provisions set out as notes under sections 1301 and 1831 of this title, and amending provisions set out as a note under section 1831 of this title] may be cited as the 'Capitol Visitor Center Act of 2008'."

§2202. Designation and naming within the Capitol Visitor Center

(a) In general

Except as provided under subsection (b), no part of the Capitol Visitor Center may be designated or named without the approval of—

(1) not less than ¾ of all members on the Capitol Preservation Commission who are members of the Democratic party; and

(2) not less than ¾ of all members on the Capitol Preservation Commission who are members of the Republican party.

(B) EXCEPTION

Subsection (a) shall not apply to any room or space under the jurisdiction of the Senate or the House of Representatives.

(Pub. L. 110–437, title I, §102, Oct. 20, 2008, 122 Stat. 4986.)

§2203. USE OF THE EMANCIPATION HALL OF THE CAPITOL VISITOR CENTER

The Emancipation Hall of the Capitol Visitor Center may not be used for any event, except upon the passage of a resolution agreed to by both houses of Congress authorizing the use of the Emancipation Hall for that event.

(Pub. L. 110–437, title I, §103, Oct. 20, 2008, 122 Stat. 4986.)

SUBCHAPTER II—OFFICE OF THE CAPITOL VISITOR CENTER

§2211. ESTABLISHMENT

There is established within the Office of the Architect of the Capitol the Office of the Capitol Visitor Center (in this chapter referred to as the "Office"), to be headed by the Chief Executive Officer for Visitor Services (in this chapter referred to as the "Chief Executive Officer").

(Pub. L. 110–437, title II, §201, Oct. 20, 2008, 122 Stat. 4986.)

§2212. APPOINTMENT AND SUPERVISION OF CHIEF EXECUTIVE OFFICER FOR VISITOR SERVICES

(A) APPOINTMENT

The Chief Executive Officer shall be appointed by the Architect of the Capitol.

(B) SUPERVISION AND OVERSIGHT

The Chief Executive Officer shall report directly to the Architect of the Capitol and shall be subject to oversight by the Committee on Rules and Administration of the Senate and the Committee on House Administration of the House of Representatives.

(C) REMOVAL

Upon removal of the Chief Executive Officer, the Architect of the Capitol shall immediately provide notice of the removal to the Committee on Rules and Administration of the Senate, the Committee on House Administration of the House of Representatives, and the Committees on Appropriations of the House of Representatives and Senate. The notice shall include the reasons for the removal.

(D) COMPENSATION

The Chief Executive Officer shall be paid at an annual rate of pay equal to the annual rate of pay of the Deputy Architect of the Capitol.

(E) TRANSITION FOR CURRENT CHIEF EXECUTIVE OFFICER FOR VISITOR SERVICES

(1) APPOINTMENT

The individual who serves as the Chief Executive Officer for Visitor Services under section 1806 of this title as of October 20, 2008, shall be the first Chief Executive Officer for Visitor Services appointed by the Architect under this section.

(2) OMITTED

(Pub. L. 110–437, title II, §202, Oct. 20, 2008, 122 Stat. 4986.)

§2213. GENERAL DUTIES OF CHIEF EXECUTIVE OFFICER

(A) ADMINISTRATION OF FACILITIES, SERVICES, AND ACTIVITIES

(1) IN GENERAL

Except to the extent otherwise provided in this chapter, the Chief Executive Officer shall be responsible for—

(A) the operation, management, and budget preparation and execution of the Capitol Visitor Center, including all long term planning and daily operational services and activities provided within the Capitol Visitor Center; and

(B) in accordance with sections 2241 and 2242 of this title, the management of guided tours of the interior of the United States Capitol.

(2) INDEPENDENT BUDGET CONSIDERATION

(A) IN GENERAL

The Architect of the Capitol, upon recommendation of the Chief Executive Officer, shall submit the proposed budget for the Office for a fiscal year in the proposed budget for that year for the Office of the Architect of the Capitol (as submitted by the Architect of the Capitol to the President). The proposed budget for the Office shall be considered independently from the other components of the proposed budget for the Architect of the Capitol.

(B) EXCLUSION OF COSTS OF GENERAL MAINTENANCE AND REPAIR OF VISITOR CENTER

In preparing the proposed budget for the Office under subparagraph (A), the Chief Executive Officer shall exclude costs attributable to the activities and services described under section 2271(b) of this title (relating to continuing jurisdiction of the Architect of the Capitol for the care and superintendence of the Capitol Visitor Center).

(B) PERSONNEL, DISBURSEMENTS, AND CONTRACTS

In carrying out this chapter, the Architect of the Capitol shall have the authority to, upon recommendation of the Chief Executive Officer—

(1) appoint, hire, and fix the compensation of such personnel as may be necessary for operations of the Office, except that no employee may be paid at an annual rate in excess of the maximum rate payable for level 15 of the General Schedule;

(2) disburse funds as may be necessary and available for the needs of the Office (consistent with the requirements of section 2233 of this title in the case of amounts in the Capitol Visitor Center Revolving Fund); and

(3) designate an employee of the Office to serve as contracting officer for the Office, subject to subsection (c).

(C) REQUIRING APPROVAL OF CERTAIN CONTRACTS

The Architect of the Capitol may not enter into a contract for the operations of the

Capitol Visitor Center for which the amount involved exceeds $250,000 without the prior approval of the Committee on Rules and Administration of the Senate and the Committee on House Administration of the House of Representatives.

(D) SEMIANNUAL REPORTS

The Chief Executive Officer shall submit a report to the Committee on Rules and Administration of the Senate and the Committee on House Administration of the House of Representatives not later than 45 days following the close of each semiannual period ending on March 31 or September 30 of each year on the financial and operational status during the period of each function under the jurisdiction of the Chief Executive Officer. Each such report shall include financial statements and a description or explanation of current operations, the implementation of new policies and procedures, and future plans for each function.

(Pub. L. 110–437, title II, §203, Oct. 20, 2008, 122 Stat. 4987.)

§2214. ASSISTANT TO THE CHIEF EXECUTIVE OFFICER

(A) IN GENERAL

The Architect of the Capitol shall—

(1) upon recommendation of the Chief Executive Officer, appoint an assistant who shall perform the responsibilities of the Chief Executive Officer during the absence or disability of the Chief Executive Officer, or during a vacancy in the position of the Chief Executive Officer; and

(2) notwithstanding section 2213(b)(1) of this title, fix the rate of basic pay for the position of the assistant appointed under subparagraph (A) [1] at a rate not to exceed the highest total rate of pay for the Senior Executive Service under subchapter VIII of chapter 53 of title 5 for the locality involved.

(B) TRANSITION FOR CURRENT ASSISTANT CHIEF EXECUTIVE OFFICER

(1) APPOINTMENT

The individual who serves as the assistant under section 1807 of this title as of October 20, 2008, shall be the first Assistant Chief Executive Officer for Visitor Services appointed by the Architect under this section.

(2) OMITTED

(Pub. L. 110–437, title II, §204, Oct. 20, 2008, 122 Stat. 4988.)

[1] *So in original. Probably should be a reference to paragraph (1).*

§2215. GIFT SHOP

(A) ESTABLISHMENT

The Architect of the Capitol, acting through the Chief Executive Officer, shall establish a Capitol Visitor Center Gift Shop within the Capitol Visitor Center for the purpose of providing for the sale of gift items. All moneys received from sales and other services by the Capitol Visitor Center Gift Shop shall be deposited in the Capitol Visitor Center Revolving Fund established under section 2231 of this title and shall be available for purposes of this section.

(B) EXCEPTION TO PROHIBITION OF SALE OR SOLICITATION ON CAPITOL GROUNDS

Section 5104(c) of title 40 shall not apply to any activity carried out under this section.

(Pub. L. 110–437, title II, §205, Oct. 20, 2008, 122 Stat. 4988.)

§2216. FOOD SERVICE OPERATIONS

(A) RESTAURANT, CATERING, AND VENDING

The Architect of the Capitol, acting through the Chief Executive Officer, shall establish within the Capitol Visitor Center a restaurant and other food service facilities, including catering services and vending machines.

(B) CONTRACT FOR FOOD SERVICE OPERATIONS

(1) IN GENERAL

The Architect of the Capitol, acting through the Chief Executive Officer, may enter into a contract for food service operations within the Capitol Visitor Center.

(2) EXISTING CONTRACT UNAFFECTED

Nothing in paragraph (1) shall be construed to affect any contract for food service operations within the Capitol Visitor Center in effect on October 20, 2008.

(C) DEPOSITS

All net profits from the food service operations within the Capitol Visitor Center and all commissions received from the contractor for such food service operations shall be deposited in the Capitol Visitor Center Revolving Fund established under section 2231 of this title.

(D) EXCEPTION TO PROHIBITION OF SALE OR SOLICITATION ON CAPITOL GROUNDS

Section 5104(c) of title 40 shall not apply to any activity carried out under this section.

(Pub. L. 110–437, title II, §206, Oct. 20, 2008, 122 Stat. 4988.)

SUBCHAPTER III—CAPITOL VISITOR CENTER REVOLVING FUND

§2231. ESTABLISHMENT AND ACCOUNTS

There is established in the Treasury of the United States a revolving fund to be known as the Capitol Visitor Center Revolving Fund (in this section referred to as the "Fund"), consisting of the following individual accounts:

(1) The Gift Shop Account.

(2) The Miscellaneous Receipts Account.

(Pub. L. 110–437, title III, §301, Oct. 20, 2008, 122 Stat. 4989.)

§2232. DEPOSITS IN THE FUND

(A) GIFT SHOP ACCOUNT

There shall be deposited in the Gift Shop Account all monies received from sales and other services by the gift shop established under section 2215 of this title, together with any interest accrued on balances in the Account.

(B) MISCELLANEOUS RECEIPTS ACCOUNT

There shall be deposited in the Miscellaneous Receipts Account each of the following (together with any interest accrued on balances in the Account):

(1) Any amounts deposited under section 2216(c) of this title.

(2) Any other receipts received from the operation of the Capitol Visitor Center.

(3) Any amounts described under section 2273(d) of this title.

(Pub. L. 110–437, title III, §302, Oct. 20, 2008, 122 Stat. 4989.)

§2233. USE OF MONIES

(A) GIFT SHOP ACCOUNT

(1) IN GENERAL

All monies in the Gift Shop Account shall be available without fiscal year limitation for disbursement by the Architect of the Capitol, upon recommendation of the Chief Executive Officer, in connection with the operation of the gift shop under section 2215 of this title, including supplies, inventories, equipment, and other expenses. In addition, such monies may be used by the Architect of the Capitol, upon recommendation of the Chief Executive Officer, to reimburse any applicable appropriations account for amounts used from such appropriations account to pay the salaries of employees of the gift shops.

(2) USE OF REMAINING FUNDS

To the extent monies in the Gift Shop Account are available after disbursements and reimbursements are made under paragraph (1), the Architect of the Capitol, upon recommendation of the Chief Executive Officer, may disburse such monies for the operation of the Capitol Visitor Center, after consultation with—

(A) the Committee on Rules and Administration of the Senate and the Committee on House Administration of the House of Representatives; and

(B) the Committees on Appropriations of the House of Representatives and Senate.

(B) MISCELLANEOUS RECEIPTS ACCOUNT

All monies in the Miscellaneous Receipts Account shall be available without fiscal year limitation for disbursement by the Architect of the Capitol, upon recommendation of the Chief Executive Officer, for the operations of the Capitol Visitor Center, after consultation with—

(1) the Committee on Rules and Administration of the Senate and the Committee on House Administration of the House of Representatives; and

(2) the Committees on Appropriations of the House of Representatives and Senate.

(Pub. L. 110–437, title III, §303, Oct. 20, 2008, 122 Stat. 4989.)

§2234. Administration of Fund

(a) Disbursements

Disbursements from the Fund may be made by the Architect of the Capitol, upon recommendation of the Chief Executive Officer.

(b) Investment authority

The Secretary of the Treasury shall invest any portion of the Fund that, as determined by the Architect of the Capitol, upon recommendation of the Chief Executive Officer, is not required to meet current expenses. Each investment shall be made in an interest-bearing obligation of the United States or an obligation guaranteed both as to principal and interest by the United States that, as determined by the Architect of the Capitol, upon recommendation of the Chief Executive Officer, has a maturity date suitable for the purposes of the Fund. The Secretary of the Treasury shall credit interest earned on the obligations to the Fund.

(c) Audit

The Fund shall be subject to audit by the Comptroller General at the discretion of the Comptroller General.

(Pub. L. 110–437, title III, §304, Oct. 20, 2008, 122 Stat. 4990.)

SUBCHAPTER IV—CAPITOL GUIDE SERVICE AND OFFICE OF CONGRESSIONAL ACCESSIBILITY SERVICES

Part A—Capitol Guide Service

§2241. Transfer of Capitol Guide Service

(a) Transfer of authorities and personnel to Office of the Capitol Visitor Center

In accordance with the provisions of this subchapter, effective on the transfer date—

(1) the Capitol Guide Service shall be an office within the Office;

(2) the contracts, liabilities, records, property, appropriations, and other assets and interests of the Capitol Guide Service, established under section 2166 of this title, and the employees of the Capitol Guide Service, are transferred to the Office, except that the transfer of any amounts appropriated to the Capitol Guide Service that remain available as of the transfer date shall occur only upon the approval of the Committees on Appropriations of the House of Representatives and Senate; and

(3) the Capitol Guide Service shall be subject to the direction of the Architect of the Capitol, upon recommendation of the Chief Executive Officer, in accordance with this part.

(b) Treatment of employees of Capitol Guide Service at time of transfer

(1) In general

Any individual who is an employee of the Capitol Guide Service on a non-temporary basis on the transfer date who is transferred to the Office under subsection (a) shall be subject to the authority of the Architect of the Capitol under section

2242(b) of this title, except that the individual's grade, compensation, rate of leave, or other benefits that apply with respect to the individual at the time of transfer shall not be reduced while such individual remains continuously so employed in the same position within the Office, other than for cause.

(2) ELIGIBILITY FOR IMMEDIATE RETIREMENT ON BASIS OF INVOLUNTARY SEPARATION

For purposes of section 8336(d) and section 8414(b) of title 5, an individual described in paragraph (1) who is separated from service with the Office shall be considered to have separated from the service involuntarily if, at the time the individual is separated from service—

(A) the individual has completed 25 years of service under such title; or

(B) the individual has completed 20 years of service under such title and is 50 years of age or older.

(C) EXCEPTION FOR CONGRESSIONAL SPECIAL SERVICES OFFICE

This section does not apply with respect to any employees, contracts, liabilities, records, property, appropriations, and other assets and interests of the Congressional Special Services Office of the Capitol Guide Service that are transferred to the Office of Congressional Accessibility Services under part B.

(Pub. L. 110–437, title IV, §401, Oct. 20, 2008, 122 Stat. 4990.)

§2242. DUTIES OF EMPLOYEES OF CAPITOL GUIDE SERVICE

(A) PROVISION OF GUIDED TOURS

(1) TOURS

In accordance with this section, the Capitol Guide Service shall provide without charge guided tours of the interior of the United States Capitol, including the Capitol Visitor Center, for the education and enlightenment of the general public.

(2) ACCEPTANCE OF FEES PROHIBITED

An employee of the Capitol Guide Service shall not charge or accept any fee, or accept any gratuity, for or on account of the official services of that employee.

(3) REGULATIONS OF THE ARCHITECT OF THE CAPITOL

All such tours shall be conducted in compliance with regulations approved by the Architect of the Capitol, upon recommendation of the Chief Executive Officer.

(B) AUTHORITY OF THE ARCHITECT OF THE CAPITOL

In providing for the direction, supervision, and control of the Capitol Guide Service, the Architect of the Capitol, upon recommendation of the Chief Executive Officer, is authorized to—

(1) subject to the availability of appropriations, establish and revise such number of positions of Guide in the Capitol Guide Service as the Architect of the Capitol considers necessary to carry out effectively the activities of the Capitol Guide Service;

(2) appoint, on a permanent basis without regard to political affiliation and solely on the basis of fitness to perform their duties, a Chief Guide and such deputies as the

Architect of the Capitol considers appropriate for the effective administration of the Capitol Guide Service and, in addition, such number of Guides as may be authorized;

(3) with the approval of the Committee on Rules and Administration of the Senate and the Committee on House Administration of the House of Representatives, with respect to the individuals appointed under paragraph (2)—

(A) prescribe the individual's duties and responsibilities; and

(B) fix, and adjust from time to time, respective rates of pay at single per annum (gross) rates;

(4) with respect to the individuals appointed under paragraph (2), take appropriate disciplinary action, including, when circumstances warrant, suspension from duty without pay, reduction in pay, demotion, or termination of employment with the Capitol Guide Service, against any employee who violates any provision of this section or any regulation prescribed by the Architect of the Capitol under paragraph (8);

(5) prescribe a uniform dress, including appropriate insignia, which shall be worn by personnel of the Capitol Guide Service;

(6) from time to time and as may be necessary, procure and furnish such uniforms to such personnel without charge to such personnel;

(7) receive and consider advice and information from any private historical or educational organization, association, or society with respect to those operations of the Capitol Guide Service which involve the furnishing of historical and educational information to the general public; and

(8) with the approval of the Committee on Rules and Administration of the Senate and the Committee on House Administration of the House of Representatives, prescribe such regulations as the Architect of the Capitol considers necessary and appropriate for the operation of the Capitol Guide Service, including regulations with respect to tour routes and hours of operation, number of visitors per guide, staff-led tours, and non-law enforcement security and special event related support.

(C) PROVISION OF ACCESSIBLE TOURS IN COORDINATION WITH OFFICE OF CONGRESSIONAL ACCESSIBILITY SERVICES

The Chief Executive Officer shall coordinate the provision of accessible tours for individuals with disabilities with the Office of Congressional Accessibility Services established under part B.

(D) DETAIL OF PERSONNEL

The Architect of the Capitol shall detail personnel of the Capitol Guide Service based on a request from the Capitol Police Board to assist the United States Capitol Police by providing ushering and informational services, and other services not directly involving law enforcement, in connection with—

(1) the inauguration of the President and Vice President of the United States;

(2) the official reception of representatives of foreign nations and other persons by the Senate or House of Representatives; or

(3) other special or ceremonial occasions in the United States Capitol or on the United States Capitol Grounds that—

(A) require the presence of additional Government personnel; and

(B) cause the temporary suspension of the performance of regular duties.

(E) EFFECTIVE DATE

This section shall take effect on the transfer date.

(Pub. L. 110–437, title IV, §402, Oct. 20, 2008, 122 Stat. 4991.)

PART B—OFFICE OF CONGRESSIONAL ACCESSIBILITY SERVICES

§2251. OFFICE OF CONGRESSIONAL ACCESSIBILITY SERVICES

(A) OMITTED

(B) SPECIFIC FUNCTIONS

The Director of Accessibility Services shall submit to the Committee on Rules and Administration of the Senate and the Committee on House Administration of the House of Representatives a list of the specific functions that the Office of Congressional Accessibility Services will perform in carrying out this part with the approval of the Committee on Rules and Administration of the Senate and the Committee on House Administration of the House of Representatives. The Director of Accessibility Services shall submit the list not later than 30 days after the transfer date.

(C) TRANSITION FOR CURRENT DIRECTOR

The individual who serves as the head of the Congressional Special Services Office as of October 20, 2008, shall be the first Director of Accessibility Services appointed by the Congressional Accessibility Services Board under section 2172 of this title.

(Pub. L. 110–437, title IV, §411, Oct. 20, 2008, 122 Stat. 4993.)

§2252. TRANSFER FROM CAPITOL GUIDE SERVICE

(A) TRANSFER OF AUTHORITIES AND PERSONNEL OF CONGRESSIONAL SPECIAL SERVICES OFFICE OF CAPITOL GUIDE SERVICE

In accordance with the provisions of this subchapter, effective on the transfer date—

(1) the contracts, liabilities, records, property, appropriations, and other assets and interests of the Congressional Special Services Office of the Capitol Guide Service, and the employees of such Office, are transferred to the Office of Congressional Accessibility Services established under section 2172(a) of this title (as amended by section 2251 of this title), except that the transfer of any amounts appropriated to the Congressional Special Services Office that remain available as of the transfer date shall occur only upon the approval of the Committees on Appropriations of the House of Representatives and Senate; and

(2) the employees of such Office shall be subject to the direction, supervision, and control of the Director of Accessibility Services.

(B) TREATMENT OF EMPLOYEES AT TIME OF TRANSFER

(1) IN GENERAL

Any individual who is an employee of the Congressional Special Services Office of the Capitol Guide Service on a non-temporary basis on the transfer date who is transferred under subsection (a) shall be subject to the authority of the Director of

Accessibility Services under section 2172(b) of this title (as amended by section 2251 of this title), except that the individual's grade, compensation, rate of leave, or other benefits that apply with respect to the individual at the time of transfer shall not be reduced while such individual remains continuously so employed in the same position within the Office of Congressional Accessibility Services established under section 2172(a) of this title (as amended by section 2251 of this title), other than for cause.

(2) ELIGIBILITY FOR IMMEDIATE RETIREMENT ON BASIS OF INVOLUNTARY SEPARATION

For purposes of section 8336(d) and section 8414(b) of title 5, an individual described in paragraph (1) who is separated from service with the Office of Congressional Accessibility Services shall be considered to have separated from the service involuntarily if, at the time the individual is separated from service—

(A) the individual has completed 25 years of service under such title; or
(B) the individual has completed 20 years of service under such title and is 50 years of age or older.

(3) PROHIBITING IMPOSITION OF PROBATIONARY PERIOD

The Director of Accessibility Services may not impose a period of probation with respect to the transfer of any individual who is transferred to the Office of Congressional Accessibility Services under subsection (a).

(Pub. L. 110–437, title IV, §412, Oct. 20, 2008, 122 Stat. 4995.)

PART C—TRANSFER DATE

§2261. TRANSFER DATE

In this subchapter, the term "transfer date" means the date occurring on the first day of the first pay period (applicable to employees transferred under section 2241 of this title) occurring on or after 30 days after October 20, 2008.

(Pub. L. 110–437, title IV, §421, Oct. 20, 2008, 122 Stat. 4996.)

SUBCHAPTER V—MISCELLANEOUS PROVISIONS

§2271. JURISDICTIONS UNAFFECTED

(A) SECURITY JURISDICTION UNAFFECTED

Nothing in this chapter granting any authority to the Architect of the Capitol or Chief Executive Officer shall be construed to affect the exclusive jurisdiction of the Capitol Police, the Capitol Police Board, the Sergeant at Arms and Doorkeeper of the Senate, and the Sergeant at Arms of the House of Representatives to provide security for the Capitol, including the Capitol Visitor Center.

(B) ARCHITECT OF THE CAPITOL JURISDICTION UNAFFECTED

(1) IN GENERAL

Nothing in this chapter granting any authority to the Chief Executive Officer shall be construed to affect the exclusive jurisdiction of the Architect of the Capitol for the care and superintendence of the Capitol Visitor Center. All maintenance services, groundskeeping services, improvements, alterations, additions, and repairs for the

Capitol Visitor Center shall be made under the direction and supervision of the Architect, subject to the approval of the Committee on Rules and Administration of the Senate and the House Office Building Commission as to matters of general policy.

(2) OMITTED

(Pub. L. 110–437, title V, §501, Oct. 20, 2008, 122 Stat. 4997.)

§2272. ACCEPTANCE OF VOLUNTEER SERVICES

Notwithstanding section 1342 of title 31, the Architect of the Capitol, upon the recommendation of the Chief Executive Officer, may accept and use voluntary and uncompensated services for the Capitol Visitor Center as the Architect of the Capitol determines necessary. No person shall be permitted to donate personal services under this section unless such person has first agreed, in writing, to waive any and all claims against the United States arising out of or connection with such services, other than a claim under the provisions of chapter 81 of title 5. No person donating personal services under this section shall be considered an employee of the United States for any purpose other than for purposes of chapter 81 of such title. In no case shall the acceptance of personal services under this subsection [1] result in the reduction of pay or displacement of any employee of the Office of the Architect of the Capitol.

(Pub. L. 110–437, title V, §503, Oct. 20, 2008, 122 Stat. 4997.)

[1] *So in original. Probably should be "section".*

§2273. COINS TREATED AS GIFTS

(A) DEFINITION

In this section, the term "covered grounds" means—

(1) the grounds described under section 5102 of title 40;

(2) the Capitol Buildings defined under section 5101 of title 40, including the Capitol Visitor Center; and

(3) the Library of Congress buildings and grounds described under section 167j of this title.

(B) TREATMENT OF COINS

In the case of any coins in any fountains on covered grounds—

(1) such coins shall be treated as gifts to the United States; and

(2) the Architect of the Capitol shall—

(A) collect such coins at such times and in such manner as the Architect determines appropriate; and

(B) except as provided under subsection (c), deposit the collected coins in accordance with subsection (d).

(C) COST REIMBURSEMENT

Any amount collected under this section shall first be used to reimburse the Architect of the Capitol for any costs incurred in the collection and processing of the coins, and maintaining fountains under the jurisdiction of the Architect of the Capitol. The amount of any such reimbursement is appropriated to the account from which such costs were paid and may be used for any authorized purpose of that account.

(D) DEPOSIT OF COINS

The Architect of the Capitol shall deposit coins collected under this section in the Miscellaneous Receipts Account of the Capitol Visitor Center Revolving Fund established under section 2231 of this title.

(E) AUTHORIZED USE AND AVAILABILITY

Amounts deposited in the Miscellaneous Receipts Account of the Capitol Visitor Center Revolving Fund under this section shall be available as provided under section 2233(b) of this title.

(Pub. L. 110–437, title V, §504, Oct. 20, 2008, 122 Stat. 4998; Pub. L. 117–103, div. I, title I, §131, Mar. 15, 2022, 136 Stat. 516.)

SUBCHAPTER VI—AUTHORIZATION OF APPROPRIATIONS

§2281. AUTHORIZATION OF APPROPRIATIONS

There are authorized to be appropriated such sums as are necessary to carry out this chapter.

(Pub. L. 110–437, title VI, §601, Oct. 20, 2008, 122 Stat. 4999.)

* * * * * * *

★

501 FIRST STREET SE., DISTRICT OF COLUMBIA SEC. 121 OF THE BALANCED BUDGE DOWNPAYMENT ACT, I

PUBLIC LAW 104–99
AS AMENDED THROUGH P.L. 105–276

THE BALANCED BUDGET DOWNPAYMENT ACT

(Sale of 501 First Street SE.)

[(Public Law 104–99; 110 Stat. 30)]

[As Amended Through P.L. 105–276, Enacted October 21, 1998]

* * * * * * *

SEC. 121. 501 FIRST STREET SE., DISTRICT OF COLUMBIA.

(a) DISPOSAL OF REAL PROPERTY.—

(1) IN GENERAL.— The Architect of the Capitol shall dispose of by sale at fair market value all right, title, and interest of the United States in and to the parcel of real property described in paragraph (9), including all improvements to such real property. Such disposal shall be made by quitclaim deed.

(2) HOUSE OFFICE BUILDING COMMISSION.— The Architect of the Capitol shall carry out this section under the direction of the House Office Building Commission.

(3) PROCEDURES.— Notwithstanding any other provision of law, the disposal under paragraph (1) shall be made in accordance with such procedures as the Architect of the Capitol determines appropriate.

(4) SENSE OF CONGRESS.— It is the sense of Congress that the child care center of the House of Representatives should remain in operation during the implementation of this section.

(5) TERMS AND CONDITIONS.— The deed of conveyance for the property to be disposed of under paragraph (1) shall contain such terms and conditions as the Architect of the Capitol determines are necessary to protect the interests of the United States.

(6) DEPOSIT OF PROCEEDS.— All proceeds from the disposal under paragraph (1) shall be deposited in the account established by subsection (b).

(7) ADVERTISING AND MARKETING.— The Architect of the Capitol shall begin advertising and marketing the property to be disposed of under paragraph (1) not later than 30 days after the date of the enactment of this Act.

(8) LOCAL ZONING AND OCCUPANCY REQUIREMENTS.— Until such date as the purchaser of the property to be disposed of under paragraph (1) takes full occupancy of such property, such property and the tenants of such property shall be deemed

to be in compliance with all applicable zoning and occupancy requirements of the District of Columbia.

(9) PROPERTY DESCRIPTION.— The parcel of real property referred to in paragraph (1) is the approximately 31,725 square feet of land located at 501 First Street, SE., on square 736 S, Lot 801 (formerly part of Reservation 17) in the District of Columbia. Such parcel is bounded by E Street, SE., to the north, First Street, SE., to the east, New Jersey Avenue, SE., to the west, and Garfield Park to the south.

(b) SEPARATE ACCOUNT IN THE TREASURY.—

(1) ESTABLISHMENT.— There is established in the Treasury of the United States a separate account which shall consist of amounts deposited into the account by the Architect of the Capitol under subsection (a).

(2) AVAILABILITY OF FUNDS.—Funds in the account established by paragraph (1) shall be available, in such amounts as are specified in appropriations Acts, to the Architect of the Capitol for—

(A)   payment of expenses associated with relocating the tenants of the property to be disposed of under subsection (a)(1);

(B)   payment of expenses associated with renovating facilities under the jurisdiction of the Architect for the purpose of accommodating such tenants;

(C)   reimbursement of expenses incurred for advertising and marketing activities related to the disposal under subsection (a)(1) in a total amount of not to exceed $75,000; and

(D)   reimbursement of expenses incurred by the Chief Administrative Officer of the House of Representatives to cover the costs of furnishings and furniture to accommodate the needs of the House of Representatives Child Care Center.

Funds made available under this paragraph shall not be subject to any fiscal year limitation.

(3) REPORTING OF TRANSACTIONS.— Receipts, obligations, and expenditures of funds in the account established by paragraph (1) shall be reported in annual estimates submitted to Congress by the Architect of the Capitol for the operation and maintenance of the Capitol Buildings and Grounds.

(4) TERMINATION OF ACCOUNT.— Not later than 2 years after the date of settlement on the property to be disposed of under subsection (a)(1), the Architect of the Capitol shall terminate the account established by paragraph (1) and all amounts remaining in the account shall be deposited into the general fund of the Treasury of the United States and credited as miscellaneous receipts.

(c) AUTHORITY TO FURNISH STEAM AND CHILLED WATER.—

(1) IN GENERAL.— The Architect of the Capitol is authorized to furnish steam and chilled water from the Capitol Power Plant to the owner of the property to be disposed of under subsection (a)(1) if the owner agrees to pay for such steam and chilled water at market rates, as determined by the Architect of the Capitol.

(2) AUTHORITY LIMITED TO EXISTING FACILITIES.— The Architect of the Capitol may furnish steam and chilled water under paragraph (1) only with respect to facilities which, on the date of the enactment of this Act, are located on the property

to be disposed of under subsection (a)(1).

(3) PROCEEDS.— All proceeds from the sale of steam and chilled water under paragraph (1) shall be deposited into the general fund of the Treasury of the United States and credited as miscellaneous receipts.

* * * * * * *

★

Laws Relating to the Smithsonian Institution

SMITHSONIAN INSTITUTION BUILDING AND GROUNDS

40 U.S.C. §6301

TITLE 40—PUBLIC BUILDINGS, PROPERTY, AND WORKS

This title was enacted by Pub. L. 107–217, §1, Aug. 21, 2002, 116 Stat. 1062

* * * * * * *

SUBTITLE II—PUBLIC BUILDINGS AND WORKS

* * * * * * *

PART C—FEDERAL BUILDING COMPLEXES

* * * * * * *

CHAPTER 63—SMITHSONIAN INSTITUTION, NATIONAL GALLERY OF ART, AND JOHN F. KENNEDY CENTER FOR THE PERFORMING ARTS

* * * * * * *

§6301. DEFINITION

In this chapter, the term "specified buildings and grounds" means—

(1) SMITHSONIAN INSTITUTION.—The Smithsonian Institution and its grounds, which include the following:

(A) SMITHSONIAN BUILDINGS AND GROUNDS ON THE NATIONAL MALL.—The Smithsonian Building, the Arts and Industries Building, the Freer Gallery of Art, the National Air and Space Museum, the National Museum of Natural History, the National Museum of American History, the National Museum of the American Indian, the Hirshhorn Museum and Sculpture Garden, the Arthur M. Sackler Gallery, the National Museum of African Art, the S. Dillon Ripley Center, and all other buildings of the Smithsonian Institution within the Mall, including the entrance walks, unloading areas, and other pertinent service roads and parking areas.

(B) NATIONAL ZOOLOGICAL PARK.—The National Zoological Park comprising all the buildings, streets, service roads, walks, and other areas within the boundary fence of the National Zoological Park in the District of Columbia and including the public space between that fence and the face of the curb lines of the adjacent city streets.

(C) OTHER SMITHSONIAN BUILDINGS AND GROUNDS.—All other buildings, service roads, walks, and other areas within the exterior boundaries of any real estate or land or interest in land (including temporary use) that the Smithsonian Institution acquires and that the Secretary of the Smithsonian Institution determines to be necessary for the adequate protection of individuals or property in the Smithsonian Institution and suitable for administration as a part of the Smithsonian Institution.

(2) NATIONAL GALLERY OF ART.—(A) The National Gallery of Art and its grounds, which extend—

(i) to the line of the face of the south curb of Constitution Avenue Northwest, between Seventh Street Northwest, and Fourth Street Northwest, to the line of the face of the west curb of Fourth Street Northwest, between Constitution Avenue Northwest, and Madison Drive Northwest; to the line of the face of the north curb of Madison Drive Northwest, between Fourth Street Northwest, and Seventh Street Northwest; and to the line of the face of the east curb of Seventh Street Northwest, between Madison Drive Northwest, and Constitution Avenue Northwest;

(ii) to the line of the face of the south curb of Pennsylvania Avenue Northwest, between Fourth Street and Third Street Northwest, to the line of the face of the west curb of Third Street Northwest, between Pennsylvania Avenue and Madison Drive Northwest, to the line of the face of the north curb of Madison Drive Northwest, between Third Street and Fourth Street Northwest, and to the line of the face of the east curb of Fourth Street Northwest, between Pennsylvania Avenue and Madison Drive Northwest; and

(iii) to the line of the face of the south curb of Constitution Avenue Northwest, between Ninth Street Northwest and Seventh Street Northwest; to the line of the face of the west curb of Seventh Street Northwest, between Constitution Avenue Northwest and Madison Drive Northwest; to the line of the face of the north curb of Madison Drive Northwest, between Seventh Street Northwest and the line of the face of the east side of the east retaining wall of the Ninth Street Expressway Northwest; and to the line of the face of the east side of the east retaining wall of the Ninth Street Expressway Northwest, between Madison Drive Northwest and Constitution Avenue Northwest.

(B) All other buildings, service roads, walks, and other areas within the exterior boundaries of any real estate or land or interest in land (including temporary use) that the National Gallery of Art acquires and that the Director of the National Gallery of Art determines to be necessary for the adequate protection of individuals or property in the National Gallery of Art and suitable for administration as a part of the National Gallery of Art.

(3) JOHN F. KENNEDY CENTER FOR THE PERFORMING ARTS.—The John F. Kennedy Center for the Performing Arts, which extends to the line of the west face of the west retaining walls and curbs of the Inner Loop Freeway on the east, the north face of the north retaining walls and curbs of the Theodore Roosevelt Bridge approaches on the south, the east face of the east retaining walls and curbs of Rock Creek Parkway on

the west, and the south curbs of New Hampshire Avenue and F Street on the north, as generally depicted on the map entitled "Transfer of John F. Kennedy Center for the Performing Arts", numbered 844/82563 and dated April 20, 1994 (as amended by the map entitled "Transfer of John F. Kennedy Center for the Performing Arts", numbered 844/82563A and dated May 22, 1997), which shall be on file and available for public inspection in the office of the National Capital Region, National Park Service.

(Pub. L. 107–217, Aug. 21, 2002, 116 Stat. 1184; Pub. L. 115–31, div. G, title IV, §426, May 5, 2017, 131 Stat. 500.)

★

ASTROPHYSICAL OBSERVATORIES

20 U.S.C. §50

SELECT PROVISIONS OF THE U.S. CODE RELATING TO THE SMITHSONIAN INSTITUTION ASTROPHYSICAL OBSERVATORIES

TITLE 20—EDUCATION

* * * * * * *

CHAPTER 3—SMITHSONIAN INSTITUTION, NATIONAL MUSEUMS AND ART GALLERIES

* * * * * * *

SUBCHAPTER I—CHARTER PROVISIONS

* * * * * * *

§50. Reception and Arrangement of Specimens and Objects of Art

Codification

R.S. §5586 derived from act Aug. 10, 1846, ch. 178, §6, 9 Stat. 105.

Statutory Notes and Related Subsidiaries

VERITAS ASTROPHYSICAL OBSERVATORY PROJECT

Veritas Astrophysical Observatory Project; Authorization of Construction and Appropriations

Pub. L. 108–331, Oct. 16, 2004, 118 Stat. 1281, as amended by Pub. L. 110–341, §1(2), Oct. 3, 2008, 122 Stat. 3738, provided that:

"SECTION 1. AUTHORIZING BOARD OF REGENTS OF SMITHSONIAN INSTITUTION TO CARRY OUT CONSTRUCTION AND RELATED ACTIVITIES IN SUPPORT OF VERITAS ASTROPHYSICAL OBSERVATORY PROJECT.

"The Board of Regents of the Smithsonian Institution is authorized to carry out construction and related activities in support of the collaborative Very Energetic Radiation Imaging Telescope Array System (VERITAS) project at the Fred Lawrence Whipple Observatory Base Camp on Mount Hopkins, Arizona, or other similar location.

"SEC. 2. AUTHORIZATION OF APPROPRIATIONS.

"There is authorized to be appropriated $1,000,000 for fiscal year 2005 to carry out section 1."

SMITHSONIAN ASTROPHYSICAL OBSERVATORY SUBMILLIMETER ARRAY

SMITHSONIAN ASTROPHYSICAL OBSERVATORY SUBMILLIMETER ARRAY; AUTHORIZATION OF CONSTRUCTION AND APPROPRIATIONS

Pub. L. 106–383, Oct. 27, 2000, 114 Stat. 1459, provided that:

"SECTION 1. FACILITY AUTHORIZED.

"The Board of Regents of the Smithsonian Institution is authorized to plan, design, construct, and equip laboratory, administrative, and support space to house base operations for the Smithsonian Astrophysical Observatory Submillimeter Array located on Mauna Kea at Hilo, Hawaii.

"SEC. 2. AUTHORIZATION OF APPROPRIATIONS.

"There are authorized to be appropriated to the Board of Regents of the Smithsonian Institution to carry out this Act, $2,000,000 for fiscal year 2001, and $2,500,000 for fiscal year 2002, which shall remain available until expended."

SMITHSONIAN ASTROPHYSICAL OBSERVATORY AND SMITHSONIAN TROPICAL RESEARCH INSTITUTE

SMITHSONIAN ASTROPHYSICAL OBSERVATORY AND SMITHSONIAN TROPICAL RESEARCH INSTITUTE; AUTHORIZATION OF CONSTRUCTION AND APPROPRIATIONS

Pub. L. 99–423, Sept. 30, 1986, 100 Stat. 963, provided: "That the Board of Regents of the Smithsonian Institution is authorized to plan and construct facilities for the Smithsonian Astrophysical Observatory and the Smithsonian Tropical Research Institute.

"SEC. 2. Effective October 1, 1986, there is authorized to be appropriated to the Board of Regents of the Smithsonian Institution:

"(a) $4,500,000 for the Smithsonian Astrophysical Observatory; and

"(b) $11,100,000 for the Smithsonian Tropical Research Institute.

"SEC. 3. Any portion of the sums appropriated to carry out the purposes of this Act may be transferred to the General Services Administration which, in consultation with the Smithsonian Institution, is authorized to enter into contracts and take such other action, to the extent of the sums so transferred to it, as may be necessary to carry out such purposes."

FRED LAWRENCE WHIPPLE OBSERVATOR

FRED LAWRENCE WHIPPLE OBSERVATORY; PURCHASE OF LAND

Pub. L. 98–73, Aug. 11, 1983, 97 Stat. 406, provided: "That the Smithsonian Institution is authorized to purchase land in Santa Cruz County, Arizona, for the permanent headquarters of the Fred Lawrence Whipple Observatory.

"SEC. 2. Effective October 1, 1984, there is authorized to be appropriated $150,000 to carry out the purposes of this Act."

★

CHARLES McC. MATHIAS, JR. LABORATORY FOR ENVIRONMENTAL RESEARCH

20 U.S.C. §50NOTE

SELECT PROVISIONS OF THE U.S. CODE RELATING TO THE CHARLES MCC. MATHIAS, JR. LABORATORY

TITLE 20—EDUCATION

* * * * * * *

CHAPTER 3—SMITHSONIAN INSTITUTION, NATIONAL MUSEUMS AND ART GALLERIES

* * * * * * *

SUBCHAPTER I—CHARTER PROVISIONS

* * * * * * *

§50. Reception and arrangement of specimens and objects of art

Codification

R.S. §5586 derived from act Aug. 10, 1846, ch. 178, §6, 9 Stat. 105.

Statutory Notes and Related Subsidiaries

CHARLES MCC. MATHIAS, JR. LABORATORY FOR ENVIRONMENTAL RESEARCH

Charles McC. Mathias, Jr. Laboratory for Environmental Research

Pub. L. 111–11, title XV, §15101, Mar. 30, 2009, 123 Stat. 1456, provided that:

"(a) Authority To Design and Construct.—The Board of Regents of the Smithsonian Institution is authorized to design and construct laboratory and support space to accommodate the Mathias Laboratory at the Smithsonian Environmental Research Center in Edgewater, Maryland.

"(b) Authorization of Appropriations.—There is authorized to be appropriated to carry out this section a total of $41,000,000 for fiscal years 2009 through 2011. Such sums shall remain available until expended."

Pub. L. 99–617, §1, Nov. 6, 1986, 100 Stat. 3488, provided that:

"(a) Construction Authorization.—The Board of Regents of the Smithsonian Institution is authorized to construct the Charles McC. Mathias, Jr. Laboratory for

Environmental Research.

"(b) Location.—The Charles McC. Mathias, Jr. Laboratory for Environmental Research shall be located at the Smithsonian Environmental Research Center, a bureau of the Smithsonian Institution, located at Edgewater, Maryland.

"(c) Authorization of Appropriations.—Effective October 1, 1986, there is authorized to be appropriated to the Board of Regents of the Smithsonian Institution $1,000,000 to carry out the purposes of this section.

"(d) Transfer of Funds.—Any portion of the sums appropriated to carry out the purposes of this section may be transferred to the General Services Administration which, in consultation with the Smithsonian Institution, is authorized to enter into contracts and take such other action, to the extent of the sums so transferred to it, as may be necessary to carry out such purposes."

★

Smithsonian Facilities

20 U.S.C. §50

SELECT PROVISIONS OF THE U.S. CODE RELATING TO ADDITIONAL SMITHSONIAN INSTITUTION FACILITIES

TITLE 20—EDUCATION

* * * * * * *

CHAPTER 3—SMITHSONIAN INSTITUTION, NATIONAL MUSEUMS AND ART GALLERIES

* * * * * * *

SUBCHAPTER I—CHARTER PROVISIONS

* * * * * * *

§50. RECEPTION AND ARRANGEMENT OF SPECIMENS AND OBJECTS OF ART

Whenever suitable arrangements can be made from time to time for their reception, all objects of art and of foreign and curious research, and all objects of natural history, plants, and geological and mineralogical specimens belonging to the United States, which may be in the city of Washington, in whosesoever custody they may be, shall be delivered to such persons as may be authorized by the Board of Regents to receive them, and shall be so arranged and classified in the building erected for the institution as best to facilitate the examination and study of them; and whenever new specimens in natural history, geology, or mineralogy are obtained for the museum of the institution, by exchanges of duplicate specimens, which the Regents may in their discretion make, or by donation, which they may receive, or otherwise, the Regents shall cause such new specimens to be appropriately classed and arranged. The minerals, books, manuscripts, and other property of James Smithson, which have been received by the Government of the United States, shall be preserved separate and apart from other property of the institution.

(R.S. §5586.)

CODIFICATION

R.S. §5586 derived from act Aug. 10, 1846, ch. 178, §6, 9 Stat. 105.

STATUTORY NOTES AND RELATED SUBSIDIARIES

LABORATORY SPACE, GAMBOA, PANAMA

LABORATORY SPACE, GAMBOA, PANAMA

Pub. L. 111–11, title XV, §15102, Mar. 30, 2009, 123 Stat. 1456, provided that:

"(a) AUTHORITY TO CONSTRUCT.—The Board of Regents of the Smithsonian Institution is authorized to construct laboratory space to accommodate the terrestrial research program of the Smithsonian tropical research institute in Gamboa, Panama.

"(b) AUTHORIZATION OF APPROPRIATIONS.—There is authorized to be appropriated to carry out this section a total of $14,000,000 for fiscal years 2009 and 2010. Such sums shall remain available until expended."

NATIONAL MUSEUM OF AFRICAN ART, CENTER FOR EASTERN ART, AND STRUCTURES FOR RELATED EDUCATIONAL FACILITIES

CONSTRUCTION OF NATIONAL MUSEUM OF AFRICAN ART, CENTER FOR EASTERN ART, AND STRUCTURES FOR RELATED EDUCATIONAL FACILITIES

Pub. L. 97–203, June 24, 1982, 96 Stat. 129, provided: "That the Board of Regents of the Smithsonian Institution is authorized to construct a building for the National Museum of African Art and a center for Eastern art together with structures for related educational activities in the area south of the original Smithsonian Institution Building adjacent to Independence Avenue at Tenth Street Southwest, in the city of Washington.

"SEC. 2. Effective October 1, 1982, there is authorized to be appropriated to the Board of Regents of the Smithsonian Institution $36,500,000 to carry out the purposes of this Act [this note]. Except for funds obligated or expended for planning, administration, and management expenses, and architectural or other consulting services, no funds appropriated pursuant to this section shall be obligated or expended until such time as there is available to such Board, from private donations or from other non-Federal sources, a sum which, when combined with the funds so appropriated, is sufficient to carry out the purposes of this Act.

"SEC. 3. Any portion of the sums appropriated to carry out the purposes of this Act [this note] may be transferred to the General Services Administration which, in consultation with the Smithsonian Institution, is authorized to enter into contracts and take such other action, to the extent of the sums so transferred to it, as may be necessary to carry out such purposes."

SMITHSONIAN INSTITUTION -- ADJACENT PROPERTY

SMITHSONIAN INSTITUTION; DEVELOPMENT OF PROPERTY ADJACENT TO ORIGINAL BUILDING

Pub. L. 96–36, July 20, 1979, 93 Stat. 94, provided: "That the Board of Regents of the Smithsonian Institution is authorized to plan for the development of the area south of the original Smithsonian Institution Building adjacent to Independence Avenue at Tenth Street, Southwest, in the city of Washington.

"Sec. 2. Effective October 1, 1979, there is authorized to be appropriated to the Board of Regents of the Smithsonian Institution $500,000 to carry out the purposes of this Act.

"Sec. 3. Any portion of the sums appropriated to carry out the purposes of this Act may be transferred to the General Services Administration which, in consultation with the Smithsonian Institution, is authorized to enter into contracts and take such other action, to the extent of the sums so transferred to it, as may be necessary to carry out such purposes."

MUSEUM SUPPORT FACILITIES

Smithsonian Institution Plans for and Construction of Museum Support Facilities; Approval of Plans and Specifications; Situs; Transfer of Land; Appropriations; Contracts by General Services Administration

Pub. L. 111–11, title XV, §15103, Mar. 30, 2009, 123 Stat. 1456, provided that:

"(a) In General.—The Board of Regents of the Smithsonian Institution is authorized to construct a greenhouse facility at its museum support facility in Suitland, Maryland, to maintain the horticultural operations of, and preserve the orchid collection held in trust by, the Smithsonian Institution.

"(b) Authorization of Appropriations.—There is authorized to be appropriated $12,000,000 to carry out this section. Such sums shall remain available until expended."

Pub. L. 94–98, Sept. 19, 1975, 89 Stat. 480, as amended by Pub. L. 95–569, Nov. 2, 1978, 92 Stat. 2444; Pub. L. 108–72, §2, Aug. 15, 2003, 117 Stat. 888, provided that: "The Regents of the Smithsonian Institution are authorized to prepare plans for, and to construct, museum support facilities to be used for (1) the care, curation, conservation, deposit, preparation, and study of the national collections of scientific, historic, and artistic objects, specimens, and artifacts; (2) the related documentation of such collections of the Smithsonian Institution; and (3) the training of museum conservators. No appropriation shall be made to construct the facilities authorized by this Act until the Committee on Public Works and Transportation of the House of Representatives and the Committee on Rules and Administration of the Senate, by resolution approve the final plans and specifications of such facilities.

"Sec. 2. The museum support facilities referred to in section 1 shall be located on federally owned land within the metropolitan area of Washington, District of Columbia. Any Federal agency is authorized to transfer land under its jurisdiction to the Smithsonian Institution for such purposes without reimbursement.

"Sec. 3. There is authorized to be appropriated to the Smithsonian Institution $21,500,000 to carry out this Act (other than section 4). Any portion of the sums appropriated for such purposes may be transferred to the General Services Administration which, in consultation with the Smithsonian Institution, is authorized to enter into contracts and take such other action, to the extent of the sums so transferred to it, as may be necessary to carry out such purposes.

"Sec. 4. Additional space and resources for national collections held by the

Smithsonian Institution.

"(a) In General.—The Board of Regents of the Smithsonian Institution may plan, design, construct, and equip additional special use storage and laboratory space at the museum support facility of the Smithsonian Institution in Suitland, Maryland, to accommodate the care, preservation, conservation, deposit, and study of national collections held in trust by the Institution.

"(b) Authorization of Appropriations.—There are authorized to be appropriated to carry out this section—

"(1) $2,000,000 for fiscal year 2003;

"(2) $10,000,000 for fiscal year 2004; and

"(3) such sums as are necessary for each of fiscal years 2005 through 2008."

[Amendment of section 3 by Pub. L. 95–569 effective Oct. 1, 1979.]

★

MUSEUM OF NATURAL HISTORY

20 U.S.C. §50

SELECT PROVISIONS OF THE U.S. CODE RELATING TO THE SMITHSONIAN INSTITUTION

TITLE 20—EDUCATION

* * * * * * *

CHAPTER 3—SMITHSONIAN INSTITUTION, NATIONAL MUSEUMS AND ART GALLERIES

* * * * * * *

SUBCHAPTER I—CHARTER PROVISIONS

* * * * * * *

§50. Reception and arrangement of specimens and objects of art

Codification

R.S. §5586 derived from act Aug. 10, 1846, ch. 178, §6, 9 Stat. 105.

Statutory Notes and Related Subsidiaries

WEST COURT OF NATIONAL MUSEUM OF NATURAL HISTORY

WEST COURT OF NATIONAL MUSEUM OF NATURAL HISTORY BUILDING

Pub. L. 103–151, Nov. 24, 1993, 107 Stat. 1515, provided that:

"SECTION 1. PLANNING, DESIGN, AND CONSTRUCTION OF WEST COURT OF NATIONAL MUSEUM OF NATURAL HISTORY BUILDING.

"The Board of Regents of the Smithsonian Institution is authorized to plan, design, and construct the West Court of the National Museum of Natural History building.

"SEC. 2. FUNDING.

"No appropriated funds may be used to pay any expense of the planning, design, and construction authorized by section 1."

EAST COURT OF NATIONAL MUSEUM OF NATURAL HISTORY

EAST COURT OF NATIONAL MUSEUM OF NATURAL HISTORY BUILDING

Pub. L. 101–455, Oct. 24, 1990, 104 Stat. 1067, as amended by Pub. L. 103–98, §1(a), Oct. 6, 1993, 107 Stat. 1015, provided that:

"SECTION 1. ADDITIONAL SPACE IN NATIONAL MUSEUM OF NATURAL HISTORY.

"The Board of Regents of the Smithsonian Institution is authorized to plan, design, construct, and equip approximately 80,000 square feet of space in the East Court of the National Museum of Natural History building.

"SEC. 2. AUTHORIZATION OF APPROPRIATIONS.

"There is authorized to be appropriated to the Smithsonian Institution for fiscal year 1991 and succeeding fiscal years not to exceed $30,000,000 to carry out this Act."

[Section 1(b) of Pub. L. 103–98 provided that: "The amendment made by subsection (a) [amending section 2 of Pub. L. 101–455, set out above] shall take effect as of October 24, 1990."]

★

NATIONAL MUSEUM OF THE AMERICAN INDIAN ACT

PUBLIC LAW 101–185
AS AMENDED THROUGH P.L. 117–286

NATIONAL MUSEUM OF THE AMERICAN INDIAN ACT

[Public Law 101–185, 103 Stat. 1336]

[As Amended Through P.L. 117–286, Enacted December 27, 2022]

AN ACT To establish the National Museum of the American Indian within the Smithsonian Institution, and for other purposes.

Be it enacted by the Senate and House of Representatives of the United States of America in Congress assembled,

SECTION 1. [20 U.S.C. 80q note] SHORT TITLE.

This Act may be cited as the "National Museum of the American Indian Act".

SEC. 2. [20 U.S.C. 80q] FINDINGS.

The Congress finds that—

(1)   there is no national museum devoted exclusively to the history and art of cultures indigenous to the Americas;

(2)   although the Smithsonian Institution sponsors extensive Native American programs, none of its 19 museums, galleries, and major research facilities is devoted exclusively to Native American history and art;

(3)   the Heye Museum in New York, New York, one of the largest Native American collections in the world, has more than 1,000,000 art objects and artifacts and a library of 40,000 volumes relating to the archaeology, ethnology, and history of Native American peoples;

(4)   the Heye Museum is housed in facilities with a total area of 90,000 square feet, but requires a minimum of 400,000 square feet for exhibition, storage, and scholarly research;

(5) the bringing together of the Heye Museum collection and the Native American collection of the Smithsonian Institution would—

(A)   create a national institution with unrivaled capability for exhibition and research;

(B)   give all Americans the opportunity to learn of the cultural legacy, historic grandeur, and contemporary culture of Native Americans;

(C)   provide facilities for scholarly meetings and the performing arts;

325

SEC. 3. [20 U.S.C. 80q–1] NATIONAL
MUSEUM OF THE AMERICAN INDIAN.

National Museum of the American Indian A

(D)   make available curatorial and other learning opportunities for Indians; and

(E)   make possible traveling exhibitions to communities throughout the Nation;

(6)   by order of the Surgeon General of the Army, approximately 4,000 Indian human remains from battlefields and burial sites were sent to the Army Medical Museum and were later transferred to the Smithsonian Institution;

(7)   through archaeological excavations, individual donations, and museum donations, the Smithsonian Institution has acquired approximately 14,000 additional Indian human remains;

(8)   the human remains referred to in paragraphs (6) and (7) have long been a matter of concern for many Indian tribes, including Alaska Native Villages, and Native Hawaiian communities which are determined to provide an appropriate resting place for their ancestors;

(9)   identification of the origins of such human remains is essential to addressing that concern; and

(10)   an extraordinary site on the National Mall in the District of Columbia (U.S. Government Reservation No. 6) is reserved for the use of the Smithsonian Institution and is available for construction of the National Museum of the American Indian.

SEC. 3. [20 U.S.C. 80q–1] NATIONAL MUSEUM OF THE AMERICAN INDIAN.

(a) ESTABLISHMENT.— There is established, within the Smithsonian Institution, a living memorial to Native Americans and their traditions which shall be known as the National Museum of the American Indian.

(b) PURPOSES.—The purposes of the National Museum are to—

(1)   advance the study of Native Americans, including the study of language, literature, history, art, anthropology, and life;

(2)   collect, preserve, and exhibit Native American objects of artistic, historical, literary, anthropological, and scientific interest;

(3)   provide for Native American research and study programs; and

(4)   provide for the means of carrying out paragraphs (1), (2), and (3) in the District of Columbia, the State of New York, and other appropriate locations.

SEC. 4. [20 U.S.C. 80q–2] AUTHORITY OF THE BOARD OF REGENTS TO ENTER INTO AN AGREEMENT PROVIDING FOR TRANSFER OF HEYE FOUNDATION ASSETS TO THE SMITHSONIAN INSTITUTION.

The Board of Regents is authorized to enter into an agreement with the Heye Foundation, to provide for the transfer to the Smithsonian Institution of title to the Heye Foundation assets. The agreement shall—

(1)   require that the use of the assets be consistent with section 3(b); and

(2)   be governed by, and construed in accordance with, the law of the State of New York.

The United States District Court for the Southern District of New York shall have original and exclusive jurisdiction over any cause of action arising under the agreement.

SEC. 5. [20 U.S.C. 80q–3] BOARD OF TRUSTEES OF THE NATIONAL MUSEUM OF THE AMERICAN INDIAN.

(a) IN GENERAL.— The National Museum shall be under a Board of Trustees with the duties, powers, and authority specified in this section.

(b) GENERAL DUTIES AND POWERS.—The Board of Trustees shall—

(1)   recommend annual operating budgets for the National Museum to the Board of Regents;

(2)   advise and assist the Board of Regents on all matters relating to the administration, operation, maintenance, and preservation of the National Museum;

(3)   adopt bylaws for the Board of Trustees;

(4)   designate a chairman and other officers from among the members of the Board of trustees;[1] and

---

[1]   So in original. Probably should be capitalized.

---

(5)   report annually to the Board of Regents on the acquisition, disposition, and display of Native American objects and artifacts and on other appropriate matters.

(c) SOLE AUTHORITY.—Subject to the general policies of the Board of Regents, the Board of Trustees shall have the sole authority to—

(1)   lend, exchange, sell, or otherwise dispose of any part of the collections of the National Museum, with the proceeds of such transactions to be used for additions to the collections of the National Museum or additions to the endowment of the National Museum, as the case may be;

(2)   purchase, accept, borrow, or otherwise acquire artifacts and other objects for addition to the collections of the Natural Museum; and

(3)   specify criteria for use of the collections of the National Museum for appropriate purposes, including research, evaluation, education, and method of display.

(d) AUTHORITY.—Subject to the general policies of the Board of Regents, the Board of Trustees shall have authority to—

(1)   provide for restoration, preservation, and maintenance of the collections of the National Museum;

(2)   solicit funds for the National Museum and determine the purposes to which such funds shall be applied; and

(3)   approve expenditures from the endowment of the National Museum for any purpose of the Museum.

(e) INITIAL APPOINTMENTS TO THE BOARD OF TRUSTEES.—

(1)   MEMBERSHIP.—The initial membership of the Board of Trustees shall consist of—

(A)   the Secretary of the Smithsonian Institution;

(B)   an Assistant Secretary of the Smithsonian Institution appointed by the Board of Regents;

(C)   8 individuals appointed by the Board of Regents; and

(D)   15 individuals, each of whom shall be a member of the board of trustees of the Heye Museum, appointed by the Board of Regents from a list of nominees recommended by the board of trustees of the Heye Museum.

(2) SPECIAL RULE.— At least 7 of the 23 members appointed under subparagraphs (C) and (D) of paragraph (1) shall be Indians.

(3) TERMS.— The trustee appointed under paragraph (1)(B) shall serve at the pleasure of the Board of Regents. The terms of the trustees appointed under subparagraph (C) or (D) of paragraph (1) shall be 3 years, beginning on the date of the transfer of the Heye Foundation assets to the Smithsonian Institution.

(4) VACANCIES.— Any vacancy shall be filled only for the remainder of the term involved. Any vacancy appointment under paragraph (1)(D) shall not be subject to the source and recommendation requirements of that paragraph, but shall be subject to paragraph (2).

(f) SUBSEQUENT APPOINTMENTS TO THE BOARD OF TRUSTEES.—

(1) MEMBERSHIP.—Upon the expiration of the terms under subsection (e), the Board of Trustees shall consist of—

(A)   the Secretary of the Smithsonian Institution;

(B)   a senior official of the Smithsonian Institution appointed by the Board of Regents; and

(C)   23 individuals appointed by the Board of Regents from a list of nominees recommended by the Board of Trustees.

(2) SPECIAL RULE.— A[1] least 12 of the 23 members appointed under paragraph (1)(C) shall be Indians.

---

[1]   So in original. Probably should be At.

---

(3) TERMS.—The trustee appointed under paragraph (1)(B) shall serve at the pleasure of the Board of Regents. Except as otherwise provided in the next sentence, the terms of members appointed under paragraph (1)(C) shall be 3 years. Of the members first appointed under paragraph (1)(C)—

(A)   7 members, 4 of whom shall be Indians, shall be appointed for a term of one year, as designated at the time of appointment; and

(B)   8 members, 4 of whom shall be Indians, shall be appointed for a term of 2 years, as designated at the time of appointment.

(4) VACANCIES.— Any vacancy shall be filled only for the remainder of the term involved.

(g) QUORUM.— A majority of the members of the Board of Trustees then in office shall constitute a quorum.

SEC. 6. [20 U.S.C. 80q–4] DIRECTOR AND
STAFF OF THE NATIONAL MUSEUM.

National Museum of the American Indian Act

(h) EXPENSES.— Members of the Board shall be entitled (to the same extent as provided in section 5703 of title 5, United States Code, with respect to employees serving intermittently in the Government service) to per diem, travel, and transportation expenses for each day (including travel time) during which they are engaged in the performance of their duties.

SEC. 6. [20 U.S.C. 80q–4] DIRECTOR AND STAFF OF THE NATIONAL MUSEUM.

(a) IN GENERAL.—The Secretary of the Smithsonian Institution shall appoint—

(1) a Director who, subject to the policies of the Board of Trustees, shall manage the National Museum; and

(2) other employees of the National Museum, to serve under the Director.

(b) OFFER OF EMPLOYMENT TO HEYE FOUNDATION EMPLOYEES.—Each employee of the Heye Museum on the day before the date of the transfer of the Heye Foundation assets to the Smithsonian Institution shall be offered employment with the Smithsonian Institution—

(1) under the usual terms of such employment; and

(2) at a rate of pay not less than the rate applicable to the employee on the day before the date of the transfer.

(c) APPLICABILITY OF CERTAIN CIVIL SERVICE LAWS.—The Secretary may—

(1) appoint the Director, 2 employees under subsection (a)(2), and the employees under subsection (b) without regard to the provisions of title 5, United States Code, governing appointments in the competitive service;

(2) fix the pay of the Director and such 2 employees without regard to the provisions of chapter 51 and subchapter III of chapter 53 of such title, relating to classification and General Schedule pay rates; and

(3) fix the pay of the employees under subsection (b) in accordance with the provisions of chapter 51 and subchapter III of chapter 53 of such title, relating to classification and General Schedule pay rates, subject to subsection (b)(2).

SEC. 7. [20 U.S.C. 80q–5] MUSEUM FACILITIES.

(a) NATIONAL MUSEUM MALL FACILITY.— The Board of Regents shall plan, design, and construct a facility on the area bounded by Third Street, Maryland Avenue, Independence Avenue, Fourth Street, and Jefferson Drive, Southwest, in the District of Columbia to house the portion of the National Museum to be located in the District of Columbia. The Board of Regents shall pay not more than ⅔ of the total cost of planning, designing, and constructing the facility from funds appropriated to the Board of Regents. The remainder of the costs shall be paid from non-Federal sources.

(b) NATIONAL MUSEUM HEYE CENTER FACILITY.—

(1) LEASE OF SPACE FROM GSA.—

(A) TERMS.— Notwithstanding section 210(j) of the Federal Property and Administrative Services Act of 1949 (40 U.S.C. 490(j)), the Administrator of General Services may lease, at a nominal charge, to the Smithsonian Institution space in the Old United States Custom House at One Bowling Green, New York,

New York, to house the portion of the National Museum to be located in the city of New York. The lease shall be subject to such terms as may be mutually agreed upon by the Administrator and the Secretary of the Smithsonian Institution. The term of the lease shall not be less than 99 years.

(B) REIMBURSEMENT OF FEDERAL BUILDINGS FUND.— The Administrator of General Services may reimburse the fund established by section 210(f) of the Federal Property and Administrative Services Act of 1949 (40 U.S.C. 490(f)) for the difference between the amount charged to the Smithsonian Institution for leasing space under this paragraph and the commercial charge under section 210(j) of such Act which, but for this paragraph, would apply to the leasing of such space. There are authorized to be appropriated to the Administrator such sums as may be necessary to carry out this subparagraph for fiscal years beginning after September 30, 1990.

(2) CONSTRUCTION.—

(A) MUSEUM FACILITY.— The Board of Regents shall plan, design, and construct a significant facility for the National Museum in the space leased under paragraph (1).

(B) AUDITORIUM AND LOADING DOCK FACILITY.— The Administrator of General Services shall plan, design, and construct an auditorium and loading dock in the Old United States Custom House at One Bowling Green, New York, New York, for the shared use of all the occupants of the building, including the National Museum.

(C) SQUARE FOOTAGE.— The facilities to be constructed under this paragraph shall have, in the aggregate, a total square footage of approximately 82,500 square feet.

(3) REPAIRS AND ALTERATIONS.— After construction of the facility under paragraph (2)(A), repairs and alterations of the facility shall be the responsibility of the Board of Regents.

(4) REIMBURSEMENT OF GSA.— The Board of Regents shall reimburse the Administrator for the Smithsonian Institution's pro rata share of the cost of utilities, maintenance, cleaning, and other services incurred with respect to the space leased under paragraph (1) and the full cost of any repairs or alterations made by the General Services Administration at the request of the Smithsonian Institution with respect to the space.

(5) COST SHARING.—

(A) GENERAL RULES.— The Board of Regents shall pay ⅓ of the costs of planning, designing, and constructing the facility under paragraph (2)(A) from funds appropriated to the Board of Regents. The remainder of the costs shall be paid from non-Federal sources.

(B) RESPONSIBILITIES OF NEW YORK CITY AND STATE.— Of the costs which are required to be paid from non-Federal sources under this paragraph, the city of New York, New York, and the State of New York have each agreed to pay $8,000,000 or an amount equal to ⅓ of the costs of planning, designing, and constructing the facility under paragraph (2)(A), whichever is less. Such payments shall be made to the Board of Regents in accordance with a payment schedule to be agreed upon by the city and State and the Board of Regents.

(C) LIMITATION ON OBLIGATIONS OF FEDERAL FUNDS.— Federal funds may not be obligated for actual construction of a facility under paragraph (2)(A) in a fiscal year until non-Federal sources have paid to the Board of Regents the non-Federal share of such costs which the Board of Regents estimates will be incurred in such year.

(6) DESIGNATION.— The facility to be constructed under paragraph (2)(A) shall be known and designated as the George Gustav Heye Center of the National Museum of the American Indian.

(c) MUSEUM SUPPORT CENTER FACILITY.— The Board of Regents shall plan, design, and construct a facility for the conservation and storage of the collections of the National Museum at the Museum Support Center of the Smithsonian Institution.

(d) MINIMUM SQUARE FOOTAGE.— The facilities to be constructed under this section shall have, in the aggregate, a total square footage of at least 400,000 square feet.

(e) AUTHORITY TO CONTRACT WITH GSA.— The Board of Regents and the Administrator of General Services may enter into such agreements as may be necessary for planning, designing, and constructing facilities under this section (other than subsection (b)(2)(B)). Under such agreements, the Board of Regents shall transfer to the Administrator, from funds available for planning, designing, and constructing such facilities, such amounts as may be necessary for expenses of the General Services Administration with respect to planning, designing, and constructing such facilities.

(f) LIMITATION ON OBLIGATION OF FEDERAL FUNDS.— Notwithstanding any other provision of this Act, funds appropriated for carrying out this section may not be obligated for actual construction of any facility under this section until the 60th day after the date on which the Board of Regents transmits to Congress a written analysis of the total estimated cost of the construction and a cost-sharing plan projecting the amount for Federal appropriations and for non-Federal contributions for the construction on a fiscal year basis.

SEC. 8. [20 U.S.C. 80q–6] CUSTOM HOUSE OFFICE SPACE AND AUDITORIUM.

(a) REPAIRS AND ALTERATIONS.— The Administrator of General Services shall make such repairs and alterations as may be necessary in the portion of the Old United States Custom House at One Bowling Green, New York, New York, which is not leased to the Board of Regents under section 7(b) and which, as of the date of the enactment of this Act, has not been altered.

(b) AUTHORIZATION OF APPROPRIATION.— There is authorized to be appropriated to the Administrator of General Services $25,000,000 from the fund established pursuant to section 210(f) of the Federal Property and Administrative Services Act of 1949 (40 U.S.C. 490(f)) to carry out this section and section 7(b)(2)(B).

SEC. 9. [20 U.S.C. 80q–7] AUDUBON TERRACE.

(a) IN GENERAL.—The Board of Regents shall—

(1) assure that, on the date on which a qualified successor to the Heye Foundation at Audubon Terrace first takes possession of Audubon Terrace, an area

of at least 2,000 square feet at that facility is accessible to the public and physically suitable for exhibition of museum objects and for related exhibition activities;

(2) upon written agreement between the Board and any qualified successor, lend objects from the collections of the Smithsonian Institution to the successor for exhibition at Audubon Terrace; and

(3) upon written agreement between the Board and any qualified successor, provide training, scholarship, technical, and other assistance (other than operating funds) with respect to the area referred to in paragraph (1) for the purposes described in that paragraph.

(b) DETERMINATION OF CHARGES.— Any charge by the Board of Regents for activities pursuant to agreements under paragraph (2) or (3) of subsection (a) shall be determined according to the ability of the successor to pay.

(c) DEFINITION.—As used in this section, the terms qualified successor to the Heye Foundation at Audubon Terrace, qualified successor, and,[1]successor mean an organization described in section 501(c)(3) of the Internal Revenue Code of 1986, and exempt from tax under section 501(a) of such Code, that, as determined by the Board of Regents—

---

[1] So in original. The comma probably should not appear.

---

(1) is a successor occupant to the Heye Foundation at Audubon Terrace, 3753 Broadway, New York, New York;

(2) is qualified to operate the area referred to in paragraph (1) for the purposes described in that paragraph; and

(3) is committed to making a good faith effort to respond to community cultural interests in such operation.

SEC. 10. [20 U.S.C. 80q–8] BOARD OF REGENTS FUNCTIONS WITH RESPECT TO CERTAIN AGREEMENTS AND PROGRAMS.

(a) PRIORITY TO BE GIVEN TO INDIAN ORGANIZATIONS WITH RESPECT TO CERTAIN AGREEMENTS.—In entering into agreements with museums and other educational and cultural organizations to—

(1) lend Native American artifacts and objects from any collection of the Smithsonian Institution;

(2) sponsor or coordinate traveling exhibitions of artifacts and objects; or

(3) provide training or technical assistance;
the Board of Regents shall give priority to agreements with Indian organizations, including Indian tribes, museums, cultural centers, educational institutions, libraries, and archives. Such agreements may provide that loans or services to such organizations may be furnished by the Smithsonian Institution at minimal or no cost.

(b) INDIAN PROGRAMS.—The Board of Regents may establish—

(1) programs to serve Indian tribes and communities; and

(2) in cooperation with educational institutions, including tribally controlled

colleges or universities (as defined in section 2(a) of the Tribally Controlled Colleges and Universities Assistance Act of 1978), programs to enhance the opportunities for Indians in the areas of museum studies, management, and research.

(c) INDIAN MUSEUM MANAGEMENT FELLOWSHIPS.— The Board of Regents shall establish an Indian Museum Management Fellowship program to provide stipend support to Indians for training in museum development and management.

(d) AUTHORIZATION OF APPROPRIATIONS.— There is authorized to be appropriated $2,000,000 for each fiscal year, beginning with fiscal year 1991, to carry out subsections (b) and (c).

SEC. 11. [20 U.S.C. 80q–9] INVENTORY, IDENTIFICATION, AND RETURN OF INDIAN HUMAN REMAINS AND INDIAN FUNERARY OBJECTS IN THE POSSESSION OF THE SMITHSONIAN INSTITUTION.

(a) INVENTORY AND IDENTIFICATION.—(1) The Secretary of the Smithsonian Institution, in consultation and cooperation with traditional Indian religious leaders and government officials of Indian tribes, shall—

(A)   inventory the Indian human remains and Indian funerary objects in the possession or control of the Smithsonian Institution; and

(B)   using the best available scientific and historical documentation, identify the origins of such remains and objects.

(2)   The inventory made by the Secretary of the Smithsonian Institution under paragraph (1) shall be completed not later than June 1, 1998.

(3)   For purposes of this subsection, the term inventory means a simple, itemized list that, to the extent practicable, identifies, based upon available information held by the Smithsonian Institution, the geographic and cultural affiliation of the remains and objects referred to in paragraph (1).

(b) NOTICE IN CASE OF IDENTIFICATION OF TRIBAL ORIGIN.— If the tribal origin of any Indian human remains or Indian funerary object is identified by a preponderance of the evidence, the Secretary shall so notify any affected Indian tribe at the earliest opportunity.

(c) RETURN OF INDIAN HUMAN REMAINS AND ASSOCIATED INDIAN FUNERARY OBJECTS.— If any Indian human remains are identified by a preponderance of the evidence as those of a particular individual or as those of an individual culturally affiliated with a particular Indian tribe, the Secretary, upon the request of the descendants of such individual or of the Indian tribe shall expeditiously return such remains (together with any associated funerary objects) to the descendants or tribe, as the case may be.

(d) RETURN OF INDIAN FUNERARY OBJECTS NOT ASSOCIATED WITH INDIAN HUMAN REMAINS.— If any Indian funerary object not associated with Indian human remains is identified by a preponderance of the evidence as having been removed from a specific burial site of an individual culturally affiliated with a particular Indian tribe, the Secretary, upon the request of the Indian tribe, shall expeditiously return such object to the tribe.

(e) INTERPRETATION.—Nothing in this section shall be interpreted as—

(1) limiting the authority of the Smithsonian Institution to return or repatriate Indian human remains or Indian funerary objects to Indian tribes or individuals; or

(2) delaying actions on pending repatriation requests, denying or otherwise affecting access to the courts, or limiting any procedural or substantive rights which may otherwise be secured to Indian tribes or individuals.

(f) AUTHORIZATION OF APPROPRIATIONS.— There is authorized to be appropriated $1,000,000 for fiscal year 1991 and such sums as may be necessary for succeeding fiscal years to carry out this section and section 11A.

SEC. 11A. [20 U.S.C. 80q–9a] SUMMARY AND REPATRIATION OF UNASSOCIATED FUNERARY OBJECTS, SACRED OBJECTS, AND CULTURAL PATRIMONY.

(a) SUMMARY.— Not later than December 31, 1996, the Secretary of the Smithsonian Institution shall provide a written summary that contains a summary of unassociated funerary objects, sacred objects, and objects of cultural patrimony (as those terms are defined in subparagraphs (B), (C), and (D), respectively, of section 2(3) of the Native American Graves Protection and Repatriation Act (25 U.S.C. 3001(3)), based upon available information held by the Smithsonian Institution. The summary required under this section shall include, at a minimum, the information required under section 6 of the Native American Graves Protection and Repatriation Act (25 U.S.C. 3004).

(b) REPATRIATION.—Where cultural affiliation of Native American unassociated funerary objects, sacred objects, and objects of cultural patrimony has been established in the summary prepared pursuant to subsection (a), or where a requesting Indian tribe or Native Hawaiian organization can show cultural affiliation by a preponderance of the evidence based upon geographical, kinship, biological, archaeological, anthropological, linguistic, folkloric, oral traditional, historical, or other relevant information or expert opinion, then the Smithsonian Institution shall expeditiously return such unassociated funerary object, sacred object, or object of cultural patrimony where—

(1) the requesting party is the direct lineal descendant of an individual who owned the unassociated funerary object or sacred object;

(2) the requesting Indian tribe or Native Hawaiian organization can show that the object was owned or controlled by the Indian tribe or Native Hawaiian organization; or

(3) the requesting Indian tribe or Native Hawaiian organization can show that the unassociated funerary object or sacred object was owned or controlled by a member thereof, provided that in the case where an unassociated funerary object or sacred object was owned by a member thereof, there are no identifiable lineal descendants of said member or the lineal descendants, upon notice, have failed to make a claim for the object.

(c) STANDARD OF REPATRIATION.— If a known lineal descendant or an Indian tribe or Native Hawaiian organization requests the return of Native American unassociated funerary objects, sacred objects, or objects of cultural patrimony pursuant to this Act and presents evidence which, if standing alone before the introduction of evidence to the contrary, would support a finding that the Smithsonian Institution did not have the right of possession, then the Smithsonian Institution shall return such objects unless it can overcome such inference and prove that it has a right of possession to the objects.

(d) MUSEUM OBLIGATION.— Any museum of the Smithsonian Institution which repatriates any item in good faith pursuant to this Act shall not be liable for claims by an aggrieved party or for claims of fiduciary duty, public trust, or violations of applicable law that are inconsistent with the provisions of this Act.

(e) STATUTORY CONSTRUCTION.— Nothing in this section may be construed to prevent the Secretary of the Smithsonian Institution, with respect to any museum of the Smithsonian Institution, from making an inventory or preparing a written summary or carrying out the repatriation of unassociated funerary objects, sacred objects, or objects of cultural patrimony in a manner that exceeds the requirements of this Act.

(f) NATIVE HAWAIIAN ORGANIZATION DEFINED.— For purposes of this section, the term Native Hawaiian organization has the meaning provided that term in section 2(11) of the Native American Graves Protection and Repatriation Act (25 U.S.C. 3001(11)).

SEC. 12. [20 U.S.C. 80q–10] SPECIAL COMMITTEE TO REVIEW THE INVENTORY, IDENTIFICATION, AND RETURN OF INDIAN HUMAN REMAINS AND INDIAN FUNERARY OBJECTS.

(a) ESTABLISHMENT; DUTIES.—Not later than 120 days after the date of the enactment of this Act, the Secretary of the Smithsonian Institution shall appoint a special committee to monitor and review the inventory, identification, and return of Indian human remains and Indian funerary objects under section 11 and unassociated funerary objects, sacred objects, and objects of cultural patrimony under section 11A. In carrying out its duties, the committee shall—

(1) with respect to the inventory and identification, ensure fair and objective consideration and assessment of all relevant evidence;

(2) upon the request of any affected party or otherwise, review any finding relating to the origin or the return of such remains or objects;

(3) facilitate the resolution of any dispute that may arise between Indian tribes with respect to the return of such remains or objects; and

(4) perform such other related functions as the Secretary may assign.

(b) MEMBERSHIP.—The committee shall consist of 7 members, of whom—

(1) 4 members shall be appointed from among nominations submitted by Indian tribes and organizations;

(2) at least 2 members shall be traditional Indian religious leaders; and

(3) the Secretary shall designate one member as chairman.
The Secretary may not appoint to the committee any individual who is an officer or employee of the Government (including the Smithsonian Institution) or any individual who is otherwise affiliated with the Smithsonian Institution.

(c) ACCESS.— The Secretary shall ensure that the members of the committee have full and free access to the Indian human remains and Indian funerary objects subject to section 11 and to any related evidence, including scientific and historical documents.

(d) PAY AND EXPENSES OF MEMBERS.—Members of the committee shall—

(1) be paid the daily equivalent of the annual rate of basic pay payable for grade

GS–18 of the General schedule under section 5332 of title 5, United States Code; and

(2) be entitled (to the same extent as provided in section 5703 of such title, with respect to employees serving intermittently in the Government service) to per diem, travel, and transportation expenses;

for each day (including travel time) during which they are engaged in the performance of their duties.

(e) RULES AND ADMINISTRATIVE SUPPORT.— The Secretary shall prescribe regulations and provide administrative support for the committee.

(f) REPORT AND TERMINATION.— At the conclusion of the work of the committee, the Secretary shall be so[1] certify by report to the Congress. The committee shall cease to exist 120 days after the submission of the report.

---

[1] So in original. Probably should be shall so.

(g) NONAPPLICABILITY OF CHAPTER 10 OF TITLE 5, UNITED STATES CODE.— Chapter 10 of title 5, United States Code, shall not apply to the committee.

(h) AUTHORIZATION OF APPROPRIATIONS.— There is authorized to be appropriated $250,000 for fiscal year 1991 and such sums as may be necessary for succeeding fiscal years to carry out this section.

SEC. 13. [20 U.S.C. 80q–11] INVENTORY, IDENTIFICATION, AND RETURN OF NATIVE HAWAIIAN HUMAN REMANS AND NATIVE HAWAIIAN FUNERARY OBJECTS IN THE POSSESSION OF THE SMITHSONIAN INSTITUTION.

(a) IN GENERAL.—The Secretary of the Smithsonian Institution shall—

(1) in conjunction with the inventory and identification under section 11, inventory and identify the Native Hawaiian human remains and Native Hawaiian funerary objects in the possession of the Smithsonian Institution;

(2) enter into an agreement with appropriate Native Hawaiian organizations with expertise in Native Hawaiian affairs (which may include the Office of Hawaiian Affairs and the Malama I Na Kupuna O Hawai'i Nei) to provide for the return of such human remains nd[2] funerary objects; and

---

[2] So in original. Probably should be and.

---

(3) to the greatest extent practicable, apply, with respect to such human remains and funerary objects, the principles and procedures set forth in sections 11 and 12 with respect to the Indian human remains and Indian funerary objects in the possession of the Smithsonian Institution.

(b) DEFINITIONS.—As used in this section—

(1) the term Malama I Na Kupuna O Hawai'i Nei means the nonprofit, Native Hawaiian organization, incorporated under the laws of the State of Hawaii by that name on April 17, 1989, the purpose of which is to provide guidance and expertise in decisions dealing with Native Hawaiian cultural issues, particularly burial issues; and

(2)   the term Office of Hawaiian Affairs means the Office of Hawaiian Affairs established by the Constitution of the State of Hawaii.

SEC. 14. [20 U.S.C. 80q–12] GRANTS BY THE SECRETARY OF THE INTERIOR TO ASSIST INDIAN TRIBES WITH RESPECT TO AGREEMENTS FOR THE RETURN OF INDIAN HUMAN REMAINS AND INDIAN FUNERARY OBJECTS.

(a) IN GENERAL.—The Secretary of the Interior may make grants to Indian tribes to assist such tribes in reaching and carrying out agreements with—

(1)   the Board of Regents for the return of Indian human remains and Indian funerary objects under section 11; and

(2)   other Federal and non-Federal entities for additional returns of Indian human remains and Indian funerary objects.

(b) AUTHORIZATION OF APPROPRIATIONS.—   There is authorized to be appropriated $1,000,000 for fiscal year 1991 and such sums as may be necessary for succeeding fiscal years for grants under subsection (a).

SEC. 15. [20 U.S.C. 80q–13] GRANTS BY THE SECRETARY OF THE INTERIOR TO ASSIST INDIAN ORGANIZATIONS WITH RESPECT TO RENOVATION AND REPAIR OF MUSEUM FACILITIES AND EXHIBIT FACILITIES.

(a) GRANTS.—   The Secretary of the Interior may make grants to Indian organizations, including Indian tribes, museums, cultural centers, educational institutions, libraries, and archives, for renovation and repair of museum facilities and exhibit facilities to enable such organizations to exhibit objects and artifacts on loan from the collections of the Smithsonian Institution or from other sources. Such grants may be made only from the Tribal Museum Endowment Fund.

(b) INDIAN ORGANIZATION CONTRIBUTION.—   In making grants under subsection (a), the Secretary may require the organization receiving the grant to contribute, in cash or in kind, not more than 50 percent of the cost of the renovation or repair involved. Such contribution may be derived from any source other than the Tribal Museum Endowment Fund.

(c) TRIBAL MUSEUM ENDOWMENT FUND.—

(1) ESTABLISHMENT.—   There is established in the Treasury a fund, to be known as the Tribal Museum Endowment Fund (hereinafter in this subsection referred to as the Fund) for the purpose of making grants under subsection (a). The Fund shall consist of (A) amounts deposited and credited under paragraph (2), (B) obligations obtained under paragraph (3), and (C) amounts appropriated pursuant to authorization under paragraph (5).

(2) DEPOSITS AND CREDITS.—   The Secretary of the Interior is authorized to accept contributions to the Fund from non-Federal sources and shall deposit such contributions in the Fund. The Secretary of the Treasury shall credit to the Fund the interest on, and the proceeds from sale and redemption of, obligations held in the Fund.

(3) INVESTMENTS.—   The Secretary of the Treasury may invest any portion of the Fund in interest-bearing obligations of the United States. Such obligations may be acquired on original issue or in the open market and may be held to maturity

or sold in the open market. In making investments for the Fund, the Secretary of the Treasury shall consult the Secretary of the Interior with respect to maturities, purchases, and sales, taking into consideration the balance necessary to meet current grant requirements.

(4) EXPENDITURES AND CAPITAL PRESERVATION.— Subject to appropriation, amounts derived from interest shall be available for expenditure from the Fund. The capital of the Fund shall not be available for expenditure.

(5) AUTHORIZATION OF APPROPRIATIONS.— There is authorized to be appropriated to the Fund $2,000,000 for each fiscal year beginning with fiscal year 1992.

(d) ANNUAL REPORT.—Not later than January 31 of each year, the Secretary of the Interior, in consultation with the Secretary of the Treasury, shall submit to the Congress a report of activities under this section, including a statement of—

(1) the financial condition of the Fund as of the end of the preceding fiscal year, with an analysis of the Fund transactions during that fiscal year; and

(2) the projected financial condition of the Fund, with an analysis of expected Fund transactions for the six fiscal years after that fiscal year.

SEC. 16. [20 U.S.C. 80q–14] DEFINITIONS.

As used in this Act—

(1) the term Board of Regents means the Board of Regents of the Smithsonian Institution;

(2) the term Board of Trustees means the Board of Trustees of the National Museum of the American Indian;

(3) the term burial site means a natural or prepared physical location, whether below, on, or above the surface of the earth, into which, as a part of a death rite or ceremony of a culture, individual human remains are deposited;

(4) the term funerary object means an object that, as part of a death rite or ceremony of a culture, is intentionally placed with individual human remains, either at the time of burial or later;

(5) the term Heye Foundation assets means the collections, endowment, and all other property of the Heye Foundation (other than the interest of the Heye Foundation in Audubon Terrace) described in the Memorandum of Understanding between the Smithsonian Institution and the Heye Foundation, dated May 8, 1989, and the schedules attached to such memorandum;

(6) the term Heye Museum means the Museum of the American Indian, Heye Foundation;

(7) the term Indian means a member of an Indian tribe;

(8) the term Indian tribe has the meaning given that term in section 4 of the Indian Self-Determination and Education Assistance Act;

(9) the term National Museum means the National Museum of the American Indian established by section 3;

SEC. 17. [20 U.S.C. 80q–15]
AUTHORIZATION OF APPROPRIATIONS.

National Museum of the American Indian Act

(10) the term Native American means an individual of a tribe, people, or culture that is indigenous to the Americas and such term includes a Native Hawaiian; and

(11) the term Native Hawaiian means a member or descendant of the aboriginal people who, before 1778, occupied and exercised sovereignty in the area that now comprises the State of Hawaii.

SEC. 17. [20 U.S.C. 80q–15] AUTHORIZATION OF APPROPRIATIONS.

(a) FUNDING.—There is authorized to be appropriated to the Board of Regents to carry out this Act (other than as provided in sections 7(b)(1)(B), 8, 10, 11, 12, 14, and 15(c)(5))—

(1) $10,000,000 for fiscal year 1990; and

(2) such sums as may be necessary for each succeeding fiscal year.

(b) PERIOD OF AVAILABILITY.— Funds appropriated under subsection (a) shall remain available without fiscal year limitation for any period prior to the availability of the facilities to be constructed under section 7 for administrative and planning expenses and for the care and custody of the collections of the National Museum.

★

NATIONAL MUSEUM OF THE AMERICAN INDIAN

20 U.S.C. §80R

TITLE 20—EDUCATION

* * * * * * *

CHAPTER 3—SMITHSONIAN INSTITUTION, NATIONAL MUSEUMS AND ART GALLERIES

* * * * * * *

SUBCHAPTER XIII—NATIONAL MUSEUM OF THE AMERICAN INDIAN

§80Q. FINDINGS

The Congress finds that—

(1) there is no national museum devoted exclusively to the history and art of cultures indigenous to the Americas;

(2) although the Smithsonian Institution sponsors extensive Native American programs, none of its 19 museums, galleries, and major research facilities is devoted exclusively to Native American history and art;

(3) the Heye Museum in New York, New York, one of the largest Native American collections in the world, has more than 1,000,000 art objects and artifacts and a library of 40,000 volumes relating to the archaeology, ethnology, and history of Native American peoples;

(4) the Heye Museum is housed in facilities with a total area of 90,000 square feet, but requires a minimum of 400,000 square feet for exhibition, storage, and scholarly research;

(5) the bringing together of the Heye Museum collection and the Native American collection of the Smithsonian Institution would—

(A) create a national institution with unrivaled capability for exhibition and research;

(B) give all Americans the opportunity to learn of the cultural legacy, historic grandeur, and contemporary culture of Native Americans;

(C) provide facilities for scholarly meetings and the performing arts;

(D) make available curatorial and other learning opportunities for Indians; and

(E) make possible traveling exhibitions to communities throughout the Nation;

(6) by order of the Surgeon General of the Army, approximately 4,000 Indian human remains from battlefields and burial sites were sent to the Army Medical

Museum and were later transferred to the Smithsonian Institution;

(7) through archaeological excavations, individual donations, and museum donations, the Smithsonian Institution has acquired approximately 14,000 additional Indian human remains;

(8) the human remains referred to in paragraphs (6) and (7) have long been a matter of concern for many Indian tribes, including Alaska Native Villages, and Native Hawaiian communities which are determined to provide an appropriate resting place for their ancestors;

(9) identification of the origins of such human remains is essential to addressing that concern; and

(10) an extraordinary site on the National Mall in the District of Columbia (U.S. Government Reservation No. 6) is reserved for the use of the Smithsonian Institution and is available for construction of the National Museum of the American Indian.

(Pub. L. 101–185, §2, Nov. 28, 1989, 103 Stat. 1336.)

STATUTORY NOTES AND RELATED SUBSIDIARIES

SHORT TITLE OF 2013 AMENDMENT

Pub. L. 113–70, §1, Dec. 26, 2013, 127 Stat. 1208, provided that: "This Act [amending provisions set out as a note under section 80q–5 of this title] may be cited as the 'Native American Veterans' Memorial Amendments Act of 2013'."

SHORT TITLE OF 1996 AMENDMENT

Pub. L. 104–278, §1(a), Oct. 9, 1996, 110 Stat. 3355, provided that: "This Act [enacting section 80q–9a of this title and amending sections 80q–3, 80q–9, and 80q–10 of this title] may be cited as the 'National Museum of the American Indian Act Amendments of 1996'."

SHORT TITLE

Pub. L. 101–185, §1, Nov. 28, 1989, 103 Stat. 1336, provided that: "This Act [enacting this subchapter] may be cited as the 'National Museum of the American Indian Act'."

§80Q–1. NATIONAL MUSEUM OF THE AMERICAN INDIAN

(A) ESTABLISHMENT

There is established, within the Smithsonian Institution, a living memorial to Native Americans and their traditions which shall be known as the "National Museum of the American Indian".

(B) PURPOSES

The purposes of the National Museum are to—

(1) advance the study of Native Americans, including the study of language, literature, history, art, anthropology, and life;

(2) collect, preserve, and exhibit Native American objects of artistic, historical, literary, anthropological, and scientific interest;

(3) provide for Native American research and study programs; and

(4) provide for the means of carrying out paragraphs (1), (2), and (3) in the District of Columbia, the State of New York, and other appropriate locations.

(Pub. L. 101–185, §3, Nov. 28, 1989, 103 Stat. 1337.)

§80Q–2. AUTHORITY OF BOARD OF REGENTS TO ENTER INTO AGREEMENT PROVIDING FOR TRANSFER OF HEYE FOUNDATION ASSETS TO SMITHSONIAN INSTITUTION

The Board of Regents is authorized to enter into an agreement with the Heye Foundation, to provide for the transfer to the Smithsonian Institution of title to the Heye Foundation assets. The agreement shall—

(1) require that the use of the assets be consistent with section 80q–1(b) of this title; and

(2) be governed by, and construed in accordance with, the law of the State of New York.

The United States District Court for the Southern District of New York shall have original and exclusive jurisdiction over any cause of action arising under the agreement.

(Pub. L. 101–185, §4, Nov. 28, 1989, 103 Stat. 1337.)

§80Q–3. BOARD OF TRUSTEES OF NATIONAL MUSEUM OF THE AMERICAN INDIAN

(A) IN GENERAL

The National Museum shall be under a Board of Trustees with the duties, powers, and authority specified in this section.

(B) GENERAL DUTIES AND POWERS

The Board of Trustees shall—

(1) recommend annual operating budgets for the National Museum to the Board of Regents;

(2) advise and assist the Board of Regents on all matters relating to the administration, operation, maintenance, and preservation of the National Museum;

(3) adopt bylaws for the Board of Trustees;

(4) designate a chairman and other officers from among the members of the Board of trustees; [1] and

(5) report annually to the Board of Regents on the acquisition, disposition, and display of Native American objects and artifacts and on other appropriate matters.

(C) SOLE AUTHORITY

Subject to the general policies of the Board of Regents, the Board of Trustees shall have the sole authority to—

(1) lend, exchange, sell, or otherwise dispose of any part of the collections of the National Museum, with the proceeds of such transactions to be used for additions to the collections of the National Museum or additions to the endowment of the National Museum, as the case may be;

(2) purchase, accept, borrow, or otherwise acquire artifacts and other objects for addition to the collections of the Natural Museum; and

(3) specify criteria for use of the collections of the National Museum for appropriate purposes, including research, evaluation, education, and method of display.

(D) AUTHORITY

Subject to the general policies of the Board of Regents, the Board of Trustees shall have authority to—

(1) provide for restoration, preservation, and maintenance of the collections of the National Museum;

(2) solicit funds for the National Museum and determine the purposes to which such funds shall be applied; and

(3) approve expenditures from the endowment of the National Museum for any purpose of the Museum.

(E) INITIAL APPOINTMENTS TO BOARD OF TRUSTEES

(1) MEMBERSHIP

The initial membership of the Board of Trustees shall consist of—

(A) the Secretary of the Smithsonian Institution;

(B) an Assistant Secretary of the Smithsonian Institution appointed by the Board of Regents;

(C) 8 individuals appointed by the Board of Regents; and

(D) 15 individuals, each of whom shall be a member of the board of trustees of the Heye Museum, appointed by the Board of Regents from a list of nominees recommended by the board of trustees of the Heye Museum.

(2) SPECIAL RULE

At least 7 of the 23 members appointed under subparagraphs (C) and (D) of paragraph (1) shall be Indians.

(3) TERMS

The trustee appointed under paragraph (1)(B) shall serve at the pleasure of the Board of Regents. The terms of the trustees appointed under subparagraph (C) or (D) of paragraph (1) shall be 3 years, beginning on the date of the transfer of the Heye Foundation assets to the Smithsonian Institution.

(4) VACANCIES

Any vacancy shall be filled only for the remainder of the term involved. Any vacancy appointment under paragraph (1)(D) shall not be subject to the source and recommendation requirements of that paragraph, but shall be subject to paragraph (2).

(F) SUBSEQUENT APPOINTMENTS TO BOARD OF TRUSTEES

(1) MEMBERSHIP

Upon the expiration of the terms under subsection (e), the Board of Trustees shall consist of—

(A) the Secretary of the Smithsonian Institution;

(B) a senior official of the Smithsonian Institution appointed by the Board of Regents; and

(C) 23 individuals appointed by the Board of Regents from a list of nominees recommended by the Board of Trustees.

(2) SPECIAL RULE

A [2] least 12 of the 23 members appointed under paragraph (1)(C) shall be Indians.

(3) TERMS

The trustee appointed under paragraph (1)(B) shall serve at the pleasure of the Board of Regents. Except as otherwise provided in the next sentence, the terms of members appointed under paragraph (1)(C) shall be 3 years. Of the members first appointed under paragraph (1)(C)—

(A) 7 members, 4 of whom shall be Indians, shall be appointed for a term of one year, as designated at the time of appointment; and

(B) 8 members, 4 of whom shall be Indians, shall be appointed for a term of 2 years, as designated at the time of appointment.

(4) VACANCIES

Any vacancy shall be filled only for the remainder of the term involved.

(G) QUORUM

A majority of the members of the Board of Trustees then in office shall constitute a quorum.

(H) EXPENSES

Members of the Board shall be entitled (to the same extent as provided in section 5703 of title 5 with respect to employees serving intermittently in the Government service) to per diem, travel, and transportation expenses for each day (including travel time) during which they are engaged in the performance of their duties.

(Pub. L. 101–185, §5, Nov. 28, 1989, 103 Stat. 1337; Pub. L. 104–278, §2, Oct. 9, 1996, 110 Stat. 3355.)

[1] *So in original. Probably should be capitalized.*

[2] *So in original. Probably should be "At".*

§80Q–4. DIRECTOR AND STAFF OF NATIONAL MUSEUM

(A) IN GENERAL

The Secretary of the Smithsonian Institution shall appoint—

(1) a Director who, subject to the policies of the Board of Trustees, shall manage the National Museum; and

(2) other employees of the National Museum, to serve under the Director.

(B) OFFER OF EMPLOYMENT TO HEYE FOUNDATION EMPLOYEES

Each employee of the Heye Museum on the day before the date of the transfer of the Heye Foundation assets to the Smithsonian Institution shall be offered employment with the Smithsonian Institution—

(1) under the usual terms of such employment; and

(2) at a rate of pay not less than the rate applicable to the employee on the day before the date of the transfer.

(C) APPLICABILITY OF CERTAIN CIVIL SERVICE LAWS

The Secretary may—

(1) appoint the Director, 2 employees under subsection (a)(2), and the employees under subsection (b) without regard to the provisions of title 5, governing appointments in the competitive service;

(2) fix the pay of the Director and such 2 employees without regard to the provisions of chapter 51 and subchapter III of chapter 53 of such title, relating to classification and General Schedule pay rates; and

(3) fix the pay of the employees under subsection (b) in accordance with the provisions of chapter 51 and subchapter III of chapter 53 of such title, relating to classification and General Schedule pay rates, subject to subsection (b)(2).

(Pub. L. 101–185, §6, Nov. 28, 1989, 103 Stat. 1339.)

§80Q–5. MUSEUM FACILITIES

(A) NATIONAL MUSEUM MALL FACILITY

The Board of Regents shall plan, design, and construct a facility on the area bounded by Third Street, Maryland Avenue, Independence Avenue, Fourth Street, and Jefferson Drive, Southwest, in the District of Columbia to house the portion of the National Museum to be located in the District of Columbia. The Board of Regents shall pay not more than 2/3 of the total cost of planning, designing, and constructing the facility from funds appropriated to the Board of Regents. The remainder of the costs shall be paid from non-Federal sources.

(B) NATIONAL MUSEUM HEYE CENTER FACILITY

(1) LEASE OF SPACE FROM GSA

(A) TERMS

Notwithstanding section 586(a) and (b) of title 40, the Administrator of General Services may lease, at a nominal charge, to the Smithsonian Institution space in the Old United States Custom House at One Bowling Green, New York, New York, to house the portion of the National Museum to be located in the city of New York. The lease shall be subject to such terms as may be mutually agreed upon by the Administrator and the Secretary of the Smithsonian Institution. The term of the lease shall not be less than 99 years.

(B) REIMBURSEMENT OF FEDERAL BUILDINGS FUND

The Administrator of General Services may reimburse the fund established by section 592 of title 40 for the difference between the amount charged to the Smithsonian Institution for leasing space under this paragraph and the commercial charge under section 586(a) and (b) of title 40 which, but for this paragraph, would apply to the leasing of such space. There are authorized to be appropriated to the Administrator such sums as may be necessary to carry out this subparagraph for fiscal years beginning after September 30, 1990.

(2) CONSTRUCTION

(A) MUSEUM FACILITY

The Board of Regents shall plan, design, and construct a significant facility for the National Museum in the space leased under paragraph (1).

(B) AUDITORIUM AND LOADING DOCK FACILITY

The Administrator of General Services shall plan, design, and construct an auditorium and loading dock in the Old United States Custom House at One Bowling Green, New York, New York, for the shared use of all the occupants of the building, including the National Museum.

(C) SQUARE FOOTAGE

The facilities to be constructed under this paragraph shall have, in the aggregate, a total square footage of approximately 82,500 square feet.

(3) REPAIRS AND ALTERATIONS

After construction of the facility under paragraph (2)(A), repairs and alterations of the facility shall be the responsibility of the Board of Regents.

(4) REIMBURSEMENT OF GSA

The Board of Regents shall reimburse the Administrator for the Smithsonian Institution's pro rata share of the cost of utilities, maintenance, cleaning, and other services incurred with respect to the space leased under paragraph (1) and the full cost of any repairs or alterations made by the General Services Administration at the request of the Smithsonian Institution with respect to the space.

(5) COST SHARING

(A) GENERAL RULES

The Board of Regents shall pay 1/3 of the costs of planning, designing, and constructing the facility under paragraph (2)(A) from funds appropriated to the Board of Regents. The remainder of the costs shall be paid from non-Federal sources.

(B) RESPONSIBILITIES OF NEW YORK CITY AND STATE

Of the costs which are required to be paid from non-Federal sources under this paragraph, the city of New York, New York, and the State of New York have each agreed to pay $8,000,000 or an amount equal to 1/3 of the costs of planning, designing, and constructing the facility under paragraph (2)(A), whichever is less. Such payments shall be made to the Board of Regents in accordance with a payment schedule to be agreed upon by the city and State and the Board of Regents.

(C) LIMITATION ON OBLIGATIONS OF FEDERAL FUNDS

Federal funds may not be obligated for actual construction of a facility under paragraph (2)(A) in a fiscal year until non-Federal sources have paid to the Board of Regents the non-Federal share of such costs which the Board of Regents estimates will be incurred in such year.

(6) DESIGNATION

The facility to be constructed under paragraph (2)(A) shall be known and designated as the "George Gustav Heye Center of the National Museum of the American Indian".

(c) MUSEUM SUPPORT CENTER FACILITY

The Board of Regents shall plan, design, and construct a facility for the conservation and storage of the collections of the National Museum at the Museum Support Center of the Smithsonian Institution.

(d) MINIMUM SQUARE FOOTAGE

The facilities to be constructed under this section shall have, in the aggregate, a total square footage of at least 400,000 square feet.

(e) AUTHORITY TO CONTRACT WITH GSA

The Board of Regents and the Administrator of General Services may enter into such agreements as may be necessary for planning, designing, and constructing facilities under this section (other than subsection (b)(2)(B)). Under such agreements, the Board of Regents shall transfer to the Administrator, from funds available for planning, designing, and constructing such facilities, such amounts as may be necessary for expenses of the General Services Administration with respect to planning, designing, and constructing such facilities.

(f) LIMITATION ON OBLIGATION OF FEDERAL FUNDS

Notwithstanding any other provision of this subchapter, funds appropriated for carrying out this section may not be obligated for actual construction of any facility under this section until the 60th day after the date on which the Board of Regents transmits to Congress a written analysis of the total estimated cost of the construction and a cost-sharing plan projecting the amount for Federal appropriations and for non-Federal contributions for the construction on a fiscal year basis.

(Pub. L. 101–185, §7, Nov. 28, 1989, 103 Stat. 1339.)

§80Q–6. CUSTOM HOUSE OFFICE SPACE AND AUDITORIUM

(a) REPAIRS AND ALTERATIONS

The Administrator of General Services shall make such repairs and alterations as may be necessary in the portion of the Old United States Custom House at One Bowling Green, New York, New York, which is not leased to the Board of Regents under section 80q–5(b) of this title and which, as of November 28, 1989, has not been altered.

(b) AUTHORIZATION OF APPROPRIATION

There is authorized to be appropriated to the Administrator of General Services $25,000,000 from the fund established pursuant to section 592 of title 40 to carry out this section and section 80q–5(b)(2)(B) of this title.

(Pub. L. 101–185, §8, Nov. 28, 1989, 103 Stat. 1341.)

§80Q–7. AUDUBON TERRACE

(A) IN GENERAL

The Board of Regents shall—

(1) assure that, on the date on which a qualified successor to the Heye Foundation at Audubon Terrace first takes possession of Audubon Terrace, an area of at least 2,000 square feet at that facility is accessible to the public and physically suitable for exhibition of museum objects and for related exhibition activities;

(2) upon written agreement between the Board and any qualified successor, lend objects from the collections of the Smithsonian Institution to the successor for exhibition at Audubon Terrace; and

(3) upon written agreement between the Board and any qualified successor, provide training, scholarship, technical, and other assistance (other than operating funds) with respect to the area referred to in paragraph (1) for the purposes described in that paragraph.

(B) DETERMINATION OF CHARGES

Any charge by the Board of Regents for activities pursuant to agreements under paragraph (2) or (3) of subsection (a) shall be determined according to the ability of the successor to pay.

(C) DEFINITION

As used in this section, the terms "qualified successor to the Heye Foundation at Audubon Terrace", "qualified successor", and,[1] "successor" mean an organization described in section 501(c)(3) of title 26, and exempt from tax under section 501(a) of title 26, that, as determined by the Board of Regents—

(1) is a successor occupant to the Heye Foundation at Audubon Terrace, 3753 Broadway, New York, New York;

(2) is qualified to operate the area referred to in paragraph (1) for the purposes described in that paragraph; and

(3) is committed to making a good faith effort to respond to community cultural interests in such operation.

(Pub. L. 101–185, §9, Nov. 28, 1989, 103 Stat. 1342.)

[1] *So in original. The comma probably should not appear.*

§80Q–8. BOARD OF REGENTS FUNCTIONS WITH RESPECT TO CERTAIN AGREEMENTS AND PROGRAMS

(A) PRIORITY TO BE GIVEN TO INDIAN ORGANIZATIONS WITH RESPECT TO CERTAIN AGREEMENTS

In entering into agreements with museums and other educational and cultural organizations to—

(1) lend Native American artifacts and objects from any collection of the Smithsonian Institution;

(2) sponsor or coordinate traveling exhibitions of artifacts and objects; or

(3) provide training or technical assistance;

the Board of Regents shall give priority to agreements with Indian organizations, including Indian tribes, museums, cultural centers, educational institutions, libraries, and archives. Such agreements may provide that loans or services to such organizations may be furnished by the Smithsonian Institution at minimal or no cost.

(b) INDIAN PROGRAMS

The Board of Regents may establish—

(1) programs to serve Indian tribes and communities; and

(2) in cooperation with educational institutions, including tribally controlled colleges or universities (as defined in section 1801(a) of title 25), programs to enhance the opportunities for Indians in the areas of museum studies, management, and research.

(c) INDIAN MUSEUM MANAGEMENT FELLOWSHIPS

The Board of Regents shall establish an Indian Museum Management Fellowship program to provide stipend support to Indians for training in museum development and management.

(d) AUTHORIZATION OF APPROPRIATIONS

There is authorized to be appropriated $2,000,000 for each fiscal year, beginning with fiscal year 1991, to carry out subsections (b) and (c).

(Pub. L. 101–185, §10, Nov. 28, 1989, 103 Stat. 1342; Pub. L. 105–244, title IX, §901(d), Oct. 7, 1998, 112 Stat. 1828; Pub. L. 110–315, title IX, §941(k)(2)(B), Aug. 14, 2008, 122 Stat. 3465.)

§80Q–9. INVENTORY, IDENTIFICATION, AND RETURN OF INDIAN HUMAN REMAINS AND INDIAN FUNERARY OBJECTS IN POSSESSION OF SMITHSONIAN INSTITUTION

(A) INVENTORY AND IDENTIFICATION

(1) The Secretary of the Smithsonian Institution, in consultation and cooperation with traditional Indian religious leaders and government officials of Indian tribes, shall—

(A) inventory the Indian human remains and Indian funerary objects in the possession or control of the Smithsonian Institution; and

(B) using the best available scientific and historical documentation, identify the origins of such remains and objects.

(2) The inventory made by the Secretary of the Smithsonian Institution under paragraph (1) shall be completed not later than June 1, 1998.

(3) For purposes of this subsection, the term "inventory" means a simple, itemized list that, to the extent practicable, identifies, based upon available information held by the Smithsonian Institution, the geographic and cultural affiliation of the remains and objects referred to in paragraph (1).

(B) NOTICE IN CASE OF IDENTIFICATION OF TRIBAL ORIGIN

If the tribal origin of any Indian human remains or Indian funerary object is identified by a preponderance of the evidence, the Secretary shall so notify any affected Indian tribe at the earliest opportunity.

(C) RETURN OF INDIAN HUMAN REMAINS AND ASSOCIATED INDIAN FUNERARY OBJECTS

If any Indian human remains are identified by a preponderance of the evidence as those of a particular individual or as those of an individual culturally affiliated with a particular Indian tribe, the Secretary, upon the request of the descendants of such individual or of the Indian tribe shall expeditiously return such remains (together with any associated funerary objects) to the descendants or tribe, as the case may be.

(D) RETURN OF INDIAN FUNERARY OBJECTS NOT ASSOCIATED WITH INDIAN HUMAN REMAINS

If any Indian funerary object not associated with Indian human remains is identified by a preponderance of the evidence as having been removed from a specific burial site of an individual culturally affiliated with a particular Indian tribe, the Secretary, upon the request of the Indian tribe, shall expeditiously return such object to the tribe.

(E) INTERPRETATION

Nothing in this section shall be interpreted as—

(1) limiting the authority of the Smithsonian Institution to return or repatriate Indian human remains or Indian funerary objects to Indian tribes or individuals; or

(2) delaying actions on pending repatriation requests, denying or otherwise affecting access to the courts, or limiting any procedural or substantive rights which may otherwise be secured to Indian tribes or individuals.

(F) AUTHORIZATION OF APPROPRIATIONS

There is authorized to be appropriated $1,000,000 for fiscal year 1991 and such sums as may be necessary for succeeding fiscal years to carry out this section and section 80q–9a of this title.

(Pub. L. 101–185, §11, Nov. 28, 1989, 103 Stat. 1343; Pub. L. 104–278, §3, Oct. 9, 1996, 110 Stat. 3355.)

§80Q–9A. SUMMARY AND REPATRIATION OF UNASSOCIATED FUNERARY OBJECTS, SACRED OBJECTS, AND CULTURAL PATRIMONY

(A) SUMMARY

Not later than December 31, 1996, the Secretary of the Smithsonian Institution shall provide a written summary that contains a summary of unassociated funerary objects, sacred objects, and objects of cultural patrimony (as those terms are defined in subparagraphs (B), (C), and (D), respectively, of section 3001(3) of title 25, based upon available information held by the Smithsonian Institution. The summary required under this section shall include, at a minimum, the information required under section 3004 of title 25.

(B) REPATRIATION

Where cultural affiliation of Native American unassociated funerary objects, sacred objects, and objects of cultural patrimony has been established in the summary prepared pursuant to subsection (a), or where a requesting Indian tribe or Native Hawaiian organization can show cultural affiliation by a preponderance of the evidence based upon geographical, kinship, biological, archaeological, anthropological, linguistic, folkloric, oral traditional, historical, or other relevant information or expert opinion, then the Smithsonian Institution shall expeditiously return such unassociated funerary object, sacred object, or object of cultural patrimony where—

(1) the requesting party is the direct lineal descendant of an individual who owned the unassociated funerary object or sacred object;

(2) the requesting Indian tribe or Native Hawaiian organization can show that the object was owned or controlled by the Indian tribe or Native Hawaiian organization; or

(3) the requesting Indian tribe or Native Hawaiian organization can show that the unassociated funerary object or sacred object was owned or controlled by a member thereof, provided that in the case where an unassociated funerary object or sacred object was owned by a member thereof, there are no identifiable lineal descendants of said member or the lineal descendants, upon notice, have failed to make a claim for the object.

(C) STANDARD OF REPATRIATION

If a known lineal descendant or an Indian tribe or Native Hawaiian organization requests the return of Native American unassociated funerary objects, sacred objects, or objects of cultural patrimony pursuant to this subchapter and presents evidence which, if standing alone before the introduction of evidence to the contrary, would support a finding that the Smithsonian Institution did not have the right of possession, then the Smithsonian Institution shall return such objects unless it can overcome such inference and prove that it has a right of possession to the objects.

(D) MUSEUM OBLIGATION

Any museum of the Smithsonian Institution which repatriates any item in good faith pursuant to this subchapter shall not be liable for claims by an aggrieved party or for claims of fiduciary duty, public trust, or violations of applicable law that are inconsistent with the provisions of this subchapter.

(E) STATUTORY CONSTRUCTION

Nothing in this section may be construed to prevent the Secretary of the Smithsonian Institution, with respect to any museum of the Smithsonian Institution, from making an inventory or preparing a written summary or carrying out the repatriation of unassociated funerary objects, sacred objects, or objects of cultural patrimony in a manner that exceeds the requirements of this subchapter.

(F) "NATIVE HAWAIIAN ORGANIZATION" DEFINED

For purposes of this section, the term "Native Hawaiian organization" has the meaning provided that term in section 3001(11) of title 25.

(Pub. L. 101–185, §11A, as added Pub. L. 104–278, §4, Oct. 9, 1996, 110 Stat. 3355.)

§80Q–10. SPECIAL COMMITTEE TO REVIEW INVENTORY, IDENTIFICATION, AND RETURN OF INDIAN HUMAN REMAINS AND INDIAN FUNERARY OBJECTS

(A) ESTABLISHMENT; DUTIES

Not later than 120 days after November 28, 1989, the Secretary of the Smithsonian Institution shall appoint a special committee to monitor and review the inventory, identification, and return of Indian human remains and Indian funerary objects under section 80q–9 of this title and unassociated funerary objects, sacred objects, and objects of cultural patrimony under section 80q–9a of this title. In carrying out its duties, the committee shall—

(1) with respect to the inventory and identification, ensure fair and objective consideration and assessment of all relevant evidence;

(2) upon the request of any affected party or otherwise, review any finding relating to the origin or the return of such remains or objects;

(3) facilitate the resolution of any dispute that may arise between Indian tribes with respect to the return of such remains or objects; and

(4) perform such other related functions as the Secretary may assign.

(B) Membership

The committee shall consist of 7 members, of whom—

(1) 4 members shall be appointed from among nominations submitted by Indian tribes and organizations;

(2) at least 2 members shall be traditional Indian religious leaders; and

(3) the Secretary shall designate one member as chairman.

The Secretary may not appoint to the committee any individual who is an officer or employee of the Government (including the Smithsonian Institution) or any individual who is otherwise affiliated with the Smithsonian Institution.

(C) Access

The Secretary shall ensure that the members of the committee have full and free access to the Indian human remains and Indian funerary objects subject to section 80q–9 of this title and to any related evidence, including scientific and historical documents.

(D) Pay and expenses of members

Members of the committee shall—

(1) be paid the daily equivalent of the annual rate of basic pay payable for grade GS–18 of the General schedule under section 5332 of title 5; and

(2) be entitled (to the same extent as provided in section 5703 of such title, with respect to employees serving intermittently in the Government service) to per diem, travel, and transportation expenses;

for each day (including travel time) during which they are engaged in the performance of their duties.

(E) Rules and administrative support

The Secretary shall prescribe regulations and provide administrative support for the committee.

(F) Report and termination

At the conclusion of the work of the committee, the Secretary shall be so [1] certify by report to the Congress. The committee shall cease to exist 120 days after the submission of the report.

(G) Nonapplicability of chapter 10 of title 5

Chapter 10 of title 5 shall not apply to the committee.

(H) Authorization of appropriations

There is authorized to be appropriated $250,000 for fiscal year 1991 and such sums as may be necessary for succeeding fiscal years to carry out this section.

(Pub. L. 101–185, §12, Nov. 28, 1989, 103 Stat. 1344; Pub. L. 104–278, §5, Oct. 9, 1996, 110 Stat. 3357; Pub. L. 117–286, §4(a)(145), Dec. 27, 2022, 136 Stat. 4321.)

[1] *So in original. Probably should be "shall so".*

§80Q–11. Inventory, identification, and return of Native Hawaiian human remains and Native Hawaiian funerary objects in possession of Smithsonian Institution

(a) In general

The Secretary of the Smithsonian Institution shall—

(1) in conjunction with the inventory and identification under section 80q–9 of this title, inventory and identify the Native Hawaiian human remains and Native Hawaiian funerary objects in the possession of the Smithsonian Institution;

(2) enter into an agreement with appropriate Native Hawaiian organizations with expertise in Native Hawaiian affairs (which may include the Office of Hawaiian Affairs and the Malama I Na Kupuna O Hawai'i Nei) to provide for the return of such human remains nd [1] funerary objects; and

(3) to the greatest extent practicable, apply, with respect to such human remains and funerary objects, the principles and procedures set forth in sections 80q–9 and 80q–10 of this title with respect to the Indian human remains and Indian funerary objects in the possession of the Smithsonian Institution.

(b) Definitions

As used in this section—

(1) the term "Malama I Na Kupuna O Hawai'i Nei" means the nonprofit, Native Hawaiian organization, incorporated under the laws of the State of Hawaii by that name on April 17, 1989, the purpose of which is to provide guidance and expertise in decisions dealing with Native Hawaiian cultural issues, particularly burial issues; and

(2) the term "Office of Hawaiian Affairs" means the Office of Hawaiian Affairs established by the Constitution of the State of Hawaii.

(Pub. L. 101–185, §13, Nov. 28, 1989, 103 Stat. 1345.)

[1] *So in original. Probably should be "and".*

§80Q–12. Grants by Secretary of the Interior to assist Indian tribes with respect to agreements for return of Indian human remains and Indian funerary objects

(a) In general

The Secretary of the Interior may make grants to Indian tribes to assist such tribes in reaching and carrying out agreements with—

(1) the Board of Regents for the return of Indian human remains and Indian funerary objects under section 80q–9 of this title; and

(2) other Federal and non-Federal entities for additional returns of Indian human remains and Indian funerary objects.

(B) AUTHORIZATION OF APPROPRIATIONS

There is authorized to be appropriated $1,000,000 for fiscal year 1991 and such sums as may be necessary for succeeding fiscal years for grants under subsection (a).

(Pub. L. 101–185, §14, Nov. 28, 1989, 103 Stat. 1345.)

§80Q–13. GRANTS BY SECRETARY OF THE INTERIOR TO ASSIST INDIAN ORGANIZATIONS WITH RESPECT TO RENOVATION AND REPAIR OF MUSEUM FACILITIES AND EXHIBIT FACILITIES

(A) GRANTS

The Secretary of the Interior may make grants to Indian organizations, including Indian tribes, museums, cultural centers, educational institutions, libraries, and archives, for renovation and repair of museum facilities and exhibit facilities to enable such organizations to exhibit objects and artifacts on loan from the collections of the Smithsonian Institution or from other sources. Such grants may be made only from the Tribal Museum Endowment Fund.

(B) INDIAN ORGANIZATION CONTRIBUTION

In making grants under subsection (a), the Secretary may require the organization receiving the grant to contribute, in cash or in kind, not more than 50 percent of the cost of the renovation or repair involved. Such contribution may be derived from any source other than the Tribal Museum Endowment Fund.

(C) TRIBAL MUSEUM ENDOWMENT FUND

(1) ESTABLISHMENT

There is established in the Treasury a fund, to be known as the "Tribal Museum Endowment Fund" (hereinafter in this subsection referred to as the "Fund") for the purpose of making grants under subsection (a). The Fund shall consist of (A) amounts deposited and credited under paragraph (2), (B) obligations obtained under paragraph (3), and (C) amounts appropriated pursuant to authorization under paragraph (5).

(2) DEPOSITS AND CREDITS

The Secretary of the Interior is authorized to accept contributions to the Fund from non-Federal sources and shall deposit such contributions in the Fund. The Secretary of the Treasury shall credit to the Fund the interest on, and the proceeds from sale and redemption of, obligations held in the Fund.

(3) INVESTMENTS

The Secretary of the Treasury may invest any portion of the Fund in interest-bearing obligations of the United States. Such obligations may be acquired on original issue or in the open market and may be held to maturity or sold in the open market. In making investments for the Fund, the Secretary of the Treasury shall consult the Secretary of the Interior with respect to maturities, purchases, and sales, taking into consideration the balance necessary to meet current grant requirements.

(4) EXPENDITURES AND CAPITAL PRESERVATION

Subject to appropriation, amounts derived from interest shall be available for expenditure from the Fund. The capital of the Fund shall not be available for expenditure.

(5) AUTHORIZATION OF APPROPRIATIONS

There is authorized to be appropriated to the Fund $2,000,000 for each fiscal year beginning with fiscal year 1992.

(Pub. L. 101–185, §15, Nov. 28, 1989, 103 Stat. 1345.)

§80Q–14. DEFINITIONS

As used in this subchapter—

(1) the term "Board of Regents" means the Board of Regents of the Smithsonian Institution;

(2) the term "Board of Trustees" means the Board of Trustees of the National Museum of the American Indian;

(3) the term "burial site" means a natural or prepared physical location, whether below, on, or above the surface of the earth, into which, as a part of a death rite or ceremony of a culture, individual human remains are deposited;

(4) the term "funerary object" means an object that, as part of a death rite or ceremony of a culture, is intentionally placed with individual human remains, either at the time of burial or later;

(5) the term "Heye Foundation assets" means the collections, endowment, and all other property of the Heye Foundation (other than the interest of the Heye Foundation in Audubon Terrace) described in the Memorandum of Understanding between the Smithsonian Institution and the Heye Foundation, dated May 8, 1989, and the schedules attached to such memorandum;

(6) the term "Heye Museum" means the Museum of the American Indian, Heye Foundation;

(7) the term "Indian" means a member of an Indian tribe;

(8) the term "Indian tribe" has the meaning given that term in section 5304 of title 25;

(9) the term "National Museum" means the National Museum of the American Indian established by section 80q–1 of this title;

(10) the term "Native American" means an individual of a tribe, people, or culture that is indigenous to the Americas and such term includes a Native Hawaiian; and

(11) the term "Native Hawaiian" means a member or descendant of the aboriginal people who, before 1778, occupied and exercised sovereignty in the area that now comprises the State of Hawaii.

(Pub. L. 101–185, §16, Nov. 28, 1989, 103 Stat. 1346.)

§80Q–15. AUTHORIZATION OF APPROPRIATIONS

(A) FUNDING

There is authorized to be appropriated to the Board of Regents to carry out this subchapter (other than as provided in sections 80q–5(b)(1)(B), 80q–6, 80q–8, 80q–9, 80q–10, 80q–12, and 80q–13(c)(5) of this title)—

(1) $10,000,000 for fiscal year 1990; and

(2) such sums as may be necessary for each succeeding fiscal year.

(B) PERIOD OF AVAILABILITY

Funds appropriated under subsection (a) shall remain available without fiscal year limitation for any period prior to the availability of the facilities to be constructed under section 80q–5 of this title for administrative and planning expenses and for the care and custody of the collections of the National Museum.

(Pub. L. 101–185, §17, Nov. 28, 1989, 103 Stat. 1347.)

* * * * * * *

★

NATIONAL AIR AND SPACE MUSEUM DULLES CENTER

20 U.S.C. §77NOTE

TITLE 20—EDUCATION

* * * * * * *

CHAPTER 3—SMITHSONIAN INSTITUTION, NATIONAL MUSEUMS AND ART GALLERIES

* * * * * * *

SUBCHAPTER VII—NATIONAL AIR AND SPACE MUSEUM

§77. NATIONAL AIR AND SPACE MUSEUM

* * * * * * *

STATUTORY NOTES AND RELATED SUBSIDIARIES

* * * * * * *

APPROPRIATIONS

Act Aug. 12, 1946, ch. 955, §6, 60 Stat. 998, as amended by Pub. L. 89–509, pt. I, §10, July 19, 1966, 80 Stat. 311, provided that: "There is hereby authorized to be appropriated the sum of $50,000 for the purposes of this Act [this subchapter] and there are hereby authorized to be appropriated annually hereafter such sums as may be necessary to maintain and administer said national air and space museum including salaries and all other necessary expenses."

* * * * * * *

CONSTRUCTION OF MUSEUM CENTER

Pub. L. 104–222, Oct. 1, 1996, 110 Stat. 3025, provided that:

"SECTION 1. CONSTRUCTION OF MUSEUM CENTER.

"The Board of Regents of the Smithsonian Institution is authorized to construct the Smithsonian Institution National Air and Space Museum Dulles Center at Washington Dulles International Airport.

"SEC. 2. LIMITATION ON USE OF FUNDS.

"No appropriated funds may be used to pay any expense of the construction authorized by section 1."

EXTENSION AT WASHINGTON DULLES INTERNATIONAL AIRPORT

Pub. L. 103–57, Aug. 2, 1993, 107 Stat. 279, provided that:

"SECTION 1. PLAN FOR NATIONAL AIR AND SPACE MUSEUM EXTENSION.

"The Board of Regents of the Smithsonian Institution shall have authority to plan and design an extension of the National Air and Space Museum at Washington Dulles International Airport.

"SEC. 2. AUTHORIZATION OF APPROPRIATIONS.

"There is authorized to be appropriated for fiscal years beginning after September 30, 1993, a total of $8,000,000 to carry out this Act."

* * * * * * *

★

JOHN F. KENNEDY CENTER

JOHN F. KENNEDY CENTER ACT

PUBLIC LAW 85–874
AS AMENDED THROUGH P.L. 117–286

JOHN F. KENNEDY CENTER ACT

[Public Law 85-874]

[As Amended Through P.L. 117–286, Enacted December 27, 2022]

AN ACT To provide for a John F. Kennedy Center for the Performing Arts which will be constructed, with funds raised by voluntary contributions, on a site made available in the District of Columbia.

Be it enacted by the Senate and House of Representatives of the United States of America in Congress assembled,

SECTION 1. [20 U.S.C. 76h note] SHORT TITLE AND FINDINGS.

(a) SHORT TITLE.— This Act may be cited as the "John F. Kennedy Center Act".

(b) FINDINGS.—Congress finds that—

(1) the late John Fitzgerald Kennedy served with distinction as President of the United States and as a Member of the Senate and the House of Representatives;

(2) by the untimely death of John Fitzgerald Kennedy the United States and the world have suffered a great loss;

(3) the late John Fitzgerald Kennedy was particularly devoted to education and cultural understanding and the advancement of the performing arts;

(4) it is fitting and proper that a living institution of the performing arts, designated as the National Center for the Performing Arts, named in the memory and honor of this great leader, shall serve as the sole national monument to his memory within the District of Columbia and its environs;

(5) such a living memorial serves all of the people of the United States by preserving, fostering, and transmitting the performing arts traditions of the people of the United States and other countries by producing and presenting music, opera, theater, dance, and other performing arts; and

(6) such a living memorial should be housed in the John F. Kennedy Center for the Performing Arts, located in the District of Columbia.

SEC. 2. [20 U.S.C. 76h] BOARD OF TRUSTEES.

(a) ESTABLISHMENT.—

(1) IN GENERAL.— There is established in the Smithsonian Institution a bureau,

which shall be directed by a board to be known as the Trustees of the John F. Kennedy Center for the Performing Arts (hereafter in this Act referred to as the Board), whose duty it shall be to maintain and administer the John F. Kennedy Center for the Performing Arts and site thereof as the National Center for the Performing Arts, a living memorial to John Fitzgerald Kennedy, and to execute such other functions as are vested in the Board by this Act.

(2) MEMBERSHIP.—The Board shall be composed of—

(A)   the Secretary of Health and Human Services;

(B)   the Librarian of Congress;

(C)   the Secretary of State;

(D)   the Chairman of the Commission of Fine Arts;

(E)   the Mayor of the District of Columbia;

(F)   the Superintendent of Schools of the District of Columbia;

(G)   the Director of the National Park Service;

(H)   the Secretary of Education;

(I)   the Secretary of the Smithsonian Institution;

(J)(i)   the Speaker and the Minority Leader of the House of Representatives;

(ii)   the chairman and ranking minority member of the Committee on Transportation and Infrastructure of the House of Representatives; and

(iii)   three additional Members of the House of Representatives appointed by the Speaker of the House of Representatives;

(K)(i)   the Majority Leader and the Minority Leader of the Senate;

(ii)   the chairman and ranking minority member of the Committee on Environment and Public Works of the Senate; and

(iii)   three additional Members of the Senate appointed by the President of the Senate; and

(L)   thirty-six general trustees, who shall be citizens of the United States, to be appointed in accordance with subsection (b).

(b) GENERAL TRUSTEES.—The general trustees shall be appointed by the President of the United States. Each trustee shall hold office as a member of the Board for a term of 6 years, except that—

(1)   any member appointed to fill a vacancy occurring before the expiration of the term for which the predecessor of the member was appointed shall be appointed for the remainder of the term;

(2)   a member shall continue to serve until the successor of the member has been appointed; and

(3)   the term of office of a member appointed before the date of enactment of the John F. Kennedy Center Act Amendments of 1994 shall expire as designated at the time of appointment.

(c) ADVISORY COMMITTEE ON THE ARTS.— There shall be an Advisory Committee

C. 3. [20 U.S.C. 76i] JOHN F. KENNEDY
:NTER FOR THE PERFORMING ARTS.

John F. Kennedy Center Act

on the Arts composed of such members as the President of the United States may designate, to serve at the pleasure of the President. Persons appointed to the Advisory Committee on the Arts, including officers or employees of the United States, shall be persons who are recognized for their knowledge of, or experience or interest in, one or more of the arts in the fields covered by the John F. Kennedy Center for the Performing Arts. The President shall designate the Chairman of the Advisory Committee on the Arts. In making such appointments the President shall give consideration to such recommendations as may from time to time be submitted to him by leading national organizations in the appropriate art fields. The Advisory Committee on the Arts shall advise and consult with the Board and make recommendations to the Board regarding existing and prospective cultural activities to be carried out by the John F. Kennedy Center for the Performing Arts. The Advisory Committee on the Arts shall assist the Board in carrying out section 5(a) of this Act. Members of the Advisory Committee on the Arts shall serve without compensation.

SEC. 3. [20 U.S.C. 76i] JOHN F. KENNEDY CENTER FOR THE PERFORMING ARTS.

(a) IN GENERAL.— The Board shall construct for the Smithsonian Institution, with funds raised by voluntary contributions, a building to be designated as the John F. Kennedy Center for the Performing Arts on a site in the District of Columbia bounded by the Inner Loop Freeway on the east, the Theodore Roosevelt Bridge approaches on the south, Rock Creek Parkway on the west, New Hampshire Avenue and F Street on the north, which shall be selected for such purpose by the National Capital Planning Commission. The National Capital Planning Commission shall acquire by purchase, condemnation, or otherwise, lands necessary to provide for the John F. Kennedy Center for the Performing Arts and related facilities. Such building shall be in accordance with plans and specifications approved by the Commission of Fine Arts.

(b) PARKING GARAGE ADDITIONS AND SITE IMPROVEMENTS.—

(1) IN GENERAL.—Substantially in accordance with the plan entitled Site Master Plan—Drawing Number 1997-2 April 29, 1997, and map number NCR 844/82571, the Board may design and construct—

(A) an addition to the parking garage at each of the north and south ends of the John F. Kennedy Center for the Performing Arts; and

(B) site improvements and modifications.

(2) AVAILABILITY.— The plan shall be on file and available for public inspection in the office of the Secretary of the Center.

(3) LIMITATION ON USE OF APPROPRIATED FUNDS.—No appropriated funds may be used to pay the costs (including the repayment of obligations incurred to finance costs) of—

(A) the design and construction of an addition to the parking garage authorized under paragraph (1)(A);

(B) the design and construction of site improvements and modifications authorized under paragraph (1)(B) that the Board specifically designates will be financed using sources other than appropriated funds; or

(C) any project to acquire large screen format equipment for an interpretive

SEC. 3. [20 U.S.C. 76i] JOHN F. KENNEDY
CENTER FOR THE PERFORMING ARTS.

John F. Kennedy Center /

theater, or to produce an interpretive film, that the Board specifically designates will be financed using sources other than appropriated funds.

(c) EXPANSION PROJECT.—

(1) AUTHORITY TO CONSTRUCT.—

(A) IN GENERAL.— Subject to the requirements of this subsection, the Board may undertake such activities as may be necessary to construct the expansion project.

(B) RESPONSIBILITIES OF THE BOARD.— The Board may construct the expansion project, and shall be responsible for the planning, design, engineering, and construction of the expansion project.

(C) LIMITATIONS.—

(i) MISSION.— All activities carried out under this paragraph shall be within the mission of the John F. Kennedy Center for the Performing Arts to serve as the national center for the performing arts.

(ii) FUNDING.— The costs of planning, design, engineering, and construction of the expansion project shall be paid for using nonappropriated funds.

(2) ANNUAL OPERATIONS AND MAINTENANCE COSTS.—

(A) ESTIMATES.— Before awarding a contract for construction of the expansion project, the Board shall estimate any additional annual operations and maintenance costs (or savings) associated with the project.

(B) BUDGET REQUESTS.— The Board shall account for any additional costs identified under subparagraph (A) in making a budget request for fiscal year 2014 and each fiscal year thereafter.

(C) BUDGET PRIORITIES.— The Board shall base a final determination on whether to proceed with the expansion project on the ability of the Board to accommodate any additional costs identified under subparagraph (A) within the other budget priorities of the Board.

(3) ACKNOWLEDGMENTS.— The Board may acknowledge private contributions used in carrying out the expansion project in the interior of the project, but may not acknowledge such private contributions on the exterior of the project. Any acknowledgment of private contributions under this paragraph shall be consistent with the requirements of section 4(b).

(4) EXPANSION PROJECT DEFINED.—In this subsection, the term expansion project means an addition to the south end of the building of the John F. Kennedy Center for the Performing Arts that—

(A) is less than 100,000 square feet;

(B) will improve the existing (as of the date of enactment of this subsection) accessibility and education functions of the Center; and

(C) will become part of the existing (as of the date of enactment of this subsection) structure of the Center.

SEC. 4. [20 U.S.C. 76j] DUTIES OF THE BOARD.

(a) PROGRAMS, ACTIVITIES, AND GOALS.—

(1) IN GENERAL.—The Board shall—

(A) present classical and contemporary music, opera, drama, dance, and other performing arts from the United States and other countries;

(B) promote and maintain the John F. Kennedy Center for the Performing Arts as the National Center for the Performing Arts—

(i) by developing and maintaining a leadership role in national performing arts education policy and programs, including developing and presenting original and innovative performing arts and educational programs for children, youth, families, adults, and educators designed specifically to foster an appreciation and understanding of the performing arts;

(ii) by developing and maintaining a comprehensive and broad program for national and community outreach, including establishing model programs for adaptation by other presenting and educational institutions; and

(iii) by conducting joint initiatives with the national education and outreach programs of the Very Special Arts, an entity affiliated with the John F. Kennedy Center for the Performing Arts which has an established program for the identification, development, and implementation of model programs and projects in the arts for disabled individuals;

(C) strive to ensure that the education and outreach programs and policies of the John F. Kennedy Center for the Performing Arts meet the highest level of excellence and reflect the cultural diversity of the United States;

(D) provide facilities for other civic activities at the John F. Kennedy Center for the Performing Arts;

(E) provide within the John F. Kennedy Center for the Performing Arts a suitable memorial in honor of the late President;

(F) develop, and update annually, a comprehensive building needs plan for the features of the John F. Kennedy Center for the Performing Arts in existence on the date of enactment of the John F. Kennedy Center Act Amendments of 1994;

(G) with respect to the building and site of the John F. Kennedy Center for the Performing Arts, plan, design, and construct each capital repair, replacement, improvement, rehabilitation, alteration, or modification necessary to maintain the functionality of the building and site at current standards of life, safety, security, and accessibility;

(H) provide—

(i) information and interpretation; and

(ii) with respect to the building and site of the John F. Kennedy Center for the Performing Arts, all necessary maintenance, repair, and alteration of, and all janitorial, security, and other services and equipment necessary for the operations of, the building and site, in a manner consistent with requirements for high quality operations; and

(I)   ensure that safe and convenient access to the site of the John F. Kennedy Center for the Performing Arts is provided for pedestrians and vehicles.

(2) ADMINISTRATIVE POWERS AND DUTIES.—

(A) AUTHORITY TO ENTER INTO CONTRACTS.—   The Board, in accordance with applicable law, may enter into contracts or other arrangements with, and make payments to, public agencies or private organizations or other private persons in order to carry out the functions of the Board under this Act. The authority described in the preceding sentence includes utilizing the services and facilities of other agencies, including the Department of the Interior, the General Services Administration, and the Smithsonian Institution.

(B) PREPARATION OF BUDGET.—   The Board shall prepare a budget pursuant to sections 1104, 1105(a), and 1513(b) of title 31, United States Code.

(C) USE OF AGENCY PERSONNEL.—   The Board may utilize or employ the services of the personnel of any agency or instrumentality of the Federal Government or the District of Columbia, with the consent of the agency or the instrumentality concerned, on a reimbursable basis, and utilize voluntary and uncompensated personnel.

(D) SELECTION OF CONTRACTORS.—In carrying out the duties of the Board under this Act, the Board may negotiate any contract—

(i)   for planning, design, engineering, or construction of buildings to be erected on the John F. Kennedy Center Plaza under section 12 and for landscaping and other improvements to the Plaza; or

(ii)   for an environmental system for, a protection system for, or a repair to, maintenance of, or restoration of the John F. Kennedy Center for the Performing Arts,

with selected contractors and award the contract on the basis of contractor qualifications as well as price.

(E) MAINTENANCE OF HALLS.—   The Board shall maintain the Hall of Nations, the Hall of States, and the Grand Foyer of the John F. Kennedy Center for the Performing Arts in a manner that is suitable to a national performing arts center that is operated as a Presidential memorial and in a manner consistent with other national Presidential memorials.

(F) MAINTENANCE OF GROUNDS.—   The Board shall manage and operate the grounds of the John F. Kennedy Center for the Performing Arts in a manner consistent with National Park Service regulations and agreements in effect on the date of enactment of the John F. Kennedy Center Act Amendments of 1994. No change in the management and operation of the grounds may be made without the express approval of Congress and of the Secretary of the Interior.

(b)(1)   Except as provided in paragraph (2) of this subsection, the Board shall assure that after the date of enactment of this subsection, no additional memorials or plaques in the nature of memorials shall be designated or installed in the public areas of the John

F. Kennedy Center for the Performing Arts.

(2) Paragraph (1) of this subsection shall not apply to—

(A) any plaque acknowledging a gift from a foreign country;

(B) any plaque on a theater chair or a theater box acknowledging the gift of such chair or box; and

(C) any inscription on the marble walls in the north or south galleries, the Hall of States, or the Hall of Nations acknowledging a major contribution;
which plaque or inscription is permitted under policies of the Board in effect on the date of enactment of this subsection.

(3) For purposes of this subsection, testimonials and benefit performances shall not be construed to be memorials.

SEC. 5. [20 U.S.C. 76k] POWERS OF THE BOARD.

(a) SOLICITATION AND ACCEPTANCE OF GIFTS.— The Board is authorized to solicit and accept for the John F. Kennedy Center for the Performing Arts, as a bureau of the Smithsonian Institution, and to hold and administer gifts, bequests, or devises of money, securities, or other property of whatsoever character for the benefit of the John F. Kennedy Center for the Performing Arts. Unless otherwise restricted by the terms of the gift, bequest, or devise, the Board is authorized to sell or exchange and to invest or reinvest in such investments as it may determine from time to time the moneys, securities, or other property composing trust funds given, bequeathed, or devised to or for the benefit of the John F. Kennedy Center for the Performing Arts. The income as and when collected shall be placed in such depositaries as the Board shall determine and shall be subject to expenditure by the Board.

(b) APPOINTMENT OF OFFICERS AND EMPLOYEES.—

(1) CHAIRPERSON AND SECRETARY.— The Board shall appoint and fix the compensation and duties of a Chairperson of the John F. Kennedy Center for the Performing Arts, who shall serve as the chief executive officer of the Center, and a Secretary of the John F. Kennedy Center for the Performing Arts. The Chairperson and Secretary shall be well qualified by experience and training to perform the duties of their respective offices.

(2) SENIOR LEVEL EXECUTIVE AND OTHER EMPLOYEES.—The Chairperson of the John F. Kennedy Center for the Performing Arts may appoint—

(A) a senior level executive who, by virtue of the background of the individual, shall be well suited to be responsible for facilities management and services and who may, without regard to the provisions of title 5, United States Code, be appointed and compensated with appropriated funds, except that the compensation may not exceed the maximum rate of pay prescribed for level IV of the Executive Schedule under section 5315 of title 5, United States Code; and

(B) such other officers and employees of the John F. Kennedy Center for the Performing Arts as may be necessary for the efficient administration of the functions of the Board.

(c) TRANSFER OF PROPERTY.— Not later than October 1, 1995, the property, liabilities, contracts, records, and unexpended balances of appropriations, authorizations, allocations, and other funds employed, held, used, arising from, available to, or to be made available in connection with the functions transferred from the Secretary of the Interior pursuant to the amendments made by the John F. Kennedy Center Act Amendments of 1994 shall be transferred, subject to section 1531 of title 31, United States Code, to the Board as the Board and the Secretary of the Interior may determine appropriate. Unexpended funds transferred pursuant to this subsection shall be used only for the purposes for which, and subject to the terms under which, the funds were originally authorized and appropriated.

(d) TRANSFER OF PERSONNEL.—

(1) IN GENERAL.— Employees of the National Park Service assigned to duties related to the functions being undertaken by the Board shall be transferred with their functions to the Board not later than October 1, 1995.

(2) RIGHTS AND BENEFITS.— Transferred employees shall remain in the Federal competitive service and retain all rights and benefits provided under title 5, United States Code. For a period of not less than 3 years after the date of transfer of an employee under paragraph (1), the transferred employee shall retain the right of priority consideration under merit promotion procedures or lateral reassignment for all vacancies within the Department of the Interior.

(3) PARK POLICE.— All United States Park Police and Park Police guard force employees assigned to the John F. Kennedy Center for the Performing Arts shall remain employees of the National Park Service.

(4) COSTS.— All usual and customary costs associated with any adverse action or grievance proceeding resulting from the transfer of functions under this section that are incurred before October 1, 1995, shall be paid from funds appropriated to the John F. Kennedy Center for the Performing Arts.

(5) REORGANIZATION AUTHORITY.— Nothing contained in this section shall prohibit the Board from reorganizing functions at the John F. Kennedy Center for the Performing Arts in accordance with laws governing reorganizations.

(e) REVIEW OF BOARD ACTIONS.— The actions of the Board relating to performing arts and to payments made or directed to be made by the Board from any trust funds shall not be subject to review by any officer or agency other than a court of law.

(f) COLLECTIVE BARGAINING.—

(1) DEFINITION.— As used in this subsection, the term theatrical employee means a nonappropriated fund employee of the Board, who is engaged in a box office, performing, or theatrical trade that is the subject of a collective bargaining agreement as of January 1, 1994, including any change in the trade as a result of a technological advance.

(2) COLLECTIVE BARGAINING.—

(A) IN GENERAL.—For the purposes of the National Labor Relations Act (29 U.S.C. 151 et seq.) and the Labor-Management Relations Act, 1947 (29 U.S.C. 141 et seq.)—

(i)   each theatrical employee shall be considered to be an employee within the meaning of section 2(3) of the National Labor Relations Act (29 U.S.C. 152(3)); and

(ii)   with respect to a theatrical employee, the Board shall be considered to be an employer within the meaning of section 2(2) of the National Labor Relations Act (29 U.S.C. 152(2)).

(B) RIGHTS AND OBLIGATIONS.— With respect to each theatrical employee, the theatrical employee and the Board shall have all of the rights and obligations specified in such Acts.

(g) PEDESTRIAN AND VEHICULAR ACCESS.— Subject to approval of the Secretary of the Interior under section 4(a)(2)(F), the Board shall develop plans and carry out projects to improve pedestrian and vehicular access to the John F. Kennedy Center for the Performing Arts.

ADMINISTRATION

SEC. 6. [20 U.S.C. 76l] (a)   The Board is authorized to adopt an official seal which shall be judicially noticed and to make such bylaws, rules, and regulations, as it deems necessary for the administration of its functions under this Act, including, among other matters, bylaws, rules, and regulations relating to the administration of its trust funds and the organization and procedure of the Board. The Board may function notwithstanding vacancies and twelve members of the Board shall constitute a quorum for the transaction of business.

(b)   The Board shall have all the usual powers and obligations of a trustee in respect of all trust funds administered by it.

(c)   The Board shall submit to the Smithsonian Institution and to Congress an annual report of the operations of the Board under this Act, including a detailed statement of all public and private moneys received and disbursed by it.

(d) INSPECTOR GENERAL.— The functions of the Board funded by funds appropriated pursuant to section 12 shall be subject to the requirements for a Federal entity under chapter 4 of title 5, United States Code. The Inspector General of the Smithsonian Institution is authorized to carry out the requirements of such chapter on behalf of the Board, on a reimbursable basis when requested by the Board.

(e) PROPERTY AND PERSONNEL COMPENSATION.—

(1) IN GENERAL.— The Board may procure insurance against any loss in connection with the property of the Board and other assets administered by the Board. Each employee and volunteer of the Board shall be considered to be a civil employee of the United States (within the meaning of the term employee as defined in section 8101(1) of title 5, United States Code), except that the Board shall continue to provide benefits with respect to any disability or death resulting from a personal injury to a nonappropriated fund employee of the Board sustained while in the performance of the duties of the employee for the Board pursuant to the workers compensation statute of the jurisdiction in which the John F. Kennedy Center for the Performing Arts is located. The disability or death benefits referred to in the preceding sentence, whether under the workers compensation statute referred to in the preceding sentence or under chapter 81 of title 5, United States Code, shall

377

continue to be the exclusive liability of the Board and the United States with respect to all employees and volunteers of the Board.

(2) FEDERAL TORT CLAIMS.— For the purposes of chapter 171 of title 28, United States Code, an employee of the Board shall be considered to be an employee of the government and the Board shall be considered to be a Federal agency. No employee of the Board may bring suit against the United States or the Board under the Federal tort claims procedure of chapter 171 of title 28, United States Code, for disability or death resulting from personal injury sustained while in the performance of the duties of the employee for the Board.

SEC. 7. [20 U.S.C.76m] PHOTOVOLTAIC SYSTEM.

(a) IN GENERAL.— The Board may study, plan, design, engineer, and construct a photovoltaic system for the main roof of the John F. Kennedy Center for the Performing Arts.

(b) REPORT.— Not later than 60 days before beginning construction of the photovoltaic system pursuant to subsection (a), the Board shall submit to the Committee on Transportation and Infrastructure of the House of Representatives and the Committee on Environment and Public Works of the Senate a report on the feasibility and design of the project.

[Section 8 repealed by P.L. 101–449]

BORROWING AUTHORITY

SEC. 9. [20 U.S.C.76o] (a)   To finance necessary parking facilities for the Center, the Board may issue revenue bonds to the Secretary of the Treasury payable from revenues accruing to the Board. The total face value of all bonds so issued shall not be greater than $20,400,000. Such obligations shall have maturities agreed upon by the Board and the Secretary of the Treasury but not in excess of fifty years. Such obligations may be redeemable at the option of the Board before maturity in such manner as may be stipulated in such obligations, but the obligations thus redeemed shall not be refinanced by the Board. The Secretary of the Treasury is authorized and directed to purchase any obligations of the Board to be issued under this section and for such purpose the Secretary of the Treasury is authorized to use as a public debt transaction the proceeds from the sale of any securities issued under chapter 31 of title 31, United States Code, and the purposes for which securities may be issued under chapter 31 of title 31, United States Code, are extended to include any purchases of the Board's obligations under this section.

(b)   Effect as of the date of enactment of this subsection the obligations of the Board incurred under subsection (a) of this section shall bear no interest, and the requirement of the Board to pay the unpaid interest which has accrued on such obligations is terminated.

(c)   There is hereby established in the Treasury of the United States a sinking fund, the Kennedy Center Revenue Bond Sinking Fund (hereinafter referred to as the Fund, which shall be used to retire the obligations of the Board incurred under subsection (a) of this section upon the respective maturities of such obligations. The Board shall pay into the Fund, beginning on January 1, 1987 and ending on January 1, 2016, the annual sum of $200,000 in amortization of the principal amount of the obligations. Such sums shall be invested by the Secretary of the Treasury in public debt securities with maturities suitable for the needs of the Fund and bearing interest at rates determined by the Secretary of the Treasury, taking into consideration the current average market yield on outstanding marketable obligations of the United States of comparable maturities. The interest on such investments shall be credited to and form a part of the Fund. Moneys in the Fund shall be used exclusively to retire the obligations of the Board incurred under subsection (a) of this section. Adjustments of not greater than plus or minus 5 per centum may be made from time to time in the annual payments to the Fund in order to correct any gains or deficiencies as a result of fluctuations in interest rates over the life of the investments: *Provided, however,* That a final adjustment shall be made between the Board and the Secretary of the Treasury at the end of the amortization period to correct any overall gain or deficiency in the Fund. The terms of this adjustment shall be covered by a memorandum of understanding between the Board and the Secretary of the Treasury to be consummated on or before the time the initial payment into the Fund is made.

GIFTS TO UNITED STATES

SEC. 10. [20 U.S.C. 76p]   The Secretary of the Treasury is authorized to accept on behalf of the United States any gift to the United States which the Secretary finds has been contributed in honor or in memory of the late President John F. Kennedy and to pay the money to such appropriation or other accounts, including the appropriation accounts established pursuant to appropriations authorized by this Act, as in the judgment of the Secretary will best effectuate the intent of the donor.

NATIONAL MEMORIAL

SEC. 11. [20 U.S.C. 76q]   The John F. Kennedy Center for the Performing Arts, designated by this Act, shall be the sole national memorial to the late John Fitzgerald Kennedy within the city of Washington and its environs.

SEC. 12. [20 U.S.C. 76q–1] JOHN F. KENNEDY CENTER PLAZA.

(a) DEFINITIONS.—In this section, the following definitions apply:

(1) AIR RIGHTS.— The term air rights means real property interests conveyed by deed, lease, or permit for the use of space between streets and alleys within the boundaries of the Project.

(2) CENTER.— The term Center means the John F. Kennedy Center for the Performing Arts.

(3) GREEN SPACES.— The term green spaces means areas within the boundaries of the Project or affected by the Project that are covered by grass, trees, or other vegetation.

(4) PLAZA.— The term Plaza means improvements to the area surrounding the John F. Kennedy Center building carried out under the Project and comprised of transportation elements (including roadways, sidewalks, and bicycle lanes) and non-transportation elements (including landscaping, green space, open public space, water, sewer, and utility connections).

(5) PROJECT.— The term Project means the Plaza project, as described in the

TEA–21 report, providing for construction of a Plaza adjacent to the Center and for improved bicycle, pedestrian, and vehicular access to and around the Center. The term includes planning, design, engineering, and construction of the Plaza, buildings to be constructed on the Plaza, and related transportation improvements and may include any other elements of the Project identified in the TEA–21 report.

(6) SECRETARY.— The term Secretary means the Secretary of Transportation.

(7) TEA–21 REPORT.— The term TEA–21 report means the report of the Secretary submitted to Congress under section 1214 of the Transportation Equity Act for the 21st Century (20 U.S.C. 76j note; 112 Stat. 204).

(b) RESPONSIBILITIES OF THE SECRETARY.—

(1) IN GENERAL.— The Secretary shall be responsible for the Project and may undertake such activities as may be necessary to construct the Project, other than buildings to be constructed on the Plaza, substantially as described in the TEA–21 report.

(2) PLANNING, DESIGN, ENGINEERING, AND CONSTRUCTION.— The Secretary shall be responsible for the planning, design, engineering, and construction of the Project, other than buildings to be constructed on the Plaza.

(3) AGREEMENTS WITH THE BOARD AND OTHER AGENCIES.— The Secretary shall enter into memoranda of agreement with the Board and any appropriate Federal or other governmental agency to facilitate the planning, design, engineering, and construction of the Project.

(4) CONSULTATION WITH THE BOARD.— The Secretary shall consult with the Board to maximize efficiencies in planning and executing the Project, including the construction of any buildings on the Plaza.

(5) CONTRACTS.— Subject to the approval of the Board, the Secretary may enter into contracts on behalf of the Center related to the planning, design, engineering, and construction of the Project.

(6) PROJECT TEAM.—

(A) ESTABLISHMENT.— To further construction of the Project, the Secretary shall establish a Project Team.

(B) MEMBERSHIP.—The Project Team shall be composed of the following members:

(i) The Secretary (or the Secretary's designee).

(ii) The Administrator of General Services (or the Administrator's designee).

(iii) The Chairman of the Board (or the Chairman's designee).

(iv) Such other individuals as the Project Team considers appropriate.

(C) PROJECT DIRECTOR.— The Project Team shall have a Project Director who shall be appointed by the Secretary, in consultation with the Administrator of General Services and the Chairman of the Board. The Project Director shall report directly to the Project Team.

(c) RESPONSIBILITIES OF THE BOARD.—

(1) IN GENERAL.— The Board, in consultation with the Project Team, may undertake such activities as may be necessary to construct buildings on the Plaza for the Project.

(2) RECEIPT OF TRANSFERS OF AIR RIGHTS.— The Board may receive from the District of Columbia such transfers of air rights as may be necessary for the planning, design, engineering, and construction of the Project.

(3) CONSTRUCTION OF BUILDINGS.— The Board, in consultation with the Project Team, may construct, with non-appropriated funds, buildings on the Plaza for the Project and shall be responsible for the planning, design, engineering, and construction of the buildings.

(4) ACKNOWLEDGMENT OF CONTRIBUTIONS.—

(A) IN GENERAL.— The Board may acknowledge private contributions used in the construction of buildings on the Plaza for the Project in the interior of the buildings, but may not acknowledge private contributions on the exterior of the buildings.

(B) APPLICABILITY OF OTHER REQUIREMENTS.— Any acknowledgment of private contributions under this paragraph shall be consistent with the requirements of section 4(b).

(5) APPROVAL BY PROJECT TEAM.— Notwithstanding section 5(e), any decision by the Board that will significantly affect, as determined by the Project Team in consultation with the Board, the scope, cost, schedule, or engineering feasibility of any element of the Project, other than buildings to be constructed on the Plaza, shall be subject to the approval of the Project Team.

(d) RESPONSIBILITIES OF THE DISTRICT OF COLUMBIA.—

(1) MODIFICATION OF HIGHWAY SYSTEM.— Notwithstanding any State or local law, the Mayor of the District of Columbia, in consultation with the National Capital Planning Commission and the Secretary, shall have exclusive authority to amend or modify the permanent system of highways of the District of Columbia as may be necessary to meet the requirements and needs of the Project.

(2) CONVEYANCES.—

(A) AUTHORITY.— Notwithstanding any State or local law, the Mayor of the District of Columbia shall have exclusive authority to convey or dispose of any interests in real estate (including air rights or air space as that term is defined by District of Columbia law) owned or controlled by the District of Columbia, as may be necessary to meet the requirements and needs of the Project.

(B) CONVEYANCE TO THE BOARD.— Not later than 90 days following the date of receipt of notification from the Secretary of the requirements and needs of the Project, the Mayor of the District of Columbia shall convey or dispose of to the Board without compensation interests in real estate described in subparagraph (A).

(3) AGREEMENTS WITH THE BOARD.— The Mayor of the District of Columbia shall have the authority to enter into memoranda of agreement with the Board

and any Federal or other governmental agency to facilitate the planning, design, engineering, and construction of the Project.

(e) OWNERSHIP.—

(1) ROADWAYS AND SIDEWALKS.— Upon completion of the Project, responsibility for maintenance and oversight of roadways and sidewalks modified or improved for the Project shall remain with the owner of the affected roadways and sidewalks.

(2) MAINTENANCE OF GREEN SPACES.— Subject to paragraph (3), upon completion of the Project, responsibility for maintenance and oversight of any green spaces modified or improved for the Project shall remain with the owner of the affected green spaces.

(3) BUILDINGS AND GREEN SPACES ON THE PLAZA.— Upon completion of the Project, the Board shall own, operate, and maintain the buildings and green spaces established on the Plaza for the Project.

(f) NATIONAL HIGHWAY BOUNDARIES.—

(1) REALIGNMENT OF BOUNDARIES.— The Secretary may realign national highways related to proposed changes to the Northern and Southern Interchanges and the E Street Approach recommended in the TEA–21 report in order to facilitate the flow of traffic in the vicinity of the Center.

(2) ACCESS TO CENTER FROM I–66.— The Secretary may improve direct access and egress between Interstate Route 66 and the Center, including its garages.

(g) GAO REVIEW.— Until completion of the Project, the Comptroller General shall review the management and oversight of construction of the Project by the Board and report periodically on the results of the review to the Committee on Transportation and Infrastructure of the House of Representatives and the Committee on Environment and Public Works of the Senate.

SEC. 13. [20 U.S.C. 76r] AUTHORIZATION OF APPROPRIATIONS.

(a) MAINTENANCE, REPAIR, AND SECURITY.—There are authorized to be appropriated to the Board to carry out section 4(a)(1)(H)—

(1) $25,690,000 for fiscal year 2020;

(2) $27,000,000 for fiscal year 2021;

(3) $28,000,000 for fiscal year 2022;

(4) $29,000,000 for fiscal year 2023; and

(5) $30,000,000 for fiscal year 2024.

(b) CAPITAL PROJECTS.—There are authorized to be appropriated to the Board to carry out subparagraphs (F) and (G) of section 4(a)(1)—

(1) $17,800,000 for fiscal year 2020;

(2) $18,000,000 for fiscal year 2021;

(3) $19,000,000 for fiscal year 2022;

(4) $20,000,000 for fiscal year 2023; and

(5) $21,000,000 for fiscal year 2024.

(c) JOHN F. KENNEDY CENTER PLAZA.— There is authorized to be appropriated to the Secretary of Transportation for capital costs incurred in the planning, design, engineering, and construction of the project authorized by section 12 (including roadway improvements related to the North and South Interchanges and construction of the John F. Kennedy Center Plaza, but not including construction of any buildings on the plaza) a total of $400,000,000 for fiscal years 2003 through 2010. Such sums shall remain available until expended.

(d) PHOTOVOLTAIC SYSTEM.— There are authorized to be appropriated to the Board such sums as are necessary to carry out section 7, to remain available until expended.

(e) LIMITATION ON USE OF FUNDS.— No funds appropriated pursuant to this section may be used for any direct expense incurred in the production of a performing arts attraction, for personnel who are involved in performing arts administration (including any supply or equipment used by the personnel), or for production, staging, public relations, marketing, fundraising, ticket sales, or education. Funds appropriated directly to the Board shall not affect nor diminish other Federal funds sought for any performing arts function and may be used to reimburse the Board for that portion of costs that are Federal costs reasonably allocated to building services and theater maintenance and repair.

SEC. 14. [20 U.S.C. 76s] DEFINITIONS.

As used in this Act, the terms building and site of the John F. Kennedy Center for the Performing Arts and grounds of the John F. Kennedy Center for the Performing Arts refer to the site in the District of Columbia on which the John F. Kennedy Center building is constructed and that extends to the line of the west face of the west retaining walls and curbs of the Inner Loop Freeway on the east, the north face of the north retaining walls and curbs of the Theodore Roosevelt Bridge approaches on the south, the east face of the east retaining walls and curbs of Rock Creek Parkway on the west, and the south curbs of New Hampshire Avenue and F Street on the north, as generally depicted on the map entitled Transfer of John F. Kennedy Center for the Performing Arts, numbered 844/82563, and dated April 20, 1994 (as amended by the map entitled Transfer of John F. Kennedy Center for the Performing Arts, numbered 844/82563A and dated May 22, 1997), which shall be on file and available for public inspection in the office of the National Capital Region, National Park Service, Department of the Interior. Upon completion of the project for establishment of the John F. Kennedy Center Plaza authorized by section 12, the Board, in consultation with the Secretary of Transportation, shall amend the map that is on file and available for public inspection under the preceding sentence.

★

John F. Kennedy Center Reauthorization Act of 2012

Public Law 112–131

JOHN F. KENNEDY CENTER REAUTHORIZATION ACT OF 2012

[(Public Law 112–131)]

[This law has not been amended]

AN ACT To amend the John F. Kennedy Center Act to authorize appropriations for the John F. Kennedy Center for the Performing Arts, and for other purposes.

Be it enacted by the Senate and House of Representatives of the United States of America in Congress assembled,

SECTION 1. SHORT TITLE.

This Act may be cited as the "John F. Kennedy Center Reauthorization Act of 2012".

SEC. 2. EXPANSION PROJECT FOR JOHN F. KENNEDY CENTER FOR THE PERFORMING ARTS.

Section 3 of the John F. Kennedy Center Act (20 U.S.C. 76i) is amended by adding at the end the following:

"(c) EXPANSION PROJECT.

"(1) AUTHORITY TO CONSTRUCT.

"(A) IN GENERAL. Subject to the requirements of this subsection, the Board may undertake such activities as may be necessary to construct the expansion project.

"(B) RESPONSIBILITIES OF THE BOARD. The Board may construct the expansion project, and shall be responsible for the planning, design, engineering, and construction of the expansion project.

"(C) LIMITATIONS.

"(i) MISSION. All activities carried out under this paragraph shall be within the mission of the John F. Kennedy Center for the Performing Arts to serve as the national center for the performing arts.

"(ii) FUNDING. The costs of planning, design, engineering, and construction of the expansion project shall be paid for using nonappropriated funds.

"(2) ANNUAL OPERATIONS AND MAINTENANCE COSTS.

"(A) ESTIMATES. Before awarding a contract for construction of the expansion project, the Board shall estimate any additional annual operations and maintenance costs (or savings) associated with the project.

"(B) BUDGET REQUESTS. The Board shall account for any additional costs identified under subparagraph (A) in making a budget request for fiscal year 2014 and each fiscal year thereafter.

"(C) BUDGET PRIORITIES. The Board shall base a final determination on whether to proceed with the expansion project on the ability of the Board to accommodate any additional costs identified under subparagraph (A) within the other budget priorities of the Board.

"(3) ACKNOWLEDGMENTS. The Board may acknowledge private contributions used in carrying out the expansion project in the interior of the project, but may not acknowledge such private contributions on the exterior of the project. Any acknowledgment of private contributions under this paragraph shall be consistent with the requirements of section 4(b).

"(4) EXPANSION PROJECT DEFINED. In this subsection, the term 'expansion project' means an addition to the south end of the building of the John F. Kennedy Center for the Performing Arts that—

"(A) is less than 100,000 square feet;

"(B) will improve the existing (as of the date of enactment of this subsection) accessibility and education functions of the Center; and

"(C) will become part of the existing (as of the date of enactment of this subsection) structure of the Center.".

SEC. 3. AUTHORIZATION OF APPROPRIATIONS.

Section 13 of the John F. Kennedy Center Act (20 U.S.C. 76r) is amended by striking subsections (a) and (b) and inserting the following:

"(a) MAINTENANCE, REPAIR, AND SECURITY. There is authorized to be appropriated to the Board to carry out section 4(a)(1)(H) $22,379,000 for each of fiscal years 2013 and 2014.

"(b) CAPITAL PROJECTS. There is authorized to be appropriated to the Board to carry out subparagraphs (F) and (G) of section 4(a)(1) $13,588,000 for each of fiscal years 2013 and 2014.".

★

OTHER LAWS RELATING TO PUBLIC BUILDINGS AND FACILITIES

40 U.S.C. CH. 61–UNITED STATES SUPREME COURT BUILDING AND GROUNDS

40 U.S.C. CODE CHAPTER 61

TITLE 40—PUBLIC BUILDINGS, PROPERTY, AND WORKS

This title was enacted by Pub. L. 107–217, §1, Aug. 21, 2002, 116 Stat. 1062

* * * * * * *

SUBTITLE II—PUBLIC BUILDINGS AND WORKS

* * * * * * *

PART C—FEDERAL BUILDING COMPLEXES

* * * * * * *

CHAPTER 61—UNITED STATES SUPREME COURT BUILDING AND GROUNDS

SUBCHAPTER I—GENERAL

§6101. DEFINITIONS AND APPLICATION

(a) DEFINITIONS.—In this chapter, the following definitions apply:

(1) OFFICIAL GUEST OF THE SUPREME COURT.—The term "official guest of the Supreme Court" means an individual who is a guest of the Supreme Court, as determined by the Chief Justice of the United States or any Associate Justice of the Supreme Court;

(2) STATE.—The term "State" means a State of the United States, the District of Columbia, Puerto Rico, the Virgin Islands, Guam, the Northern Mariana Islands, the Federated States of Micronesia, the Marshall Islands, Palau, and any territory or possession of the United States; and

(b) APPLICATION.—For purposes of section 6102 of this title and subchapters III and IV, the Supreme Court grounds—

(1) extend to the line of the face of—

(A) the east curb of First Street Northeast, between Maryland Avenue Northeast and East Capitol Street;

(B) the south curb of Maryland Avenue Northeast, between First Street Northeast and Second Street Northeast;

(C) the west curb of Second Street Northeast, between Maryland Avenue Northeast and East Capitol Street; and

(D) the north curb of East Capitol Street between First Street Northeast and Second Street Northeast; and

(2) comprise any property under the custody and control of the Supreme Court as part of the Supreme Court grounds, including property acquired as provided by law on behalf of the Federal Government in lots 2, 3, 800, 801, and 802 in square 758 in the District of Columbia as an addition to the grounds of the Supreme Court Building and that parcel transferred under the Supreme Court Grounds Transfer Act of 2005.

(Pub. L. 107–217, Aug. 21, 2002, 116 Stat. 1180; Pub. L. 109–214, §1(c)(2), Apr. 11, 2006, 120 Stat. 326.)

§6102. REGULATIONS

(a) AUTHORITY OF THE MARSHAL.—In addition to the restrictions and requirements specified in subchapter IV, the Marshal of the Supreme Court may prescribe regulations, approved by the Chief Justice of the United States, that are necessary for—

(1) the adequate protection of the Supreme Court Building and grounds and of individuals and property in the Building and grounds; and

(2) the maintenance of suitable order and decorum within the Building and grounds.

(b) POSTING REQUIREMENT.—All regulations prescribed under this section shall be posted in a public place at the Building and shall be made reasonably available to the public in writing.

(Pub. L. 107–217, Aug. 21, 2002, 116 Stat. 1180.)

SUBCHAPTER II—BUILDINGS AND GROUNDS

§6111. SUPREME COURT BUILDING

(a) IN GENERAL.—

(1) STRUCTURAL AND MECHANICAL CARE.—The Architect of the Capitol shall have charge of the structural and mechanical care of the Supreme Court Building, including—

(A) the care and maintenance of the grounds; and

(B) the supplying of all mechanical furnishings and mechanical equipment for the Building.

(2) OPERATION AND MAINTENANCE.—The Architect shall direct the operation and maintenance of the mechanical equipment and repair of the building.

(3) CONTRACT AUTHORITY.—The Architect may enter into all necessary contracts to carry out this subsection.

(b) AVAILABILITY OF APPROPRIATIONS.—Amounts appropriated under—

(1) subsection (a) and sections 6112 and 6113 of this title are available for—

(A) expenses of heating and air-conditioning refrigeration supplied by the Capitol Power Plant, advancements for which shall be made and deposited in the Treasury to the credit of appropriations provided for the Capitol Power Plant; and

(B) the purchase of electrical energy; and

(2) the heading "Supreme Court of the United States" and "care of the building and grounds" are available for—

(A) improvements, maintenance, repairs, equipment, supplies, materials, and appurtenances;

(B) special clothing for workers;

(C) personal and other services (including temporary labor without regard to chapter 51, subchapter III of chapter 53, and subchapter III of chapter 83, of title 5); and

(D) without compliance with section 6101(b) to (d) of title 41—

(i) for snow removal (by hire of personnel and equipment or under contract); and

(ii) for the replacement of electrical transformers containing polychlorinated biphenyls.

(Pub. L. 107–217, Aug. 21, 2002, 116 Stat. 1180; Pub. L. 109–284, §6(18), Sept. 27, 2006, 120 Stat. 1213; Pub. L. 111–350, §5(l)(22), Jan. 4, 2011, 124 Stat. 3852.)

§6112. SUPREME COURT BUILDING AND GROUNDS EMPLOYEES

Employees required to carry out section 6111(a) of this title shall be—

(1) appointed by the Architect of the Capitol with the approval of the Chief Justice of the United States;

(2) compensated in accordance with chapter 51 and subchapter III of chapter 53 of title 5; and

(3) subject to subchapter III of chapter 83 of title 5.

(Pub. L. 107–217, Aug. 21, 2002, 116 Stat. 1181.)

§6113. DUTIES OF THE SUPERINTENDENT OF THE SUPREME COURT BUILDING

Except as provided in section 6111(a) of this title, all duties and work required for the operation, domestic care, and custody of the Supreme Court Building shall be performed under the direction of the Marshal of the Supreme Court. The Marshal serves as the superintendent of the Building.

(Pub. L. 107–217, Aug. 21, 2002, 116 Stat. 1181.)

§6114. OLIVER WENDELL HOLMES GARDEN

The Architect of the Capitol shall maintain and care for the Oliver Wendell Holmes Garden in accordance with the provisions of law on the maintenance and care of the grounds of the Supreme Court Building.

(Pub. L. 107–217, Aug. 21, 2002, 116 Stat. 1181.)

SUBCHAPTER III—POLICING AUTHORITY

§6121. GENERAL

(a) AUTHORITY OF MARSHAL OF THE SUPREME COURT AND SUPREME COURT POLICE.—In accordance with regulations prescribed by the Marshal of the Supreme Court and approved by the Chief Justice of the United States, the Marshal and the Supreme Court Police shall have authority—

(1) to police the Supreme Court Building and grounds and adjacent streets to protect individuals and property;

(2) in any location, to protect—

(A) the Chief Justice, any Associate Justice of the Supreme Court, and any official guest of the Supreme Court;

(B) any officer or employee of the Supreme Court while that officer or employee is performing official duties; and

(C) any member of the immediate family of the Chief Justice, any Associate Justice, or any officer of the Supreme Court if the Marshal determines such protection is necessary.[1]

(3) while performing duties necessary to carry out paragraph (1) or (2), to make arrests for any violation of Federal or State law and any regulation under Federal or State law; and

(4) to carry firearms as may be required while performing duties under section 6102 of this title, this subchapter, and subchapter IV.

(b) AUTHORIZATION TO CARRY FIREARMS—[2] Duties under subsection (a)(2)(A) with respect to an official guest of the Supreme Court in any location (other than the District of Columbia, Maryland, and Virginia) shall be authorized in writing by the Chief Justice or an Associate Justice, if those duties require the carrying of firearms under subsection (a)(4).

(Pub. L. 107–217, Aug. 21, 2002, 116 Stat. 1182; Pub. L. 108–356, §1, Oct. 21, 2004, 118 Stat. 1416; Pub. L. 110–402, §1(a), Oct. 13, 2008, 122 Stat. 4254; Pub. L. 113–62, §1, Dec. 20, 2013, 127 Stat. 666; Pub. L. 116–75, §2, Nov. 27, 2019, 133 Stat. 1160; Pub. L. 117–148, §2, June 16, 2022, 136 Stat. 1288.)

§122. Designation of members of the Supreme
Court Police   CHAPTER 61—UNITED STATES SUPREME
COURT BUILDING AND GROUNDS

[1] *So in original. The period probably should be a semicolon.*

[2] *So in original. The dash probably should be preceded by a period.*

§6122. DESIGNATION OF MEMBERS OF THE SUPREME COURT POLICE

Under the general supervision and direction of the Chief Justice of the United States, the Marshal of the Supreme Court may designate employees of the Supreme Court as members of the Supreme Court Police, without additional compensation.

(Pub. L. 107–217, Aug. 21, 2002, 116 Stat. 1182.)

§6123. AUTHORITY OF METROPOLITAN POLICE OF THE DISTRICT OF COLUMBIA

The Metropolitan Police of the District of Columbia may make arrests within the Supreme Court Building and grounds for a violation of federal or state law or any regulation under federal or state law. This section does not authorize the Metropolitan Police to enter the Supreme Court Building to make an arrest in response to a complaint, serve a warrant, or patrol the Supreme Court Building or grounds, unless the Metropolitan Police have been requested to do so by, or have received the consent of, the Marshal of the Supreme Court or an assistant to the Marshal.

(Pub. L. 107–217, Aug. 21, 2002, 116 Stat. 1182.)

SUBCHAPTER IV—PROHIBITIONS AND PENALTIES

§6131. PUBLIC TRAVEL IN SUPREME COURT GROUNDS

Public travel in, and occupancy of, the Supreme Court grounds is restricted to the sidewalks and other paved surfaces.

(Pub. L. 107–217, Aug. 21, 2002, 116 Stat. 1182.)

§6132. SALE OF ARTICLES, SIGNS, AND SOLICITATION IN SUPREME COURT BUILDING AND GROUNDS

It is unlawful—

(1) to offer or expose any article for sale in the Supreme Court Building or grounds;

(2) to display a sign, placard, or other form of advertisement in the Building or grounds; or

(3) to solicit fares, alms, subscriptions, or contributions in the Building or grounds.

(Pub. L. 107–217, Aug. 21, 2002, 116 Stat. 1183.)

§6133. PROPERTY IN THE SUPREME COURT BUILDING AND GROUNDS

It is unlawful to step or climb on, remove, or in any way injure any statue, seat, wall, fountain, or other erection or architectural feature, or any tree, shrub, plant, or turf, in the Supreme Court Building or grounds.

(Pub. L. 107–217, Aug. 21, 2002, 116 Stat. 1183.)

§6134. FIREARMS, FIREWORKS, SPEECHES, AND OBJECTIONABLE LANGUAGE IN THE SUPREME COURT BUILDING AND GROUNDS

It is unlawful to discharge a firearm, firework or explosive, set fire to a combustible, make a harangue or oration, or utter loud, threatening, or abusive language in the Supreme Court Building or grounds.

(Pub. L. 107–217, Aug. 21, 2002, 116 Stat. 1183.)

§6135. Parades, assemblages, and display of flags in the Supreme Court Building and grounds

It is unlawful to parade, stand, or move in processions or assemblages in the Supreme Court Building or grounds, or to display in the Building and grounds a flag, banner, or device designed or adapted to bring into public notice a party, organization, or movement.

(Pub. L. 107–217, Aug. 21, 2002, 116 Stat. 1183.)

§6136. Suspension of prohibitions against use of Supreme Court grounds

To allow the observance of authorized ceremonies in the Supreme Court Building and grounds, the Marshal of the Supreme Court may suspend for those occasions any of the prohibitions contained in this subchapter as may be necessary for the occasion if—

(1) responsible officers have been appointed; and

(2) the Marshal determines that adequate arrangements have been made—

(A) to maintain suitable order and decorum in the proceedings; and

(B) to protect the Supreme Court Building and grounds and individuals and property in the Building and grounds.

(Pub. L. 107–217, Aug. 21, 2002, 116 Stat. 1183.)

§6137. Penalties

(a) In General.—An individual who violates this subchapter, or a regulation prescribed under section 6102 of this title, shall be fined under title 18, imprisoned not more than 60 days, or both.

(b) Venue and Procedure.—Prosecution for a violation described in subsection (a) shall be in the United States District Court for the District of Columbia or in the Superior Court of the District of Columbia, on information by the United States Attorney or an Assistant United States Attorney.

(c) Offenses Involving Property Damage Over $100.—If during the commission of a violation described in subsection (a), public property is damaged in an amount exceeding $100, the period of imprisonment for the offense may be not more than five years.

(Pub. L. 107–217, Aug. 21, 2002, 116 Stat. 1183; Pub. L. 108–356, §2, Oct. 21, 2004, 118 Stat. 1416.)

★

Provisions of 40 U.S.C. Relating to Public Buildings, Grounds, and Parks in the District of Columbia

40 U.S.C.

TITLE 40—PUBLIC BUILDINGS, PROPERTY, AND WORKS

This title was enacted by Pub. L. 107–217, §1, Aug. 21, 2002, 116 Stat. 1062

* * * * * * *

SUBTITLE II—PUBLIC BUILDINGS AND WORKS

* * * * * * *

Chap. Sec.

* * * * * * *

* * * * * * *

* * * * * * *

PART D—PUBLIC BUILDINGS, GROUNDS, AND PARKS IN THE DISTRICT OF COLUMBIA

CHAPTER 81—ADMINISTRATIVE

SUBCHAPTER I—GENERAL

SUBCHAPTER II—JURISDICTION

SUBCHAPTER III—SERVICES FOR FACILITIES

SUBCHAPTER IV—MISCELLANEOUS

SUBCHAPTER I—GENERAL

§8101. SUPERVISION OF PUBLIC BUILDINGS AND GROUNDS IN DISTRICT OF COLUMBIA NOT OTHERWISE PROVIDED FOR BY LAW

(a) IN GENERAL.—Under regulations the President prescribes, the Administrator of General Services shall have charge of the public buildings and grounds in the District of Columbia, except those buildings and grounds which otherwise are provided for by law.

(b) NOTICE OF UNLAWFUL OCCUPANCY.—If the Administrator, or the officer under the direction of the Administrator who is in immediate charge of those public buildings and grounds, decides that an individual is unlawfully occupying any part of that public land, the Administrator or officer in charge shall notify the United States marshal for the District of Columbia in writing of the unlawful occupation.

(c) Ejection of Trespasser.—The marshal shall have the trespasser ejected from the public land and shall restore possession of the land to the officer charged by law with the custody of the land.

(Pub. L. 107–217, Aug. 21, 2002, 116 Stat. 1204.)

§8102. Protection of Federal Government buildings in District of Columbia

The Attorney General and the Secretary of the Treasury may prohibit—

(1) a vehicle from parking or standing on a street or roadway adjacent to a building in the District of Columbia—

(A) at least partly owned or possessed by, or leased to, the Federal Government; and

(B) used by law enforcement authorities subject to their jurisdiction; and

(2) a person or entity from conducting business on property immediately adjacent to a building described in paragraph (1).

(Pub. L. 107–217, Aug. 21, 2002, 116 Stat. 1205.)

§8103. Application of District of Columbia laws to public buildings and grounds

(a) Application of Laws.—Laws and regulations of the District of Columbia for the protection of public or private property and the preservation of peace and order are extended to all public buildings and public grounds belonging to the Federal Government in the District of Columbia.

(b) Penalties.—A person shall be fined under title 18, imprisoned for not more than six months, or both if the person—

(1) is guilty of disorderly and unlawful conduct in or about those public buildings or public grounds;

(2) willfully injures the buildings or shrubs;

(3) pull downs, impairs, or otherwise injures any fence, wall, or other enclosure;

(4) injures any sink, culvert, pipe, hydrant, cistern, lamp, or bridge; or

(5) removes any stone, gravel, sand, or other property of the Government, or any other part of the public grounds or lots belonging to the Government in the District of Columbia.

(Pub. L. 107–217, Aug. 21, 2002, 116 Stat. 1205.)

§8104. Regulation of private and semipublic buildings adjacent to public buildings and grounds

(a) Factors for Development.—In view of the provisions of the Constitution respecting the establishment of the seat of the National Government, the duties it imposed on Congress in connection with establishing the seat of the National Government, and the solicitude shown and the efforts exerted by President Washington in the planning and development of the Capital City, the development should proceed along the lines of good order, good taste, and with due regard to the public interests involved, and a reasonable degree of control should be exercised over the architecture of private or semipublic buildings adjacent to public buildings and grounds of major importance.

(b) Submission of Application to Commission of Fine Arts.—The Mayor of the

District of Columbia shall submit to the Commission of Fine Arts an application for a permit to erect or alter any building, a part of which fronts or abuts on the grounds of the Capitol, the grounds of the White House, the part of Pennsylvania Avenue extending from the Capitol to the White House, Lafayette Park, Rock Creek Park, the Zoological Park, the Rock Creek and Potomac Parkway, Potomac Park, or The Mall Park System and public buildings adjacent to the System, or abuts on any street bordering any of those grounds or parks, so far as the plans relate to height and appearance, color, and texture of the materials of exterior construction.

(c) REPORT TO MAYOR.—The Commission shall report promptly its recommendations to the Mayor, including any changes the Commission decides are necessary to prevent reasonably avoidable impairment of the public values belonging to the public building or park. If the Commission fails to report its approval or disapproval of a plan within 30 days, the report is deemed approved and a permit may be issued.

(d) ACTION BY THE MAYOR.—The Mayor shall take action the Mayor decides is necessary to effect reasonable compliance with the recommendation under subsection (c).

(Pub. L. 107–217, Aug. 21, 2002, 116 Stat. 1205; Pub. L. 109–284, §6(22), Sept. 27, 2006, 120 Stat. 1213.)

§8105. APPROVAL BY ADMINISTRATOR OF GENERAL SERVICES

Subject to applicable provisions of existing law relating to the functions in the District of Columbia of the National Capital Planning Commission and the Commission of Fine Arts, only the Administrator of General Services is required to approve sketches, plans, and estimates for buildings to be constructed by the Administrator, except that the Administrator and the United States Postal Service must approve buildings designed for post office purposes.

(Pub. L. 107–217, Aug. 21, 2002, 116 Stat. 1206; Pub. L. 109–284, §6(23), Sept. 27, 2006, 120 Stat. 1213.)

§8106. BUILDINGS ON RESERVATIONS, PARKS, OR PUBLIC GROUNDS

A building or structure shall not be erected on any reservation, park, or public grounds of the Federal Government in the District of Columbia without express authority of Congress.

(Pub. L. 107–217, Aug. 21, 2002, 116 Stat. 1206.)

§8107. ADVERTISEMENTS AND SALES IN OR AROUND WASHINGTON MONUMENT

Except on the written authority of the Director of the National Park Service, advertisements of any kind shall not be displayed, and articles of any kind shall not be sold, in or around the Washington Monument.

(Pub. L. 107–217, Aug. 21, 2002, 116 Stat. 1206.)

§8108. USE OF PUBLIC BUILDINGS FOR PUBLIC CEREMONIES

Except as expressly authorized by law, public buildings in the District of Columbia (other than the Capitol Building and the White House), and the approaches to those public buildings, shall not be used or occupied in connection with ceremonies for the inauguration of the President or other public functions.

(Pub. L. 107–217, Aug. 21, 2002, 116 Stat. 1206.)

SUBCHAPTER II—JURISDICTION

§8121. IMPROPER APPROPRIATION OF STREETS

(a) AUTHORITY.—The Secretary of the Interior shall—

(1) prevent the improper appropriation or occupation of any public street, avenue, square, or reservation in the District of Columbia that belongs to the Federal Government;

(2) reclaim the street, avenue, square, or reservation if unlawfully appropriated;

(3) prevent the erection of any permanent building on property reserved to or for the use of the Government, unless plainly authorized by law; and

(4) report to Congress at the beginning of each session on the Secretary's proceedings in the premises, together with a full statement of all property described in this subsection, and how, and, and by what authority, the property is occupied or claimed.

(b) APPLICATION.—This section does not interfere with the temporary and proper occupation of any part of the property described in subsection (a), by lawful authority, for the legitimate purposes of the Government.

(Pub. L. 107–217, Aug. 21, 2002, 116 Stat. 1206.)

§8122. JURISDICTION OVER PORTION OF CONSTITUTION AVENUE

The Director of the National Park Service has jurisdiction over that part of Constitution Avenue west of Virginia Avenue that was under the control of the Commissioners of the District of Columbia prior to May 27, 1908.

(Pub. L. 107–217, Aug. 21, 2002, 116 Stat. 1207.)

§8123. RECORD OF TRANSFER OF JURISDICTION BETWEEN DIRECTOR OF NATIONAL PARK SERVICE AND MAYOR OF DISTRICT OF COLUMBIA

When in accordance with law or mutual legal agreement, spaces or portions of public land are transferred between the jurisdiction of the Director of the National Park Service, as established by the Act of July 1, 1898 (ch. 543, 30 Stat. 570), and the Mayor of the District of Columbia, the letters of transfer and acceptance exchanged between them are sufficient authority for the necessary change in the official maps and for record when necessary.

(Pub. L. 107–217, Aug. 21, 2002, 116 Stat. 1207.)

§8124. TRANSFER OF JURISDICTION BETWEEN FEDERAL AND DISTRICT OF COLUMBIA AUTHORITIES

(a) TRANSFER OF JURISDICTION.—Federal and District of Columbia authorities administering properties in the District that are owned by the Federal Government or by the District may transfer jurisdiction over any part of the property among or between themselves for purposes of administration and maintenance under conditions the parties agree on. The National Capital Planning Commission shall recommend the transfer before it is completed.

(b) REPORT TO CONGRESS.—The District authorities shall report all transfers and agreements to Congress.

(c) CERTAIN LAWS NOT REPEALED.—Subsection (a) does not repeal any law in effect on May 20, 1932, which authorized the transfer of jurisdiction of certain land among and between federal and District authorities.

(Pub. L. 107–217, Aug. 21, 2002, 116 Stat. 1207.)

§8125. PUBLIC SPACES RESULTING FROM FILLING OF CANALS

The Director of the National Park Service has jurisdiction over all public spaces resulting from the filling of canals in the original city of Washington that were not under the jurisdiction of the Chief of Engineers of the United States Army as of August 1, 1914, except spaces included in the navy yard or in actual use as roadways and sidewalks and spaces assigned by law to the District of Columbia for use as a property yard and the location of a sewage pumping station. The spaces shall be laid out as reservations as a part of the park system of the District of Columbia.

(Pub. L. 107–217, Aug. 21, 2002, 116 Stat. 1207.)

§8126. TEMPORARY OCCUPANCY OF POTOMAC PARK BY SECRETARY OF AGRICULTURE

(a) NOT MORE THAN 75 ACRES.—The Director of the National Park Service may allow the Secretary of Agriculture to temporarily occupy as a testing ground not more than 75 acres of Potomac Park not needed in any one season for reclamation or park improvement. The Secretary shall vacate the area at the close of any season on the request of the Director.

(b) CONTINUE AS PUBLIC PARK UNDER DIRECTOR.—This section does not change the essential character of the land used, which shall continue to be a public park under the charge of the Director.

(Pub. L. 107–217, Aug. 21, 2002, 116 Stat. 1207.)

§8127. PART OF WASHINGTON AQUEDUCT FOR PLAYGROUND PURPOSES

(a) JURISDICTION OF MAYOR.—The Mayor of the District of Columbia has possession, control, and jurisdiction of the land of the Washington Aqueduct adjacent to the Champlain Avenue pumping station and lying outside of the fence around the pumping station as it—

(1) existed on August 31, 1918; and

(2) was transferred by the Chief of Engineers for playground purposes.

(b) JURISDICTION OF SECRETARY OF THE ARMY NOT AFFECTED.—This section does not affect the superintendence and control of the Secretary of the Army over the Washington Aqueduct and the rights, appurtenances, and fixtures connected with the Aqueduct.

(Pub. L. 107–217, Aug. 21, 2002, 116 Stat. 1208.)

SUBCHAPTER III—SERVICES FOR FACILITIES

§8141. CONTRACT TO RENT BUILDINGS IN THE DISTRICT OF COLUMBIA NOT TO BE MADE UNTIL APPROPRIATION ENACTED

A contract shall not be made for the rent of a building, or part of a building, to be used for the purposes of the Federal Government in the District of Columbia until Congress enacts an appropriation for the rent. This section is deemed to be notice to all contractors or lessors of the building or a part of the building.

(Pub. L. 107–217, Aug. 21, 2002, 116 Stat. 1208.)

§8142. RENT OF OTHER BUILDINGS

An executive department of the Federal Government renting a building for public use in the District of Columbia may rent a different building instead if it is in the public interest to do so. This section does not authorize an increase in the number of buildings in use or in the amount paid for rent.

(Pub. L. 107–217, Aug. 21, 2002, 116 Stat. 1208.)

§8143. HEAT

(a) CORCORAN GALLERY OF ART.—The Administrator of General Services may furnish heat from the central heating plant to the Corcoran Gallery of Art, if the Corcoran Gallery of Art agrees to—

(1) pay for heat furnished at rates the Administrator determines; and

(2) connect the building with the Federal Government mains in a manner satisfactory to the Administrator.

(b) BOARD OF GOVERNORS OF THE FEDERAL RESERVE SYSTEM.—The Administrator may furnish steam from the central heating plant for the use of the Board of Governors of the Federal Reserve System on the property which the Board acquired in squares east of 87 and east of 88 in the District of Columbia if the Board agrees to—

(1) pay for the steam furnished at reasonable rates the Administrator determines but that are at least equal to cost; and

(2) provide the necessary connections with the Government mains at its own expense and in a manner satisfactory to the Administrator.

(c) NON-FEDERAL PUBLIC BUILDINGS.—The Administrator shall determine the rates to be paid for steam furnished to the Corcoran Gallery of Art, the Pan American Union Buildings, the American Red Cross Buildings, and other non-federal public buildings authorized to receive steam from the central heating plant.

(Pub. L. 107–217, Aug. 21, 2002, 116 Stat. 1208.)

§8144. DELIVERY OF FUEL FOR USE DURING ENSUING FISCAL YEAR

During April, May, and June of each year, the Administrator of General Services may deliver to all branches of the Federal Government and the government of the District of Columbia as much fuel for their use during the following fiscal year as may be practicable to store at the points of consumption. The branches of the Federal Government and the government of the District of Columbia shall pay for the fuel from their applicable appropriations for that fiscal year.

(Pub. L. 107–217, Aug. 21, 2002, 116 Stat. 1209.)

SUBCHAPTER IV—MISCELLANEOUS

§8161. RESERVATION OF PARKING SPACES FOR MEMBERS OF CONGRESS

The Council of the District of Columbia shall designate, reserve, and properly mark appropriate and sufficient parking spaces on the streets adjacent to all public buildings in the District for the use of Members of Congress engaged in public business.

(Pub. L. 107–217, Aug. 21, 2002, 116 Stat. 1209.)

§8162. AILANTHUS TREES PROHIBITED

Ailanthus trees shall not be purchased for, or planted in, the public grounds.

(Pub. L. 107–217, Aug. 21, 2002, 116 Stat. 1209.)

§8163. USE OF GREENHOUSES AND NURSERY FOR TREES, SHRUBS, AND PLANTS

The greenhouses and nursery shall be used only for the propagation of trees, shrubs, and plants suitable for planting in the public reservations. Only those trees, shrubs, and plants shall be planted in the public reservations.

(Pub. L. 107–217, Aug. 21, 2002, 116 Stat. 1209.)

§8164. E. BARRETT PRETTYMAN UNITED STATES COURTHOUSE

(a) OPERATION, MAINTENANCE, AND REPAIR.—The operation, maintenance, and repair of the E. Barrett Prettyman United States Courthouse, used by the United States Court of Appeals for the District of Columbia and the United States District Court for the District of Columbia, is under the control of the Administrator of General Services.

(b) ALLOCATION OF SPACE.—The allocation of space in the Courthouse is vested in the chief judge of the United States Court of Appeals for the District of Columbia and the chief judge of the United States District Court for the District of Columbia.

(Pub. L. 107–217, Aug. 21, 2002, 116 Stat. 1209.)

§8165. SERVICES FOR OFFICE OF PERSONNEL MANAGEMENT

For carrying out the work of the Director of the Office of Personnel Management and the examinations provided for in sections 3304 and 3305 of title 5, the Administrator of General Services shall—

(1) assign or provide suitable and convenient rooms and accommodations, which are furnished, heated, and lighted, in Washington, D.C.;

(2) supply necessary stationery and other articles; and

(3) arrange for or provide necessary printing.

(Pub. L. 107–217, Aug. 21, 2002, 116 Stat. 1210.)

CHAPTER 83—WASHINGTON METROPOLITAN REGION DEVELOPMENT

§8301. DEFINITION

In this chapter, the term "Washington metropolitan region" includes the District of Columbia, the counties of Montgomery and Prince Georges in Maryland, and the counties of Arlington and Fairfax and the cities of Alexandria and Falls Church in Virginia.

(Pub. L. 107–217, Aug. 21, 2002, 116 Stat. 1210.)

§8302. NECESSITY FOR COORDINATION IN THE DEVELOPMENT OF THE WASHINGTON METROPOLITAN REGION

Because the District of Columbia is the seat of the Federal Government and has become the urban center of a rapidly expanding Washington metropolitan region, the necessity for the continued and effective performance of the functions of the Government in the District of Columbia, the general welfare of the District of Columbia, the health and living standards of the people residing or working in the District of Columbia, and the conduct of industry, trade, and commerce in the District of Columbia require that to the fullest extent possible the development of the District of Columbia and the management of its public affairs, and the activities of the departments, agencies, and instrumentalities of the Government which may be carried out in, or in relation to, the other areas of the Washington metropolitan region, shall be coordinated with the development of those other areas and with the management of their public affairs so that, with the cooperation and assistance of those other areas, all of the areas in the Washington metropolitan area shall be developed and their public affairs shall be managed so as to contribute effectively toward the solution of the community development problems of the Washington metropolitan region on a unified metropolitan basis.

(Pub. L. 107–217, Aug. 21, 2002, 116 Stat. 1210.)

§8303. DECLARATION OF POLICY OF COORDINATED DEVELOPMENT AND MANAGEMENT

The policy to be followed for the attainment of the objective established by section 8302 of this title, and for the more effective exercise by Congress, the executive branch of the Federal Government, the Mayor of the District of Columbia, and all other officers, agencies, and instrumentalities of the District of Columbia of their respective functions, powers, and duties in respect of the Washington metropolitan region, shall be that the functions, powers, and duties shall be exercised and carried out in a manner that (with proper recognition of the sovereignty of Maryland and Virginia in respect of those areas of the Washington metropolitan region that are located within their respective jurisdictions) will best facilitate the attainment of the coordinated development of the areas of the Washington metropolitan area and the coordinated management of their public affairs so as to contribute effectively to the solution of the community development problems of the Washington metropolitan region on a unified metropolitan basis.

(Pub. L. 107–217, Aug. 21, 2002, 116 Stat. 1210.)

§8304. PRIORITY PROJECTS

In carrying out the policy pursuant to section 8303 of this title for the attainment of the objective established by section 8302 of this title, priority should be given to the solution, on a unified metropolitan basis, of the problems of water supply, sewage disposal, and water pollution and transportation.

(Pub. L. 107–217, Aug. 21, 2002, 116 Stat. 1211.)

CHAPTER 85—NATIONAL CAPITAL SERVICE AREA AND DIRECTOR

Sec.

§8501. NATIONAL CAPITAL SERVICE AREA

(a) ESTABLISHMENT.—

(1) BOUNDARIES.—The National Capital Service Area is in the District of Columbia and includes the principal federal monuments, the White House, the Capitol Building, the United States Supreme Court Building, and the federal executive, legislative, and judicial office buildings located adjacent to the Mall and the Capitol Building, and is more particularly described as the area bounded as follows:

Beginning at that point on the present Virginia-District of Columbia boundary due west of the northernmost point of Theodore Roosevelt Island and running due east to the eastern shore of the Potomac River;

thence generally south along the shore at the mean high water mark to the northwest corner of the Kennedy Center;

thence east along the northern side of the Kennedy Center to a point where it reaches the E Street Expressway;

thence east on the expressway to E Street Northwest and thence east on E Street Northwest to Eighteenth Street Northwest;

thence south on Eighteenth Street Northwest to Constitution Avenue Northwest;

thence east on Constitution Avenue to Seventeenth Street Northwest;

thence north on Seventeenth Street Northwest to Pennsylvania Avenue Northwest;

thence east on Pennsylvania Avenue to Jackson Place Northwest;

thence north on Jackson Place to H Street Northwest;

thence east on H Street Northwest to Madison Place Northwest;

thence south on Madison Place Northwest to Pennsylvania Avenue Northwest;

thence east on Pennsylvania Avenue Northwest to Fifteenth Street Northwest;

thence south on Fifteenth Street Northwest to Pennsylvania Avenue Northwest;

thence southeast on Pennsylvania Avenue Northwest to John Marshall Place Northwest;

thence north on John Marshall Place Northwest to C Street Northwest;

thence east on C Street Northwest to Third Street Northwest;

thence north on Third Street Northwest to D Street Northwest;

thence east on D Street Northwest to Second Street Northwest;

thence south on Second Street Northwest to the intersection of Constitution Avenue Northwest and Louisiana Avenue Northwest;

thence northeast on Louisiana Avenue Northwest to North Capitol Street;

thence north on North Capitol Street to Massachusetts Avenue Northwest;

thence southeast on Massachusetts Avenue Northwest so as to encompass Union Square;

thence following Union Square to F Street Northeast;

thence east on F Street Northeast to Second Street Northeast;

thence south on Second Street Northeast to D Street Northeast;

thence west on D Street Northeast to First Street Northeast;

thence south on First Street Northeast to Maryland Avenue Northeast;

thence generally north and east on Maryland Avenue to Second Street Northeast;

thence south on Second Street Northeast to C Street Southeast;

thence west on C Street Southeast to New Jersey Avenue Southeast;

thence south on New Jersey Avenue Southeast to D Street Southeast;

thence west on D Street Southeast to Canal Street Parkway;

thence southeast on Canal Street Parkway to E Street Southeast;

thence west on E Street Southeast to the intersection of Washington Avenue Southwest and South Capitol Street;

thence northwest on Washington Avenue Southwest to Second Street Southwest;

thence south on Second Street Southwest to Virginia Avenue Southwest;

thence generally west on Virginia Avenue to Third Street Southwest;

thence north on Third Street Southwest to C Street Southwest;

thence west on C Street Southwest to Sixth Street Southwest;

thence north on Sixth Street Southwest to Independence Avenue;

thence west on Independence Avenue to Twelfth Street Southwest;

thence south on Twelfth Street Southwest to D Street Southwest;

thence west on D Street Southwest to Fourteenth Street Southwest;

thence south on Fourteenth Street Southwest to the middle of the Washington Channel;

thence generally south and east along the mid-channel of the Washington Channel to a point due west of the northern boundary line of Fort Lesley McNair;

thence due east to the side of the Washington Channel;

thence following generally south and east along the side of the Washington Channel at the mean high water mark, to the point of confluence with the Anacostia River, and along the northern shore at the mean high water mark to the northern most point of the Eleventh Street Bridge;

thence generally south and east along the northern side of the Eleventh Street Bridge to the eastern shore of the Anacostia River;

thence generally south and west along such shore at the mean high water mark to the point of confluence of the Anacostia and Potomac Rivers;

thence generally south along the eastern shore at the mean high water mark of the Potomac River to the point where it meets the present southeastern boundary line of the District of Columbia;

thence south and west along such southeastern boundary line to the point where it meets the present Virginia-District of Columbia boundary;

thence generally north and west up the Potomac River along the Virginia-District of Columbia boundary to the point of beginning.

(2) STREETS AND SIDEWALKS INCLUDED.—Where the area in paragraph (1) is bounded by a street, the street, and any sidewalk of the street, are included in the area.

(3) FEDERAL PROPERTY THAT AFFRONTED OR ABUTTED THE AREA DEEMED TO BE IN THE AREA.—Federal real property that on December 24, 1973, affronted or abutted the

414

area described in paragraph (1) is deemed to be in the area. For the purposes of this paragraph, federal real property affronting or abutting the area described in paragraph (1)—

(A) is deemed to include Fort Lesley McNair, the Washington Navy Yard, the Anacostia Naval Annex, the United States Naval Station, Bolling Air Force Base, and the Naval Research Laboratory; and

(B) does not include any area situated outside of the District of Columbia boundary as it existed immediately prior to December 24, 1973, any part of the Anacostia Park situated east of the northern side of the Eleventh Street Bridge, or any part of the Rock Creek Park.

(b) APPLICABILITY OF OTHER PROVISIONS.—

(1) PROVISIONS COVERING BUILDINGS AND GROUNDS IN AREA NOT AFFECTED.—Except to the extent specifically provided by this section, this section does not—

(A) apply to the United States Capitol Buildings and Grounds as defined and described in sections 5101 and 5102 of this title, any other buildings and grounds under the care of the Architect of the Capitol, the Supreme Court Building and grounds as described in section 6101 of this title, and the Library of Congress buildings and grounds as defined in section 11 of the Act of August 4, 1950 (2 U.S.C. 167j); and

(B) repeal, amend, alter, modify, or supersede—

(i) chapter 51 of this title, section 9, 9A, 9B, 9C or 14 of the Act of July 31, 1946 (ch. 707, 60 Stat. 719, 720), any other general law of the United States, any law enacted by Congress and applicable exclusively to the District of Columbia, or any rule or regulation prescribed pursuant to any of those provisions, that was in effect on January 1, 1975, and that pertained to those buildings and grounds; or

(ii) any authority which existed on December 24, 1973, with respect to those buildings and grounds and was vested on January 1, 1975, in the Senate, the House of Representatives, Congress, any committee, commission, or board of the Senate, the House of Representatives, or Congress, the Architect of the Capitol or any other officer of the legislative branch, the Chief Justice of the United States, the Marshal of the Supreme Court, or the Librarian of Congress.

(2) CONTINUED APPLICATION OF LAWS, REGULATIONS, AND RULES.—Except to the extent otherwise specifically provided in this section, all general laws of the United States and all laws enacted by the Congress and applicable exclusively to the District of Columbia, including regulations and rules prescribed pursuant to any of those laws, that were in effect on January 1, 1975, and which applied to and in the areas included in the National Capital Service Area pursuant to this section continue to be applicable to and in the National Capital Service Area in the same manner and to the same extent as if this section had not been enacted and remain applicable until repealed, amended, altered, modified, or superseded.

(c) AVAILABILITY OF SERVICES AND FACILITIES.—As far as practicable, any service or facility authorized by the District of Columbia Home Rule Act (Public Law 93–198, 87 Stat. 774) to be rendered or furnished (including maintenance of streets and highways, and services under section 1537 of title 31) shall be made available to the Senate, the House of Representatives, Congress, any committee, commission, or board of the Senate, the House of Representatives, or Congress, the Architect of the Capitol, any other officer of the legislative branch who on January 1, 1975, was vested with authority over those buildings and grounds, the Chief Justice of the United States, the Marshal of the Supreme Court, and the Librarian of Congress on their request. If payment would be required for the rendition or furnishing of a similar service or facility to any other federal agency, the recipient, on presentation of proper vouchers and as agreed on by the parties, shall pay for the service or facility in advance or by reimbursement.

(d) RIGHT TO PARTICIPATE IN ELECTION NOT AFFECTED BY RESIDENCY.—An individual may not be denied the right to vote or otherwise participate in any manner in any election in the District of Columbia solely because the individual resides in the National Capital Service Area.

(Pub. L. 107–217, Aug. 21, 2002, 116 Stat. 1211; Pub. L. 109–284, §6(24), Sept. 27, 2006, 120 Stat. 1213.)

§8502. NATIONAL CAPITAL SERVICE DIRECTOR

(a) ESTABLISHMENT AND COMPENSATION.—There is in the Executive Office of the President the National Capital Service Director who shall be appointed by the President. The Director shall receive compensation at the maximum rate established for level IV of the Executive Schedule under section 5315 of title 5.

(b) PERSONNEL.—The Director may appoint and fix the rate of compensation of necessary personnel, subject to chapters 33 and 51 and subchapter III of chapter 53 of title 5.

(c) DUTIES.—

(1) PRESIDENT.—The President, through the Director and using District of Columbia governmental services to the extent practicable, shall ensure that there is provided in the area described in section 8501(a) of this title adequate fire protection and sanitation services.

(2) DIRECTOR.—Except with respect to that part of the National Capital Service Area comprising the United States Capitol Buildings and Grounds as defined and described in sections 5101 and 5102 of this title, the Supreme Court Building and grounds as described in section 6101 of this title, and the Library of Congress buildings and grounds as defined in section 11 of the Act of August 4, 1950 (2 U.S.C. 167j), the Director shall ensure that there is provided in the remainder of the area described in section 8501(a) of this title adequate police protection and maintenance of streets and highways.

(Pub. L. 107–217, Aug. 21, 2002, 116 Stat. 1215; Pub. L. 109–284, §6(25), (26), Sept. 27, 2006, 120 Stat. 1213.)

CHAPTER 87—PHYSICAL DEVELOPMENT OF NATIONAL CAPITAL REGION

SUBCHAPTER I—GENERAL

SUBCHAPTER I—GENERAL

§8701. FINDINGS AND PURPOSES

(a) FINDINGS.—Congress finds that—

(1) the location of the seat of government in the District of Columbia has brought about the development of a metropolitan region extending well into adjoining territory in Maryland and Virginia;

(2) effective comprehensive planning is necessary on a regional basis and of continuing importance to the federal establishment;

(3) the distribution of federal installations throughout the region has been and will continue to be a major influence in determining the extent and character of development;

(4) there is needed a central planning agency for the National Capital region to coordinate certain developmental activities of the many different agencies of the Federal and District of Columbia Governments so that those activities may conform with general objectives;

(5) there is an increasing mutuality of interest and responsibility between the various levels of government that calls for coordinate and unified policies in planning

both federal and local development in the interest of order and economy;

(6) there are developmental problems of an interstate character, the planning of which requires collaboration between federal, state, and local governments in the interest of equity and constructive action; and

(7) the instrumentalities and procedures provided in this chapter will aid in providing Congress with information and advice requisite to legislation.

(b) PURPOSES.—

(1) IN GENERAL.—The purposes of this chapter (except sections 8733–8736) are—

(A) to secure comprehensive planning for the physical development of the National Capital and its environs;

(B) to provide for the participation of the appropriate planning agencies of the environs in the planning; and

(C) to establish the agency and procedures requisite to the administration of the functions of the Federal and District Governments related to the planning.

(2) OBJECTIVE.—The general objective of this chapter (except sections 8733–8736) is to enable appropriate agencies to plan for the development of the federal establishment at the seat of government in a manner—

(A) consistent with the nature and function of the National Capital and with due regard for the rights and prerogatives of the adjoining States and local governments to exercise control appropriate to their functions; and

(B) which will, in accordance with present and future needs, best promote public health, safety, morals, order, convenience, prosperity, and the general welfare, as well as efficiency and economy in the process of development.

(Pub. L. 107–217, Aug. 21, 2002, 116 Stat. 1216.)

§8702. DEFINITIONS

In this chapter—

(1) ENVIRONS.—The term "environs" means the territory surrounding the District of Columbia included in the National Capital region.

(2) NATIONAL CAPITAL.—The term "National Capital" means the District of Columbia and territory the Federal Government owns in the environs.

(3) NATIONAL CAPITAL REGION.—The term "National Capital region" means—

(A) the District of Columbia;

(B) Montgomery and Prince Georges Counties in Maryland;

(C) Arlington, Fairfax, Loudoun, and Prince William Counties in Virginia; and

(D) all cities in Maryland or Virginia in the geographic area bounded by the outer boundaries of the combined area of the counties listed in subparagraphs (B) and (C).

(4) PLANNING AGENCY.—The term "planning agency" means any city, county, bi-county, part-county, or regional planning agency authorized under state and local laws to make and adopt comprehensive plans.

(Pub. L. 107–217, Aug. 21, 2002, 116 Stat. 1216.)

SUBCHAPTER II—PLANNING AGENCIES

§8711. National Capital Planning Commission

(a) Establishment and Purpose.—The National Capital Planning Commission is the central federal planning agency for the Federal Government in the National Capital, created to preserve the important historical and natural features of the National Capital, except for the United States Capitol Buildings and Grounds (as defined and described in sections 5101 and 5102 of this title), any extension of, or additions to, those Buildings and Grounds, and buildings and grounds under the care of the Architect of the Capitol.

(b) Composition.—

(1) Membership.—The National Capital Planning Commission is composed of—

(A) ex officio, the Secretary of the Interior, the Secretary of Defense, the Administrator of General Services, the Mayor of the District of Columbia, the Chairman of the Council of the District of Columbia, the chairman of the Committee on Governmental Affairs of the Senate, and the chairman of the Committee on Government Reform of the House of Representatives, or an alternate any of those individuals designates; and

(B) five citizens with experience in city or regional planning, three of whom shall be appointed by the President and two of whom shall be appointed by the Mayor.

(2) Residency requirement.—The citizen members appointed by the Mayor shall be residents of the District of Columbia. Of the three appointed by the President, at least one shall be a resident of Virginia and at least one shall be a resident of Maryland.

(3) Terms.—An individual appointed by the President serves for six years. An individual appointed by the Mayor serves for four years. An individual appointed to fill a vacancy shall be appointed only for the unexpired term of the individual being replaced.

(4) Pay and expenses.—Citizen members are entitled to $100 a day when performing duties vested in the Commission and to reimbursement for necessary expenses incurred in performing those duties.

(c) Chairman and Officers.—The President shall designate the Chairman of the National Capital Planning Commission. The Commission may elect from among its members other officers as it considers desirable.

(d) Personnel.—The National Capital Planning Commission may employ a Director, an executive officer, and other technical and administrative personnel as it considers necessary. Without regard to section 6101(b) to (d) of title 41 and section 3109, chapters 33 and 51, and subchapter III of chapter 53, of title 5, the Commission may employ, by contract or otherwise, the temporary or intermittent (not more than one year) services of city planners, architects, engineers, appraisers, and other experts or organizations of experts, as may be necessary to carry out its functions. The Commission shall fix the rate of compensation so as not to exceed the rate usual for similar services.

(e) Principal Duties.—The principal duties of the National Capital Planning Commission include—

(1) preparing, adopting, and amending a comprehensive plan for the federal activities in the National Capital and making related recommendations to the

appropriate developmental agencies; and

(2) serving as the central planning agency for the Government within the National Capital region and reviewing the development programs of the developmental agencies to advise as to consistency with the comprehensive plan.

(f) TRANSFER OF OTHER FUNCTIONS, POWERS, AND DUTIES.—The National Capital Planning Commission shall carry out all other functions, powers, and duties of the National Capital Park and Planning Commission, including those formerly vested in the Highway Commission established by the Act of March 2, 1893 (ch. 197, 27 Stat. 532), and those formerly vested in the National Capital Park Commission by the Act of June 6, 1924 (ch. 270, 43 Stat. 463).

(g) ESTIMATE.—The National Capital Planning Commission shall submit to the Office of Management and Budget before December 16 of each year its estimate of the total amount to be appropriated for expenditure under this chapter (except sections 8732–8736) during the next fiscal year.

(h) FEES.—The National Capital Planning Commission may charge fees to cover the full cost of Geographic Information System products and services the Commission supplies. The fees shall be credited to the applicable appropriation account as an offsetting collection and remain available until expended.

(Pub. L. 107–217, Aug. 21, 2002, 116 Stat. 1217; Pub. L. 109–284, §6(27), Sept. 27, 2006, 120 Stat. 1213; Pub. L. 111–350, §5(l)(23), Jan. 4, 2011, 124 Stat. 3852.)

§8712. MAYOR OF THE DISTRICT OF COLUMBIA

(a) PLANNING RESPONSIBILITIES.—The Mayor of the District of Columbia is the central planning agency for the government of the District of Columbia in the National Capital and is responsible for coordinating the planning activities of the District government and for preparing and implementing the District elements of the comprehensive plan for the National Capital, which may include land use elements, urban renewal and redevelopment elements, a multiyear program of public works for the District, and physical, social, economic, transportation, and population elements. The Mayor's planning responsibility shall not extend to—

(1) federal or international projects and developments in the District, as determined by the National Capital Planning Commission; or

(2) the United States Capitol Buildings and Grounds as defined and described in sections 5101 and 5102 of this title, any extension of, or additions to, those Buildings and Grounds, and buildings and grounds under the care of the Architect of the Capitol.

(b) PARTICIPATION AND CONSULTATION.—In carrying out the responsibilities under this section and section 8721 of this title, the Mayor shall establish procedures for citizen participation in the planning process and for appropriate meaningful consultation with any state or local government or planning agency in the National Capital region affected by any aspect of a comprehensive plan, including amendments, affecting or relating to the District.

(Pub. L. 107–217, Aug. 21, 2002, 116 Stat. 1218; Pub. L. 109–284, §6(28), Sept. 27, 2006, 120 Stat. 1213.)

SUBCHAPTER III—PLANNING PROCESS

§8721. Comprehensive plan for the National Capital

(a) Preparation and Adoption by Commission.—The National Capital Planning Commission shall prepare and adopt a comprehensive, consistent, and coordinated plan for the National Capital. The plan shall include the Commission's recommendations or proposals for federal developments or projects in the environs and District elements of the comprehensive plan, or amendments to the elements, adopted by the Council of the District of Columbia and with respect to which the Commission has not determined a negative impact exists. Those elements or amendments shall be incorporated into the comprehensive plan without change. The Commission may include in its plan any part of a plan adopted by any planning agency in the environs and may make recommendations of collateral interest to the agencies. The Commission may adopt any part of an element. The Commission shall review and may amend or extend the plan so that its recommendations may be kept up to date.

(b) Review by District of Columbia.—The Mayor of the District of Columbia shall submit each District element of the comprehensive plan, and any amendment, to the Council for revision or modification, and adoption, by act, following public hearings. Following adoption and prior to implementation, the Council shall submit each element or amendment to the Commission for review and comment with regard to the impact of the element or amendment on the interests or functions of the federal establishment in the National Capital.

(c) Commission Response to Council Action.—

(1) Period of review.—Within 60 days after receiving an element or amendment from the Council, the Commission shall certify to the Council whether the element or amendment has a negative impact on the interests or functions of the federal establishment in the National Capital.

(2) No negative impact.—If the Commission takes no action in the 60-day period, the element or amendment is deemed to have no negative impact and shall be incorporated into the comprehensive plan for the National Capital and implemented.

(3) Negative impact.—

(A) Certification to council.—If the Commission finds a negative impact, it shall certify its findings and recommendations to the Council.

(B) Response of council.—On receipt of the Commission's findings and recommendations, the Council may—

(i) accept the findings and recommendations and modify the element or amendment accordingly; or

(ii) reject the findings and recommendations and resubmit a modified form of the element or amendment to the Commission for reconsideration.

(C) Findings and recommendations accepted.—If the Council accepts the findings and recommendations and modifies the element or amendment, the Council shall submit the element or amendment to the Commission for the Commission to determine whether the modification has been made in accordance with the Commission's findings and recommendations. If the Commission does not act on the modified element or amendment within 30 days after receiving it, the element or amendment is deemed to have been modified in accordance with the findings and recommendations and shall be incorporated into the comprehensive plan for the National Capital and implemented. If within the 30-day period the Commission again determines the element or amendment has a negative impact on the functions or interests of the federal establishment in the National Capital, the element or amendment shall not be implemented.

(D) FINDINGS AND RECOMMENDATIONS REJECTED.—If the Council rejects the findings and recommendations and resubmits a modified element or amendment, the Commission, within 60 days after receiving it, shall decide whether the modified element or amendment has a negative impact on the interests or functions of the federal establishment within the National Capital. If the Commission does not act within the 60-day period, the modified element or amendment is deemed to have no negative impact and shall be incorporated into the comprehensive plan and implemented. If the Commission finds a negative impact, it shall certify its findings (in sufficient detail that the Council can understand the basis of the objection of the Commission) and recommendations to the Council and the element or amendment shall not be implemented.

(d) RESUBMISSION DEEMED NEW ELEMENT OR AMENDMENT.—Any element or amendment which the Commission has determined has a negative impact on the federal establishment in the National Capital which is submitted again in a modified form not less than one year from the day it was last rejected by the Commission is deemed to be a new element or amendment for purposes of the review procedure specified in this section.

(e) REVIEW, HEARINGS, AND CITIZEN ADVISORY COUNCILS.—

(1) REVIEW.—Before the comprehensive plan, any element of the plan, or any revision is adopted, the Commission shall present the plan, element, or revision to the appropriate federal or District of Columbia authorities for comment and recommendations. The Commission may present the proposed revisions annually in a consolidated form. Recommendations by federal and District of Columbia authorities are not binding on the Commission, but the Commission shall give careful consideration to any views and recommendations submitted prior to final adoption.

(2) HEARINGS AND CITIZEN ADVISORY COUNCILS.—The Commission—

(A) may provide periodic opportunity for review and comments by nongovernmental agencies or groups through public hearings, meetings, or conferences, exhibitions, and publication of its plans; and

(B) in consultation with the Council, may encourage the formation of citizen advisory councils.

(f) EXTENSION OF TIME LIMITATIONS.—On request of the Commission, the Council may grant an extension of any time limitation contained in this section.

(g) PUBLISHING COMPREHENSIVE PLAN.—As appropriate, the Commission and the Mayor jointly shall publish a comprehensive plan for the National Capital, consisting of the elements of the comprehensive plan for the federal activities in the National Capital developed by the Commission and the District elements developed by the Mayor and the Council in accordance with this section.

(h) PROCEDURES FOR CONSULTATION.—

(1) COMMISSION AND MAYOR.—The Commission and the Mayor jointly shall

establish procedures for appropriate meaningful continuing consultation throughout the planning process for the National Capital.

(2) GOVERNMENT AGENCIES.—In order that the National Capital may be developed in accordance with the comprehensive plan, the Commission, with the consent of each agency concerned as to its representation, may establish advisory and coordinating committees composed of representatives of agencies of the Federal and District of Columbia Governments as may be necessary or helpful to obtain the maximum amount of cooperation and correlation of effort among the various agencies. As it considers appropriate, the Commission may invite representatives of the planning and developmental agencies of the environs to participate in the work of the committees.

(Pub. L. 107–217, Aug. 21, 2002, 116 Stat. 1219.)

§8722. PROPOSED FEDERAL AND DISTRICT DEVELOPMENTS AND PROJECTS

(a) AGENCIES TO USE COMMISSION AS CENTRAL PLANNING AGENCY.—Agencies of the Federal Government responsible for public developments and projects shall cooperate and correlate their efforts by using the National Capital Planning Commission as the central planning agency for federal activities in the National Capital region. To aid the Commission in carrying out this function, federal and District of Columbia governmental agencies on request of the Commission shall furnish plans, data, and records the Commission requires. The Commission on request shall furnish related plans, data, and records to federal and District of Columbia governmental agencies.

(b) CONSULTATION BETWEEN AGENCIES AND COMMISSION.—

(1) BEFORE CONSTRUCTION PLANS PREPARED.—To ensure the comprehensive planning and orderly development of the National Capital, a federal or District of Columbia agency, before preparing construction plans the agency originates for proposed developments and projects or before making a commitment to acquire land, to be paid for at least in part from federal or District amounts, shall advise and consult with the Commission as the agency prepares plans and programs in preliminary and successive stages that affect the plan and development of the National Capital. After receiving the plans, maps, and data, the Commission promptly shall make a preliminary report and recommendations to the agency. If the agency, after considering the report and recommendations of the Commission, does not agree, it shall advise the Commission and provide the reasons why it does not agree. The Commission then shall submit a final report. After consultation and suitable consideration of the views of the Commission, the agency may proceed to take action in accordance with its legal responsibilities and authority.

(2) EXCEPTIONS.—

(A) IN GENERAL.—Paragraph (1) does not apply to projects within the Capitol grounds or to structures erected by the Department of Defense during wartime or national emergency within existing military, naval, or Air Force reservations, except that the appropriate defense agency shall consult with the Commission as to any developments which materially affect traffic or require coordinated planning of the surrounding area.

(B) ADVANCE DECISIONS OF COMMISSION.—The Commission shall determine in advance the type or kinds of plans, developments, projects, improvements, or acquisitions which do not need to be submitted for review by the Commission as to conformity with its plans.

(c) ADDITIONAL PROCEDURE FOR DEVELOPMENTS AND PROJECTS WITHIN ENVIRONS.—

(1) SUBMISSION TO COMMISSION.—Within the environs, general plans showing the location, character, and extent of, and intensity of use for, proposed federal and District developments and projects involving the acquisition of land shall be submitted to the Commission for report and recommendations before a final commitment to the acquisition is made, unless the matter specifically has been approved by law.

(2) COMMISSION ACTION.—Before acting on any general plan, the Commission shall advise and consult with the appropriate planning agency having jurisdiction over the affected part of the environs. When the Commission decides that proposed developments or projects submitted to the Commission under subsection (b) involve a major change in the character or intensity of an existing use in the environs, the Commission shall advise and consult with the planning agency. The report and recommendations shall be submitted within 60 days and shall be accompanied by any reports or recommendations of the planning agency.

(3) WORKING WITH STATE OR LOCAL AUTHORITY OR AGENCY.—In carrying out its planning functions with respect to federal developments or projects in the environs, the Commission may work with, and make agreements with, any state or local authority or planning agency as the Commission considers necessary to have a plan or proposal adopted and carried out.

(d) APPROVAL OF FEDERAL PUBLIC BUILDINGS.—The provisions of the Act of June 20, 1938 (ch. 534, 52 Stat. 797) shall not apply to federal public buildings. In order to ensure the orderly development of the National Capital, the location, height, bulk, number of stories, and size of federal public buildings in the District of Columbia and the provision for open space in and around federal public buildings in the District of Columbia are subject to the approval of the Commission.

(e) APPROVAL OF DISTRICT GOVERNMENT BUILDINGS IN CENTRAL AREA.—Subsection (d) is extended to include public buildings erected by any agency of the Government of the District of Columbia in the central area of the District (as defined by concurrent action of the Commission and the Council of the District of Columbia), except that the Commission shall transmit its approval or disapproval within 30 days after the day the proposal was submitted to the Commission.

(Pub. L. 107–217, Aug. 21, 2002, 116 Stat. 1221; Pub. L. 109–284, §6(29), Sept. 27, 2006, 120 Stat. 1213.)

§8723. CAPITAL IMPROVEMENTS

(a) SIX-YEAR PROGRAM OF PUBLIC WORKS PROJECTS.—The National Capital Planning Commission shall recommend a six-year program of public works projects for the Federal Government which the Commission shall review annually with the agencies concerned. Each federal agency shall submit to the Commission in the first quarter of each fiscal year a copy of its advance program of capital improvements within the National Capital and its environs.

(b) SUBMISSION OF MULTIYEAR CAPITAL IMPROVEMENT PLAN.—By February 1 of each year, the Mayor of the District of Columbia shall submit to the Commission a copy of the multiyear capital improvements plan for the District of Columbia that the Mayor develops under section 444 of the District of Columbia Home Rule Act (Public Law 93–198, 87 Stat. 800). The Commission has 30 days in which to comment on the plan but may not change or disapprove of the plan.

(Pub. L. 107–217, Aug. 21, 2002, 116 Stat. 1223.)

§8724. ZONING REGULATIONS AND MAPS

(a) AMENDMENTS OF ZONING REGULATIONS AND MAPS.—The National Capital Planning Commission may make a report and recommendation to the Zoning Commission of the District of Columbia, as provided in section 5 of the Act of June 20, 1938 (ch. 534, 52 Stat. 798), on the relation, conformity, or consistency of proposed amendments of the zoning regulations and maps with the comprehensive plan for the National Capital. The Planning Commission may also submit to the Zoning Commission proposed amendments or general revisions to the zoning regulations or the zoning map for the District of Columbia.

(b) ADDITIONAL REPORT BY PLANNING COMMISSION.—When requested by an authorized representative of the Planning Commission, the Zoning Commission may recess for a reasonable period of time any public hearing it is holding to consider a proposed amendment to the zoning regulations or map so that the Planning Commission may have an opportunity to present to the Zoning Commission an additional report on the proposed amendment.

(c) ZONING COMMITTEE OF NATIONAL CAPITAL PLANNING COMMISSION.—

(1) ESTABLISHMENT AND COMPOSITION.—There is a Zoning Committee of the National Capital Planning Commission. The Committee consists of at least three members of the Planning Commission the Planning Commission designates for that purpose. The number of members serving on the Committee may vary.

(2) DUTIES.—The Committee shall carry out the functions vested in the Planning Commission under this section and section 8725 of this title—

(A) to the extent the Planning Commission decides; and

(B) when requested by the Zoning Commission and approved by the Planning Commission.

(Pub. L. 107–217, Aug. 21, 2002, 116 Stat. 1223.)

§8725. RECOMMENDATIONS ON PLATTING AND SUBDIVIDING LAND

(a) BY COUNCIL OF THE DISTRICT OF COLUMBIA.—The Council of the District of Columbia shall submit any proposed change in, or addition to, the regulations or general orders regulating the platting and subdividing of lands and grounds in the District of Columbia to the National Capital Planning Commission for report and recommendation before the Council adopts the change or addition. The Council shall advise the Commission when it does not agree with the recommendations of the Commission and shall give the reasons why it disagrees. The Commission then shall submit a final report within 30 days. After considering the final report, the Council may act in accordance with its legal responsibilities and authority.

(b) BY PLANNING COMMISSION.—The Commission shall submit to the Council any proposed change in, or amendment to, the general orders that the Commission considers appropriate. The Council shall treat the amendments proposed in the same manner as other proposed amendments.

(Pub. L. 107–217, Aug. 21, 2002, 116 Stat. 1224.)

§8726. AUTHORIZATION OF APPROPRIATIONS

Amounts necessary to carry out this subchapter may be appropriated from money in the Treasury not otherwise appropriated and from any appropriate appropriation law, except the annual District of Columbia Appropriation Act.

(Pub. L. 107–217, Aug. 21, 2002, 116 Stat. 1224.)

SUBCHAPTER IV—ACQUIRING AND DISPOSING OF LAND

§8731. ACQUIRING LAND FOR PARK, PARKWAY, OR PLAYGROUND PURPOSES

(a) AUTHORITY TO ACQUIRE LAND.—The National Capitol Planning Commission shall acquire land the Planning Commission believes is necessary and desirable in the District of Columbia and adjacent areas in Maryland and Virginia for suitable development of the National Capital park, parkway, and playground system. The acquisition must be within the limits of the appropriations made for those purposes. The Planning Commission shall request the advice of the Commission of Fine Arts in selecting land to be acquired.

(b) HOW LAND MAY BE ACQUIRED.—

(1) PURCHASE OR CONDEMNATION PROCEEDING.—The National Capital Planning Commission may buy land when the land can be acquired at a price the Planning Commission considers reasonable or by a condemnation proceeding when the land cannot be bought at a reasonable price.

(2) LAND IN THE DISTRICT OF COLUMBIA.—A condemnation proceeding to acquire land in the District of Columbia shall be conducted in accordance with section 1 of the Act of December 23, 1963 (Public Law 88–241, 77 Stat. 571).

(3) LAND IN MARYLAND OR VIRGINIA.—The Planning Commission may acquire land in Maryland or Virginia under arrangements agreed to by the Commission and the proper officials of Maryland or Virginia.

(c) CONTROL OF LAND.—

(1) LAND IN THE DISTRICT OF COLUMBIA.—Land acquired in the District of Columbia shall be a part of the park system of the District of Columbia and be under the control of the Director of the National Park Service. The National Capital Planning Commission may assign areas suitable for playground purposes to the control of the Mayor of the District of Columbia for playground purposes.

(2) LAND IN MARYLAND OR VIRGINIA.—Land acquired in Maryland or Virginia shall be controlled as determined by agreement between the Planning Commission and the proper officials of Maryland or Virginia.

(d) PRESIDENTIAL APPROVAL REQUIRED.—The designation of all land to be acquired by condemnation, all contracts to purchase land, and all agreements between the National Capital Planning Commission and the officials of Maryland and Virginia are subject to the approval of the President.

(Pub. L. 107–217, Aug. 21, 2002, 116 Stat. 1224.)

§8732. Acquiring Land Subject to Limited Rights Reserved to Grantor and Limited Permanent Rights in Land Adjoining Park Property

(a) In General.—The National Capital Planning Commission in accordance with this chapter may acquire, for and on behalf of the Federal Government, by gift, devise, purchase, or condemnation—

(1) fee title to land subject to limited rights, but not for business purposes, reserved to the grantor; and

(2) permanent rights in land adjoining park property sufficient to prevent the use of the land in certain specified ways which would essentially impair the value of the park property for its purposes.

(b) Prerequisites to Acquisition.—

(1) Fee title to land subject to limited rights.—The reservation of rights to the grantor shall not continue beyond the life of the grantor of the fee. The Commission must decide that the permanent public park purposes for which control over the land is needed are not essentially impaired by the reserved rights and that there is a substantial saving in cost by acquiring the land subject to the limited rights as compared with the cost of acquiring unencumbered title to the land.

(2) Permanent rights in land adjoining park property.—The Commission must decide that the protection and maintenance of the essential public values of the park can be secured more economically by acquiring the permanent rights than by acquiring the land.

(c) Presidential Approval Required.—All contracts to acquire land or rights under this section are subject to the approval of the President.

(Pub. L. 107–217, Aug. 21, 2002, 116 Stat. 1225.)

§8733. Lease of Land Acquired for Park, Parkway, or Playground Purposes

The Secretary of the Interior may lease, for not more than five years, land or an existing building or structure on land acquired for park, parkway, or playground purposes, and may renew the lease for an additional five years. A lease or renewal under this section is—

(1) subject to the approval of the National Capital Planning Commission;

(2) subject to the need for the immediate use of the land, building, or structure in other ways by the public; and

(3) on terms the Administrator decides.

(Pub. L. 107–217, Aug. 21, 2002, 116 Stat. 1225.)

§8734. Sale of Land by Mayor

(a) Authority To Sell.—With the approval of the National Capital Planning Commission, the Mayor of the District of Columbia, for the best interests of the District of Columbia, may sell to the highest bidder at public or private sale real estate in the District of Columbia owned in fee simple by the District of Columbia for municipal use that the Council of the District of Columbia and the Commission find to be no longer required for public purposes.

(b) Paying Expenses and Depositing Proceeds.—The Mayor—

(1) may pay the reasonable and necessary expenses of the sale of each parcel of

land sold; and

(2) shall deposit the net proceeds of each sale in the Treasury to the credit of the District of Columbia.

(Pub. L. 107–217, Aug. 21, 2002, 116 Stat. 1226.)

§8735. SALE OF LAND BY SECRETARY OF THE INTERIOR

(a) AUTHORITY TO SELL.—With the approval of the National Capital Planning Commission, the Secretary of the Interior, for the best interests of the Federal Government, may sell, by deed or instrument, real estate held by the Government in the District of Columbia and under the jurisdiction of the National Park Service which may be no longer needed for public purposes. The land may be sold for cash or on a deferred-payment plan the Secretary approves, at a price not less than the Government paid for it and not less than its present appraised value as determined by the Secretary.

(b) SALE TO HIGHEST BIDDER.—In selling any parcel of land under this section, the Secretary shall have public or private solicitation for bids or offers be made as the Secretary considers appropriate. The Secretary shall sell the parcel to the party agreeing to pay the highest price if the price is otherwise satisfactory. If the price offered or bid by the owner of land abutting the land to be sold equals the highest price offered or bid by any other party, the parcel may be sold to the owner of the abutting land.

(c) PAYING EXPENSES AND DEPOSITING PROCEEDS.—The Secretary—

(1) may pay the reasonable and necessary expenses of the sale of each parcel of land sold; and

(2) shall deposit the net proceeds of each sale in the Treasury to the credit of the Government and the District of Columbia in the proportion that each—

(A) paid the appropriations used to acquire the parcels; or

(B) was obligated to pay the appropriations, at the time of acquisition, by reimbursement.

(Pub. L. 107–217, Aug. 21, 2002, 116 Stat. 1226.)

§8736. EXECUTION OF DEEDS

The Mayor of the District of Columbia may execute deeds of conveyance for real estate sold under this subchapter. The deeds shall contain a full description of the land sold as required by law.

(Pub. L. 107–217, Aug. 21, 2002, 116 Stat. 1227.)

§8737. AUTHORIZATION OF APPROPRIATIONS

An amount equal to not more than one cent for each inhabitant of the continental United States as determined by the last preceding decennial census may be appropriated each year in the District of Columbia Appropriation Act for the National Capital Planning Commission to use for the payment of its expenses and for the acquisition of land the Commission may acquire under section 8731 of this title for the purposes named, including compensation for the land, surveys, ascertainment of title, condemnation proceedings, and necessary conveyancing. The appropriated amounts shall be paid from the revenues of the District of Columbia and the general amounts of the Treasury in the same proportion as other expenses of the District of Columbia.

(Pub. L. 107–217, Aug. 21, 2002, 116 Stat. 1227.)

CHAPTER 89—NATIONAL CAPITAL MEMORIALS AND COMMEMORATIVE WORKS

[1] *Section catchline amended by Pub. L. 108–126 without corresponding amendment of analysis.*

§8901. PURPOSES

The purposes of this chapter are—

(1) to preserve the integrity of the comprehensive design of the L'Enfant and McMillan plans for the Nation's Capital;

(2) to ensure the continued public use and enjoyment of open space in the District of Columbia and its environs, and to encourage the location of commemorative works within the urban fabric of the District of Columbia;

(3) to preserve, protect and maintain the limited amount of open space available to residents of, and visitors to, the Nation's Capital; and

(4) to ensure that future commemorative works in areas administered by the National Park Service and the Administrator of General Services in the District of Columbia and its environs—

(A) are appropriately designed, constructed, and located; and

(B) reflect a consensus of the lasting national significance of the subjects involved.

(Pub. L. 107–217, Aug. 21, 2002, 116 Stat. 1227; Pub. L. 108–126, title II, §203(a), Nov. 17, 2003, 117 Stat. 1349.)

§8902. DEFINITIONS AND NONAPPLICATION

(a) DEFINITIONS.—In this chapter:

(1) COMMEMORATIVE WORK.—The term "commemorative work" means any statue, monument, sculpture, memorial, plaque, inscription, or other structure or landscape feature, including a garden or memorial grove, designed to perpetuate in a permanent manner the memory of an individual, group, event or other significant element of American history, except that the term does not include any such item which is located within the interior of a structure or a structure which is primarily used for other purposes.

(2) THE DISTRICT OF COLUMBIA AND ITS ENVIRONS.—The term "the District of Columbia and its environs" means those lands and properties administered by the National Park Service and the General Services Administration located in the Reserve, Area I, and Area II as depicted on the map entitled "Commemorative Areas

Washington, DC and Environs", numbered 869/86501 B, and dated June 24, 2003.

(3) RESERVE.—The term "Reserve" means the great cross-axis of the Mall, which generally extends from the United States Capitol to the Lincoln Memorial, and from the White House to the Jefferson Memorial, as depicted on the map referenced in paragraph (2).

(4) SPONSOR.—The term "sponsor" means a public agency, or an individual, group or organization that is described in section 501(c)(3) of the Internal Revenue Code of 1986 and exempt from tax under section 501(a) of such Code, and which is authorized by Congress to establish a commemorative work in the District of Columbia and its environs.

(b) NONAPPLICATION.—This chapter does not apply to commemorative works authorized by a law enacted before January 3, 1985.

(Pub. L. 107–217, Aug. 21, 2002, 116 Stat. 1227; Pub. L. 108–126, title II, §203(b), Nov. 17, 2003, 117 Stat. 1350.)

§8903. CONGRESSIONAL AUTHORIZATION OF COMMEMORATIVE WORKS

(a) IN GENERAL.—Commemorative works—

(1) may be established on federal lands referred to in section 8901(4) of this title only as specifically authorized by law; and

(2) are subject to applicable provisions of this chapter.

(b) MILITARY COMMEMORATIVE WORKS.—A military commemorative work may be authorized only to commemorate a war or similar major military conflict or a branch of the armed forces. A commemorative work solely commemorating a limited military engagement or a unit of an armed force may not be authorized. Commemorative works to a war or similar major military conflict may not be authorized until at least 10 years after the officially designated end of such war or conflict.

(c) WORKS COMMEMORATING EVENTS, INDIVIDUALS, OR GROUPS.—A commemorative work commemorating an event, individual, or group of individuals, except a military commemorative work as described in subsection (b), may not be authorized until after the 25th anniversary of the event, death of the individual, or death of the last surviving member of the group.

(d) CONSULTATION WITH NATIONAL CAPITAL MEMORIAL ADVISORY COMMISSION.—In considering legislation authorizing commemorative works in the District of Columbia and its environs, the Committee on Natural Resources of the House of Representatives and the Committee on Energy and Natural Resources of the Senate shall solicit the views of the National Capital Memorial Advisory Commission.

(e) EXPIRATION OF LEGISLATIVE AUTHORITY.—Any legislative authority for a commemorative work shall expire at the end of the seven-year period beginning on the date of the enactment of such authority, or at the end of the seven-year period beginning on the date of the enactment of legislative authority to locate the commemorative work within Area I, if such additional authority has been granted, unless—

(1) the Secretary of the Interior or the Administrator of General Services (as appropriate) has issued a construction permit for the commemorative work during that period; or

(2) the Secretary or the Administrator (as appropriate), in consultation with the National Capital Memorial Advisory Commission, has made a determination that—

(A) final design approvals have been obtained from the National Capital Planning Commission and the Commission of Fine Arts; and

(B) 75 percent of the amount estimated to be required to complete the commemorative work has been raised.

If these two conditions have been met, the Secretary or the Administrator (as appropriate) may extend the seven-year legislative authority for a period not to exceed three additional years. Upon expiration of the legislative authority, any previous site and design approvals shall also expire.

(Pub. L. 107–217, Aug. 21, 2002, 116 Stat. 1228; Pub. L. 108–126, title II, §203(c), Nov. 17, 2003, 117 Stat. 1350; Pub. L. 111–11, title VII, §7116(e)(1), Mar. 30, 2009, 123 Stat. 1203.)

§8904. NATIONAL CAPITAL MEMORIAL ADVISORY COMMISSION

(a) ESTABLISHMENT AND COMPOSITION.—There is established the National Capital Memorial Advisory Commission, which shall be composed of—

(1) the Director of the National Park Service;

(2) the Architect of the Capitol;

(3) the Chairman of the American Battle Monuments Commission;

(4) the Chairman of the Commission of Fine Arts;

(5) the Chairman of the National Capital Planning Commission;

(6) the Mayor of the District of Columbia;

(7) the Commissioner of the Public Buildings Service of the General Services Administration; and

(8) the Secretary of Defense.

(b) CHAIRMAN.—The Director is the Chairman of the National Capital Memorial Advisory Commission.

(c) ADVISORY ROLE.—The National Capital Memorial Advisory Commission shall advise the Secretary of the Interior and the Administrator of General Services (as appropriate) on policy and procedures for establishment of, and proposals to establish, commemorative works in the District of Columbia and its environs and on other matters concerning commemorative works in the Nation's Capital as the Commission considers appropriate.

(d) MEETINGS.—The National Capital Memorial Advisory Commission shall meet at least twice annually.

(Pub. L. 107–217, Aug. 21, 2002, 116 Stat. 1229; Pub. L. 108–126, title II, §203(d), Nov. 17, 2003, 117 Stat. 1351; Pub. L. 111–11, title VII, §7116(e)(2), Mar. 30, 2009, 123 Stat. 1203.)

§8905. SITE AND DESIGN APPROVAL

(a) CONSULTATION ON, AND SUBMISSION OF, PROPOSALS.—A sponsor authorized by law to establish a commemorative work in the District of Columbia and its environs may request a permit for construction of the commemorative work only after the following requirements are met:

(1) CONSULTATION.—The sponsor must consult with the National Capital Memorial Advisory Commission regarding the selection of alternative sites and design concepts for the commemorative work.

(2) SUBMITTAL.—Following consultation in accordance with clause (1), the Secretary of the Interior or the Administrator of General Services, as appropriate,

must submit, on behalf of the sponsor, site and design proposals to the Commission of Fine Arts and the National Capital Planning Commission for their approval.

(b) DECISION CRITERIA.—In considering site and design proposals, the Commission of Fine Arts, National Capital Planning Commission, and the Secretary or Administrator (as appropriate) shall be guided by, but not limited by, the following criteria:

(1) SURROUNDINGS.—To the maximum extent possible, a commemorative work shall be located in surroundings that are relevant to the subject of the work.

(2) LOCATION.—A commemorative work shall be located so that—

(A) it does not interfere with, or encroach on, an existing commemorative work; and

(B) to the maximum extent practicable, it protects open space, existing public use, and cultural and natural resources.

(3) MATERIAL.—A commemorative work shall be constructed of durable material suitable to the outdoor environment.

(4) LANDSCAPE FEATURES.—Landscape features of commemorative works shall be compatible with the climate.

(5) MUSEUMS.—No commemorative work primarily designed as a museum may be located on lands under the jurisdiction of the Secretary in Area I or in East Potomac Park as depicted on the map referenced in section 8902(2).[1]

(6) SITE-SPECIFIC GUIDELINES.—The National Capital Planning Commission and the Commission of Fine Arts may develop such criteria or guidelines specific to each site that are mutually agreed upon to ensure that the design of the commemorative work carries out the purposes of this chapter.

(c) DONOR CONTRIBUTIONS.—

(1) ACKNOWLEDGMENT OF DONOR CONTRIBUTION.—Except as otherwise provided in this subsection, the Secretary of the Interior or Administrator of General Services, as applicable, may permit a sponsor to acknowledge donor contributions at the commemorative work.

(2) REQUIREMENTS.—An acknowledgment under paragraph (1) shall—

(A) be displayed—

(i) inside an ancillary structure associated with the commemorative work; or

(ii) as part of a manmade landscape feature at the commemorative work; and

(B) conform to applicable National Park Service or General Services Administration guidelines for donor recognition, as applicable.

(3) LIMITATIONS.—An acknowledgment under paragraph (1) shall—

(A) be limited to an appropriate statement or credit recognizing the contribution;

(B) be displayed in a form in accordance with National Park Service and General Services Administration guidelines;

(C) be displayed for a period of up to 10 years, with the display period to be commensurate with the level of the contribution, as determined in accordance with the plan and guidelines described in subparagraph (B);

(D) be freestanding; and

(E) not be affixed to—

(i) any landscape feature at the commemorative work; or

(ii) any object in a museum collection.

(4) Cost.—The sponsor shall bear all expenses related to the display of donor acknowledgments under paragraph (1).

(5) Applicability.—This subsection shall apply to any commemorative work dedicated after January 1, 2010.

(Pub. L. 107–217, Aug. 21, 2002, 116 Stat. 1229; Pub. L. 108–126, title II, §§203(e), 204, Nov. 17, 2003, 117 Stat. 1351, 1352; Pub. L. 113–291, div. B, title XXX, §3054(c), Dec. 19, 2014, 128 Stat. 3807.)

[1] So in original. Probably should be section "8902(a)(2)."

§8906. Criteria for issuance of construction permit

(a) Criteria for Issuing Permit.—Before issuing a permit for the construction of a commemorative work in the District of Columbia and its environs, the Secretary of the Interior or Administrator of General Services, as appropriate, shall determine that—

(1) the site and design have been approved by the Secretary or Administrator, the National Capital Planning Commission and the Commission of Fine Arts;

(2) knowledgeable individuals qualified in the field of preservation and maintenance have been consulted to determine structural soundness and durability of the commemorative work and to ensure that the commemorative work meets high professional standards;

(3) the sponsor authorized to construct the commemorative work has submitted contract documents for construction of the commemorative work to the Secretary or Administrator; and

(4) the sponsor authorized to construct the commemorative work has available sufficient amounts to complete construction of the project.

(b) Donation for Perpetual Maintenance and Preservation.—

(1) In addition to the criteria described above in subsection (a), no construction permit shall be issued unless the sponsor authorized to construct the commemorative work has donated an amount equal to 10 percent of the total estimated cost of construction to offset the costs of perpetual maintenance and preservation of the commemorative work. All such amounts shall be available for those purposes pursuant to the provisions of this subsection. The provisions of this subsection shall not apply in instances when the commemorative work is constructed by a Department or agency of the Federal Government and less than 50 percent of the funding for such work is provided by private sources.

(2) Notwithstanding any other provision of law, money on deposit in the Treasury on the date of enactment of the Commemorative Works Clarification and Revision Act of 2003 provided by a sponsor for maintenance pursuant to this subsection shall be credited to a separate account in the Treasury.

(3) Money provided by a sponsor pursuant to the provisions of this subsection after the date of enactment of the Commemorative Works Clarification and Revision Act of 2003 shall be credited to a separate account with the National Park Foundation.

(4) Upon request of the Secretary or Administrator (as appropriate), the Secretary of the Treasury or the National Park Foundation shall make all or a portion of such moneys available to the Secretary or the Administrator (as appropriate) for the maintenance of a commemorative work. Under no circumstances may the Secretary or Administrator request funds from a separate account exceeding the total money

in the account established under paragraph (2) or (3). The Secretary and the Administrator shall maintain an inventory of funds available for such purposes. Funds provided under this paragraph shall be available without further appropriation and shall remain available until expended.

(c) SUSPENSION FOR MISREPRESENTATION IN FUNDRAISING.—The Secretary of the Interior or Administrator may suspend any activity under this chapter that relates to the establishment of a commemorative work if the Secretary or Administrator determines that fundraising efforts relating to the work have misrepresented an affiliation with the work or the Federal Government.

(d) ANNUAL REPORT.—The person authorized to construct a commemorative work under this chapter must submit to the Secretary of the Interior or Administrator an annual report of operations, including financial statements audited by an independent certified public accountant. The person shall pay for the report.

(Pub. L. 107–217, Aug. 21, 2002, 116 Stat. 1230; Pub. L. 108–126, title II, §203(f), Nov. 17, 2003, 117 Stat. 1351.)

§8907. TEMPORARY SITE DESIGNATION

(a) CRITERION FOR DESIGNATION.—If the Secretary of the Interior, in consultation with the National Capital Memorial Commission, determines that a site where commemorative works may be displayed on a temporary basis is necessary to aid in the preservation of the limited amount of open space available to residents of, and visitors to, the Nation's Capital, a site may be designated on land the Secretary administers in the District of Columbia.

(b) PLAN.—A designation may be made under subsection (a) only if, at least 120 days before the designation, the Secretary, in consultation with the Commission, prepares and submits to Congress a plan for the site. The plan shall include specifications for the location, construction, and administration of the site and criteria for displaying commemorative works at the site.

(c) RISK AND AGREEMENT TO INDEMNIFY.—A commemorative work displayed at the site shall be installed, maintained, and removed at the sole expense and risk of the person authorized to display the work. The person shall agree to indemnify the United States for any liability arising from the display of the commemorative work under this section.

(Pub. L. 107–217, Aug. 21, 2002, 116 Stat. 1231.)

§8908. AREAS I AND II

(a) AVAILABILITY OF MAP.—The Secretary of the Interior or the Administrator of General Services (as appropriate) shall make available, for public inspection at appropriate offices of the National Park Service and the General Services Administration, the map entitled "Commemorative Areas Washington, DC and Environs", numbered 869/86501 B, and dated June 24, 2003.

(b) SPECIFIC CONDITIONS APPLICABLE TO AREA I AND AREA II.—

(1) AREA I.—After seeking the advice of the National Capital Memorial Advisory Commission, the Secretary or Administrator, as appropriate, may recommend the location of a commemorative work in Area I only if the Secretary or Administrator decides that the subject of the commemorative work is of preeminent historical and lasting significance to the United States. The Secretary or Administrator shall

notify the Commission, the Committee on Natural Resources of the House of Representatives, and the Committee on Energy and Natural Resources of the Senate of the recommendation that a commemorative work should be located in Area I. The location of a commemorative work in Area I is deemed to be authorized only if the recommendation is approved by law not later than 150 calendar days after the notification.

(2) AREA II.—Commemorative works of subjects of lasting historical significance to the American people may be located in Area II.

(c) RESERVE.—After the date of enactment of the Commemorative Works Clarification and Revision Act of 2003, no commemorative work or visitor center shall be located within the Reserve.

(Pub. L. 107–217, Aug. 21, 2002, 116 Stat. 1231; Pub. L. 108–126, title II, §§202(b), 203(g), Nov. 17, 2003, 117 Stat. 1349, 1352; Pub. L. 111–11, title VII, §7116(e)(3), Mar. 30, 2009, 123 Stat. 1203.)

§8909. ADMINISTRATIVE

(a) MAINTENANCE OF DOCUMENTATION OF DESIGN AND CONSTRUCTION.—Complete documentation of design and construction of each commemorative work located in the District of Columbia and its environs shall be provided to the Secretary of the Interior or Administrator of General Services, as appropriate, and shall be permanently maintained in the manner provided by law.

(b) RESPONSIBILITY FOR MAINTENANCE OF COMPLETED WORK.—On completion of any commemorative work in the District of Columbia and its environs, the Secretary or Administrator, as appropriate, shall assume responsibility for maintaining the work.

(c) REGULATIONS OR STANDARDS.—The Secretary and Administrator shall prescribe appropriate regulations or standards to carry out this chapter.

(Pub. L. 107–217, Aug. 21, 2002, 116 Stat. 1231.)

CHAPTER 91—COMMISSION OF FINE ARTS

§9101. ESTABLISHMENT, COMPOSITION, AND VACANCIES

(a) ESTABLISHMENT.—There is a Commission of Fine Arts.

(b) COMPOSITION.—The Commission is composed of seven well-qualified judges of the fine arts, appointed by the President, who serve for four years each or until their successors are appointed and qualified.

(c) VACANCIES.—The President shall fill vacancies on the Commission.

(d) EXPENSES.—Members of the Commission shall be paid actual expenses in traveling to and from the District of Columbia to attend Commission meetings and while attending those meetings.

(Pub. L. 107–217, Aug. 21, 2002, 116 Stat. 1232.)

§9102. DUTIES

(a) IN GENERAL.—The Commission of Fine Arts shall advise on—

(1) the location of statues, fountains, and monuments in the public squares, streets, and parks in the District of Columbia;

(2) the selection of models for statues, fountains, and monuments erected under the authority of the Federal Government;

(3) the selection of artists to carry out clause (2); and

(4) questions of art generally when required to do so by the President or a committee of Congress.

(b) DUTY TO REQUEST ADVICE.—The officers required to decide the questions described in subsection (a)(1)–(3) shall request the Commission to provide the advice.

(c) NONAPPLICATION.—This section does not apply to the Capitol Building and the Library of Congress buildings.

(Pub. L. 107–217, Aug. 21, 2002, 116 Stat. 1232.)

§9103. PERSONNEL

The Commission of Fine Arts has a secretary and other assistance the Commission authorizes. The secretary is the executive officer of the Commission.

(Pub. L. 107–217, Aug. 21, 2002, 116 Stat. 1232.)

§9104. AUTHORIZATION OF APPROPRIATIONS

Necessary amounts may be appropriated to carry out this chapter.

(Pub. L. 107–217, Aug. 21, 2002, 116 Stat. 1232.)

CHAPTER 93—THEODORE ROOSEVELT ISLAND

§9301. MAINTENANCE AND ADMINISTRATION

The Director of the National Park Service shall maintain and administer Theodore Roosevelt Island as a natural park for the recreation and enjoyment of the public.

(Pub. L. 107–217, Aug. 21, 2002, 116 Stat. 1233.)

§9302. CONSENT OF THEODORE ROOSEVELT ASSOCIATION REQUIRED FOR DEVELOPMENT

(a) GENERAL PLAN FOR DEVELOPMENT.—The Theodore Roosevelt Association must approve every general plan for the development of Theodore Roosevelt Island.

(b) DEVELOPMENT INCONSISTENT WITH PLAN.—As long as the Association remains in existence, development inconsistent with the general plan may not be carried out without the Association's consent.

(Pub. L. 107–217, Aug. 21, 2002, 116 Stat. 1233; Pub. L. 109–284, §6(30), Sept. 27, 2006, 120 Stat. 1213.)

§9303. ACCESS TO THEODORE ROOSEVELT ISLAND

Subject to the approval of the National Capital Planning Commission and the availability of appropriations, the Director of the National Park Service may provide suitable means of access to and on Theodore Roosevelt Island.

(Pub. L. 107–217, Aug. 21, 2002, 116 Stat. 1233.)

§9304. SOURCE OF APPROPRIATIONS

The appropriations needed for construction of suitable means of access to and on Theodore Roosevelt Island and annually for the care, maintenance, and improvement of the land and improvements may be made from amounts not otherwise appropriated from the Treasury.

(Pub. L. 107–217, Aug. 21, 2002, 116 Stat. 1233.)

CHAPTER 95—WASHINGTON AQUEDUCT AND OTHER PUBLIC WORKS IN THE DISTRICT OF COLUMBIA

§9501. CHIEF OF ENGINEERS

(a) SUPERINTENDENCE DUTIES.—

(1) WASHINGTON AQUEDUCT AND OTHER PUBLIC WORKS AND IMPROVEMENTS IN THE DISTRICT OF COLUMBIA.—The Chief of Engineers has the immediate superintendence of—

(A) the Washington Aqueduct, together with all rights, appurtenances, and fixtures connected with the Aqueduct and belonging to the Federal Government; and

(B) all other public works and improvements in the District of Columbia in which the Government has an interest and which are not otherwise specially provided for by law.

(2) OBEYING REGULATIONS.—In carrying out paragraph (1), the Chief of Engineers shall obey regulations the President prescribes, through the Secretary of the Army.

(b) NO INCREASE IN COMPENSATION.—The Chief of Engineers shall not receive additional compensation for the services required under this chapter.

(c) OFFICE.—The Chief of Engineers shall be furnished an office in one of the public buildings in the District of Columbia, as the Administrator of General Services directs, and shall be supplied by the Federal Government with stationery, instruments, books, and furniture which may be required for the performance of the duties of the Chief of Engineers.

(Pub. L. 107–217, Aug. 21, 2002, 116 Stat. 1233.)

§9502. AUTHORITY OF CHIEF OF ENGINEERS

(a) IN GENERAL.—The Chief of Engineers and necessary assistants may use all lawful means to carry out their duties.

(b) SUPPLY OF WATER IN DISTRICT OF COLUMBIA.—

(1) PROVIDING WATER.—The Chief of Engineers has complete control over the Washington Aqueduct to regulate the manner in which the authorities of the District of Columbia may tap the supply of water to the inhabitants of the District of Columbia.

(2) STOPPAGE OF WATER FLOW.—The Chief of Engineers shall stop the authorities of the District of Columbia from tapping the supply of water when the supply is no more than adequate to the wants of the public buildings and grounds.

(3) APPEAL OF DECISION.—The decision of the Chief of Engineers on all questions

concerning the supply of water under this subsection may be appealed only to the Secretary of the Army.

(Pub. L. 107–217, Aug. 21, 2002, 116 Stat. 1234.)

§9503. RECORD OF PROPERTY

The Chief of Engineers shall keep in the office a complete record of all land and other property connected with or belonging to the Washington Aqueduct and other public works under the charge of the Chief of Engineers, together with accurate plans and surveys of the public grounds and reservations in the District of Columbia.

(Pub. L. 107–217, Aug. 21, 2002, 116 Stat. 1234.)

§9504. REPORTS

As superintendent of the Washington Aqueduct, the Chief of Engineers annually shall submit to the Secretary of the Army, within nine months after the end of the fiscal year, a report of the Chief of Engineers' operations for that year and a report of the condition, progress, repairs, casualties, and expenditures of the Washington Aqueduct and other public works under the charge of the Chief of Engineers.

(Pub. L. 107–217, Aug. 21, 2002, 116 Stat. 1234.)

§9505. PAYING FOR MAIN PIPES

(a) FEDERAL GOVERNMENT.—The Federal Government shall only pay for the number of main pipes of the Washington Aqueduct needed to furnish public buildings, offices, and grounds with the necessary supply of water.

(b) DISTRICT OF COLUMBIA.—The District of Columbia shall pay the cost of any main pipe of the Washington Aqueduct which supplies water to the inhabitants of the District of Columbia, in the manner provided by law.

(Pub. L. 107–217, Aug. 21, 2002, 116 Stat. 1234.)

§9506. CIVIL PENALTY

A person that, without the consent of the Chief of Engineers, taps or opens the mains or pipes laid by the Federal Government is liable to the Government for a civil penalty of at least $50 and not more than $500.

(Pub. L. 107–217, Aug. 21, 2002, 116 Stat. 1234.)

§9507. CONTROL OF EXPENDITURES

Unless expressly provided for by law, the Secretary of the Army shall direct the expenditure of amounts appropriated for the Washington Aqueduct and for other public works in the District of Columbia.

(Pub. L. 107–217, Aug. 21, 2002, 116 Stat. 1235.)

★

NATIONAL GALLERY OF ART

40 U.S.C. CH. 3, SUBCH. II

TITLE 20—EDUCATION

* * * * * * *

CHAPTER 3—SMITHSONIAN INSTITUTION, NATIONAL MUSEUMS AND ART GALLERIES

* * * * * * *

* * * * * * *

SUBCHAPTER II—NATIONAL GALLERY OF ART

§71. DESIGNATION OF SITE

The area bounded by Seventh Street, Constitution Avenue, Fourth Street, and North Mall Drive, Northwest, in the District of Columbia, is appropriated to the Smithsonian Institution as a site for a National Gallery of Art. The Smithsonian Institution is authorized to permit the A. W. Mellon Educational and Charitable Trust (hereinafter referred to as the donor) to construct on said site for the Smithsonian Institution a building to be designated the National Gallery of Art, and to remove any existing structure and landscape the grounds within said area. The adjoining area bounded by Fourth Street, Pennsylvania Avenue, Third Street, and North Mall Drive, Northwest, in the District of Columbia, is reserved as a site for future additions to the National Gallery of Art. The project shall be in accordance with plans and specifications approved by the Commission of Fine Arts.

(Mar. 24, 1937, ch. 50, §1, 50 Stat. 51.)

STATUTORY NOTES AND RELATED SUBSIDIARIES

SMITHSONIAN AMERICAN ART MUSEUM

Pub. L. 106–385, Oct. 27, 2000, 114 Stat. 1463, provided that:

"SECTION 1. RENAMING OF NATIONAL MUSEUM OF AMERICAN ART.

"(a) IN GENERAL.—The National Museum of American Art, as designated under section 1 of Public Law 96–441 (20 U.S.C. 71 note), shall be known as the 'Smithsonian American Art Museum'.

"(b) REFERENCES IN LAW.—Any reference in any law, regulation, document, or paper to the National Museum of American Art shall be considered to be a reference to the Smithsonian American Art Museum.

"SEC. 2. EFFECTIVE DATE.

"Section 1 shall take effect on the day after the date of enactment of this Act [Oct. 27, 2000]."

Pub. L. 96–441, §§1, 3, 4, Oct. 13, 1980, 94 Stat. 1884, provided: "That the bureau of the Smithsonian Institution designated as the National Collection of Fine Arts by section 6(c) of the joint resolution entitled 'Joint Resolution providing for the construction and maintenance of a National Gallery of Art', approved March 24, 1937 (20 U.S.C. 71 note), shall be known as the 'National Museum of American Art'.

"SEC. 3. Any reference in any law, regulation, document, or paper to the National Collection of Fine Arts or the Museum of History and Technology shall on and after the effective date of this Act [Oct. 13, 1980] be considered to be a reference to the National Museum of American Art and the National Museum of American History, respectively.

"SEC. 4. This Act shall take effect on the day after the date of the enactment of this Act [Oct. 13, 1980]."

Act Mar. 24, 1937, ch. 50, 50 Stat. 51, sections 1 to 5 of which are incorporated as sections 71, 72 to 74, and 75 of this title, provided in section 6(c) that: "The existing bureau of the Smithsonian Institution now designated as a national gallery of art shall hereafter be known as the National Collection of Fine Arts."

GENERAL POST OFFICE BUILDING; TRANSFER TO SMITHSONIAN INSTITUTION FOR USE AS ART GALLERIES; RELOCATION OF UNITED STATES INTERNATIONAL TRADE COMMISSION

Pub. L. 98–523, Oct. 19, 1984, 98 Stat. 2433, provided: "That at such time as it is declared to be excess property pursuant to section 2(d) of this Act, the Administrator of General Services (hereinafter in this Act referred to as the 'Administrator') is authorized to transfer to the Smithsonian Institution, in accordance with section 202 of the Federal Property and Administrative Services Act of 1949 (40 U.S.C. 483) [now 40 U.S.C. 521–527, 529], without reimbursement, and for use by the Smithsonian Institution for certain art galleries and related functions, the General Post Office Building with any attached underground structures and the site of such building, located between Seventh and Eighth Streets Northwest and E and F Streets Northwest, in the District of Columbia.

"SEC. 2. (a) The Administrator, at the earliest practicable date, shall relocate all operations of the United States International Trade Commission (hereinafter in this Act referred to as the 'Commission') to a building in downtown Washington, District of Columbia. The Administrator's determination as to such relocation shall be based on studies and investigations in which the Chairman of the Commission shall have full opportunity to consult and cooperate with the Administrator. Such consultation shall include opportunity for the Chairman to participate jointly with the Administrator in surveys of available buildings and to submit views and recommendations to the Administrator with respect to space suitable for the Commission's operations. The Administrator shall advise the Chairman in writing of the building to which the operations of the Commission are to be relocated. The Administrator's determination of such relocation shall not take effect for a period of at least sixty days after the date such determination is made and the Chairman is advised of the building to which the operations of the Commission are to be relocated. In the event the Chairman disagrees with the Administrator's determination of such relocation, the Chairman, within thirty days after the Chairman is advised of the building to which the operations of the Commission are to be relocated, may make a written request for review of such determination to the Administrator, and the Administrator shall conduct a formal review of such determination.

"(b) The Administrator and the Chairman shall each report separately in writing to the Committees on Environment and Public Works, Finance, Rules and Administration, and Governmental Affairs [now Committee on Homeland Security and Governmental Affairs] of the Senate and to the Committees on Public Works and Transportation, Ways and Means, House Administration, and Government Operations [now Committee on Oversight and Accountability] of the House of Representatives not later than sixty days after the date of enactment of this Act [Oct. 19, 1984] and every thirty days thereafter on the status of the relocation required by this section.

"(c) During the period in which the Commission and the United States Postal Service continue to occupy the General Post Office Building referred to in the first section of this Act, the Administrator shall maintain such building in order to prevent its deterioration and to assure that conditions therein are safe and the building is presentable and suitable to the normal operations of the Commission and such Service.

"(d) Upon accomplishment of the relocation required by subsection (a) of this section, the Administrator shall declare the property referred to in the first section of this Act to be excess property as defined in section 3 of the Federal Property and Administrative Services Act of 1949 (40 U.S.C. 472) [now 40 U.S.C. 102].

"SEC. 3. There is authorized to be appropriated to the Board of Regents of the Smithsonian Institution $40,000,000 for fiscal years beginning after September 30, 1984, for renovation and repair, after the transfer made under the first section of this Act, of the General Post Office Building referred to in such section. Any portion of the sums appropriated under this section may be transferred to the General Services Administration which, in consultation with the Smithsonian Institution, is authorized to enter into contracts and take such other action, to the extent of the sums so transferred to it, as may be necessary to carry out such renovation and repair. No contract for such renovation or repair shall be advertised or entered into before the end of the period of thirty days of continuous session of Congress beginning on the date the Smithsonian

Institution submits to the Committees on Public Works and Transportation and House Administration of the House of Representatives and the Committees on Environment and Public Works and Rules and Administration of the Senate the plans and advanced engineering and design for such renovation and repair. For purposes of this section, continuity of session is broken only by an adjournment of Congress sine die, and the days on which either House is not in session because of an adjournment of more than three days to a day certain are excluded in the computation of any period of time in which Congress is in continuous session."

§71A. ADDITIONS; PAYMENT OF CONSTRUCTION COSTS FROM TRUST FUNDS

The Trustees of the National Gallery of Art are authorized to construct within the area reserved as a site for future additions by the third sentence of section 71 of this title one or more buildings to serve as additions to the National Gallery of Art. The cost of constructing any such building shall be paid from trust funds administered by such Trustees. The plans and specifications for any such building shall be approved by the Commission of Fine Arts and the National Capital Planning Commission.

(Pub. L. 90–376, §1, July 5, 1968, 82 Stat. 286.)

EDITORIAL NOTES

CODIFICATION

Section was not enacted as part of act Mar. 24, 1937, ch. 50, 50 Stat. 51, which comprises this subchapter.

STATUTORY NOTES AND RELATED SUBSIDIARIES

TRANSFER OF JURISDICTION

Pub. L. 90–376, §4, July 5, 1968, 82 Stat. 286, provided that: "The Commissioner [Mayor] of the District of Columbia is authorized to transfer to the United States such jurisdiction as the District of Columbia may have over any of the property within the area referred to in the first section of this Act [this section]."

PUBLIC UTILITY: PAYMENT OF COST OF RELOCATION OR PROTECTION FROM TRUST FUNDS

Pub. L. 90–376, §5, July 5, 1968, 82 Stat. 286, provided that: "If any public utility (whether privately or publicly owned) located within the area referred to in the first section of this Act [this section] is required to be relocated or protected by reason of the construction within such area of any addition to the National Gallery of Art, the cost of such relocation or protection shall be paid from trust funds administered by the Trustees of the National Gallery of Art."

§71B. STATUS OF COMPLETED ADDITION

Any building constructed under authority of section 71a of this title shall, upon completion, be a part of the National Gallery of Art.

(Pub. L. 90–376, §2, July 5, 1968, 82 Stat. 286.)

Editorial Notes

Codification

Section was not enacted as part of act Mar. 24, 1937, ch. 50, 50 Stat. 51, which comprises this subchapter.

§72. Board of Trustees

(a) Establishment

There is established in the Smithsonian Institution a bureau, which shall be directed by a board to be known as the Trustees of the National Gallery of Art, whose duty it shall be to maintain and administer the National Gallery of Art and site thereof and to execute such other functions as are vested in the board by this subchapter. The board shall be composed as follows: The Chief Justice of the United States, the Secretary of State, the Secretary of the Treasury, and the Secretary of the Smithsonian Institution, ex officio; and five general trustees who shall be citizens of the United States, to be chosen as hereinafter provided. No officer or employee of the Federal Government shall be eligible to be chosen as a general trustee.

(b) Method of selection; term of office

The general trustees first taking office shall be chosen by the Board of Regents of the Smithsonian Institution, subject to the approval of the donor, and shall have terms expiring one each on July 1 of 1939, 1941, 1943, 1945, and 1947, as designated by the Board of Regents. A successor shall be chosen by a majority vote of the general trustees and shall have a term expiring ten years from the date of the expiration of the term for which his predecessor was chosen, except that a successor chosen to fill a vacancy occurring prior to the expiration of such term shall be chosen only for the remainder of such term.

(Mar. 24, 1937, ch. 50, §2, 50 Stat. 52.)

Statutory Notes and Related Subsidiaries

Delegation of Functions by Secretary of State to Director of United States Information Agency

Pub. L. 95–426, title II, §205, Oct. 7, 1978, 92 Stat. 975, as amended by Pub. L. 97–241, title III, §303(b), Aug. 24, 1982, 96 Stat. 291, provided that: "The Secretary of State may delegate to the Director of the United States Information Agency, with the consent of the Director, the functions vested in the Secretary by section 2(a) of the joint resolution entitled 'Joint Resolution providing for the construction and maintenance of a National Gallery of Art', approved March 24, 1937 (20 U.S.C. 72(a))."

[For abolition of United States Information Agency (other than Broadcasting Board of Governors and International Broadcasting Bureau), transfer of functions, and treatment of references thereto, see sections 6531, 6532, and 6551 of Title 22, Foreign Relations and Intercourse.]

§73. Acceptance of gift from A. W. Mellon

Upon completion of the National Gallery of Art, the board shall accept for the

Smithsonian Institution as a gift from the donor a collection of works of art which shall be housed and exhibited in the National Gallery of Art.

(Mar. 24, 1937, ch. 50, §3, 50 Stat. 52.)

§74. Maintenance

(a) Pledge of funds for upkeep; authorization of appropriations

The faith of the United States is pledged that, on completion of the National Gallery of Art by the donor in accordance with the terms of this subchapter and the acquisition from the donor of the collection of works of art, the United States will provide such funds as may be necessary for the upkeep of the National Gallery of Art and the administrative expenses and costs of operation thereof, including the protection and care of works of art acquired by the board, so that the National Gallery of Art shall be at all times properly maintained and the works of art contained therein shall be exhibited regularly to the general public free of charge. For these purposes, and to provide, prior to the completion of the National Gallery of Art, for the protection and care of the works of art in said Gallery and for administrative and operating expenses and equipment preparatory to the opening of the Gallery to the public, there are authorized to be appropriated such sums as may be necessary.

(b) Acceptance of gifts and other property; investment of funds

The board is authorized to accept for the Smithsonian Institution and to hold and administer gifts, bequests, or devises of money, securities, or other property of whatsoever character for the benefit of the National Gallery of Art. Unless otherwise restricted by the terms of the gift, bequest, or devise, the board is authorized to sell or exchange and to invest or reinvest in such investments as it may determine from time to time the moneys, securities, or other property composing trust funds given, bequeathed, or devised to or for the benefit of the National Gallery of Art. The income as and when collected shall be placed in such depositaries as the board shall determine and shall be subject to expenditure by the board.

(c) Appointment and compensation of officers and employees

The board shall appoint and fix the compensation and duties of a director, an assistant director, a secretary, and a chief curator of the National Gallery of Art, and of such other officers and employees of the National Gallery of Art as may be necessary for the efficient administration of the functions of the board. Such director, assistant director, secretary, and chief curator shall be compensated from trust funds available to the board for the purpose, and their appointment and salaries shall not be subject to the civil-service laws or chapter 51 and subchapter III of chapter 53 of title 5. The director, assistant director, secretary, and chief curator shall be well qualified by experience and training to perform the duties of their office and the original appointment to each such office shall be subject to the approval of the donor.

(d) Review of actions of board

The actions of the board, including any payment made or directed to be made by it from any trust funds, shall not be subject to review by any officer or agency other than a court of law.

(Mar. 24, 1937, ch. 50, §4, 50 Stat. 52; Apr. 13, 1939, ch. 61, 53 Stat. 577; Oct. 28, 1949, ch. 782, title XI, §1106(a), 63 Stat. 972.)

CODIFICATION

In subsec. (c), "chapter 51 and subchapter III of chapter 53 of title 5" substituted for "the Classification Act of 1949, as amended" on authority of Pub. L. 89–554, §7(b), Sept. 6, 1966, 80 Stat. 631, the first section of which enacted Title 5, Government Organization and Employees.

AMENDMENTS

1949—Act Oct. 28, 1949, substituted "Classification Act of 1949" for "Classification Act of 1923".

1939—Subsec. (a). Act Apr. 13, 1939, inserted in last sentence "and to provide, prior to the completion of the National Gallery of Art, for the protection and care of the works of art in said Gallery and for administrative and operating expenses and equipment preparatory to the opening of the Gallery to the public".

REPEALS

Act Oct. 28, 1949, ch. 782, cited as a credit to this section, was repealed (subject to a savings clause) by Pub. L. 89–554, Sept. 6, 1966, §8, 80 Stat. 632, 655.

§74A. PERMANENT LOAN OF FUNDS BY BOARD OF TRUSTEES TO TREASURY; SEMIANNUAL INTEREST PAYMENTS TO BOARD

The Secretary of the Treasury is authorized and directed to receive into the Treasury from time to time as a permanent loan by the Board of Trustees of the National Gallery of Art to the United States sums in cash of not to exceed $5,000,000 in the aggregate, and to pay interest on the principal amount of such loan at a rate which is the higher of the rate of 4 per centum per annum or a rate which is .25 percentage points less than a rate determined by the Secretary of the Treasury, taking into consideration the current average market yield on outstanding long-term marketable obligations of the United States, adjusted to the nearest one-eighth of 1 per centum, payable semiannually. Such interest is permanently appropriated for payment to the Board of Trustees of the National Gallery of Art.

(Apr. 10, 1943, ch. 46, 57 Stat. 62; Pub. L. 94–418, Sept. 21, 1976, 90 Stat. 1278.)

CODIFICATION

Section was not enacted as part of act Mar. 24, 1937, ch. 50, 50 Stat. 51, which comprises this subchapter.

AMENDMENTS

1976—Pub. L. 94–418 inserted provision authorizing alternate interest rate to existing interest rate of 4 per centum per annum.

§75. AUTHORITY AND FUNCTIONS OF THE BOARD

(A) OFFICIAL SEAL; BYLAWS, RULES, AND REGULATIONS; QUORUM

The board is authorized to adopt an official seal which shall be judicially noticed and to make such bylaws, rules, and regulations, as it deems necessary for the administration of its functions under this subchapter, including, among other matters, bylaws, rules, and regulations relating to the acquisition, exhibition, and loan of works of art, the administration of its trust funds, and the organization and procedure of the board. The board may function notwithstanding vacancies, and three members of the board shall constitute a quorum for the transaction of business.

(B) QUALITY OF WORKS OF ART

In order that the collection of the National Gallery of Art shall always be maintained at a high standard and in order to prevent the introduction therein of inferior works of art, no work of art shall be included in the permanent collection of the National Gallery of Art unless it be of similar high standard of quality to those in the collection acquired from the donor.

(C) POWERS AND OBLIGATIONS

The board shall have all the usual powers and obligations of a trustee in respect of all trust funds administered by it and all works of art acquired by it.

(D) ANNUAL REPORTS

The board shall submit to the Smithsonian Institution an annual report of its operations under this subchapter, including a detailed statement of all acquisitions and loans of works of art and of all public and private moneys received and disbursed.

(Mar. 24, 1937, ch. 50, §5, 50 Stat. 53.)

★

Selected Provisions of 54 U.S.C.–National Park Service and Related Programs Ch. 3055 National Building Museum

54 U.S.C. Ch. 3055

TITLE 54—NATIONAL PARK SERVICE AND RELATED PROGRAMS

This title was enacted by Pub. L. 113–287, §3, Dec. 19, 2014, 128 Stat. 3094

* * * * * * *

Subtitle I—National Park System

DIVISION A—ESTABLISHMENT AND GENERAL ADMINISTRATION

CHAPTER 1001—GENERAL PROVISIONS

Sec.

* * * * * * *

100102.   Definitions.

* * * * * * *

§100102. DEFINITIONS

In this title:

(1) DIRECTOR.—The term "Director" means the Director of the National Park Service.

* * * * * * *

(3) SECRETARY.—The term "Secretary" means the Secretary of the Interior.

* * * * * * *

(Pub. L. 113–287, §3, Dec. 19, 2014, 128 Stat. 3096.)

§305502. COOPERATIVE AGREEMENT TO OPERATE MUSEUM

To provide a national center to commemorate and encourage the building arts and to preserve and maintain a nationally significant building that exemplifies the great achievements of the building arts in the United States, the Secretary and the Administrator of General Services shall enter into a cooperative agreement with the Committee for the operation of a National Building Museum in the Federal building located in the block bounded by Fourth Street, Fifth Street, F Street, and G Street, Northwest in Washington, District of Columbia. The cooperative agreement shall include provisions that—

(1) make the site available to the Committee without charge;

(2) provide, subject to available appropriations, such maintenance, security, information, janitorial, and other services as may be necessary to ensure the preservation and operation of the site; and

(3) prescribe reasonable terms and conditions by which the Committee can fulfill its responsibilities under this division.

(Pub. L. 113–287, §3, Dec. 19, 2014, 128 Stat. 3223.)

§305503. ACTIVITIES AND FUNCTIONS

The National Building Museum shall—

(1) collect and disseminate information concerning the building arts, including the establishment of a national reference center for current and historic documents, publications, and research relating to the building arts;

(2) foster educational programs relating to the history, practice, and contribution to society of the building arts, including promotion of imaginative educational approaches to enhance understanding and appreciation of all facets of the building arts;

(3) publicly display temporary and permanent exhibits illustrating, interpreting and demonstrating the building arts;

(4) sponsor or conduct research and study into the history of the building arts and their role in shaping our civilization; and

(5) encourage contributions to the building arts.

(Pub. L. 113–287, §3, Dec. 19, 2014, 128 Stat. 3223.)

§305504. MATCHING GRANTS TO COMMITTEE

The Secretary shall provide matching grants to the Committee for its programs related to historic preservation. The Committee shall match the grants in such a manner and with such funds and services as shall be satisfactory to the Secretary, except that not more than $500,000 may be provided to the Committee in any one fiscal year.

(Pub. L. 113–287, §3, Dec. 19, 2014, 128 Stat. 3224.)

§305505. ANNUAL REPORT

The Committee shall submit an annual report to the Secretary and the Administrator of General Services concerning its activities under this chapter and shall provide the Secretary and the Administrator of General Services with such other information as the Secretary may consider necessary or advisable.

(Pub. L. 113–287, §3, Dec. 19, 2014, 128 Stat. 3224.)

* * * * * * *

★

INTERNATIONAL CENTER ACT

PUBLIC LAW 90–553
AS AMENDED THROUGH P.L. 110–249

INTERNATIONAL CENTER ACT

[Public Law 90–553; 82 Stat. 958]

[As Amended Through P.L. 110–249, Enacted June 26, 2008]

AN ACT To authorize the transfer, conveyance, lease, and improvement of, and construction on, certain property in the District of Columbia, for use as a headquarters site for the Organization of American States, as sites for governments of foreign countries, and for other purposes.

Be it enacted by the Senate and House of Representatives of the United States of America in Congress assembled,

That (a) in order to facilitate the conduct of foreign relations by the Department of State in Washington, District of Columbia, through the creation of a more propitious atmosphere for the establishment of foreign government and international organization offices and other facilities, the Secretary of State is authorized to develop in coordination with the Administrator of General Services for, or to sell, exchange, or lease to foreign governments and international organizations property owned by the United States in the Northwest section of the District of Columbia bounded by Connecticut Avenue, Yuma Street, 36th Street, Reno Road, and Tilden Street, except that portion of lot 802 in square 1964, the jurisdiction over which was transferred to the District of Columbia for use as an educational facility, upon such terms and conditions as the Secretary may prescribe. Every lease, contract of sale, deed, and other document of transfer shall provide (1) that the foreign government shall devote the property transferred to use for legation purposes, or (2) sthat the international organization shall devote the property transferred to its official uses.

(b)   There is established in the Treasury of the United States an account into which may be deposited funds provided as advance payments pursuant to subsection (a).

(c)   The Secretary of State may request the Secretary of the Treasury to invest such portion of the funds deposited in that account as is not, in the judgment of the Secretary of State, required to meet the current needs of the account. Such investments shall be made by the Secretary of the Treasury in public debt securities with maturities suitable to the needs of the account, as determined by the Secretary of State, and bearing interest at a rate determined by the Secretary of the Treasury, taking into consideration the current market yields on outstanding marketable obligations of the United States of comparable maturity. Notwithstanding the foregoing limitations, the property identified by the District of Columbia as tax lots 803, 804, 805, and 806 within the area described in this section may be leased or subleased to an entity other than a foreign government or international organization, so long as the Secretary maintains the right to approve the occupant and the intended use of the property.

SEC. 2.   Upon the request of any foreign government or international organization and with funds provided by such government or organization in advance, the Secretary of State, in consultation with the Administrator of General Services, is authorized to design, construct, and equip a headquarters building or legation building or related facilities on property described in the first section of this Act.

SEC. 3.   The Act of June 20, 1938 (D.C. Code, secs. 5–413 to 5–428), shall not apply to buildings constructed on property transferred or conveyed pursuant to this Act including section 3 of this Act as in effect January 1, 1980. Plans showing the location, height, bulk, number of stories, and size of, and the provisions for open spaceand offstreet parking in and around, such buildings shall be approved by the National Capital Planning Commission, and plans showing the height and appearance, color, and texture of the materials of exterior construction of such buildings shall be approved by the Commission of Fine Arts prior to the construction thereof.

SEC. 4. (a)   The demolition or removal of existing structures, site preparation, and the construction, reconstruction, rebuilding of (1) public streets and sidewalks, (2) public sewers and their appurtenances, (3) water mains, fire hydrants, and other parts of the public water supply and distribution system, (4) the fire alarm system, (5) other utilities, (6) facilities for security and maintenance, and (7) related improvements necessary to accomplish the purposes of this Act, which are within or contiguous to the area described in section 1 of this Act and which are occasioned in carrying out the provisions of this Act, shall be provided by the Secretary of State, in coordination with the Administrator of General Services and the government of the District of Columbia.

(b)   The Secretary of State shall periodically advise the Committee on Foreign Affairs and Public Works and Transportation of the House of Repesentatives[1] and the Committee on Foreign Relations of the Senate on construction of facilities for security or maintenance under this section.

---

[1]

Section 1 of Public Law 104–14 (109 Stat. 163) provides as follows:

SECTION 1. REFERENCES IN LAW TO COMMITTEES OF THE HOUSE OF REPRESENTATIVES.

(a) References to Committees With New Names.—Except as provided in subsection (c), any reference in any provision of law enacted before January 4, 1995, to—

(1)

* * *

* * * * * * *

(5) the Committee on Foreign Affairs of the House of Representatives shall be treated as referring to the Committee on International Relations of the House of Representatives;

* * * * * * *

(9) the Committee on Public Works and Transportation of the House of Representatives shall be treated as referring to the Committee on Transportation and Infrastructure of the House of Representatives; and

* * * * * * *

(c)(1)(A)   The Department of State is authorized to require the payment of a fee by other executive agencies of the United States for the lease or use of facilities located at the International Center which are used for the purposes of security and maintenance. Any payments received for lease or use of such facilities shall be credited to the account entitled International Center, Washington, District of Columbia and shall be available, without fiscal year limitation, to cover the operation and maintenance expenses of such facilities, including administration, maintenance, utilities, repairs, and alterations.

(B)   The authority of subparagraph (A) shall be exercised only to such extent or in such amounts as are provided in advance in an appropriation Act.

(2)   For purposes of paragraph (1), the term Executive agencies is used within the meaning of section 105 of title 5, United States Code.

SEC. 5.   There is hereby authorized to be appropriated, without fiscal year limitation, not to exceed $2,200,000 to carry out the purposes of section 5 of this Act: *Provided*, That such sums as may be appropriated hereunder shall be reimbursed to the Treasury from proceeds of the sale, exchange, or lease of property to foreign governments and international organizations as provided for in the first section of this Act. All proceeds received from such sales, exchanges, or leases shall, notwithstanding the provisions of section 3617 of the Revised Statutes (31 U.S.C. 484) or any other law, be paid into a special account with the Treasurer of the United States, such account to be administered by the Secretary of State for the purposes set out in section 5 of this Act. All sums remaining in such special account after completion of the projects authorized in section 5 shall be covered into the Treasury as miscellaneous receipts. The Secretary may retain therefrom a reserve for maintenance and security of those public improvements authorized by this Act which have not been conveyed to a government or international organization under the first section of this Act, and for surveys and plans related to development of additional areas within the Nation's Capital for chancery and diplomatic purposes. Amounts in the reserve will be available only to the extent and in such amounts as provided in advance in appropriations Acts.

SEC. 6.   This Act may be cited as the "International Center Act".

★

40 U.S.C. Ch. 69–Union Station Redevelopment

40 U.S.C. Ch. 69

TITLE 40—PUBLIC BUILDINGS, PROPERTY, AND WORKS

This title was enacted by Pub. L. 107–217, §1, Aug. 21, 2002, 116 Stat. 1062

* * * * * * *

SUBTITLE II—PUBLIC BUILDINGS AND WORKS

* * * * * * *

PART C—FEDERAL BUILDING COMPLEXES

* * * * * * *

CHAPTER 69—UNION STATION REDEVELOPMENT

SUBCHAPTER I—UNION STATION COMPLEX

§6901. DEFINITION

In this subchapter, the term "Union Station complex" means real property, air rights, and improvements the Secretary of the Interior leased under sections 101–110 of the National Visitors Center Facilities Act of 1968 (Public Law 90–264, 82 Stat. 43) and property acquired and improvements made in accordance with this subchapter.

(Pub. L. 107–217, Aug. 21, 2002, 116 Stat. 1201.)

§6902. ASSIGNMENT OF RIGHT, TITLE, AND INTEREST IN THE UNION STATION COMPLEX TO THE SECRETARY OF TRANSPORTATION

The Secretary of Transportation has the right, title, and interest in and to the Union Station complex, including all agreements and leases made under sections 101–110 of the National Visitors Center Facilities Act of 1968 (Public Law 90–264, 82 Stat. 43). To the extent the Secretary of Transportation and the Secretary of the Interior agree, the Secretary of the Interior may lease space for visitor services.

(Pub. L. 107–217, Aug. 21, 2002, 116 Stat. 1201.)

§6903. AGREEMENTS AND CONTRACTS

The Secretary of Transportation may make agreements and contracts, except an agreement or contract to sell property rights at the Union Station complex, with a person, a federal, regional, or local agency, or the Architect of the Capitol that the Secretary considers necessary or desirable to carry out the purposes of this subchapter.

(Pub. L. 107–217, Aug. 21, 2002, 116 Stat. 1201.)

§6904. ACQUISITION, MAINTENANCE, AND USE OF PROPERTY

(a) ACQUISITION.—The Secretary of Transportation may acquire for the Federal Government an interest in real property (including easements or reservations) and any other property interest (including contract rights) in or relating or adjacent to the Union Station complex that the Secretary considers necessary to carry out the purposes of this subchapter.

(b) MAINTENANCE AND USE.—The Secretary may maintain, use, operate, manage, and lease, either directly, by contract, or through development agreements, any property interest the Secretary holds or acquires for the Government under this subchapter in the manner and subject to the terms, conditions, covenants, and easements that the Secretary considers necessary or desirable to carry out the purposes of this subchapter.

(Pub. L. 107–217, Aug. 21, 2002, 116 Stat. 1201.)

§6905. SERVICE ON BOARD OF DIRECTORS OF UNION STATION REDEVELOPMENT CORPORATION

To further the rehabilitation, redevelopment, and operation of the Union Station complex, the Secretary of Transportation and the Administrator of the Federal Railroad Administration may serve as ex officio members of the board of directors of the Union Station Redevelopment Corporation.

(Pub. L. 107–217, Aug. 21, 2002, 116 Stat. 1202.)

§6906. Union Station Fund

(a) Establishment.—There is a special deposit account in the Treasury known as the "Union Station Fund", which shall be administered as a revolving fund.

(b) Content.—The account shall be credited with receipts of the Secretary of Transportation from activities authorized by this subchapter.

(c) Use of Amounts.—The Secretary may use income and proceeds received from activities authorized by this subchapter, including operating and leasing income and payments made to the Federal Government under development agreements, to pay expenses the Secretary incurs in carrying out the purposes of this subchapter, including construction, acquisition, leasing, operation, and maintenance expenses and payments made to developers under development agreements.

(d) Availability of Amounts.—The balance in the account is available in amounts specified in annual appropriation laws for making expenditures authorized by this subchapter.

(Pub. L. 107–217, Aug. 21, 2002, 116 Stat. 1202.)

§6907. Use of other appropriated amounts

(a) Waiver of Cost Sharing Requirement.—The Secretary of Transportation may use amounts appropriated under section 24909(a)(2)(A) of title 49 to carry out the purposes of this subchapter.

(b) Ban on Using Amounts for Heliport.—Amounts appropriated under section 24909 of title 49 may not be used for design, construction, or operation of a heliport at or near Union Station.

(Pub. L. 107–217, Aug. 21, 2002, 116 Stat. 1202.)

§6908. Parking facility

(a) Title.—The Federal Government has the right, title, and interest in and to the parking facility at Union Station.

(b) Fees.—The rate of fees charged for use of the facility may exceed the rate required for maintenance and operation of the facility. The rate shall be established in a manner that encourages use of the facility by rail passengers and participants in activities in the Union Station complex and area.

(Pub. L. 107–217, Aug. 21, 2002, 116 Stat. 1202.)

§6909. Supplying steam or chilled water to Union Station complex

The Architect of the Capitol may make agreements with the Secretary of Transportation to furnish steam, chilled water, or both from the Capitol Power Plant to the Union Station complex, at no expense to the legislative branch.

(Pub. L. 107–217, Aug. 21, 2002, 116 Stat. 1202.)

§6910. Authorization of appropriations

Amounts necessary to meet lease and other obligations, including maintenance requirements, incurred by the Secretary of the Interior and assigned to the Secretary of Transportation under this subchapter may be appropriated to the Secretary of Transportation.

(Pub. L. 107–217, Aug. 21, 2002, 116 Stat. 1202.)

SUBCHAPTER II—NATIONAL VISITOR FACILITIES ADVISORY COMMISSION

§6921. Establishment, composition, and meetings

(a) Establishment.—There is a National Visitor Facilities Advisory Commission.

(b) Composition.—

(1) Membership.—The Commission is composed of—

(A) the Secretary of the Interior;

(B) the Administrator of General Services;

(C) the Secretary of the Smithsonian Institution;

(D) the Chairman of the National Capital Planning Commission;

(E) the Chairman of the Commission of Fine Arts;

(F) six Members of the Senate, three from each party, to be appointed by the President of the Senate;

(G) six Members of the House of Representatives, three from each party, to be appointed by the Speaker of the House of Representatives; and

(H) three individuals appointed by the President, at least two of whom shall not be officers of the Federal Government, and one member of whom shall be a representative of the District of Columbia government.

(2) Chairman.—The Secretary of the Interior serves as the Chairman of the Commission.

(3) Service of non-federal members.—Non-federal members serve at the pleasure of the President.

(c) Meetings.—The Commission shall meet at the call of the Chairman.

(Pub. L. 107–217, Aug. 21, 2002, 116 Stat. 1203.)

§6922. Duties

(a) In General.—The National Visitor Facilities Advisory Commission shall—

(1) conduct continuing investigations and studies of sites and plans to provide additional facilities and services for visitors and students coming to the Nation's Capital; and

(2) advise the Secretary of the Interior and the Administrator of General Services on the planning, construction, acquisition, and operation of those visitor facilities.

(b) Staff and Facilities.—The Director of the National Park Service, in consultation with the Administrator, shall provide the necessary staff and facilities to assist the Commission in carrying out its duties under this subchapter.

(Pub. L. 107–217, Aug. 21, 2002, 116 Stat. 1203.)

§6923. Compensation and expenses

Members of the National Visitor Facilities Advisory Commission who are not officers or employees of the Federal Government or the government of the District of Columbia are entitled to receive compensation under section 3109 of title 5 and expenses under section 5703 of title 5.

(Pub. L. 107–217, Aug. 21, 2002, 116 Stat. 1203.)

§6924. REPORTS AND RECOMMENDATIONS

The National Visitor Facilities Advisory Commission shall report to the Secretary of the Interior and the Administrator of General Services the results of its studies and investigations. A report recommending additional facilities for visitors shall include the Commission's recommendations as to sites for the facilities to be provided, preliminary plans, specifications, and architectural drawings for the facilities, and the estimated cost of the recommended sites and facilities.

(Pub. L. 107–217, Aug. 21, 2002, 116 Stat. 1203.)

* * * * * *

★

DETAIL OF CAPITOL POLICE

PUBLIC LAW 106–58

INDEPENDENT AGENCIES APPROPRIATIONS ACT, 2000

(Sec. 410 - Conveyance of Land to the Columbia Hospital for Women)

[Public Law 106–58; 113 Stat. 454]

[As Amended Through P.L. 106–58, Enacted September 29, 1999]

SEC. 410. CONVEYANCE OF LAND TO THE COLUMBIA HOSPITAL FOR WOMEN.

(a) ADMINISTRATOR OF GENERAL SERVICES.— Upon receipt of written notice and the consideration specified herein from the Columbia Hospital for Women (formerly Columbia Hospital for Women and Lying-In Asylum, located in Washington, District of Columbia; in this section referred to as Columbia Hospital), subject to subsection (f) and such other terms and conditions as the Administrator of General Services (in this section referred to as the Administrator) shall require, the Administrator shall convey to Columbia Hospital, all right, title, and interest of the United States in and to those pieces or parcels of land in the District of Columbia, described in subsection (b), together with all improvements thereon and appurtenances thereto (in this section referred to as the Property). The purchase price for the Property shall be $14,000,000 (not including any accrued interest) to be paid in accordance with the terms set forth in subsection (d). The purpose of this conveyance is to provide hospital, medical and healthcare services and related uses, including but not limited to the expansion by Columbia Hospital of its Ambulatory Care Center, Betty Ford Breast Center, and the Columbia Hospital Center for Teen Health and Reproductive Toxicology Center.

(b) PROPERTY DESCRIPTION.—

(1) IN GENERAL.— The land referred to in subsection (a) was conveyed to the United States of America by deed dated May 2, 1888, from David Fergusson, widower, recorded in liber 1314, folio 102, of the land records of the District of Columbia, and is that portion of square numbered 25 in the city of Washington in the District of Columbia which was not previously conveyed to such hospital by the Act of June 28, 1952 (66 Stat. 287; chapter 486).

(2) PARTICULAR DESCRIPTION.— The Property is more particularly described as square 25, lot 803, or as follows: all that piece or parcel of land situated and lying in the city of Washington in the District of Columbia and known as part of square numbered 25, as laid down and distinguished on the plat or plan of said city as follows: beginning for the same at the northeast corner of the square being the corner formed by the intersection of the west line of Twenty-fourth Street Northwest, with the south line of north M Street Northwest and running thence south with

the line of said Twenty-fourth Street Northwest for the distance of two hundred and thirty-one feet ten inches, thence running west and parallel with said M Street Northwest for the distance of two hundred and thirty feet six inches and running thence north and parallel with the line of said Twenty-fourth Street Northwest for the distance of two hundred and thirty-one feet ten inches to the line of said M Street Northwest and running thence east with the line of said M Street Northwest to the place of beginning two hundred and thirty feet and six inches together with all the improvements, ways, easements, rights, privileges, and appurtenances to the same belonging or in anywise appertaining.

(c) DATE OF CONVEYANCE.—

(1) DATE.— The date of the conveyance of the Property shall be no later than 90 days from the date upon which the Administrator receives from Columbia Hospital written notice of its intent to purchase the Property during which time the parties shall execute all necessary purchase and sale documents, and shall pay the initial cash consideration in an amount at minimum equal to the first of 30 equal annual installment payments of the purchase price as contemplated in subsection (d)(2) hereinbelow.

(2) DEADLINE FOR CONVEYANCE OF THE PROPERTY.— Written notification and payment of the consideration set forth under subsection (c)(1) from Columbia Hospital shall be ineffective, and all rights granted Columbia Hospital under this section to purchase the Property shall lapse, and become void and of no further force and effect, if that written notification and installment payment are not received by the Administrator before the date which is one (1) year after the date of the enactment of this section.

(3) QUITCLAIM DEED.— Any conveyance of the Property to Columbia Hospital under this section shall be by quitclaim deed.

(d) CONVEYANCE TERMS.—

(1) IN GENERAL.—The conveyance of the Property shall be consistent with the terms and conditions set forth in this section and such other terms and conditions as the Administrator deems to be in the interest of the United States, including but not limited to—

(A) credit and payment provisions, including the provision for the prepayment of the full purchase price if mutually acceptable to the parties;

(B) restrictions on the use of the Property for the purposes set forth in subsection (a);

(C) conditions under which the Property or interests therein may be sold, mortgaged, assigned, or otherwise conveyed in order to facilitate financing to fulfill its intended use; and

(D) consequences in the event of default by Columbia Hospital for failing to pay all installments payments toward the total purchase price when due, including reversion of the described property to the United States.

(2) PAYMENT OF PURCHASE PRICE.— Columbia Hospital shall pay the total purchase price of $14,000,000.00 for the Property. The terms and conditions of the sale shall be as deemed by the Administrator to be in the best interests of the

United States. Such terms may include financing the payment of the purchase price in annual installments for a term not to exceed 30 years with interest on the unpaid balance not to exceed four and five-tenths percent (4.5%) per annum (except during periods of default or upon entry of a final judgment amount).

(3)   The Administrator shall have full authority to administer the credit granted to Columbia Hospital in accordance with this section including, without limitation, the authority to adjust, settle, or compromise the amounts specified in this section or in the documents of conveyance.

(4) EXECUTION OF DOCUMENTS.— The Columbia Hospital shall execute and provide to the Administrator such written instruments including but not limited to contracts for purchase and sale, notes, mortgages, deeds of trust, restrictive covenants, indenture deeds, and assurances as the Administrator may reasonably request to effect this transaction and to protect the interests of the United States under this section.

(e) TREATMENT OF AMOUNTS RECEIVED.— Amounts received by the United States as payments under this section shall be paid into the fund established by section 210(f) of the Federal Property and Administrative Services Act of 1949 (40 U.S.C. 490(f)), and may be expended by the Administrator for real property management and related activities not otherwise provided for, without further authorization.

(f) REVERSIONARY INTEREST.—

(1) IN GENERAL.—The Property, once conveyed as authorized under subsection (a), shall revert to the United States, together with any improvements thereon—

(A)   One (1) year from the date on which Columbia Hospital defaults in paying to the United States any amount when due; or

(B)   immediately, upon any attempt by Columbia Hospital to assign, sell, mortgage, or convey the Property without the Administrator's prior written consent before the United States has received full purchase price, plus accrued interest.

(2) RELEASE OF REVERSIONARY INTEREST.— The Administrator may release, upon request, any restriction imposed on the use of the Property authorized in subsection (d)(1)(B) for the purposes set forth in subsection (a), and release any reversionary interest of the United States in the Property upon receipt by the United States of full payment of the purchase price, including any accrued interest, specified under subsection (d)(2), or such other terms and conditions as may be determined by the Administrator to be in the best interests of the United States as set forth in subsection (d).

(3) PROPERTY RETURNED TO THE GENERAL SERVICES ADMINISTRATION.— Any portion of the Property that reverts to the United States under this subsection shall be under the jurisdiction, custody and control of the General Services Administration and shall be available for use or disposition by the Administrator in accordance with applicable Federal law.

★

54 U.S.C. LAND AND WATER CONSERVATION FUND PROVISIONS

54 U.S.C.–NATIONAL PARK SERVICE AND RELATED PROGRAMS
§200301-03

TITLE 54—NATIONAL PARK SERVICE AND RELATED PROGRAMS

This title was enacted by Pub. L. 113-287, §3, Dec. 19, 2014, 128 Stat. 3094

* * * * * * *

Subtitle II—Outdoor Recreation Programs

* * * * * * *

CHAPTER 2003—LAND AND WATER CONSERVATION FUND

* * * * * * *

§200301. DEFINITIONS

In this chapter:

(1) FUND.—The term "Fund" means the Land and Water Conservation Fund established under section 200302 of this title.

(2) STATE.—The term "State" means a State, the District of Columbia, Puerto Rico, Guam, American Samoa, the Virgin Islands, and the Northern Mariana Islands.

(Pub. L. 113-287, §3, Dec. 19, 2014, 128 Stat. 3171.)

§200302. ESTABLISHMENT OF LAND AND WATER CONSERVATION FUND

(a) ESTABLISHMENT.—There is established in the Treasury the Land and Water Conservation Fund.

(b) DEPOSITS.—There shall be deposited in the Fund the following revenues and collections:

(1) All proceeds (except so much thereof as may be otherwise obligated, credited, or paid under authority of the provisions of law set forth in section 572(a) or 574(a) to (c) of title 40 or under authority of any appropriation Act that appropriates an amount, to be derived from proceeds from the transfer of excess property and the

479

disposal of surplus property, for necessary expenses, not otherwise provided for, incident to the utilization and disposal of excess and surplus property) received from any disposal of surplus real property and related personal property under chapter 5 of title 40, notwithstanding any provision of law that such proceeds shall be credited to miscellaneous receipts of the Treasury. Nothing in this chapter shall affect existing laws or regulations concerning disposal of real or personal surplus property to schools, hospitals, and States and their political subdivisions.

(2) The amounts provided for in section 200310 of this title.

(c) AUTHORIZATION OF APPROPRIATIONS.—

(1) IN GENERAL.—In addition to the sum of the revenues and collections estimated by the Secretary to be deposited in the Fund pursuant to this section, there are authorized to be appropriated annually to the Fund out of any money in the Treasury not otherwise appropriated such amounts as are necessary to make the income of the Fund not less than $900,000,000 for each fiscal year.

(2) RECEIPTS UNDER OUTER CONTINENTAL SHELF LANDS ACT.—To the extent that amounts appropriated under paragraph (1) are not sufficient to make the total annual income of the Fund equivalent to the amounts provided in paragraph (1), an amount sufficient to cover the remainder shall be credited to the Fund from revenues due and payable to the United States for deposit in the Treasury as miscellaneous receipts under the Outer Continental Shelf Lands Act (43 U.S.C. 1331 et seq.).

(Pub. L. 113–287, §3, Dec. 19, 2014, 128 Stat. 3171; Pub. L. 114–113, div. O, title VIII, §801(a), Dec. 18, 2015, 129 Stat. 3030; Pub. L. 116–9, title III, §3001(a), Mar. 12, 2019, 133 Stat. 754; Pub. L. 116–152, §3(b)(1), Aug. 4, 2020, 134 Stat. 687.)

§200303. AVAILABILITY OF FUNDS

(a) IN GENERAL.—Any amounts deposited in the Fund under section 200302 for fiscal year 2020 and each fiscal year thereafter shall be made available for expenditure for fiscal year 2021 and each fiscal year thereafter, without further appropriation or fiscal year limitation, to carry out the purposes of the Fund (including accounts and programs made available from the Fund pursuant to the Further Consolidated Appropriations Act, 2020 (Public Law 116–94; 133 Stat. 2534)).

(b) ADDITIONAL AMOUNTS.—Amounts made available under subsection (a) shall be in addition to amounts made available to the Fund under section 105 of the Gulf of Mexico Energy Security Act of 2006 (43 U.S.C. 1331 note; Public Law 109–432) or otherwise appropriated from the Fund.

(c) ALLOCATION AUTHORITY.—

(1) SUBMISSION OF COST ESTIMATES.—The President shall submit to Congress detailed account, program, and project allocations of the full amount made available under subsection (a)—

(A) for fiscal year 2021, not later than 90 days after the date of enactment of the Great American Outdoors Act; and

(B) for each fiscal year thereafter, as part of the annual budget submission of the President.

(2) ALTERNATE ALLOCATION.—

(A) IN GENERAL.—Appropriations Acts may provide for alternate allocation of amounts made available under subsection (a), including allocations by account, program, and project.

(B) ALLOCATION BY PRESIDENT.—

(i) NO ALTERNATE ALLOCATIONS.—If Congress has not enacted legislation establishing alternate allocations by the date on which the Act making full-year appropriations for the Department of the Interior, Environment, and Related Agencies for the applicable fiscal year is enacted into law, amounts made available under subsection (a) shall be allocated by the President.

(ii) INSUFFICIENT ALTERNATE ALLOCATION.—If Congress enacts legislation establishing alternate allocations for amounts made available under subsection (a) that are less than the full amount appropriated under that subsection, the difference between the amount appropriated and the alternate allocation shall be allocated by the President.

(3) RECREATIONAL PUBLIC ACCESS.—Amounts expended from the Fund under this section shall be consistent with the requirements for recreational public access for hunting, fishing, recreational shooting, or other outdoor recreational purposes under section 200306(c).

(4) ANNUAL REPORT.—The President shall submit to Congress an annual report that describes the final allocation by account, program, and project of amounts made available under subsection (a), including a description of the status of obligations and expenditures.

(Pub. L. 113–287, §3, Dec. 19, 2014, 128 Stat. 3172; Pub. L. 116–152, §3(a), Aug. 4, 2020, 134 Stat. 686.)

* * * * * *

★

ENERGY POLICY ACT OF 1992 §310

PUBLIC LAW 102–486

AS AMENDED THROUGH P.L. 117–286

ENERGY POLICY ACT OF 1992

[Pub. L. 102–486; Approved onOct. 24, 1992;106 Stat. 2776]

[As Amended ThroughP.L. 117–286, EnactedDecember 27, 2022]
[This Act consists of Pub. L. 102–486 (106 Stat. 2776) enacted on Oct. 24, 1992, and generally appears in title 42, United States Code. Bracketed notes are used at the end of each section for the convenience of the reader to indicate the United States Code citation.]

An Act to provide for improved energy efficiency.

Be it enacted by the Senate and House of Representatives of the United States of America in Congress assembled,

* * * * * * *

* * * * * * *

TITLE III— ALTERNATIVE FUELS—GENERAL

* * * * * * *

SEC. 310. REPORTS.

(a) GENERAL SERVICE ADMINISTRATION PROGRAM REPORT.— Not later than one year after the date of the enactment of this Act, and biennially thereafter, the Administrator of General Services shall report to the Congress on the General Services Administration's alternative fueled vehicle program under this Act. The report shall contain information on—

(1) the number and type of alternative fueled vehicles procured;

(2) the location of alternative fueled vehicles by standard Federal region;

(3) the total number of alternative fueled vehicles used by each Federal agency;

(4) arrangements with commercial entities for refueling and maintenance of alternative fueled vehicles;

(5) future alternative fueled vehicle procurement and placement strategy;

(6) the difference in cost between the purchase, maintenance, and operation of alternative fueled vehicles and the purchase, maintenance, and operation of

comparable conventionally fueled motor vehicles;

(7)   coordination among Federal, State, and local governments for alternative fueled vehicle procurement and placement;

(8)   the percentage of alternative fuel use in dual-fueled vehicles procured by the Administrator of General Services as measured under section 308;

(9)   a description of the representative sample of alternative fueled vehicles as determined under section 400AA(b)(1)(A) of the Energy Policy and Conservation Act; and

(10)   award recipients under this title.

(b) COMPLIANCE REPORT.—

(1) IN GENERAL.— Not later than February 15, 2006, and annually thereafter for the next 14 years, the head of each Federal agency which is subject to this Act and Executive Order No. 13031 shall prepare, and submit to Congress, a report that—

(A)   summarizes the compliance by such Federal agency with the alternative fuel purchasing requirements for Federal fleets under this Act and Executive Order No. 13031; and

(B)   includes a plan of compliance that contains specific dates for achieving compliance using reasonable means.

(2) CONTENTS.—

(A) IN GENERAL.— Each report submitted under paragraph (1) shall include—

(i)   any information on any failure to meet statutory requirements or requirements under Executive Order No. 13031;

(ii) (I)   any plan of compliance that the agency head is required to submit under Executive Order No. 13031; or

(II)   if a plan of compliance referred to in subclause (I) does not contain specific dates by which the Federal agency is to achieve compliance, a revised plan of compliance that contains specific dates for achieving compliance; and

(iii)   any related information the agency head is required to submit to the Director of the Office of Management and Budget under Executive Order No. 13031.

(B) PENULTIMATE REPORT.—   The penultimate report submitted under paragraph (1) shall include an announcement that the report for the next year shall be the final report submitted under paragraph (1).

(3) PUBLIC DISSEMINATION OF REPORT.— Each report submitted under paragraph (1) shall be made public, including—

(A)   placing such report on a publicly available website on the Internet; and

(B)   publishing the availability of the report, including such website address, in the Federal Register.

[42 U.S.C. 13218]

* * * * * *

★

ENERGY POLICY ACT OF 2005

PUBLIC LAW 109–58
AS AMENDED THROUGH P.L. 118–159

ENERGY POLICY ACT OF 2005

[Public Law 109–58, Enacted August 8, 2005]

[As Amended Through P.L. 118–159, Enacted December 23, 2024]

AN ACT To ensure jobs for our future with secure, affordable, and reliable energy.

Be it enacted by the Senate and House of Representatives of the United States of America in Congress assembled,

SECTION 1. [42 U.S.C. 15801 note] SHORT TITLE; TABLE OF CONTENTS.

(a) SHORT TITLE.— This Act may be cited as the "Energy Policy Act of 2005".

(b) TABLE OF CONTENTS.— The table of contents for this Act is as follows:

---

[1]   So in law. There is no item relating to section 2 (definitions) in the table of contents.

TITLE I—ENERGY EFFICIENCY

Subtitle A—Federal Programs

TITLE II—RENEWABLE ENERGY

Subtitle A—General Provisions

SEC. 2. [42 U.S.C. 15801] DEFINITIONS.

Except as otherwise provided, in this Act:

(1) DEPARTMENT.— The term Department means the Department of Energy.

(2) INSTITUTION OF HIGHER EDUCATION.—

(A) IN GENERAL.— The term institution of higher education has the meaning given the term in section 101(a) of the Higher Education Act of 1065 (20 U.S.C. 1001(a)).

(B) INCLUSION.—The term institution of higher education includes an organization that—

(i) is organized, and at all times thereafter operated, exclusively for the benefit of, to perform the functions of, or to carry out the functions of one or more organizations referred to in subparagraph (A); and

(ii) is operated, supervised, or controlled by or in connection with one or more of those organizations.

(3) NATIONAL LABORATORY.—The term National Laboratory means any of the following laboratories owned by the Department:

(A)   Ames Laboratory.

(B)   Argonne National Laboratory.

(C)   Brookhaven National Laboratory.

(D)   Fermi National Accelerator Laboratory.

(E)   Idaho National Laboratory.

(F)   Lawrence Berkeley National Laboratory.

(G)   Lawrence Livermore National Laboratory.

(H)   Los Alamos National Laboratory.

(I)   National Energy Technology Laboratory.

(J)   National Renewable Energy Laboratory.

(K)   Oak Ridge National Laboratory.

(L)   Pacific Northwest National Laboratory.

(M)   Princeton Plasma Physics Laboratory.

(N)   Sandia National Laboratories.

(O)   Savannah River National Laboratory.

(P)   Stanford Linear Accelerator Center.

(Q)   Thomas Jefferson National Accelerator Facility.

(4) SECRETARY.— The term Secretary means the Secretary of Energy.

(5) SMALL BUSINESS CONCERN.— The term small business concern has the meaning given the term in section 3 of the Small Business Act (15 U.S.C. 632).

TITLE I—ENERGY EFFICIENCY

Subtitle A—FEDERAL PROGRAMS

* * * * * * *

SEC. 102. ENERGY MANAGEMENT REQUIREMENTS.

(a) ENERGY REDUCTION GOALS.—

(1) AMENDMENT.— Section 543(a)(1) of the National Energy Conservation Policy Act (42 U.S.C. 8253(a)(1)) is amended by striking its Federal buildings so that and all that follows through the end and inserting ``the Federal buildings of the agency (including each industrial or laboratory facility) so that the energy consumption per gross square foot of the Federal buildings of the agency in fiscal years 2006 through 2015 is reduced, as compared with the energy consumption per gross square foot of the Federal buildings of the agency in fiscal year 2003, by the percentage specified in the following table:

``Fiscal Year	Percentage reduction
2006	2
2007	4
2008	6
2009	8
2010	10
2011	12
2012	14
2013	16
2014	18
2015	20.''.

(2) REPORTING BASELINE.— The energy reduction goals and baseline established in paragraph (1) of section 543(a) of the National Energy Conservation Policy Act (42 U.S.C. 8253(a)(1)), as amended by this subsection, supersede all previous goals and baselines under such paragraph, and related reporting requirements.

(b) REVIEW AND REVISION OF ENERGY PERFORMANCE REQUIREMENT.— Section 543(a) of the National Energy Conservation Policy Act (42 U.S.C. 8253(a)) is further amended by adding at the end the following:

"(3)   Not later than December 31, 2014, the Secretary shall review the results of the implementation of the energy performance requirement established under paragraph (1) and submit to Congress recommendations concerning energy performance requirements for fiscal years 2016 through 2025.".

(c) EXCLUSIONS.— Section 543(c)(1) of the National Energy Conservation Policy Act (42 U.S.C. 8253(c)(1)) is amended by striking An agency may exclude and all that follows through the end and inserting ``(A) An agency may exclude, from the energy performance requirement for a fiscal year established under subsection (a) and the energy management requirement established under subsection (b), any Federal building or collection of Federal buildings, if the head of the agency finds that—

"(i)   compliance with those requirements would be impracticable;

"(ii)   the agency has completed and submitted all federally required energy management reports;

"(iii)   the agency has achieved compliance with the energy efficiency requirements of this Act, the Energy Policy Act of 1992, Executive orders, and other Federal law; and

"(iv)   the agency has implemented all practicable, life cycle cost-effective projects with respect to the Federal building or collection of Federal buildings to be excluded.

"(B) A finding of impracticability under subparagraph (A)(i) shall be based on—

"(i)   the energy intensiveness of activities carried out in the Federal building or collection of Federal buildings; or

"(ii)   the fact that the Federal building or collection of Federal buildings is used in the performance of a national security function.".

(d) REVIEW BY SECRETARY.—Section 543(c)(2) of the National Energy Conservation Policy Act (42 U.S.C. 8253(c)(2)) is amended—

(1)   by striking impracticability standards and inserting standards for exclusion;

(2)   by striking a finding of impracticability and inserting the exclusion; and

(3)   by striking energy consumption requirements and inserting requirements of subsections (a) and (b)(1).

(e) CRITERIA.— Section 543(c) of the National Energy Conservation Policy Act (42 U.S.C. 8253(c)) is further amended by adding at the end the following:

"(3)   Not later than 180 days after the date of enactment of this paragraph, the Secretary shall issue guidelines that establish criteria for exclusions under paragraph (1).".

(f) RETENTION OF ENERGY AND WATER SAVINGS.— Section 546 of the National Energy Conservation Policy Act (42 U.S.C. 8256) is amended by adding at the end the following new subsection:

"(e) RETENTION OF ENERGY AND WATER SAVINGS.— An agency may retain any funds appropriated to that agency for energy expenditures, water expenditures, or wastewater treatment expenditures, at buildings subject to the requirements of section 543(a) and (b), that are not made because of energy savings or water savings. Except as otherwise provided by law, such funds may be used only for energy efficiency, water conservation, or unconventional and renewable energy resources projects. Such projects shall be subject to the requirements of section 3307 of title 40, United States Code.".

(g) REPORTS.—Section 548(b) of the National Energy Conservation Policy Act (42 U.S.C. 8258(b)) is amended—

(1)   in the subsection heading, by inserting the President and before Congress; and

(2)   by inserting President and before Congress.

(h) CONFORMING AMENDMENT.— Section 550(d) of the National Energy

Conservation Policy Act (42 U.S.C. 8258b(d)) is amended in the second sentence by striking the 20 percent reduction goal established under section 543(a) of the National Energy Conservation Policy Act (42 U.S.C. 8253(a)). and inserting each of the energy reduction goals established under section 543(a)..

* * * * * * *

SEC. 105. ENERGY SAVINGS PERFORMANCE CONTRACTS.

(a) EXTENSION.— Section 801(c) of the National Energy Conservation Policy Act (42 U.S.C. 8287(c)) is amended by striking 2006 and inserting 2016.

(b) EXTENSION OF AUTHORITY.— Any energy savings performance contract entered into under section 801 of the National Energy Conservation Policy Act (42 U.S.C. 8287) after October 1, 2003, and before the date of enactment of this Act, shall be considered to have been entered into under that section.

SEC. 106. [42 U.S.C. 15811] VOLUNTARY COMMITMENTS TO REDUCE INDUSTRIAL ENERGY INTENSITY.

(a) DEFINITION OF ENERGY INTENSITY.— In this section, the term energy intensity means the primary energy consumed for each unit of physical output in an industrial process.

(b) VOLUNTARY AGREEMENTS.— The Secretary may enter into voluntary agreements with one or more persons in industrial sectors that consume significant quantities of primary energy for each unit of physical output to reduce the energy intensity of the production activities of the persons.

(c) GOAL.— Voluntary agreements under this section shall have as a goal the reduction of energy intensity by not less than 2.5 percent each year during the period of calendar years 2007 through 2016.

(d) RECOGNITION.— The Secretary, in cooperation with other appropriate Federal agencies, shall develop mechanisms to recognize and publicize the achievements of participants in voluntary agreements under this section.

(e) TECHNICAL ASSISTANCE.— A person that enters into an agreement under this section and continues to make a good faith effort to achieve the energy efficiency goals specified in the agreement shall be eligible to receive from the Secretary a grant or technical assistance, as appropriate, to assist in the achievement of those goals.

(f) REPORT.—Not later than each of June 30, 2012, and June 30, 2017, the Secretary shall submit to Congress a report that—

(1) evaluates the success of the voluntary agreements under this section; and

(2) provides independent verification of a sample of the energy savings estimates provided by participating firms.

SEC. 107. [42 U.S.C. 15812] ADVANCED BUILDING EFFICIENCY TESTBED.

(a) ESTABLISHMENT.— The Secretary, in consultation with the Administrator of General Services, shall establish an Advanced Building Efficiency Testbed program for the development, testing, and demonstration of advanced engineering systems, components, and materials to enable innovations in building technologies. The program shall evaluate efficiency concepts for government and industry buildings, and demonstrate the ability of next generation buildings to support individual and organizational productivity and health (including by improving indoor air quality) as well as flexibility and technological change to improve environmental sustainability. Such program shall complement and not duplicate existing national programs.

(b) PARTICIPANTS.— The program established under subsection (a) shall be led by a university with the ability to combine the expertise from numerous academic fields including, at a minimum, intelligent workplaces and advanced building systems and engineering, electrical and computer engineering, computer science, architecture, urban design, and environmental and mechanical engineering. Such university shall partner with other universities and entities who have established programs and the capability of advancing innovative building efficiency technologies.

(c) AUTHORIZATION OF APPROPRIATIONS.— There are authorized to be appropriated to the Secretary to carry out this section $6,000,000 for each of the fiscal years 2006 through 2008, to remain available until expended. For any fiscal year in which funds are expended under this section, the Secretary shall provide one-third of the total amount to the lead university described in subsection (b), and provide the remaining two-thirds to the other participants referred to in subsection (b) on an equal basis.

* * * * * * *

SEC. 110. DAYLIGHT SAVINGS.

(a) AMENDMENT.—Section 3(a) of the Uniform Time Act of 1966 (15 U.S.C. 260a(a)) is amended—

(1) by striking first Sunday of April and inserting second Sunday of March; and

(2) by striking last Sunday of October and inserting first Sunday of November.

(b) EFFECTIVE DATE.— Subsection (a) shall take effect 1 year after the date of enactment of this Act or March 1, 2007, whichever is later.

(c) REPORT TO CONGRESS.— Not later than 9 months after the effective date stated in subsection (b), the Secretary shall report to Congress on the impact of this section on energy consumption in the United States.

(d) RIGHT TO REVERT.— Congress retains the right to revert the Daylight Saving Time back to the 2005 time schedules once the Department study is complete.

SEC. 111. [42 U.S.C. 15813] ENHANCING ENERGY EFFICIENCY IN MANAGEMENT OF FEDERAL LANDS.

(a) SENSE OF THE CONGRESS.— It is the sense of the Congress that Federal agencies should enhance the use of energy efficient technologies in the management of natural resources.

(b) ENERGY EFFICIENT BUILDINGS.— To the extent practicable, the Secretary of the Interior, the Secretary of Commerce, and the Secretary of Agriculture shall seek to incorporate energy efficient technologies in public and administrative buildings associated with management of the National Park System, National Wildlife Refuge System, National Forest System, National Marine Sanctuaries System, and other public lands and resources managed by the Secretaries.

(c) ENERGY EFFICIENT VEHICLES.— To the extent practicable, the Secretary of the Interior, the Secretary of Commerce, and the Secretary of Agriculture shall seek to use energy efficient motor vehicles, including vehicles equipped with biodiesel or hybrid engine technologies, in the management of the National Park System, National Wildlife Refuge System, National Forest System, National Marine Sanctuaries System, and other public lands and resources managed by the Secretaries.

* * * * * * *

TITLE II—RENEWABLE ENERGY

Subtitle A—GENERAL PROVISIONS

* * * * * * *

SEC. 203. [42 U.S.C. 15852] FEDERAL PURCHASE REQUIREMENT.

(a) REQUIREMENT.—The President, acting through the Secretary, shall seek to ensure that, to the extent economically feasible and technically practicable, of the total amount of electric energy the Federal Government consumes during any fiscal year, the following amounts shall be renewable energy:

(1)   Not less than 3 percent in fiscal years 2007 through 2009.

(2)   Not less than 5 percent in fiscal years 2010 through 2012.

(3)   Not less than 7.5 percent in fiscal year 2013 and each fiscal year thereafter.

(b) DEFINITIONS.—In this section:

(1) BIOMASS.—The term biomass means any lignin waste material that is segregated from other waste materials and is determined to be nonhazardous by the Administrator of the Environmental Protection Agency and any solid, nonhazardous, cellulosic material that is derived from—

(A)   any of the following forest-related resources: mill residues, precommercial thinnings, slash, and brush, or nonmerchantable material;

(B)   solid wood waste materials, including waste pallets, crates, dunnage, manufacturing and construction wood wastes (other than pressure-treated, chemically-treated, or painted wood wastes), and landscape or right-of-way tree trimmings, but not including municipal solid waste (garbage), gas derived from the biodegradation of solid waste, or paper that is commonly recycled;

(C)   agriculture wastes, including orchard tree crops, vineyard, grain, legumes, sugar, and other crop by-products or residues, and livestock waste nutrients; or

(D)   a plant that is grown exclusively as a fuel for the production of electricity.

(2) RENEWABLE ENERGY.— The term renewable energy means marine energy (as defined in section 632 of the Energy Independence and Security Act of 2007),

or electric energy produced from solar, wind, biomass, landfill gas, geothermal, municipal solid waste, or new hydroelectric generation capacity achieved from increased efficiency or additions of new capacity at an existing hydroelectric project.

(c) CALCULATION.—

(1) IN GENERAL.—For purposes of determining compliance with the requirement of this section, the amount of renewable energy shall be doubled if

(A) the renewable energy is produced and used on-site at a Federal facility;

(B) the renewable energy is produced on Federal lands and used at a Federal facility; or

(C) the renewable energy is produced on Indian land as defined in title XXVI of the Energy Policy Act of 1992 (25 U.S.C. 3501 et seq.) and used at a Federal facility.

(2) SEPARATE CALCULATION.—

(A) IN GENERAL.— For purposes of determining compliance with the requirement of this section, any energy consumption that is avoided through the use of geothermal energy shall be considered to be renewable energy produced.

(B) EFFICIENCY ACCOUNTING.— Energy consumption that is avoided through the use of geothermal energy that is considered to be renewable energy under this section shall not be considered energy efficiency for the purpose of compliance with Federal energy efficiency goals, targets, and incentives.

(d) REPORT.— Not later than April 15, 2007, and every 2 years thereafter, the Secretary shall provide a report to Congress on the progress of the Federal Government in meeting the goals established by this section.

★

ENERGY INDEPENDENCE AND SECURITY ACT

OF 2007

AS CONTAINED WITHIN THE U.S.C.

42 U.S.C. §§6834, 8259B, 17001, 17081–17083, 17091–17096, 17131, 17141, 17143, 17144; 2 U.S.C. §§1824, 2162A, 2169.

SELECTED PROVISIONS OF THE ENERGY INDEPENDENCE AND SECURITY ACT OF 2007 AS IN THE U.S.C.

TITLE 42—THE PUBLIC HEALTH AND WELFARE

Pub. L. 114–11, §1(a), Apr. 30, 2015, 129 Stat. 182, provided that: "This Act [enacting sections 17062, 17063, 17084, and 17085 of this title, amending sections 6295, 6302 to 6304, and 17091 of this title, and enacting provisions set out as a note under this section] may be cited as the 'Energy Efficiency Improvement Act of 2015'."

Pub. L. 114–11, title I, §101, Apr. 30, 2015, 129 Stat. 182, provided that: "This title [enacting sections 17062, 17084, and 17085 of this title] may be cited as the 'Better Buildings Act of 2015'."

* * * * * * *

CHAPTER 81—ENERGY CONSERVATION AND RESOURCE RENEWAL

* * * * * * *

SUBCHAPTER II—ENERGY CONSERVATION STANDARDS FOR NEW BUILDINGS

* * * * * * *

§6834. FEDERAL BUILDING ENERGY EFFICIENCY STANDARDS

(Pub. L. 94–385, title III, §305, as added Pub. L. 102–486, title I, §101(a)(2), Oct. 24, 1992, 106 Stat. 2784; amended Pub. L. 109–58, title I, §109, Aug. 8, 2005, 119 Stat. 614; Pub. L. 110–140, title IV, §433(a), title V, §523, Dec. 19, 2007, 121 Stat. 1612, 1662.)

STATUTORY NOTES AND RELATED SUBSIDIARIES

EFFECTIVE DATE OF 2007 AMENDMENT

REVISION OF FEDERAL ACQUISITION REGULATION; ISSUANCE OF GUIDANCE

Pub. L. 110–140, title IV, §433(c), (d), Dec. 19, 2007, 121 Stat. 1614, provided that:

"(c) REVISION OF FEDERAL ACQUISITION REGULATION.—Not later than 2 years after the date of the enactment of this Act [Dec. 19, 2007], the Federal Acquisition Regulation shall be revised to require Federal officers and employees to comply with this section [amending this section and section 6832 of this title] and the amendments made by this section in the acquisition, construction, or major renovation of any facility. The members of the Federal Acquisition Regulatory Council (established under section 25 of the Office of Federal Procurement Policy Act ([former] 41 U.S.C. 421) [see 41 U.S.C. 1302]) shall consult with the Federal Director and the Commercial Director before promulgating regulations to carry out this subsection.

"(d) GUIDANCE.—Not later than 90 days after the date of promulgation of the revised regulations under subsection (c), the Administrator for Federal Procurement Policy shall issue guidance to all Federal procurement executives providing direction and instructions to renegotiate the design of proposed facilities and major renovations for existing facilities to incorporate improvements that are consistent with this section."

* * * * * * *

SUBCHAPTER III—FEDERAL ENERGY INITIATIVE

* * * * * * *

PART B—FEDERAL ENERGY MANAGEMENT

* * * * * * *

§8259B. FEDERAL PROCUREMENT OF ENERGY EFFICIENT PRODUCTS

(Pub. L. 95–619, title V, §553, as added Pub. L. 109–58, title I, §104(a), Aug. 8, 2005, 119 Stat. 609; amended Pub. L. 110–140, title V, §§524, 525(a), Dec. 19, 2007, 121 Stat. 1662, 1663.)

STATUTORY NOTES AND RELATED SUBSIDIARIES

CATALOGUE LISTING DEADLINE

Pub. L. 110–140, title V, §525(b), Dec. 19, 2007, 121 Stat. 1663, provided that: "Not later than 9 months after the date of enactment of this Act [Dec. 19, 2007], the General Services Administration and the Defense Logistics Agency shall ensure that the requirement established by the amendment made by subsection (a)(2)(A) [amending this section] has been fully complied with."

* * * * * * *

CHAPTER 152—ENERGY INDEPENDENCE AND SECURITY

* * * * * * *

§17001. DEFINITIONS

In this Act:

(1) DEPARTMENT

The term "Department" means the Department of Energy.

(2) INSTITUTION OF HIGHER EDUCATION

The term "institution of higher education" has the meaning given the term in section 1001(a) of title 20.

(3) SECRETARY

The term "Secretary" means the Secretary of Energy.

(Pub. L. 110–140, §2, Dec. 19, 2007, 121 Stat. 1498.)

* * * * * * *

SUBCHAPTER III—ENERGY SAVINGS IN BUILDINGS AND INDUSTRY

§17061. DEFINITIONS

In this title:

(1) ADMINISTRATOR

The term "Administrator" means the Administrator of General Services.

(2) ADVISORY COMMITTEE

The term "Advisory Committee" means the Green Building Advisory Committee established under section 484.

(3) COMMERCIAL DIRECTOR

The term "Commercial Director" means the individual appointed to the position established under section 17081 of this title.

(4) CONSORTIUM

The term "Consortium" means the High-Performance Green Building Partnership Consortium created in response to section 17092(c)(1) of this title to represent the private sector in a public-private partnership to promote high-performance green buildings and zero-net-energy commercial buildings.

(5) COST-EFFECTIVE LIGHTING TECHNOLOGY

(A) IN GENERAL

The term "cost-effective lighting technology" means a lighting technology

that—
    (i) will result in substantial operational cost savings by ensuring an installed consumption of not more than 1 watt per square foot; or
    (ii) is contained in a list under—
        (I) section 8259b of this title;
        (II) Federal acquisition regulation 23–203; and
        (III) is at least as energy-conserving as required by other provisions of this Act, including the requirements of this title and title III which shall be applicable to the extent that they would achieve greater energy savings than provided under clause (i) or this clause.>

(B) INCLUSIONS

The term "cost-effective lighting technology" includes—
    (i) lamps;
    (ii) ballasts;
    (iii) luminaires;
    (iv) lighting controls;
    (v) daylighting; and
    (vi) early use of other highly cost-effective lighting technologies.

(6) COST-EFFECTIVE TECHNOLOGIES AND PRACTICES

The term "cost-effective technologies and practices" means a technology or practice that—
    (A) will result in substantial operational cost savings by reducing electricity or fossil fuel consumption, water, or other utility costs, including use of geothermal heat pumps;
    (B) complies with the provisions of section 8259b of this title and Federal acquisition regulation 23–203; and
    (C) is at least as energy and water conserving as required under this title, including sections 431 through 435, and title V, including sections 511 through 525, which shall be applicable to the extent that they are more stringent or require greater energy or water savings than required by this section.

(7) FEDERAL DIRECTOR

The term "Federal Director" means the individual appointed to the position established under section 17092(a) of this title.

(8) FEDERAL FACILITY

The term "Federal facility" means any building that is constructed, renovated, leased, or purchased in part or in whole for use by the Federal Government.

(9) OPERATIONAL COST SAVINGS

(A) IN GENERAL

The term "operational cost savings" means a reduction in end-use operational costs through the application of cost-effective technologies and practices or geothermal heat pumps, including a reduction in electricity consumption relative to consumption by the same customer or at the same facility in a given year, as defined in guidelines promulgated by the Administrator pursuant to section 7628(b) of this title, that achieves cost savings sufficient to pay the incremental additional costs of using cost-effective technologies and practices including geothermal heat pumps by not later than the later of the date established under sections 431 through 434, or—

(i) for cost-effective technologies and practices, the date that is 5 years after the date of installation; and

(ii) for geothermal heat pumps, as soon as practical after the date of installation of the applicable geothermal heat pump.

(B) INCLUSIONS

The term "operational cost savings" includes savings achieved at a facility as a result of—

(i) the installation or use of cost-effective technologies and practices; or

(ii) the planting of vegetation that shades the facility and reduces the heating, cooling, or lighting needs of the facility.

(C) EXCLUSION

The term "operational cost savings" does not include savings from measures that would likely be adopted in the absence of cost-effective technology and practices programs, as determined by the Administrator.

(10) GEOTHERMAL HEAT PUMP

The term "geothermal heat pump" means any heating or air conditioning technology that—

(A) uses the ground or ground water as a thermal energy source to heat, or as a thermal energy sink to cool, a building; and

(B) meets the requirements of the Energy Star program of the Environmental Protection Agency applicable to geothermal heat pumps on the date of purchase of the technology.

(11) GSA FACILITY

(A) IN GENERAL

The term "GSA facility" means any building, structure, or facility, in whole or in part (including the associated support systems of the building, structure, or facility) that—

(i) is constructed (including facilities constructed for lease), renovated, or purchased, in whole or in part, by the Administrator for use by the Federal Government; or

(ii) is leased, in whole or in part, by the Administrator for use by the Federal Government—

(I) except as provided in subclause (II), for a term of not less than 5 years; or

(II) for a term of less than 5 years, if the Administrator determines that use of cost-effective technologies and practices would result in the payback of expenses.

(B) INCLUSION

The term "GSA facility" includes any group of buildings, structures, or facilities described in subparagraph (A) (including the associated energy-consuming support systems of the buildings, structures, and facilities).

(C) EXEMPTION

The Administrator may exempt from the definition of "GSA facility" under this paragraph a building, structure, or facility that meets the requirements of section 8253(c) of this title.

(12) HIGH-PERFORMANCE BUILDING

The term "high-performance building" means a building that integrates and optimizes on a life cycle basis all major high performance attributes, including energy conservation, environment, safety, security, durability, accessibility, cost-benefit, productivity, sustainability, functionality, and operational considerations.

(13) HIGH-PERFORMANCE GREEN BUILDING

The term "high-performance green building" means a high-performance building that, during its life-cycle, as compared with similar buildings (as measured by Commercial Buildings Energy Consumption Survey or Residential Energy Consumption Survey data from the Energy Information Agency)—

(A) reduces energy, water, and material resource use;

(B) improves indoor environmental quality, including reducing indoor pollution, improving thermal comfort, and improving lighting and acoustic environments that affect occupant health and productivity;

(C) reduces negative impacts on the environment throughout the life-cycle of the building, including air and water pollution and waste generation;

(D) increases the use of environmentally preferable products, including biobased, recycled content, and nontoxic products with lower life-cycle impacts;

(E) increases reuse and recycling opportunities;

(F) integrates systems in the building;

(G) reduces the environmental and energy impacts of transportation through building location and site design that support a full range of transportation choices for users of the building; and

(H) considers indoor and outdoor effects of the building on human health and the environment, including—

(i) improvements in worker productivity;

(ii) the life-cycle impacts of building materials and operations; and

(iii) other factors that the Federal Director or the Commercial Director consider to be appropriate.

(14) LIFE-CYCLE

The term "life-cycle", with respect to a high-performance green building, means all stages of the useful life of the building (including components, equipment, systems, and controls of the building) beginning at conception of a high-performance green building project and continuing through site selection, design, construction, landscaping, commissioning, operation, maintenance, renovation, deconstruction or demolition, removal, and recycling of the high-performance green building.

(15) LIFE-CYCLE ASSESSMENT

The term "life-cycle assessment" means a comprehensive system approach for measuring the environmental performance of a product or service over the life of the product or service, beginning at raw materials acquisition and continuing through manufacturing, transportation, installation, use, reuse, and end-of-life waste management.

(16) LIFE-CYCLE COSTING

The term "life-cycle costing", with respect to a high-performance green building, means a technique of economic evaluation that—

(A) sums, over a given study period, the costs of initial investment (less resale value), replacements, operations (including energy use), and maintenance and repair of an investment decision; and

(B) is expressed—

(i) in present value terms, in the case of a study period equivalent to the longest useful life of the building, determined by taking into consideration the typical life of such a building in the area in which the building is to be located; or

(ii) in annual value terms, in the case of any other study period.

(17) OFFICE OF COMMERCIAL HIGH-PERFORMANCE GREEN BUILDINGS

The term "Office of Commercial High-Performance Green Buildings" means the Office of Commercial High-Performance Green Buildings established under section 17081(a) of this title.

(18) OFFICE OF FEDERAL HIGH-PERFORMANCE GREEN BUILDINGS

The term "Office of Federal High-Performance Green Buildings" means the Office of Federal High-Performance Green Buildings established under section 17092(a) of this title.

(19) PRACTICES

The term "practices" means design, financing, permitting, construction, commissioning, operation and maintenance, and other practices that contribute to achieving zero-net-energy buildings or facilities.

(20) ZERO-NET-ENERGY COMMERCIAL BUILDING

The term "zero-net-energy commercial building" means a commercial building that is designed, constructed, and operated to—

(A) require a greatly reduced quantity of energy to operate;

(B) meet the balance of energy needs from sources of energy that do not produce greenhouse gases;

(C) therefore result in no net emissions of greenhouse gases; and

(D) be economically viable.

(Pub. L. 110–140, title IV, §401, Dec. 19, 2007, 121 Stat. 1596.)

* * * * * * *

PART B—HIGH-PERFORMANCE COMMERCIAL BUILDINGS

§17081. COMMERCIAL HIGH-PERFORMANCE GREEN BUILDINGS

(A) DIRECTOR OF COMMERCIAL HIGH-PERFORMANCE GREEN BUILDINGS

Notwithstanding any other provision of law, the Secretary, acting through the Assistant Secretary of Energy Efficiency and Renewable Energy, shall appoint a Director of Commercial High-Performance Green Buildings to a position in the career-reserved Senior Executive service, with the principal responsibility to—

(1) establish and manage the Office of Commercial High-Performance Green Buildings; and

(2) carry out other duties as required under this part.

(B) QUALIFICATIONS

The Commercial Director shall be an individual, who by reason of professional background and experience, is specifically qualified to carry out the duties required under this part.

(C) DUTIES

The Commercial Director shall, with respect to development of high-performance green buildings and zero-energy commercial buildings nationwide—

(1) coordinate the activities of the Office of Commercial High-Performance Green Buildings with the activities of the Office of Federal High-Performance Green Buildings;

(2) develop the legal predicates and agreements for, negotiate, and establish one or more public-private partnerships with the Consortium, members of the Consortium, and other capable parties meeting the qualifications of the Consortium, to further such development;

(3) represent the public and the Department in negotiating and performing in accord with such public-private partnerships;

(4) use appropriated funds in an effective manner to encourage the maximum investment of private funds to achieve such development;

(5) promote research and development of high-performance green buildings, consistent with section 17083 of this title; and

(6) jointly establish with the Federal Director a national high-performance green building clearinghouse in accordance with section 17083(1) of this title, which shall provide high-performance green building information and disseminate research results through—

(A) outreach;

(B) education; and

(C) the provision of technical assistance.

(D) REPORTING

The Commercial Director shall report directly to the Assistant Secretary for Energy Efficiency and Renewable Energy, or to other senior officials in a way that facilitates the integrated program of this part for both energy efficiency and renewable energy and both technology development and technology deployment.

(E) COORDINATION

The Commercial Director shall ensure full coordination of high-performance green building information and activities, including activities under this part, within the Federal Government by working with the General Services Administration and all relevant agencies, including, at a minimum—

(1) the Environmental Protection Agency;
(2) the Office of the Federal Environmental Executive;
(3) the Office of Federal Procurement Policy;
(4) the Department of Energy, particularly the Federal Energy Management Program;
(5) the Department of Health and Human Services;
(6) the Department of Housing and Urban Development;
(7) the Department of Defense;
(8) the National Institute of Standards and Technology;
(9) the Department of Transportation;
(10) the Office of Science Technology and Policy; and
(11) such nonprofit high-performance green building rating and analysis entities as the Commercial Director determines can offer support, expertise, and review services.

(F) HIGH-PERFORMANCE GREEN BUILDING PARTNERSHIP CONSORTIUM

(1) RECOGNITION

Not later than 90 days after December 19, 2007, the Commercial Director shall formally recognize one or more groups that qualify as a high-performance green building partnership consortium.

(2) REPRESENTATION TO QUALIFY

To qualify under this section, any consortium shall include representation from—
(A) the design professions, including national associations of architects and of professional engineers;
(B) the development, construction, financial, and real estate industries;
(C) building owners and operators from the public and private sectors;
(D) academic and research organizations, including at least one national laboratory with extensive commercial building energy expertise;
(E) building code agencies and organizations, including a model energy code-setting organization;
(F) independent high-performance green building associations or councils;
(G) experts in indoor air quality and environmental factors;
(H) experts in intelligent buildings and integrated building information systems;
(I) utility energy efficiency programs;

(J) manufacturers and providers of equipment and techniques used in high-performance green buildings;

(K) public transportation industry experts; and

(L) nongovernmental energy efficiency organizations.

(3) FUNDING

The Secretary may make payments to the Consortium pursuant to the terms of a public-private partnership for such activities of the Consortium undertaken under such a partnership as described in this part directly to the Consortium or through one or more of its members.

(G) REPORT

Not later than 2 years after December 19, 2007, and biennially thereafter, the Commercial Director, in consultation with the Consortium, shall submit to Congress a report that—

(1) describes the status of the high-performance green building initiatives under this part and other Federal programs affecting commercial high-performance green buildings in effect as of the date of the report, including—

(A) the extent to which the programs are being carried out in accordance with this part; and

(B) the status of funding requests and appropriations for those programs; and

(2) summarizes and highlights development, at the State and local level, of high-performance green building initiatives, including executive orders, policies, or laws adopted promoting high-performance green building (including the status of implementation of those initiatives).

(Pub. L. 110–140, title IV, §421, Dec. 19, 2007, 121 Stat. 1602.)

§17082. ZERO NET ENERGY COMMERCIAL BUILDINGS INITIATIVE

(A) DEFINITIONS

In this section:

(1) CONSORTIUM

The term "consortium" means a High-Performance Green Building Consortium selected by the Commercial Director.

(2) INITIATIVE

The term "initiative" means the Zero-Net-Energy Commercial Buildings Initiative established under subsection (b)(1).

(3) ZERO-NET-ENERGY COMMERCIAL BUILDING

The term "zero-net-energy commercial building" means a high-performance commercial building that is designed, constructed, and operated—

(A) to require a greatly reduced quantity of energy to operate;

(B) to meet the balance of energy needs from sources of energy that do not produce greenhouse gases;

(C) in a manner that will result in no net emissions of greenhouse gases; and

(D) to be economically viable.

(B) ESTABLISHMENT

(1) IN GENERAL

The Commercial Director shall establish an initiative, to be known as the "Zero-Net-Energy Commercial Buildings Initiative"—

(A) to reduce the quantity of energy consumed by commercial buildings located in the United States; and

(B) to achieve the development of zero net energy commercial buildings in the United States.

(2) CONSORTIUM

(A) IN GENERAL

Not later than 180 days after December 19, 2007, the Commercial Director shall competitively select, and enter into an agreement with, a consortium to develop and carry out the initiative.

(B) AGREEMENTS

In entering into an agreement with a consortium under subparagraph (A), the Commercial Director shall use the authority described in section 7256(g) of this title, to the maximum extent practicable.

(C) GOAL OF INITIATIVE

The goal of the initiative shall be to develop and disseminate technologies, practices, and policies for the development and establishment of zero net energy commercial buildings for—

(1) any commercial building newly constructed in the United States by 2030;

(2) 50 percent of the commercial building stock of the United States by 2040; and

(3) all commercial buildings in the United States by 2050.

(D) COMPONENTS

In carrying out the initiative, the Commercial Director, in consultation with the consortium, may—

(1) conduct research and development on building science, design, materials, components, equipment and controls, operation and other practices, integration, energy use measurement, and benchmarking;

(2) conduct pilot programs and demonstration projects to evaluate replicable approaches to achieving energy efficient commercial buildings for a variety of building types in a variety of climate zones;

(3) conduct deployment, dissemination, and technical assistance activities to encourage widespread adoption of technologies, practices, and policies (including demand-response technologies, practices, and policies) to achieve energy efficient commercial buildings;

(4) conduct other research, development, demonstration, and deployment activities necessary to achieve each goal of the initiative, as determined by the Commercial Director, in consultation with the consortium;

(5) develop training materials and courses for building professionals and trades on achieving cost-effective high-performance energy efficient buildings;

(6) develop and disseminate public education materials to share information on the benefits and cost-effectiveness of high-performance energy efficient buildings;

(7) support code-setting organizations and State and local governments in developing minimum performance standards in building codes that recognize the ready availability of many technologies utilized in high-performance energy efficient buildings;

(8) develop strategies for overcoming the split incentives between builders and purchasers, and landlords and tenants, to ensure that energy efficiency and high-performance investments are made that are cost-effective on a lifecycle basis; and

(9) develop improved means of measurement and verification of energy savings and performance for public dissemination.

(E) COST SHARING

In carrying out this section, the Commercial Director shall require cost sharing in accordance with section 16352 of this title.

(F) AUTHORIZATION OF APPROPRIATIONS

There are authorized to be appropriated to carry out this section—

(1) $20,000,000 for fiscal year 2008;

(2) $50,000,000 for each of fiscal years 2009 and 2010;

(3) $100,000,000 for each of fiscal years 2011 and 2012; and

(4) $200,000,000 for each of fiscal years 2013 through 2018.

(Pub. L. 110–140, title IV, §422, Dec. 19, 2007, 121 Stat. 1604; Pub. L. 117–58, div. D, title I, §40104(d), Nov. 15, 2021, 135 Stat. 933.)

§17083. PUBLIC OUTREACH

The Commercial Director and Federal Director, in coordination with the Consortium, shall carry out public outreach to inform individuals and entities of the information and services available governmentwide by—

(1) establishing and maintaining a national high-performance green building clearinghouse, including on the Internet, that—

(A) identifies existing similar efforts and coordinates activities of common interest; and

(B) provides information relating to high-performance green buildings, including hyperlinks to Internet sites that describe the activities, information, and resources of—

(i) the Federal Government;

(ii) State and local governments;

(iii) the private sector (including nongovernmental and nonprofit entities and organizations); and

(iv) international organizations;

(2) identifying and recommending educational resources for implementing high-performance green building practices, including security and emergency benefits and practices;

(3) providing access to technical assistance, tools, and resources for constructing high-performance green buildings, particularly tools to conduct life-cycle costing and life-cycle assessment;

(4) providing information on application processes for certifying a high-performance green building, including certification and commissioning;

(5) providing to the public, through the Commercial Director, technical and research information or other forms of assistance or advice that would be useful in planning and constructing high-performance green buildings;

(6) using such additional methods as are determined by the Commercial Director to be appropriate to conduct public outreach;

(7) surveying existing research and studies relating to high-performance green buildings; and

(8) coordinating activities of common interest.

(Pub. L. 110–140, title IV, §423, Dec. 19, 2007, 121 Stat. 1606.)

* * * * * * *

Part C—High-Performance Federal Buildings

§17091. Leasing

(a) In general

Except as provided in subsection (b), effective beginning on the date that is 3 years after December 19, 2007, no Federal agency shall enter into a contract to lease space in a building that has not earned the Energy Star label in the most recent year.

(b) Exception

(1) Application

This subsection applies if—

(A) no space is available in a building described in subsection (a) that meets the functional requirements of an agency, including locational needs;

(B) the agency proposes to remain in a building that the agency has occupied previously;

(C) the agency proposes to lease a building of historical, architectural, or cultural significance (as defined in section 3306(a)(4) of title 40) or space in such a building; or

(D) the lease is for not more than 10,000 gross square feet of space.

(2) Buildings without Energy Star label

If one of the conditions described in paragraph (1) is met, the agency may enter into a contract to lease space in a building that has not earned the Energy Star label in the most recent year if the lease contract includes provisions requiring that, prior to occupancy or, in the case of a contract described in paragraph (1)(B), not later than 1 year after signing the contract, the following requirements are met:

(A) The space is renovated for all energy efficiency and conservation improvements that would be cost effective over the life of the lease, including improvements in lighting, windows, and heating, ventilation, and air conditioning systems.

(B)(i) Subject to clause (ii), the space is benchmarked under a nationally recognized, online, free benchmarking program, with public disclosure, unless the space is a space for which owners cannot access whole building utility consumption data, including spaces—

(I) that are located in States with privacy laws that provide that utilities shall not provide such aggregated information to multitenant building owners; and

(II) for which tenants do not provide energy consumption information to the commercial building owner in response to a request from the building owner.

(ii) A Federal agency that is a tenant of the space shall provide to the building owner, or authorize the owner to obtain from the utility, the energy consumption information of the space for the benchmarking and disclosure required by this subparagraph.

(C) REVISION OF FEDERAL ACQUISITION REGULATION

(1) IN GENERAL

Not later than 3 years after December 19, 2007, the Federal Acquisition Regulation described in section 1121(b) and (c)(1) of title 41 shall be revised to require Federal officers and employees to comply with this section in leasing buildings.

(2) CONSULTATION

The members of the Federal Acquisition Regulatory Council established under section 1302(a) of title 41 shall consult with the Federal Director and the Commercial Director before promulgating regulations to carry out this subsection.

(Pub. L. 110–140, title IV, §435, Dec. 19, 2007, 121 Stat. 1615; Pub. L. 114–11, title III, §301(a), Apr. 30, 2015, 129 Stat. 189.)

§17092. HIGH-PERFORMANCE GREEN FEDERAL BUILDINGS

(A) ESTABLISHMENT OF OFFICE

Not later than 60 days after December 19, 2007, the Administrator shall establish within the General Services Administration an Office of Federal High-Performance Green Buildings, and appoint an individual to serve as Federal Director in, a position in the career-reserved Senior Executive service, to—

(1) establish and manage the Office of Federal High-Performance Green Buildings; and

(2) carry out other duties as required under this part.

(B) COMPENSATION

The compensation of the Federal Director shall not exceed the maximum rate of basic pay for the Senior Executive Service under section 5382 of title 5, including any applicable locality-based comparability payment that may be authorized under section 5304(h)(2)(C) of that title.

(C) DUTIES

The Federal Director shall—

(1) coordinate the activities of the Office of Federal High-Performance Green Buildings with the activities of the Office of Commercial High-Performance Green Buildings, and the Secretary, in accordance with section 6834(a)(3)(D) of this title;

(2) ensure full coordination of high-performance green building information and activities within the General Services Administration and all relevant agencies, including, at a minimum—

(A) the Environmental Protection Agency;

(B) the Office of the Federal Environmental Executive;

(C) the Office of Federal Procurement Policy;

(D) the Department of Energy;

(E) the Department of Health and Human Services;

(F) the Department of Defense;

(G) the Department of Transportation;

(H) the National Institute of Standards and Technology; and

(I) the Office of Science and Technology Policy;

(3) establish a senior-level Federal Green Building Advisory Committee under section 474, which shall provide advice and recommendations in accordance with that section and subsection (d);

(4) identify and every 5 years reassess improved or higher rating standards recommended by the Advisory Committee;

(5) ensure full coordination, dissemination of information regarding, and promotion of the results of research and development information relating to Federal high-performance green building initiatives;

(6) identify and develop Federal high-performance green building standards for all types of Federal facilities, consistent with the requirements of this part and section 6834(a)(3)(D) of this title;

(7) establish green practices that can be used throughout the life of a Federal facility;

(8) review and analyze current Federal budget practices and life-cycle costing issues, and make recommendations to Congress, in accordance with subsection (d); and

(9) identify opportunities to demonstrate innovative and emerging green building technologies and concepts.

(D) ADDITIONAL DUTIES

The Federal Director, in consultation with the Commercial Director and the Advisory Committee, and consistent with the requirements of section 6834(a)(3)(D) of this title shall—

(1) identify, review, and analyze current budget and contracting practices that affect achievement of high-performance green buildings, including the identification of barriers to high-performance green building life-cycle costing and budgetary issues;

(2) develop guidance and conduct training sessions with budget specialists and contracting personnel from Federal agencies and budget examiners to apply life-cycle cost criteria to actual projects;

(3) identify tools to aid life-cycle cost decisionmaking; and

(4) explore the feasibility of incorporating the benefits of high-performance green

buildings, such as security benefits, into a cost-budget analysis to aid in life-cycle costing for budget and decisionmaking processes.

(E) INCENTIVES

Within 90 days after December 19, 2007, the Federal Director shall identify incentives to encourage the expedited use of high-performance green buildings and related technology in the operations of the Federal Government, in accordance with the requirements of section 6834(a)(3)(D) of this title, including through—

(1) the provision of recognition awards; and

(2) the maximum feasible retention of financial savings in the annual budgets of Federal agencies for use in reinvesting in future high-performance green building initiatives.

(F) REPORT

Not later than 2 years after December 19, 2007, and biennially thereafter, the Federal Director, in consultation with the Secretary, shall submit to Congress a report that—

(1) describes the status of compliance with this part, the requirements of section 6834(a)(3)(D) of this title, and other Federal high-performance green building initiatives in effect as of the date of the report, including—

(A) the extent to which the programs are being carried out in accordance with this part and the requirements of section 6834(a)(3)(D) of this title; and

(B) the status of funding requests and appropriations for those programs;

(2) identifies within the planning, budgeting, and construction process all types of Federal facility procedures that may affect the certification of new and existing Federal facilities as high-performance green buildings under the provisions of section 6834(a)(3)(D) of this title and the criteria established in subsection (h);

(3) identifies inconsistencies, as reported to the Advisory Committee, in Federal law with respect to product acquisition guidelines and high-performance product guidelines;

(4) recommends language for uniform standards for use by Federal agencies in environmentally responsible acquisition;

(5) in coordination with the Office of Management and Budget, reviews the budget process for capital programs with respect to alternatives for—

(A) restructuring of budgets to require the use of complete energy and environmental cost accounting;

(B) using operations expenditures in budget-related decisions while simultaneously incorporating productivity and health measures (as those measures can be quantified by the Office of Federal High-Performance Green Buildings, with the assistance of universities and national laboratories);

(C) streamlining measures for permitting Federal agencies to retain all identified savings accrued as a result of the use of life-cycle costing for future high-performance green building initiatives; and

(D) identifying short-term and long-term cost savings that accrue from high-performance green buildings, including those relating to health and productivity;

(6) identifies green, self-sustaining technologies to address the operational needs of Federal facilities in times of national security emergencies, natural disasters, or other

dire emergencies;

(7) summarizes and highlights development, at the State and local level, of high-performance green building initiatives, including executive orders, policies, or laws adopted promoting high-performance green building (including the status of implementation of those initiatives); and

(8) includes, for the 2-year period covered by the report, recommendations to address each of the matters, and a plan for implementation of each recommendation, described in paragraphs (1) through (7).

(G) IMPLEMENTATION

The Office of Federal High-Performance Green Buildings shall carry out each plan for implementation of recommendations under subsection (f)(8).

(H) IDENTIFICATION OF CERTIFICATION SYSTEM

(1) IN GENERAL

For the purpose of this section, not later than 60 days after December 19, 2007, the Federal Director shall identify and shall provide to the Secretary pursuant to section 6834(a)(3)(D) of this title, a certification system that the Director determines to be the most likely to encourage a comprehensive and environmentally-sound approach to certification of green buildings.

(2) BASIS

The system identified under paragraph (1) shall be based on—

(A) a study completed every 5 years and provided to the Secretary pursuant to section 6834(a)(3)(D) of this title, which shall be carried out by the Federal Director to compare and evaluate standards;

(B) the ability and availability of assessors and auditors to independently verify the criteria and measurement of metrics at the scale necessary to implement this part;

(C) the ability of the applicable standard-setting organization to collect and reflect public comment;

(D) the ability of the standard to be developed and revised through a consensus-based process;

(E) an evaluation of the robustness of the criteria for a high-performance green building, which shall give credit for promoting—

(i) efficient and sustainable use of water, energy, and other natural resources;

(ii) use of renewable energy sources;

(iii) improved indoor environmental quality through enhanced indoor air quality, thermal comfort, acoustics, day lighting, pollutant source control, and use of low-emission materials and building system controls;

(iv) reduced impacts from transportation through building location and site design that promote access by public transportation; and

(v) such other criteria as the Federal Director determines to be appropriate; and

(F) national recognition within the building industry.

(Pub. L. 110–140, title IV, §436, Dec. 19, 2007, 121 Stat. 1616.)

§17093. FEDERAL GREEN BUILDING PERFORMANCE

(A) IN GENERAL

Not later than October 31 of each of the 2 fiscal years following the fiscal year in which this Act is enacted, and at such times thereafter as the Comptroller General of the United States determines to be appropriate, the Comptroller General of the United States shall, with respect to the fiscal years that have passed since the preceding report—

(1) conduct an audit of the implementation of this part, section 6834(a)(3)(D) of this title, and section 17091 of this title; and

(2) submit to the Federal Director, the Advisory Committee, the Administrator, and Congress a report describing the results of the audit.

(B) CONTENTS

An audit under subsection (a) shall include a review, with respect to the period covered by the report under subsection (a)(2), of—

(1) budget, life-cycle costing, and contracting issues, using best practices identified by the Comptroller General of the United States and heads of other agencies in accordance with section 17092(d) of this title;

(2) the level of coordination among the Federal Director, the Office of Management and Budget, the Department of Energy, and relevant agencies;

(3) the performance of the Federal Director and other agencies in carrying out the implementation plan;

(4) the design stage of high-performance green building measures;

(5) high-performance building data that were collected and reported to the Office; and

(6) such other matters as the Comptroller General of the United States determines to be appropriate.

(C) ENVIRONMENTAL STEWARDSHIP SCORECARD

The Federal Director shall consult with the Advisory Committee to enhance, and assist in the implementation of, the Office of Management and Budget government efficiency reports and scorecards under section 17144 of this title and the Environmental Stewardship Scorecard announced at the White House summit on Federal sustainable buildings in January 2006, to measure the implementation by each Federal agency of sustainable design and green building initiatives.

(Pub. L. 110–140, title IV, §437, Dec. 19, 2007, 121 Stat. 1619.)

§17094. STORM WATER RUNOFF REQUIREMENTS FOR FEDERAL DEVELOPMENT PROJECTS

The sponsor of any development or redevelopment project involving a Federal facility with a footprint that exceeds 5,000 square feet shall use site planning, design, construction, and maintenance strategies for the property to maintain or restore, to the maximum extent technically feasible, the predevelopment hydrology of the property with regard to the temperature, rate, volume, and duration of flow.

(Pub. L. 110–140, title IV, §438, Dec. 19, 2007, 121 Stat. 1620.)

STATUTORY NOTES AND RELATED SUBSIDIARIES

EFFECTIVE DATE

Section effective on the date that is 1 day after Dec. 19, 2007, see section 1601 of Pub. L. 110–140, set out as a note under section 1824 of Title 2, The Congress.

§17095. COST-EFFECTIVE TECHNOLOGY ACCELERATION PROGRAM

(A) DEFINITION OF ADMINISTRATOR

In this section, the term "Administrator" means the Administrator of General Services.

(B) ESTABLISHMENT

(1) IN GENERAL

The Administrator shall establish a program to accelerate the use of more cost-effective technologies and practices at GSA facilities.

(2) REQUIREMENTS

The program established under this subsection shall—

(A) ensure centralized responsibility for the coordination of cost reduction-related recommendations, practices, and activities of all relevant Federal agencies;

(B) provide technical assistance and operational guidance to applicable tenants to achieve the goal identified in subsection (c)(2)(B)(ii);

(C) establish methods to track the success of Federal departments and agencies with respect to that goal; and

(D) be fully coordinated with and no less stringent nor less energy-conserving or water-conserving than required by other provisions of this Act and other applicable law, including sections 321 through 324, 431 through 438, 461, 511 through 518, and 523 through 525 and amendments made by those sections.

(C) ACCELERATED USE OF TECHNOLOGIES

(1) REVIEW

(A) IN GENERAL

As part of the program under this section, not later than 90 days after December 19, 2007, the Administrator shall conduct a review of—

(i) current use of cost-effective lighting technologies and geothermal heat pumps in GSA facilities; and

(ii) the availability to managers of GSA facilities of cost-effective lighting technologies and geothermal heat pumps.

(B) REQUIREMENTS

The review under subparagraph (A) shall—

(i) examine the use of cost-effective lighting technologies, geothermal heat pumps, and other cost-effective technologies and practices by Federal agencies in GSA facilities; and

(ii) as prepared in consultation with the Administrator of the Environmental

Protection Agency, identify cost-effective lighting technology and geothermal heat pump technology standards that could be used for all types of GSA facilities.

(2) REPLACEMENT

(A) IN GENERAL

As part of the program under this section, not later than 180 days after December 19, 2007, the Administrator shall establish, using available appropriations and programs implementing sections 432 and 525 (and amendments made by those sections), a cost-effective lighting technology and geothermal heat pump technology acceleration program to achieve maximum feasible replacement of existing lighting, heating, cooling [1] technologies with cost-effective lighting technologies and geothermal heat pump technologies in each GSA facility. Such program shall fully comply with the requirements of sections 321 through 324, 431 through 438, 461, 511 through 518, and 523 through 525 and amendments made by those sections and any other provisions of law, which shall be applicable to the extent that they are more stringent or would achieve greater energy savings than required by this section.

(B) ACCELERATION PLAN TIMETABLE

(I) IN GENERAL

To implement the program established under subparagraph (A), not later than 1 year after December 19, 2007, the Administrator shall establish a timetable of actions to comply with the requirements of this section and sections 431 through 435, whichever achieves greater energy savings most expeditiously, including milestones for specific activities needed to replace existing lighting, heating, cooling technologies with cost-effective lighting technologies and geothermal heat pump technologies, to the maximum extent feasible (including at the maximum rate feasible), at each GSA facility.

(II) GOAL

The goal of the timetable under clause (i) shall be to complete, using available appropriations and programs implementing sections 431 through 435 (and amendments made by those sections), maximum feasible replacement of existing lighting, heating, and cooling technologies with cost-effective lighting technologies and geothermal heat pump technologies consistent with the requirements of this section and sections 431 through 435, whichever achieves greater energy savings most expeditiously. Notwithstanding any provision of this section, such program shall fully comply with the requirements of the Act [2] including sections 321 through 324, 431 through 438, 461, 511 through 518, and 523 through 525 and amendments made by those sections and other provisions of law, which shall be applicable to the extent that they are more stringent or would achieve greater energy or water savings than required by this section.

(D) GSA FACILITY TECHNOLOGIES AND PRACTICES

(1) IN GENERAL

Not later than 180 days after December 19, 2007, and annually thereafter, the Administrator shall—

(A) ensure that a manager responsible for implementing section 432 and for accelerating the use of cost-effective technologies and practices is designated for each GSA facility; and

(B) submit to Congress a plan to comply with section 432, this section, and other applicable provisions of this Act and applicable law with respect to energy and water conservation at GSA facilities.

(2) MEASURES

The plan shall implement measures required by such other provisions of law in accordance with those provisions, and shall implement the measures required by this section to the maximum extent feasible (including at the maximum rate feasible) using available appropriations and programs implementing sections 431 through 435 and 525 (and amendments made by those sections), by not later than the date that is 5 years after December 19, 2007.

(3) CONTENTS OF PLAN

The plan shall—

(A) with respect to cost-effective technologies and practices—

(i) identify the specific activities needed to comply with sections 431 through 435;

(ii) identify the specific activities needed to achieve at least a 20-percent reduction in operational costs through the application of cost-effective technologies and practices from 2003 levels at GSA facilities by not later than 5 years after December 19, 2007;

(iii) describe activities required and carried out to estimate the funds necessary to achieve the reduction described in clauses (i) and (ii);

(B) include an estimate of the funds necessary to carry out this section;

(C) describe the status of the implementation of cost-effective technologies and practices at GSA facilities, including—

(i) the extent to which programs, including the program established under subsection (b), are being carried out in accordance with this part; and

(ii) the status of funding requests and appropriations for those programs;

(D) identify within the planning, budgeting, and construction processes, all types of GSA facility-related procedures that inhibit new and existing GSA facilities from implementing cost-effective technologies;

(E) recommend language for uniform standards for use by Federal agencies in implementing cost-effective technologies and practices;

(F) in coordination with the Office of Management and Budget, review the budget process for capital programs with respect to alternatives for—

(i) implementing measures that will assure that Federal agencies retain all identified savings accrued as a result of the use of cost-effective technologies, consistent with section 8253(a)(1) of this title, and other applicable law; and

(ii) identifying short- and long-term cost savings that accrue from the use of cost-effective technologies and practices;

(G) with respect to cost-effective technologies and practices, achieve substantial operational cost savings through the application of the technologies; and

(H) include recommendations to address each of the matters, and a plan for implementation of each recommendation, described in subparagraphs (A) through (G).

(4) ADMINISTRATION

Notwithstanding any provision of this section, the program required under this section shall fully comply with the requirements of sections 321 through 324, 431 through 438, 461, 511 through 518, and 523 through 525 and amendments made by those sections, which shall be applicable to the extent that they are more stringent or would achieve greater energy or water savings than required by this section.

(E) AUTHORIZATION OF APPROPRIATIONS

There are authorized to be appropriated such sums as are necessary to carry out this section, to remain available until expended.

(Pub. L. 110–140, title IV, §439, Dec. 19, 2007, 121 Stat. 1620.)

[1] So in original. Probably should be "and cooling".

[2] So in original. Probably should be "this Act".

§17096. AUTHORIZATION OF APPROPRIATIONS

There is authorized to be appropriated to carry out sections 434 through 439 and 482 $4,000,000 for each of fiscal years 2008 through 2012, to remain available until expended.

(Pub. L. 110–140, title IV, §440, Dec. 19, 2007, 121 Stat. 1623.)

* * * * * * *

SUBCHAPTER IV—ENERGY SAVINGS IN GOVERNMENT AND PUBLIC INSTITUTIONS

PART A—ENERGY SAVINGS PERFORMANCE CONTRACTING

§17131. TRAINING FEDERAL CONTRACTING OFFICERS TO NEGOTIATE ENERGY EFFICIENCY CONTRACTS

(A) PROGRAM

The Secretary shall create and administer in the Federal Energy Management Program a training program to educate Federal contract negotiation and contract management personnel so that the contract officers are prepared to—

(1) negotiate energy savings performance contracts;

(2) conclude effective and timely contracts for energy efficiency services with all

companies offering energy efficiency services; and

(3) review Federal contracts for all products and services for the potential energy efficiency opportunities and implications of the contracts.

(B) SCHEDULE

Not later than 1 year after December 19, 2007, the Secretary shall plan, staff, announce, and begin training under the Federal Energy Management Program.

(C) PERSONNEL TO BE TRAINED

Personnel appropriate to receive training under the Federal Energy Management Program shall be selected by and sent for the training from—

(1) the Department of Defense;

(2) the Department of Veterans Affairs;

(3) the Department;

(4) the General Services Administration;

(5) the Department of Housing and Urban Development;

(6) the United States Postal Service; and

(7) all other Federal agencies and departments that enter contracts for buildings, building services, electricity and electricity services, natural gas and natural gas services, heating and air conditioning services, building fuel purchases, and other types of procurement or service contracts determined by the Secretary, in carrying out the Federal Energy Management Program, to offer the potential for energy savings and greenhouse gas emission reductions if negotiated with taking into account those goals.

(D) TRAINERS

Training under the Federal Energy Management Program may be conducted by—

(1) attorneys or contract officers with experience in negotiating and managing contracts described in subsection (c)(7) from any agency, except that the Secretary shall reimburse the related salaries and expenses of the attorneys or contract officers from amounts made available for carrying out this section to the extent the attorneys or contract officers are not employees of the Department; and

(2) private experts hired by the Secretary for the purposes of this section, except that the Secretary may not hire experts who are simultaneously employed by any company under contract to provide energy efficiency services to the Federal Government.

(E) AUTHORIZATION OF APPROPRIATIONS

There are authorized to be appropriated to the Secretary to carry out this section $750,000 for each of fiscal years 2008 through 2012.

(Pub. L. 110–140, title V, §517, Dec. 19, 2007, 121 Stat. 1659.)

PART B—ENERGY EFFICIENCY IN FEDERAL AGENCIES

§17141. PROHIBITION ON INCANDESCENT LAMPS BY COAST GUARD

(A) PROHIBITION

Except as provided by subsection (b), on and after January 1, 2009, a general service incandescent lamp shall not be purchased or installed in a Coast Guard facility by or on behalf of the Coast Guard.

(B) EXCEPTION

A general service incandescent lamp may be purchased, installed, and used in a Coast Guard facility whenever the application of a general service incandescent lamp is—

(1) necessary due to purpose or design, including medical, security, and industrial applications;

(2) reasonable due to the architectural or historical value of a light fixture installed before January 1, 2009; or

(3) the Commandant of the Coast Guard determines that operational requirements necessitate the use of a general service incandescent lamp.

(C) LIMITATION

In this section, the term "facility" does not include a vessel or aircraft of the Coast Guard.

(Pub. L. 110–140, title V, §522, Dec. 19, 2007, 121 Stat. 1662.)

§17142. PROCUREMENT AND ACQUISITION OF ALTERNATIVE FUELS

No Federal agency shall enter into a contract for procurement of an alternative or synthetic fuel, including a fuel produced from nonconventional petroleum sources, for any mobility-related use, other than for research or testing, unless the contract specifies that the lifecycle greenhouse gas emissions associated with the production and combustion of the fuel supplied under the contract must, on an ongoing basis, be less than or equal to such emissions from the equivalent conventional fuel produced from conventional petroleum sources.

(Pub. L. 110–140, title V, §526, Dec. 19, 2007, 121 Stat. 1663.)

STATUTORY NOTES AND RELATED SUBSIDIARIES

EFFECTIVE DATE

Section effective on the date that is 1 day after Dec. 19, 2007, see section 1601 of Pub. L. 110–140, set out as a note under section 1824 of Title 2, The Congress.

WAIVER AUTHORITY FOR ALTERNATIVE FUEL PROCUREMENT REQUIREMENT

Pub. L. 114–328, div. A, title III, §312, Dec. 23, 2016, 130 Stat. 2073, provided that:

"(a) IN GENERAL.—The Secretary of Defense may waive the requirement under section 526 of the Energy Independence and Security Act of 2007 (Public Law 110–140; 42 U.S.C. 17142) if the Secretary determines it is in the national security interest of the United States.

"(b) NOTIFICATION REQUIREMENT.—The Secretary of Defense shall notify the congressional defense committees [Committees on Armed Services and Appropriations of the Senate and the House of Representatives] not later than 15 days after exercising the waiver authority under subsection (a)."

§17143. GOVERNMENT EFFICIENCY STATUS REPORTS

(A) IN GENERAL

Each Federal agency subject to any of the requirements of this title or the amendments made by this title shall compile and submit to the Director of the Office of Management and Budget an annual Government efficiency status report on—

(1) compliance by the agency with each of the requirements of this title and the amendments made by this title;

(2) the status of the implementation by the agency of initiatives to improve energy efficiency, reduce energy costs, and reduce emissions of greenhouse gases; and

(3) savings to the taxpayers of the United States resulting from mandated improvements under this title and the amendments made by this title.

(B) SUBMISSION

The report shall be submitted—

(1) to the Director at such time as the Director requires;

(2) in electronic, not paper, format; and

(3) consistent with related reporting requirements.

(Pub. L. 110–140, title V, §527, Dec. 19, 2007, 121 Stat. 1663.)

§17144. OMB GOVERNMENT EFFICIENCY REPORTS AND SCORECARDS

(A) REPORTS

Not later than April 1 of each year, the Director of the Office of Management and Budget shall submit an annual Government efficiency report to the Committee on Oversight and Government Reform of the House of Representatives and the Committee on Governmental Affairs of the Senate, which shall contain—

(1) a summary of the information reported by agencies under section 17143 of this title;

(2) an evaluation of the overall progress of the Federal Government toward achieving the goals of this title and the amendments made by this title; and

(3) recommendations for additional actions necessary to meet the goals of this title and the amendments made by this title.

(B) SCORECARDS

The Director of the Office of Management and Budget shall include in any annual energy scorecard the Director is otherwise required to submit a description of the compliance of each agency with the requirements of this title and the amendments made by this title./p>

(Pub. L. 110–140, title V, §528, Dec. 19, 2007, 121 Stat. 1664.)

Provisions of Public Law 110-140 included in 2 U.S.C.

TITLE 2—THE CONGRESS

* * * * * * *

CHAPTER 28—ARCHITECT OF THE CAPITOL

* * * * * * *

SUBCHAPTER I—GENERAL

* * * * * * *

§1824. ENERGY AND ENVIRONMENTAL MEASURES IN CAPITOL COMPLEX MASTER PLAN

(A) IN GENERAL

To the maximum extent practicable, the Architect of the Capitol shall include energy efficiency and conservation measures, greenhouse gas emission reduction measures, and other appropriate environmental measures in the Capitol Complex Master Plan.

(B) REPORT

Not later than 6 months after December 19, 2007, the Architect of the Capitol shall submit to the Committee on Transportation and Infrastructure of the House of Representatives and the Committee on Rules and Administration of the Senate, a report on the energy efficiency and conservation measures, greenhouse gas emission reduction measures, and other appropriate environmental measures included in the Capitol Complex Master Plan pursuant to subsection (a).

(Pub. L. 110–140, title V, §503, Dec. 19, 2007, 121 Stat. 1655.)

* * * * * * *

CHAPTER 30—OPERATION AND MAINTENANCE OF CAPITOL COMPLEX

* * * * * * *

SUBCHAPTER VII—OTHER ENTITIES AND SERVICES

* * * * * * *

§2162A. Promoting maximum efficiency in operation of Capitol Power Plant

(A) Steam boilers

(1) In general

The Architect of the Capitol shall take such steps as may be necessary to operate the steam boilers at the Capitol Power Plant in the most energy efficient manner possible to minimize carbon emissions and operating costs, including adjusting steam pressures and adjusting the operation of the boilers to take into account variations in demand, including seasonality, for the use of the system.

(2) Effective date

The Architect shall implement the steps required under paragraph (1) not later than 30 days after December 19, 2007.

(B) Chiller plant

(1) In general

The Architect of the Capitol shall take such steps as may be necessary to operate the chiller plant at the Capitol Power Plant in the most energy efficient manner possible to minimize carbon emissions and operating costs, including adjusting water temperatures and adjusting the operation of the chillers to take into account variations in demand, including seasonality, for the use of the system.

(2) Effective date

The Architect shall implement the steps required under paragraph (1) not later than 30 days after December 19, 2007.

(C) Meters

Not later than 90 days after December 19, 2007, the Architect of the Capitol shall evaluate the accuracy of the meters in use at the Capitol Power Plant and correct them as necessary.

(D) Report on implementation

Not later than 180 days after December 19, 2007, the Architect of the Capitol shall complete the implementation of the requirements of this section and submit a report describing the actions taken and the energy efficiencies achieved to the Committee on Transportation and Infrastructure of the House of Representatives, the Committee on Commerce, Science, and Transportation of the Senate, the Committee on House

Administration of the House of Representatives, and the Committee on Rules and Administration of the Senate.

(Pub. L. 110–140, title V, §504, Dec. 19, 2007, 121 Stat. 1656.)

* * * * * * *

§2169. Capitol complex E–85 refueling station

(a) Construction

The Architect of the Capitol may construct a fuel tank and pumping system for E–85 fuel at or within close proximity to the Capitol Grounds Fuel Station.

(b) Use

The E–85 fuel tank and pumping system shall be available for use by all legislative branch vehicles capable of operating with E–85 fuel, subject to such other legislative branch agencies reimbursing the Architect of the Capitol for the costs of E–85 fuel used by such other legislative branch vehicles.

(c) Authorization of appropriations

There is authorized to be appropriated to carry out this section $640,000 for fiscal year 2008.

(Pub. L. 110–140, title V, §502, Dec. 19, 2007, 121 Stat. 1655.)

Provisions of Public Law 110-140 not included in U.S.C.

Title V—Energy savings in government and public institutions

Subtitle A—United States Capitol complex

§501. CAPITOL COMPLEX PHOTOVOLTAIC ROOF FEASIBILITY STUDIES

(A) STUDIES

The Architect of the Capitol may conduct feasibility studies regarding construction of photovoltaic roofs for the Rayburn House Office Building and the Hart Senate Office Building.

(B)REPORT

Not later than 6 months after the date of enactment of this Act, the Architect of the Capitol shall transmit to the Committee on Transportation and Infrastructure of the House of Representatives and the Committee on Rules and Administration of the Senate a report on the results of the feasibility studies and recommendations regarding construction of photovoltaic roofs for the buildings referred to in subsection (a).

(C) AUTHORIZATION OF APPROPRIATIONS

There is authorized to be appropriated to carry out this section $500,000.

§502. [2 U.S.C. 2169]CAPITOL COMPLEX E–85 REFUELING STATION

§503. [2 U.S.C. 1824]ENERGY AND ENVIRONMENTAL MEASURES IN CAPITOL COMPLEX MASTER PLAN

§504. PROMOTING MAXIMUM EFFICIENCY IN OPERATION OF CAPITOL POWER PLANT

(A) STEAM BOILERS

(1) IN GENERAL

The Architect of the Capitol shall take such steps as may be necessary to operate the steam boilers at the Capitol Power Plant in the most energy efficient manner possible to minimize carbon emissions and operating costs, including adjusting steam pressures and adjusting the operation of the boilers to take into account variations in demand, including seasonality, for the use of the system.

(2) EFFECTIVE DATE

The Architect shall implement the steps required under paragraph (1) not later than 30 days after the date of the enactment of this Act.

(B) CHILLER PLANT

(1) IN GENERAL

The Architect of the Capitol shall take such steps as may be necessary to operate the chiller plant at the Capitol Power Plant in the most energy efficient manner possible to minimize carbon emissions and operating costs, including adjusting water temperatures and adjusting the operation of the chillers to take into account variations in demand, including seasonality, for the use of the system.

(2) EFFECTIVE DATE

The Architect shall implement the steps required under paragraph (1) not later than 30 days after the date of the enactment of this Act.

(C) METERS

Not later than 90 days after the date of the enactment of this Act, the Architect of the Capitol shall evaluate the accuracy of the meters in use at the Capitol Power Plant and correct them as necessary.

(D) REPORT ON IMPLEMENTATION

Not later than 180 days after the date of the enactment of this Act, the Architect of the Capitol shall complete the implementation of the requirements of this section and submit a report describing the actions taken and the energy efficiencies achieved to the Committee on Transportation and Infrastructure of the House of Representatives, the Committee on Commerce, Science, and Transportation of the Senate, the Committee on House Administration of the House of Representatives, and the Committee on Rules and Administration of the Senate.

* * * * * * *

Subtitle B—Energy savings performance contracting

* * * * * * *

§517. [2 U.S.C. 1824] TRAINING FEDERAL CONTRACTING OFFICERS TO NEGOTIATE ENERGY EFFICIENCY CONTRACTS

§518. STUDY OF ENERGY AND COST SAVINGS IN NONBUILDING APPLICATIONS

(A) DEFINITIONS

In this section:

(1) NONBUILDING APPLICATION

The term nonbuilding application means—

(A) any class of vehicles, devices, or equipment that is transportable under the power of the applicable vehicle, device, or equipment by land, sea, or air and that consumes energy from any fuel source for the purpose of—

(i) that transportation; or

(ii) maintaining a controlled environment within the vehicle, device, or equipment; and

(B) any federally-owned equipment used to generate electricity or transport water.

(2) SECONDARY SAVINGS

(A) In general

The term secondary savings means additional energy or cost savings that are a direct consequence of the energy savings that result from the energy efficiency improvements that were financed and implemented pursuant to an energy savings performance contract.

(B) Inclusions

The term secondary savings includes—

(i) energy and cost savings that result from a reduction in the need for fuel delivery and logistical support;

personnel cost savings and environmental benefits; and

(iii) in the case of electric generation equipment, the benefits of increased efficiency in the production of electricity, including revenues received by the Federal Government from the sale of electricity so produced.

(B) STUDY

(1) IN GENERAL

TAs soon as practicable after the date of enactment of this Act, the Secretary and the Secretary of Defense shall jointly conduct, and submit to Congress and the President a report of, a study of the potential for the use of energy savings performance contracts to reduce energy consumption and provide energy and cost savings in nonbuilding applications.

(2) REQUIREMENTS

The study under this subsection shall include—

(A) an estimate of the potential energy and cost savings to the Federal Government, including secondary savings and benefits, from increased efficiency in nonbuilding applications;

(B) an assessment of the feasibility of extending the use of energy savings performance contracts to nonbuilding applications, including an identification of any regulatory or statutory barriers to that use; and

(C) such recommendations as the Secretary and Secretary of Defense determine to be appropriate.

Subtitle C—Energy efficiency in Federal agencies

§521. INSTALLATION OF PHOTOVOLTAIC SYSTEM AT DEPARTMENT OF ENERGY HEADQUARTERS BUILDING

(A) IN GENERAL

The Administrator of General Services shall install a photovoltaic system, as set forth in the Sun Wall Design Project, for the headquarters building of the Department located at 1000 Independence Avenue, SW., Washington, DC, commonly known as the Forrestal Building.

(B) FUNDING

There shall be available from the Federal Buildings Fund established by section 592 of title 40, United States Code, $30,000,000 to carry out this section. Such sums shall be derived from the unobligated balance of amounts made available from the Fund for fiscal year 2007, and prior fiscal years, for repairs and alternations and other activities (excluding amounts made available for the energy program). Such sums shall remain available until expended.

★

BETTER BUILDINGS ACT

40 U.S.C. §§17062–63.

Provisions of the Better Buildings Act of 2015

TITLE 42—THE PUBLIC HEALTH AND WELFARE

* * * * * * *

CHAPTER 152—ENERGY INDEPENDENCE AND SECURITY

§17001. Definitions

Short Title of 2015 Amendment

Pub. L. 114–11, §1(a), Apr. 30, 2015, 129 Stat. 182, provided that: "This Act [enacting sections 17062, 17063, 17084, and 17085 of this title, amending sections 6295, 6302 to 6304, and 17091 of this title, and enacting provisions set out as a note under this section] may be cited as the 'Energy Efficiency Improvement Act of 2015'."

Pub. L. 114–11, title I, §101, Apr. 30, 2015, 129 Stat. 182, provided that: "This title [enacting sections 17062, 17084, and 17085 of this title] may be cited as the 'Better Buildings Act of 2015'."

* * * * * * *

CHAPTER 152—ENERGY INDEPENDENCE AND SECURITY

* * * * * * *

SUBCHAPTER III—ENERGY SAVINGS IN BUILDINGS AND INDUSTRY

SUBCHAPTER III—ENERGY SAVINGS IN BUILDINGS AND INDUSTRY

* * * * * * *

* * * * * * *

§17062. ENERGY EFFICIENCY IN FEDERAL AND OTHER BUILDINGS

(A) DEFINITIONS

In this section:

(1) ADMINISTRATOR

The term "Administrator" means the Administrator of General Services.

(2) COST-EFFECTIVE ENERGY EFFICIENCY MEASURE

The term "cost-effective energy efficiency measure" means any building product, material, equipment, or service, and the installing, implementing, or operating thereof, that provides energy savings in an amount that is not less than the cost of such installing, implementing, or operating.

(3) COST-EFFECTIVE WATER EFFICIENCY MEASURE

The term "cost-effective water efficiency measure" means any building product, material, equipment, or service, and the installing, implementing, or operating thereof, that provides water savings in an amount that is not less than the cost of such installing, implementing, or operating.

(B) MODEL PROVISIONS, POLICIES, AND BEST PRACTICES

(1) IN GENERAL

Not later than 180 days after April 30, 2015, the Administrator, in consultation with the Secretary of Energy and after providing the public with an opportunity for notice and comment, shall develop model commercial leasing provisions and best practices in accordance with this subsection.

(2) COMMERCIAL LEASING

(A) IN GENERAL

The model commercial leasing provisions developed under this subsection shall, at a minimum, align the interests of building owners and tenants with regard to investments in cost-effective energy efficiency measures and cost-effective water efficiency measures to encourage building owners and tenants to collaborate to invest in such measures.

(B) Use of model provisions

The Administrator may use the model commercial leasing provisions developed under this subsection in any standard leasing document that designates a Federal agency (or other client of the Administrator) as a landlord or tenant.

(C) Publication

The Administrator shall periodically publish the model commercial leasing provisions developed under this subsection, along with explanatory materials, to encourage building owners and tenants in the private sector to use such provisions and materials.

(3) Realty services

The Administrator shall develop policies and practices to implement cost-effective energy efficiency measures and cost-effective water efficiency measures for the realty services provided by the Administrator to Federal agencies (or other clients of the Administrator), including periodic training of appropriate Federal employees and contractors on how to identify and evaluate those measures.

(4) State and local assistance

The Administrator, in consultation with the Secretary of Energy, shall make available model commercial leasing provisions and best practices developed under this subsection to State, county, and municipal governments for use in managing owned and leased building space in accordance with the goal of encouraging investment in all cost-effective energy efficiency measures and cost-effective water efficiency measures.

(Pub. L. 114–11, title I, §102, Apr. 30, 2015, 129 Stat. 182.)

§17063. Energy information for commercial buildings

(a) Omitted

(b) Study

(1) In general

Not later than 2 years after April 30, 2015, the Secretary of Energy, in collaboration with the Administrator of the Environmental Protection Agency, shall complete a study—

    (A) on the impact of—

        (i) State and local performance benchmarking and disclosure policies, and any associated building efficiency policies, for commercial and multifamily buildings; and

        (ii) programs and systems in which utilities provide aggregated information regarding whole building energy consumption and usage information to owners of multitenant commercial, residential, and mixed-use buildings;

(B) that identifies best practice policy approaches studied under subparagraph (A) that have resulted in the greatest improvements in building energy efficiency; and

(C) that considers—

(i) compliance rates and the benefits and costs of the policies and programs on building owners, utilities, tenants, and other parties;

(ii) utility practices, programs, and systems that provide aggregated energy consumption information to multitenant building owners, and the impact of public utility commissions and State privacy laws on those practices, programs, and systems;

(iii) exceptions to compliance in existing laws where building owners are not able to gather or access whole building energy information from tenants or utilities;

(iv) the treatment of buildings with—

(I) multiple uses;

(II) uses for which baseline information is not available; and

(III) uses that require high levels of energy intensities, such as data centers, trading floors, and televisions [1] studios;

(v) implementation practices, including disclosure methods and phase-in of compliance;

(vi) the safety and security of benchmarking tools offered by government agencies, and the resiliency of those tools against cyber attacks; and

(vii) international experiences with regard to building benchmarking and disclosure laws and data aggregation for multitenant buildings.

(2) SUBMISSION TO CONGRESS

At the conclusion of the study, the Secretary shall submit to the Committee on Energy and Commerce of the House of Representatives and Committee on Energy and Natural Resources of the Senate a report on the results of the study.

(C) CREATION AND MAINTENANCE OF DATABASE

(1) IN GENERAL

Not later than 18 months after April 30, 2015, and following opportunity for public notice and comment, the Secretary of Energy, in coordination with other relevant agencies, shall maintain, and if necessary create, a database for the purpose of storing and making available public energy-related information on commercial and multifamily buildings, including—

(A) data provided under Federal, State, local, and other laws or programs regarding building benchmarking and energy information disclosure;

(B) information on buildings that have disclosed energy ratings and certifications; and

(C) energy-related information on buildings provided voluntarily by the owners of the buildings, only in an anonymous form unless the owner provides otherwise.

(2) COMPLEMENTARY PROGRAMS

The database maintained pursuant to paragraph (1) shall complement and not duplicate the functions of the Environmental Protection Agency's Energy Star Portfolio Manager tool.

(D) INPUT FROM STAKEHOLDERS

The Secretary of Energy shall seek input from stakeholders to maximize the effectiveness of the actions taken under this section.

(E) REPORT

Not later than 2 years after April 30, 2015, and every 2 years thereafter, the Secretary of Energy shall submit to the Committee on Energy and Commerce of the House of Representatives and Committee on Energy and Natural Resources of the Senate a report on the progress made in complying with this section.

(Pub. L. 114–11, title III, §301, Apr. 30, 2015, 129 Stat. 189.)

^{1} *So in original. Probably should be "television".*

★

PENNSYLVANIA AVENUE DEVELOPMENT

40 U.S.C. CH. 67

TITLE 40—PUBLIC BUILDINGS, PROPERTY, AND WORKS

This title was enacted by Pub. L. 107–217, §1, Aug. 21, 2002, 116 Stat. 1062

* * * * * * *

SUBTITLE II—PUBLIC BUILDINGS AND WORKS

* * * * * * *

PART C—FEDERAL BUILDING COMPLEXES

* * * * * * *

CHAPTER 67—PENNSYLVANIA AVENUE DEVELOPMENT

SUBCHAPTER I—TRANSFER AND ASSIGNMENT OF RIGHTS, AUTHORITIES, TITLE, AND INTERESTS

§6701. TRANSFER OF RIGHTS AND AUTHORITIES OF PENNSYLVANIA AVENUE DEVELOPMENT CORPORATION

(a) IN GENERAL.—The Administrator of General Services—

(1) may make and perform transactions with an agency or instrumentality of the Federal Government, a State, the District of Columbia, or any person as necessary to carry out the trade center plan at the Federal Triangle Project; and

(2) has all the rights and authorities of the former Pennsylvania Avenue Development Corporation with regard to property transferred from the Corporation to the General Services Administration in fiscal year 1996.

(b) USE OF AMOUNTS AND INCOME.—

(1) ACTIVITIES ASSOCIATED WITH TRANSFERRED RESPONSIBILITIES.—The Administrator may use amounts transferred from the Corporation or income earned on Corporation property for activities associated with carrying out the responsibilities of the Corporation transferred to the Administrator. Any income earned after October 1, 1998, shall be deposited to the Federal Buildings Fund to be available for the purposes authorized under this subchapter, notwithstanding section 592(c)(1) of this title.

(2) EXCESS AMOUNTS OR INCOME.—Any amounts or income the Administrator considers excess to the amount needed to fulfill the responsibilities of the Corporation transferred to the Administrator shall be applied to any outstanding debt the Corporation incurred when acquiring real estate, except debt associated with the Ronald Reagan Building and International Trade Center.

(c) PAYMENT TO DISTRICT OF COLUMBIA.—With respect to real property transferred from the Corporation to the Administrator under section 6702 of this title, the Administrator shall pay to the District of Columbia government, in the same way as previously paid by the Corporation, an amount equal to the amount of real property tax which would have been payable to the government beginning on the date the Corporation acquired the real property if legal title to the property had been held by a private citizen on that date and during all periods to which that date relates.

(Pub. L. 107–217, Aug. 21, 2002, 116 Stat. 1193.)

§6702. TRANSFER AND ASSIGNMENT OF RIGHTS, TITLE, AND INTERESTS IN PROPERTY

(a) IN GENERAL.—

(1) LEASES, COVENANTS, AGREEMENTS, AND EASEMENTS.—As provided in this section, the General Services Administration, the National Capital Planning Commission, and the National Park Service have the rights, title, and interest of the Pennsylvania Avenue Development Corporation in and to all leases, covenants, agreements, and easements the Corporation executed before April 1, 1996, in carrying out its powers and duties under the Pennsylvania Avenue Development Corporation Act of 1972 (Public Law 92–578, 86 Stat. 1266) and the Federal Triangle Development Act (Public Law 100–113, 101 Stat. 735).

(2) PROPERTY.—The Administration has the rights, title, and interest of the Corporation in and to all property held in the name of the Corporation, except as

provided in subsection (c).

(b) GENERAL SERVICES ADMINISTRATION.—

(1) RESPONSIBILITIES.—The responsibilities of the Corporation transferred to the Administration under subsection (a) include—

(A) the collection of revenue owed the Federal Government as a result of real estate sales or lease agreements made by the Corporation and private parties, including—

(i) the Willard Hotel property on Square 225;

(ii) the Gallery Row project on Square 457;

(iii) the Lansburgh's project on Square 431; and

(iv) the Market Square North project on Square 407;

(B) the collection of sale or lease revenue owed the Government from the sale or lease before April 1, 1996, of two undeveloped sites owned by the Corporation on Squares 457 and 406;

(C) the application of collected revenue to repay Treasury debt the Corporation incurred when acquiring real estate;

(D) performing financial audits for projects in which the Corporation has actual or potential revenue expectation, as identified in subparagraphs (A) and (B), in accordance with procedures described in applicable sale or lease agreements;

(E) the disposition of real estate properties which are or become available for sale and lease or other uses;

(F) payment of benefits in accordance with the Uniform Relocation Assistance and Real Property Acquisition Policies Act of 1970 (42 U.S.C. 4601 et seq.) to which persons in the project area squares are entitled as a result of the Corporation's acquisition of real estate; and

(G) carrying out the responsibilities of the Corporation under subchapter III and the Federal Triangle Development Act (Public Law 100–113, 101 Stat. 735), including responsibilities for managing assets and liabilities of the Corporation under subchapter III and the Act.

(2) POWERS.—In carrying out the responsibilities of the Corporation transferred under this section, the Administrator of General Services may—

(A) acquire land, improvements, and property by purchase, lease or exchange, and sell, lease, or otherwise dispose of any property, as necessary to complete the development plan developed under section 5 of the Pennsylvania Avenue Development Corporation Act of 1972 (Public Law 92–578, 86 Stat. 1269) if a notice of intention to carry out the acquisition or disposal is first transmitted to the Committee on Transportation and Infrastructure and the Committee on Appropriations of the House of Representatives and the Committee on Environment and Public Works and the Committee on Appropriations of the Senate and at least 60 days elapse after the date of the transmission;

(B) modify the plan referred to in subparagraph (A) if the modification is first transmitted to the Committee on Transportation and Infrastructure and the Committee on Appropriations of the House of Representatives and the Committee on Environment and Public Works and the Committee on Appropriations of the Senate and at least 60 days elapse after the date of the transmission;

(C) maintain any existing Corporation insurance programs;

(D) make and perform transactions with an agency or instrumentality of the Federal Government, a State, the District of Columbia, or any person as necessary to carry out the responsibilities of the Corporation under subchapter III and the Federal Triangle Development Act (Public Law 100–113, 101 Stat. 735);

(E) request the Council of the District of Columbia to close any alleys necessary for the completion of development in Square 457; and

(F) use all of the amount transferred from the Corporation or income earned on Corporation property to complete any pending development projects.

(c) NATIONAL PARK SERVICE.—

(1) PROPERTY.—The National Park Service has the right, title, and interest in and to the property located in the Pennsylvania Avenue National Historic Site, including the parks, plazas, sidewalks, special lighting, trees, sculpture, and memorials, depicted on a map entitled "Pennsylvania Avenue National Historic Park", dated June 1, 1995, and numbered 840–82441. The map shall be on file and available for public inspection in the offices of the Service.

(2) RESPONSIBILITIES.—The Service is responsible for management, administration, maintenance, law enforcement, visitor services, resource protection, interpretation, and historic preservation at the Site.

(3) SPECIAL EVENTS, FESTIVALS, CONCERTS, OR PROGRAMS.—The Service may—

(A) make transactions with an agency or instrumentality of the Government, a State, the District of Columbia, or any person as considered necessary or appropriate for the conduct of special events, festivals, concerts, or other art and cultural programs at the Site; or

(B) establish a nonprofit foundation to solicit amounts for those activities.

(4) JURISDICTION OF DISTRICT OF COLUMBIA.—Jurisdiction of Pennsylvania Avenue and all other roadways from curb to curb remains with the District of Columbia but vendors are not permitted to occupy street space except during temporary special events.

(d) NATIONAL CAPITAL PLANNING COMMISSION.—The National Capital Planning Commission is responsible for ensuring that development in the Pennsylvania Avenue area is carried out in accordance with the Pennsylvania Avenue Development Corporation Plan—1974.

(Pub. L. 107–217, Aug. 21, 2002, 116 Stat. 1194.)

SUBCHAPTER II—PENNSYLVANIA AVENUE DEVELOPMENT

§6711. DEFINITION

In this subchapter, the term "development area" means the area to be developed, maintained, and used in accordance with this subchapter and the Pennsylvania Avenue Development Corporation Act of 1972 (Public Law 92–578, 86 Stat. 1266) and is the area bounded as follows:

Beginning at a point on the southwest corner of the intersection of Fifteenth Street and E Street Northwest;

thence proceeding east along the southern side of E Street to the southwest corner of the intersection of Thirteenth Street and Pennsylvania Avenue Northwest;

thence southeast along the southern side of Pennsylvania Avenue to a point being the southeast corner of the intersection of Pennsylvania Avenue and Third Street Northwest;

thence north along the eastern side of Third Street to the northeast corner of the intersection of C Street and Third Street Northwest;

thence west along the northern side of C Street to the northeast corner of the intersection of C Street and Sixth Street Northwest;

thence north along the eastern side of Sixth Street to the northeast corner of the intersection of E Street and Sixth Street Northwest;

thence west along the northern side of E Street to the northeast corner of the intersection of E Street and Seventh Street Northwest;

thence north along the eastern side of Seventh Street to the northeast corner of the intersection of Seventh Street and F Street Northwest;

thence west along the northern side of F Street to the northwest corner of the intersection of F Street and Ninth Street Northwest;

thence south along the western side of Ninth Street to the northwest corner of the intersection of Ninth Street and E Street Northwest;

thence west along the northern side of E Street to the northeast corner of the intersection of E Street and Thirteenth Street Northwest;

thence north along the eastern side of Thirteenth Street to the northeast corner of the intersection of F Street and Thirteenth Street Northwest;

thence west along the northern side of F Street to the northwest corner of the intersection of F Street and Fifteenth Street Northwest;

thence north along the western side of Fifteenth Street to the northwest corner of the intersection of Pennsylvania Avenue and Fifteenth Street Northwest;

thence west along the southern side of Pennsylvania Avenue to the southeast corner of the intersection of Pennsylvania Avenue and East Executive Avenue Northwest;

thence south along the eastern side of East Executive Avenue to the intersection of South Executive Place and E Street Northwest;

thence east along the southern side of E Street to the point of beginning.

(Pub. L. 107–217, Aug. 21, 2002, 116 Stat. 1196.)

§6712. Powers of other agencies and instrumentalities in the development area

This subchapter and the Pennsylvania Avenue Development Corporation Act of 1972 (Public Law 92–578, 86 Stat. 1266) do not preclude other agencies or instrumentalities of the Federal Government or of the District of Columbia from exercising any lawful powers in the development area consistent with the development plan described in section 5(a) of the Act (86 Stat. 1269) or the provisions and purposes of this subchapter and the Act. However, the agency or instrumentality shall not release, modify, or depart from any feature or detail of the development plan without the prior approval of the Administrator of General Services.

(Pub. L. 107–217, Aug. 21, 2002, 116 Stat. 1197.)

§6713. Certification of new construction

New construction (including substantial remodeling, conversion, rebuilding, enlargement, extension, or major structural improvement of existing building, but not including ordinary maintenance or remodeling or changes necessary to continue occupancy) shall not be authorized or conducted within the development area except on prior certification by the Administrator of General Services that the construction is, or may reasonably be expected to be, consistent with the carrying out of the development plan described in section 5(a) of the Pennsylvania Avenue Development Corporation Act of 1972 (Public Law 92–578, 86 Stat. 1269).

(Pub. L. 107–217, Aug. 21, 2002, 116 Stat. 1197.)

§6714. RELOCATION SERVICES

(a) USE OF DISTRICT OF COLUMBIA GOVERNMENT.—The Administrator of General Services may use the services of the District of Columbia government in the administration of a relocation program pursuant to the Uniform Relocation Assistance and Real Property Acquisition Policies Act of 1970 (42 U.S.C. 4601 et seq.). The Administrator shall reimburse the government for the cost of the services.

(b) COORDINATION OF RELOCATION PROGRAMS.—All relocation services performed by or on behalf of the Administrator shall be coordinated with the District of Columbia's central relocation programs.

(c) PREFERENTIAL RIGHTS OF DISPLACED OWNERS AND TENANTS.—An owner or tenant of real property whose residence or business is terminated as a result of acquisitions made pursuant to this subchapter or the Pennsylvania Avenue Development Corporation Act of 1972 (Public Law 92–578, 86 Stat. 1266) shall be granted a preferential right to lease or purchase from the Administrator similar real property as may become available for a similar use. The preferential right is limited to the parties in interest and is not transferable or assignable.

(Pub. L. 107–217, Aug. 21, 2002, 116 Stat. 1197.)

§6715. COORDINATION WITH DISTRICT OF COLUMBIA

(a) LOCAL NEEDS, INITIATIVE, AND PARTICIPATION.—In carrying out the purposes of this subchapter and the Pennsylvania Avenue Development Corporation Act of 1972 (Public Law 92–578, 86 Stat. 1266), the Administrator of General Services shall—

(1) consult and cooperate with District of Columbia officials and community leaders at the earliest practicable time;

(2) give primary consideration to local needs and desires and to local and regional goals and policies as expressed in urban renewal, community renewal, and comprehensive land use plans and regional plans; and

(3) foster local initiative and participation in connection with the planning and development of projects.

(b) COMPLIANCE WITH LOCAL REQUIREMENTS.—To the extent the Administrator constructs, rehabilitates, alters, or improves any project under this subchapter, the Administrator shall comply with all District of Columbia laws, ordinances, codes, and regulations. Section 8722(d) of this title applies to all construction, rehabilitation, alteration, and improvement of all buildings by the Administrator under this subchapter. Construction, rehabilitation, alteration, and improvement of any project by non-Federal Government sources is subject to the District of Columbia Official Code and zoning regulations.

(Pub. L. 107–217, Aug. 21, 2002, 116 Stat. 1198.)

§6716. Reports

(a) Reports to President and Congress.—The Administrator of General Services shall transmit comprehensive and detailed reports of the Administrator's operations, activities, and accomplishments under this subchapter to the President and Congress. The Administrator shall transmit a report to the President each January and to the President and Congress at other times that the Administrator considers desirable.

(b) Protection and Enhancement of Significant Historic and Architectural Values.—A report under subsection (a) shall include a detailed discussion of the actions the Administrator has taken in the reporting period to protect and enhance the significant historic and architectural values of structures within the boundaries of the Administrator's jurisdiction under this subchapter and shall indicate similar actions the Administrator plans to take and issues the Administrator anticipates dealing with during the upcoming fiscal year related to historic and architectural preservation. The report shall indicate the degree to which public concern has been considered and incorporated into decisions the Administrator made relative to historic and architectural preservation.

(Pub. L. 107–217, Aug. 21, 2002, 116 Stat. 1198.)

SUBCHAPTER III—FEDERAL TRIANGLE DEVELOPMENT

§6731. Definitions

In this subchapter—

(1) Federal triangle development area.—The term "Federal Triangle development area" means the area bounded as follows:

Beginning at a point on the southwest corner of the intersection of Fourteenth Street and Pennsylvania Avenue (formerly E Street), Northwest;

thence south along the western side of Fourteenth Street to the northwest corner of the intersection of Fourteenth Street and Constitution Avenue, Northwest;

thence east along the northern side of Constitution Avenue to the northeast corner of the intersection of Twelfth Street and Constitution Avenue, Northwest;

thence north along the eastern side of Twelfth Street and Constitution Avenue, Northwest;

thence north along the eastern side of Twelfth Street to the southeast corner of the intersection of Twelfth Street and Pennsylvania Avenue, Northwest;

thence west along the southern side of Pennsylvania Avenue to the point of beginning.

(2) Federal triangle property.—The term "Federal Triangle property" means—

(A) the property owned by the Federal Government in the District of Columbia, known as the "Great Plaza" site, which consists of squares 256, 257, 258, parts of squares 259 and 260, and adjacent closed rights-of-way as shown on plate IV of the King Plats of 1803 located in the Office of the Surveyor of the District of Columbia; and

(B) except for purposes of section 6733(a) of this title, any property the Pennsylvania Avenue Development Corporation acquired under section 3(b) of the Federal Triangle Development Act (Public Law 100–113, 101 Stat. 736).

(Pub. L. 107–217, Aug. 21, 2002, 116 Stat. 1198.)

§6732. FEDERAL TRIANGLE DEVELOPMENT AREA

The Federal Triangle development area is deemed to be part of the development area described in section 6711 of this title. The Administrator of General Services has the same authority over the Federal Triangle development area as over the development area described in section 6711.

(Pub. L. 107–217, Aug. 21, 2002, 116 Stat. 1199.)

§6733. FEDERAL TRIANGLE PROPERTY

(a) TITLE.—Title to the Federal Triangle property reverts to the Administrator of General Services not later than the date on which ownership of the Ronald Reagan Building and International Trade Center vests in the Federal Government.

(b) NONAPPLICABILITY OF CERTAIN LAWS.—

(1) BUILDING PERMITS AND INSPECTION.—For purposes of development of the Federal Triangle property, the person selected to develop the property is not subject to any state or local law relating to building permits and inspection.

(2) TAXES AND ASSESSMENTS.—The property and improvements to the property are not subject to real and personal property taxation or to special assessments.

(Pub. L. 107–217, Aug. 21, 2002, 116 Stat. 1199.)

§6734. RONALD REAGAN BUILDING AND INTERNATIONAL TRADE CENTER

(a) ESTABLISHMENT AND DESIGNATION.—The building constructed on the Federal Triangle property shall be known and designated as the Ronald Reagan Building and International Trade Center.

(b) TITLE.—The person selected to develop the Federal Triangle property may own the Building for not more than 35 years from the date construction of the Building began. The title to the Building shall be in the Administrator of General Services from the date title to the Federal Triangle property reverts to the Administrator.

(c) LIMITATIONS.—

(1) SIZE OF BUILDING.—The Building (including parking facilities) may not exceed 3,100,000 gross square feet in size.

(2) HEIGHT OF BUILDING.—The height of the Building shall be compatible with the height of surrounding Federal Government buildings.

(3) DESIGN.—The Building shall—

(A) be designed in harmony with historical and Government buildings in the vicinity;

(B) reflect the symbolic importance and historic character of Pennsylvania Avenue and the Nation's Capital; and

(C) represent the dignity and stability of the Government.

(d) CONSTRUCTION STANDARDS.—The Building shall meet all standards applicable to construction of a federal building.

(e) ACCOUNTING SYSTEM.—The Administrator shall maintain an accounting system for operation and maintenance of the Building which will allow accurate projections of the dates and cost of major repairs, improvements, reconstructions, and replacements of the Building and other capital expenditures on the Building. The Administrator shall act as necessary to ensure that amounts are available to cover the projected cost and expenditures.

(f) LEASE OF BUILDING.—

(1) LEASE AGREEMENT.—Under an agreement with the person selected to construct the Ronald Reagan Building and International Trade Center, the Administrator shall lease the Building for federal office space and the international cultural and trade center space.

(2) MINIMUM REQUIREMENTS OF LEASE AGREEMENT.—The agreement includes at a minimum the following:

(A) LIMIT ON LENGTH OF LEASE.—The Administrator will lease the Building for the period of time that the person selected to construct the Building owns the Building.

(B) RENTAL RATE.—The rental rate per square foot of occupiable space for all space in the Building will be in the best interest of the Government and will carry out the objectives of this subchapter and the Federal Triangle Development Act (Public Law 100–113, 101 Stat. 735). The aggregate rental rate for all space in the Building shall produce an amount at least equal to the amount necessary to amortize the cost of development of the Federal Triangle property over the life of the lease.

(C) OBLIGATION OF AMOUNTS.—Obligation of amounts from the Federal Building Fund shall only be made on an annual basis to meet lease payments.

(3) AUTHORIZATION TO OBLIGATE AMOUNTS.—Amounts may be obligated as described in paragraph (2)(C).

(Pub. L. 107–217, Aug. 21, 2002, 116 Stat. 1199.)

* * * * * * *

★

FEDERAL ASSETS SALE AND TRANSFER ACT OF 2016

PUBLIC LAW 114–287
AS AMENDED THROUGH P.L. 118–272

FEDERAL ASSETS SALE AND TRANSFER ACT OF 2016

[(Public Law 114–287)]

[As Amended Through P.L. 118–272, Enacted January 4, 2025]

AN ACT To decrease the deficit by consolidating and selling Federal buildings and other civilian real property, and for other purposes.

Be it enacted by the Senate and House of Representatives of the United States of America in Congress assembled,

SECTION 1. [40 U.S.C. 1303 note] SHORT TITLE; TABLE OF CONTENTS.

(a) SHORT TITLE.— This Act may be cited as the "Federal Assets Sale and Transfer Act of 2016".

(b) TABLE OF CONTENTS.— The table of contents for this Act is as follows:

SEC. 2. PURPOSES.

The purpose of this Act is to reduce the costs of Federal real estate by—

(1) consolidating the footprint of Federal buildings and facilities;

(2) maximizing the utilization rate of Federal buildings and facilities;

(3) reducing the reliance on leased space;

(4) selling or redeveloping high value assets that are underutilized to obtain the highest and best value for the taxpayer and maximize the return to the taxpayer;

(5) reducing the operating and maintenance costs of Federal civilian real properties;

(6) reducing redundancy, overlap, and costs associated with field offices;

(7) creating incentives for Federal agencies to achieve greater efficiency in their inventories of civilian real property;

(8) facilitating and expediting the sale or disposal of unneeded Federal civilian real properties;

(9) improving the efficiency of real property transfers for the provision of services to the homeless;

(10) assisting Federal agencies in achieving the Government's sustainability goals by reducing excess space, inventory, and energy consumption, as well as by leveraging new technologies; and

(11) implementing innovative methods for the sale, redevelopment, consolidation, or lease of Federal buildings and facilities, including the use of no cost, nonappropriated contracts for expert real estate services to obtain the highest and best value for the taxpayer.

SEC. 3. DEFINITIONS.

In this Act, unless otherwise expressly stated, the following definitions apply:

(1) ADMINISTRATOR.— The term Administrator means the Administrator of General Services.

(2) BOARD.— The term Board means the Public Buildings Reform Board established by section 4.

(3) CERCLA.— The term CERCLA means the Comprehensive Environmental Response, Compensation, and Liability Act of 1980 (42 U.S.C. 9601 et seq.).

(4) FEDERAL AGENCY.— The term Federal agency means an executive department or independent establishment in the executive branch of the Government, and a wholly owned Government corporation.

(5) FEDERAL CIVILIAN REAL PROPERTY AND CIVILIAN REAL PROPERTY.—

(A) IN GENERAL.— The terms Federal civilian real property and civilian real property refer to Federal real property assets, including public buildings as defined in section 3301(a) of title 40, United States Code, occupied and improved grounds, leased space, or other physical structures under the custody and control of any Federal agency.

(B) EXCLUSIONS.—Subparagraph (A) shall not be construed as including any of the following types of property:

(i)   Properties that are on military installations (including any fort, camp, post, naval training station, airfield proving ground, military supply depot, military school, or any similar facility of the Department of Defense).

(ii)   A base, camp, post, station, yard, center, or homeport facility for any ship or activity under the jurisdiction of the Coast Guard.

(iii)   Properties that are excluded for reasons of national security by the Director of the Office of Management and Budget.

(iv)   Properties that are excepted from the definition of the term property under section 102 of title 40, United States Code.

(v) Indian and Native Alaskan properties, including—

(I)   any property within the limits of an Indian reservation to which the United States owns title for the benefit of an Indian tribe; and

(II)   any property title that is held in trust by the United States for the benefit of an Indian tribe or individual or held by an Indian tribe or individual subject to restriction by the United States against alienation.

(vi)   Properties operated and maintained by the Tennessee Valley Authority pursuant to the Tennessee Valley Authority Act of 1933 (16 U.S.C. 831 et seq.).

(vii)   Postal properties owned by the United States Postal Service.

(viii)   Properties, other than office buildings and warehouses, used in connection with Federal programs for agricultural, recreational, or conservation purposes, including research in connection with the programs.

(ix)   Properties used in connection with river, harbor, flood control, reclamation, or power projects.

(x)   Properties located outside the United States operated or maintained by the Department of State or the United States Agency for International Development.

(6) FIELD OFFICE.— The term field office means any Federal office that is not the headquarters office location for the Federal agency.

(7) HUD.— The term HUD means the Department of Housing and Urban Development.

(8) OMB.— The term OMB means the Office of Management and Budget.

(9) VALUE OF TRANSACTIONS.— The term value of transactions means the sum of the estimated proceeds and estimated costs, based on the accounting system developed

or identified under section 12(f), associated with the transactions included in Board recommendations.

SEC. 4. BOARD.

(a) ESTABLISHMENT.— There is established an independent board to be known as the Public Buildings Reform Board.

(b) DUTIES.— The Board shall carry out the duties as specified in this Act.

(c) MEMBERSHIP.—

(1) IN GENERAL.— The Board shall be composed of a Chairperson appointed by the President, by and with the advice and consent of the Senate, and 6 members appointed by the President.

(2) APPOINTMENTS.— In selecting individuals for appointments to the Board, the President shall appoint members in the following manner:

(A) Two members recommended by the Speaker of the House of Representatives.

(B) Two members recommended by the majority leader of the Senate.

(C) One member recommended by the minority leader of the House of Representatives.

(D) One member recommended by the minority leader of the Senate.

(3) TERMS.—

(A) IN GENERAL.— Subject to subparagraph (B), the term for each member of the Board shall be 6 years.

(B) LIMITATION.— Notwithstanding subparagraph (A), the term of a member of the Board shall continue beyond 6 years until such time as the President appoints a replacement member of the Board.

(4) VACANCIES.— Vacancies shall be filled in the same manner as the original appointment.

(5) QUALIFICATIONS.—In selecting individuals for appointment to the Board, the President shall ensure that the Board contains individuals with expertise representative of the following:

(A) Commercial real estate and redevelopment.

(B) Space optimization and utilization.

(C) Community development, including transportation and planning.

SEC. 5. BOARD MEETINGS.

(a) OPEN MEETINGS.— Each meeting of the Board, other than meetings in which classified information is to be discussed, shall be open to the public. Any open meeting shall be announced in the Federal Register and the Federal Web site established by the Board at least 14 calendar days in advance of a meeting. For all public meetings, the Board shall release an agenda and a listing of materials relevant to the topics to be discussed.

(b) QUORUM AND MEETINGS.— 4 Board members shall constitute a quorum for the purposes of conducting business and three or more Board members shall constitute a meeting of the Board.

(c) TRANSPARENCY OF INFORMATION.—All the proceedings, information, and deliberations of the Board shall be open, upon request, to the Chairperson and ranking minority party member, and their respective subcommittee Chairperson and subcommittee ranking minority party member, of—

(1) the Committee on Transportation and Infrastructure of the House of Representatives;

(2) the Committee on Oversight and Government Reform of the House of Representatives;

(3) the Committee on Homeland Security and Governmental Affairs of the Senate;

(4) the Committee on Environment and Public Works of the Senate; and

(5) the Committees on Appropriations of the House of Representatives and the Senate.

(d) GOVERNMENT ACCOUNTABILITY OFFICE.— All proceedings, information, and deliberations of the Board shall be open, upon request, to the Comptroller General of the United States.

SEC. 6. COMPENSATION AND TRAVEL EXPENSES.

(a) COMPENSATION.—

(1) RATE OF PAY FOR MEMBERS.— Each member, other than the Chairperson, shall be paid at a rate equal to the daily equivalent of the minimum annual rate of basic pay payable for level IV of the Executive Schedule under section 5315 of title 5, United States Code, for each day (including travel time) during which the member is engaged in the actual performance of duties vested in the Board.

(2) RATE OF PAY FOR CHAIRPERSON.— The Chairperson shall be paid for each day referred to in paragraph (1) at a rate equal to the daily equivalent of the minimum annual rate of basic pay payable for level III of the Executive Schedule under section 5314 of title 5, United States Code.

(b) TRAVEL.— Members shall receive travel expenses, including per diem in lieu of subsistence, in accordance with sections 5702 and 5703 of title 5, United States Code.

SEC. 7. EXECUTIVE DIRECTOR.

(a) APPOINTMENT.— The Board shall appoint an Executive Director, who may be appointed without regard to the provisions of title 5, United States Code, governing appointments in the competitive service.

(b) RATE OF PAY.— The Executive Director shall be paid at the rate of basic pay payable for level IV of the Executive Schedule under section 5315 of title 5, United States Code.

(c) RETURN TO CIVIL SERVICE.— An Executive Director selected from the civil service (as defined in section 2101 of title 5, United States Code) shall be entitled to

SEC. 8. [40 U.S.C. 1303 note] SHORT TITLE;
TABLE OF CONTENTS.

Federal Assets Sale and Transfer Act of 20

return to the civil service (as so defined) after service to the Board ends if the service of the Executive Director to the Board ends for reasons other than misconduct, neglect of duty, or malfeasance.

SEC. 8. STAFF.

(a) ADDITIONAL PERSONNEL.— Subject to subsection (b), the Executive Director may request additional personnel detailed from Federal agencies.

(b) REQUESTS FOR DETAIL EMPLOYEES.— Upon request of the Executive Director and approval of the Board, the head of any Federal agency shall detail the requested personnel of that agency to the Board for a period of not less than 1 year to assist the Board in carrying out its duties under this Act.

(c) HIRING OF TERM EMPLOYEES.— The Executive Director, with approval of the Board, may use the Office of Personnel Management to hire employees for terms not to exceed 2 years pursuant to the Office of Personnel Management guidance for nonstatus appointments in the competitive service.

(d) QUALIFICATIONS.— Appointments shall be made with consideration of a balance of expertise consistent with the qualifications of representatives described in section 4(c)(5).

SEC. 9. CONTRACTING AUTHORITY.

(a) EXPERTS AND CONSULTANTS.— The Board, to the extent practicable and subject to appropriations Acts, shall use contracts, including nonappropriated contracts, entered into by the Administrator for services necessary to carry out the duties of the Board.

(b) OFFICE SPACE.— The Administrator, in consultation with the Board, shall identify and provide, without charge, suitable office space within the existing Federal space inventory to house the operations of the Board.

(c) PERSONAL PROPERTY.— The Board shall use personal property already in the custody and control of the Administrator.

SEC. 10. TERMINATION.

The Board shall cease operations and terminate on December 31, 2026.

SEC. 11. DEVELOPMENT OF RECOMMENDATIONS TO BOARD.

(a) SUBMISSIONS OF AGENCY INFORMATION AND RECOMMENDATIONS.—Not later than 120 days after the date of enactment of this Act, and not later than 120 days after the first day of each fiscal year thereafter until the termination of the Board, the head of each Federal agency shall submit to the Administrator, the Director of OMB, and the Board the following:

(1) CURRENT DATA.— Current data of all Federal civilian real properties owned, leased, or controlled by the agency, including all relevant information prescribed by the Administrator and the Director of OMB, including data related to the age and condition of the property, operating costs, history of capital expenditures, sustainability metrics, number of Federal employees and functions housed in the respective property, number of Federal employees physically reporting to the respective property each work day, square footage (including gross, rentable, and

SEC. 11. [40 U.S.C. 1303 note] SHORT TITLE; TABLE OF CONTENTS.

Federal Assets Sale and Transfer Act of 2016

usable), amount of acreage associated with the respective property, and whether the respective property is on a campus or larger facility.

(2) AGENCY RECOMMENDATIONS.—Recommendations of the agency on the following:

(A)   Federal civilian real properties that can be sold for proceeds or otherwise disposed of, reported as excess, declared surplus, outleased, or otherwise no longer meeting the needs of the agency, excluding leasebacks or other such exchange agreements where the property continues to be used by the agency.

(B)   Federal civilian real properties that can be transferred, exchanged, consolidated, co-located, reconfigured, or redeveloped, so as to reduce the civilian real property inventory, reduce the operating costs of the Government, and create the highest value and return for the taxpayer.

(C)   Operational efficiencies that the Government can realize in its operation and maintenance of Federal civilian real properties.

(3) CONSOLIDATION PLANS.— Any Federal agency plans to consolidate, reconfigure, or otherwise reduce the use of owned and leased Federal civilian real property of the Federal agency.

(b) STANDARDS AND CRITERIA.—

(1) DEVELOPMENT OF STANDARDS AND CRITERIA.—Not later than 60 days after the deadline for submissions of agency recommendations under subsection (a), the Director of OMB, in consultation with the Administrator, shall—

(A)   review the agency recommendations;

(B)   develop consistent standards and criteria against which the agency recommendations will be reviewed; and

(C)   submit to the Board the recommendations developed pursuant to paragraph (2).

(2) RECOMMENDATIONS TO BOARD.— The Director of OMB and the Administrator shall jointly develop recommendations to the Board based on the standards and criteria developed under paragraph (1).

(3) FACTORS.—In developing the standards and criteria under paragraph (1), the Director of OMB, in consultation with the Administrator, shall incorporate the following factors:

(A)   The extent to which the civilian real property could be sold (including property that is no longer meeting the needs of the Government), redeveloped, outleased, or otherwise used to produce the highest and best value and return for the taxpayer.

(B)   The extent to which the operating and maintenance costs are reduced through consolidating, co-locating, and reconfiguring space, and through realizing other operational efficiencies.

(C)   The extent to which the utilization rate is being maximized and is consistent with non-governmental industry standards for the given function or operation.

SEC. 11. [40 U.S.C. 1303 note] SHORT TITLE;
TABLE OF CONTENTS.

Federal Assets Sale and Transfer Act of 20

(D)   The extent and timing of potential costs and savings, including the number of years, beginning with the date of completion of the proposed recommendation.

(E)   The extent to which reliance on leasing for long-term space needs is reduced.

(F)   The extent to which a civilian real property aligns with the current mission of the Federal agency.

(G)   The extent to which there are opportunities to consolidate similar operations across multiple agencies or within agencies.

(H)   The economic impact on existing communities in the vicinity of the civilian real property.

(I)   The extent to which energy consumption is reduced.

(J)   The extent to which public access, including access by members of federally recognized Indian Tribes, to agency services is maintained or enhanced.

(c) SPECIAL RULE FOR UTILIZATION RATES.— Standards developed by the Director of OMB pursuant to subsection (b) shall incorporate and apply clear standard utilization rates to the extent that such standard rates increase efficiency and provide performance data. The utilization rates shall be consistent throughout each applicable category of space and with nongovernment space utilization rates. To the extent the space utilization rate of a given agency exceeds the utilization rates to be applied under this subsection, the Director of OMB may recommend realignment, co-location, consolidation, or other type of action to improve space utilization.

(d) SUBMISSION TO BOARD.—

(1) IN GENERAL.— The Director of OMB shall submit the standards, criteria, and recommendations developed pursuant to subsection (b) to the Board with all supporting information, data, analyses, and documentation.

(2) PUBLICATION.— The standards, criteria, and recommendations developed pursuant to subsection (b) shall be published in the Federal Register and transmitted to the committees listed in section 5(c) and to the Comptroller General of the United States.

(3) ACCESS TO INFORMATION.— The Board shall also have access to all information pertaining to the recommendations developed pursuant to subsection (b), including supporting information, data, analyses, and documentation submitted pursuant to subsection (a). Upon request, a Federal agency shall provide to the Board any additional information pertaining to the civilian real properties under the custody, control, or administrative jurisdiction of the Federal agency. The Board shall notify the committees listed in section 5(c) of any failure by an agency to comply with a request of the Board.

(e) DISCLOSURE OF INFORMATION.—

(1) IN GENERAL.— Except as provided in paragraph (2), the Board may not publicly disclose any information received under paragraph (2) or (3) of subsection (a) until the Board, the Administrator, and the Director of OMB enter into an

agreement describing what information is ready to be publicly disclosed.

(2) APPLICATION.— Paragraph (1) shall not apply to any disclosure of information to the Committee on Environment and Public Works of the Senate or the Committee on Transportation and Infrastructure of the House of Representatives.

SEC. 12. BOARD DUTIES.

(a) IDENTIFICATION OF PROPERTY REDUCTION OPPORTUNITIES.— The Board shall identify opportunities for the Government to reduce significantly its inventory of civilian real property and reduce costs to the Government.

(b) IDENTIFICATION OF HIGH VALUE ASSETS.—

(1) IDENTIFICATION OF CERTAIN PROPERTIES.—Not later than 180 days after Board members are appointed pursuant to section 4, the Board shall—

(A)   identify not fewer than five Federal civilian real properties that are not on the list of surplus or excess as of such date with a total fair market value of not less than $500,000,000 and not more than $750,000,000; and

(B)   transmit the list of the Federal civilian real properties to the Director of OMB and Congress as Board recommendations and subject to the approval process described in section 13.

(2) INFORMATION AND DATA.— In order to meet the goal established under paragraph (1), each Federal agency shall provide, upon request, any and all information and data regarding its civilian real properties to the Board. In the case of a failure by a Federal agency to comply with a request of the Board, the Board shall notify the committees listed in section 5(c), the relevant congressional committees of jurisdiction for the Federal agency, and the inspector general of the Federal agency of that failure.

(3) FACTORS.— In identifying properties pursuant to paragraph (1), the Board shall consider the factors listed in section 11(b)(3).

(4) LEASEBACK RESTRICTIONS.—

(A) IN GENERAL.— None of the existing improvements on properties sold under this subsection may be leased back to the Government for a period of greater than 3 years.

(B) REQUIREMENTS.—A leaseback under this paragraph—

(i)   shall expire on or before the last day of the 3-year period beginning on the date of the sale of the respective property;

(ii)   may not contain any options to extend or renew the leaseback;

(iii)   may only be entered into once for purposes of temporarily housing the Federal agency in the property at the time of the sale; and

(iv)   shall only be for the purpose of facilitating the sale of the respective property.

(5) REPORT OF EXCESS.— Not later than 60 days after the approval of Board recommendations pursuant to paragraph (1), Federal agencies with custody, control, or administrative jurisdiction over the identified properties shall submit a Report of

SEC. 12. [40 U.S.C. 1303 note] SHORT TITLE;
TABLE OF CONTENTS.

Federal Assets Sale and Transfer Act of 20

Excess to the General Services Administration.

(6) SALE.—

(A) INITIATION OF SALE.— Not later than 120 days after the acceptance by the Administrator of the Report of Excess and notwithstanding any other provision of law (including section 501 of the McKinney-Vento Homeless Assistance Act (42 U.S.C. 11411), but except as provided in section 14(g)), the General Services Administration shall initiate the sale of the civilian real properties described in paragraph (1).

(B) COMPLETION OF SALE.— Not later than 1 year after the acceptance of the Report of Excess, the Administrator shall sell the civilian real properties at fair market value at highest and best use, unless the Director of OMB determines it is in the financial interest of the Government to execute a sale more than a year after the acceptance of the Report of Excess, but not greater than 2 years after the acceptance of the Report of Excess.

(c) ANALYSIS OF INVENTORY.— The Board shall perform an independent analysis of the inventory of Federal civilian real property and the recommendations submitted pursuant to section 11. The Board shall not be bound or limited by the recommendations submitted pursuant to section 11. If, in the opinion of the Board, an agency fails to provide needed information, data, or adequate recommendations that meet the standards and criteria, the Board shall develop such recommendations as the Board considers appropriate based on existing data contained in the Federal Real Property Profile or other relevant information.

(d) PREPARATION OF PROPERTIES FOR DISPOSAL.— At the request of, and in coordination with, the Board, a Federal agency may undertake any analyses and due diligence as necessary, to supplement the independent analysis of the Board under subsection (c), to prepare a property for disposition so that the property may be included in the recommendations of the Board under subsection (h), including completion of the requirements of section 306108 of title 54, United States Code, for historic preservation and identification of the likely highest and best use of the property subsequent to disposition.

(e) INFORMATION AND PROPOSALS.—

(1) RECEIPT.— Notwithstanding any other provision of law, the Board may receive and consider proposals, information, and other data submitted by State, Tribal, and local officials and the private sector.

(2) CONSULTATION.— The Board shall consult with State, Tribal, and local officials on information, proposals, and other data that the officials submit to the Board.

(3) AVAILABILITY.— Information submitted to the Board shall be made publicly available.

(f) ACCOUNTING SYSTEM.— Not later than 120 days after the date on which the Board members are appointed pursuant to section 4, the Board shall identify or develop and implement a system of accounting to be used to independently evaluate the costs of and returns on the recommendations. Such accounting system shall be applied in developing the Board's recommendations and determining the highest return to the taxpayer. In applying the accounting system, the Board shall set a standard performance period of not less than 15 years.

(g) PUBLIC HEARING.— The Board shall conduct public hearings. All testimony before the Board at a public hearing under this subsection shall be presented under oath.

(h) REPORTING OF INFORMATION AND RECOMMENDATIONS.—

(1) IN GENERAL.—Subject to the schedule and limitations specified in paragraph (2), the Board shall transmit to the Director of OMB, and publicly post on a Federal Web site maintained by the Board, reports containing the Board's findings, conclusions, and recommendations for—

(A) the consolidation, exchange, co-location, reconfiguration, lease reductions, sale, outlease, and redevelopment of Federal civilian real properties;

(B) the process to be followed by Federal agencies to carry out the actions described in subparagraph (A), including the use of no cost, nonappropriated contracts for expert real estate services and other innovative methods, to obtain the highest and best value for the taxpayer; and

(C) other operational efficiencies that can be realized in the Government's operation and maintenance of such properties.

(2) SCHEDULE AND LIMITATIONS.—

(A) FIRST ROUND.— Not later than 2 years after the date of transmittal of the list of properties recommended pursuant to subsection (b), the Board shall transmit to the Director of OMB the first report required under paragraph (1). The total value of transactions contained in the first report may not exceed $2,500,000,000.

(B) SECOND ROUND.— Not earlier than 3 years after the date of transmittal of the first report, the Board shall transmit to the Director of OMB the second report required under paragraph (1). The total value of transactions contained in the second report may not exceed $4,750,000,000.

(C) THIRD ROUND.— During the period beginning on the day after the transmittal of the second report and ending on the day before the date on which the Board terminates under section 10, the Board shall transmit to the Director of OMB a third report required under paragraph (1).

(3) CONSENSUS IN MAJORITY.— The Board shall seek to develop consensus recommendations, but if a consensus cannot be obtained, the Board may include in the reports required under this subsection recommendations that are supported by a majority of the Board.

(4) COMMUNITY NOTIFICATION.—45 days before the date on which the Board transmits the third report required under paragraph (1), the Board shall notify—

(A) any State or local government of any findings, conclusions, or recommendations contained in that report that relate to a Federal civilian real property located in the State or locality, as applicable; and

(B) any federally recognized Indian Tribe of any findings, conclusions, or recommendations contained in that report that relate to a Federal civilian real property that—

(i)   is in close geographic proximity to a property described in section 3(5)(B)(v); or

(ii)   relates to a Federal civilian real property that is known to be accessed at regular frequency by members of the federally recognized Indian Tribe for other reasons.

(i) FEDERAL WEB SITE.— The Board shall establish and maintain a Federal Web site for the purposes of making relevant information publicly available.

(j) REVIEW BY GAO.— The Comptroller General of the United States shall transmit to Congress and the Board a report containing a detailed analysis of the recommendations and selection process.

(k) REPORT TO CONGRESS.— The Board shall periodically submit to the Committee on Environment and Public Works of the Senate and the Committee on Transportation and Infrastructure of the House of Representatives a report containing any recommendations on consolidations, exchanges, sales, lease reductions, and redevelopments that are not included in the transmissions submitted under subsection (h), or approved by the Director of OMB under section 13, but that the majority of the Board concludes meets the goals of this Act.

SEC. 13. REVIEW BY OMB.

(a) REVIEW OF RECOMMENDATIONS.— Upon receipt of the Board's recommendations pursuant to subsections (b) and (h) of section 12, the Director of OMB shall conduct a review of the recommendations.

(b) REPORT TO BOARD AND CONGRESS.— Not later than 30 days after the receipt of the Board's recommendations, the Director of OMB shall transmit to the Board and Congress a report that sets forth the Director of OMB's approval or disapproval of the Board's recommendations.

(c) APPROVAL AND DISAPPROVAL.—

(1) APPROVAL.— If the Director of OMB approves the Board's recommendations, the Director of OMB shall transmit a copy of the recommendations to Congress, together with a certification of such approval.

(2) DISAPPROVAL.— If the Director of OMB disapproves the Board's recommendations, in whole or in part, the Director of OMB shall transmit a copy of the recommendations to Congress and the reasons for disapproval of the recommendations to the Board and Congress.

(3) REVISED RECOMMENDATIONS.— Not later than 30 days after the receipt of reasons for disapproval under paragraph (2), the Board shall transmit to the Director of OMB revised recommendations for approval.

(4) APPROVAL OF REVISED RECOMMENDATIONS.— If the Director of OMB approves the revised recommendations, in whole or in part, received under paragraph (3), the Director of OMB shall transmit a copy of the recommendations to Congress, together with a certification of such approval.

EC. 14. [40 U.S.C. 1303 note] SHORT TITLE;
ABLE OF CONTENTS.

Federal Assets Sale and Transfer Act of 2016

(d) TERMINATION OF PROCESS FOR GIVEN ROUND.— If the Director of OMB does not transmit to Congress an approval and certification described in paragraph (1) or (4) of subsection (c) on or before the 30th day following the receipt of the Board's recommendations or revised recommendations, as the case may be, the process shall terminate until the following round, as described in section 12.

SEC. 14. IMPLEMENTATION OF BOARD RECOMMENDATIONS.

(a) DEADLINES.—

(1) PREPARATION.—Federal agencies shall—

(A) not later than 60 days after the Director of OMB transmits the Board's recommendations to Congress pursuant to paragraph (1) or (4) of section 13(c), immediately begin preparations to carry out the Board's recommendations; and

(B) not later than 2 years after such transmittal, initiate all activities necessary to carry out the Board's recommendations.

(2) COMPLETION.— Not later than 6 years after the Director of OMB transmits the Board's recommendations to Congress pursuant to paragraph (1) or (4) of section 13(c), Federal agencies shall complete all recommended actions. All actions shall be economically beneficial, cost neutral, or otherwise favorable to the Government.

(3) EXTENUATING CIRCUMSTANCES.— For actions that will take longer than the 6-year period described in paragraph (2) due to extenuating circumstances, Federal agencies shall notify the Director of OMB and Congress, as soon as the extenuating circumstance presents itself, with an estimated time to complete the relevant action.

(b) ACTIONS OF FEDERAL AGENCIES RELATED TO CIVILIAN REAL PROPERTIES.—In taking actions related to any civilian real property under this Act, Federal agencies may take, pursuant to subsection (c), all such necessary and proper actions, including—

(1) acquiring land, constructing replacement facilities, performing such other activities, and conducting advance planning and design as may be required to transfer functions from a Federal asset or property to another Federal civilian property;

(2) reimbursing other Federal agencies for actions performed at the request of the Board; and

(3) taking such actions as are practicable to maximize the value of Federal civilian real property to be sold by clarifying zoning and other limitations on use of such property.

(c) ACTIONS OF FEDERAL AGENCIES TO IMPLEMENT BOARD RECOMMENDATIONS.—

(1) USE OF EXISTING LEGAL AUTHORITIES.—

(A) IN GENERAL.—Except as provided in paragraph (2), when acting on a recommendation of the Board, a Federal agency shall—

(i) in consultation with the Administrator, continue to act within the Federal agency's existing legal authorities, including legal authorities delegated to the Federal agency by the Administrator; or

(ii)   work in partnership with the Administrator to carry out such actions.

(B) NECESSARY AND PROPER ACTIONS.— The Administrator may take such necessary and proper actions, including the sale, conveyance, or exchange of civilian real property, as required to implement the Board's recommendations in the time period required under subsection (a).

(2) EXPERTS.— A Federal agency may enter into no cost, nonappropriated contracts for expert commercial real estate services to carry out the Federal agency's responsibilities pursuant to the recommendations.

(d) DISCRETION OF ADMINISTRATOR REGARDING TRANSACTIONS.— For any transaction identified, recommended, or commenced as a result of this Act, any otherwise required legal priority given to, or requirement to enter into, a transaction to convey a Federal civilian real property for less than fair market value, for no consideration at all, or in a transaction that mandates the exclusion of other market participants, shall be at the discretion of the Administrator.

(e) RELATIONSHIP TO OTHER LAWS.—Any recommendation or commencement of a sale, disposal, consolidation, reconfiguration, co-location, or realignment of civilian real property under this Act shall not be subject to—

(1)   section 545(b)(8) of title 40, United States Code;

(2)   sections 550, 553, and 554 of title 40, United States Code;

(3)   any section of the Act entitled An Act Authorizing the transfer of certain real property for wildlife, or other purposes (16 U.S.C. 667b);

(4)   section 47151 of title 49, United States Code;

(5)   sections 107 and 317 of title 23, United States Code;

(6)   section 1304(b) of title 40, United States Code;

(7)   section 13(d) of the Surplus Property Act of 1944 (50 U.S.C. App. 1622(d));

(8)   any other provision of law authorizing the conveyance of real property owned by the Government for no consideration; and

(9)   any congressional notification requirement other than that in section 545 of title 40, United States Code.

(f) PUBLIC BENEFIT.—

(1) SUBMISSION OF INFORMATION TO HUD.— The Director of OMB shall submit to the Secretary of HUD, on the same day the Director of OMB submits the Board's recommendations to Congress pursuant to paragraphs (1) and (4) of section 13(c), all known information on Federal civilian real properties that are included in the recommendations (except those recommended under section 12(b)).

(2) HUD TO REPORT TO BOARD.— Not later than 30 days after the submission of information on Federal properties under paragraph (1), the Secretary shall identify any suitable civilian real properties for use as a property benefiting the mission of assistance to the homeless for the purposes of further screening pursuant to section 501 of the McKinney-Vento Homeless Assistance Act (42 U.S.C. 11411).

(3) ADDITIONAL AUTHORITY.— Following the review under paragraph (2), with respect to a civilian real property that is not identified by the Secretary as suitable for use as a property benefiting the mission of assistance to the homeless and that has been recommended for sale by the Board, the Director of OMB may exclude the property from the Board's recommendations if the Director determines that the property is suitable for use as a public park or recreation area by a State or local government and it is in the best interest of taxpayers.

(g) ENVIRONMENTAL CONSIDERATIONS.—

(1) TRANSFERS OF REAL PROPERTY.—

(A) IN GENERAL.— When implementing the recommended actions for civilian real properties that have been identified in the Board's report, as specified in section 12(h), and subject to paragraph (2) and in compliance with CERCLA, including section 120(h) of CERCLA (42 U.S.C. 9620(h)), Federal agencies may enter into an agreement to transfer by deed, pursuant to section 120(h)(3) of that Act (42 U.S.C. 9620(h)(3)), civilian real property with any person.

(B) ADDITIONAL TERMS AND CONDITIONS.— The head of the disposing agency may require any additional terms and conditions in connection with an agreement authorized by subparagraph (A) as the head of the disposing agency considers appropriate to protect the interests of the United States. Such additional terms and conditions shall not affect or diminish any rights or obligations of the Federal agencies under section 120(h) of CERCLA (including, without limitation, the requirements of subsections (h)(3)(A) and (h)(3)(C)(iv) of that section).

(2) CERTIFICATION CONCERNING COSTS.—A transfer of Federal civilian real property may be made under paragraph (1) only if the head of the disposing agency certifies to the Board and Congress that—

(A) the costs of all environmental restoration, waste management, and environmental compliance activities otherwise to be paid by the disposing agency with respect to the property are equal to or greater than the fair market value of the property to be transferred, as determined by the head of the disposing agency; or

(B) if such costs are lower than the fair market value of the property, the recipient of the property agrees to pay the difference between the fair market value and such costs.

(3) PAYMENTS TO RECIPIENTS.—In the case of a civilian real property covered by a certification under paragraph (2)(A), the disposing agency may pay the recipient of such property an amount equal to the lesser of—

(A) the amount by which the costs incurred by the recipient of such property for all environmental restoration, waste management, and environmental compliance activities with respect to such property exceed the fair market value of such property as specified in such certification; or

(B) the amount by which the costs (as determined by the head of the disposing agency) that would otherwise have been incurred by the Secretary for

SEC. 15. [40 U.S.C. 1303 note] SHORT TITLE;
TABLE OF CONTENTS.

Federal Assets Sale and Transfer Act of 20

such restoration, waste management, and environmental compliance activities with respect to such property exceed the fair market value of such property as so specified.

(4) INFORMATION TO BE PROVIDED TO RECIPIENTS.— As part of an agreement under paragraph (1), the head of the disposing agency shall disclose, in accordance with applicable law, to the person to whom the civilian real property will be transferred information possessed by the disposing agency regarding the environmental restoration, waste management, and environmental compliance activities that relate to the property. The head of the disposing agency shall provide such information before entering into the agreement.

(5) CONSIDERATION OF ENVIRONMENTAL REMEDIATION IN GRANTING TIME EXTENSIONS.— For the purposes of granting time extensions under subsection (a), the Director of OMB shall give the need for significant environmental remediation to a civilian real property more weight than any other factor in determining whether to grant an extension to implement a Board recommendation.

(6) LIMITATION ON STATUTORY CONSTRUCTION.— Nothing in this Act may be construed to modify, alter, or amend CERCLA, the National Environmental Policy Act of 1969, or the Solid Waste Disposal Act (42 U.S.C. 6901 et seq.).

SEC. 15. AUTHORIZATION OF APPROPRIATIONS.

There is authorized to be appropriated to carry out this Act an initial appropriation of—

(1) $2,000,000 for salaries and expenses of the Board; and

(2) $40,000,000 to be deposited into the Asset Proceeds and Space Management Fund for activities related to the implementation of the Board's recommendations.

SEC. 16. FUNDING.

(a) SALARIES AND EXPENSES ACCOUNT.—

(1) ESTABLISHMENT.— There is established in the Treasury of the United States an account to be known as the Public Buildings Reform Board Salaries and Expenses Account (in this subsection referred to as the Account). The Account shall be under the custody and control of the Chairperson of the Board and deposits in the Account shall remain available until expended.

(2) NECESSARY PAYMENTS.— There shall be deposited into the Account such amounts, as are provided in appropriations Acts, for those necessary payments for salaries and expenses to accomplish the administrative needs of the Board.

(b) ASSET PROCEEDS AND SPACE MANAGEMENT FUND.—

(1) ESTABLISHMENT.— There is established in the Treasury of the United States an account to be known as the Public Buildings Reform Board—Asset Proceeds and Space Management Fund (in this subsection referred to as the Fund). The Fund shall be under the custody and control of the Administrator and deposits in the Fund shall remain available until expended.

(2) USE OF AMOUNTS.— Amounts in the Fund shall be used solely for the purposes of carrying out actions pursuant to the Board recommendations approved

under section 13.

(3) DEPOSITS.—The following amounts shall be deposited into the Fund and made available for obligation or expenditure only as provided in advance in appropriations Acts (subject to section 3307 of title 40, United States Code, to the extent an appropriation normally covered by that section exceeds $20,000,000) for the purposes specified:

(A)   Such amounts as are provided in appropriations Acts, to remain available until expended, for the consolidation, co-location, exchange, redevelopment, reconfiguration of space, disposal, and other actions recommended by the Board for Federal agencies.

(B)   Amounts received from the sale of any civilian real property action taken pursuant to a recommendation of the Board.

(4) USE OF AMOUNTS TO COVER COSTS.—As provided in appropriations Acts, amounts in the Fund may be made available to cover necessary costs associated with implementing the recommendations pursuant to section 14, including costs associated with—

(A)   sales transactions;

(B)   acquiring land, construction, constructing replacement facilities, and conducting advance planning and design as may be required to transfer functions from a Federal asset or property to another Federal civilian property;

(C)   co-location, redevelopment, disposal, and reconfiguration of space; and

(D)   other actions recommended by the Board for Federal agencies.

(c) ADDITIONAL REQUIREMENT FOR BUDGET CONTENTS.— The President shall transmit along with the President's budget submitted pursuant to section 1105 of title 31, United States Code, an estimate of proceeds that are the result of the Board's recommendations and the obligations and expenditures needed to support such recommendations.

SEC. 17. CONGRESSIONAL APPROVAL OF PROPOSED PROJECTS.

Section 3307(b) of title 40, United States Code, is amended—

(1)   by striking and at the end of paragraph (6);

(2)   by striking the period at the end of paragraph (7) and inserting ; and; and

(3)   by adding at the end the following:

"(8)   a statement of how the proposed project is consistent with the standards and criteria developed under section 11(b) of the Federal Assets Sale and Transfer Act of 2016.".

SEC. 18. PRECLUSION OF JUDICIAL REVIEW.

The following actions shall not be subject to judicial review:

(1)   Actions taken pursuant to sections 12 and 13.

(2)   Actions of the Board.

SEC. 19. [40 U.S.C. 1303 note] SHORT TITLE; TABLE OF CONTENTS.

Federal Assets Sale and Transfer Act of 201

SEC. 19. IMPLEMENTATION REVIEW BY GAO.

Upon transmittal of the Board's recommendations from the Director of OMB to Congress under section 13, the Comptroller General of the United States at least annually shall monitor and review the implementation activities of Federal agencies pursuant to section 14, and report to Congress any findings and recommendations.

SEC. 20. AGENCY RETENTION OF PROCEEDS.

(a) IN GENERAL.— Section 571 of title 40, United States Code, is amended by striking subsections (a) and (b) and inserting the following:

"(a) PROCEEDS FROM TRANSFER OR SALE OF REAL PROPERTY.—

"(1) DEPOSIT OF NET PROCEEDS.— Net proceeds described in subsection (c) shall be deposited into the appropriate real property account of the agency that had custody and accountability for the real property at the time the real property is determined to be excess.

"(2) EXPENDITURE OF NET PROCEEDS.— The net proceeds deposited pursuant to paragraph (1) may only be expended, as authorized in annual appropriations Acts, for activities described in sections 543 and 545, including paying costs incurred by the General Services Administration for any disposal-related activity authorized by this chapter.

"(3) DEFICIT REDUCTION.— Any net proceeds described in subsection (c) from the sale, lease, or other disposition of surplus real property that are not expended under paragraph (2) shall be used for deficit reduction. Any net proceeds not obligated within 3 years after the date of deposit and not expended within 5 years after such date shall be deposited as miscellaneous receipts in the Treasury.

"(b) EFFECT ON OTHER SECTIONS.— Nothing in this section is intended to affect section 572(b), 573, or 574.

"(c) NET PROCEEDS.—The net proceeds described in this subsection are proceeds under this chapter, less expenses of the transfer or disposition as provided in section 572(a), from a—

"(1) transfer of excess real property to a Federal agency for agency use; or

"(2) sale, lease, or other disposition of surplus real property.".

(b) EFFECTIVE DATE.—The provisions of this section, including the amendments made by this section, shall take effect on the date on which the Board transmits the second report under section 12(h)(2)(B) and shall apply to proceeds from—

(1) transactions contained in that report; and

(2) any transactions conducted after the date on which the Board terminates under section 10.

SEC. 21. FEDERAL REAL PROPERTY DATABASE.

(a) DATABASE REQUIRED.— Not later than 1 year after the date of enactment of this section, the Administrator shall publish a single, comprehensive, and descriptive database of all Federal real property under the custody and control of all executive agencies, other than Federal real property excluded for reasons of national security, in accordance with subsection (b).

(b) REQUIRED INFORMATION FOR DATABASE.—The Administrator shall collect from the head of each executive agency descriptive information, except for classified information, of the nature, use, and extent of the Federal real property of each such agency, including the following:

(1)   The geographic location of each Federal real property of each such agency, including the address and description for each such property.

(2)   The total size of each Federal real property of each such agency, including square footage and acreage of each such property.

(3)   Whether the Federal real property is currently, or will in the future be, needed to support agency's mission or function.

(4)   The utilization of each Federal real property for each such agency, including whether such property is excess, surplus, underutilized, or unutilized.

(5)   The number of days each Federal real property is designated as excess, surplus, underutilized, or unutilized.

(6)   The annual operating costs of each Federal real property.

(7)   The replacement value of each Federal real property.

(8)   The ability of the Federal real property to support a communications facility installation.

(9)(A)   Whether the Federal real property is on a campus or similar facility; and

(B)   if applicable, identification of the campus or facility and related details, including total acreage of the campus or facility.

(c) ACCESS TO DATABASE.—

(1) FEDERAL AGENCIES.— The Administrator, in consultation with the Director of OMB, shall make the database established and maintained under this section available to other Federal agencies.

(2) PUBLIC ACCESS.— To the extent consistent with national security and procurement laws, the database shall be accessible by the public at no cost through the Web site of the General Services Administration.

(d) TRANSPARENCY OF DATABASE.—To the extent practicable, the Administrator shall ensure that the database—

(1)   uses an open, machine-readable format;

(2)   permits users to search and sort Federal real property data; and

(3)   includes a means to download a large amount of Federal real property data and a selection of such data retrieved using a search.

(e) APPLICABILITY.— Nothing in this section may be construed to require an agency to make available to the public information that is exempt from disclosure pursuant to section 552(b) of title 5, United States Code.

SEC. 22. [40 U.S.C. 1303 note] SHORT TITLE;
TABLE OF CONTENTS.

Federal Assets Sale and Transfer Act of 20

(f) DEFINITION OF COMMUNICATIONS FACILITY INSTALLATION.—In this section, the term communications facility installation means—

(1) any infrastructure, including any transmitting device, tower, or support structure, and any equipment, switches, wiring, cabling, power sources, shelters, or cabinets associated with the licensed or permitted unlicensed wireless or wireline transmission of writings, signs, signals, data, images, pictures, and sounds of any kind; and

(2) any antenna or apparatus that—

(A) is designed for the purpose of emitting radio frequency;

(B) is designed to be operated, or is operating, from a fixed location pursuant to authorization by the Federal Communications Commission or is using duly authorized devices that do not require individual licenses; and

(C) is added to a tower, building, or other structure.

SEC. 22. STREAMLINING MCKINNEY-VENTO HOMELESS ASSISTANCE ACT.

Section 501 of the McKinney-Vento Homeless Assistance Act (42 U.S.C. 11411) is amended—

(1) in subsection (b)(2)—

(A) by striking (2)(A) and inserting (2);

(B) by redesignating clauses (i) and (ii) as subparagraphs (A) and (B), respectively;

(C) in subparagraph (A) (as so redesignated) by striking and at the end;

(D) in subparagraph (B) (as so redesignated) by striking the period at the end and inserting ; and; and

(E) by adding at the end the following:

"(C) in the case of surplus property, the provision of permanent housing with or without supportive services is an eligible use to assist the homeless under this section.";

(2) in subsection (c)(1)(A) by striking in the Federal Register and inserting on the Web site of the Department of Housing and Urban Development or the General Services Administration;

(3) in subsection (d)—

(A) in paragraph (1) by striking period of 60 days and inserting period of 30 days;

(B) in paragraphs (2) and (4) by striking 60-day period and inserting 30-day period; and

(C) in paragraph (3) by adding at the end the following: If no such review of the determination is requested within the 20-day period, such property will not be included in subsequent publications unless the landholding agency makes changes to the property (e.g. improvements) that may change the unsuitable determination and the Secretary subsequently determines the property is

EC. 23. [40 U.S.C. 1303 note] SHORT TITLE;
ABLE OF CONTENTS.

Federal Assets Sale and Transfer Act of 2016

suitable.;

(4) in subsection (e)—

(A) in paragraph (2)—

(i)   by striking (2) and inserting (2)(A);

(ii) in subparagraph (A) (as so designated)—

(I)   by striking 90 days and inserting 75 days; and

(II)   by striking a complete application and inserting an initial application; and

(iii)   by adding at the end the following:

"(B) An initial application shall set forth—

"(i)   the services that will be offered;

"(ii)   the need for the services; and

"(iii)   the experience of the applicant that demonstrates the ability to provide the services.";

(B)   in paragraph (3) by striking 25 days after receipt of a completed application and inserting 10 days after receipt of an initial application; and

(C)   by adding at the end the following:

"(4)   If the Secretary of Health and Human Services approves an initial application, the applicant has 45 days in which to provide a final application that sets forth a reasonable plan to finance the approved program.

"(5)   No later than 15 days after receipt of the final application, the Secretary of Health and Human Services shall review, make a final determination, and complete all actions on the final application. The Secretary of Health and Human Services shall maintain a public record of all actions taken in response to an application."; and

(5)   in subsection (f)(1) by striking available by and inserting available, at the applicant's discretion, by.

SEC. 23. ADDITIONAL PROPERTY.

Section 549(c)(3)(B)(vii) of title 40, United States Code, is amended to read as follows:

"(vii)   a museum attended by the public, and, for purposes of determining whether a museum is attended by the public, the Administrator shall consider a museum to be public if the nonprofit educational or public health institution or organization, at minimum, accedes to any request submitted for access during business hours;".

SEC. 24. SALE OF 12TH AND INDEPENDENCE.

(a) DEFINITION.— In this section, the term property means the property located in the District of Columbia, subject to survey and as determined by the Administrator,

SEC. 25. [40 U.S.C. 1303 note] SHORT TITLE;
TABLE OF CONTENTS.

Federal Assets Sale and Transfer Act of 20

generally consisting of Squares 325 and 326 and a portion of Square 351 and generally bounded by 12th Street, Independence Avenue, C Street, and the James Forrestal Building, all in Southwest Washington, District of Columbia, and shall include all associated air rights, improvements thereon, and appurtenances thereto.

(b) SALE.— Not later than December 31, 2018, the Administrator shall sell the property at fair market value at highest and best use.

(c) REQUIREMENT.— Notwithstanding any other provision of law, the sale of the property by the Administrator shall ensure continuity of security measures, parking access, and infrastructure requirements of the James Forrestal Building while it is occupied by the Department of Energy.

(d) NET PROCEEDS.— Any net proceeds received shall be paid into an account in the Federal Buildings Fund established under section 592 of title 40, United States Code. Upon deposit, the net proceeds from the sale may be expended only subject to a specific future appropriation.

SEC. 25. SALE OF COTTON ANNEX.

(a) DEFINITION.— In this section, the term property means property located in the District of Columbia, subject to survey and as determined by the Administrator, generally consisting of Square 326 south of C Street, all in Southwest Washington, District of Columbia, including the building known as the Cotton Annex.

(b) SALE.— Not later than December 31, 2018, the Administrator shall sell the property at fair market value at highest and best use.

(c) NET PROCEEDS.— Any net proceeds received shall be paid into an account in the Federal Buildings Fund established under section 592 of title 40, United States Code. Upon deposit, the net proceeds from the sale may be expended only subject to a specific future appropriation.

SEC. 26. ACCESS TO FEDERAL REAL PROPERTY COUNCIL MEETINGS AND REPORTS.

(a) IN GENERAL.— The Federal Real Property Council established by subsection (a) of section 623 of title 40, United States Code, shall ensure that the Board has access to any meetings of the Federal Real Property Council and any reports required under that section, subject to the condition that the Board enters into a memorandum of understanding relating to public disclosure with the Administrator and the Federal Real Property Council before the Board has access to those meetings and reports.

(b) NOTIFICATION.— The Board shall notify the Committee on Environment and Public Works of the Senate and the Committee on Transportation and Infrastructure of the House of Representatives if the Administrator and the Federal Real Property Council described in subsection (a) have not entered into a memorandum of understanding pursuant to that subsection by the date that is 60 days after the date of enactment of this section, and every 60 days thereafter until the memorandum of understanding is entered into.

★

THOMAS R. CARPER WATER RESOURCES DEVELOPMENT ACT OF 2024 DIV. B, TITLE III–PUBLIC BUILDINGS REFORMS

PUBLIC LAW 118–272

THOMAS R. CARPER WATER RESOURCES DEVELOPMENT ACT OF 2024

[(Public Law 118–272)]

[This law has not been amended]

AN ACT To provide for improvements to the rivers and harbors of the United States, to provide for the conservation and development of water and related resources, and for other purposes.

Be it enacted by the Senate and House of Representatives of the United States of America in Congress assembled,

* * * * * * *

DIVISION B—OTHER MATTERS

* * * * * * *

TITLE III—PUBLIC BUILDINGS REFORMS

SEC. 2301. AMENDMENTS TO THE FEDERAL ASSETS SALE AND TRANSFER ACT OF 2016.

(a) PURPOSES.—Section 2 of the Federal Assets Sale and Transfer Act of 2016 (40 U.S.C. 1303 note; Public Law 114-287) is amended—

(1) in paragraph (9), by striking and at the end;

(2) in paragraph (10), by striking the period at the end and inserting ; and; and

(3) by adding at the end the following:

"(11) implementing innovative methods for the sale, redevelopment, consolidation, or lease of Federal buildings and facilities, including the use of no cost, nonappropriated contracts for expert real estate services to obtain the highest and best value for the taxpayer.".

(b) DEFINITIONS.— Section 3(5)(B)(viii) of the Federal Assets Sale and Transfer Act of 2016 (40 U.S.C. 1303 note; Public Law 114-287) is amended by inserting , other than office buildings and warehouses, after Properties.

(c) BOARD.—Section 4(c)(3) of the Federal Assets Sale and Transfer Act of 2016 (40 U.S.C. 1303 note; Public Law 114-287) is amended—

(1) by striking The term and inserting the following:

"(A) IN GENERAL.— Subject to subparagraph (B), the term"; and

(2) by adding at the end the following:

"(B) LIMITATION.— Notwithstanding subparagraph (A), the term of a member of the Board shall continue beyond 6 years until such time as the President appoints a replacement member of the Board.".

(d) BOARD MEETINGS.— Section 5(b) of the Federal Assets Sale and Transfer Act of 2016 (40 U.S.C. 1303 note; Public Law 114-287) is amended by striking Five Board members and inserting 4 Board members.

(e) EXECUTIVE DIRECTOR.— Section 7 of the Federal Assets Sale and Transfer Act of 2016 (40 U.S.C. 1303 note; Public Law 114-287) is amended by adding at the end the following:

"(c) RETURN TO CIVIL SERVICE.— An Executive Director selected from the civil service (as defined in section 2101 of title 5, United States Code) shall be entitled to return to the civil service (as so defined) after service to the Board ends if the service of the Executive Director to the Board ends for reasons other than misconduct, neglect of duty, or malfeasance.".

(f) STAFF.—Section 8 of the Federal Assets Sale and Transfer Act of 2016 (40 U.S.C. 1303 note; Public Law 114-287) is amended—

(1) in subsection (b)—

(A) by striking and the Director of OMB; and

(B) by inserting for a period of not less than 1 year before to assist the Board;

(2) by redesignating subsection (c) as subsection (d); and

(3) by inserting after subsection (b) the following:

"(c) HIRING OF TERM EMPLOYEES.— The Executive Director, with approval of the Board, may use the Office of Personnel Management to hire employees for terms not to exceed 2 years pursuant to the Office of Personnel Management guidance for nonstatus appointments in the competitive service.".

(g) TERMINATION.— Section 10 of the Federal Assets Sale and Transfer Act of 2016 (40 U.S.C. 1303 note; Public Law 114-287) is amended by striking 6 years after the date on which the Board members are appointed pursuant to section 4 and inserting on December 31, 2026.

(h) DEVELOPMENT OF RECOMMENDATIONS TO BOARD.—Section 11 of the Federal Assets Sale and Transfer Act of 2016 (40 U.S.C. 1303 note; Public Law 114-287) is amended—

(1) in subsection (a)—

(A) in the matter preceding paragraph (1), by striking the Administrator and the Director of OMB and inserting the Administrator, the Director of OMB, and the Board;

(B) in paragraph (1)—

(i) by striking and square and inserting number of Federal employees physically reporting to the respective property each work day, square; and

  (ii) by inserting , amount of acreage associated with the respective property, and whether the respective property is on a campus or larger facility before the period at the end; and

  (C) by adding at the end the following:

  "(3) CONSOLIDATION PLANS.— Any Federal agency plans to consolidate, reconfigure, or otherwise reduce the use of owned and leased Federal civilian real property of the Federal agency.";

 (2) in subsection (b)(3)(J), by inserting , including access by members of federally recognized Indian Tribes, after public access; and

 (3) by adding at the end the following:

  "(e) DISCLOSURE OF INFORMATION.—

  "(1) IN GENERAL.— Except as provided in paragraph (2), the Board may not publicly disclose any information received under paragraph (2) or (3) of subsection (a) until the Board, the Administrator, and the Director of OMB enter into an agreement describing what information is ready to be publicly disclosed.

  "(2) APPLICATION.— Paragraph (1) shall not apply to any disclosure of information to the Committee on Environment and Public Works of the Senate or the Committee on Transportation and Infrastructure of the House of Representatives.".

 (i) BOARD DUTIES.—Section 12 of the Federal Assets Sale and Transfer Act of 2016 (40 U.S.C. 1303 note; Public Law 114-287) is amended—

 (1) in subsection (b)(2), by striking the second sentence and inserting the following: In the case of a failure by a Federal agency to comply with a request of the Board, the Board shall notify the committees listed in section 5(c), the relevant congressional committees of jurisdiction for the Federal agency, and the inspector general of the Federal agency of that failure.;

 (2) in subsection (d)—

  (A) in paragraph (1), by inserting , Tribal, after State; and

  (B) in paragraph (2), by inserting , Tribal, after State;

 (3) by redesignating subsections (d) through (i) as subsections (e) through (j), respectively;

 (4) by inserting after subsection (c) the following:

  "(d) PREPARATION OF PROPERTIES FOR DISPOSAL.— At the request of, and in coordination with, the Board, a Federal agency may undertake any analyses and due diligence as necessary, to supplement the independent analysis of the Board under subsection (c), to prepare a property for disposition so that the property may be included in the recommendations of the Board under subsection (h), including completion of the requirements of section 306108 of title 54, United States Code, for historic preservation and identification of the likely highest and best use of the property subsequent to disposition.";

 (5) in subsection (h) (as so redesignated)—

(A) in paragraph (1)—

(i)   in subparagraph (A), by striking and at the end;

(ii)   by redesignating subparagraph (B) as subparagraph (C); and

(iii)   by inserting after subparagraph (A) the following:

"(B)   the process to be followed by Federal agencies to carry out the actions described in subparagraph (A), including the use of no cost, nonappropriated contracts for expert real estate services and other innovative methods, to obtain the highest and best value for the taxpayer; and"; and

(B)   in paragraph (2), by adding at the end the following:

"(C) THIRD ROUND.— During the period beginning on the day after the transmittal of the second report and ending on the day before the date on which the Board terminates under section 10, the Board shall transmit to the Director of OMB a third report required under paragraph (1)."; and

(C)   by adding at the end the following:

"(4) COMMUNITY NOTIFICATION.—45 days before the date on which the Board transmits the third report required under paragraph (1), the Board shall notify—

"(A)   any State or local government of any findings, conclusions, or recommendations contained in that report that relate to a Federal civilian real property located in the State or locality, as applicable; and

"(B)   any federally recognized Indian Tribe of any findings, conclusions, or recommendations contained in that report that relate to a Federal civilian real property that—

"(i)   is in close geographic proximity to a property described in section 3(5)(B)(v); or

"(ii)   relates to a Federal civilian real property that is known to be accessed at regular frequency by members of the federally recognized Indian Tribe for other reasons."; and

(6)   by adding at the end the following:

"(k) REPORT TO CONGRESS.— The Board shall periodically submit to the Committee on Environment and Public Works of the Senate and the Committee on Transportation and Infrastructure of the House of Representatives a report containing any recommendations on consolidations, exchanges, sales, lease reductions, and redevelopments that are not included in the transmissions submitted under subsection (h), or approved by the Director of OMB under section 13, but that the majority of the Board concludes meets the goals of this Act.".

(j) REVIEW BY OMB.—Section 13 of the Federal Assets Sale and Transfer Act of 2016 (40 U.S.C. 1303 note; Public Law 114-287) is amended—

(1)   in subsection (a), by striking subsections (b) and (g) and inserting subsections (b) and (h); and

(2) in subsection (c)(4)—

(A)   by inserting , in whole or in part, before received under paragraph (3); and

(B)   by striking revised the second place it appears.

(k) AGENCY RETENTION OF RECORDS.— Section 20 of the Federal Assets Sale and Transfer Act of 2016 (40 U.S.C. 1303 note; Public Law 114-287) is amended by striking subsection (b) and inserting the following:

"(b) EFFECTIVE DATE.—The provisions of this section, including the amendments made by this section, shall take effect on the date on which the Board transmits the second report under section 12(h)(2)(B) and shall apply to proceeds from—

"(1)   transactions contained in that report; and

"(2)   any transactions conducted after the date on which the Board terminates under section 10.".

(l) FEDERAL REAL PROPERTY DATABASE.— Section 21(b) of the Federal Assets Sale and Transfer Act of 2016 (40 U.S.C. 1303 note; Public Law 114-287) is amended by adding at the end the following:

"(9)(A)   Whether the Federal real property is on a campus or similar facility; and

"(B)   if applicable, identification of the campus or facility and related details, including total acreage of the campus or facility.".

(m) ACCESS TO FEDERAL REAL PROPERTY COUNCIL MEETINGS AND REPORTS.—

(1) IN GENERAL.— The Federal Assets Sale and Transfer Act of 2016 (40 U.S.C. 1303 note; Public Law 114-287) is amended by adding at the end the following:

"SEC. 26. ACCESS TO FEDERAL REAL PROPERTY COUNCIL MEETINGS AND REPORTS

"(a) IN GENERAL.— The Federal Real Property Council established by subsection (a) of section 623 of title 40, United States Code, shall ensure that the Board has access to any meetings of the Federal Real Property Council and any reports required under that section, subject to the condition that the Board enters into a memorandum of understanding relating to public disclosure with the Administrator and the Federal Real Property Council before the Board has access to those meetings and reports.

"(b) NOTIFICATION.— The Board shall notify the Committee on Environment and Public Works of the Senate and the Committee on Transportation and Infrastructure of the House of Representatives if the Administrator and the Federal Real Property Council described in subsection (a) have not entered into a memorandum of understanding pursuant to that subsection by the date that is 60 days after the date of enactment of this section, and every 60 days thereafter until the memorandum of understanding is entered into.".

(2) CLERICAL AMENDMENT.— The table of contents in section 1(b) of the Federal Assets Sale and Transfer Act of 2016 (Public Law 114-287; 130 Stat. 1463) is amended by inserting after the item relating to section 25 the following:

"Sec.?26.?Access to Federal Real Property Council meetings and reports."

.

(n) CONFORMING AMENDMENTS.—

(1)   Section 3(9) of the Federal Assets Sale and Transfer Act of 2016 (40 U.S.C. 1303 note; Public Law 114-287) is amended by striking section 12(e) and inserting section 12(f).

(2)   Section 14(g)(1)(A) of the Federal Assets Sale and Transfer Act of 2016 (40 U.S.C. 1303 note; Public Law 114-287) is amended by striking section 12(g) and inserting section 12(h).

(o) TECHNICAL AMENDMENTS.—

(1)   Section 16(b)(1) of the Federal Assets Sale and Transfer Act of 2016 (40 U.S.C. 1303 note; Public Law 114-287) is amended, in the second sentence, by striking of General Services.

(2)   Section 21(a) of the Federal Assets Sale and Transfer Act of 2016 (40 U.S.C. 1303 note; Public Law 114-287) is amended by striking of General Services.

(3)   Section 24 of the Federal Assets Sale and Transfer Act of 2016 (40 U.S.C. 1303 note; Public Law 114-287) is amended, in each of subsections (a), (b), and (c), by striking of General Services.

(4)   Section 25(b) of the Federal Assets Sale and Transfer Act of 2016 (40 U.S.C. 1303 note; Public Law 114-287) is amended by striking of General Services.

SEC. 2302. [40 U.S.C. 584 note] UTILIZING SPACE EFFICIENTLY AND IMPROVING TECHNOLOGIES ACT.

(a) DEFINITIONS.—In this section:

(1) ACTUAL UTILIZATION RATE.— The term actual utilization rate means the total usable square footage of a public building or federally-leased space divided by the occupancy.

(2) ADMINISTRATOR.— The term Administrator means the Administrator of General Services.

(3) BUILDING UTILIZATION.— The term building utilization means the percentage of utilization generated by comparing the actual utilization rate with the capacity based on a utilization benchmark of 150 useable square feet per person.

(4) CAPACITY.— The term capacity means the total usable square footage of a public building or federally-leased space divided by a utilization benchmark.

(5) DIRECTOR.— The term Director means the Director of the Office of Management and Budget.

(6) FEDERAL AGENCY.— The term Federal agency means an executive department covered by the Chief Financial Officers Act of 1990 (Public Law 101-576; 104 Stat. 2838).

(7) OCCUPANCY.— The term occupancy means the average number of employees actually performing duties in person in a public building or federally-leased space at

least 40 hours per week over a 2-month period.

(8) PUBLIC BUILDING.— The term public building has the meaning given the term in section 3301(a) of title 40, United States Code.

(b) IDENTIFICATION AND DEPLOYMENT OF BUILDING USAGE TECHNOLOGY.—

(1) IN GENERAL.— Not later than 60 days after the date of enactment of this Act, the Administrator, in coordination with the Director, shall establish standard methodologies and identify technologies available for measuring occupancy in public buildings and federally-leased space.

(2) MEASUREMENT OF UTILIZATION.— Not later than 180 days after the date of enactment of this Act, the heads of Federal agencies shall work with the Administrator to identify, deploy, and use Personal Identity Verification badge swipe data isolating only the first credential use of the day for each cardholder and other technologies that the Administrator determines to be appropriate, such as sensors, in public buildings and federally-leased space where the Federal agency occupies space to measure the occupancy of public buildings and federally-leased space.

(3) PROTECTION OF PERSONALLY IDENTIFIABLE INFORMATION.— In carrying out paragraph (2), the Administrator shall ensure any sensors used for the purposes of determining occupancy are designed to protect of all personally identifiable information.

(c) REPORTING ON USAGE OF REAL PROPERTY.—

(1) IN GENERAL.—Not later than 1 year after the date of enactment of this Act, and annually thereafter, the heads of Federal agencies shall submit to the Director, the Administrator, the Committee on Transportation and Infrastructure of the House of Representatives, the Committee on Environment and Public Works of the Senate, and the Committees on Appropriations of the House of Representatives and the Senate a report on—

(A) the occupancy and the actual utilization rates of space in public buildings and federally-leased space occupied by the respective agency of the Federal agency head broken down by building and lease;

(B) the methodology used for determining occupancy, including the period of time and other parameters used to determine occupancy on a regular basis;

(C) the utilization percentage of each public building and federally-leased space by the respective agency of the Federal agency head, comparing the capacity to the actual utilization rate based on a utilization benchmark of 150 usable square feet per person; and

(D) any costs associated with capacity that exceeds occupancy with respect to the respective agency of the Federal agency head.

(2) PUBLISHING REQUIREMENT.—

(A) IN GENERAL.— Except as provided in subparagraph (B), the heads of Federal agencies shall make each report required under paragraph (1) available on a publicly accessible website of the General Services Administration.

(B) EXCEPTION.— The publishing requirements of subparagraph (A) shall not apply if the head of the respective Federal agency makes a determination that making the report required under paragraph (1) available on a publicly accessible website would be detrimental to national security.

(d) REDUCING UNNEEDED SPACE.—

(1) TARGET UTILIZATION METRICS.— Not later than 1 year after the date of enactment of this Act, and annually thereafter, the Director, in consultation with the Administrator, shall ensure building utilization in each public building and federally-leased space is not less than 60 percent on average over each 1-year period.

(2) ACTIONS.—In the event that building utilization is below 60 percent on average over a 1-year period described in paragraph (1) for any particular public building or federally-leased space, the Administrator shall—

(A)   provide notice to the tenant agency informing the agency of the excess in capacity along with associated costs of such excess; and

(B)   notify the Committee on Transportation and Infrastructure of the House of Representatives, the Committee on Environment and Public Works of the Senate, and the Committees on Appropriations of the House of Representatives and the Senate of the excess capacity and associated costs.

(3) SUBSEQUENT FAILURE.— If the tenant agency fails to meet the 60 percent target under paragraph (1) in the reporting period subsequent to the reporting period under paragraph (2), the Administrator shall, in consultation with the Director, take steps to reduce the space of the tenant agency, including consolidating the tenant agency with another agency, selling or disposing of excess capacity space, and adjusting space requirements, as appropriate, for any replacement space.

(4) PRIORITIZATION.— The Administrator, in coordination with the Director, shall prioritize to the maximum extent practicable capital investments in public buildings where Federal agencies meet or exceed building utilization metrics, except that prioritization may be given to projects that will result in building utilization of 60 percent or more.

(5) EXCEPTIONS.—

(A) IN GENERAL.— The Director may provide exceptions to building utilization metrics based on the amount of non-standard office space a Federal agency demonstrates is required to meet the mission of the agency, including warehouse space, laboratories critical to the mission of the agency, and public customer-facing spaces driven by agency missions.

(B) REPORTING.— The Administrator shall submit to the Committee on Transportation and Infrastructure of the House of Representatives, the Committee on Environment and Public Works of the Senate, and the Committees on Appropriations of the House of Representatives and the Senate a report on any exceptions granted under subparagraph (A), including the justification for the exception.

(e) HEADQUARTERS BUILDINGS.—

(1) HEADQUARTERS CONSOLIDATIONS.— Not later than 1 year after the date of enactment of this Act, the Director, in consultation with the Administrator, shall

submit to the Committee on Transportation and Infrastructure of the House of Representatives, the Committee on Environment and Public Works of the Senate, and the Comptroller General of the United States a plan to consolidate department and agency headquarters buildings in the National Capital Region that will result in building utilizations of 60 percent or greater.

(2) CONTENTS.—The plan submitted under paragraph (1) shall include details on the following:

(A)   Which departments and agencies will collocate and consolidate and into which buildings and associated details before and after plan implementation related to building utilization, building capacities, and actual utilization.

(B)   Details on the strategies for the sale or disposal of buildings that will no longer be needed for Federal use.

(C)   A detailed breakdown of any costs associated with the proposed consolidations and collocations.

(D)   An estimate of future savings as a result of space reductions and consolidations, including costs associated with energy savings and building operations.

(3) IMPLEMENTATION.— Not later than 1 year after the submission of the plan under paragraph (1), the Administrator and Director shall begin implementing the plan.

(f) FEDERAL USE IT OR LOSE IT LEASES ACT.—

(1) DEFINITIONS.—In this subsection:

(A) FEDERAL TENANT.—

(i) IN GENERAL.— The term Federal tenant means a Federal agency that has an occupancy agreement with the Administrator to occupy a commercial lease for office space secured by the Administrator on behalf of the Federal Government.

(ii) EXCLUSION.— The term Federal tenant does not include an element of the intelligence community.

(B) INTELLIGENCE COMMUNITY.— The term intelligence community has the meaning given the term in section 3 of the National Security Act of 1947 (50 U.S.C. 3003).

(2) REPORTING OF SPACE UTILIZATION AND OCCUPANCY DATA FOR OFFICE SPACE.—An occupancy agreement between the Administrator and a Federal tenant for office space shall—

(A) include language that requires the Federal tenant to submit to the Administrator an annual report for the duration of the agreement containing data on—

(i)   monthly total occupancy of such office space;

(ii)   the actual utilization of such office space;

(iii)   monthly space utilization rates; and

(iv)   any other office space utilization data considered important by the Administrator; and

(B)   include language that requires the Federal tenant to have written procedures in place governing the return of office space to the Administrator if the occupancy of the Federal tenant falls below a 60 percent space utilization rate for 6 months within any 1-year period, beginning on the date on which the agreement takes effect.

(3) REQUIREMENTS FOR FEDERAL AGENCIES WITH INDEPENDENT LEASING AUTHORITIES.—The head of any agency with independent leasing authorities with leases for office space shall submit to the Committee on Transportation and Infrastructure of the House of Representatives, the Committee on Environment and Public Works of the Senate, and each congressional committee of jurisdiction of the applicable independent leasing authority an annual report for the duration of the agreement containing data on—

(A)   monthly total occupancy of the office space;

(B)   the actual utilization of the office space;

(C)   monthly space utilization rates; and

(D)   any other office space utilization data considered important for collection by Congress.

(4) EXCEPTIONS TO REPORTING AND OCCUPANCY AGREEMENT REQUIREMENTS.— This subsection shall not apply to properties used by an element of the intelligence community.

(5) APPLICABILITY.— The requirements of this subsection shall apply to any occupancy or novation agreement entered into on or after the date that is 180 days after the date of enactment of this Act.

(g) GAO REPORT.—

(1) IN GENERAL.— Not later than 1 year after the date of enactment of this Act, the Comptroller General of the United States shall submit to Congress a report on the cost to each Federal agency of measuring the occupancy and actual utilization rates of space in public buildings and federally-leased space to prepare the reports required under subsection (d).

(2) REQUIREMENTS.— The Comptroller General of the United States shall include in the report required under paragraph (1) the cost of deploying sensors and technologies pursuant to subsection (c) but shall exclude any such technologies that were in place before the date of enactment of this Act.

(h) INVESTIGATION OF UNDERUTILIZED SPACE.—

(1) REPORTING REQUIREMENT.— Not later than 90 days after the submission of each report under subsection (d), the head of each Federal agency shall submit to the inspector general of each respective agency a report detailing any public building or federally-leased space with a capacity of 500 or more employees under the jurisdiction of the agency that has a utilization rate below 20 percent during the reporting period that is not a vacant office building.

(2) INSPECTOR GENERAL INVESTIGATION.— On receipt of a report under paragraph (1), the inspector general of the relevant Federal agency shall conduct an investigation to determine whether there is any evidence of fraud, waste, abuse, or mismanagement with respect to the use of the public building or federally-leased space identified in the report.

SEC. 2303. IMPACT OF CRIME ON PUBLIC BUILDING USAGE ACT.

(a) REPORT ON IMPACT OF CRIME ON PUBLIC BUILDING USAGE.—Not later than 1 year after the date of enactment of this Act, the Comptroller General of the United States shall conduct a review and submit to the Committee on Environment and Public Works of the Senate and the Committee on Transportation and Infrastructure of the House of Representatives a report outlining—

(1) the effects of increased crime rates and safety concerns, including the use of fentanyl and other illicit drugs and substances, in areas surrounding Federal buildings on building usage for in-person work at Federal buildings;

(2) how usage of different commuting modes of transportation to Federal buildings are affected by increased crime rates;

(3) the effects of low office utilization rates on safety around Federal buildings;

(4) any agency exceptions given to the policy set forth in the memorandum of the Office of Management and Budget entitled "Measuring, Monitoring, and Improving Organizational Health and Organizational Performance in the Context of Evolving Agency Work Environments" and issued on April 13, 2023, due to unsafe commuting conditions; and

(5) any costs associated with safety issues impacting Federal building.

(b) REPORT ON COSTS OF CRIME AROUND PUBLIC BUILDINGS.— Not later than 1 year after the date of enactment of this Act, the inspector general of the General Services Administration, in coordination with inspectors general of other relevant Federal agencies, shall submit to the Committee on Environment and Public Works of the Senate and the Committee on Transportation and Infrastructure of the House of Representatives a report on the impacts on and costs associated with building operations related to crime and public safety in and around Federal buildings.

SEC. 2304. FEDERAL OVERSIGHT OF CONSTRUCTION USE AND SAFETY ACT.

(a) ELIMINATING PROJECT ESCALATIONS.— Section 3307(c) of title 40, United States Code, is amended by adding at the end the following: The Administrator shall notify, in writing, the Committee on Transportation and Infrastructure of the House of Representatives and the Committee on Environment and Public Works of the Senate of any increase of more than 5 percent of an estimated maximum cost or of any increase or decrease in the scope or size of a project of 5 or more percent. Such notification shall include an explanation regarding any such increase or decrease. Prospectus.The scope or size of a project shall not increase or decrease by more than 10 percent unless an amended prospectus is submitted and approved pursuant to this section.

(b) PUBLIC SAFETY AT FEDERAL BUILDINGS.—

(1) DATA COLLECTION.— The Administrator of General Services shall collect

data from tenant Federal agencies reports of any safety incidents as a result of criminal or other activity impacting public safety in and around public buildings, as defined in section 3301 of title 40, United States Code.

(2) REPORT.—Not later than 180 days after the date of enactment of this Act, the Administrator shall submit to the Committee on Transportation and Infrastructure of the House of Representatives and the Committee on Environment and Public Works of the Senate a report that—

(A) contains the data collected under paragraph (1); and

(B) describes any actions taken or planned, if necessary, to improve building management and operations to address such incidents.

(c) REDUCING WASTE IN NEW PROJECTS.—Section 3307(b) of title 40, United States Code, is amended—

(1) in the matter preceding paragraph (1), by inserting (referred to in this section as the 'Administrator') after Administrator of General Services;

(2) in paragraph (7), by striking and at the end;

(3) in paragraph (8), by striking the period at the end and inserting a semicolon; and

(4) by adding at the end the following:

"(9) information on any space occupied by the relevant agency in the geographical area of the proposed facility, including uses, utilization rates, any proposed consolidations, and, if not proposed to be consolidated, a justification for such determination;

"(10) a statement by the Administrator of whether the public building needs of the Government for the proposed space to be leased were formerly met by a federally owned building, including any building identified for disposal or sale; and

"(11) details on actual utilization rates, including number of personnel assigned to the facility, number of personnel expected to work in-person at the facility and whether all personnel identified reflect filled and authorized positions.".

(d) REVIEW OF SPECIAL USE SPACE.—

(1) REVIEW.— The Comptroller General of the United States shall review the use of special use spaces in Federal buildings, including conference centers, fitness centers, and similar spaces to determine levels of utilization, opportunities for sharing, collocating, and other efficiencies.

(2) REPORT.— Not later than 1 year after the date of enactment of this Act, the Comptroller General of the United States shall submit to the Committee on Transportation and Infrastructure of the House of Representatives and the Committee on Environment and Public Works of the Senate a report containing the review under paragraph (1).

(e) INTERAGENCY SPACE COORDINATION.—

(1) IN GENERAL.— Chapter 33 of title 40, United States Code, is amended by adding at the end the following:

"SEC. 3319. [40 U.S.C. 3319] INTERAGENCY SPACE COORDINATION

"Unless a Federal agency specifically restricts the sharing of the information described in this section for national security purposes, the Administrator of General Services shall share with tenant Federal agencies pursuing new or replacement office space information on any other Federal agencies located in the same geographical area for purposes of determining opportunities for consolidations, collocations, or other space sharing to reduce the costs of space and maximize space utilization.".

(2) CLERICAL AMENDMENT.— The analysis for chapter 33 of title 40, United States Code, is amended by adding at the end the following:

"3319.   Interagency space coordination."

(f) NOTIFICATION OF MILESTONES.— Section 3307 of title 40, United States Code, is amended by adding at the end the following:

"(i) NOTIFICATION REQUIRED.—For each project approved under this section, the Administrator shall notify, in writing, the Committee on Transportation and Infrastructure of the House of Representatives and the Committee on Environment and Public Works of the Senate of any project milestones that are accomplished, including—

"(1)   the solicitation and award of design and construction services;

"(2)   the completion of any actions required for the project pursuant to the National Environmental Policy Act of 1969 (42 U.S.C. 4321 et seq.);

"(3)   any ceremonies for the beginning or completion of the project;

"(4)   a naming ceremony for the project; and

"(5)   the completion of the project.".

SEC. 2305. PUBLIC BUILDINGS ACCOUNTABILITY ACT.

Not later than 1 year after the date of enactment of this Act, the Comptroller General of the United States shall conduct a review of the Public Buildings Service and submit to the Committee on Transportation and Infrastructure of the House of Representatives and the Committee on Environment and Public Works of the Senate a report containing the results of that review, including—

(1) a review of the administration and management of all Public Buildings Service real estate programs and activities, including—

(A)   a review and accounting of the number of employees and contract workers, including functions and the sources of funding (for example building operations, reimbursable work, project-specific funding) categorized by region and organizational, management, and oversight structure within the Public Building Service, including identification of components, programs, and reporting structures;

(B)   an accounting of in-person attendance by employee category and function;

(C)   an analysis, trends, and comparisons of staffing numbers and associated costs and other administrative costs over the 10 years preceding the review; and

(D)   an analysis of the effectiveness of organizational structure, management, and oversight in carrying out the mission of the Public Buildings Service; and

(2)   a review of the building operations account of the Federal Buildings Fund established by section 592(a) of title 40, United States Code, including activities and costs associated with conferences, training, and travel and transportation.

SEC. 2306. SALE OF WEBSTER SCHOOL.

(a) SALE.— Not later than December 31, 2025, the Administrator of General Services (referred to in this section as the "Administrator") shall sell the property described in subsection (b) at fair market value and for the highest and best use.

(b) PROPERTY DESCRIBED.— The property referred to in subsection (a) is the property generally consisting of Lot 822 of Square 375 at 940 H Street Northwest in Washington, District of Columbia, including the building known as the Webster School, subject to a survey, as determined appropriate by the Administrator.

(c) TREATMENT OF NET PROCEEDS; FUTURE APPROPRIATION.—

(1) IN GENERAL.— Any net proceeds received from the sale under this section shall be deposited into an account in the Federal Buildings Fund established by section 592(a) of title 40, United States Code (referred to in this subsection as the "Fund").

(2) FUTURE APPROPRIATION.— On deposit of net proceeds into the Fund under paragraph (1), those net proceeds may only be expended pursuant to a specific future appropriation.

SEC. 2307. REAL PROPERTY CONVEYANCE.

(a) IN GENERAL.— Not later than 2 years after the date of enactment of this Act, the Administrator of General Services, on behalf of the Director of the Bureau of Prisons of the Department of Justice, shall sell, by quitclaim deed, the property described in subsection (b) at fair market value and at highest and best use.

(b) PROPERTY DESCRIBED.— The property to be sold under this section is all property, including all buildings and improvements thereon, located in the State of Missouri in connection with the United States Penitentiary, Leavenworth, Kansas, and administered by the United States Bureau of Prisons.

(c) SURVEY REQUIRED.— As soon as practicable after the date of enactment of this Act, the exact legal description, including buildings, improvements, and acreage of the property to be sold under this section shall be determined by a survey that is satisfactory to the Administrator.

(d) DEFERRED MAINTENANCE.— Any deferred maintenance required pursuant to the agreement between the United States and the Farley-Beverly Drainage District and entered into on April 18, 1967, shall be addressed before sale of the property under this section.

(e) Costs.— Any costs incurred for the completion of the survey or other activities undertaken to prepare the property for sale under this section, including costs related to the deferred maintenance requirements described in subsection (d), shall be reimbursed from the gross proceeds of the sale.

(f) Net Proceeds.—

(1) In general.— Any net proceeds received from the sale of the property under this section shall be deposited into an account in the Federal Buildings Fund established by section 592(a) of title 40, United States Code.

(2) Future appropriation.— On deposit of net proceeds into the Fund under paragraph (1), the net proceeds may be expended only subject to a specific future appropriation.

(g) Prohibition on Foreign Ownership.—

(1) Definitions.— In this subsection, the terms "beneficial owner", "foreign entity", and "foreign person" have the meanings given those terms in section 2 of the Secure Federal LEASEs Act (40 U.S.C. 585 note; Public Law 116-276).

(2) Prohibition.— The property described in subsection (b) may not be sold to any foreign person or foreign entity, including if the foreign person or foreign entity is a beneficial owner of the foreign person or foreign entity.

SEC. 2308. THINK DIFFERENTLY ABOUT BUILDING ACCESSIBILITY ACT.

Not later than 1 year after the date of enactment of this Act, the Comptroller General of the United States shall report to the Committee on Transportation and Infrastructure of the House of Representatives and the Committee on Environment and Public Works of the Senate on the compliance under the Architectural Barriers Act of 1968 (42 U.S.C. 4151 et seq.) of all office buildings under the jurisdiction, custody, or control of the General Services Administration.

SEC. 2309. [40 U.S.C. 3101 note] REVISION OF DESIGN STANDARDS.

(a) In General.— Not later than 6 months after the date of enactment of this Act, the Administrator of General Services (referred to in this section as the "Administrator") shall revise the process by which the Administrator updates or changes the P100 facilities standards guidance document for federally owned buildings under the custody and control of the General Services Administration.

(b) Process.—The Administrator shall ensure that the process revised under subsection (a) requires—

(1) a public comment period for any updates or changes to the documents described in such subsection;

(2) publication of those updates or changes in the Federal Register and on the website of the General Services Administration; and

(3) a summary of any comments received during the public comment period.

(c) Report.— The Administrator shall submit to the Committee on Transportation and Infrastructure of the House of Representatives and the Committee on Environment and Public Works of the Senate a report describing the revisions to the process required under subsection (a).

SEC. 2310. [40 U.S.C. 3101 note] REVISION
OF DESIGN STANDARDS.

Thomas R. Carper Water Resourc
Development Act of 20:

SEC. 2310. LIMITATION ON AUTHORIZATIONS.

Section 3307 of title 40, United States Code (as amended by section 2304(f)), is amended by adding at the end the following:

"(j) EXPIRATION OF COMMITTEE RESOLUTIONS.—

"(1) IN GENERAL.— Unless a lease is awarded or a construction, alteration, repair, design, or acquisition project is initiated not later than 5 years after the resolution approvals adopted by the Committee on Transportation and Infrastructure of the House of Representatives and the Committee on Environment and Public Works of the Senate pursuant to subsection (a), the resolutions shall be deemed expired.

"(2) APPLICATION.— This subsection shall only apply to resolutions approved after the date of enactment of this subsection.".

SEC. 2311. CONVEYANCE OF FEDERAL COURTHOUSE TO THE CITY OF HUNTSVILLE, ALABAMA.

(a) IN GENERAL.— Not later than 60 days after the date of enactment of this Act, the Administrator of General Services shall offer to convey to the City of Huntsville, Alabama, all right, title, and interest of the United States in and to the property described in subsection (b).

(b) PROPERTY DESCRIPTION.— The property referred to in subsection (a) is the parcel of land and building located at 101 E. Holmes Avenue, Huntsville, Alabama, which is known as the "Huntsville Courthouse and Post Office".

(c) CONSIDERATION.— In exchange for the conveyance of the Huntsville Courthouse and Post Office to the City of Huntsville, Alabama under this title, the Administrator of General Services shall require the City of Huntsville, Alabama, to pay to the Administrator of General Services, subject to subsection (d), consideration in an amount equal to the fair market value of the Huntsville Courthouse and Post Office, as determined based on an appraisal that is acceptable to the Administrator of General Services.

(d) CREDITS.— In lieu of all or a portion of the amount of consideration for the Huntsville Courthouse and Post Office, the Administrator of General Services shall accept as consideration for the conveyance of such Huntsville Courthouse and Post Office any credits related to the appraised value of the 4.76-acre parcel of land located at 660 Gallatin Street, Huntsville, Alabama.

(e) COSTS.— As a condition of the conveyance under this section, the City shall pay all costs associated with the conveyance.

SEC. 2312. WILBUR J. COHEN FEDERAL BUILDING.

(a) SALE.— Not later than 2 years after the vacancy of existing Federal agencies, the Administrator of General Services shall sell for fair market value at highest and best use, the Wilbur J. Cohen Federal building located at 330 Independence Avenue SW in Washington, D.C.

(b) NET PROCEEDS.—

(1) IN GENERAL.— Any net proceeds received from the sale of the property

under this section shall be deposited into an account in the Federal Buildings Fund established by section 592(a) of title 40, United States Code.

(2) FUTURE APPROPRIATION.— On deposit of net proceeds into the Fund under paragraph (1), such net proceeds may be expended only subject to a specific future appropriation.

(c) PROHIBITION ON FOREIGN OWNERSHIP.—

(1) DEFINITIONS.— In this subsection, the terms "beneficial owner", "foreign entity", and "foreign person" have the meanings given those terms in section 2 of the Secure Federal LEASEs Act (40 U.S.C. 585 note; Public Law 116-276).

(2) PROHIBITION.— The property described in subsection (a) may not be sold to any foreign person or foreign entity, including if the foreign person or foreign entity is a beneficial owner of the foreign person or foreign entity.

SEC. 2313. EUGENE E. SILER, JR. UNITED STATES COURTHOUSE ANNEX.

(a) DESIGNATION.— The United States courthouse annex located at 310 South Main Street in London, Kentucky, shall be known and designated as the "Eugene E. Siler, Jr. United States Courthouse Annex".

(b) REFERENCES.— Any reference in a law, map, regulation, document, paper, or other record of the United States to the United States courthouse annex referred to in subsection (a) shall be deemed to be a reference to the "Eugene E. Siler, Jr. United States Courthouse Annex".

SEC. 2314. SENATOR DIANNE FEINSTEIN FEDERAL BUILDING.

(a) DESIGNATION.— The Federal building located at 50 United Nations Plaza in San Francisco, California, shall be known and designated as the "Senator Dianne Feinstein Federal Building".

(b) REFERENCES.— Any reference in a law, map, regulation, document, paper, or other record of the United States to the Federal building referred to in subsection (a) shall be deemed to be a reference to the "Senator Dianne Feinstein Federal Building".

SEC. 2315. REUBEN E. LAWSON FEDERAL BUILDING.

(a) FINDINGS.—Congress finds that—

(1) Reuben E. Lawson dedicated his life and career to promoting the ideals of equality and inclusion as a lawyer for the Roanoke chapter of the National Association for the Advancement of Colored People (commonly known as the "NAACP") who actively worked to end segregation in Southwest Virginia;

(2) arguing a number of significant cases in the Western District of Virginia, Reuben E. Lawson fought to ensure the enforcement of Brown v. Board of Education of Topeka, 347 U.S. 483 (1954), so that schools in the Roanoke region would be fully integrated; and

(3) Southwest Virginians are indebted to Reuben E. Lawson for his important work in ending segregation, and it is fitting that he be remembered in the current home of the court in which he valiantly fought.

(b) REDESIGNATION.— The Richard H. Poff Federal Building located at 210 Franklin

SEC. 2316. [40 U.S.C. 3101 note] REVISION
OF DESIGN STANDARDS.

Thomas R. Carper Water Resource
Development Act of 202

Road Southwest in Roanoke, Virginia, shall be known and designated as the "Reuben E. Lawson Federal Building".

(c) REFERENCES.— Any reference in a law, map, regulation, document, paper, or other record of the United States to the Richard H. Poff Federal Building shall be deemed to be a reference to the "Reuben E. Lawson Federal Building".

SEC. 2316. IRENE M. KEELEY UNITED STATES COURTHOUSE.

(a) DESIGNATION.— The United States courthouse located at 500 West Pike Street in Clarksburg, West Virginia, shall be known and designated as the "Irene M. Keeley United States Courthouse".

(b) REFERENCES.— Any reference in a law, map, regulation, document, paper, or other record of the United States to the United States courthouse referred to in subsection (a) shall be deemed to be a reference to the "Irene M. Keeley United States Courthouse".

SEC. 2317. VIRGINIA SMITH FEDERAL BUILDING.

(a) DESIGNATION.— The Federal building located at 300 E. 3rd Street in North Platte, Nebraska, shall be known and designated as the "Virginia Smith Federal Building".

(b) REFERENCES.— Any reference in a law, map, regulation, document, paper, or other record of the United States to the Federal building referred to in subsection (a) shall be deemed to be a reference to the "Virginia Smith Federal Building".

SEC. 2318. HAROLD L. MURPHY FEDERAL BUILDING AND UNITED STATES COURTHOUSE.

(a) FINDINGS.—Congress finds that—

(1) Judge Harold L. Murphy was born in Felton, Georgia, in 1927;

(2) Judge Murphy attended West Georgia College before serving in the United States Navy during the closing years of World War II;

(3) Judge Murphy resumed his studies at the University of Mississippi and the University of Georgia School of Law, where he graduated in 1949;

(4) Judge Murphy began a law practice in Haralson County, Georgia, and in 1950 was elected to the Georgia House of Representatives as the youngest Member at the time;

(5) Judge Murphy served five consecutive terms before stepping down in 1961 to focus on practicing law;

(6) in 1971, Judge Murphy was appointed by Governor Jimmy Carter to the Superior Court for the Tallapoosa Judicial Circuit, and following his election in 1976, President Carter nominated Judge Murphy to the United States District Court for the Northern District of Georgia;

(7) Judge Murphy was confirmed by the United States Senate on July 28, 1977;

(8) for 45 years, Judge Murphy served his country on the Federal bench and became an acclaimed jurist and legal icon with a stellar reputation that extended far beyond Georgia;

(9) Judge Murphy always displayed a quick wit and a keen sense of humor, was

kind and empathetic, and treated all those who appeared before him with courtesy and respect;

(10) Judge Murphy worked tirelessly and carried a full docket until the age of 90, when he took senior judge status in the Northern District of Georgia;

(11) Judge Murphy continued to preside over cases until his death on December 28, 2022;

(12) Judge Murphy received many professional awards and recognitions, including from the State Bar of Georgia and the University of Georgia School of Law;

(13) in 2014, Alabama State University renamed its graduate school after Judge Murphy in recognition of his landmark ruling in Knight v. Alabama, a long-running case that the Eleventh Circuit Court of Appeals asked him to handle involving the vestiges of racial segregation then present in the Alabama University System; and

(14) above all else, Judge Murphy was a loving and devoted husband and father—and a strong role model.

(b) DESIGNATION.— The Federal building and United States courthouse located at 600 East First Street in Rome, Georgia, shall be known and designated as the "Harold L. Murphy Federal Building and United States Courthouse".

(c) REFERENCES.— Any reference in a law, map, regulation, document, paper, or other record of the United States to the Federal building and United States courthouse referred to in subsection (b) shall be deemed to be a reference to the "Harold L. Murphy Federal Building and United States Courthouse".

SEC. 2319. FELICITAS AND GONZALO MENDEZ UNITED STATES COURTHOUSE.

(a) DESIGNATION.— The United States courthouse located at 350 W. 1st Street, Los Angeles, California, shall be known and designated as the "Felicitas and Gonzalo Mendez United States Courthouse".

(b) REFERENCES.— Any reference in a law, map, regulation, document, paper, or other record of the United States to the United States courthouse referred to in subsection (a) shall be deemed to be a reference to the "Felicitas and Gonzalo Mendez United States Courthouse".

SEC. 2320. HELEN EDWARDS ENGINEERING RESEARCH CENTER.

(a) DESIGNATION.— The Department of Energy Integrated Engineering Research Center Federal Building located at the Fermi National Accelerator Laboratory in Batavia, Illinois, shall be known and designated as the "Helen Edwards Engineering Research Center".

(b) REFERENCES.— Any reference in a law, map, regulation, document, paper, or other record of the United States to the Federal building referred to in subsection (a) shall be deemed to be a reference to the "Helen Edwards Engineering Research Center".

★